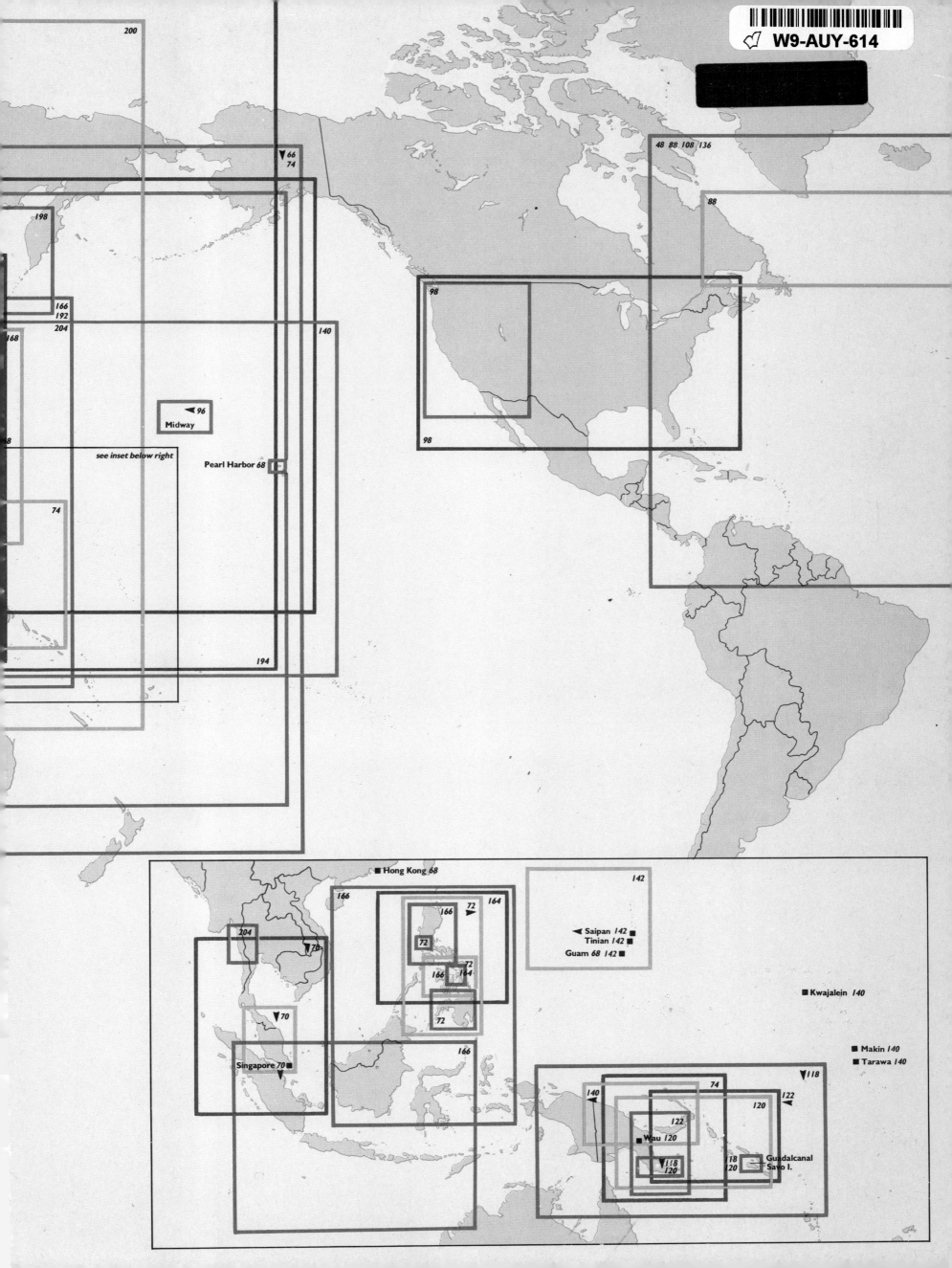

200

198

166
192

168

204

▼66
74

48 88 108 136

88

98

98

◄96

Midway

see inset below right

Pearl Harbor 68

74

194

■ Hong Kong 68

166

204

▼76

142

◄ Saipan 142 ■
Tinian 142 ■
Guam 68 142 ■

72

166   164

72

72

166   164

72

■ Kwajalein 140

▼70

■ Makin 140
■ Tarawa 140

Singapore 70 ■

166

▼118

140

74

122

120

◄

122
▼

120
◄

■ Wau 120

118
120

118
120

Guadalcanal
Savo I.

THE TIMES
ATLAS OF THE
SECOND WORLD WAR

ATLAS OF THE SECOND

THE ✦ TIMES

WORLD WAR

EDITED BY JOHN KEEGAN

1817

HARPER & ROW, PUBLISHERS, New York

Grand Rapids, Philadelphia, St. Louis, San Francisco
London, Singapore, Sydney, Tokyo

This book is published in Great Britain
by Times Books Limited.

FIRST EDITION

Editorial Direction
Andrew Heritage
Barry Winkleman

Ian Castello-Cortes
Rosemary Aspinwall
Paul Middleton
Ailsa Heritage
Elizabeth Wyse
Miranda Smith

Design
Ivan Dodd *art direction*
Malcolm Swanston
Tracy Enever

Maps and typesetting
Swanston Graphics, Derby

Malcolm Swanston
James Mills-Hicks
Andrea Fairbrass
Melvyn Pickering
Jeanne Radford
Andrew Bright
Malcolm Porter
Graham Malkin
Adrian Van Weerdenburg

Duncan Mackay

Colour Processing
Colourscan, Singapore

Place names consultant, index
P J M Geelan

Picture research
Mark Seaman

Glossary
Anthony Livesey

Chronology
Matthew Bennett

Printed in Italy by
Arnoldo Mondadori, Verona

The publishers would also like to thank the following:
Keith Simpson *formerly Dept. of War Studies, Sandhurst*;
N.C. de Lee *Senior Lecturer, Dept. of War Studies, Sandhurst*;
H.A.G. Lewis *formerly of the Directorate of Military Survey*;
Oleg Alexandrovich Rzheshevsky *Academy of Sciences,
Institute of General History, Moscow*; Major T.J. Gregson;
Col. Fred Clark Boli *United States Air Force*.

Library of Congress Cataloging-in-Publication Data

The Times atlas of the Second World War / [edited by] John
Keegan. — 1st ed.
    p.   cm.
    Includes index.
    ISBN 0-06-016178-7
    1. World War, 1939–1945—Maps. 2. Geography,
Historical—Maps. I. Keegan, John, 1934–
II. Times Books (Firm) III. Title: Times atlas of the
2nd World War.
  G1038.T6 1989 <G&M>
  911—dc20   89-45070
                                        CIP
                                     MAP

89 90 91 92 93 10 9 8 7 6 5 4 3 2 1

Contents

Contents *continued*

Contents *continued*

Contributors

Editor:

JOHN KEEGAN Defence Correspondent of *The Daily Telegraph*, formerly Senior Lecturer in War Studies, Royal Military Academy, Sandhurst

Consultant editors:

CHRISTOPHER BELLAMY Research Analyst specializing in Soviet military and strategic affairs, Centre for Defence Studies, University of Edinburgh

MICHAEL ORR Lecturer in Strategic Studies, Centre for Soviet Studies, Royal Military Academy, Sandhurst

RICHARD OVERY Reader in Modern History, King's College, University of London

NORMAN STONE Professor of Modern History, University of Oxford

H P WILLMOTT Senior Lecturer in War Studies, Royal Military Academy, Sandhurst

Contributors:

Matthew Bennett
Lecturer in Communication Studies
Royal Military Academy
Sandhurst

Norman Davies
Professor of Polish History
School of Slavonic and East European Studies
London University

John Erickson
Director, Centre for Defence Studies
Edinburgh University

Martin Gilbert
Merton College
Oxford University

Anthony Glees
Lecturer in Modern Political History
Brunel University

Keith Hayward
Department of International Relations and Politics
Staffordshire Polytechnic

Norman Longmate
Historical Researcher and Author
London

James Lucas
Formerly Imperial War Museum
London

Alan Milward
Professor of Economics
London School of Economics

Charles Messenger
Historical Researcher and Author
London

Mark Seaman
Imperial War Museum
London

Keith Sword
Research Fellow
School of Slavonic and East European Studies
London University

Mark Wheeler
Lecturer in History
School of Slavonic and East European Studies
London University

Introduction

THE SECOND WORLD WAR is the largest event in the history of mankind. No populated continent was untouched by its operations. The majority of states exercising sovereign government in 1939 took part in it, as did the colonial empires of Britain, France, Italy and Holland which then comprehended most of the non-sovereign area of the world, and the political structure of the post-war world has been largely determined by the war's outcome.

The period between 1936 and 1946 saw the largest and most extraordinary movements of people across the face of the globe. Hundreds of thousands of Europeans and Asians fled from war zones, were forcibly relocated or sought political refuge in other countries. The war sent Brazilians to campaign in Italy, Indian subjects of the British King-Emperor to fight under British colours in North Africa and Europe and under Japanese colours in Burma, German soldiers who had been Austrian before 1938 to invade Crete, Australians to fight Frenchmen in Syria, Polish fighter pilots to defend London in the Battle of Britain, Belgians to die in Nazi uniform in the Battle of Berlin, Russian Cossacks to defend the beaches of Normandy against Americans and Maoris from New Zealand to attack Italians in Libya.

The war was also fought and suffered by civilians, who may have numbered half of the estimated fifty million people killed between 1939 and 1945. The worst and most unique aspect of this was the organized exterminations of entire populations and communities in both Europe and China. The war also demanded the mobilization of civilian labour on an unprecedented scale, and in some countries – notably Britain, the Soviet Union and the United States – women took the place of men in the labour force in significant numbers. Strategic bombing was one of the major threats to civilians on the home fronts; in Germany more women than men were killed by the Allied combined bomber offensive. A high proportion of the victims of terror, reprisal and internecine fighting in the cruel guerrilla warfare carried on in Yugoslavia and Greece were also female. Material deprivation – most marked in German-occupied Russia and Japanese-occupied China – affected women, children and civilian males indifferently.

The global nature of the war, and the ambitions of the belligerents, meant that it was fought on a scale which, even today, confounds the imagination. It stimulated in the combatant states, and those which supplied them, the largest and most sustained economic effort ever undertaken. The world economy was not merely revived after the depression of the inter-war years. Demand for raw materials, manufactures and agricultural produce was stimulated by the war; state direction of the economies of the combatant states, together with the fiscal and credit policies that their governments imposed, caused them to grow at a rate and to a size which was unprecedented. In Germany, Britain, Japan and the Soviet Union, which all suffered heavy damage to their economies through bombing or invasion, much of the increased output was immediately consumed by the war effort, but in the United States the size of the economy increased by over 50 per cent between 1939 and 1945, thus ensuring that America would dominate the world's economy for the next 30 years.

The war was not only a stimulus to unparalleled economic activity. It also provoked the most important clash of ideologies experienced by the world since the Crusades, though a clash of a more complex kind. The ultra-nationalist malcontents of the Axis – German, Italy and Japan – loosely labelled as Fascist, confronted on the one hand a Soviet Marxist dictatorship which differed little from them in its methods of government (though greatly in its proclaimed political purposes), and on the other the major democracies. The eventual victory of the Allied anti-Axis powers, determined largely by their superior economic strength, did not solve the contradictions of that uneasy alliance, some of which are beginning to be resolved directly only as this Atlas goes to press.

The war, however it had ended, would have changed the world irreversibly. The proximate causes of its conclusion – America's detonation of atomic bombs at Hiroshima and Nagasaki and the Red Army's victory over Germany – ensured that world politics would be utterly altered after 1945. Wisely no war leader of 1939-45 promised his followers that they were fighting 'a war to end war', as some had done in 1914-18. That, as far as total war between great powers goes, was nevertheless the apparent outcome of the victory of 1945.

This Atlas has been conceived as a means of conveying to its users both the totality and complexity of the Second World War. It does not seek to portray, as so many histories of the war do, the inevitable triumph of the anti-Axis alliance. It does not accord predominance to any one theatre: the campaigns in Russia and in the Pacific are treated as of equal importance with those in western Europe. Its coverage is not exclusively military. Economic and political factors are recognized as having the importance they did, as are the enormous material and human costs of the conflict.

This Atlas could not have been completed without the dedicated attention of the consultant editors, each of whom assumed responsibility for a particular part of the Atlas, and without the specialized knowledge and willing enthusiasm of the contributors.

John Keegan
May 1989

Military formations and units

A military unit is a force composed of troops of the same arm of service, e.g. an infantry company or an artillery battery. A formation is a force composed of units of different arms of service. The smallest true formation is a division, though brigades usually contain units of different arms and are conventionally regarded as formations.

A battalion is a unit 600-1000 strong; a regiment, composed of three battalions, is about 3000 strong; a brigade, which contains two regiments or several battalions, varies in strength between 3000 and 6000; a division has three brigades with supporting troops and is about 15,000 strong; a corps contains at least two divisions, an army at least two corps and an army group at least two armies.

Battalions are commanded by lieutenant-colonels, regiments by colonels, brigades by brigadiers, divisions by major-generals and corps by lieutenant-generals; armies and army groups are commanded by lieutenant-generals, generals or (field) marshals as appropriate. Conventionally, the ranks from brigadier to marshal are represented by one, two, three, four or five stars.

There are many national exceptions to these broad rules. The British Army, for example, calls armoured and artillery battalions regiments; a British infantry regiment, on the other hand, is not a tactical unit but a historical parent unit of independent battalions. In the German Army, battalions were often commanded by majors and divisions by lieutenant-generals. In many armies the brigade does not exist or else is an independent organization outside a division. The Soviet Union, in the Second World War, called army groups 'fronts'; there were higher headquarters called 'theatres' or 'directions'. The United States Army called infantry brigades 'regimental combat teams' and armoured brigades 'combat commands'.

Size also varied greatly from country to country. Japanese formations were generally smaller than their western equivalents; Chinese formations were often so weak as not to deserve their designations. German formations grew smaller during the war, as losses had their effect; Russian formations, by contrast, were often skeletal in 1941-42 but regained strength as the war progressed. The formations and units of all armies, even those with ample manpower, lost strength significantly during periods of intense fighting.

The units and formations shown on the maps in *The Times Atlas of the Second World War* are adapted from standard NATO symbols. The size and organization of formations shown on the maps reflects the order of battle at the beginning of any particular action. In certain instances, the size of a military unit has been rationalized to give a clear indication of the numbers of combatants involved.

KEY TO MAP SYMBOLS

Many of the colours and symbols used in this atlas are common to each map. This general key should be used as a guide to understanding them. Exceptions and additional symbols are keyed on the individual maps.

National colours

land colours	arrow/unit/ symbol colours	
		British & Commonwealth
		American
		French
		Russian
		Chinese
		German/German satellites
		Italian
		Japanese
		others, specified on map

Military weaponry

- bomber
- fighter bomber
- fighter
- troop carrier
- heavy aircraft carrier
- light aircraft carrier
- battleship
- heavy cruiser
- light cruiser
- destroyer
- patrol/escort vessel
- auxiliary vessel
- landing craft
- merchantman
- oil tanker
- submarine

General military symbols
(mostly coloured according to nationality)

- army/navy movement
- retreat (unless otherwise specified)
- air track
- defensive positions
- air raid (coloured according to nationality of raider)
- airborne landing
- sinking (coloured according to nationality of vessel)
- minefield
- storage depot
- gun emplacement
- battle

Military units: types

- infantry
- cavalry
- armour
- airborne
- naval troops
- airforce unit

Military units: sizes

XXXXX / NAME/NUMBER / COMMANDER	army group
XXXX / NAME/NUMBER / COMMANDER	army/fleet/air force
XXX / TYPE/NUMBER	corps (number in roman numerals)
XX / TYPE	division (nationality/number in arabic numerals outside unit box)
X / TYPE	brigade (nationality/number in arabic numerals outside unit box)
III / TYPE	regiment
II / TYPE	battalion

e.g. the German Army Group South, commanded by Rundstedt appears as:

XXXXX
SOUTH
RUNDSTEDT

the 9th Australian armoured division appears as:

XX
9 AUS.

- xxx —— boundary between units (with appropriate size qualification)
- army base
- airforce base
- naval base

General cartographic symbols

- o village/town/city
- built-up area
- road
- railway
- river
- canal
- national border
- temporary/altered border
- swamp/marsh
- oilfield
- compass direction showing orientation of map

W EUROPE

1919
JUNE 28 Treaty of Versailles

1920
League of Nations assembles at Geneva

1923
JANUARY 11 French and Belgians occupy the Ruhr
NOVEMBER 8 Munich *Putsch* fails; Hitler imprisoned

1925
APRIL 26 Hindenburg becomes President of Germany
JULY 18 Mein Kampf published in Munich
DECEMBER 1 Germany, France and Belgium pledge non-aggression in Locarno Pact

1926
SEPTEMBER 8 Germany admitted to League of Nations

1929
JUNE Hitler opposes Young Plan on reparation; becomes national figure

1930
SEPTEMBER 14 German Election – the Nazi party becomes the second largest

1932
MARCH/APRIL Hitler defeated in presidential elections. *Sturm Abteilung* (SA), radical Nazi para-military force, banned
JUNE 30 SA ban lifted
JULY Election. Nazis largest party but without majority

1933
JANUARY Hitler becomes Chancellor of National Coalition Government
FEBRUARY 27 Reichstag Fire; Nazis blame Communists and suspend civil liberties
MARCH 28 Enabling Act gives Hitler dictatorial powers
OCTOBER 14 Germany leaves League of Nations

1934
FEBRUARY 6 Fascist riots in Paris
JUNE 30 'Night of Long Knives' – Nazis purge SA
AUGUST 1 Hindenburg dies. Hitler becomes *Führer* and Supreme Commander
OCTOBER 1 Hitler orders creation of air force, and expansion of army and navy
23 London Disarmament Conference

1935
JANUARY 13 Saar votes to return to Germany
FEBRUARY 1 Anglo-German Conference in London
MARCH 7 Saar restored to Germany
16 Germany repudiates disarmament clauses in Versailles Treaty

JUNE 18 Anglo-German Naval Pact

SEPTEMBER 15 Anti-Jewish Nuremberg Laws. Swastika becomes official German flag

N & E EUROPE

1922
APRIL 16 Rapallo Pact between Germany and USSR

1934
JANUARY 26 German-Polish non-aggression pact
JULY 25 Austrian Nazi assassination of Chancellor Dolfuss
SEPTEMBER 18 USSR joins League of Nations
OCTOBER 9 King Alexander of Yugoslavia assassinated

1935

MAY 2 Franco-Soviet Mutual Assistance Pact
MAY 16 Czech-Soviet Pact

MEDITERRANEAN & AFRICA

1922
OCTOBER 30 March on Rome. Mussolini becomes Italian Prime Minister

1935
JANUARY 7 Franco-Italian agreement

JUNE 3 Mussolini rejects British concessions on Ethiopia

OCTOBER 3 Italy invades Ethiopia

MAINLAND ASIA

1924
JANUARY 21 First National Congress of the Kuomintang

1927
APRIL 18 Nationalist government established at Nanking under Chiang Kai-shek

1931
SEPTEMBER 18 Mukden Incident. Japanese occupy Manchuria
1932
JANUARY 28 Shanghai riots; Japanese take control of the city

1933
FEBRUARY 23 (to 12 March) Japanese occupy China north of Great Wall
March 1 Japanese establish puppet state of Manchukuo under Chief Executive, Pu Yi

1934
OCTOBER (to Nov. 1935) Long March of the Chinese Communists

1935

DECEMBER 1 Chiang Kai-shek elected Chinese president (Nanking Government). Anti-Japanese riots by Peking students

PACIFIC & OCEANIA

1930
MAY 15 Japanese Prime Minister assassinated for supporting London Treaty

1933
MARCH 27 Japan leaves League of Nations

1934
DECEMBER 19 Japanese refuse to be bound by additions to the Washington Naval Treaty

ATLANTIC & AMERICAS

1920
USA absent from League of Nations

1928
AUGUST 27 Kellogg-Briand Pact; USA, Great Britain, Germany. Italy and Japan pledge non-aggression

1930
APRIL 22 London Naval Treaty restricts warship construction

1935

DECEMBER 24 US Neutrality Act passed

W EUROPE	N & E EUROPE	MEDITERRANEAN & AFRICA	MAINLAND ASIA	PACIFIC & OCEANIA	ATLANTIC & AMERICAS
1936 **MARCH 7** Germany reoccupies the Rhineland **31** British Civil Defence opens anti-gas school **JULY 18** Spanish Civil War starts **AUGUST 24** Compulsory 2-year military service in Germany **OCTOBER 14** Belgium ends military alliance with France	**1936** **MARCH 23** Italy, Austria and Hungary sign Rome Pact	**1936** **MAY 26** Anglo-Egyptian Alliance **AUGUST 3** Italy annexes Ethiopia **OCTOBER 25** Berlin-Rome Axis agreement	**1936** **APRIL 8** USSR-Mongolia Mutual Assistance Treaty **DECEMBER 12** Sian Incident-Chiang Kai-shek declares war on Japan	**1936** **JANUARY 15** Japan leaves London Naval Conference **FEBRUARY 16** Military faction appoints Hiroto Japanese Prime Minister **NOVEMBER 25** German-Japanese Anti-Comintern Pact	**1936** **MARCH 25** Great Britain, USA and France sign London Naval Convention **NOVEMBER 1** Roosevelt becomes US President **DECEMBER 1** Pan-American Peace Conference in Buenos Aires
1937 **FEBRUARY 8** Franco's forces take Málaga **APRIL 27** Axis bombing destroys Guernica **MAY 28** Chamberlain becames British Prime Minister **JUNE 12** Heydrich issues 'Racial Violence' decrees **JULY 17** Anglo-German Naval agreement **SEPTEMBER 25-28** Mussolini visits Berlin **NOVEMBER 5** Air Raid Precautions Bill introduced in British House of Commons **17-21** Lord Halifax meets Hitler on Sudetenland issue	**1937** **JANUARY 24** Bulgarian-Yugoslav Peace Treaty **JUNE 12** Stalin purges Russian generals **OCTOBER 16** Fascist Party formed in Hungary **NOVEMBER 20** Italo-Austro-Hungarian Pact extended	**1937** **MARCH 25** Italy-Yugoslav 5-year assistance pact **NOVEMBER 6** Italy joins Anti-Comintern Pact **DECEMBER 11** Italy withdraws from the League of Nations	**1937** **JULY 7** Sino-Japanese War starts **28** Japanese seize Peking **NOVEMBER 9** Japanese take Shanghai **DECEMBER 12-13** Japanese take Nanking and massacre population	**1937** **JUNE 1** Prince Konoye becomes Japanese Prime Minister and Hiroto Foreign Minister	**1937** **MAY 1** Roosevelt signs US Neutrality Act
1938 **MARCH 12** The *Anschluss*: German troops enter Austria **APRIL 15** Franco's troops take Vinaroz Republican Spain severed in two **AUGUST 12** Germany mobilizes **SEPTEMBER 30** Great Britain, France, Germany and Italy agree to transfer of Sudetenland to Germany **NOVEMBER 9** *Kristallnacht* anti-Jewish pogrom **DECEMBER 6** Franco-German Non-aggression pact	**1938** **APRIL 23** Sudeten Germans demand full autonomy **SEPTEMBER 7** Sudeten Germans break off talks with Czech government **22** Czech government resigns **OCTOBER 1** Germans enter Sudetenland **5** President Beneš resigns	**1938** **APRIL 16** Anglo-Italian Pact **27** Greco-Turkish Treaty **MAY 3-9** Hitler visits Mussolini in Rome **17** Anglo-Turkish agreement secures Turkish neutrality **DECEMBER 17** Italy denounces 1935 agreement with France	**1938** **MARCH 28** Japanese instal puppet government in Nanking **JULY 11** Russo-Japanese clash on border of Manchuria (Manchukuo) **OCTOBER 21** Japanese take Canton **25** Japanese take Hankow		
1939 **JANUARY 26** Franco's troops take Barcelona **27** Great Britain and France recognize Franco's government **APRIL 7** Germany, Italy, Spain and Japan sign Anti-Comintern Pact **MAY 22** German-Italian Pact of Steel **23** Nazi-Soviet Non-aggression (Molotov) Pact signed **AUGUST 26** Hitler guarantees neutrality of Belgium, Holland, Luxembourg and Sweden **31** British fleet mobilizes; 1.5m women and children evacuated from London **SEPTEMBER 3** Great Britain, France, New Zealand and Australia declare war on Germany **10** BEF moves to France **12** Chamberlain rejects Hitler's peace plans **30** General Sikorski sets up Polish government in exile in Paris **OCTOBER 14** HMS *Royal Oak* sunk in Scapa Flow by *U.47* **NOVEMBER 18** German magnetic mines inflict heavy damage on British shipping **23** Magnetic mine analyzed by British: counter-measures taken	**1939** **FEBRUARY** Hungary joins Anti-Comintern Pact **MARCH 15-16** Germany dismembers Czechoslovakia **22** Germans annexe Memel **23** Poland rejects German proposals on Danzig. Nazi-Soviet Pact signed, containing clauses about the partition of Poland **AUGUST 23** Anglo-Polish Mutual Assistance Pact **SEPTEMBER 1** Germans invade Poland, annex Danzig; Great Britain and France demand withdrawal **5** Germans cross R. Vistula **17** Russians invade eastern Poland **23** German-Russian demarcation line reached **27** Warsaw surrenders **29** Partition of Poland **OCTOBER 6** End of fighting in Poland **12** First deportation of Austrian and Czech Jews to Poland **NOVEMBER 30** USSR invades Finland **DECEMBER 22** Strong Finnish counter-attack **29** Finnish victory at Suommusalmi	**1939** **APRIL 7** Italy occupies Albania **29** Spain joins Anti-Comintern Pact **AUGUST 2** Wavell made Commander-in-Chief in Near East **SEPTEMBER 3** Wavell's command extended to E.Africa, Iraq and Persian Gulf	**1939** **FEBRUARY 10** Japanese take Hainan **JUNE 14** Japanese blockade British concession at Tientsin **AUGUST 23** Nazi-Soviet Non-aggression (Molotov) Pact signed	**1939** **APRIL 7** Germany, Italy, Spain and Japan sign Anti-Comintern Pact **AUGUST 25** Japan quits Anti-Comintern Pact	**1939** **SEPTEMBER 5** USA neutrality **10** Canada declares war on Germany. Battle of the Atlantic begins. Allied losses: 53 ships for 2 U-boats; 41 of 153,800 tons to U-boats **30** *Graf Spee* sinks first ship **OCTOBER 27** US Neutrality Bill passed in Senate. Allied shipping losses: 196,000 tons for 5 U-boats **NOVEMBER** Allied shipping losses: 21 ships of 51,600 tons **DECEMBER 13** Battle of River Plate **16** *Graf Spee* scuttled. Allied shipping losses: 73 ships of 189,900 tons, U-boats sink 25 for loss of 1

W EUROPE

JANUARY

4 Goering takes control of German war production
8 Butter, bacon and sugar rationed in Great Britain

15 Belgium refuses Allied request to pass through her territory

FEBRUARY
1-28 British *Ultra* team breaks *Enigma* Code

14 British arm merchant ships in North Sea
15 Germany announces she will treat them as warships

27 Churchill claims half of German U-boat fleet destroyed

MARCH
1 French government offers to purchase 'heavy water' from Norway

10 Exiled German scientists produce atom plans in Britain
11 Meat rationing begins in Great Britain

18 Hitler and Mussolini meet at the Brenner Pass
19 RAF bomb installations at Hörnum

31 First German armed merchant ship *Atlantis* begins cruise
APRIL
2 German planes raid Scapa Flow. RAF takes decision to conduct bombing operations at night

27 Men aged 26 registered for military service in Great Britain

MAY

5 Norwegian government in exile set up in London
10 Chamberlain resigns; Churchill new Prime Minister. Germany attacks Holland, Belgium and Luxembourg
11 Rapid German advances. Fort Eben Emael taken by airborne assault
14 German air raid on Rotterdam
15 Holland capitulates; government in exile set up in London. German forces cross R.Meuse
18 Antwerp captured
20 Somme battle: German forces reach the Channel
26 Dunkirk evacuation begins
27 Belgian army capitulates

JUNE
3 Dunkirk evacuation ends; 350,000 rescued
4 Germans take 40,000 prisoners at Dunkirk

14 Germans enter Paris
16 Reynaud resigns; Marshal Pétain forms new French government

22 Franco-German Armistice signed (effective 25th) at Compiègne
23 First British Commando raid on Boulogne
28 Britain recognizes General de Gaulle as Free French leader
30 Germans occupy Guernsey

N & E EUROPE

JANUARY
1 Russian offensive against Finns

8-12 Finnish successes in Karelian Isthmus

FEBRUARY
1 Russians attack in Karelia

11 German-Soviet economic pact
12 Finnish defences crack

15-16 *Altmark* incident
17 Finns retreat

MARCH

5-12 Finns negotiate with Russians

13 Treaty of Moscow ends the 'Winter War'

29 Molotov announces Soviet neutrality
APRIL

7 Allied forces sail for Norway

9 Germans occupy Denmark, invade Norway
10-13 Two battles at Narvik, RN sinks German destroyer force (10)

16-19 Allied landings near Namsos: British are driven back

30 King Haakon of Norway evacuated
MAY
1 Norway surrenders
2 Allies evacuate Namsos

8 Timoshenko becomes Soviet Defence Commisar

13 Allied landings near Narvik

28 Allies take Narvik
29 German-Rumanian arms and oil pact
JUNE

4-8 Allies evacuate Norway

10 Norway capitulates

18 Russians begin to occupy Baltic states

28 Russians occupy Bessarabia and Bukovina

MEDITERRANEAN & AFRICA

FEBRUARY

12 Australian and New Zealand troops land at Suez

MAY

16 British Admiralty closes Mediterranean to merchant shipping

JUNE

10 Italy declares war on Britain and France
11-29 Italian air raids on Malta

MAINLAND ASIA

JUNE

20 France allows Japanese military mission into northern Indo-China

24 France closes Indo-Chinese frontier

PACIFIC & OCEANIA

JUNE

18 British gold carrier *Aliagara* sunk off Auckland, New Zealand

ATLANTIC & AMERICAS

JANUARY
Allied shipping losses: 73 ships of 214,500 tons

FEBRUARY
Allied shipping losses: 226,900 tons, 45 ships of 169,500 tons to U-boats

MARCH
U-boat losses (3) and redeployment reduces shipping losses to 45

APRIL
Allied shipping losses: 58 of 158,200 tons. U-boats only sink 7 ships and lose 5 in Norwegian campaign

MAY

31 Roosevelt's 'Million-Dollar' defence programme. Allied shipping losses: 101 ships of 288,400 tons. U-boats only sink 13 of 55,500
JUNE
Allied shipping losses: 140 ships of 585,500 tons, many in association with the Dunkirk evacuation, 58 ships of 284,100 tons to U-boats

W EUROPE	N & E EUROPE	MEDITERRANEAN & AFRICA	MAINLAND ASIA	PACIFIC & OCEANIA	ATLANTIC & AMERICAS
JULY	**JULY**	**JULY**	**JULY**	**JULY**	**JULY**
10 Battle of Britain begins. *Luftwaffe* attack Channel convoys **11** Pétain becomes head of French State	**5** Rumania establishes closer links with Axis				**5** U-boats extend campaign in Atlantic
21 Czech government in exile set up in London	**14** Russia absorbs Lithuania, Latvia and Estonia		**18** Britain closes Burma Road	**16** Prince Konoye becomes Japanese Prime Minister	**17** All Atlantic convoys routed north of Ireland **19** Roosevelt signs 'Two Navy Expansion Act'. Allied shipping losses: 105 ships, 38 to U-boats; beginning of the 'Happy Time' for U-boats (23 in training)
		30 French North African and Syrian armies demobilized	**27** Arrest of British subjects in Japan		
AUGUST		**AUGUST**	**AUGUST**	**AUGUST**	**AUGUST**
		3-19 Italy occupies British Somaliland	**9** Britain agrees to withdraw troops from Shanghai and north China	**1** Japanese establish New Order in Far East	
12 Portsmouth heavily bombed **13** Eagle Day of Battle of Britain					
15 Mass daylight raids over England					**16** U-51 sunk by depth charge from plane **17** Hitler declares blockade of British Isles. Allied shipping losses: 397,200 tons, 256 ships of 267,600 tons to U-boats
19 Hitler's peace terms rejected by Great Britain					
25 First RAF raid on Berlin					
SEPTEMBER	**SEPTEMBER**	**SEPTEMBER**	**SEPTEMBER**	**SEPTEMBER**	**SEPTEMBER**
3 Hitler plans invasion of Britain – Operation *Sea Lion* (for 21st) **7** Battle of London – 'The Blitz' begins	**4-15** General Antonescu organizes coup in Rumania		**13** Japanese *Zero* fighters have great success in first action		**3** Britain receives 50 US destroyers in return for granting US leases on naval bases on Bermuda, Jamaica, Trinidad, British Guiana and Newfoundland
15 Battle of Britain Sunday		**13** Italians invade Egypt, take Sollum			**16** US Conscription Bill passed
17 Hitler postpones Operation *Sea Lion*					**20-22** U-boat Wolf Packs attack Convoy HX-72 sinking 12 ships of 78,000 tons. Allied losses: 100 ships of 448,600 tons, 59 to U-boats
	25 Quisling government in Norway	**23-25** Abortive Gaullist coup at Dakar	**22** Japanese forces enter Indo-China	**26** US bans iron exports to Japan **27** Germany, Italy and Japan sign Tripartite Pact	
27 Germany, Italy and Japan sign Tripartite (Axis) Pact **29** 'Mother and Child' evacuation; 500,000 leave London		**27** Germany, Italy and Japan sign Tripartite Pact			
OCTOBER	**OCTOBER**	**OCTOBER**	**OCTOBER** **1** Japanese occupy Weihaiwei	**OCTOBER**	**OCTOBER**
	7 Germans enter Rumania		**8** Churchill announces re-opening of Burma Road		
12 Hitler postpones *Sea Lion* until Spring 1941					
15 400-bomber raid on London			**18** Japanese bomb Burma Road		**17-19** Convoy SC-7 loses 21 of 30 ships to U-boats **19-20** Convoy HX-79 loses 12 of 49 ships. Allied shipping losses: 103 ships of 443,000 tons, 352,400 to U-boats
	20 Hungary signs Tripartite Pact				
	22 Slovakia joins Pact; first deportation of Jews from Alsace-Lorraine and Rhineland to Poland				
NOVEMBER	**NOVEMBER** **1** Jews forbidden to leave walled Warsaw ghetto	**28** Italians invade Greece **29** British troops sail for Crete **NOVEMBER**	**NOVEMBER**	**NOVEMBER**	**NOVEMBER**
7 RAF raids Krupp works in Essen		**11-12** Taranto Raid; Fleet Air Arm cripples Italian fleet			**5** Roosevelt re-elected US President for fourth term
14 Coventry bombing opens Night Blitz – Germans use *Knickebein* radar system for greater accuracy		**14** Greeks throw Italians back into Albania			**15** US flying boats begin patrols from Bermuda
19 Heavy bombing of Birmingham		**22** Greeks defeat Italian 9th Army			**18-19** Sunderland flying boat detects U-boat using ASV1 radar for first time. Allied shipping losses: 97 ships of 385,000 tons, 32 to U-boats
28 300 planes bomb Liverpool	**29** Draft plan for German Eastern campaign		**30** Japanese and Nanking governments sign treaty		
DECEMBER	**DECEMBER**	**DECEMBER**			**DECEMBER** Allied shipping losses: 82, of which U-boats only sink 37 owing to bad weather
8 400-plane fire raid on London		**6** Badoglio resigns. Cavallo becomes Italian Commander-in-Chief			
		9 British Western desert offensive Operation *Compass*			
		11 British capture Sidi Barrani			
20 Heavy raid on Liverpool	**18** Secret Hitler memo on Operation *Barbarossa*	**17** British reoccupy Sollum			
23 Eden becomes Foreign Secretary					**23** Lord Halifax Ambassador in Washington **25** *Admiral Hipper* driven off from troop convoy. Allied shipping losses, year total: 1,059 ships of 4,055,706 tons
29 Worst fire raid on London to date					

W EUROPE

FEBRUARY

3 German battle cruisers *Scharnhorst* and *Gneisenau* break into North Sea in Operation *Berlin*

11 Darlan appointed deputy and successor to Pétain

24 Britain agrees to send forces to Greece

MARCH
1 RAF 1000-bomber raid on Cologne; first use of AI air-to-air radar

13 Devastating night raids on Glasgow and Clydeside leave two-thirds of the population homeless

MAY
1-9 Liverpool Blitz

10 Climax of London Blitz. Hess flies to Scotland

15 Gloster E28/39 flight powered by Whittle jet engine

JUNE
2 Vichy government orders census of Jews

13 12,000 Jews 'interned' in France

N & E EUROPE

MARCH
1 Bulgaria joins Axis and German troops enter country

4 Commando raid on Lofoten Is. (Norway)

19 German ultimatum to Yugoslavia

25 Yugoslavia signs Tripartite Pact
27 Coup in Yugoslavia

APRIL
6 Germans invade Yugoslavia
10 Germans capture Zagreb
12 Germans take Belgrade
17 Yugoslav army capitulates

JUNE

22 Germany invades Russia. Italy and Rumania declare war on USSR.
23 Hungary and Slovakia declare war on USSR.
23 Hungary and Slovakia.
23 Germans cross R.Bug. Destruction of Soviet Air Force
26 Finland declares war on USSR
28 Germans capture Minsk
30 Germans encircle Russian forces in Bialystok 'pocket'

MEDITERRANEAN & AFRICA

JANUARY
1-2 British sea and air bombardment of Bardia

5 Australians capture Bardia; 48,000 prisoners

11 HMS *Southampton* sunk by Stuka attack

22 Tobruk falls to British and Australians; 25,000 prisoners

FEBRUARY

2 Rommel arrives in Tripoli
7 Italian collapse at Beda Fomm
6 British and Australians take Benghazi

10 Mussolini accepts offer of a German armoured division, British forces advance into East Africa
12 Rommel arrives in Tripoli
14 German troops join him

25 British forces occupy Mogadishu

MARCH
1 Free French forces capture Kufra Oasis

7 British and Australian forces land in Greece
9-25 Greeks repel Italian counter-offensive in Albania

28-29 Battle of Cape Matapan RN sinks 3 Italian cruisers
30 Afrika Korps offensive in Cyrenaica

APRIL
1 Raschid Ali seizes power in Iraq
4 Afrika Korps captures Benghazi
6 Germans invade Greece and Yugoslavia
13 Rommel's forces surround Tobruk
16 German troop convoy wiped out off Kerkennah Is.
22 Greek army surrenders to Germans at Thessalonika; British withdrawal begins
24 Germans break through at Thermopylae
25 Germans occupy Halfaya pass
27 Germans enter Athens. British evacuate Greece
28 Germans take Sollum
30 Iraqi troops surround RAF base at Habbaniya

MAY
1 German attack on Tobruk repulsed
2 Iraq demands British withdrawal
5-9 *Tiger* convoy carries tanks to Alexandria
6-10 British forces defeat Iraqis and march on Baghdad

15 Operation *Brevity*: British retake Sollum and Halfaya
20-31 Operation *Merkur*: German invasion of Crete. 6000 paratroops dropped

30 Iraqi revolt ends

31 British thrown out of Crete

JUNE
1 British enter Baghdad
5 Germans claim 15,000 prisoners on Crete
8 British, Australian, Indian and Free French forces invade Syria
11 Italians occupy Greece
14-17 British Operation *Battleaxe* fails to relieve Tobruk
21 Free French occupy Damascus. Auchinleck replaces Wavell as Commander-in-Chief in Middle East

MAINLAND ASIA

FEBRUARY

19 Australian 8th Division lands in Singapore

APRIL

21 Japanese occupy Foochow

MAY

9 Thailand and French Indo-China sign peace treaty in Tokyo

14 British reinforcements land in Singapore

PACIFIC & OCEANIA

FEBRUARY

27 New Zealand cruiser sinks Italian ship off Maldives

APRIL

13 Japan and USSR sign 5-year neutrality pact, freeing Soviet forces to fight the Germans

MAY

8 RN cruiser *Cornwall* sinks German raider *Pinguin* near Seychelles

JUNE

11 USSR-Japanese trade pact

17 Japanese-Dutch negotiations fail

27 Japan declares 'Greater East Asia Co-prosperity Sphere'

ATLANTIC & AMERICAS

JANUARY
1-23 First Washington Conference

10 Lend-Lease Bill introduced to Congress

20 Roosevelt's third inauguration. Allied shipping losses: 76 ships of 320,200 tons, 21 to U-boats

FEBUARY
1-14 German Pocket battleship *Admiral Hipper* sinks 7 ships in raid from Brest

MARCH

6 Churchill gives Battle of Atlantic Directive
7 HMS *Wolverine* sinks U-47
8 Senate passes Lend-Lease Bill
11 Roosevelt signs Lend-Lease Bill

16-17 U-99 and U-100 sunk
22 End of Operation *Berlin*, Germans sink 22 vessels

30 US Navy begins to patrol west Atlantic. Allied shipping losses: 139 ships of 529,700 tons, 41 to U-boats, 41 to aircraft, with 6 U-boats sunk

APRIL
4 German raider *Thor* sinks armed merchant cruiser *Voltaire*

11 USN covers to 26° W, British cover to 35° W
15 RAF Coastal Command under RN control increases cover. Allied shipping losses: 195 ships of 687,000 tons, 43 to U-boats, 116 to aircraft

MAY

7 Captured German ship provides secret *Enigma* code papers
9 Captured U-boat provides British with *Hydra* naval code

18-27 Voyage of the *Prinz Eugen* and *Bismarck*

24 They engage *Hood* and *Prince of Wales*; *Hood* sunk
27 *Bismarck* sunk
27 Newfoundland Escort Force accompanies convoy HX-129. Allied shipping losses: 139 ships, 58 of 325,500 tons to U-boats

JUNE
1 *Prinz Eugen* reaches Brest. US Coastguard begins patrols from southern Greenland

23-29 Battle of Convoy HX-133, 5 ships lost for 2 U-boats (out of 10). Allied shipping losses: 109 ships of 432,000 tons, 61 ships of 310,000 tons to U-boats

W EUROPE

JULY

8 First daylight raid by RAF 'Flying Fortresses' on Wilhelmshaven

16 RAF bomb shipping in Rotterdam
19 BBC broadcasts 'V' for Victory declaring Resistance in occupied Europe

AUGUST

7 RAF fighter-sweeps over northern France begin

18 National Fire Service formed in Britain

OCTOBER

20 German commander of Nantes shot by Resistance; 50 hostages shot in reprisal

NOVEMBER

18 Sir Alan Brooke appointed Chief of the Imperial General Staff

N & E EUROPE

JULY

1 Germans capture Riga
3 Stalin calls for 'scorched earth' policy in broadcast
4 Tito announces resistance in Yugoslavia
8 Germany and Italy partition Yugoslavia
10 Germans cross R.Dnieper.

12 Anglo-Soviet Mutual Assistance Agreement
15 Germans capture Smolensk
21 Moscow bombed
22 German advance halted through exhaustion

31 Hitler's 'Final solution' order

AUGUST

5 Siege of Odessa begins

7 Stalin becames Supreme Commander

16 Germans take Novgorod

19 Germans surround Leningrad

24 Finns surround Russians at Viipuri

29 Russians evacuate Karelian Isthmus
SEPTEMBER
1 Russians counter-attack at Gomel
2 Three Power Conference in Moscow (to 29th)
3 First use of Auschwitz gas chambers
5 Germans occupy Estonia

12 First snows slow German offensive
15 Siege of Leningrad begins
16 Germans to shoot 50 to 100 hostages in retaliation for the death of one of their own
19 Germans take Kiev and Poltava

25 German paratroops land in Crimea
30 Massacre of Jews at Kiev
OCTOBER

7 Panzers seal off Briansk and Vyazma pockets
8 Germans take Orel
10 Britain to supply USSR on Lend-Lease terms
14 Deportation of German Jews to Poland
16 Germans take Odessa. Soviet government moved to Kuibyshev
20 Germans take Briansk
21 General Zhukov takes charge of Moscow defence
24 Germans take Kharkov
27 Russians counter-attack at Moscow
29 Germans break through in Crimea

NOVEMBER
1 Germans take Simferopol. Marshal Shaposhnikov becomes Soviet Chief of Staff
2 Tito's partisans and Chetniks fight each other in Yugoslavia
3 Germans capture Kursk
9 Germans take Yalta
15 German advance halted by extreme cold
16 Germans take Kerch

22 Germans take Rostov
25 German attack on Moscow, Panzers get within 20 miles of city
28 Germans lose Rostov

DECEMBER
5 Germans abandon attack on Moscow

17 Hitler issues 'Halt Order' on general offensive
19 Hitler assumes direct command of armies in field

29 Russians retake Kerch

MEDITERRANEAN & AFRICA

JULY

3 End of Vichy resistance in Syria

11 Ceasefire in Syria

14 Acre Convention between Allied and Vichy forces

26 Italian E-boats attack Valetta harbour
31 (to 2 Aug.) *Style* convoy reinforces Malta garrison

AUGUST

25-28 British and Russians enter Persia to secure oil supply

SEPTEMBER

4 Heavy air raids on Malta

9 RAF raids Turin. Persian government accepts Anglo-Soviet terms
15 Hitler orders U-boats to operate in the Mediterranean

20 Italian 'human torpedoes' sink 3 British ships at Gibraltar
23-28 *Halberd* convoy to Malta

OCTOBER
RAF night raids:
4 on Benghazi
5 on Tripoli
6 on Piraeus

NOVEMBER

8-9 British force K from Malta destroys Italian convoy
14 RN carrier *Ark Royal* sunk by U-boat
17 Keyes Raid - abortive Commando raid on Rommel's HQ
18 8th Army launches Operation *Crusader*
20 Tank battle at Sidi Rezegh
23 Afrika Korps destroys S.African 5th Brigade but is forced to retreat
27 Mass Italian surrender at Gondar, Ethiopia
29 Rommel counter-attacks
DECEMBER

10-11 Siege of Tobruk raised; Rommel retreats to Gazala

14-23 Convoy HG76 reaches Malta
16 British advance to Gazala; Rommel retreats to El Agheila

25 British retake Benghazi

MAINLAND ASIA

JULY

28 Japanese troops land in Indo-China to occupy Vichy bases

AUGUST

8-13 Japanese air-raids on Chungking

SEPTEMBER

28 Japanese occupy Changsha

NOVEMBER

28 *Prince of Wales* and *Repulse* arrive at Colombo
DECEMBER

7 Japanese land in Siam and Malaya, bomb Singapore

10 Japanese sink *Repulse* and *Prince of Wales*

15 British forces fall back in Burma, Malaya and Kowloon

18 Japanese land on Hong Kong

25 Hong Kong surrenders

PACIFIC & OCEANIA

JULY

10 Germany urges Japan to fight USSR

16 Japanese Cabinet resigns

AUGUST

5 US and Great Britain impose embargoes on sale of raw materials to Japan

SEPTEMBER

13 Japanese Combined Fleet on exercises

18 Japanese prepare Southern Area operation

OCTOBER

17 Konoye resigns, Tojo takes over

20 Japanese prepare Pearl Harbor attack

26 Japanese carrier fleet sets sail

NOVEMBER

19 HMAS *Sidney* fights German raider *Kormoran*; both sink

25 USN begins compulsory convoying of merchant ships
29 Japan decides on war
DECEMBER

7 Japanese bomb Pearl Harbor, declare war on US

10 Japanese land on Luzon, capture Guam

17 Japanese land in North Borneo

22 Japanese land in Lingayen Gulf
24 Japanese capture Wake I.
25 Hong Kong falls to Japanese. Allied shipping losses: 430,000 tons

ATLANTIC & AMERICAS

JULY

1 USN aircraft start anti-sub patrols from Newfoundland

7 US Marines arrive in Iceland

19 USN TF1 protects all ships sailing to Iceland

26 Japanese assets frozen in US and UK. Allied shipping losses: 121,000 tons, 22 of 94,200 to U-boats

AUGUST
1 US oil embargo against 'aggressor' states

9-12 Placentia Bay Conference
12 Atlantic Charter signed by Roosevelt and Churchill

19 (to 3 Sept.) British Spitzbergen expedition
27 U-570 captured by Coastal Command bomber. Allied shipping losses: 41 ships of 130,700 tons, 23 of 80,300 to U-boats
SEPTEMBER

4 USS *Greer* attacked by U-boat

11 US Navy told to 'shoot on sight'

15 U-boats diverted to Mediterranean
20 First successful shooting-down of German plane from escort carrier HMS *Audacity* (OG-74 still loses 6 from 27)
29 British convoy PQ1 Reykjavik to Archangel. 84 ships of 285,900 tons lost. 53 to U-boats.

OCTOBER

16-17 U-boat damages US destroyer *Kearney*

31 U-boat sinks US destroyer *Reuben James*, first American loss. Allied shipping losses: 218,300 tons, 156,500 tons to U-boats
NOVEMBER

3 HMS *Indomitable* carrier intended for Far East damaged at Bermuda
6 Roosevelt announces $1bn loan to USSR

22 HMS *Devonshire* sinks German raider *Atlantis* off West African coast

30 British bomber sinks *U-206* using ASV radar. Allied shipping losses: 104,600 tons, 13 ships of 62,200 to U-boats
DECEMBER

8 Allies declare war on Japan. USSR remains neutral

11 US declares war on Italy and Germany

14-23 Convoy HG-76 Gibraltar to London fights off 12 U-boat attack (5 sunk) for the loss of escort carrier *Audacity*
22 (to 7 Jan.) Churchill and Roosevelt decide strategy at the Arcadia Conference in Washington. Allies shipping losses: 153,000 tons, year total: 1229 ships of 4,300,000 tons

W EUROPE

JANUARY

18 Germany, Italy and Japan sign new military pact

FEBRUARY

4 Lord Beaverbrook becomes British Minister of Production
8 Speer made German Arms Minister
11-12 *Scharnhorst* and *Gneisenau* reach Brest
14 Area bombing directive shifts RAF from specific to general urban targets

27 Bruneval commando raid captures secret 'W' system

MARCH

20 Midget submarine trials in Great Britain
24 Army Air Corps – paratroops and gliders – set up in Great Britain
28 Commando raid on St.Nazaire. RAF destroy Lübeck with aid of *Gee* radar system

APRIL

14 New Vichy government under Laval

23 *Baedeker* raids against Britain's cathedral cities begin
24 Germans smash spy ring 'A' in Paris

MAY

30 1000-bomber raid on Cologne

JUNE
1 Work begins at Peenemünde on V1 flying bomb

13 First V2 flight a failure

25 General Eisenhower made Commander-in-Chief Europe

N & E EUROPE

JANUARY

5 Russians control Kerch peninsula; Stalin orders general offensive

13 Russians recapture Kiev
15 *Tirpitz* sails to Norway

28 Timoshenko's forces advance in the Ukraine

FEBRUARY

13 Russian advance slows in White Russia

23 Russians reach R. Dnieper

MARCH
1 Russian offensive in Crimea

30 Russian counter-offensive ends; Germans much weakened

MAY

8 German Summer offensive begins
9 Russians attack Kharkov

16-17 Germans capture Kerch and halt Russians east of Kharkov
20 Germans recapture Kerch peninsula

27 Attempted assasination of Heydrich in Prague (dies of wounds 4 June)
28 German victory at Kharkov

JUNE

5 Germans besiege Sevastopol

10 Reprisal massacre at Lidice for Heydrich's death

24 Tito's partisans driven into retreat
28 Axis summer offensive on southern front
30 Germans break into Sevastopol

MEDITERRANEAN & AFRICA

JANUARY

2 British and S.Africans recapture Bardia
5 British attack Halfaya

11 British recapture Sollum

17 Germans surrender in Cyrenaica

21 Rommel begins surprise attack to reconquer Cyrenaica

29 Germans recapture Benghazi
29 Anglo-Persian agreement
FEBRUARY

4 Germans take Derna
5 Rommel's advance halted at Gazala

MARCH

6 HMS *Eagle* carrier ferries 18 Spitfires to Malta

20-23 Second Alexandria convoy to Malta wiped out
22 British defeat Italians in naval battle at Sirte

APRIL

7 2000 plane air raid on Malta

16 Malta awarded George Cross

20 USS *Wasp* ferries Spitfires to Malta, but many are destroyed

MAY

5-6 British capture Madagascar

9 64 Spitfires arrive on Malta

26-30 Rommel attacks and outflanks Gazala line
28 Bir Hakeim tank battle - Free French hold out

JUNE

10 Free French retreat from Bir Hakeim
13 Gibraltar convoy *Harpoon* and Alexandria convoy *Vigorous* set out for Malta
16 *Harpoon* gets through, *Vigorous* turns back
17 British garrison Tobruk and retreat to Egypt
20-21 Germans attack and take Tobruk
25 Auchinleck made Commander-in-Chief in Desert
30 Germans reach El Alamein

MAINLAND ASIA

JANUARY

7 Japanese defeated by Chinese at Changsha, but break through into central Malaya
11 Japanese enter Kuala Lumpur

16 Japanese invade Burma from Siam

30 British withdraw into Singapore, destroying the causeway
FEBRUARY

7 Japanese land on Singapore I.

15 British surrender at Singapore: 130,000 prisoners

29 Britain promises full dominion status to India after the war
MARCH

8 Japanese enter Rangoon

10 General Stilwell appointed Chief of Staff in China

19 General Slim takes charge in Burma

APRIL

4 Fires sweep Mandalay after Japanese bombing

9 Japanese carriers attack Trincomalee. British warships sunk.

29 Japanese seize Lashio and cut Burma Road
30 Japanese control central Burma. Allied shipping losses: 150,000 tons in Indian Ocean
MAY
1 British evacuate Mandalay
2 British retreat over Irrawaddy

11 Japanese offensives in Yunnan and Chekiang provinces

20 Japanese take up defensive positions in Burma

24 General Stilwell arrives in Delhi after 20 days trek through jungle

JUNE

4 Japanese attack Chuhsien

PACIFIC & OCEANIA

JANUARY

2 Japanese occupy Manila and Cavite naval bases

11 Japanese capture Tarakan in Dutch East Indies

22 Japanese planes attack New Guinea; Americans retreat on Bataan
23 Japanese land on Rabaul
24 Battle of Macassar Strait
25 Australia mobilizes fully
26 Japanese land on Solomon Is.
FEBRUARY
1 US carrier attack on Gilbert and Marshall Is.

14 Japanese parachute drop on south Sumatra
19 Japanese invade Bali, carrier aircraft bomb Darwin
20 Japanese land on Portuguese Timor

27 Japanese win battle of Java Sea
28 Japanese invade Java. Allied shipping losses: 54 ships of 181,200 tons
MARCH
2 Japanese land on Mindanao

9 Dutch East Indies capitulates, General Yamashita appointed Commander-in-Chief in Philippines

18 Mountbatten appointed Chief of Combined Operations. Allied shipping losses: 252,000 tons

APRIL
1 Japanese land on Dutch New Guinea
3 New Japanese offensive on Bataan
4 Japanese sink HMSS *Dorsetshire*, *Cornwall*, *Hermes* and *Hollyhock* in Indian Ocean
9 General King surrenders at Bataan
11 (to 5 May) 'Bataan Death March'. Japanese bomb Trincomalee

18 Surprise 'Doolittle Raid': B25s bomb Japan

MAY

4-8 First carrier versus carrier battle of Coral Sea; Japanese lose the *Shoho*, US the *Lexington*
5-6 Japanese land on Corregidor and American garrison surrenders; General Wainwright surrenders all forces on the Philippines

30 US task force sets out for Midway
31 Japanese midget submarines fail in attack in Sidney harbour
JUNE
4 Battle of Midway; USN sinks 4 Japanese carriers and destroys 300 aircraft
7 Japanese invade Aleutian Is.

ATLANTIC & AMERICAS

JANUARY
1 UN Declaration signed by 26 nations in Washington
6 American forces to be stationed in Great Britain
13 German U-boats commence Operation *Paukenschlag* on east coast of America, sinking 150,000 tons
13 Conference of Allied governments pledges to punish war criminals
15-28 Rio de Janeiro Conference

25 America mobilizes
27 Formation of Chief of Staffs Committee. Allied shipping losses: 106 ships of 419,900 tons
FEBRUARY

6 Announcement of British and US joint command in Washington

16 German U-boats shell oil installations on Aruba; also sink 3 tankers

20 USA grants billion dollar loan to USSR
23 Signing of Mutual Aid agreement between Great Britain, USA, Australia and New Zealand. Allied shipping losses: 154 ships of 679,600, 85 of 476,500 to U-boats
MARCH

30 Pacific War Council set up in Washington. Allied shipping losses: 273 ships of 834,000 tons, 98 to U-boats
APRIL
1 Beginning of US convoy system

14 US destroyer *Roper* sinks first U-boat U 85

27 Roosevelt announces war economy measures. Allied shipping losses: 132 ships of 674,500 tons, 74 to U-boats
MAY
Allied shipping losses: 705,000 tons, 125 of 607,200 tons to U-boats

JUNE

18-19 Churchill in meeting with Roosevelt on Second Front and the Manhattan Project working on the atom bomb

27 Convoy PQ17 leaves Reykjavik. Allied shipping losses: 173 ships of 834,200 tons, 144 of 700,200 tons to U-boats

W EUROPE

JULY

18 First flight of Me262 jet fighter

AUGUST

15 *Pathfinder* force created in Great Britain
17 First all-American bombing raid in Europe
19 Dieppe raid; 6000 men suffer 50% casualties

OCTOBER

2 Successful V2 launch
4 British commando raid on Sark
7 Dieppe prisoners put in chains - British retaliate (rescinded 10 Dec.)

18 Hitler orders execution of all captured commandos

NOVEMBER

11 Darlan surrenders to Allies. Germans occupy southern France

DECEMBER

2 Beveridge Report plans Welfare State in Great Britain

7-12 Royal Marine Commando raids on Bordeaux and SW France (Cockleshell Heroes)

20 First operation using navigational radar aid *Oboe*

N & E EUROPE

JULY

3 Germans take Sevastopol
4 Germans reach R. Don on a wide front
4-9 Convoy PQ17 is attacked and scattered with two-thirds losses. Arctic convoys postponed

17 Germans take Voronezh

22 First deportations from Warsaw Ghetto to concentration camps; Treblinka opens

31 Germans cross R.Don on 150-mile front

AUGUST

9 Germans capture Krasnodar and Maikop
12 Germans advance in Kuban region; First Moscow Conference; Stalin and Churchill meet

19 General Paulus orders 6th Army to take Stalingrad

SEPTEMBER

1 Fierce fighting around Stalingrad

13-18 Allied Convoy PQ18 successful
13 'Final' German offensive at Stalingrad

OCTOBER

14 Hitler orders East Front troops to stand fast. Second 'Final' offensive at Stalingrad
22 Unsuccessful German assaults on Leningrad
26 Heavy fighting in Stalingrad

NOVEMBER

19 Russians counter-attack at Stalingrad, now with air superiority

23 German 6th Army surrounded

28 Russian offensive on Central Front

DECEMBER

16 Russian offensive on R.Don - Italian 8th Army collapses

28 Hitler withdraws Army Group A from the Caucasus
31 Russians advance to Zimovniki

MEDITERRANEAN & AFRICA

JULY

2 Germans driven back from El Alamein

14 Rommel attacks at Tel El Eisa; 8th Army counter-attacks at Ruweisat Ridge
14-19 Malta re-supplied and HMS *Eagle* flies in 31 spitfires

AUGUST

10-15 *Pedestal* convoy to Malta badly mauled; HMS *Eagle* sunk
13 Montgomery made Commander-in-Chief 8th Army
15 General Alexander takes charge of Middle East Forces

30 (to 2 Sept.) Battle of Alam Halfa

SEPTEMBER

18 British land in Eastern Madagasgar

30 8th Army probing attacks at El Alamein

OCTOBER

22 Heavy RAF raid on Turin
23 Beginning of Battle of El Alamein

27 8th Army regroups for breakout attack
28 RAF breaks up German tank formations south of El Alamein
30 Germans driven back

NOVEMBER

1 Operation *Supercharge* : breakout from El Alamein begins
4 Axis forces retreat
8 (to 29 Nov.) Operation *Torch* : US invasion of North Africa begins
11 Axis troops enter unoccupied France and Corsica
12 8th Army reaches Tobruk
15-18 Convoy *Stoneage* reaches Malta without opposition
18 8th Army enters Cyrene
20 Allies take Benghazi

25 SOE and Greek Resistance blow up Gorgopotamos railway bridge

DECEMBER

1-2 Italians recall 3 out of 4 supply convoys. 50% loss of supplies throughout month

13 Rommel withdraws from El Agheila

21 8th Army overtakes German rearguard at Sirte
25 8th Army occupies Sirte

MAINLAND ASIA

AUGUST

9 Gandhi is arrested

OCTOBER

19 US War Department offers to equip 30 more Chinese divisions

DECEMBER

17 Japanese withdraw to Gwedauk-Kondan line

21 British and Indian forces advance into Burma

PACIFIC & OCEANIA

JULY

12 Australians reach Kokoda

AUGUST

7 US Marines land on Guadalcanal
8 Battle of Savo I. US fleet defeated

21 Japanese driven back on Guadalcanal
23-24 Sea battle of east Solomon Is.

26 Japanese land at Milne Bay

SEPTEMBER

1 Tojo resigns as Japanese Foreign Minister
5 Australians force Japanese withdrawal from Milne Bay
11 Japanese halted in Owen Stanley Range
13 Japanese attack on Guadalcanal airfield heavily defeated
15 Japanese sink US aircraft carrier *Wasp*

29 Richard Sorge, Soviet master spy, convicted in Japan

OCTOBER

11-12 Battle of Cape Esperance off Guadalcanal
14-17 Australians meet heavy resistance on the Kokoda Trail

26 Battle of Santa Cruz off Guadalcanal, Japanese carrier *Yara* and USS *Hornet* sunk

NOVEMBER

2 Kokoda recaptured by Australians

30 (to 1 Dec.) Naval battle of Tassafaronga. Allied shipping losses: 131,000 tons

DECEMBER

14 Japanese reinforce New Guinea

31 Japanese plan to evacuate Guadalcanal

ATLANTIC & AMERICAS

JULY

19 German U-boats concentrate on Atlantic shipping. abandon US coast
21 Admiral Leahy becomes Roosevelt's Chief of Staff

30 Full conscription in Canada. Allied shipping losses: 128 ships of 618,100, 96 of 476,100 tons to U-boats, 11 U-boats sunk

AUGUST

22 Brazil declares war on Germany and Italy, providing bases for convoy protection. Allied shipping losses: 123 ships of 661,100 tons, 108 of 544,400 to U-boats

SEPTEMBER

9 First (and only) Japanese bombing of USA
10-14 Convoy ON-127 loses 12 ships to U-boat attack

23 First 'Liberty Ship' produced 10 days after laying keel
24 USS *Stephen Hopkins* fights German raider *Stier*, both ships sink. Allied shipping losses: 114 ships of 567,300 tons, 98 of 485,400 to U-boats

OCTOBER

7 UN Commission to investigate Axis war crimes

13 German sea-raider *Komet* sunk. Allied shipping losses: 637,800 tons, 94 ships of 619,000 to U-boats

NOVEMBER

4 Churchill co-ordinates anti-U-boat warfare

19 Admiral Horton takes over British Western Approaches Command. Allied shipping losses: 119 ships of 729,100 tons, nearly all to U-boats

DECEMBER

2 Professor Fermi sets up atomic reactor in Chicago

14 U-boat code *Triton* broken but information not available to operational units yet
17 UN declares Nazi crimes against the Jews will be avenged

31 Battle of Barents Sea - German surface fleet humiliated in attack on Convoy JW-51B. Hitler orders concentration on U-boats. Allied shipping losses: 60 of 330,000 tons to U-boats; year's total: 7,990,000; replacements 1m tons short

W EUROPE

JANUARY

14 (to Jan.24) Casablanca conference

16 First RAF raids on Berlin since Nov. 1941

27 First USAAF bombing raid on Germany at Wilhelmshaven
30 First RAF raids using H S bomb-aiming radar. Vichy government forms *Milice* under Joseph Damand

FEBRUARY

28 Norwegian commandos destroy 'heavy water' factory at Vemork

MARCH
1 HS radar used by Allied Coastal Command

5 First flight of Gloster Meteor jet

26 Laval assumes reins of power in France; Pétain a figurehead

APRIL
1 Invasion of Europe plans begin

5 Air raids open battle of the Ruhr
7 Hitler and Mussolini meet in Germany

26 Russia severs relations with Polish government in London over Katyn massacre

MAY

9 German Ju88 equipped with *Lichtenstein* radar captured intact in Great Britain

16-17 The Dams Raid – RAF's 'bouncing bombs' breach Möhne and Eder dams

22 Test flight of German Me262 jet fighter

JUNE

3 Formation of French Committee for National Liberation
4 Second RAF Tactical Air Force formed in Great Britain

10 'Point Blank' directive improves Allied bombing strategy

15 First flight German Arado Ar 234 jet bomber

20 First Allied 'shuttle' raid

N & E EUROPE

JANUARY

3 Germans begin withdrawal from Caucasus

8 German 6th Army refuses surrender demand

18 Siege of Leningrad raised

21 Russians capture airfield supplying Stalingrad
26 Russians capture Voronezh
31 General Paulus surrenders 6th Army at Stalingrad

FEBRUARY
2 Remaining Germans surrender at Stalingrad
6 Russians reach Sea of Azov and cut off German Army Group A
8 Russians take Kursk

14 Russians take Rostov

16 Russians take Kharkov

28 Guderian reorganizes Panzer forces

MARCH

2-4 Germans defeat Russian 3rd Tank Army at Kharkov

15 Germans recapture Kharkov

26 Spring thaw halts fighting around Kharkov

31 Russians advance in Kuban
APRIL

12 Germans announce discovery of Katyn Massacre graves

19 Beginning of Warsaw Ghetto up-rising

MAY

15 (to 9 June) 5th Axis offensive versus Yugoslav Partisans; Tito's forces almost destroyed
16 Warsaw Rising defeated

22 Comintern dissolved

27 British mission to aid Tito lands
JUNE

2 Air battle over Kursk
4 Night raid by Germans on Gorki tank factory

11 Russians raid airfields west of Kursk

MEDITERRANEAN & AFRICA

JANUARY

14-24 Casablanca Conference: Roosevelt demands unconditional surrender
15 8th Army attacks at Buerat

18 First Tiger tanks in Tunisia

28 8th Army captures Tripoli

FEBRUARY
5 Mussolini dismisses Ciano and Grandi

8 8th Army enters Tunisia

14-25 Kasserine Campaign

14 Heavy German counter-attack. Battle of Kasserine Pass

20 Germans break through

24 Allies recover Kasserine Pass

27 Battle of Hunt's Gap

MARCH

2 German withdrawal begins in Tunisia

6 Rommel leaves Afrika Korps

9 Arnim takes command of Afrika Korps

20-28 8th Army attacks and breaks through Mareth line
29 Allies take Gabès
30 (to 1 April) Adana Conference

APRIL

9 British push through Fondouk Pass

21 8th Army takes Enfidaville Line
22 US 1st Army attacks at Bou Arada, pressing on Tunis

MAY

4-12 Last Allied offensive in North Africa
7 18th Army Group takes Tunis
12 Arnim surrenders all Axis troops in North Africa
13 Marshal Messe surrenders Italian 1st Army

30 (to 11 June) Fortress island of Pantelleria taken after heavy bombardment prior to invasion of Sicily
JUNE

12 Lampedusa surrenders

MAINLAND ASIA

FEBRUARY

8 First Chindit raids of Wingate's 77th Indian Brigade

MARCH

13 Chinese push Japanese back over R.Yangtze

17 Japanese attack on Arakan Front

APRIL

8 General Kawabe takes over from General Iida as Japanese Commander-in-Chief Burma

MAY

14 Japanese occupy Maungdaw in Burma

17 Japanese attack across R.Yangtze

21 Japanese attack in central China

JUNE

18 Announced Wavell to be Viceroy of India, installed Oct.; Auchinleck becomes Commander-in-Chief of the Indian Army

PACIFIC & OCEANIA

JANUARY
2 Allies capture Buna

4 Japanese begin evacuation of Guadalcanal
8-9 Battle of Huon Gulf

15 US offensive in Guadalcanal

22 End of fighting in New Guinea

FEBRUARY
1-19 Japanese 17th Army evacuated from Guadalcanal
6 First Allied air success in Pacific, 26 Japanese planes shot down for no loss

MARCH
2-5 Battle of Bismarck Sea, destruction of Japanese troop convoy to New Guinea

26 Sea battle of Komandorski Is.

APRIL

18 Admiral Yamamoto shot down and killed by US fighters
21 US airmen captured in Japan are beheaded. Admiral Koga commands Japanese combined fleet

MAY

11 Americans land on Attu

JUNE
1 Beginning of US submarine war against Japanese shipping

8 Japanese begin to evacuate Kiska

16 Japanese suffer heavy air losses in attacks on Guadalcanal
20 Japanese attack Australians in New Guinea
21 US troops land on New Georgia in Solomon Is.

30 Amphibious Operation *Cartwheel* against Japanese on Rabaul, landings on New Guinea

ATLANTIC & AMERICAS

JANUARY

6 Admiral Raeder resigns as Commander-in-Chief German Navy

11 Roosevelt asks Congress for $100 bn budget

31 USA announces first gaseous diffusion plant. Allied shipping losses: 50 ships of 261,400 tons, 37 of 203,100 to U-boats

FEBRUARY

18 U-boat Pack attacks Convoy ON-166, sinking 14 ships of 850,000 tons. Allied shipping losses: 73 ships of 403,100 tons, 63 of 359,300 to U-boats

MARCH

5-20 Biggest convoy battle of the war; SC122 and HX229 lose 22 ships for 1 U-boat, 21 ships of 140,800 tons - crisis of Atlantic Battle

12 Washington Military Conference on the Pacific. Closing of Atlantic 'air gap' with first escort carriers

31 Atlantic escorts fitted with 'Hedgehog'. Allied shipping losses: 120 ships of 693,000 tons, 108 of 627,000 to U-boats
APRIL
1 Convoy protection improved; British and Canadians in north, USN in south

28 (to 6 May) Battle of Convoy ONS-5, the turning point in Atlantic. 7 U-boats sunk
30 RN 'Support Groups' provide improved convoy protection. Allied shipping losses: 64 ships of 334,700 tons, 56 of 327,900 to U-boats
MAY

5 U-513 sinks 4 ships off Brazil

12-25 Second Washington Conference

22 Admiral Dönitz suspends U-boat operations in North Atlantic. Allied shipping losses: 58 ships of 299,400 tons, 50 of 264,900 tons to U-boats, 41 U-boats sunk
JUNE
Allied shipping losses: down to 28, 20 to U-boats

W EUROPE	N & E EUROPE	MEDITERRANEAN & AFRICA	MAINLAND ASIA	PACIFIC & OCEANIA	ATLANTIC & AMERICAS
JULY	**JULY**	**JULY**		**JULY**	**JULY**
	5 Operation *Zitadelle* last German offensive at Kursk	**4** General Sikorski killed in air crash		**1** US troops capture Viru Harbour, New Guinea	
	12 Largest tank battle in history at Kursk	**9** Allied airborne troops land by night on Sicily			
	15 Russian counter-attacks at Orel	**10** Operation *Husky*: main Allied landings on Sicily		**12-13** Sea battle of Kolombangara, Japanese defeated	
17 Hitler and Mussolini meet at Feltre		**19** First Allied air raids on Rome		**15** US wins air battle over the Solomon Is.	**20** Roosevelt orders US atom research to be shared with British scientists
24 'Window' metallic strips used to baffle German radar		**22** Americans capture Palermo		**16** Australians defeat Japanese in New Guinea and Solomon Is.	**28** Roosevelt broadcasts surrender terms to Italy
24 (to 2 Aug.) RAF raids Hamburg, destroying 70% of city; 30,000 casualties		**25** Mussolini resigns and is arrested, Fascist government dissolved			**31** New Allied shipping tonnage overtakes losses. Allied shipping losses: 61 ships of 365,400 tons, 46 to U-boats, 37 U-boats sunk
27 Fire storm in Hamburg		**26** Badoglio takes over, establishes martial law			
AUGUST	**AUGUST**	**AUGUST**	**AUGUST**	**AUGUST**	**AUGUST**
1 De Gaulle made President of French Committee of National Defence, Giraud Commander-in-Chief		**2** Italians make peace moves through their embassy in Lisbon	**1** Burma declares war on Great Britain and USA		**3** U-boats abandon Wolf Packs for independent patrols
	5 Russians capture Orel and Bielgorod	**10** First use of penicillin during invasion of Sicily		**6-7** Battle of Vella Gulf, successful US naval ambush	**10-11** Churchill in Quebec for War Committee Conference with Canadian government
		12-17 Germans evacuate Sicily			
17 First Schweinfurt raid, 60 B17s lost		**14** Rome declared an open city		**15** US troops invade Kiska I.	**14-24** Quadrant Conference in Quebec. Allied shipping losses: only 100,000 tons, 25 U-boats lost including 10 U-tankers
21 First photos of V1 reach Great Britain from Denmark		**17** Allies take Messina		**21** Australians capture Mt. Tamba in New Guinea	
	23 Russians recapture Kharkov		**25** Mountbatten becomes Supreme Commander South East Asia	**28** End of Japanese resistance on New Guinea	
31 First test firing of German *Rheintochter* anti-aircraft rocket	**26** Russian Four Front offensive in Ukraine		**28** Japanese bomb Chungking (first time since 1941)	**31** US Fast Carrier Force raids Marcus I.	
SEPTEMBER	**SEPTEMBER**	**SEPTEMBER**	**SEPTEMBER**	**SEPTEMBER**	**SEPTEMBER**
	1 (to 1 Nov.) Russians take Dorogobuzh. Partisan campaign against railways begins	**3** Armistice signed with Italy; Allies land in Calabria		Japanese shipping losses: 160,000 tons to US submarines	
7 V-weapon sites bombed	**7** Germans begin evacuation of Ukraine	**8** Eisenhower and Badoglio announce Italy's surrender			
	8 Yugoslav Partisans round up and disarm Italian forces	**9** Allies land at Salerno; British Airborne Division lands at Taranto			
	9 Russian Black Sea fleet outflanks German Blue Line on Taman peninsula	**10** Germans occupy Rome; British take Taranto, landings in Dodecanese			
	12 Germans evacuate Kuban peninsula	**12** Mussolini rescued by Germans	**13** Chiang Kai-shek becomes President of Chinese Republic		
	16 Partisans seize Split	**14** British occupy Kos			
	17 Russians take Briansk	**17-18** Allied breakout at Salerno			**18** Wolf Pack raids resumed in North Atlantic. Allied shipping losses: 29 ships of 156,400 tons, 9 to U-boats, 3 U-boats sunk
	21 Russians take Chernigov				
	22 Russians take Poltava and cross R. Dnieper	**22** Allied landings at Bari			
	25 Russians take Smolensk	**23** Mussolini re-establishes Fascist government			
	28 Germans recapture Split				
OCTOBER	**OCTOBER**	**OCTOBER**	**OCTOBER**	**OCTOBER**	**OCTOBER**
1 Fifth Army captures Naples and Benevento	**2** Russian offensive halted	**2** British Commandos land at Termoli and link up with 8th Army	**3** Japanese attack in central China	**2** Australians take Finschhafen	
		4 Corsica liberated		**6** Americans land on Kolombangara I.	
	9 Russians control Kuban peninsula	**12** Allies cross R. Volturno but offensive is halted			
14 Second Schweinfurt raid; heavy losses (60 B17s) halt US daylight raids	**14** Russians recapture Zaporozhe	**13** Italy declares war on Germany		**17** German raider *Michel* sunk off Japan by US submarines	**20** US Commission on War Crimes set up. Allied shipping losses: only 9 merchant ships in North Atlantic
	18 (to 1 Nov.) Second Moscow Conference Second Panzer Army occupies Yugoslavia		**25** Burma-Siam 'Death' Railway completed	**27** New Zealand forces land on Treasury I. in Solomon Is.	
		30 Germans counter-attack on R. Trigno			
NOVEMBER	**NOVEMBER**	**NOVEMBER**		**NOVEMBER**	**NOVEMBER**
	1 Russians cut land routes to Germans in Crimea			**1** US Marines land on Bougainville	
	6 Russians take Kiev	**8** 8th Army takes Sangro Heights		**2** Naval battle of Empress Augusta Bay secures Bougainville landings	
	10 Start of battle of Cherkassy; Russian paratroops and partisans link up				**15** Germans abandon U-boat operations in Atlantic
18 Heaviest RAF raid of war so far opens Battle of Berlin				**20** US troops land on Makin and Tarawa Atolls, Gilbert Is.	
		22-26 First Cairo Conference		**24** US carrier *Liscombe Bay* sunk by submarine off Makin	
	28 Teheran Conference begins	**28** (to 1 Dec.) Teheran Conference meeting of 'Big Three'		**25-26** Sea battle of St.George	
DECEMBER	**DECEMBER**	**DECEMBER**	**DECEMBER**	**DECEMBER** Japanese shipping losses: 265,000 tons; merchant fleet reduced to 80% of 1941	**DECEMBER**
2 Hitler calls up German youth	**3** Russians advance on a wide front	**3** 5th Army opens new offensive			
	4 Yugoslavs announce Provisional Government	**4-7** Second Cairo Conference			
12 Rommel appointed Commander-in-Chief *Fortress Europe*	**12** Czech-Soviet alliance signed in Moscow				**11** British Admiralty announce 2-day battle against U-boats
	14 Cherkassy captured, Russians begin Winter offensive				
	15 First trial of Nazi war criminals	**17** 5th Army takes San Pietro	**18** Stilwell appointed to command Chinese troops in India and northern Burma		
	26 Russians attack in Kiev salient				**25-26** Battle of North Cape, RN sinks the *Scharnhorst*. Allied shipping losses: in Nov.-Dec.; 60 ships of 313,000 tons, 12 of 17 U-tanker boats sunk, 17 U-boats
	28 Russians make rapid advances on a wide front, cut Polotsk-Vitebsk railway	**28** 8th Army captures Ortona			
	31 Russians take Zhitomir				

W EUROPE

JANUARY

1 Rommel takes command of Army Group B

16 Eisenhower assumes command as Supreme Commander Allied Expeditionary Forces

FEBRUARY

1 French Forces of the Interior formed to co-ordinate Resistance

8 *Overlord* plan agreed

14 Eisenhower sets up SHAEF HQ

20-27 'Big Week' bombing of German fighter factories

MARCH

6 First major Allied daylight raid on Berlin

12 Czech government in London calls for Resistance in Slovakia

18 Heaviest RAF raid so far on Hamburg; 3000 tons of bombs dropped

APRIL

26 E-boats attack Force U in Channel during D-Day Exercises

MAY

1-16 Commonwealth Prime Ministers Conference in London
2 Spain guarantees continued neutrality

8 Eisenhower chooses June 5 for D-Day
9 Allied Bombing prepares for D-Day

16 First operational flight of German Me163 rocket fighter

JUNE

2 First air 'shuttle' raid
4-6 Resistance disrupts communications in France
6 D-Day landings between Cherbourg and Le Havre; use of Mulberry artificial harbours
9 Allied aircraft begin operating from French airstrips
10 Massacre at Oradour-sur-Glane near Limoges by SS
11 French Resistance rising at Vercors begins (to 29 July)
12 All Normandy landing zones linked up
13 First V-1s land in Great Britain
15 First use of 22,000lb. 'Tallboy' bomb by RAF
25 General Koenig appointed to command the French Forces of the Interior
27 Americans capture Cherbourg

N & E EUROPE

JANUARY

3 Russians take Olevsk and cut railway to Warsaw
4 Yugoslav Partisans capture Banja Luka
6 Russians advance into Poland
7 Russians advance in Ukraine
8 Russians take Kirovograd
14 Russians break through on a broad front

19 Russians take Novgorod

27 Leningrad finally relieved after almost 900-day siege

FEBRUARY

1 Polish Resistance assassinate Major Kutschera, Chief of Gestapo in Poland

MARCH

1 Russians attack across R. Narva

6 Russians advance on 100km front in Ukraine

13 Russians take Kherson
14 Germans trapped in Nikolayev pocket

19 Germans occupy Hungary
20 Russians take Vinnitsa

24 Russians reach R. Dniester
25 Russians capture Proskurov

31 Russians take Ochakov on Black

APRIL

10 Russians take Odessa
11 Russians take Kerch. Germans retreat into Sevastopol
13 Russians capture Feodosiya and Simferopol
14-17 Russians take Tarnopol and cut German front in two
16 Yalta falls. Eichmann begins round up of 800,000 Hungarian Jews

22 Tito's partisans take Korčula I.

MAY

9 Russians capture Sevastopol

31 Germans counter-attack north of Jassy

JUNE

9 Russian offensive begins on Finnish front

18 Russians break through Mannerheim Line

23 Russian offensive in Byelorussia
24 Russians reach R.Drina

27 Russians cross R.Dnieper
30 Finns halt Russian attack. General Strike in Copenhagen

MEDITERRANEAN & AFRICA

JANUARY

8 Verona trial of Italians involved in deposing Mussolini

15 5th Army takes Mt.Trocchio; Germans withdraw across R.Rapido

17 Allies cross R. Garigliano

20 Americans reach R. Rapido

22 6th Army landings at Anzio

30 5th Army breaks into Gustav Line

FEBRUARY

7 German counter-attack at Anzio

10 Italian rule returned over Sicily, south Italy and Sardinia
15 Monastery of Cassino destroyed by artillery and bombing
16 Second German counter-attack at Anzio almost cuts Allied forces in two
19 Allied air power halts Germans at Anzio

MARCH

3 German attacks at Anzio cease; Greek Resistance fights Germans

13 Russo-Italian agreement

15 New Zealanders and Indians attack Monte Cassino

22 Allied attacks at Cassino halted

MAY

11 Allies attack Gustav Line
15 Germans withdraw to Adolf Hitler Line
18 Poles capture Monastery Hill at Cassino; last U-boat sinking in Mediterranean
20 US troops clear up Gaeta Peninsula
23 Breakout from Anzio begins
25 Germans retreat from Anzio

JUNE

5 5th Army enters Rome
7 5th Army takes Civitavecchia, 8th Army takes Subiaco
10 8th Army advances up Adriatic coast

20 8th Army takes Perugia

MAINLAND ASIA

JANUARY

6 'Merrill's Marauders' set up in Burma

9 British capture Maungdaw in Burma

13 Chinese occupy Hukawng Valley

FEBRUARY

4 Japanese offensive in Arakan drives Allies back into India; Chinese attack in Hukawng Valley
7 Allied forces cut-off in 'Admin Box'

25 British relieve 'Admin Box'

MARCH

1 Chindit 16th Brigade crosses R.Chindwin
4 US and Chinese troops combine in Hukawng Valley
5 Chindit airdrops north of Indaw
8 Battle of Imphal begins
14 British fall back from Imphal
16 Japanese cross R.Chindwin and cut Kohima-Imphal Road

24 Major-General Wingate killed in air crash
27 Lentaigne takes over Chindits
29 Siege of Imphal begins

APRIL

4-20 Japanese besiege Kohima

18 Operation *Ichi-go*; Japanese attack to control Peking-Hankow railway

28 Japanese advance in Honan province

MAY

4 Chinese overrun Inkangahtawng on Kamaing road
5 14th Army counter-attacks at Imphal
8 Japanese attack 14th Army in Manipur Hills
9 Japanese capture Lushan and cut Peking-Hankow railway
10 Chinese attack across R. Salween

26 Japanese offensive against US airbases in China
27 Monsoons curtail fighting in Burma

JUNE

2 Chinese besiege Myitkyina
3 End of Kohima battle

18 Japanese take Changsha

22 Siege of Imphal lifted

26 Chinese take Mogaung

PACIFIC & OCEANIA

JANUARY

31 US troops invade Kwajalein and Majura Atolls (Marshall Is.)

FEBRUARY

14-17 US and New Zealand forces take Green I.

17-18 Truk Raid - severe damage to Japanese navy and air base
19 US troops land on Eniwetok I.
21 Tojo made Chief of Japanese Army General Staff

MARCH

6 US Marines land at Talasea in New Britain
9 Japanese attack on Bougainville
12 US Marines occupy Wotho Atoll
15 US landing on Manus I. (Admiralty Is.)

20 US Marines land on Emirau I. in Bismarck Arch

24 Japanese counter-offensive on Bougainville defeated

APRIL

11 Japanese give up Gasmata and Cape Hopkins

22 Americans land unopposed at Hollandia, Dutch New Guinea
26 Australians take Alexishafen, Americans advance in Hollandia and Aitape
29-30 US TF58 attacks Truk Atoll

MAY

19 Last fighting on Wakde Is.

27 Americans land on Biak I.

JUNE

7 Americans capture airfield on Biak

11 US TF58 begins bombardment of Marianas
14 First B29 Superfortress raid on Japan
15 US Marines land on Saipan

19-20 Battle of the Philippine Sea: Japanese lose 300 aircraft and 14 ships sunk or damaged

27 Heavy fighting on Saipan

ATLANTIC & AMERICAS

JANUARY

1-31 First test flights US XP80 jet fighter

FEBRUARY

7 First use of *Snorkel* equipment on U-boat

MARCH

22 Admiral Dönitz orders U-boats to operate singly and to give up convoy attacks. Allied shipping losses: Jan.-March 54 ships, but 60 U-boats sunk

APRIL

24 US War Department considers invasion of Japan necessary

JUNE

30 USA severs relations with Finland

W EUROPE

JULY

2 Kluge replaces von Runstedt as Commander-in-Chief West

9 Second Army takes Caen

17 Rommel badly wounded
18 Operation *Goodwood* begun by Second Army; US troops take St. Lô
20 Von Stauffenberg's plot to blow up Hitler fails

25-30 Operation *Cobra* achieves breakthrough west of St. Lô

29 (to 1 Aug.) Germans counter-attack on R.Odon

AUGUST

4-8 German bomb plotters tried and executed
6 Third Army takes Nantes and reaches Brest
12 PLUTO pipeline provides oil across English Channel
15 Operation *Anvil/Dragoon* begins; Allied 7th Army invades southern France
16 Canadians surround Falaise
20 Falaise Gap closed, bridgehead established over R.Seine
22 Rising in Paris
25 Allied forces liberate Paris
28 Allies take Marseilles and Toulon
29 US troops take Soissons; French cross the Rhine
31 British 1st Army reaches Amiens, captures Somme bridgeheads. Montgomery made Field Marshal

SEPTEMBER

1 Artois, Dieppe and Rouen taken; US troops cross R. Meuse
3/4 Allies liberate Antwerp and Brussels
7 US troops cross R. Moselle
8 First V2s land in London
12 US 1st Army enters Germany. Le Havre surrenders
15 US 1st Army reaches Siegfried Line
17-21 Operation *Market Garden* results in destruction of Allied airborne forces
22 Boulogne surrenders

28 Calais surrenders

OCTOBER

3 Me262 fighter operational

13 1st Army enters Aachen
14 Allies liberate Athens. Rommel commits suicide
18 *Volksturm*, the last ditch people's army, created in Germany
21 Germans surrender Aachen
23 De Gaulle recognized as ruler of France

31 RAF Mosquitoes destroy Gestapo HQ at Aarhus

NOVEMBER

9 US 3rd Army crosses R. Moselle

12 RAF sink *Tirpitz* in Tromso Fjord

14 London Agreement on the organization of Occupied Europe

20 French 1st Army drives through Belfort Gap

24 Allies cross R.Saar; French take Strasbourg

30 New Polish cabinet formed in London

DECEMBER

3 British Home Guard stands down

10 Franco-Russian Treaty of Alliance

12 Americans capture V-weapon factory at Wittring

16-25 Battle of the Bulge in the Ardennes; Barstogne holds out
17 Malmédy Massacre of US prisoners of war by SS

22 Final German attempt to reach R. Meuse
26 US 3rd Army tanks under General Patton relieve Bastogne

30 RAF Mosquitoes bomb Gestapo HQ in Oslo

N & E EUROPE

JULY

1 Russians cross the Berezina
3 Russians recapture Minsk

11 Russians attack 'Panther Line'

17 Russians cross R.Bug into Poland

24 Russians liberate first concentration camp at Maidanek

28 Russians take Brest-Litovsk
31 Russians 10 miles from Warsaw. Baltic Fleet lands troops on Hiiumaa and Saaremaa

AUGUST

1 Polish Underground Army revolts in Warsaw
6 Russians take Drohobycz oil centre

14 Russians begin ofensive from Vistula bridgehead

17 Russians reach east Prussian border
20 Russian fleet lands troops in mouth of Danube, attacking Rumania

23 Russians surround German 7th Army at Kishinev

29 Slovak uprising begins
30 Russians take Ploeşti. Germans abandon Bulgaria
31 Russians take Bucharest

SEPTEMBER

2 Provisional Russo-Finnish treaty ends fighting
5 USSR declares war on Bulgaria
6 Russians reach Yugoslav border

8 Russians enter Bulgaria unopposed

14 Russians enter Warsaw subsurbs

18 USAAF supplies Polish resistance

21 Tito meets Stalin

23 Russians reach Gulf of Riga
26 Russians occupy Estonia

OCTOBER

1 Russians enter Yugoslavia
2 End of Warsaw Resistance
4 Russians and Tito's partisans link up

9-19 Moscow Conference
10 Russians capture Riga; tank battle at Debrecen, 3 Russian corps destroyed

20 Belgrade liberated

23 Russians enter East Prussia

28 Germans begin evacuation of Albania. Russo-Bulgarian armistice
30 Last extermination gassing at Auschwitz

NOVEMBER

21 Albanians take Tirana and Durazzo

23 Germans evacuate Finnish Lapland

DECEMBER

18 Russians cross R. Sajó

27 Siege of Budapest begins

MEDITERRANEAN & AFRICA

JULY

1 5th Army captures Cecina

16 8th Army takes Arezzo and reaches R.Arno

AUGUST

4 8th Army enters Florence

31 8th Army attacks Gothic Line
SEPTEMBER
2 5th Army enters Pisa

8 5th Army breaks through Gothic Line

26 8th Army crosses R. Rubicon

29 SS Massacre at Mt. Sole

OCTOBER

4 British troops land in Greece

12 British paratroops take Athens airfield
14 Athens liberated

21 8th Army crosses R. Savio

24 British capture Lamia

NOVEMBER

4 Liberation of Greece completed

10 8th Army takes Forlì

23 Germans evacuate Macedonia

30 British submarines redeployed from Mediterranean; end of naval war there

DECEMBER

1 Germans withdraw to evacuation points in Crete
4 Athens under martial law
6 8th Army crosses R. Lamone

MAINLAND ASIA

JULY

18 Japanese retreat from Imphal-Kohima

AUGUST

3 Chinese take Myitkyina

16 Last Japanese resistance in India ends

OCTOBER

19 British capture Japanese supply depot at Mohnyin in Burma

NOVEMBER

2 14th Army takes Mawlu in Burma

10 Japanese capture US air base at Kweilin in Kwangsi province
13 Japanese capture Linchow air base

DECEMBER

6 Japanese retake Tushan

10 14th Army reaches Indaw

15 Chinese take Bhamo in Burma

20 14th Army takes Kandaung

30 14th Army takes Kaduma

PACIFIC & OCEANIA

JULY

7 Japanese wiped out on Saipan; Admirals Nagumo and Yano die
10 Japanese counter-attack near Aitape on New Guinea
18 Tojo's Cabinet resigns: Kaso replaces Tojo, Umeza becomes Army Commander-in-Chief
21 US Marines land on Guam
24 US Marines land on Tinian

28 End of resistance on Biak

AUGUST

1 Tinian secured by US troops

9 Destruction of Japanese on Guam

SEPTEMBER

2 Wakde operation completed

10-11 US 3rd Fleet attacks Palaus

OCTOBER

9 US 3rd Fleet bombards Marcus I.
11 3rd Fleet aircraft attack Okinawa
12-18 3rd Fleet air operations against Formosa
17 US Rangers land in Leyte Gulf
20 US 6th Army invades Leyte

24-26 Naval air battle over Leyte destroys remains of Japanese carrier fleet

27 *Kamikaze* attacks on US TF38 in Philippines

NOVEMBER

11 US Navy bombards Iwo Jima

15 US 8th Army lands on Mapia Is.

24 First B29 raid on Tokyo

DECEMBER

15 Mindoro airfield construction begun by US forces

18 Typhoon severely damages TF38

22 End of Japanese resistance on Leyte
28 Mindoro airfield fully operational
30 10 US vessels lost to air attack off Mindoro

ATLANTIC & AMERICAS

AUGUST

21-29 Dumbarton Oaks Conference

SEPTEMBER

11 Second Quebec Conference

NOVEMBER

27 Cordell Hall resigns. Edward Stettinius becomes US Secretary of State

W EUROPE

JANUARY

1-17 Germans withdraw in the Ardennes
3 US 1st Army attacks Ardennes salient

16 Ardennes salient eliminated

25 De Gaulle demands permanent occupation of Rhineland

FEBRUARY

1 US 7th Army reaches Siegfried Line

9 Allies break through Siegfried Line

11 US 3rd Army enters Prüm

13-14 Destruction of Dresden in fire storm, 100,000 civilians killed

22 Air Operation *Clarion* against German communications network

25 US 1st Army captures Düren

MARCH

1 US 1st Army takes München-Gladbach
2 US 3rd Army takes Trier
5 Cologne captured, US 9th and 1st Armies reach the Rhine
7 1st Army crosses R. Rhine by Remagen Bridge

17 3rd Army takes Coblenz
20 US 7th Army takes Saarbrücken
25 3rd Army crosses R. Rhine
27 Last V2 lands in Great Britain. Allied armies link up near Coblenz (1st and 3rd) and Darmstadt (3rd and 7th)
28 Eisenhower shifts emphasis of Allied advance away from Berlin

APRIL

1 US 1st and 9th Armies complete encirclement of German Army Group B in Ruhr
4 US troops reach and cross R. Weser

10 US 9th Army takes Hanover
12 Allies liberate Belsen and Buchenwald
15 Arnhem captured
18 Ruhr pocket forces surrender
20 Nuremberg taken

29 Allies liberate Dachau

MAY

4 German forces in Holland, Denmark and NW Germany surrender
5 Ceasefire in West
7 General Jodl signs unconditional surrender
8 VE Day
9 German surrender ratified in Berlin
9-12 Channel Is. liberated

23 German High Command imprisoned; Himmler commits suicide

JUNE

5 Occupying powers partition Germany and Berlin

N & E EUROPE

JANUARY

2 Germans counter-attack at Budapest

17 Russians take Warsaw
18 Polish Provisional government set up
19 Russians take Tilsit
20 Hungarian armistice
26 Russians liberate Auschwitz
27 Russians cross R. Vistula
29 Poznań surrounded; Germans evacuate 2 million troops and civilians from East Prussia

FEBRUARY

4-11 Yalta Conference

11 Russians advance towards Breslau and Dresden, overrun Budapest
15 Russians attack Danzig, surround Breslau
17-24 Germans wipe out Russian Hron bridgehead

23 Russians take Poznań

MARCH

5 Tito forms new Yugoslav government
6 Germans counter-attack toward Budapest

11 Czech government in exile leaves London for Slovakia
16 German peace overtures via Sweden
22 Russians besiege Danzig and Gdynia

28 Gdynia falls

30 Danzig taken

APRIL

4 Last Germans leave Hungary
6 Yugoslav Partisans take Sarajevo
7-13 Russians attack and occupy Vienna
9 Russians take Königsberg
11 Soviet-Yugoslav treaty
16 (to 2 May) Russian final offensive on Berlin

23 Russians enter Berlin

26 US 1st Army and Russian patrols meet at Torgau

30 Hitler commits suicide

MAY

2 Russians hold Berlin, German casualties in battle for city 150,000 dead, 300,000 captured

9 Russians occupy Prague

MEDITERRANEAN & AFRICA

JANUARY

3 New Greek government under President Plastivas

30 (to 2 Feb.) Malta Conference

APRIL

11 8th Army crosses R. Santerno

14 5th Army attacks in Po Valley

24 5th and 8th Armies cross R. Po
26 Allies cross R. Adige

28 Mussolini captured by partisans and hanged

MAY

2 German armies in Italy surrender

MAINLAND ASIA

JANUARY

4 British attack in Arakan and break through to Akyab I.

7 14th Army reaches Shwebo, occupies Kinu

21 14th Army takes Monywa
22 Burma Road reopened

26 Japanese troops ordered to withdraw to Chinese coast
28 Supply convoy reaches China over Ledo Burma Road

FEBRUARY

13 14th Army establishes bridgeheads over R. Irrawaddy south of Mandalay

17 Bridgeheads hold out against Japanese counter-attacks

MARCH

4 Allies take Meiktila

7 Chinese take Lashio
8 Indians enter Mandalay

9 Japanese attack French forces in Indo-China, set up Empire of Annam
13 14th Army captures Maymyo, cutting Japanese escape route from Mandalay
15 Indian 17th Division besieged at Meiktila
17 14th Army takes Sagaing and Ava
19 Japanese evacuate Mandalay

APRIL

9 14th Army captures Thazi

19 14th Army takes Magwe and Myingan

MAY

1 British airborne troops land south of Rangoon
2 14th Army rescues Pegu
3 Indians capture Rangoon

10 14th Army links up with troops from Arakan

18 Chinese occupy Foochow

26 Chinese occupy Yung-ning, cutting Japanese land route to Indo-China

PACIFIC & OCEANIA

JANUARY

3 US TF38 attacks aircraft and ships at Formosa

6 *Kamikaze* attacks against invasion forces approaching Lingayen Gulf

25 Americans capture airfield on Luzon

FEBRUARY

1 US 6th Army advances on Manila

16 Iwo Jima bombarded from sea and air
16-17 Fast carrier raid on Japan
17 Americans occupy Bataan peninsula
19-26 US Marines land on Iwo Jima
21 US Carrier *Saratoga* badly damaged in *Kamikaze* attack
23 US Marines take Mt. Suribachi on Iwo Jima
24 Manila secured
27 Americans land on Verde I.
28 Corregidor secured

MARCH

1 US infantry land on Lubang I.
3 US troops land on Burias I. and Ticao I.
4 Manila falls
8 Americans land at Zamboanga on Mindanao
9-10 Fire blitz on Tokyo

27 Americans take Cebu City. Operation *Starvation* against Japanese shipping

APRIL

1 US 10th Army invades Okinawa
3 General MacArthur becomes Commander-in-Chief US Armed Forces, Pacific with Nimitz as Naval commander
5 Russia denounces neutrality pact with Japan; Japanese Cabinet resigns
7 Battle of East China Sea
11 *Kamikaze* attacks on US TF38 at Okinawa

23 Americans control central Philippines

27 US 6th Army takes Baguio on Luzon

MAY

1 Australians land on Tarakan I.

11 US 10th Army attacks on Okinawa

14 Daylight fire raid on Nagoya

18 US Marines take Sugar Loaf Hill on Okinawa

27 US 6th Army takes Santa Fe on Luzon

JUNE

4 US Marines land on north Oroku Peninsula

10 Australian 9th Division invades Borneo

18 Last resistance on Mindanao ends

22 End of resistance on Okinawa

27 US 6th Army reaches Apani, ending Luzon campaign

ATLANTIC & AMERICAS

APRIL

12 President Roosevelt dies. Truman becomes President

MAY

4 Dönitz orders U-boats to surrender

JUNE

25-26 World Charter of Security signed in San Francisco

W EUROPE

JULY

1 US, British and French troops move into Berlin

17 (to 2 Aug.) Potsdam Conference on reparation, peace treaties, Austria and Poland

25 Potsdam declaration on Japan
26 Labour Party wins British election; Atlee becomes Prime Minister

NOVEMBER

20 Nuremberg trials begin

N & E EUROPE

DECEMBER

27 Great Britain, USA and USSR hold meeting in Moscow to discuss Korea

MEDITERRANEAN & AFRICA

MAINLAND ASIA

JULY

31 British midget submarine attack at Singapore
AUGUST

8 Russia declares war on Japan and invades Manchuria (Manchukuo)

18 Manchuria overrun

21 Japanese surrender in Manchuria

28 Mao Tse-tung and Chang Kai-shek meet in Chungking, Japanese sign surrender documents in Rangoon
SEPTEMBER

5 British land in Singapore

7 Japanese surrender in Shanghai

9 Japanese surrender in China signed

13 Japanese surrender in Burma signed
16 Japanese surrender in Hong Kong signed

OCTOBER

10 Agreement between Mao Tse-tung and Chang Kai-shek

PACIFIC & OCEANIA

JULY

10 1000 bomber raid on Japanese mainland

17 1500 plane raid on Tokyo meets no air opposition; British Pacific Fleet and US 3rd Fleet raid Japan

30 Japan rejects Potsdam ultimatum
AUGUST
3 Complete blockade of Japan in effect

6 Atomic bomb dropped on Hiroshima
8 Russia declares war on Japan
9 Atom bomb dropped on Nagasaki

14 Japanese agree to unconditional surrender terms
15 VJ Day

27 US and Allied naval units enter Japanese ports

SEPTEMBER
2 Japanese sign instrument of surrender on board USS *Missouri* in Tokyo Bay

ATLANTIC & AMERICAS

JULY

16 First atom bomb test at Alamogordo in Mexican Desert

NOVEMBER

27 UN Charter ratified by 29 nations

DECEMBER

4 US Senate approves America's participation in UN

Europe after the First World War

THE FIRST WORLD WAR ceased with the armistice of 11 November 1918. Germany gave in – her empire in collapse, her towns in uproar, her army in retreat. The terms of the peace, decided at Paris in 1919, were such that Germany would not be able to fight again. Her overseas empire was confiscated. The navy was impounded, and at Scapa Flow it was to be sunk by the crews themselves. Allied troops occupied strategic points on the western German border. Imports of food were strictly controlled; cities starved, and an epidemic in Central Europe which killed some 10 million more people than the war itself.

The aftermath of the war was apparent for some time. In Russia the civil war effectively came to an end only in February 1921, when the last anti-Bolshevik forces evacuated the Crimea, bound for exile. The Habsburg monarchy in Central Europe had disintegrated in October 1918, and warring went on between its 'successor-states'. The two dominant nationalities had been the Germans, in the western part, and the Hungarians in the east. The rule of both was now overthrown: the Czechs and Slovaks asserted independence, ruling over a new state which, mainly in its western part (the Sudetenland) contained three million Germans. Poland re-emerged with many Germans living within its borders. Yugoslavia combined Serbs, Croats, Slovenes and others; Rumania took Transylvania, Bessarabia and southern Dobruja in eastern Hungary. Hungary, reduced by almost two-thirds of her historic area, briefly passed under Communist rule until counter-revolutionary forces regained control in 1919.

The victorious powers held a peace conference in Paris in 1919 to establish the shape of the post-war world. Under the Treaty of Versailles, signed on 28 June 1919, Germany lost Alsace-Lorraine to France, and territories in the east, to the newly-reconstituted Polish Republic, as well as areas to Denmark, Lithuania and Belgium. She had to accept limitation of her armed forces to 100,000 men – a police-force, in effect –

and occupation of strategic places on the east bank of the Rhine by Allied forces for fifteen years. The Saar, with important mineral reserves, was handed to France for the same period. In principle (confirmed in 1921), Germany had to agree to pay 'reparations' – an annual sum ostensibly designed to compensate the victims of German aggression, but really intended, by removing gold reserves, to prevent the German economy from ever recovering. To justify this, the Allies made the German delegates agree that Germany (as distinct from the imperial régime of 1914) had caused the war in 1914.

Other treaties in 1919-22 were similarly felt by the losing parties to represent injustice. The Treaty of Saint Germain, in September 1919, settled the fate of most Germans – now known as *Volksdeutsche* – living in the old Habsburg monarchy. Austria was created, more or less by fiat of the Allies, to prevent Germans there from joining the German Republic (as they had almost overwhelmingly voted to do); other parts of the monarchy were consigned to Italy, Yugoslavia, Rumania, Czechoslovakia and Poland. Although independent, Austria was also required to pay reparations. Hungary's new borders were dictated by the Treaty of Trianon in June 1920. Turkey and Bulgaria, former allies of Germany, also lost territory – in the Turkish case a vast amount, to newly-devised states in the Middle East, including Palestine, which, as a 'Jewish national home', was passed to Britain as a League of Nations mandate. The various wars came to an end with recognition by the new Soviet state of national borders with Poland, the Baltic states and Finland (the Treaty of Riga, 1921).

Europe had been dramatically redrawn, but national hatreds had not been overcome – very far from it. The Western Powers claimed superior morality, and devised the League of Nations at Geneva, at American instigation, as a means of sustaining the political and moral *status quo*. But the question remained: would the combined weight of the victorious Allies

be strong enough to enforce the post-war settlement?

This proved not to be the case. The USA had entered into war with Germany in 1917 and soon relapsed into isolation, keen only to recoup her outstanding loans in Europe. The French wanted to keep Germany down, insisting on full reparations, and allying with the new 'successor' states; the British now wished to restore her gradually to the European comity of nations. German reparations could only be paid by an export surplus, which would dent Britain's own exports. Britain, therefore, opposed French demands for reparations, and was upset when the French occupied the Ruhr in 1922-23.

Germany was in a state of internal chaos. The empire had gone – the Kaiser in exile in Holland – and an uneasy republic took its place, named after the town of Weimar, where the republican government went to escape rebellion in Berlin. An ultra-democratic constitution was devised, in February 1919. But it was assailed from the Left (Spartakists in 1918-19, Comintern in 1921 and 1923) and the Right (Friekorps rebellion and Kapp Putsch, 1919-20: Hitler's Munich Putsch, November 1923); further, the parties which operated the republic were themselves badly divided. Lack of central control and the occupation of much of Germany's industrial heartland by the Allies meant that finances became a nightmare. By November 1923, when a new, stable currency was introduced, there were over 50 thousand million marks to the pound sterling.

In 1924 the mark stabilized and the Weimar Republic entered a period of relative calm. Germany was admitted to the League of Nations: she agreed to new plans on reparations – the Dawes Plan of 1924, and the Young Plan of 1929 – and co-operated in world affairs. Economic recovery went ahead just the same, and in 1925 there was an accord of the Western Powers, which led to the Treaty of Locarno. By this, German statesmen – Gustav Stresemann in particular – 'accepted'

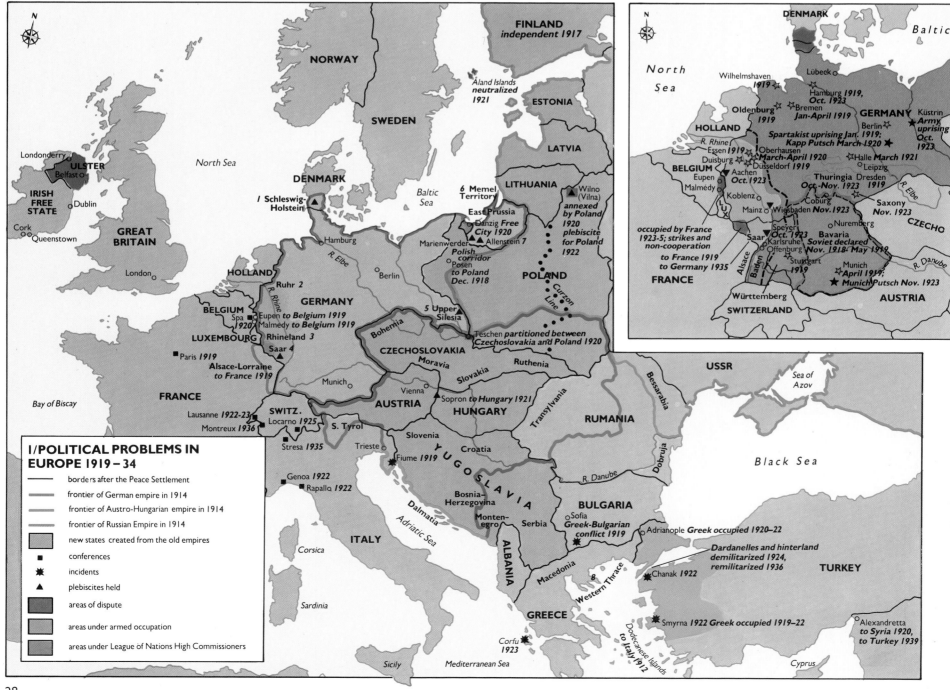

I/POLITICAL PROBLEMS IN EUROPE 1919–34

— borders after the Peace Settlement
— frontier of German empire in 1914
— frontier of Austro-Hungarian empire in 1914
— frontier of Russian Empire in 1914
▨ new states created from the old empires
■ conferences
✳ incidents
▲ plebiscites held
▨ areas of dispute
▨ areas under armed occupation
▨ areas under League of Nations High Commissioners

reparations and the new western borders, though not the eastern ones. The states of Europe agreed for a few years. The Soviet Union had even concluded a pact with Germany in 1922 (the Treaty of Rapallo). In the 1920s, there was extensive economic collaboration between the Communist government of the Soviet Union and the West. But nationalist hatreds were ever-present and the economic recovery of the 1920s was only able to keep them in check for a few years. In the 1930s European rivalries would once again break out.

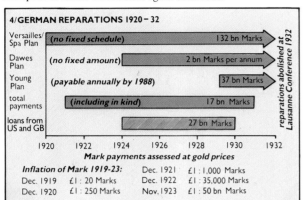

4/GERMAN REPARATIONS 1920-32

Versailles/ Spa Plan	(no fixed schedule)	132 bn Marks	
Dawes Plan	(no fixed amount)	2 bn Marks per annum	
Young Plan	(payable annually by 1988)	37 bn Marks	
total payments	(including in kind)	17 bn Marks	
loans from US and GB		27 bn Marks	

reparations abolished at Lausanne Conference 1932

1920 1922 1924 1926 1928 1930 1932
Mark payments assessed at gold prices

Inflation of Mark 1919-23:
Dec. 1919 £1 : 20 Marks
Dec. 1920 £1 : 250 Marks
Dec. 1921 £1 : 1,000 Marks
Dec. 1922 £1 : 35,000 Marks
Nov. 1923 £1 : 50 bn Marks

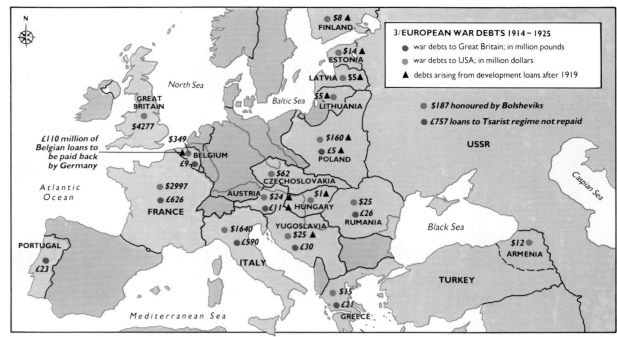

3/EUROPEAN WAR DEBTS 1914-1925
- ● war debts to Great Britain; in million pounds
- ● war debts to USA; in million dollars
- ▲ debts arising from development loans after 1919

● $187 honoured by Bolsheviks
● £757 loans to Tsarist regime not repaid

£110 million of Belgian loans to be paid back by Germany

2/WEIMAR GERMANY 1919-23
- – – boundary of de-militarized zone
- areas of Allied occupation
- plebiscite areas
- ▼ separatist declarations
- ☆ Left-Wing uprising
- ★ Right-Wing uprising
- Communist government 1923
- area of Nazi Putsch 1923

TERRITORIAL CHANGES in Europe, decided at a series of post-war conferences, seemed to create more problems than they solved. In addition to those annotated on map (1), the following measures were taken (numbered on map 1):

1 plebiscite Feb. 1920 divided between Denmark and Germany
2 occupied by France 1923-25
3 evacuated 1930, remilitarized 1936
4 League of Nations Mandate, by plebiscite to Germany 1935
5 divided between Germany and Poland, plebiscite March 1921
6 Allied occupation 1920-23, annexed to Lithuania 1923, autonomous 1924
7 Marienwerder and Allenstein plebiscite for Germany July 1920
8 to Greece from Bulgaria 1919

The dismemberment of Germany, the heavy economic restrictions imposed on her, and the question of reparation payments (4) led to economic collapse and political turmoil under the Weimar

Republic (2). The creation of a belt of new states out of the cadaver of the Austro-Hungarian empire left vast numbers under alien rule, their rights ostensibly protected under the minority clauses of the respective treaties. Despite these, there were enormous movements of refugees (6), from Bolshevism and Fascism, as well as from alien rule. The post-war conferences did little to solve Europe's economic problems resulting from the war, which in addition to Germany's problems included vast debts to both America and Great Britain (3). But the peace settlements of 1919 were underpinned by a series of pacts which appeared to maintain the *status quo*. These alliances had three main aims: to prevent Germany from seeking to reverse the verdict of the First World War; to build up a *cordon sanitaire* against Bolshevik Russia; to maintain the territorial settlement in Eastern Europe and forestall treaty revision, particularly on the part of Hungary. France, in alliance with Poland, was the main support of the Little Entente; Germany (which only recovered freedom of manoeuvre after 1934) and the Soviet Union remained in comparative isolation. Italy under Mussolini was keen to play a major role in the Mediterranean and in the Danubian basin. Nevertheless, the French security system operated effectively until the onset of Depression (page 30), which weakened France and after 1936, if not before, undercut its alliances in Eastern Europe. The decisive change came with the German-Polish Neutrality Pact (1934), which knocked the lynch pin out of France's defensive system. After 1936, when Germany repudiated the Locarno treaties of 1925, a new period began, which – ultimately – led to the outbreak of war in 1939.

Picture: Galloping inflation in Weimar Germany produced a situation where even paper, rags and bones commanded huge prices.

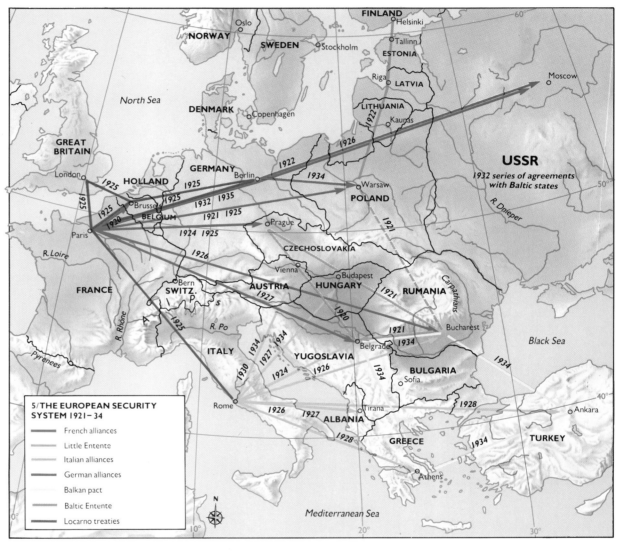

5/THE EUROPEAN SECURITY SYSTEM 1921-34
- French alliances
- Little Entente
- Italian alliances
- German alliances
- Balkan pact
- Baltic Entente
- Locarno treaties

USSR
1932 series of agreements with Baltic states

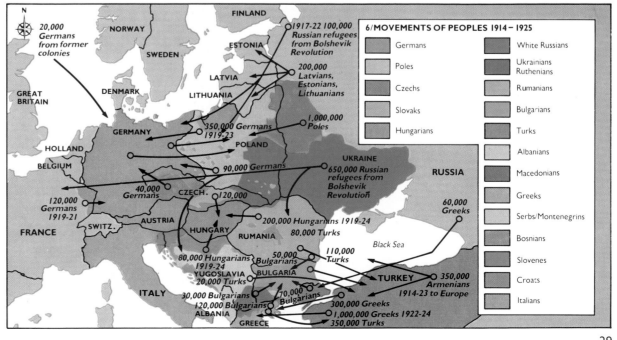

20,000 Germans from former colonies

6/MOVEMENTS OF PEOPLES 1914-1925
- Germans
- Poles
- Czechs
- Slovaks
- Hungarians
- White Russians
- Ukrainians Ruthenians
- Rumanians
- Bulgarians
- Turks
- Albanians
- Macedonians
- Greeks
- Serbs/Montenegrins
- Bosnians
- Slovenes
- Croats
- Italians

1917-22 100,000 Russian refugees from Bolshevik Revolution
200,000 Latvians, Estonians, Lithuanians
1,000,000 Poles
350,000 Germans 1919-23
90,000 Germans
40,000 Germans
120,000 Germans 1919-21
120,000
650,000 Russian refugees from Bolshevik Revolution
60,000 Greeks
200,000 Hungarians 1919-24
80,000 Turks
80,000 Hungarians 1919-24
50,000 Bulgarians
110,000 Turks
20,000 Bulgarians
30,000 Bulgarians
120,000 Bulgarians
70,000 Bulgarians
300,000 Greeks
1,000,000 Greeks 1922-24
350,000 Turks
350,000 Armenians 1914-23 to Europe

Europe 1929~1939

By the Summer of 1929, the West had returned to guarded optimism: the disasters following upon the First World War appeared to be at an end. The world's economy was recovering and, internally, the various new states created after 1919 were becoming more stable. This situation came to an end in October 1929, when the US Stock Exchange on Wall Street dramatically collapsed. Now an unreal speculative boom turned into an equally unreal collapse. Exports, everywhere, ran down – by the Autumn of 1932 to one-third of their level in 1929. This meant worldwide unemployment. In the first instance, it affected the ship-building and heavy-industrial areas. But since these, in turn, then purchased less of the necessities of life, it affected food production – farmers soon found that they had no takers for their products and, in the first half of the 1930s, people went hungry while farmers destroyed their produce. This, then, was the 'Great Depression'.

Unemployment, bitter farmers, and the instability of foreign exchange resulted in the widespread disruption of political patterns. In the more prosperous countries of the West, which had reserves upon which to fall, Right and Centre, or moderate Left and Centre, held the ring. Liberal economics, whether in the form of Roosevelt's 'New Deal' or the National Government in Great Britain, kept consensus, supplied employment, and recovered. Elsewhere the solutions were more extreme. Outstanding among them were those of Adolf Hitler in Germany and Josef Stalin in Russia. Hitler, long a nationalist agitator, had steered his national socialist (Nazi) party into a position of parliamentary dominance in Germany by 1932. He became Chancellor of Germany in 1933. Stalin emerged after Lenin's death in 1924, as the dominant figure in the USSR; in 1929 he proclaimed as the original idea of Communism the collectivization of agriculture and the forced industrialization of the Soviet Union, to be effected by a programme of Five Year Plans. Both leaders turned towards radical solutions. In March 1933 Hitler received almost forty-five per cent of the votes and, together with the few per cent awarded to the conservative Right, ran Germany. Stalin was equally determined to show that the original Communist alternative to capitalism was not dead.

Hitler wanted to restore Germany to her former glory as the lynch pin of a modern European superstate and as the effective ruler of Eastern and Central Europe. Stalin seemed to be set on a Communist empire, its frontiers unclear, but undoubtedly oriented to the West. Both leaders voiced strong dissatisfaction with the apparent weakness of the belt of new states which, since 1919, had forced a buffer zone between them. Britain and France, now cast in the role of forces of moderation, were faced with a dilemma. The British Prime Minister, Neville Chamberlain, thought he was dealing with 'two mad dogs'. Which dictator would be the most amenable to reason? At first, this seemed to be Hitler; after all, enlightened British opinion had said for some years that Germany ought to be given her rightful place in Europe. Thus, Hitler's strong arm tactics were tolerated. He was allowed to re-arm, by conscription, in 1935;

he was allowed to re-occupy the Rhineland, militarily, in 1936. He was variously told that Germany might, in due course, have her colonies in Africa back again, and when in March 1938 Germany re-occupied Austria (the *Anschluss*), this too passed without more than paper protest. In September 1938 Hitler was also granted the (mainly) German populated parts of Czechoslovakia, at the agreement of Munich, where Chamberlain and the French Prime Minister, Daladier, met Hitler, with Mussolini's mediation.

Later on, the Munich agreement counted as shameful – the hand-over of an ally. At the time, it made sense to most people. There seemed to be a fascist conspiracy, of Mussolini, Franco and Hitler. Everyone dreaded another world war. The French had built a huge defensive wall, the Maginot line, but had no plans to attack. The British needed time to build up their airforce and their air-defence, whilst also facing colonial rivalry with Italy in Africa and in the Mediterranean and Japan in the Far East. But Hitler now showed that he regarded Munich not as a settlement but as a payment on account. German rearmament proceeded and in March 1939 Hitler seized Bohemia and Moravia, Slovakia becoming a client state. The British now saw Hitler as marching towards world conquest – an impression reinforced by Nazi atrocities against Jews and non-Germans. British guarantees were given to Poland and Rumania; the French reluctantly followed; the USA refused to be involved.

If the Western Powers were seriously to resist Hitler, they could only do so practically if they had an alliance with the Soviet Union. They did approach Stalin, but it remains unclear whether their approach was seriously made, or seriously entertained. The Red Army at this time was very weak, Stalin having purged much of its higher officer-corps, and in any case the Western Powers were reluctant to upset Nazism only to put Communism in its place. In the event, Hitler approached Stalin offering to partition Poland and Eastern Europe, and a pact was concluded in late August 1939. With the assurance of Stalin's help, Hitler invaded Poland on 1 September. The British and French saw no option but to declare war, which they did on 3 September, after their ultimatum had been rejected.

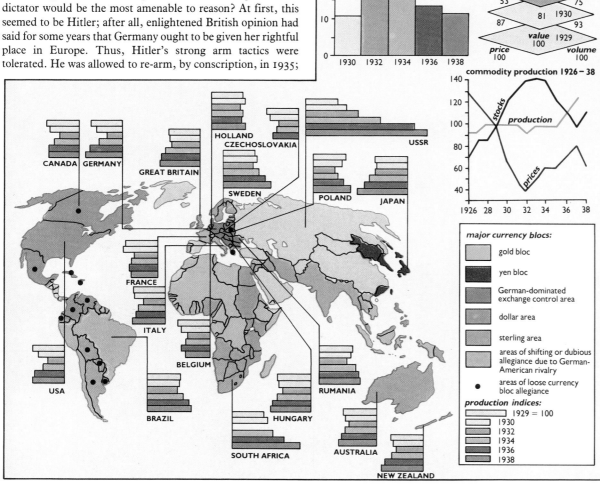

1/THE WORLD ECONOMY 1929–38

world unemployment

indices of world trade

	price 100	value 100	volume 100
1929	87		93
1930		81	75
1932	53	39	78
1934	44	34	86
1936	46	38	89
1938		40	

commodity production 1926–38

major currency blocs:
- gold bloc
- yen bloc
- German-dominated exchange control area
- dollar area
- sterling area
- areas of shifting or dubious allegiance due to German-American rivalry
- areas of loose currency bloc allegiance

production indices:
- 1929 = 100
- 1930
- 1932
- 1934
- 1936
- 1938

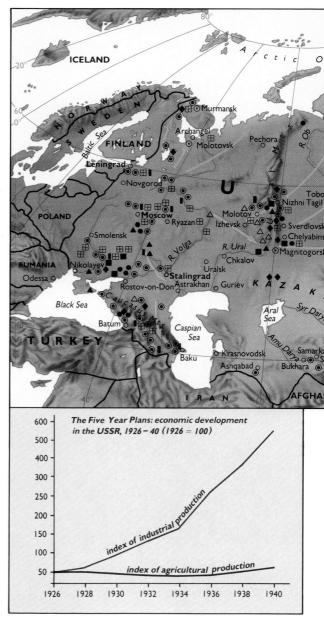

The Five Year Plans: economic development in the USSR, 1926–40 (1926 = 100)

index of industrial production

index of agricultural production

2/POLITICAL AND SOCIAL CHANGE IN EUROPE 1929–39

FINLAND
Communist Party banned, 1930
Attempted Fascist (Lapua) coups, Oct. 1930 and Feb. 1932

NORWAY 30.8
Strike waves, 1931, 1936-8

SWEDEN 22.8

ESTONIA

LATVIA

DENMARK 31.7
North Schleswig German agitation, 1933

LITHUANIA
Nationalist Union becomes openly fascist, 1932

POLAND 15.6
Major strike waves affecting peasants and workers, 1935-8

LUX

GERMANY 30.1
Unstable, pre-revolutionary period, 1930-33
Sudetendeutsche Partei formed, 1935

CZECHOSLOVAKIA 13.5

AUSTRIA 26.1
Unsuccessful Nazi coup, Dollfuss killed, July 1934
Pro-Nazi demonstrations, April 1933

SWITZ 21.3
9 Nov. (1932 – Labour disturbances at Geneva

HUNGARY

RUMANIA
Fascist 'Iron Guard' tolerated and financed by Carol II, 1930-38
Jiu Valley strikers massacred, 1929
Bucharest railway strike bloodily suppressed, 1934

YUGOSLAVIA
Strike wave, 1935-8

ITALY

Corsica

Sardinia

BULGARIA

ALBANIA
Muslim insurrection, May 1937

Rubber workers sit-down, Salonika, 1934

GREECE
Depression fuels monarchist resurgence, 1932
Metaxas dictator, 1936-41

TURKEY
Dervish rising near Izmir, Dec. 1930

U S S R

Baltic Sea

Black Sea

Sea

Sicily

TUNISIA

Rhodes

Cyprus

Legend

political regimes:
- fascist
- repressive or conservative
- democratic
- 22.5 percentage of industrial workers unemployed

major movements of protest and dissatisfaction
- ◆ strike wave
- ▲ sit-down strike(s)
- ■ riot, demonstration or single strike
- ● right-wing activity

THE GREAT BULL MARKET of 1928 gave way to a precipitous fall in stock prices in Oct. 1929. The Slump (1) saw a drastic drop in the level of prices coupled with a moderate decrease in volume, which produced a decline in the value of world trade. The consequent slump in commodity prices caused severe hardship and dislocation in many countries. Multilateral trade and payment was replaced by a system of increasingly closed currency and trading blocs. In Soviet Russia (3) Stalin had inaugurated a series of Five Year Plans, development programmes which saw an invigoration of industry at the cost of massive collectivization – especially of agriculture – and a ruthless relocation or eradication of imbalances of population. Protest movements of the Right and Left arose in almost every country, severely testing the social and political fabric. In Europe there occurred a widespread polarization to extremes (2), and in countries where democratic traditions and institutions were weak some form of Right-Wing dictatorship invariably resulted. The elaborate security system established by the victorious Allies after the First World War (page 28) was soon undermined, and a new series of agreements (4) emerged by which France and Great Britain attempted to contain the dual threat posed by Soviet Communism and the emergent Fascist governments in Italy, Germany and Spain. At first they sought associates to deter German or Italian aggression. Hitler tried either to isolate or, as with the Axis and the Anti-Comintern Pacts, to distract his political opponents. Mussolini hoped to control Hitler's rate of expansion to match Italy's capabilities. Other countries concluded non-aggression pacts with Hitler or joined in the 'neutralist' Declaration of Copenhagen. But underpinning the increasing desperation of these measures was the common realization by most European countries that re-armament (5) on a massive scale was unavoidable.

Picture below left: The Proclamation of Freedom to Rearm rally, Berlin 1935. Although Hitler had ordered secret rearmament programmes in 1934, he was sufficiently confident of his position to make his policies public the following year.

1934-35

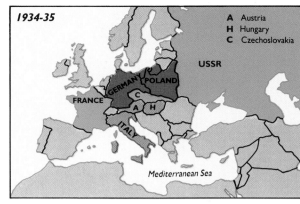

A Austria
H Hungary
C Czechoslovakia

USSR
GERMANY
POLAND
FRANCE
C
A H
ITALY
Mediterranean Sea

1936-37

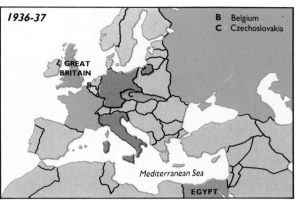

B Belgium
C Czechoslovakia

GREAT BRITAIN
C
Mediterranean Sea
EGYPT

1938-39

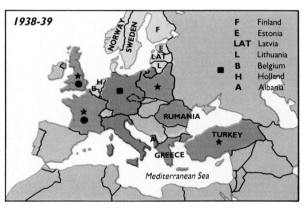

F Finland
E Estonia
LAT Latvia
L Lithuania
B Belgium
H Holland
A Albania

NORWAY SWEDEN
F
E
LAT
L
B
H
A
RUMANIA
GREECE
TURKEY
Mediterranean Sea

4/EUROPEAN POLITICAL AGREEMENTS 1934–39 (above)

1934-35:
- German–Polish non-aggression pact, 1934
- Rome protocols, March 1934
- Franco–Soviet/Soviet–Czech. pact, May 1935 (see also 1936-37)

1936-37:
- Axis, Nov. 1936 and May 1939
- declaration of neutrality, 1936
- Anglo–Egyptian treaty, 1936

1938-39:
- British and French guarantees for Poland, Greece, Rumania and Turkey, 1939
- ★ Anglo–Franco–Polish and Anglo–Franco–Turkish alliances, Sept. 1939
- Copenhagen declaration of neutrality, July 1938
- ● Anglo–French staff talks, Apr. 1936
- ■ German–Soviet non-aggression pact, 1939

3/THE SOVIET UNION 1926–40

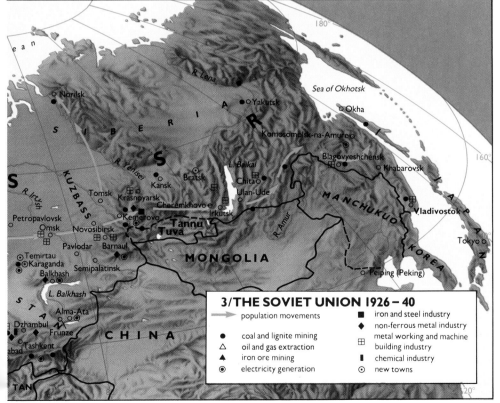

Norilsk
R. Lena
Yakutsk
Sea of Okhotsk
Okha
Komosomolsk-na-Amure
Blagovyeshchensk
Khabarovsk
R. Yenisei
Kansk
Bratsk
L. Baikal
Chita
Ulan-Ude
R. Amur
MANCHUKUO
Tomsk
Krasnoyarsk
Cheremkhovo
Irkutsk
Vladivostok
KOREA
KUZBASS
Kemerovo
Tokyo
Petropavlovsk
Omsk
Novosibirsk
Pavlodar
Barnaul
MONGOLIA
Temirtau
Karaganda
Semipalatinsk
Peiping (Peking)
Balkhash
L. Balkhash
Alma-Ata
Dzhambul
Frunze
CHINA
Tashkent

population movements
- ● coal and lignite mining
- △ oil and gas extraction
- ▲ iron ore mining
- ⊙ electricity generation
- ■ iron and steel industry
- ◆ non-ferrous metal industry
- ⊞ metal working and machine building industry
- ▮ chemical industry
- ⊙ new towns

5/EUROPEAN REARMAMENT 1930–39

The figures below are from a variety of sources. In certain instances estimates are only based on government publications
* battleships, battlecruisers, cruisers, aircraft carriers, destroyers, submarines; excludes ships under construction, demilitarized ships
† peacetime armies only, including conscripts, but not reserves

armaments		GREAT BRITAIN	FRANCE	USSR	GERMANY	ITALY
* major warships	1932	284	175	89	26	150
	1939	290	161	101	88	240
military aircraft	1932	445	under 400	2 595	36	not available
	1939	7940	3163	10,382	8295	not available
† army	1932	192,000	c. 350,000	562,000	100,000	234,000
	1939	237,000	500,000	1,900,000	730,000	400,000
military expenditure	1931/32	£107.5m	13.8fr.bn	1.4m.roubles	RM 0.61bn	5.01bn lire
	1938/39	£397.4m	29.1fr.bn	27m.roubles	RM 17.24 bn	15.02bn lire

China 1920~1931

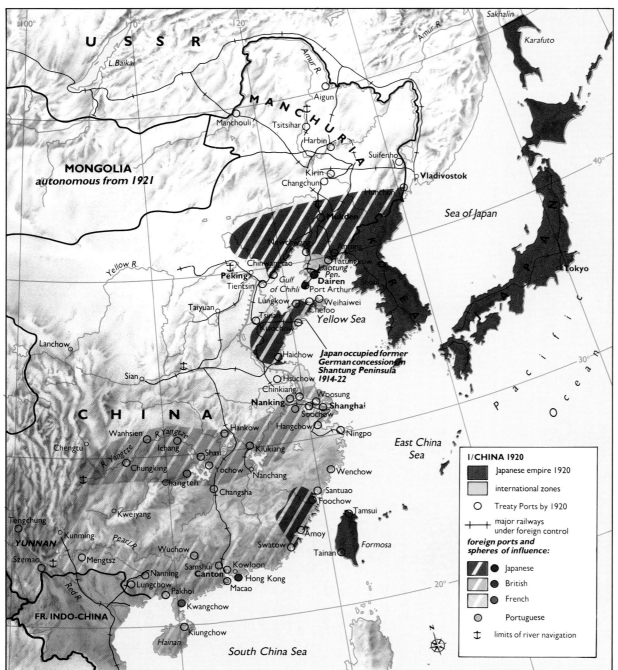

2/THE ANHWEI-CHIHLI WAR, 1920

1/CHINA 1920

- ▨ Japanese empire 1920
- ▦ international zones
- ○ Treaty Ports by 1920
- ╬ major railways under foreign control

foreign ports and spheres of influence:

- ◣ ● Japanese
- ◣ ● British
- ◣ ● French
- ○ Portuguese
- ⚓ limits of river navigation

warlord powers (maps 2–6):

- Fengtien Clique (from 1926 war under Chang Tso-lin)
- Anhwei Clique
- Chihli Clique
- T'ang Chi-yao warlord of Yunnan
- Liu Hsien-shih warlord of Kweichow
- Kwangsi Clique
- Kuominchun Clique under Feng Yu-hsiang
- Chihli faction under Sun Ch'uan-fang
- Chihli faction under Wu P'ei-fu
- area of Kuomintang (Nationalist)
- → Kuomintang (Nationalist) forces control
- → pro-Nationalist forces

THE PRIVILEGED POSITIONS that the Great Powers had established in China survived the revolution of 1911-12, (1) but president Yüan Shih-k'ai's attempt in 1915 to install himself as emperor destroyed the authority of central government. Secession by Kwangsi and revolt throughout the country left provincial military governors with effective local power as Yüan's party, the Peiyang, split between Anhwei and Chihli factions. Chang Tso-lin, later head of the Fengtien, established himself in Manchuria, and the most important of the old-guard revolutionaries, Sun Yat-sen, began to create a power base in the south. After 1918, virtually every province was beset by local power struggles as the main factions fought for control of north China and the Yangtze valley; but a clear split emerged between these warlord factions and the south. By the time of the Anhwei-Chihli war

IN THE OPENING DECADES of the twentieth century, China was to play a part in East Asian politics not dissimilar to that played by the Balkan states in European politics: it was a forum for Great Power rivalry, dissent and – eventually – open hostilities. In the last six decades of the nineteenth century various European powers and the United States compromised China's sovereignty and integrity by a series of unequal treaties that exacted from China territorial, commercial, financial and extra-territorial concessions. Although the Western Powers wanted the ruling Manchu dynasty to survive as guarantor of their privileges, they wanted it sufficiently weak to be unable to challenge them; the effect of their actions, however, was to undermine the authority of the dynasty and to generate political pressures within China that erupted in the revolution of October 1911, the overthrow of the 250-year-old Manchu dynasty and the inauguration of a republic in February 1912.

The erosion of Manchu authority after 1900 coincided with an intensification of Great Power rivalries within China, the most important of which was the conflict of interest between Russia and Japan. The latter, which had escaped subjugation to the Western Powers largely because China attracted so much of their predatory attention, emerged upon the China scene in 1895 when she defeated Manchu forces in Korea and Manchuria. However, the gains she made, ratified at the Treaty of Shimonoseki, were stripped from her by the Triple Intervention of France, Germany and Russia. Thereafter Russo-Japanese estrangement deepened as Russia sought to secure for herself an exclusive sphere of influence in Korea and Manchuria, both of which Japan considered vital to her own security and economic interests. The Russo-Japanese war of 1904–05 saw Japanese forces victorious in both Korea and southern Manchuria and paved the way for a post-war *rapprochement* that allowed Japan to take control of Korea (1910) whilst Manchuria was divided between Japan and Russia. Here they worked together against other powers in the

preservation of their respective spheres of interest, and after 1912 arranged for a division of Mongolia between themselves in the event of a disintegration of China.

The First World War witnessed both the eclipse of European power and influence and the progressive weakening of central authority in China, developments which Japan sought to put to her advantage in the form of the 'Twenty-one Demands' of 1915. Though forced by international pressure to moderate her position, the 'Twenty-one Demands' revealed the extent of Japanese ambitions: in effect, Japan aimed at reducing China to a position of dependency upon her. Japan secured from China recognition of certain of her claims, but their acceptance by the government of Yüan Shih-k'ai, fatally compromised the latter's hopes of founding his own dynasty and set in train a series of revolts and mass demonstrations that were to lead to the collapse of central authority in China after Yüan's death in 1916.

Between 1918 and 1928 China was savaged by a series of violent clashes between a variety of individuals and factions that made and broke a bewildering sequence of alliances with one another in a naked struggle for power. Motivated more by self-interest than by political idealism, rival warlords sought to ensure their own power bases through the prevention of the emergence of a single centralizing authority. Yet in terms of the events that were to lead to the outbreak of the Second World War, the period between 1918 and 1928 was critical, for this 'warlord era' presented all the Powers with the problem of deciding which individual or faction to support at any particular time, and to what purpose.

For Japan this problem was particularly acute, because her extensive interests in China were mainly concentrated in Manchuria, which was the fief of Chang Tso-lin who hoped to establish his authority throughout northern China, but whose capacity to rule Manchuria effectively weakened in the period. As a result, the Japanese Army in Manchuria and northern

China became gradually involved in China's interminable wars in defence of what were felt to be Japan's national interests. These were both undefined and constantly widened as the Japanese Army sought to take further advantage of Chinese weakness. Further, after 1921, there emerged at Canton a nationalist authority – the Kuomintang – under Sun Yat-sen, which embraced a genuine, if conveniently vague political programme, dominated by an ambition to end the state of civil war in China by a twin policy of conquest and political mobilization. With Soviet support, the Canton government spent the period before 1926 consolidating its authority in the south before beginning the Northern Expedition against the warlords on and beyond the Yangtze.

Within six months Nationalist armies secured the upper Yangtze, Nanking and Shanghai, but in mid-1927, faced by military reverses around Hsüchow and the realization that its Communist allies were intent on a seizure of power on their own behalf, the Kuomintang turned upon the Communists and thereafter sought a series of arrangements with northern warlords that would preserve the existing political and social order, whilst ensuring at least nominal Kuomintang authority throughout China.

Various wars continued into 1929 and even beyond, but in October 1928 the Kuomintang authorities established themselves in Nanking as the National Government of China and in so doing presented the prospect of bringing some form of order to China as a whole. Its attempts to bring Manchuria into its fold led to an ill-judged war with the Soviet Union in 1929 that was to be very significant for the future: it revealed Chinese ambitions and the threat these presented to all the powers that depended upon Chinese divisions for the preservation of their interests; it also revealed Chinese weaknesses. By 1930 the Japanese decided that it was time to act decisively to defend their interests in mainland Asia, firstly in Manchuria, then in China itself.

3/THE FIRST CHIHLI-FENGTIEN WAR, 1922

4/THE SECOND CHIHLI-FENGTIEN WAR, 1924

5/CHINA 1926

of 1920 (2), China had fragmented; but with Sun Yat-sen establishing a provisional government at Canton in 1921, he, Chang and Anhwei survivors planned to destroy Chihli dominance. Sun Yat-sen, however, was undermined by various warlords in the south, and the Fengtien were badly beaten in May 1922 (3). Thereafter the Chihli sought to restore a single national authority. In the second Fengtien-Chihli war (4) it was defeated as a result of betrayals and desertions. In the south, Sun Yat-sen created a radical party based on mass support, enlisting Soviet aid. After Sun's death (1925) Chiang Kai-shek emerged as military leader of a National (Kuomintang) Government uneasily divided between Left and Right. At the same time Chang Tso-lin sought to expand his power into the lower Yangtze, but was outmanoeuvred and was even subjected to attack inside Manchuria. After stemming this invasion (with Japanese assistance) Chang joined forces with two other warlords, Wu P'ei-fu and Sun Ch'uan-fang (5), to divide northern and central China between them. But Chiang Kai-shek had secured his base around Canton and on 9 July 1926 launched The Northern Expedition (6), Wu being beaten around Changsha and Sun at Nanchang. Nationalist armies secured Shanghai and Nanking in March 1927; then the Nationalist camp split between a Left-Wing government in Hankow and a Right-wing government headed by Chiang in Nanking. After a massacre of Communists in Shanghai in April, Chiang, now independent of Soviet assistance, treated with various northern warlords in order to isolate both the Hankow government and Chang Tso-lin, whose forces were badly defeated in May. Complex negotiations and campaigning followed until mid-1928, when Chang was murdered by the Japanese. In Oct. 1928 a Nationalist government was formally inaugurated at Nanking (7) which, despite a Communist threat, gained the nominal allegiance of most warlords. But this new order was soon to be challenged by the Japanese.

Picture above right: Chinese warlord armies, badly equipped and raised by feudal levy, nevertheless relied on modern trains, heavy artillery and occasional air support.

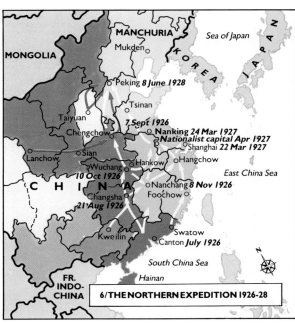

6/THE NORTHERN EXPEDITION 1926-28

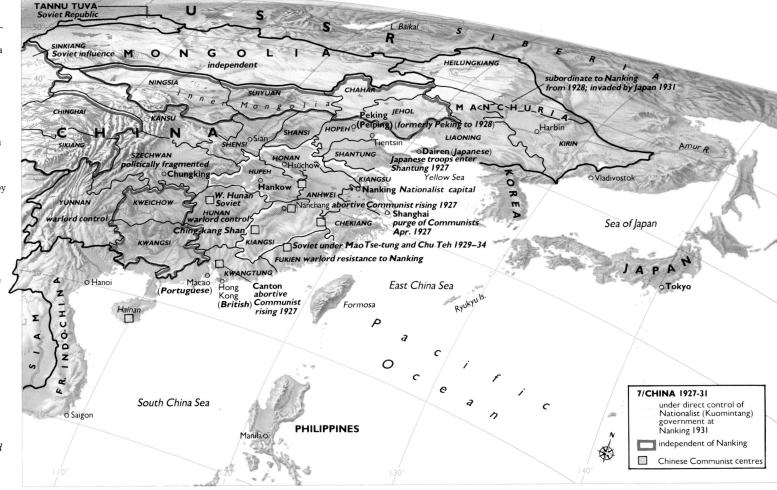

7/CHINA 1927-31

under direct control of Nationalist (Kuomintang) government at Nanking 1931

☐ independent of Nanking

☐ Chinese Communist centres

Japanese expansion 1931~1941

THE DECADE following the end of the First World War saw Japan observe considerable restraint towards China and the Western Powers (page 32). This moderation, however, survived neither the emergence of a nationalist government in Nanking nor the onset of the Great Depression in 1929. The former was an explicit threat to Japan's existing privileges and future ambitions in China; the latter intensified Japan's search for raw materials and markets in a drive towards self-sufficiency. These developments, combined with the Japanese Army's acquired habit of intervention in Chinese affairs without reference to Tokyo and a hardening nationalist view that Manchuria and Mongolia were natural areas of Japanese interest, led to the Japanese occupation of Manchuria.

A five-month campaign brought the Japanese effective control of the Chinese province, and on 18 February 1932, a Japanese puppet assembly proclaimed the independence of Manchuria; in March a new state, Manchukuo, was promulgated with the last emperor of China, Pu-yi, the successor to the Manchu throne, installed at its head. This declaration of independence, however, defined the neighbouring Chinese province, Jehol, as part of this new state, and in January and February 1933 the Japanese occupied the irredentist territory. Over the next two years a policy of alternating inducements and threats was used to force extensive concessions from the Chinese in the areas beyond the Great Wall.

After July 1937, the Japanese Army embarked upon the full-scale invasion and conquest of northern and central China. As in 1931, however, the driving force behind Japanese aggression was the suspicion that China was attempting to settle her domestic quarrels in order to resist her neighbour; following the Long March (1934-35) when the Communists withdrew from their southern bases to the north-west, the Sian

agreement (Dec. 1936) brought an uneasy end to nearly a decade of civil war between the Nationalists and Communists (page 32). In northern China the Japanese made extensive gains, but on the lower Yangtze they were bitterly opposed around Shanghai and it was not taken until November. Nanking fell the following month amidst scenes of mass butchery and rape on the part of Japanese. It was not until May 1938, however, that the capture of Tungshan allowed the Japanese to link their conquests in northern and central China: thereafter the Japanese advanced up the Yangtze to secure Hankow and Wuchang in October. Having lost Canton in the same month, the Chinese made no attempt to defend the great cities of the middle Yangtze.

Chiang refused various overtures for peace, and Japan sought to counter Chiang's obstinacy by sponsoring Chinese regimes at both Peking and Nanking, but these were too weak to make them genuine alternatives to Chiang's regime at Chungking. The Japanese were without the means of fully occupying the areas they already held, and further conquests only threatened further complications. In 1941 the Japanese nevertheless occupied the major coastal cities south of the Yangtze, as their attention turned to the possibility of isolating Chungking from all outside sources of support. The defeat of France in 1940 placed Indo-China in pledge to the Japanese, and in September 1940 Japanese forces moved into northern Indo-China; in July 1941 Japan forced the Vichy authorities to accept a joint protectorate over Indo-China. These moves prompted the United States to impose sanctions on Japan (page 66), thereby setting in train the events that were to lead to the outbreak of the Pacific war in December. But the war in China was to continue (page 144) under its own complex terms of conduct, until the final Japanese capitulation in August 1945.

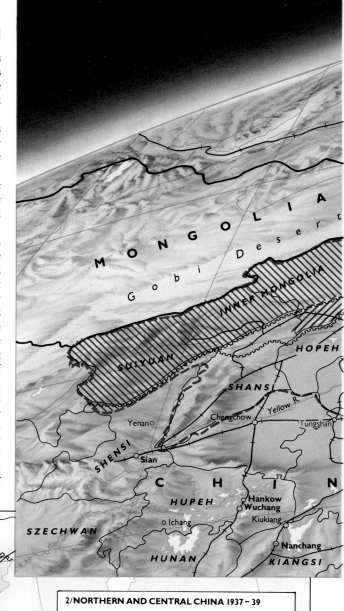

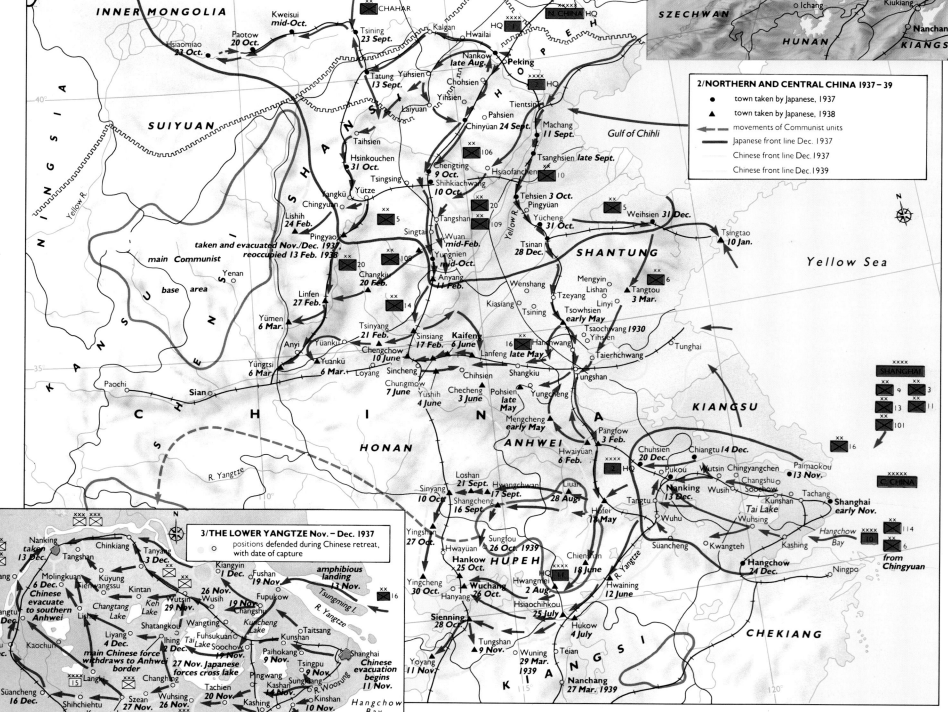

2/NORTHERN AND CENTRAL CHINA 1937-39

- ● town taken by Japanese, 1937
- ▲ town taken by Japanese, 1938
- ←- - movements of Communist units
- —— Japanese front line Dec. 1937
- —— Chinese front line Dec. 1937
- —— Chinese front line Dec.1939

3/THE LOWER YANGTZE Nov. – Dec. 1937

- ○ positions defended during Chinese retreat, with date of capture

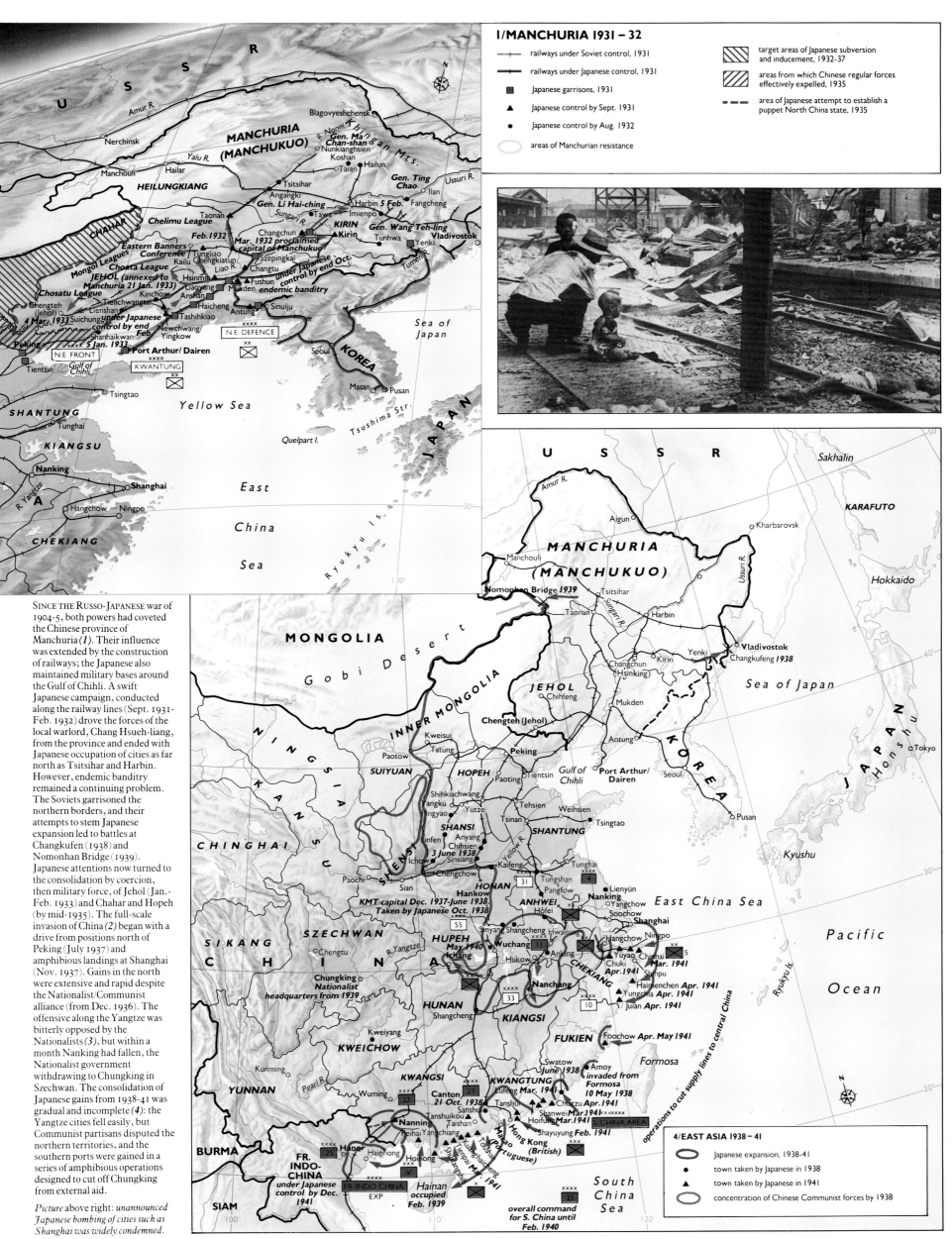

I/MANCHURIA 1931–32

railways under Soviet control, 1931
railways under Japanese control, 1931
■ Japanese garrisons, 1931
▲ Japanese control by Sept. 1931
● Japanese control by Aug. 1932
areas of Manchurian resistance

target areas of Japanese subversion and inducement, 1932-37
areas from which Chinese regular forces effectively expelled, 1935
— — area of Japanese attempt to establish a puppet North China state, 1935

SINCE THE RUSSO-JAPANESE war of 1904-5, both powers had coveted the Chinese province of Manchuria (*1*). Their influence was extended by the construction of railways; the Japanese also maintained military bases around the Gulf of Chihli. A swift Japanese campaign, conducted along the railway lines (Sept. 1931-Feb. 1932) drove the forces of the local warlord, Chang Hsueh-liang, from the province and ended with Japanese occupation of cities as far north as Tsitsihar and Harbin. However, endemic banditry remained a continuing problem. The Soviets garrisoned the northern borders, and their attempts to stem Japanese expansion led to battles at Changkufen (1938) and Nomonhan Bridge (1939). Japanese attentions now turned to the consolidation by coercion, then military force, of Jehol (Jan.-Feb. 1933) and Chahar and Hopeh (by mid-1935). The full-scale invasion of China (*2*) began with a drive from positions north of Peking (July 1937) and amphibious landings at Shanghai (Nov. 1937). Gains in the north were extensive and rapid despite the Nationalist/Communist alliance (from Dec. 1936). The offensive along the Yangtze was bitterly opposed by the Nationalists (*3*), but within a month Nanking had fallen, the Nationalist government withdrawing to Chungking in Szechwan. The consolidation of Japanese gains from 1938-41 was gradual and incomplete (*4*): the Yangtze cities fell easily, but Communist partisans disputed the northern territories, and the southern ports were gained in a series of amphibious operations designed to cut off Chungking from external aid.

Picture above right: unannounced Japanese bombing of cities such as Shanghai was widely condemned.

4/EAST ASIA 1938–41

Japanese expansion, 1938-41
● town taken by Japanese in 1938
▲ town taken by Japanese in 1941
concentration of Chinese Communist forces by 1938

Fascism in Europe 1922~1939

FASCISM WAS FOUNDED by Benito Mussolini, a Left-Wing agitator in Italy who, in 1915, broke with the main strain of Italian socialism and became a nationalist. Fascism was characterized by extreme nationalism and dictatorship with the concomitants of militarism, secret police and violent anti-Marxism (although several of the leading Fascists began as figures of the Left, and continued to preach egalitarianism and anti-capitalism). The externals of Fascism everywhere were much the same, usually derived from Italian models: 'the Roman Salute', with arm outstretched, as answer to the Marxists' clenched-fist-in-anger; black shirts, as counterpart to Garibaldi's red ones. There was a Fascist style in architecture (a bombastic classicism), broad-ranging propaganda, youth-organization and a commitment to remodelling all social institutions. All Fascist movements had their 'Leader' – Duce, Führer, Jefe. Beyond these externals, however, Fascism varied greatly in character and violence: German Fascism – Nazism – was unique in the extent of its aggression and dictatorship.

Fascists came to power by different means, but in all cases the background was of severe economic dislocation – inflation, followed by unemployment. Established political parties failed to agree to a solution and political life disintegrated. In Italy unemployed ex-soldiers supplied the backbone of Mussolini's Fascist movement; though small in terms of electoral support (7% in 1920) it was successful in street-fighting. By 1922,

Mussolini could take power with a threat of violence and the connivance of Right-Wing elements. At bottom, the Fascist answer to political problems was simple: force. The economy would be made to work by suppression of strikes, by tariffs against foreign goods, often by re-employment through armaments and the conquest of new markets in an empire (which would also supply cheap raw materials and a place in which to deposit surplus proletarians). Anyone arguing with this programme at home would be imprisoned, and if foreigners got in the way there would be war.

When the Great Slump came after 1929 (page 30), economies disintegrated – those with high proportions of peasants being, in the main, the worst affected. In Germany, however, a unique economic imbalance, arising from mismanagement, the Western Powers' demand for endless reparations (page 28) and an excessive reliance on foreign investment, drove unemployment up to nearly one-third of the working population. The party system collapsed, and in January 1933, Hitler, who promised drastic solutions, and with one-third of the electorate behind him, became Chancellor. His first acts were to take up alliance with the orthodox Right, which gave him a majority at the next election; then he arranged for the Reichstag to vote him dictatorial powers (the Enabling Act, March 1933). A secret police, the Gestapo, with para-military auxiliaries in two Nazi adjuncts, the SA and the SS, harried

opponents, putting them in concentration camps. Eventually, the chief of the SS, Heinrich Himmler, extended his power over the entire police force; in 1934, he was authorized by Hitler to carry out a murderous purge of his rivals in the SA (the Night of the Long Knives, 30 June). Anti-semitism was a main platform for the Nazis, who blamed economic troubles on the Jews, who were alleged to be un-German parasites.

Hitler became increasingly popular. The economy recovered remarkably quickly: by 1936 there was little unemployment, and by 1938 there were labour shortages. A great many Germans of humble origin were taken through the Party to rank and office and many others prospered with the economic recovery. The Nazis claimed, perhaps plausibly, that this was caused by their new economic system: a virtual prohibition of cheap foreign goods, price-stops, state-led cartels in industry and agriculture, and a paper-currency which could be 'spent' to promote employment. Such an enclosed economic system offended international economics, but Hitler meant to make Germany self-sufficient. Further, he intended to take over countries to the east, particularly the Soviet Union, which would become German colonies. To this end, re-armament was launched as soon as Hitler was able. By 1936, Hitler was able to re-occupy the Rhineland, the first in a number of audacious manoeuvres – backed up by force – designed to restore to Germany her 'traditional' territories.

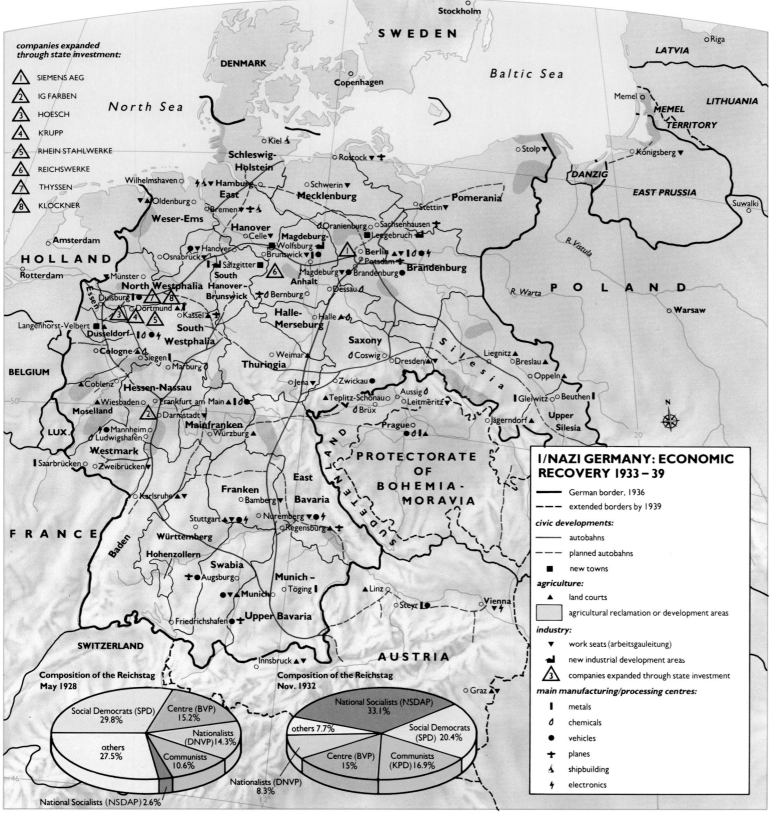

THE NAZIS ACHIEVED a dramatic increase in political support between 1928 and 1932 (1, diagram); after Hitler became Chancellor (1933) he introduced a wide range of economic development measures (1), backed up by protectionist foreign trade policies. Under-developed areas, major companies and flagging industries enjoyed state support and investment; a motorway network (autobahnen), new towns and industrial sites were created, which with a reinvigorated armaments industry (page 30) led to a massive boost to the Germany economy. By comparison, the older Fascist state of Italy, although announcing similar plans, failed to effect them as successfully (5). Hitler also revived Germany's political fortunes (2). First he eliminated the national restrictions imposed at Versailles (page 28): the Saarland was recovered by plebiscite, the Rhineland remilitarized, Austria annexed. Then, pretending to advocate self-determination for German minorities, he turned on France's allies, Czechoslovakia and Poland. Czechoslovakia's multi-racial composition facilitated, with British and French acquiescence at Munich, its progressive partition. Polish resistance to German claims (Danzig, the 'Corridor') led to war (page 38). Mussolini's colonial ambitions led to the invasion of Ethiopia (on the pretext of disputed border territories) (4), and the annexation of Albania. The Fascist challenge in Europe, however, first boiled over into violence in Spain, where a revolt of military officers in Spanish Morocco led to civil war (3). The military, political right and Roman Catholic Church (with German and Italian 'volunteers' and military aid) grouped against the 'Popular Front' government, republicans, anti-clericals, anarchists, socialists and Communists, Basque and Catalan separatists (with Soviet military aid). Against widespread criticism Britain and France initiated an international Non-Intervention Agreement – a measure mirrored in later years when the Fascist leader Franco refused to join Hitler's Axis, Spain remaining neutral throughout the Second World War.

Picture above right: A mass Nazi rally at the Zeppelinfeld, Nuremberg, 1936.

While Hitler was re-arming and increasing his domestic power, many European countries emulated the models of Fascism. In 1936 much of the Spanish Army revolted against a Left-inclined Republican government. General Franco was widely (though wrongly) supposed to be the agent of a Fascist conspiracy, but Hitler and Mussolini supplied him with weapons and men (the *Luftwaffe* saw its first action there). By Summer 1939 Franco had won.

Hitler rapidly threw Mussolini and Franco into his shadow. Italian Fascism proved much less successful, in economic terms, in the 1930s. Mussolini looked to foreign triumphs, and in 1935 launched a vicious war to conquer Abyssinia. This, and his support for Franco, provided cheap victories but shut off Mussolini from the Western Powers. In 1936, Hitler and Mussolini drew together, forming the 'axis' between Berlin and Rome, around which the politics of Europe were supposed to revolve. With Italian adhesion guaranteed, Hitler was now free to undermine the independence of the Eastern and Central European countries which he regarded as stepping-stones to the empire he planned in Russia.

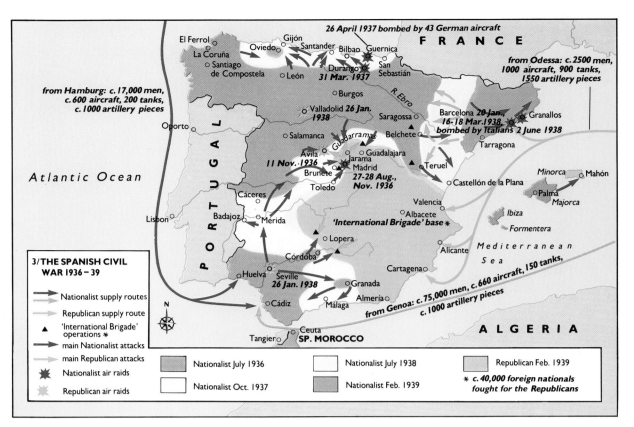

3/THE SPANISH CIVIL WAR 1936–39

- ⟶ Nationalist supply routes
- ⟶ Republican supply route
- ▲ 'International Brigade' operations ✳
- → main Nationalist attacks
- → main Republican attacks
- ✴ Nationalist air raids
- ✴ Republican air raids

Nationalist July 1936
Nationalist Oct. 1937
Nationalist July 1938
Nationalist Feb. 1939
Republican Feb. 1939

✳ c. 40,000 foreign nationals fought for the Republicans

26 April 1937 bombed by 43 German aircraft

from Hamburg: c. 17,000 men, c. 600 aircraft, 200 tanks, c. 1000 artillery pieces

from Odessa: c. 2500 men, 1000 aircraft, 900 tanks, 1550 artillery pieces

Barcelona 20 Jan., 16-18 Mar. 1938, bombed by Italians 2 June 1938

'International Brigade' base ✳

from Genoa: c. 75,000 men, c. 660 aircraft, 150 tanks, c. 1000 artillery pieces

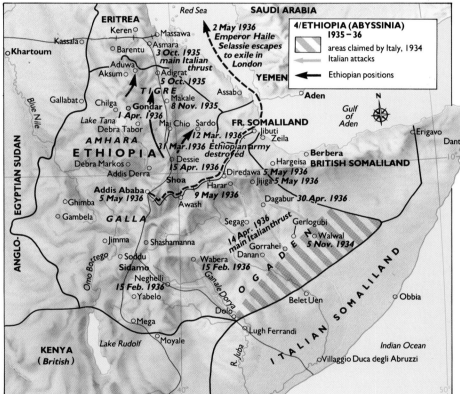

4/ETHIOPIA (ABYSSINIA) 1935–36

- areas claimed by Italy, 1934
- Italian attacks
- ← Ethiopian positions

2 May 1936 Emperor Haile Selassie escapes to exile in London

2/FASCIST EXPANSION 1934–39

⑧ annexed to Germany (E. Prussia) Mar. 1939
② reoccupied by Germany Mar. 1936
④ Czechoslovak territory given to Germany by Munich agreement Sept. 1938
⑤ Czechoslovakian territory annexed to Poland Sept. 1938
⑦ occupied by Hungary Mar. 1939
① plebiscite (Jan.) to join Germany Mar. 1935
③ annexed to Germany Mar. 1938 (Anschluss)
⑥ Slovak territory to Hungary Nov. 1938
⑨ occupied by Italy Apr. 1939

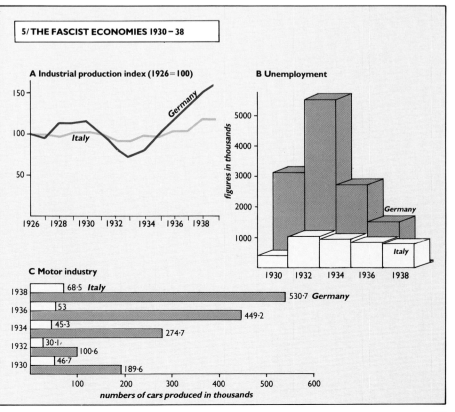

5/ THE FASCIST ECONOMIES 1930 – 38

A Industrial production index (1926=100)

Germany
Italy

B Unemployment

figures in thousands

Germany
Italy

1930 1932 1934 1936 1938

C Motor industry

Year	Italy	Germany
1938	68·5	530·7
1936	53	449·2
1934	45·3	274·7
1932	30·1	100·6
1930	46·7	189·6

numbers of cars produced in thousands

Poland SEPTEMBER 1939

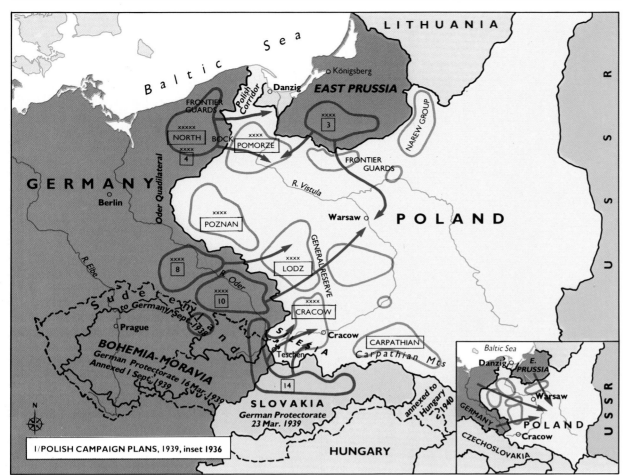

I/POLISH CAMPAIGN PLANS, 1939, inset 1936

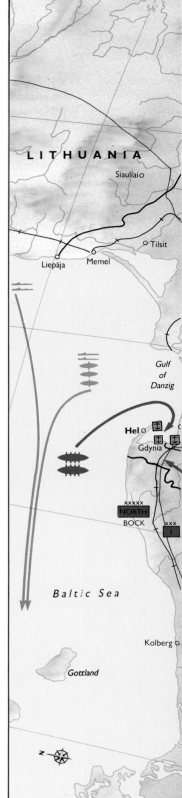

THE POLISH DEFENCE PLAN of 1936, (*1, inset*), designed to counter German aggression, was to mass forces on the western frontier, whilst simultaneously attacking East Prussia. German annexation of Czech Sudetenland (1938) and the subsequent placing of German troops in Slovakia enforced a revision (*1*), which spread the Poles thinly along the frontier from the Carpathians to Lithuania. The 1939 German plan involved a textbook breakthrough, the cutting of the Polish Corridor, encirclement of the Poles and annihilation within pincer jaws centred on Warsaw. In practice, the breakthrough followed the plan perfectly (*2*). At 0440, 1 Sept., the *Luftwaffe* destroyed much of the air force on the ground, whilst the 4th Army crossed the Polish Corridor, linking with the 3rd Army in East Prussia (3 Sept.) and joining its advance on Warsaw. Despite the primitive state of the Polish road network some units in the south advanced 15 miles on the first day and by 5 Sept. the 14th Army was at Cracow, the 10th beyond Częstochowa and the 8th near Lodz. The Polish front line, with the exception of the Poznan Army, were all retreating. By 7 Sept. German Army Groups North (Bock) and South (Rundstedt) were within 40 and 25 miles of Warsaw respectively. Their original provision for encirclement of the Poles along the River Vistula was revised when, hearing of the Polish eastward escape, the envelopment was extended to the River Bug. The Poznan Army, isolated by the initial German advance, turned east on 10 Sept. and attempted to break across the River Bzura (*3*) through the German envelopment to reach Warsaw. This initiative was contained by the Germans around Kutno and the pocket surrendered on 17 September. Meanwhile, Guderian's panzers took Brest (17 Sept.), while Lwów fell on 19 Sept. Warsaw, heavily bombed, capitulated on 27 Sept., the last Polish combatants surrendered on 6 Oct. The Russians invaded on 17 Sept., German advance units withdrawing behind a pre-agreed partition line. At this stage many Polish combatants surrendered to the Germans in preference to confronting the Soviet Army.

Picture left: the German Army advancing along a typical, unmetalled Polish road.

THE POLISH CAMPAIGN was the shortest and most decisive of all German aggressions of the Second World War, of which it marked the opening stage. Between 1 and 19 September, 1939 German armies broke through Poland's northern, western and southern frontiers and completed whirlwind advances which overwhelmed the much weaker Polish forces; their destruction was consummated by the intervention of the Soviet army, which began to advance into eastern Poland on 17 September.

The concessions of territory under the Versailles treaty to the reborn state of Poland were the most resented grievances felt by Germany in the inter-war years (page 28). Resentment focussed particularly on the loss of direct access to East Prussia, through the creation of the Polish Corridor to the Baltic, of the German-speaking city of Danzig and of the largely German-speaking regions of Silesia. Hitler placed the repossession of these areas high on his list of 'territorial ambitions', even though the integrity of Poland was guaranteed by France (1921) and, from 31 March 1939, by Britain (page 30).

On 25 March 1939, Hitler told the German Army Staff that the time had come to consider solving the 'Polish problem' by military means. On 3 April he set 1 September as the date for an attack. On 28 April he abrogated the German-Polish non-aggression treaty of 1934 and on 23 May he warned his generals to expect war. Simultaneous negotiations with the Western Allies and with Russia, beginning in April, ostensibly designed to solve the 'Polish problem' without conflict, culminated in the signing of the Molotov-Ribbentrop Pact on 23 August. This agreed spheres of influence in Eastern Europe and freed Germany to attack Poland without risking a Russian counter-offensive.

Germany deployed five armies totalling 1,500,000 men for the offensive. The Poles, who began military preparations in July, had succeeded in mobilizing one million when, following German-staged frontier incidents, the Germans attacked at dawn on 1 September. The *Luftwaffe* attacked Polish air bases throughout the country: many obsolete aircraft were destroyed although the Polish airforce destroyed or damaged over 500 German planes. Aerial attacks against Polish defences and cities continued throughout the campaign. A German naval bombardment destroyed the defences of Gdynia, near Danzig, and much of the Polish Fleet on the first day.

On the ground, the German advance was quick. The Polish High Command, in the hope of preserving its western industrial region, had rejected the option of making a stand on the river line of the Narew-Vistula-San. Instead the Polish armies were deployed at the frontiers, which the Germans quickly broke through, thereafter encircling the isolated Polish forces. Without armour or mechanical transport, the Poles were unable to manoeuvre on the battlefield against invaders armed with nearly 2000 modern tanks.

The German penetration of the frontiers was complete by 5 September. By 7 September 10th Army, advancing from the south, was within forty miles of Warsaw, which the Polish government had left the day before. 8th and 14th Armies had kept pace to the west, capturing the Silesian industrial region. From the north, 4th and 3rd Armies had advanced rapidly, the latter being 25 miles from Warsaw by 7 September. Most of the Polish forces were then confined within their encircling pincers, concentrated in two large pockets around Kutno and Warsaw. The German plan had expected this outcome. Reports that Polish forces were escaping eastwards prompted a revision on 11 September, to extend the envelopment beyond the River Vistula. A spirited Polish counter-offensive west of Warsaw on the River Bzura was crushed by 17 September.

On that day, two Soviet Fronts, the Byelorussian and Ukrainian, marched into Poland from the east. The Soviets apparently overcame their initial unreadiness in order to prevent German occupation of eastern Poland. They met little resistance.

This first example of German *blitzkrieg* tactics – fast moving armoured thrusts supported by air strikes, penetrating deep behind enemy defences to create encirclements which could be mopped up later – had proved a total success.

The Germans took 694,000 prisoners; 100,000 Poles escaped into Lithuania, Hungary and Rumania, many eventually joining the Allies in the west. German losses were 13,000 killed and 30,000 wounded, Polish losses 70,000 killed and 133,000 wounded against the Germans. Losses at Russian hands have never been accurately calculated.

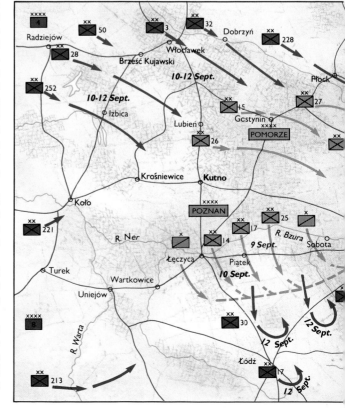

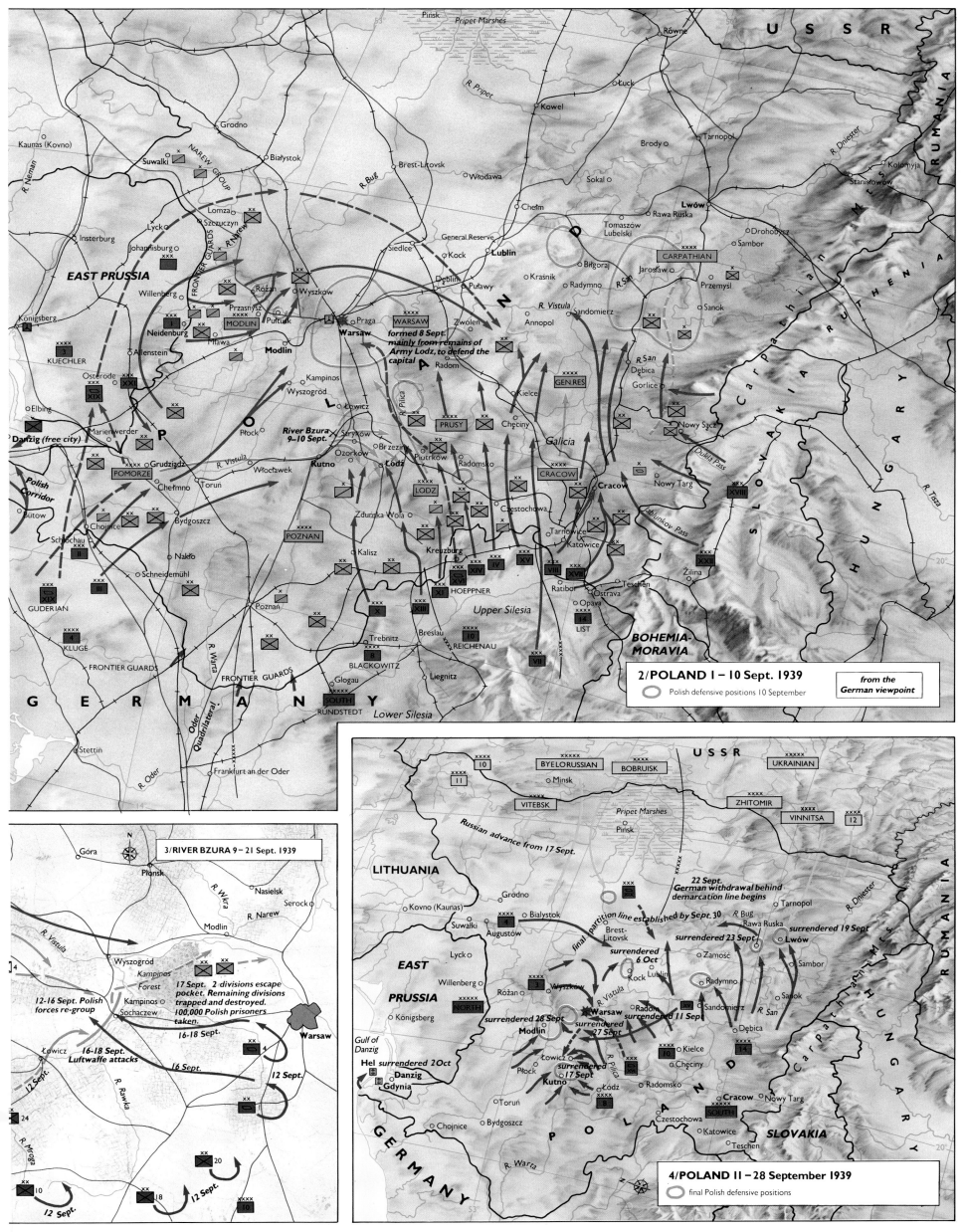

2/POLAND 1 – 10 Sept. 1939
from the German viewpoint
◯ Polish defensive positions 10 September

3/RIVER BZURA 9 – 21 Sept. 1939

4/POLAND 11 – 28 September 1939
◯ final Polish defensive positions

Scandinavia 1939~1940

BETWEEN THE INVASION of Poland, in September 1939, and the campaign in the West, in May 1940, Germany and the USSR transformed, by force or diplomacy, the political geography of the Baltic. The Baltic states, together with Finland, had been allocated to the Soviet sphere of influence by a secret protocol to the Ribbentrop-Molotov Pact of 23 August 1939 (page 36). From late September, they were forced to sign treaties allowing the basing of Soviet troops on their territory and in June 1940 were definitively occupied, and subsequently annexed as Soviet republics. Finland was confronted on 12 October by Soviet demands to cede a 30-year lease on bases in Karelia, Hangö on the Baltic, and the Rybachi Peninsula and Petsamo in the Arctic. On 26 November Russia staged an incident which provided the pretext for attack along the whole Russo-Finnish border. The Finns had time to mobilize 200,000 men against one million Soviets. Mannerheim, the Finnish commander, put six of his nine divisions in Karelia, two north of Lake Ladoga with one in reserve. The northern front was held by scattered units. Encirclement tactics (*motti*), and pinpoint assaults on targets such as field kitchens, allowed Finnish units to inflict humiliating defeats on the Red Army north of Lake Ladoga in December, particularly at Tolvayarvi and Suomussalmi. Meanwhile, Mannerheim held Karelia and counterattacked on 23 December. The Soviets regrouped and on 1 February opened a final offensive. Its sheer weight forced the Finns to sue for peace on 6 March; a treaty of 12 March ceded to Russia all the territory demanded before the outbreak. Finnish fatal casualties exceeded 24,000, Soviet 200,000, many killed by cold or deprivation.

Soviet aggression against Finland focussed Allied and Axis attention on Scandinavia. The German navy was anxious to acquire bases there, both to protect the iron ore trade with Sweden and to outflank the Royal Navy's dominance of the North Sea. Angered by British violation of neutral Norwegian waters to recover British prisoners from a German merchantman (the *Altmark* incident 16 February 1940) and encouraged by the Norwegian Nazi Vidkun Quisling's claim of local enthusiasm for the German cause, Hitler ordered General Falkenhorst to plan for an invasion of Norway on 21 February.

The British and French considered their own plans for landings in Norway. They were forestalled, however, by the Germans on 9 April who launched a brilliantly conceived combined operation. Denmark capitulated immediately. Norway, where German sea and airborne forces landed at Oslo, Kristiansand, Stavanger, Bergen, Trondheim and Narvik, held out longer. Norwegian troops resisted resolutely in the north and were joined by Franco-British forces at Trondheim (18 April) and Narvik (14 April). In two battles in the Narvik fjords (10 and 13 April), the Royal Navy inflicted heavy losses on the German covering force. In fierce fighting around Trondheim, British, French and Polish troops were forced to evacuate or surrender by 3 May. The battle at Narvik persisted until 4 June (Allied attention by then turning to events in the Low Countries), and reinforcements forced an Allied evacuation on 8 June. The withdrawal turned into near disaster as the Allied convoys were harried by German battleships in the North Sea, resulting in the loss of six British vessels; the cruiser evacuating the King and government of Norway narrowly escaped. The Norwegian army concluded an armistice on 9 June and Quisling was installed as puppet ruler.

GERMANY INVADED NORWAY on 9 Apr. (3). At Oslo, Norwegian shore batteries sank the cruiser *Blücher* before it could land troops, allowing the government to escape north, and then to England. The city was captured by an airborne landing. At Stavanger, Kristiansand, Bergen, Trondheim and Narvik, the Germans got ashore on schedule. A British naval force which observed the Narvik and Trondheim groups at sea concluded that they were making for the Atlantic. Once the Germans were established, however, the small Norwegian army (15,000) resisted, reinforced by British and French troops who landed at Andalsnes (17-19 Apr.) and Namsos (14-15 Apr.) near Trondheim and at Narvik (14 Apr.). German reinforcements from the south defeated the British at Tretten on 23 Apr. and forced the evacuation of both Andalsnes and Trondheim on 2-3 May. At Narvik, the German invaders were isolated by the British defeat of their naval supports (4) on 10 and 13 Apr. By the end of May the outnumbered Germans were forced to the Swedish border, but the Allied collapse in France decided the evacuation of Narvik by 8 June, the transports and their escorts running the gauntlet of German surface raiders in the North Sea (5).

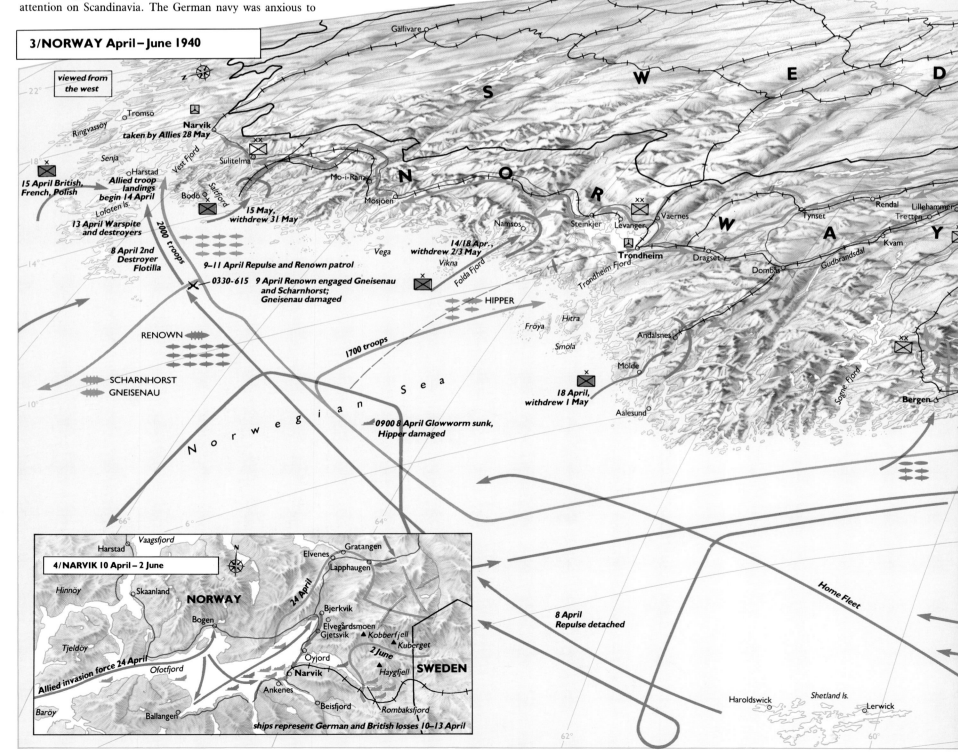

1/FINLAND Nov. 1939 – Mar. 1940
▓ area occupied by USSR from Mar. 1940

Norwegian Sea
L. Väner
Stockholm
Baltic Sea
Vaasa
Pori
Tampere
Turku
Hangö
Helsinki
Tallinn
ESTONI[A]

3/NORWAY April – June 1940

viewed from the west

Lulea
Gällivare
SWEDEN
Tromso
Narvik — taken by Allies 28 May
Ringvassöy
Senja
Sulitelma
15 April British, French, Polish
Harstad — Allied troop landings begin 14 April
Lofoten Is.
13 April Warspite and destroyers
8 April 2nd Destroyer Flotilla
2000 t troops
Bodö
Saltfjord
15 May, withdrew 31 May
Mo-i-Rana
Mosjöen
NORWAY
9–11 April Repulse and Renown patrol
0330-615 9 April Renown engaged Gneisenau and Scharnhorst; Gneisenau damaged
Vega
Namsos
Vikna
14/18 Apr., withdrew 2/3 May
Folda Fjord
HIPPER
RENOWN
1700 troops
Fröya
Hitra
Smöla
SCHARNHORST
GNEISENAU
Norwegian Sea
0900 8 April Glowworm sunk, Hipper damaged
18 April, withdrew 1 May
Molde
Aalesund
Vaernes
Steinkjer
Levanger
Trondheim
Dragset
Dombas
Andalsnes
Gudbrandsdal
Tynset
Rendal
Lillehammer
Tretten
Kvam
Sogne Fjord
Bergen
Home Fleet

4/NARVIK 10 April – 2 June

Harstad
Vaagsfjord
Gratangen
Elvenes
Lapphaugen
Hinnöy
Skaanland
NORWAY
Bogen
Tjeldöy
24 April
Bjerkvik
Elvegårdsmoen
Gjetsvik
Kobberfjell
Kuberget
2 June
Haygfjell
SWEDEN
Öyjord
Narvik
Ankenes
Allied invasion force 24 April
Ofotfjord
Baröy
Ballangen
Beisfjord
Rombaksfjord
8 April Repulse detached
ships represent German and British losses 10–13 April

Haroldswick
Shetland Is.
Lerwick

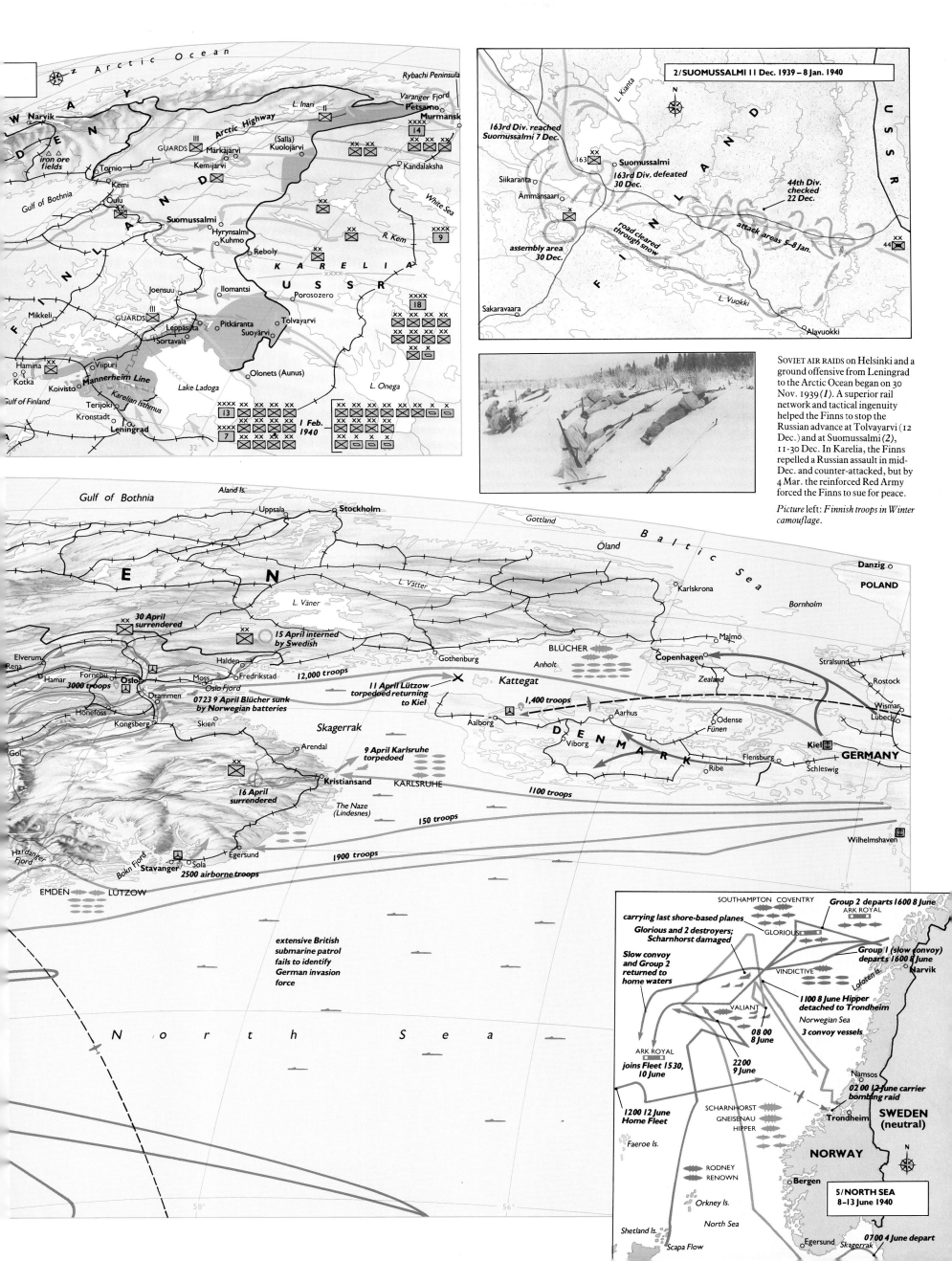

Map 1 (left - Finland/Scandinavia)

Arctic Ocean
Rybachi Peninsula
Varanger Fjord
Narvik
L. Inari
Petsamo
Murmansk
14
Arctic Highway
GUARDS
Markäjärvi
(Salla)
Kuolojärvi
Kandalaksha
Kemijarvi
iron ore fields
Tornio
Kemi
Oulu
White Sea
Gulf of Bothnia
9
Suomussalmi
Hyrynsalmi
Kuhmo
R. Kem
Reboly
KARELIA
Mikkeli
USSR
Joensuu
Ilomantsi
Porosozero
18
GUARDS
Leppäsiltä
Pitkäranta
Tolvayarvi
Suoyärvi
Sortavala
Hamina
Kotka
Viipuri
Koivisto
Olonets (Aunus)
L. Onega
Mannerheim Line
Karelian Isthmus
Lake Ladoga
Gulf of Finland
Terijoki
Kronstadt
Leningrad
13
7
1 Feb. 1940

Map 2 (top right)

2/SUOMUSSALMI 11 Dec. 1939 – 8 Jan. 1940

L. Kianta
163rd Div. reached Suomussalmi 7 Dec.
163
Suomussalmi
163rd Div. defeated 30 Dec.
44th Div. checked 22 Dec.
Siikaranta
Ämmänsaari
attack areas 5-8 Jan.
assembly area 30 Dec.
road cleared through snow
F I N L A N D
USSR
Sakaravaara
L. Vuokki
Alavuokki
44

Caption (right)

SOVIET AIR RAIDS on Helsinki and a ground offensive from Leningrad to the Arctic Ocean began on 30 Nov. 1939 (*1*). A superior rail network and tactical ingenuity helped the Finns to stop the Russian advance at Tolvayarvi (12 Dec.) and at Suomussalmi(*2*), 11-30 Dec. In Karelia, the Finns repelled a Russian assault in mid-Dec. and counter-attacked, but by 4 Mar. the reinforced Red Army forced the Finns to sue for peace.

Picture left: Finnish troops in Winter camouflage.

Map 3 (centre - North Sea / Denmark / Norway)

Gulf of Bothnia
Aland Is.
Uppsala
Stockholm
Gottland
Baltic Sea
Öland
Danzig
POLAND
L. Vätter
Karlskrona
Bornholm
SWEDEN
L. Väner
Malmö
30 April surrendered
15 April interned by Swedish
BLÜCHER
Copenhagen
Stralsund
Elverum
Rena
Fornebu
Oslo
Halden
Gothenburg
Anholt
Zealand
Rostock
Hamar
3000 troops
Moss
Fredrikstad
12,000 troops
11 April Lützow torpedoed returning to Kiel
Kattegat
1,400 troops
Wismar
Lübeck
Drammen
Oslo Fjord
0723 9 April Blücher sunk by Norwegian batteries
Aalborg
Aarhus
Odense
Fünen
Kiel
Hönefoss
Kongsberg
Skien
Skagerrak
9 April Karlsruhe torpedoed
DENMARK
Viborg
GERMANY
Gol
Arendal
Kristiansand
KARLSRUHE
Flensburg
Schleswig
Ribe
16 April surrendered
The Naze (Lindesnes)
1100 troops
150 troops
Wilhelmshaven
Hardanger Fjord
Bokn Fjord
Sola
Stavanger
Egersund
1900 troops
2500 airborne troops
EMDEN LÜTZOW

extensive British submarine patrol fails to identify German invasion force

North Sea

Map 5 (bottom right)

SOUTHAMPTON COVENTRY
Group 2 departs 1600 8 June
ARK ROYAL
carrying last shore-based planes
GLORIOUS
Glorious and 2 destroyers; Scharnhorst damaged
VINDICTIVE
Group 1 (slow convoy) departs 1600 8 June
Narvik
Slow convoy and Group 2 returned to home waters
1100 8 June Hipper detached to Trondheim
Lofoten Is.
Norwegian Sea
VALIANT
3 convoy vessels
08 00 8 June
ARK ROYAL
joins Fleet 1530, 10 June
2200 9 June
02 00 12 June carrier bombing raid
1200 12 June Home Fleet
SCHARNHORST
GNEISENAU
HIPPER
Trondheim
SWEDEN (neutral)
Faeroe Is.
NORWAY
RODNEY
RENOWN
Bergen
Orkney Is.
North Sea
Shetland Is.
Scapa Flow
Egersund
Skagerrak
0700 4 June depart

5/NORTH SEA 8–13 June 1940

The Low Countries 1940

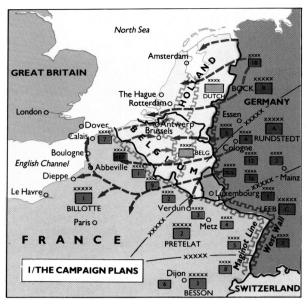

HITLER ANNOUNCED HIS INTENTION to attack in the west to his generals on 27 Sept. 1939, the day Poland capitulated. He wanted the campaign completed before winter and demanded a plan. That was submitted by OKH on 19 October – *Yellow* was for a drive to the Dutch and Belgium coasts, to secure a base for further operations by land, sea and air against the French and British. It dissatisfied Hitler, who wanted a more decisive outcome. OKH demurred, while bad weather forced successive postponements. *Yellow* was finally cancelled when German officers carrying secret documents compromised it by force-landing at Mechelen in Belgium on 9 January 1940. The plan replacing it (*Sicklestroke*) was the brainchild of a critic of OKH, General Manstein. It coincided with Hitler's own ideas and, with his backing, was transformed by OKH into a grand design (24 February) to encircle and destroy the Anglo-French armies in northern France.

The French, with their British Allies, depended on the Maginot Line to defend the Franco-German frontier. That, with neutral Belgium, was to be covered, in the event of a German invasion, by rushing the Allies' mobile forces to the line of the river Dyle, and hinging their right flank on the Ardennes forest, which was believed 'untankable'. This latter assumption proved dangerously ignorant. The Germans had performed extensive exercises to test the viability of an armoured thrust through the Ardennes forest, allowing them to bypass the Maginot Line. In fact their tactical thinking was based on the combined use of armoured thrusts and advance units of mobile sappers. *Sicklestroke* planned to drive the armoured columns of Army Group A across the Ardennes and across the Meuse, most formidable of the river obstacles, at Sedan, Monthermé and Dinant. The columns were then to swing north-west and drive for the Channel coast near Abbeville, trapping the French First Army Group and the British Expeditionary Force (BEF) with their backs to the sea. Airborne and ground forces would, meanwhile, overwhelm the defences of neutral Holland, while the main weight of Army Group B fell on the Belgians. The role of Army Group C, which had been allotted no armour, was to engage the garrison of the Maginot Line, which it was to penetrate if possible.

Numbers on each side were approximately equal. The Germans deployed 136 divisions against 94 French, 12 British (comprising almost the whole of Britain's military strength), 22 Belgian and 9 Dutch. Allied tanks numbered 3000 to 2500, though the Germans were superior in aircraft, 3200 to 1800. The Allied divisions, however, were of very uneven quality, and few were pure tank formations. The Germans, by contrast,

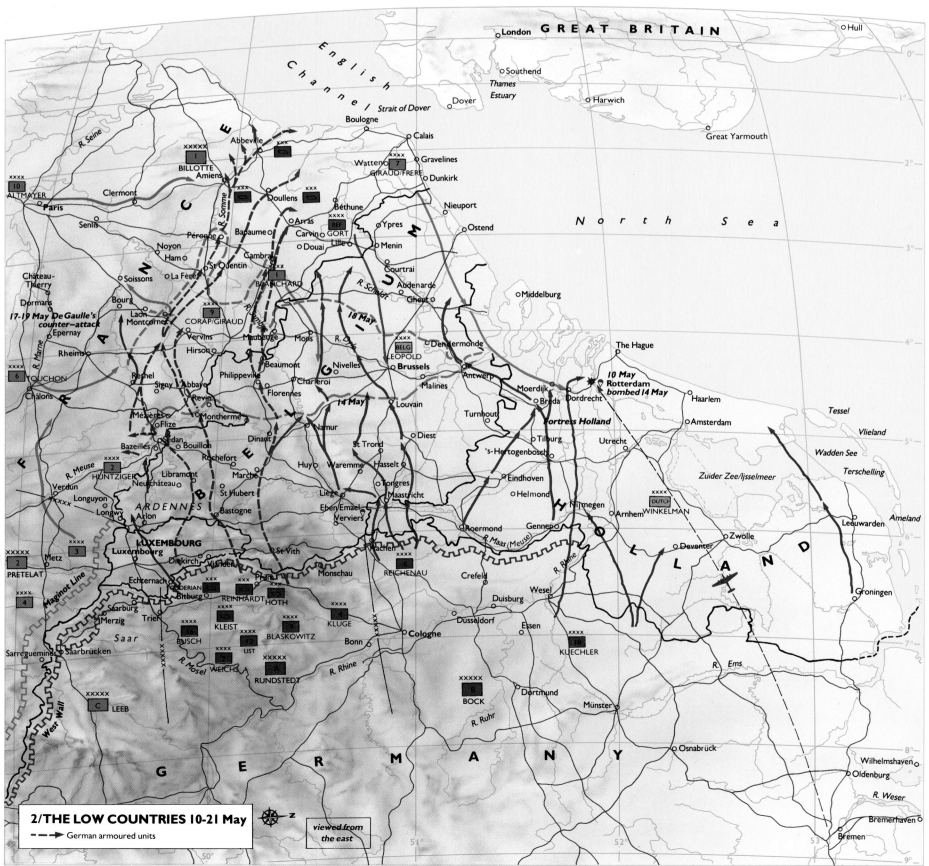

2/THE LOW COUNTRIES 10-21 May

- - - → German armoured units

viewed from the east

had organised their tanks into ten panzer divisions, strongly supported by tactical air forces, massing the majority under Army Group A for the Meuse crossings. The German army also had a clearcut offensive doctrine, later to be called *Blitzkrieg* ('lightning war'), while the Allies thought in defensive terms. They also had a muddled chain of command, while there was little enthusiasm for the war among the rank and file.

Germany began its attack on 10 May. In Holland the Dutch army was organized around Rotterdam, Amsterdam and Utrecht (Fortress Holland). It had not fought since 1830. German parachutists penetrated Fortress Holland and secured bridgeheads for airborne troops and tank columns. French relieving columns were turned back and on 14 May, after the Luftwaffe had carried out a threat to bomb Rotterdam, causing 30,000 civilian casualties, and German ground troops had made contact with the parachutists, Holland surrendered.

The Belgian army was also committed to the defence of the national fortresses, particularly on the Meuse; it was to fight with great bravery after the defences of Belgium were compromised on 10 May, when German glider troops neutralised the fortress defending the Meuse crossing at Eben Emael. On the next day the Belgian army began to fall back to the Dyle, where the French First Army Group (with most of the French mobile and armour divisions and the BEF under its command) had arrived. But by 15 May the German Eighteenth Army was outflanking them from Holland on the north, while the Sixth was pressing against the Dyle Line itself. Meanwhile, Army Group A had crossed the Meuse at Dinant and Sedan on 13 May, and Monthermé on 15 May. As French resistance collapsed on that sector, Army Group A's 8 panzer divisions drove into northern France.

Gamelin, French supreme commander, acquiesced in the withdrawal of the First Army Group and the BEF from the Dyle to the Scheldt on 16 May and tried to organise realignments and counter-attacks to save his crumbling front. Armoured thrusts by the French, under de Gaulle, at Laon (17-19 May) and by the British at Arras (21 May) dented but did not cut the German panzer corridor. The latter illustrated the lack of German awareness of their enemy's weakness, as the German divisional commander, Rommel, believed he had been attacked by 5 tank divisions. Nevertheless, the German panzers had reached St Quentin on 18 May and Abbeville on 20 May. French counter-attacks, ordered by Waygand (who succeeded Gamelin on 19 May) also failed at Cambrai and Amiens on 22-23 May.

A German attack separated the Belgian army from the BEF on 25 May, forcing Belgium's capitulation on 28 May. Meanwhile, the BEF and the French forces in the north were being forced back into what would become the Dunkirk perimeter. The succession of water lines surrounding the port was judged by Hitler so serious an obstacle to his tanks that he ordered their halt on 23 May. This apparent error of judgement gave the trapped armies a glimmer of hope. On 26 May, the British government authorised Gort to withdraw the BEF to Britain, and evacuation (Operation *Dynamo*) began next day. A portion of the French army continued to defend Lille until 1 June. The rest, with the BEF, was shipped from the Dunkirk beaches. By 4 June, when evacuation ceased, 338,226 men had been taken off, two-thirds British. German pressure on the pocket, resumed on 26 May, was relentless but was restrained by brave resistance and fierce intervention by the RAF, which flew 2739 sorties. Almost all the heavy equipment of the BEF and First Army Group was lost or left behind, but Britain at least had the core of an army with which to prepare the defence of the United Kingdom. The Germans, meanwhile, turned south.

THE CAMPAIGN in the Low Countries was, on the German part, a masterly piece of detailed planning (*1*) and accurate execution (*2*). It pinpointed the weakness of the Allied response, although it provoked extraordinary acts of courageous improvization. The German attack, Operation *Sichelschnitt* (*Sicklestroke*), bypassed the Maginot Line to the west, encircled the Dutch and Belgian armies and pinned the BEF and the First French Army Group against the Channel. The overall success of the campaign relied upon a series of detailed airborne and river crossing manoeuvres: paratroops were dropped at key points around Rotterdam, whilst at Eben Emael, a modern fortress, guarding the crossing of the Albert Canal between Liège and Maastricht, was assaulted by German glider troops on 10 May (*3*). Landing on the roof, they blasted their way inside with beehive charges, forcing the garrison to surrender on 11 May. The first crossing of the Meuse was acheived by 7th Panzer Division (Rommel) early on 13 May at Dinant. Later that day a larger crossing was made by Guderian's Panzer Group at Sedan (*4*). Dive-bombing by Stukas prepared the assault and panicked the French defenders. German losses were nevertheless heavy but three of their four attempted crossings succeeded. By midnight the Meuse had been bridged and next day Guderian's tanks, deflecting a French counter-attack, seized two bridges across the Ardennes Canal and began the advance into France. On 21 May the British mounted an armoured counter-attack on the spearhead of the German panzer corridor at Arras (*5*). Planned in divisional strength, it was eventually launched with only two tank and two infantry battalions. Nevertheless it halted the advance of the 7th Panzer Division, bit ten miles into its flank, causing heavy losses of men and equipment. The panzer thrust managed, however, to reach the coast by 21 May. Operation *Dynamo*, begun on 27 May, was designed to withdraw the survivors of the BEF and as many of the French as possible to Britain (*6*). Fierce defence of the water lines surrounding Dunkirk allowed 338,226 soldiers (including 110,000 French) to be taken off by 4 June. The Germans were then within 1¼ miles of the sea. An armada of small boats participated in *Dynamo*, but most troops were evacuated by the Royal Navy which, despite RAF cover, bore both fighter-bomber attack and coastal battery fire.

Picture right: *British troops awaiting evacuation at Dunkirk.*

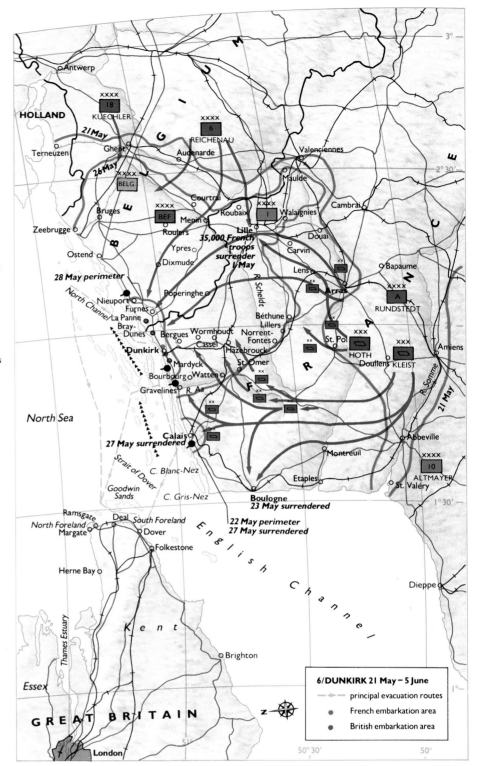

6/DUNKIRK 21 May – 5 June
- - - principal evacuation routes
● French embarkation area
● British embarkation area

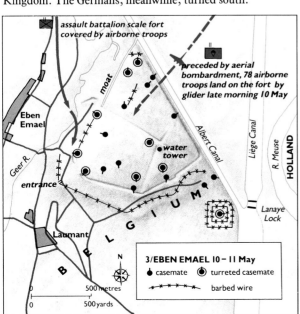

3/EBEN EMAEL 10–11 May
● casemate ● turreted casemate
╪╪╪ barbed wire

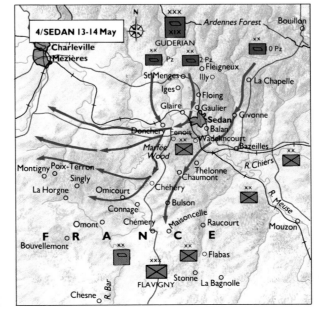

4/SEDAN 13-14 May

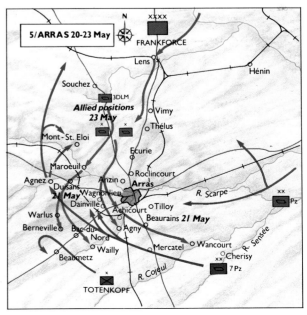

5/ARRAS 20-23 May

France JUNE 1940

WHILE WEYGAND'S PLAN to halt the German advance to the sea by counter-attacks towards Arras and Amiens had been tried and failed (21 May, 1 June, page 42), he had been organizing a new defensive line (the Weygand Line) along the Somme and Aisne. Reinforcements and surviving elements of the battle in the north had been deployed in a new Fourth Army Group (Huntziger) which, together with Second and a reorganized Third, was ordered to hold 225 miles of front with only 50 divisions. German strength, at over 120 divisions, was unimpaired. The French air force had received reinforcements from the RAF and still operated 1000 aircraft, but more than half the French tanks had been lost in the defence of Belgium where the morale of the army had been severely dented.

The Germans aligned most of their panzer divisions in two groups (Kleist and Guderian) opposite Amiens and Rheims, as the spearheads of Army Groups B and A. They attacked on 5 and 9 June respectively. The French, in the path of Army Group B, resisted valiantly – as did those in the coastal pocket around St Valéry-en-Caux (surrendered 12 June; the defenders included the British 51st Highland Division). But by the night of 8 June, Bock had broken through towards Paris and next day Rundstedt attacked towards Rheims. He met three days of fierce resistance also but on 11 June the collapse of the French in front of Bock forced Rundstedt's opponents to retreat behind the Marne. Next day Guderian's panzer group (now joined by Kleist) broke through to the east of Paris.

Reynaud's government had left Paris for Tours on 10 June, at the head of a vast efflux of fugitives (l'exode) which was to leave the city apparently almost deserted when the Germans entered on 14 June. Churchill, making his fourth visit to France since he had become Prime Minister on 10 May, visited Reynaud at Tours on 11 June to urge continued resistance. When he returned to England he took with him General Charles de Gaulle, whom Reynaud had appointed Under-Secretary for War, after his valiant effort to blunt the German advance at Laon (17-19 May, page 42), as an ally against the peace party in his cabinet. At de Gaulle's prompting, Churchill proposed on 16 June 'an indissoluble union' of Britain and France as a testimony of their determination to fight Germany to the end. But the proposal was unacceptable to the peace party which, on the night of 16 June, appointed Marshall Philippe Pétain, the hero of Verdun in 1916, head of government. Early the following morning he decided to re-negotiate for an armistice. On 18 June de Gaulle made his historic broadcast from London establishing a 'Free France' to carry on the fight.

Within France, however, the advance of the German army proceeded almost unchecked. Bordeaux had become the seat of French government on 14 June, and by that date Army Groups

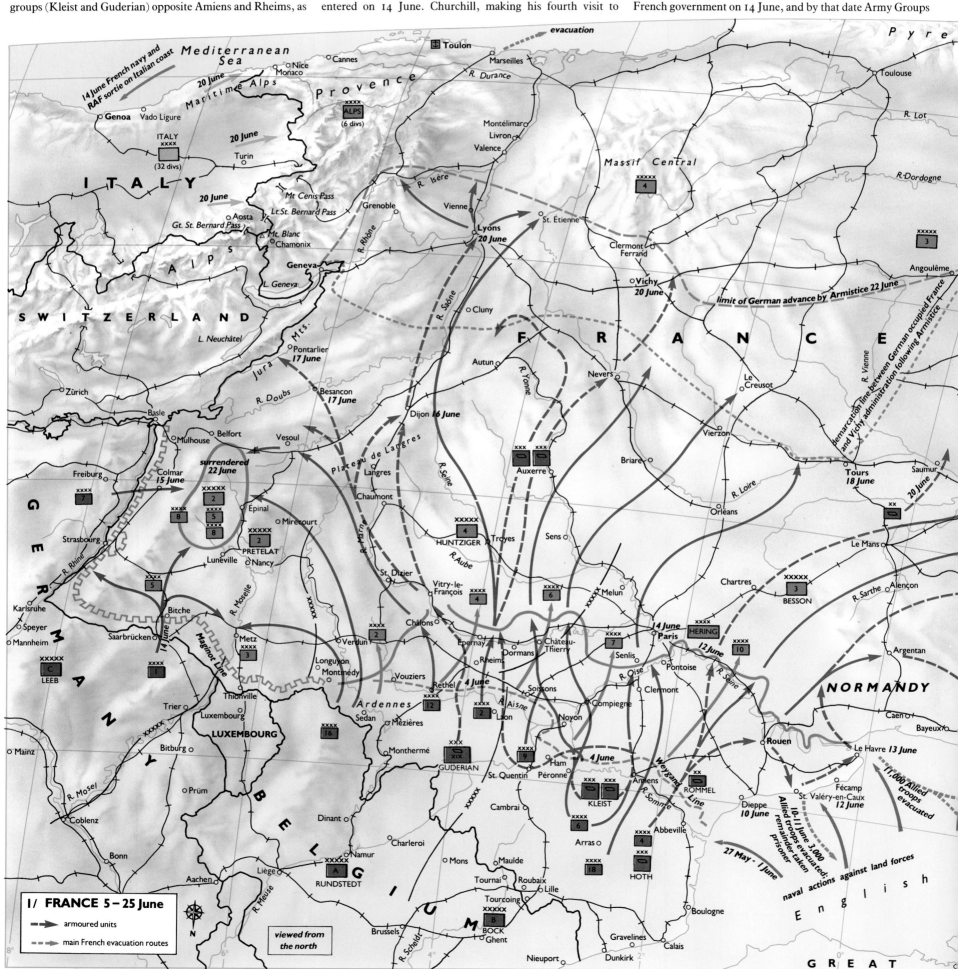

1/ FRANCE 5 – 25 June

- - → armoured units
- - → main French evacuation routes

viewed from the north

B and A had crossed the Seine and were pressing forward towards the Loire, while C had broken the Maginot Line near Saarbrücken. On 15 June it was broken again near Colmar and the remnants of the French Second Army Group, encircled by Army Group C near Epinal, surrendered on 22 June.

In places the French continued to resist the advance of Army Groups B and A, notably at Saumur on the Loire, where the students of the famous cavalry school held the bridges against the tanks of Army Group B, 19-20 June. On 19 June, however, Pétain had formally petitioned the Germans for an armistice. On 21 June a French armistice delegation was taken by the Germans to the forest near Compiègne, site of the German armistice of November 1918, where, on the next day, in a conspicuously humiliating gesture, Hitler signed the terms in the same railway carriage in which the Germans had agreed to the end of the First World War.

The armistice did not take effect until 25 June, when Italy, which had come into the war on 10 June, also signed. Mussolini, hoping for victories as spectacular as the German,

attacked the French defenders of the Alps on 20 June but achieved no success at all. Italy was nevertheless allotted a zone of occupation in Provence. The German zone of occupation delineated by the armistice was smaller than that captured by the German armies which, by 22 June, had advanced almost to Bordeaux and south of Lyons. The *zone libre*, with its seat of government at Vichy, eventually comprised France south of the Loire, less its Atlantic and Alpine frontiers. The French empire and the French fleet, which based itself in the Mediterranean and North African ports, remained under the control of Pétain's Vichy government. Vichy remained in name a sovereign government and was permitted an 'armistice army' of 100,000 men, but Paris and the territory outside the *zone libre* came under the German military administration. Nevertheless, substantial numbers of French troops and naval vessels had been evacuated to Britain (although many later returned to Vichy territories). Meanwhile, de Gaulle and his adherents, who now began to rally French colonies to Free France, were declared traitors by the Vichy government.

THE BATTLE OF FRANCE was, like that for the Low Countries, a swift victory for the Germans (*1*) despite valiant resistance at many points by the French army. The German Army Groups B and A, which had secured bridgeheads across the Somme and Aisne before the opening of the second stage in the campaign in the west, reached the Seine-Marne Line by 12 June. Hoth's panzer group then turned west into Brittany, capturing Brest on 19 June. Guderian's panzer group turned east, helping Army Group C to encircle the remnants of the French Second Army Group (surrendered 22 June). Kleist's panzer group spearheaded the advance into central France. The line of the Loire was reached on 17 June and the Gironde and lower Rhône by 25 June. Some of Kleist's tanks penetrated as far as the Pyrenees before withdrawing. The Italian army, which attacked on 20 June, was held at the border by six French divisions. The conquered territory was swiftly reorganized (*2*). By the terms of the armistice of 25 June, the parts of French Alsace-Lorraine which had been German from 1871-1914

were reincorporated in the Reich (so too were Belgian border districts annexed at Versailles). Nice and Savoy, French since 1859, were returned to Italy. France as far north as the Loire, together with the Atlantic coast, was placed under German military administration – also extended to Belgium and Holland. The capital of Pétain's *Etat français* was established at Vichy. The French empire (*3*) remained under the control of Vichy. It included Syria-Lebanon, Algeria, Tunisia and Morocco, French West Africa, Madagascar, French Guiana and Indo-China, (where the Japanese negotiated basing rights with Vichy in July 1941, page 66). The French city ports in India and the French Pacific territories were soon to declare their support for the Free French. However, it required some diplomatic pressure to align the French Caribbean territories with the Allies, who feared the establishment of U-Boat bases there.

Picture above right: A German armoured division manoeuvring on a plain in N. France, June 1940.

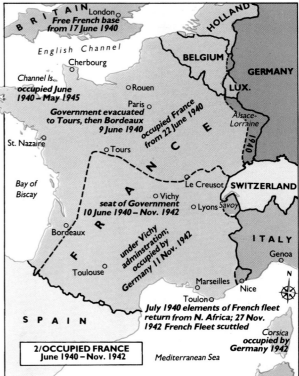

2/OCCUPIED FRANCE
June 1940 – Nov. 1942

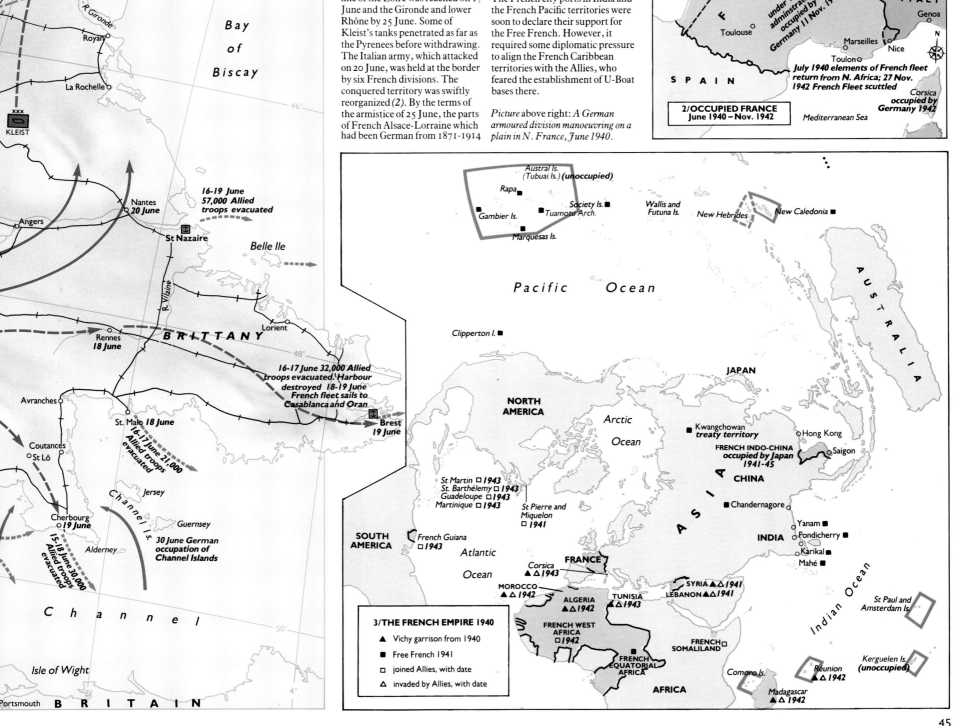

3/THE FRENCH EMPIRE 1940
▲ Vichy garrison from 1940
■ Free French 1941
□ joined Allies, with date
△ invaded by Allies, with date

Britain 1939~1945

THE COMPULSORY MOBILIZATION of the British people for war began in July 1939. The first-ever peacetime conscripts, young men aged twenty, were called up for supposedly six months' military training. It was to be six years before the survivors returned to civilian life.

On 1 September, the day Hitler invaded Poland, a nationwide black-out was imposed and the official evacuation of the cities began. The declaration of war two days later, and the 'phoney war' which followed, came almost as an anti-climax, when the expected air raids failed to materialize. Morale, under a feeble, peace-minded government, sagged but the German invasion of France, on 10 May 1940, and the creation, on the same day, of a coalition government under Winston Churchill transformed the situation. On 22 May a short Emergency Powers (Defence) Act passed all its stages in a single day. It required all citizens to place 'themselves, their services and their property' at the disposal of His Majesty.

Plans for the evacuation of children from target areas and the creation of Civil Defence organizations and measures had been placed in hand in 1939, but in 1940 the government's first aim was to keep the armed forces up to strength and well equipped. The various government departments now prepared each year a 'manpower budget', as crucial as their financial plans. The sum of these anticipated needs had then to be reconciled with the available supply of labour. The War Office, Admiralty and Air Ministry had first claim and eventually all

men aged 18 to 50 became liable to military service. The limiting factor in the expansion of the forces was, however, lack of equipment rather than men. The first Schedule of Reserved Occupations exempted certain types of craftsmen *en bloc* and members of other occupations over a certain age. The age-limits were, however, steadily raised, some types of work were de-reserved, and eventually every application for reservation was judged according to the individual circumstances.

In August 1940 it was calculated that 58% of the additional workers required by the munitions factories by August 1941 would need to be women and a publicity campaign to attract recruits, on the theme of 'Your duty now is war work', followed. In December 1941, the month of Pearl Harbor, a new Act made women, as well as men, between the ages of 18 and 50 liable to some form of national service and it was steadily applied to one age group after another. By October 1942 it was affecting women aged up to 45, who could be directed into factory work unless they had children under 14, and any classed as 'mobile' could be sent away from home to live in lodgings. In July 1943 the registration began of women up to 50.

The country's material resources were mobilized as effectively as its labour. Civilian consumption of every kind was cut to the bone to set free labour and factory capacity, and to leave shipping space for essential food and munitions. To damp

down spending at a time of full (and often well-paid) employment, a continuous publicity campaign exhorted the public instead to 'Hit Back with National Savings', interest being maintained by special 'Wings for Victory' and 'Salute the Soldier' weeks. To waste anything became socially unacceptable as well as a criminal offence. Paper, rags, rubber, bones, tin cans, even razor blades, were all salvaged. The drive to produce more home-grown food encompassed not only the farmer but the ordinary householder, who was from 1939 onwards urged to 'Dig for Victory' on every patch of waste land and to turn his flower-beds over to onions or cabbages.

The most important measure in restricting civilian demand was rationing. Petrol went 'on coupons' first, from 23 September 1939, but there was no petrol, except for essential users, from 1 July 1942. Food rationing, highly successful in maintaining the nation's health as well as in saving imports, began on 8 January 1940, when bacon, ham, sugar and butter became available only with a ration book, followed in March by meat, in July by tea, margarine and fats, in March 1941 by jam, in May by cheese and in December 1941 by most tinned food and other packaged products. Soap was rationed in February 1942 and sweets in July. Bulky imported products of low nutritional value, like lemons and bananas, totally disappeared, but 'spam' was a welcome newcomer, and dried eggs – dehydrated egg powder – saved shipping space. Clothes were rationed, in June 1941, to release labour and provide manufacturing space. New furniture and bed linen, and then only in a simple 'Utility' style, were available on 'dockets' confined to the newly-wed and bombed-out. Alarm clocks,

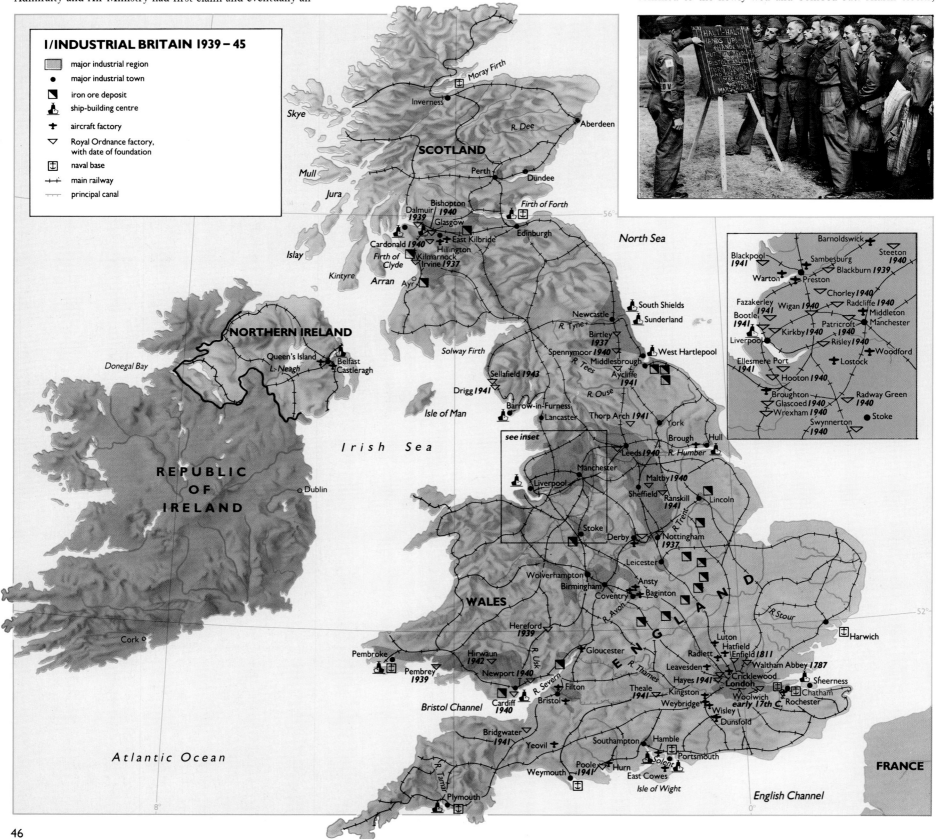

essential to shift workers, required a special permit, while such semi-necessities as a new toothbrush or saucepan meant a long and often fruitless search through the shops.

Fuel supply proved to be the weakest aspect of the wartime economy. Short-sightedly, miners had been encouraged to join the forces or transfer to other industries so that the labour force dwindled, from 766,000 in 1939 to 698,000 in 1941, while coal output slumped from 231 to 206 million tons. But as the war effort got into its stride the factories needed more, not less, fuel and a serious shortage threatened. Ex-miners were now directed back into the industry; from 1942 anyone called up for the forces could opt to go down the mines instead and from December 1943 a selection by ballot compelled a number of those registering to do so. Industrial output was maintained but the civilian consumer, at the end of every queue, came off badly. In June 1942, a voluntary system of restraint was launched, with each household expected to set itself a 'fuel target' which it was honour-bound not to exceed. Cold, however, triumphed over principle and the real control was imposed by coal merchants who could supply only a fraction of most orders.

Thus the nation shivered its way through the last dismal, rocket-ridden Winter of the war to Victory in Europe Day, on 8 May 1945. By then it could congratulate itself on having been more fully mobilized for war than any other combatant nation, except Russia, and having mustered its resources far more efficiently than Nazi Germany. Further, the rationale had been established for the creation of a Welfare State, the primary achievement of Britain's post-war Labour government.

THE PRE-WAR NEEDS of the British armed forces had been met by the government-owned Royal Ordnance Factories and a few private manufacturers. Only by involving most of the country's industrial capacity (1) was it possible to begin to equip the vastly-expanded fighting services. The output of .303 rifles was raised from 34,416 in 1939 to 909,785 in 1943, that of tanks from 969 in 1939 to 8611 in 1942, that of torpedoes from 939 in 1940 to 7288 in 1943. The greatest expansion was in the aircraft industry (pages 52, 112, 138), whose principle was 'disperse to manufacture, concentrate to build'. Britain needed large imports of oil, raw materials and food (2D). Pre-war estimates had put her annual requirements (excluding oil products) at 47 million tons. Britain actually survived on far less: 30.5 million tons in 1941 and no more than 22.9 million (plus 10.7 million tons of tanker imports) in 1942. The total began to rise again in 1943. The mobilization of resources in Britain was total (2C): the working population (males 14-64 years, female 14-59 years) was divided into Group I: shipbuilding, heavy industry, aircraft production – the spine of the war effort; Group II: supporting industries such as agriculture, mining, government, transport, communications etc.; and Group III, service industries, building, food processing, textiles, banking and commerce. The latter sector was steadily squeezed to supply labour for war factories, and after the Blitz (1940/41) even Civil Defence and Fire Services were run down to meet the Forces' demands for recruits and by mid-1943 over 3.5 million women were doing full or part-time paid work and a million more giving voluntary service. A policy of reducing food consumption, through rationing, accompanied a vigorous drive to increase home production of food (2A, B). Acreage under the plough was dramatically increased to produce wheat and potatoes (unrationed 'fillers'), and barley. Much of the meat ration was met from home-reared beef. Before the war Britain was divided into 3 categories of risk from enemy bombing. In high risk areas, schoolchildren and some other priority classes qualified for official evacuation (4) to safer 'reception' (low risk) areas. The classification changed with the conditions of war, the South-East becoming an evacuation zone by June 1940; the advent of V-1 and V-2 bombing raids led to the evacuation of previously neutral areas of London to previously high risk cities such as Manchester. Britain was also divided into 12 Civil Defence regions (3). Within these regions, Regional Commissions controlled by the Ministry of Home Security ensured local authorities could deal with air raids and organized air raid wardens; if national communications and central government broke down, each Regional headquarters would become a mini-government with almost unlimited local powers. The vast destruction caused by fire during the Blitz led to the creation of the centrally controlled National Fire Service; Britain was divided into 39 Fire Areas.

Picture left: the British Home Guard (Local Defence Volunteers, formed May 1940), poorly equipped and trained, were raised to combat the threat of German invasion.
Right: British propaganda extended from subversive publications distributed in enemy territory to innumerable domestic homilies to encourage the civilian war effort.

GROW YOUR OWN FOOD

3/CIVIL DEFENCE 1939 – 1945

— regional boundary
● regional headquarters (list below)
— fire service divisions
▬ planned GHQ line
--- other stop line

1 Scotland
2 Northern
3 North Western
4 North Eastern
5 Wales
6 Midland
7 North Midland
8 Eastern
9 South Western
10 Southern
11 London
12 South Eastern

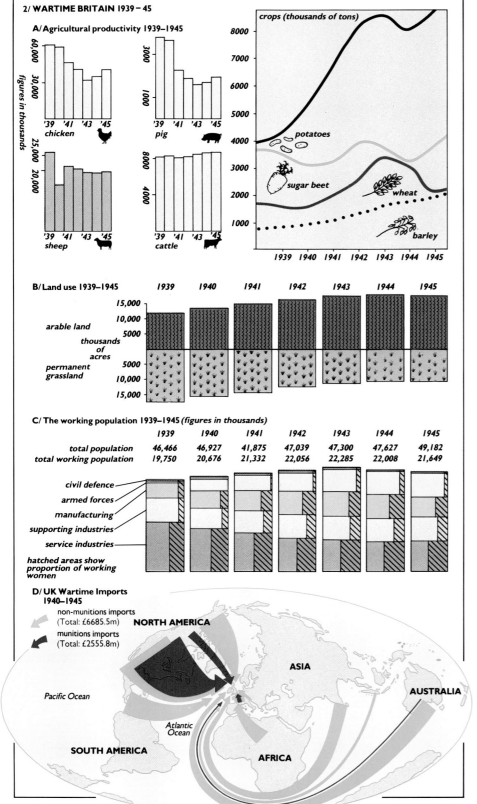

2/ WARTIME BRITAIN 1939 – 45

A/ Agricultural productivity 1939–1945

B/ Land use 1939–1945

	1939	1940	1941	1942	1943	1944	1945
arable land							
permanent grassland							

C/ The working population 1939–1945 *(figures in thousands)*

	1939	1940	1941	1942	1943	1944	1945
total population	46,466	46,927	41,875	47,039	47,300	47,627	49,182
total working population	19,750	20,676	21,332	22,056	22,285	22,008	21,649

civil defence
armed forces
manufacturing
supporting industries
service industries

hatched areas show proportion of working women

D/ UK Wartime Imports 1940–1945

non-munitions imports (Total: £6685.5m)
munitions imports (Total: £2555.8m)

NORTH AMERICA
SOUTH AMERICA
Pacific Ocean
Atlantic Ocean
ASIA
AFRICA
AUSTRALIA

4/EVACUATION 1939 – 1945

● ◗ evacuation area
▢ reception area
▢ neutral area

total number of evacuees throughout Great Britain

the Blitz — Sept. 1940
V-1s — June 1944
V-2s — Sept. 1944

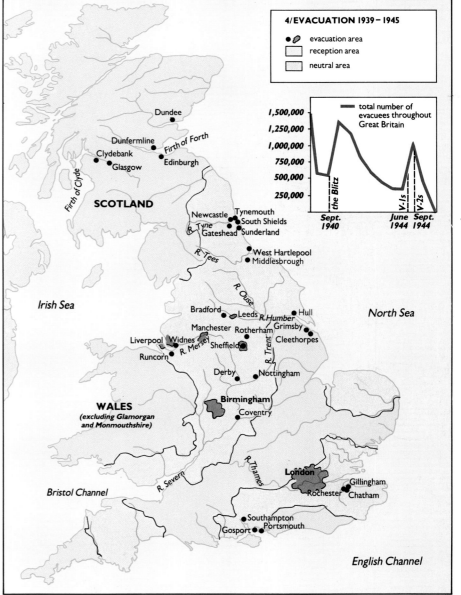

THE DEFEAT OF THE GERMAN NAVY in the First World War stemmed from its attempt to conduct a campaign against Allied merchant shipping from a position of strategic and numerical weakness. Despite its awareness of the reasons for its previous defeat, the German Navy entered the Second World War committed to the same attritional doctrine that had failed it after 1917 and was forced to operate under the same handicaps as in the First World War.

German naval strategy in 1939 – tonnage warfare – was based on a simple calculation: if 750,000 tons of British shipping could be sunk every month, over a twelve-month period, then Britain would be forced to surrender. At this time Britain, totally dependent upon the sea for over 60 million tons per annum of imports, had some 22 million tons of shipping, over half of which was available after September 1939 for oceanic trade. Germany began the war with 57 submarines (not the 350 deemed necessary to complete Britain's defeat) but it was her intention to develop her campaign against shipping by using mines, aircraft and warship and auxiliary raiders. It was after June 1940, when the acquisition of bases in Norway and France allowed German aircraft and submarines to reach into the Atlantic far beyond the range of effective escort cover, that

the campaign against Allied shipping was joined on a significant scale by aircraft and raiders for the first time. The peak of their efforts, however, was passed very quickly. Though five warships broke into the Atlantic in the first half of 1941 the loss of the *Bismarck* revealed the danger of operating surface units without air support in waters patrolled by Allied aircraft; RAF raids on Brest led to the withdrawal of major warships to Germany in February 1942. Auxiliary raiders disguised as unarmed merchantmen continued to set sail until October 1942 and to operate until October 1943, but their activities after 1941 were largely neutralized by the extension of convoys throughout the Atlantic; thereafter they were exiled to the more distant and less rewarding waters of the Indian and Pacific Oceans. The *Luftwaffe* ceased to be a major factor in the Battle of the Atlantic after June 1941 because of its commitments on the Eastern Front.

After the German use of magnetic mines in Autumn 1939 and of acoustic mines in Autumn 1940 in British home waters

was countered, U-boats were the primary instrument in the German campaign against Allied commerce throughout the war. In this initial period the Allies were at their weakest. There was no comprehensive convoy system throughout the Atlantic; and with convoys poorly protected there was no good reason for the German Navy and *Luftwaffe* to run risks by directing their main efforts against escorted merchantmen when so much shipping remained outside convoy. Of the 1787 Allied and neutral merchantmen sunk between September 1939 and June 1941 only 362 were sunk in convoy.

Only in this initial period of the war, therefore, were the Germans able to conduct a balanced campaign against Allied shipping; but even though at this time German submarines commanded considerable success, most notably in Autumn 1940, various developments indicated that Germany's tonnage warfare strategy was failing at this early stage. The invasions of Norway and the Netherlands had forced their shipping into

THE EUROPEAN WAR BEGAN in Sept. 1939 with the German Navy, apart from two raiders in the Atlantic, unable to carry the campaign against Allied shipping outside the North Sea, the English Channel and the Western Approaches; as a consequence, the bulk of Allied shipping losses were incurred in these areas, with German mining activity causing a severe disruption of coastal shipping in the North Sea (*1, 4*). By having virtually the whole of the U-boat arm available for operations in Sept. 1939, however, the German Navy trapped itself in a pattern of operations that hindered the long-term expansion of the U-boat service in the first phase of the war (*5*). As a result, sinkings by submarines in the first ten months of the war fluctuated considerably. The German conquest of France (page 44), however, changed the strategic pattern of the war at sea; possession of naval bases on the French Atlantic coast gave German submarines and aircraft direct access into the Atlantic and forced the British to divert shipping from the southwest approaches to the northwest. With isolated exceptions, the southwest approaches remained closed to Allied shipping until 1944 (*4*).

I/THE NORTH ATLANTIC
Sept. 1939 – May 1940
- Allied merchant ships sunk by U-boats
- • U-boats sunk
- --- major convoy routes
- ---·--- air escort cover

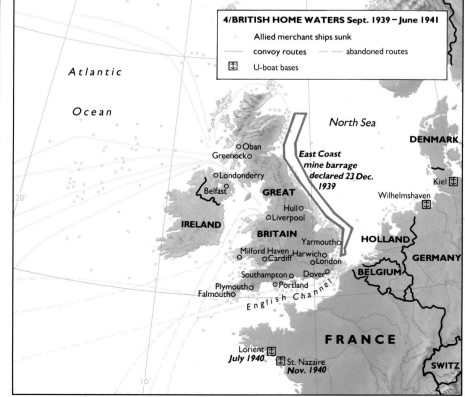

4/BRITISH HOME WATERS Sept. 1939 – June 1941
- Allied merchant ships sunk
- —— convoy routes   - - - abandoned routes
- ⊞ U-boat bases

East Coast mine barrage declared 23 Dec. 1939

Lorient July 1940
St. Nazaire Nov. 1940

3/ALLIED MERCHANT SHIPPING LOSSES Sept. 1939 – Mar. 1941

date	U-boat	aircraft	mine	warship raider	merchant raider	E-boat	unknown and other causes	quarterly totals
Sept. - Dec. 1939	421,156 (114)	2,949 (10)	262,697 (79)	61,337 (15)	none	none	7,253 (4)	755,392 (222)
Jan. - Mar. 1940	343,610 (108)	33,240 (20)	167,357 (50)	1,761 (1)	none	none	2,467 (2)	548,435 (181)
Apr. - June 1940	372,160 (78)	276,950 (77)	153,591 (53)	25,506 (2)	40,631 (6)	7,701 (5)	155,636 (78)	1,032,175 (299)
July - Sept. 1940	758,778 (153)	179,804 (63)	55,300 (26)	none	194,647 (30)	29,836 (15)	14,398 (10)	1,232,763 (297)
Oct. - Dec. 1940	711,610 (132)	90,080 (32)	133,641 (72)	69,719 (14)	131,366 (18)	10,448 (3)	31,404 (11)	1,178,268 (282)
Jan. - Mar. 1941	566,585 (101)	281,216 (88)	57,199 (39)	187,662 (37)	114,222 (25)	23,340 (12)	23,115 (15)	1,253,339 (317)

totals by theatre Sept. 1939 – Mar. 1941

Atlantic Ocean	Mediterranean	Indian Ocean	Pacific Ocean
5,605,449 (1,533)	84,394 (17)	210,005 (31)	99,531 (15)

figures show tonnages, with number of ships in brackets

British ports; further, rationing and the strict control of shipping space reduced Britain's import needs by more than half in the course of the war. Moreover, despite German success – which in this period peaked in April 1941 with the fourth highest Allied losses of the entire war – sinkings registered per operational U-boat began to decline in 1941, as did the direct exchange rate between sinkings of merchantmen and U-boats. In effect, therefore, as convoys became more widespread and better protected, the U-boats found it increasingly difficult to sink merchantmen and throughout this period they were never able to sustain a rate of sinkings that approximated to the original tonnage warfare requirements. Meanwhile, problems of extending the U-boat arm meant that after eighteen months of war, its operational strength was less than half that of September 1939. Lastly, as British counter-measures in the eastern Atlantic became increasingly effective – the convoy system in the North Atlantic being extended in Spring 1941 – the U-boats were forced both to turn their attention to convoys and to move westwards in an attempt to find victims beyond the range of British aircraft. As they did so, however, there emerged the danger of a German clash with the United States, a clash which, despite the increasingly obvious American determination to ensure Britain's survival, Hitler desperately wished to avoid.

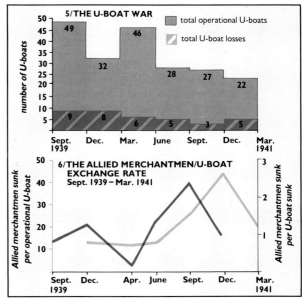

5/THE U-BOAT WAR

number of U-boats

- total operational U-boats
- total U-boat losses

49, 32, 46, 28, 27, 22

9, 8, 6, 6, 7, 5

Sept. 1939 — Dec. — Mar. — June — Sept. — Dec. — Mar. 1941

6/THE ALLIED MERCHANTMEN/U-BOAT EXCHANGE RATE
Sept. 1939 – Mar. 1941

Allied merchantmen sunk per operational U-boat

Allied merchantmen sunk per U-boat sunk

Sept. 1939 — Dec. — Apr. — June — Sept. — Dec. — Mar. 1941

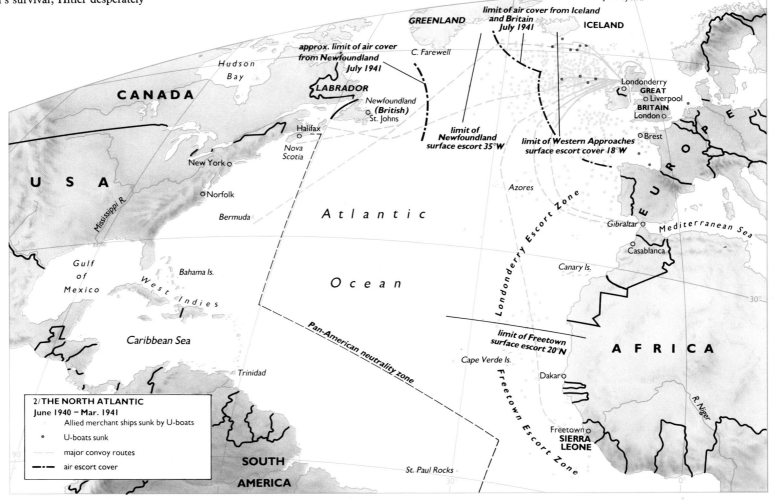

2/THE NORTH ATLANTIC
June 1940 – Mar. 1941

- Allied merchant ships sunk by U-boats
- • U-boats sunk
- major convoy routes
- ▬▬ air escort cover

AFTER JUNE 1940 the campaign against Allied shipping was joined on a significant scale by aircraft and raiders. The peak of the warship effort was made in the first half of 1941 when five ships broke into the Atlantic, but the loss of the *Bismarck* and RAF raids on Brest led to the withdrawal of heavy warships to Germany in Feb. 1942; thereafter German warships were used as a threat to Arctic convoys. The last of the disguised raiders was sunk in Oct. 1943, though their activities were dissipated after 1941 by the extension of the Atlantic convoy. German submarines, however, now commanded increasing success, reaching a high point in Oct. 1940 when they sank 352,407 tons of shipping. The gradual extension of convoy and the development of British air bases in Iceland after 1940, however, forced the U-boats westwards.

Picture top right: The German pocket battleship Graf Spee *at the Spithead Review, 1937. One of the more successful German commerce raiders, she sank 9 ships totalling 50,089 tons in the South Atlantic and Indian Oceans, before being disabled by a British cruiser force off the River Plate; she was scuttled off Montevideo, 17 Dec. 1939.*

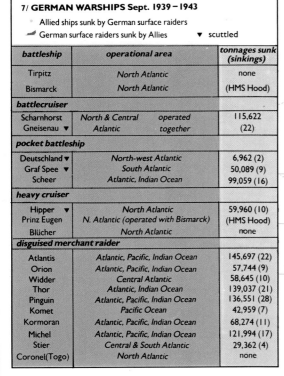

7/ GERMAN WARSHIPS Sept. 1939 – 1943

- ∙ Allied ships sunk by German surface raiders
- ▬ German surface raiders sunk by Allies
- ▼ scuttled

battleship	operational area		tonnages sunk (sinkings)
Tirpitz	North Atlantic		none
Bismarck	North Atlantic		(HMS Hood)
battlecruiser			
Scharnhorst	North & Central	operated	115,622
Gneisenau ▼	Atlantic	together	(22)
pocket battleship			
Deutschland ▼	North-west Atlantic		6,962 (2)
Graf Spee ▼	South Atlantic		50,089 (9)
Scheer	Atlantic, Indian Ocean		99,059 (16)
heavy cruiser			
Hipper ▼	North Atlantic		59,960 (10)
Prinz Eugen	N. Atlantic (operated with Bismarck)		(HMS Hood)
Blücher	North Atlantic		none
disguised merchant raider			
Atlantis	Atlantic, Pacific, Indian Ocean		145,697 (22)
Orion	Atlantic, Pacific, Indian Ocean		57,744 (9)
Widder	Central Atlantic		58,645 (10)
Thor	Atlantic, Indian Ocean		139,037 (21)
Pinguin	Atlantic, Pacific, Indian Ocean		136,551 (28)
Komet	Pacific Ocean		42,959 (7)
Kormoran	Atlantic, Pacific, Indian Ocean		68,274 (11)
Michel	Atlantic, Pacific, Indian Ocean		121,994 (17)
Stier	Central & South Atlantic		29,362 (4)
Coronel (Togo)	North Atlantic		none

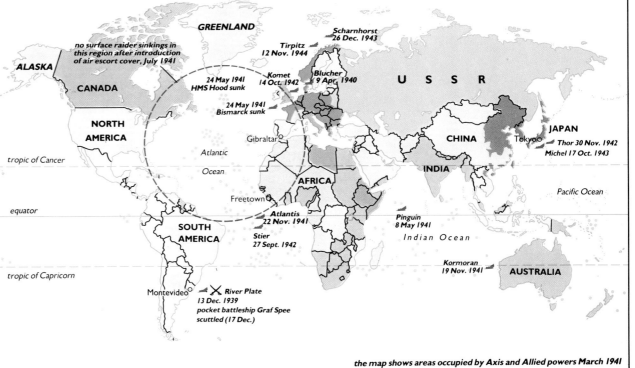

the map shows areas occupied by Axis and Allied powers March 1941

Africa 1940~1941

THE STRATEGIC SITUATION in the Mediterranean and North Africa was transformed by the German invasion of France in June 1940 (page 44). Hitherto the overwhelming naval and military power of the French and British in the region, assured by their respective fleet bases spanning the Mediterranean, had deterred Italy from intervening on the side of her ally, Germany. Mussolini's decision to join in the defeat of France (10 June) was partly prompted by his desire to profit from an altered balance of power in the Mediterranean.

The neutralization of French naval power left the Italian navy the largest in the Mediterranean. Further, Italian ground forces, stationed in Libya, Ethiopia, Eritrea and Italian Somaliland, formed the largest combatant group in North Africa. Britain was confronted with a possible cross-Channel invasion and seemed unlikely to be able effectively to support her forces beyond Europe. Seizing what he perceived as an initiative, Mussolini ordered offensives against the frontiers of the Sudan (Kassala and Gallabat captured, 4 July), Kenya (Moyale captured 15 July) and British Somaliland (occupied 5-19 August). On 13 September a large Italian army entered

Egypt from Libya but halted on 18 September, after advancing 60 miles, to construct a forward base at Sidi Barrani. These early successes were soon to be reversed.

The British and de Gaulle's Free French began taking action against the Vichy government's forces in Africa soon after the French capitulation, the better to consolidate their control of the continent. Under the terms of the armistice with Germany, Vichy retained control of the French overseas empire and the forces within it, including the French Fleet, which had taken refuge at Oran and Mers-el-Kebir in Algeria. On 3 July the British Mediterranean Fleet, following Vichy's refusal to immobilize its navy, bombarded those ports, sinking a battleship, damaging 3 other large warships, and killing 1300 French sailors, an act which outraged France. However, the

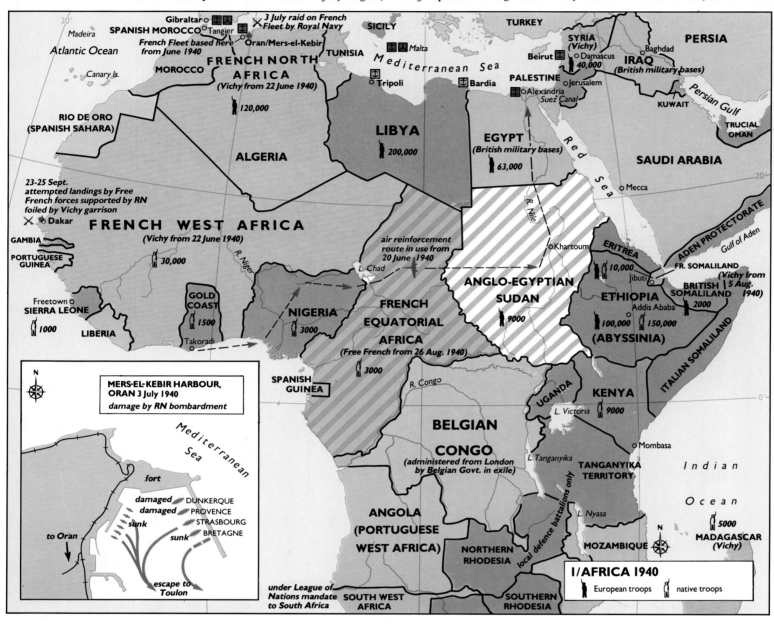

HITLER HAD NO PLANS for involvement in Africa (1), but the terms of the French armistice in June 1940 allowed France to retain control of her colonies and protectorates in North and West Africa, and her mandated territories in Syria and Lebanon, together with local military forces. These posed a potential threat to British control of the Mediterranean, exercized through her bases at Gibraltar and Malta and the garrison in Egypt; Britain also had colonial forces in the Sudan, Kenya and British Somaliland. With the entry of Germany's ally, Italy, into the war (10 June) the struggle for control of Africa broke out. The Free French leader de Gaulle, through his emissary Leclerc, succeeded in rallying French colonies in Equatorial Africa (Aug.-Oct. 1940), but an attempt to seize Senegal (23-25 Sept.) failed. The French Fleet in Mers-el-Kebir and Oran (1, inset) was bombarded by the British (3 July) on its refusal to scuttle, join forces or sail to a British or French Caribbean port. Of its battleships Bretagne was sunk, Dunkerque and Provence damaged and Strasbourg escaped to Toulon. Mussolini, keen to take

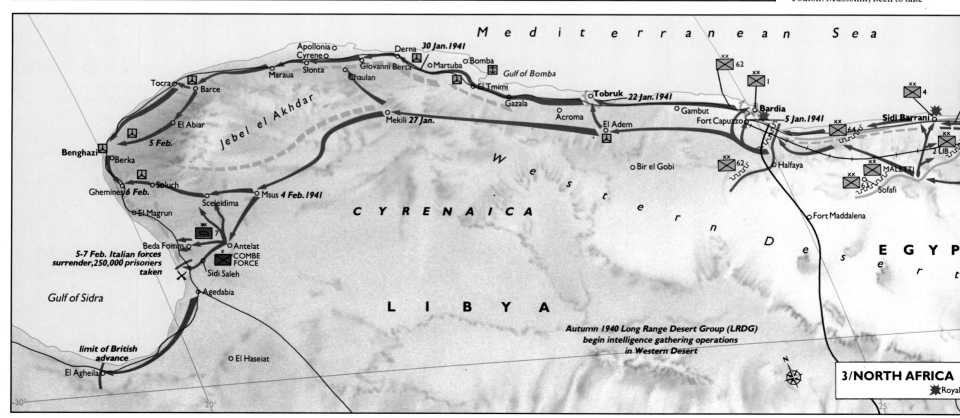

French squadron in Alexandria was surrendered to the British without loss, and various French warships still in British ports were seized. When on 23-25 September a British naval force, with de Gaulle on board, approached Dakar in French West Africa (Senegal) and landed a force, it was driven off. Free France's only success at this stage of the war was to rally the remote colonies of Equatorial Africa and Congo (page 44).

On land the British went over to the offensive in Egypt on 9 December. The operation had been planned to last only five days but its success led Wavell, the desert commander, to enter Libya in early January 1941 and thereafter to capture Bardia (5 January) and Tobruk (22 January). He then divided his force, sending the 7th Armoured Division across the desert to meet the 6th Australian Division advancing along the coast. On 5 February they joined hands at Beda Fomm, having advanced 500 miles capturing 130,000 prisoners and much equipment.

The British offensive in East Africa opened on 19-20 January 1941, when forces in the Sudan invaded Eritrea and northern Ethiopia. Three weeks later, a second front was opened when Cunningham's offensive from Kenya into Italian Somaliland and southern Ethiopia was launched on 11 February. British Somaliland was reoccupied by a force which landed from Aden at Berbera on 16 March. By 25 February most of Italian Somaliland had been occupied. Addis Ababa, the Ethiopian capital, fell on 6 April. Italian resistance was strongest in the north, where a bitter battle for the mountain position of Keren did not end until 26 March. The Duke of Aosta, Italian Commander-in-Chief, then withdrew to Amba Alagi where, after more fighting, he surrendered on 16 May. Isolated forces continued resistance until 3 July. Some 420,000 Italian troops, including Africans, had been killed or captured in East Africa, against 3100 British Commonwealth casualties. The victory restored the Emperor Haile Selassie of Ethiopia to his throne.

The initiative had now returned to British hands. The problem of supply and coordination between London and eastern Africa still remained, as did substantial areas of Vichy territory. But if the latter could be contained, and the substantial Commonwealth troops east of Aden be fully exploited, Allied control of the eastern Mediterranean and the Middle East might be assured. But the advent of German forces in the Balkans and Mediterranean would alter this balance.

advantage of British weakness in the area in order to expand his Africa colonies launched offensives in East Africa from July (2). With the exception of the occupation of British Somaliland (5-19 Aug.) these failed. A British counter-offensive provoked heavy fighting around Keren in mountainous northern Eritrea. The first battle (3-13 Feb. 1941) was an Italian defensive victory; in the second (15-26 Mar. 1941) the British took the position and began a victorious advance. The Italian offensive into Egypt (3) began on 13 Sept., but was not followed up, allowing a British counter-offensive (9 Dec.) to gain the initiative, forcing the surrender by Feb. 1941 of large Italian forces. In the Mediterranean (4) there were indecisive clashes between the British and Italian fleets in 1940 – the only clear-cut success being the attack on Taranto harbour (11-12 Nov. page 54). But the advent of the Luftwaffe, which attacked a British Gibraltar/Malta convoy (6-10 Jan.), signalled the beginning of a sustained offensive against Malta itself.

Picture above: The aftermath of the British raid on Mers-el-Kebir, 3 July, 1940

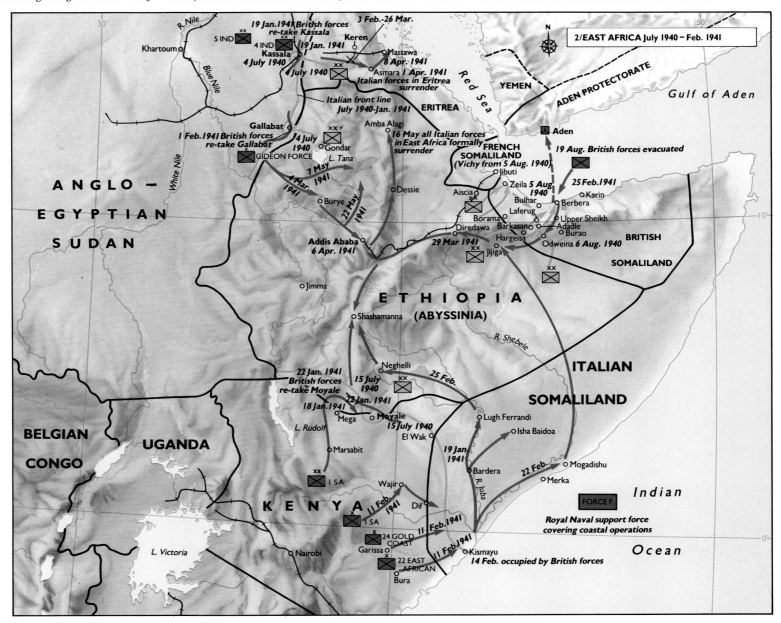

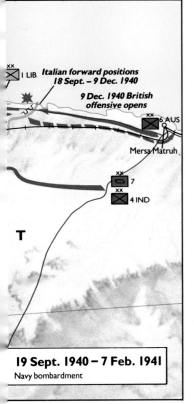

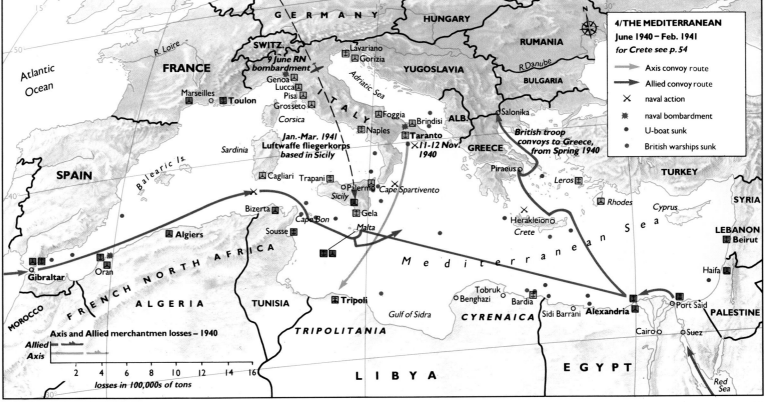

51

Air War in Europe I 1940~1941

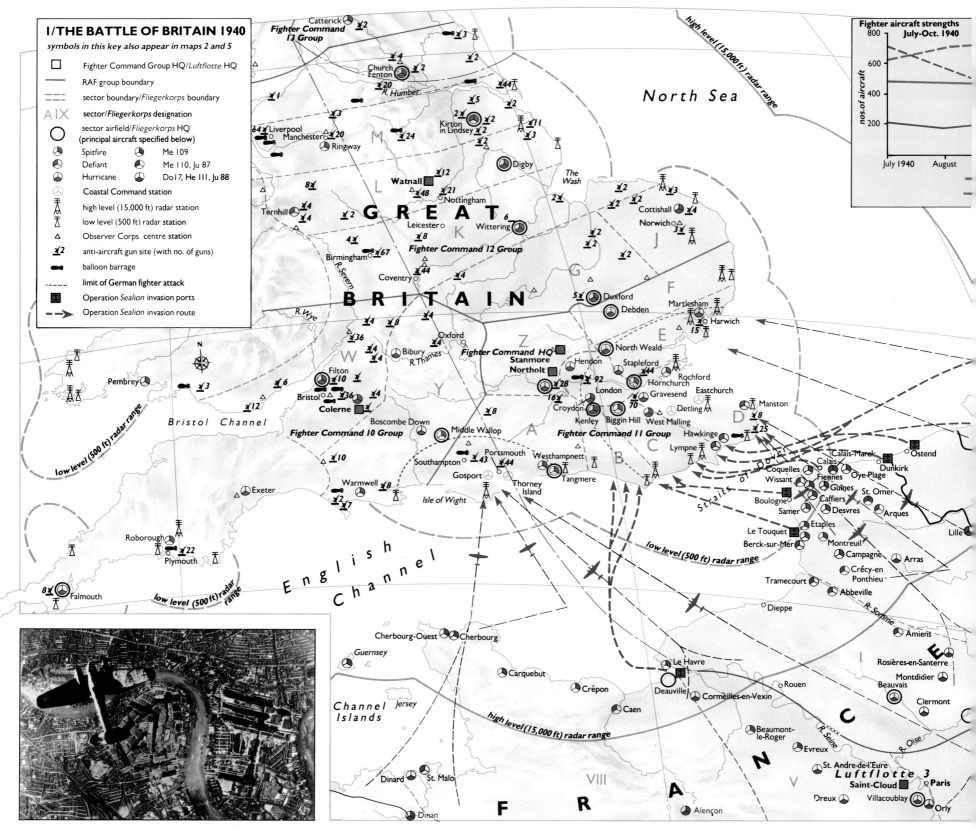

Fighter aircraft strengths July-Oct. 1940

WITH THE DEFEAT OF FRANCE in June 1940 Hitler hoped that Britain would sue for peace. When Britain refused any offer to end the war, Hitler ordered an invasion of the British Isles. On 16 July the directive for Operation *Sealion* was issued. The directive ordered the German airforce (*Luftwaffe*) to overpower the RAF as the prelude to a cross-Channel invasion. For the first time a battle was to be fought between aircraft that would alter the course of the war.

The *Luftwaffe* was poorly prepared for the conflict. Heavy losses were sustained in the invasion of France. German aircraft lacked sufficient range or bomb-carrying capacity to mount a major campaign over hostile territory against a well-armed adversary. German airmen lacked experience of this kind of campaign, and, most important of all, German fighter range was too short to cover more than a small part of southern England for even limited periods, allowing the RAF to stay out of range and to regroup in relative safety to the north and west.

The British had been preparing since 1937, though the RAF was still short of pilots and of combat experience. Britain now possessed radar and a comprehensive air defence organization. British fighter units were at last stocked with the fast monoplane fighters, Hurricanes and Spitfires, in large numbers – almost 700 by June 1940. Moreover, British factories, bullied by Lord Beaverbrook, Minister for Aircraft

Production, were turning out over 400 fighters a month by late 1940; Germany produced on average less than 200 a month.

From July 1940 mixed groups of German bombers and dive-bombers, escorted by fighters, attacked British airfields, air depots and radar stations within range of their bases in France and the Low Countries. *Luftwaffe* intelligence reported, incorrectly, by mid-August that the task was almost complete. Though there were times when the sheer weight of German forces threatened to overwhelm the defences of the Kent and Sussex sectors, airfields were rapidly repaired and a stream of replacement aircraft and pilots ensured that the overall strength of Fighter Command actually rose during August and September. By contrast, German fighter units declined in operational strength from over 700 in July to 275 by 1 October. The Ju-87 dive-bomber, so effective in the land battles, proved vulnerable and was withdrawn. Nor was any target system attacked with sufficient intensity to create a critical situation for the defenders. By mid-September, after high losses of pilots and planes, the *Luftwaffe* halted its offensive and *Sealion* was postponed indefinitely. From July to October the RAF lost 915 aircraft: the German air force 1733.

Hitler, preparing to turn east against the Soviet Union, agreed to try a heavy bombing offensive. In mid-September the *Luftwaffe* switched from day to night attacks against military

and economic targets in Britain's major cities. Helped by good electronic navigation aids, German airmen made devastating attacks on 16 major cities and ports over a six-month period. But the *Luftwaffe* suffered continued attrition of aircraft and crews, lacked pilots and navigators with training for long-range flying and bombardment, and lacked aircraft with sufficient range and lifting-power to deliver a crucial blow. Though heavy damage and high civilian casualties were sustained, neither was as great as the British government had planned for (page 46). British war production was not greatly affected and morale remained intact. In the early Spring, Hitler ordered an end to the bombing. The first strategic air campaign was a failure.

The defeat of the *Luftwaffe* in 1940 saved Britain from an invasion which her badly depleted army could hardly have repelled. But British air leaders did not learn from the German failure. Instead they began a limited offensive against German targets using similar medium, twin-engined bombers. During 1941 the campaign built up steadily, directed first at strategic economic and military targets. These attacks proved so inaccurate that Bomber Command was compelled to switch to 'area bombing'. Churchill saw this as the only way Britain could fight back in 1940 and 1941, and wanted the German civilians to 'feel the weight of the war'. Thus, the foundations were laid for the great bombing offensives conducted later in the war.

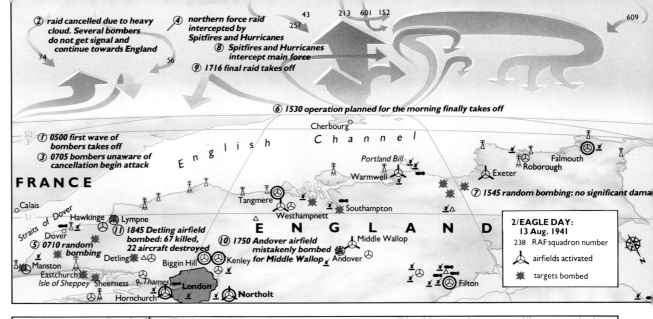

② raid cancelled due to heavy cloud. Several bombers do not get signal and continue towards England

④ northern force raid intercepted by Spitfires and Hurricanes

43   213 601 152
257
74   56

⑧ Spitfires and Hurricanes intercept main force
⑨ 1716 final raid takes off

⑥ 1530 operation planned for the morning finally takes off

① 0500 first wave of bombers takes off
③ 0705 bombers unaware of cancellation begin attack

Cherbourg

English Channel

FRANCE

Portland Bill
Warmwell
Portland Bill

Roborough   Falmouth
Exeter

⑦ 1545 random bombing: no significant damage

Calais   Hawkinge   Lympne   Tangmere   Westhampnett   Southampton

Straits of Dover   Dover   Westhampnett

⑤ 0710 random bombing

⑪ 1845 Detling airfield bombed: 67 killed, 22 aircraft destroyed

Detling   Biggin Hill   Kenley   Andover

⑩ 1750 Andover airfield mistakenly bombed for Middle Wallop

Middle Wallop   Filton

Manston   Eastchurch   Sheerness   Isle of Sheppey
Hornchurch   R. Thames   London   Northolt

ENGLAND

2/EAGLE DAY: 13 Aug. 1941
238 RAF squadron number
airfields activated
targets bombed

UNTIL THE SUMMER of 1940 air warfare in Europe had largely consisted of close support for ground armies, and the bombing of 'defended' cities (Warsaw, Rotterdam) by the *Luftwaffe*. The 'knock-out blow' from the air, initially feared by all participants, did not materialize. After the invasion of France, the situation altered, and aircraft came into their own. Between late July and mid-Sept. 1940 the *Luftwaffe* sought to defeat the RAF to pave the way for Operation *Sealion*, a German invasion of southern England. The resulting engagement – the Battle of Britain – proved to be the first serious setback the Germans encountered (1). The Germans underestimated the tenacity and complexity of the British defence (6). When radar and Observer Corps intelligence showed approaching German aircraft, details were sent directly to Fighter Command HQ and the Fighter Group operations rooms. The Group then gave instructions to Sector commanders who put their squadrons on alert. On a final order from Group HQ, the Sector commander ordered combat. The Sector retained control over the aircraft in the air when in radio contact. After that squadron leaders took operational control. This proved a quick and effective chain of command and contributed much to the eventual success of the RAF in the battle. Despairing of a continual battle of attrition, on 13th Aug. 1940 the German air force launched an all-out attack on the RAF, code-named *Adlertag* ('Eagle Day', 2). 5 waves of bombers and escort fighters were sent against 9 major airfields from Eastchurch to Portland. Bad visibility and fierce fighter defence brought poor results. The *Luftwaffe* lost 45 aircraft, the RAF only 13. Nevertheless, the campaign to destroy the RAF continued for another month, although the Germans failed to develop sufficient tactical or economic programmes to make a sustained air attack effective. Frustrated at lack of success against the RAF, the *Luftwaffe* switched to night bombing of cities in Sept. (5). Over 35,000 tons of bombs were dropped for the loss of 650 German aircraft. London (4) was attacked 19 times between Sept. 1940 and May 1941 with about 19,000 tons of bombs. The bombers were sent to attack rail centres, docks, munitions works and government buildings. Much of the destruction occurred instead in civilian residential areas close to strategic targets. The campaign was finally cancelled in order to conserve

forces for the coming Russian offensive. The Blitz failed to force Britain out of the war, and resulted in further improvements in British defences. The RAF began bombing strategic economic sites (oil, transport, docks etc.) in Germany in May 1940 (3). The campaign was soon extended to cover German-occupied territory. The difficulty in locating sites at night resulted in general attacks on industrial areas rather than specific targets – the origin of 'area bombing'. By the end of 1941 the RAF had dropped 50,000 tons on Europe, almost as much as Germany had dropped on Britain.

Picture left: A German Heinkel III medium bomber passing over the Isle of Dogs in London's docklands.

from 10 July to 31 Oct. 1940, 1733 German and 915 British fighters were destroyed

September   October   November

aircraft output
British   German   *front line strength*

Inland Sea

Amsterdam
The Hague   Soesterberg

Rotterdam

HOLLAND

Antwerp
Ghent   R. Scheldt

BELGIUM
Brussels

Luftflotte 2

Cambrai

Couvron
Compiègne   Laon   ××××

Atlantic Ocean   IRELAND

SWEDEN   DENMARK   Baltic Sea

Newcastle upon Tyne
York   Manchester
Liverpool
Grantham
GREAT BRITAIN
Huntingdon
Abingdon   Exning
Bristol   High Wycombe   London
English Channel   Dunkirk
Cherbourg   Boulogne   Calais
Dieppe
Le Havre
R. Seine
St. Nazaire   Paris   OCCUPIED FRANCE
R. Loire
La Pallice   Mannheim   Karlsruhe
Bordeaux airfield   Ambès   Bordeaux   Geneva   SWITZERLAND
VICHY FRANCE
R. Garonne   R. Rhône   Turin   ITALY   Genoa

North Sea
Sylt   Flensburg
Cuxhaven   Kiel   Warnemünde   Rostock
Wilhelmshaven   Lübeck   Wismar
Texel   Emden   Hamburg   Stettin
Oldenburg   Bremen   Bremerhaven
Amsterdam   HOLLAND   Salzbergen   Osnabrück   Hanover   Brunswick   Berlin   POLAND
8   10   Münster   Soest   Magdeburg
4 5   9   Hamm   Paderborn
3   Antwerp   Monheim   Kassel   Merseburg
BELGIUM   Cologne
1 2   Brussels   Bonn   Frankfurt
Aachen   Coblenz   BOHEMIA   MORAVIA
LUXEMBOURG   Nuremberg   SLOVAKIA
Stuttgart
Munich
München Gladbach

see inset

GERMANY

EAST PRUSSIA

1 Hazebrouck
2 Merville
3 Ostend
4 Zeebrugge
5 Flushing
6 Haamstede
7 Schipol
8 Rotterdam
9 Eindhoven
10 Soesterberg

3/BRITISH BOMBING OF EUROPE 1939–41
■ Bomber Command HQ
● Bomber Group HQ
● Bomber Command station
targets attacked, with weight of bombs:
25–1000 tons
1000–3000 tons
3000–4000 tons

Emmerich   Gelsenkirchen
R. Rhine   Wanne-Eickel   Dortmund
Wesel   Lünen
Bottrop
Sterkrade   Homberg   Essen   Schwerte
Hüls   Duisburg   R. Ruhr
Krefeld
Düsseldorf   Reisholz

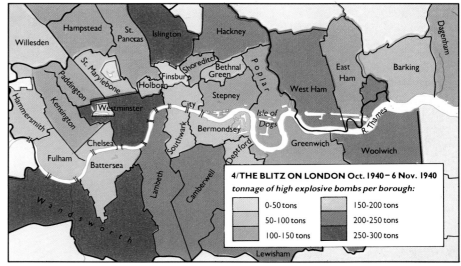

Hampstead   St. Pancras   Islington   Hackney
Willesden
Paddington   Dagenham
St. Marylebone   Shoreditch   Bethnal Green   Poplar
Kensington   Finsbury   East Ham   Barking
Hammersmith   Holborn   Stepney   West Ham
City   Isle of Dogs
Westminster
Chelsea   Southwark   Bermondsey   Deptford   Greenwich   Woolwich
Fulham   Lambeth   Camberwell
Battersea   R. Thames
Wandsworth
Lewisham

4/THE BLITZ ON LONDON Oct. 1940 – 6 Nov. 1940
tonnage of high explosive bombs per borough:
0–50 tons   150–200 tons
50–100 tons   200–250 tons
100–150 tons   250–300 tons

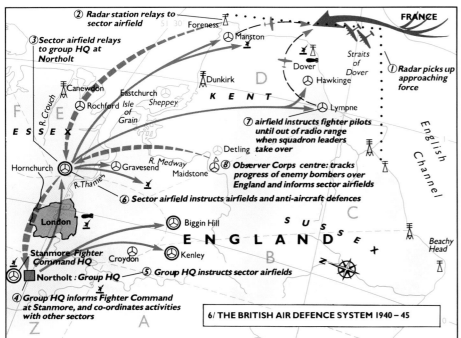

② Radar station relays to sector airfield
Foreness
FRANCE
③ Sector airfield relays to group HQ at Northolt
Manston
Straits of Dover
① Radar picks up approaching force
Canewdon   Dover
Eastchurch   Dunkirk
Rochford   Isle of Grain   Hawkinge
R. Crouch   Sheppey   KENT
ESSEX   Lympne
⑦ airfield instructs fighter pilots until out of radio range when squadron leaders take over
Hornchurch   R. Medway   Detling
Gravesend   Maidstone
R. Thames   ⑧ Observer Corps centre: tracks progress of enemy bombers over England and informs sector airfields
⑥ Sector airfield instructs airfields and anti-aircraft defences
London   English Channel
SUSSEX
Biggin Hill
Croydon   Kenley   ENGLAND   Beachy Head
Stanmore: Fighter Command HQ
Northolt : Group HQ
⑤ Group HQ instructs sector airfields
④ Group HQ informs Fighter Command at Stanmore, and co-ordinates activities with other sectors

6/ THE BRITISH AIR DEFENCE SYSTEM 1940 – 45

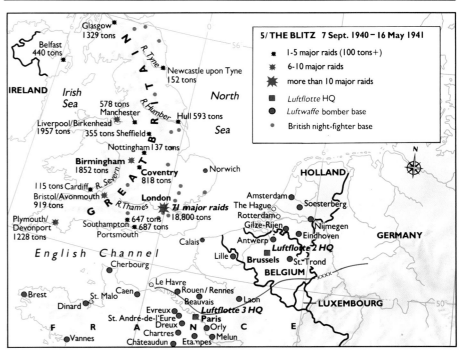

Glasgow 1329 tons
Belfast 440 tons   R. Tyne
IRELAND   Newcastle upon Tyne 152 tons
Irish Sea   North Sea
578 tons   Manchester   R. Humber   Hull 593 tons
Liverpool/Birkenhead 1957 tons   355 tons Sheffield
Nottingham 137 tons
Birmingham 1852 tons   Coventry 818 tons   Norwich
115 tons Cardiff   647 tons
Bristol/Avonmouth 919 tons   R. Severn   London 18,800 tons   71 major raids
Plymouth/Devonport 1228 tons   Southampton 647 tons   Portsmouth 687 tons   R. Thames
English Channel
Cherbourg   HOLLAND
Amsterdam   The Hague   Soesterberg
Calais   Rotterdam   Gilze-Rijen   Nijmegen
Le Havre   Lille   Antwerp   *Luftflotte 2 HQ*   GERMANY
St. Malo   Rouen/Rennes   Brussels   St-Trond
Dinard   Caen   BELGIUM   LUXEMBOURG
Evreux   Beauvais
St. André-de-l'Eure   Dreux   *Luftflotte 3 HQ*
Vannes   Chartres   Paris   Orly   Melun
Châteaudun   Etampes

5/ THE BLITZ 7 Sept. 1940 – 16 May 1941
1–5 major raids (100 tons+)
6–10 major raids
more than 10 major raids
■ Luftflotte HQ
● Luftwaffe bomber base
● British night-fighter base

The Balkans 1941

1/THE BALKANS Apr. 1939 – Apr. 1941
▲ membership of Tripartite Pact, originally between Germany, Italy and Japan in Sept. 1940

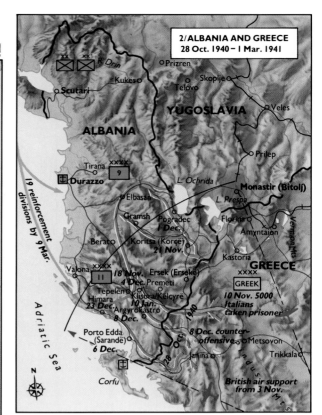

2/ALBANIA AND GREECE 28 Oct. 1940 – 1 Mar. 1941

UNTIL 1940, various diplomatic moves and territorial changes in the Balkans (*1*) failed to maintain the *status quo* of the major European powers. Hitler's plans for peacefully securing the area for Axis, in the Tripartite Pact, were undermined by Mussolini's invasion of Greece (28 Oct. 1940) from his new colonial stepping stone Albania (*2*). Unexpectedly, the Greeks fought back, driving the Italians deep into Albania by 23 Dec. British forces occupied Crete and Lemnos (31 Oct.) and RAF units arrived in the Peloponnese (3 Nov.) to provide support. British carrier aircraft attacked the Italian Fleet in harbour at Taranto (11 Nov.), damaging 3 battleships and forcing its withdrawal to Italy's west coast. Hitler determined (4 Nov.) to divert resources to contain the problem. A German offensive (*3*) opened (6 April) with advance bombing and armoured units entering Yugoslavia, forcing a surrender by 14 April. A two-pronged assault on Greece, into Thrace and through Macedonia, forced through the Greek defensive lines. British troops, landed on Greece on 4 March, were evacuated to Crete on 30 April as German armoured divisions poured south, supporting advance airborne landings at Corinth. The airborne forces under Student were then used to invade Crete (20 May) (*4*), which the British were forced to abandon (28-31 May) after fierce resistance. The British lost over 25,000 troops dead or captured in the Balkans, a total not enhanced by the loss of 6 cruisers and 7 destroyers, and damage to 5 battleships and an aircraft carrier, during the campaign and evacuation (*5*). In exchange, the Royal Navy destroyed 2 German convoys bringing reinforcements to Crete, killing 5000 troops. Nevertheless, Allied control of the eastern Mediterranean was now jeopardized, and the Axis had secured, by military means, the whole of south-eastern Europe.

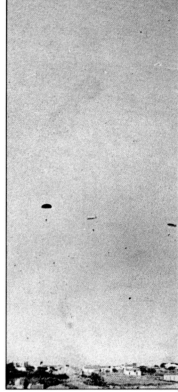

Picture right: German paratroops descending on Crete, May 1941. The 7 Parachute Div. landed in 2 waves, capturing Maleme airfield after 2 days fighting, thereby securing a base for airborne supply and reinforcement. But the high casualties (5678 dead) made Hitler avoid any future airborne operations.

4/CRETE 21–31 May 1941

THE BALKANS, source of the disagreements which had precipitated the First World War, remained isolated from the course of the Second throughout the first year. In June 1940, however, the Soviet Union made on Rumania the territorial claims agreed with Germany in the Ribbentrop-Molotov Pact of 22 August, 1939 (page 30). It annexed the provinces of Bessarabia and northern Bukovina (the former had been Russian before 1917; the latter had not). Germany and Italy accepted these annexations in the Vienna Award of 30 August, 1940, which also returned northern Transylvania to Hungary and southern Dobruja (September 7) to Bulgaria. Rumania's shrunken frontiers were, however, at the same time guaranteed by Italy and Germany. Hitler was anxious to secure access to Rumania's oil fields at Ploeşti, which were to remain Germany's main source of supply throughout the war. He was also suspicious of Soviet ambitions in the Balkans, particularly as his intention to attack Russia grew during the Autumn of 1940; in September he sent a 'military mission' of an army division to Rumania and Hungary, binding them into the Tripartite Pact (signed between Germany, Italy and Japan on 27 September). Bulgaria, which Hitler was simultaneously wooing away from dependence on Russia, joined the pact on 1 March, 1941.

Hitler's aim of transforming the Balkans into a satellite region by peaceful diplomacy was disturbed on 28 October, 1940, by Mussolini's unprovoked invasion of Greece from Albania. Mussolini, whose part in the defeat of France had been inglorious (page 44), hoped to confront his fellow dictator with a military triumph of his own. He believed Greece would collapse when attacked. On the contrary, the Greeks resisted stiffly and then, with the assistance of British air units landed in the Peloponnese (from 3 November), counter-attacked. By mid-December, the Italians had been driven back fifty miles within Albania and by 1 March most of the south was in Greek hands. Mussolini's initiative infuriated Hitler: it both provided Britain with a pretext to intervene and heightened Russian suspicions of his policy towards Bulgaria, which the Soviet government had earmarked as a satellite of its own. At Hitler's meeting with Molotov in Berlin on 11-12 November the Soviet Foreign Minister declared Russia's intention of extending a unilateral guarantee of Bulgaria's frontiers, with the aim of securing bases from which it could exercise closer control over the exit from the Black Sea. It was Molotov's attitude here which stiffened Hitler's resolve to attack Russia.

In the meantime, however, Hitler had ordered the Army General Staff (4 November) to prepare plans for an attack on Greece (Operation *Marita*). This was to be mounted from Bulgaria, where German engineers began to bridge the Danube

on 28 February 1941, to permit the attack force in Rumania to reach its attack positions. Yugoslavia, across which he also required transit rights, had resisted his diplomacy thus far, but on 25 March agreed to join the Tripartite Pact. Two days later, the Yugoslav government was deposed by a military coup. Hitler at once included the invasion of Yugoslavia in his general plan. The military government of Yugoslavia sought, but was denied, Soviet assistance; its mission to Moscow secured a meaningless treaty of friendship on 5 April. On the next day, German forces opened an attack from southern Germany, Rumania and Bulgaria. An air attack on Belgrade (6 April) killed 17,000 citizens and on 10 April Yugoslav resistance began to collapse when the predominantly Croatian 4th and 7th Armies mutinied. An autonomous Croat government welcomed the Germans into Zagreb the same day. Belgrade fell two days later and the government asked for an armistice on 14 April. Serbian resistance began almost at once, with the formation of royalist *Chetnik* groups in the mountains.

In Greece the government was committed, for political reasons, to defending the Metaxas Line along the Bulgarian frontier with Thrace (promised to Bulgaria as a bribe for joining the Tripartite Pact). Its main force was therefore in the wrong place to resist the Germans when they crossed the Yugoslav frontier on 10 April. A British expeditionary force, which had been sent to Greece from Egypt in March, also found itself in the wrong place and was quickly forced to retreat. German troops captured Athens on 27 April and the British evacuated the Peloponnese, with heavy loss, on 30 April. The British fugitives joined a garrison which had been sent to Crete the previous October. Hitler decided to take the island from them and, in the airborne Operation *Mercury* (20-31 May), captured the Maleme airstrip and forced the British to evacuate to Egypt from the southern harbour of Sphakia. German seaborne reinforcements suffered heavily from British naval attack, although losses were not as severe as those of the British.

Hitler's Balkan *blitzkrieg* not only inflicted humiliation and heavy casualties on the British. It also compromised their strategic position in the eastern Mediterranean. It opened up the immediate danger that Hitler would establish a centre of power in the Levant, threatening the British forces in Egypt and the Middle East; it put paid to hopes that Turkey might soon be brought into the war on the Allied side. The extension of Axis control over the Balkans also robbed Britain of its last potential foothold in Europe and committed it to acting against the *Wehrmacht* on land only through guerrilla and resistance forces (pages 84, 110). For the Germans, however, the guerrilla war in Yugoslavia (page 128) would prove the costliest that it had to fight in occupied western Europe.

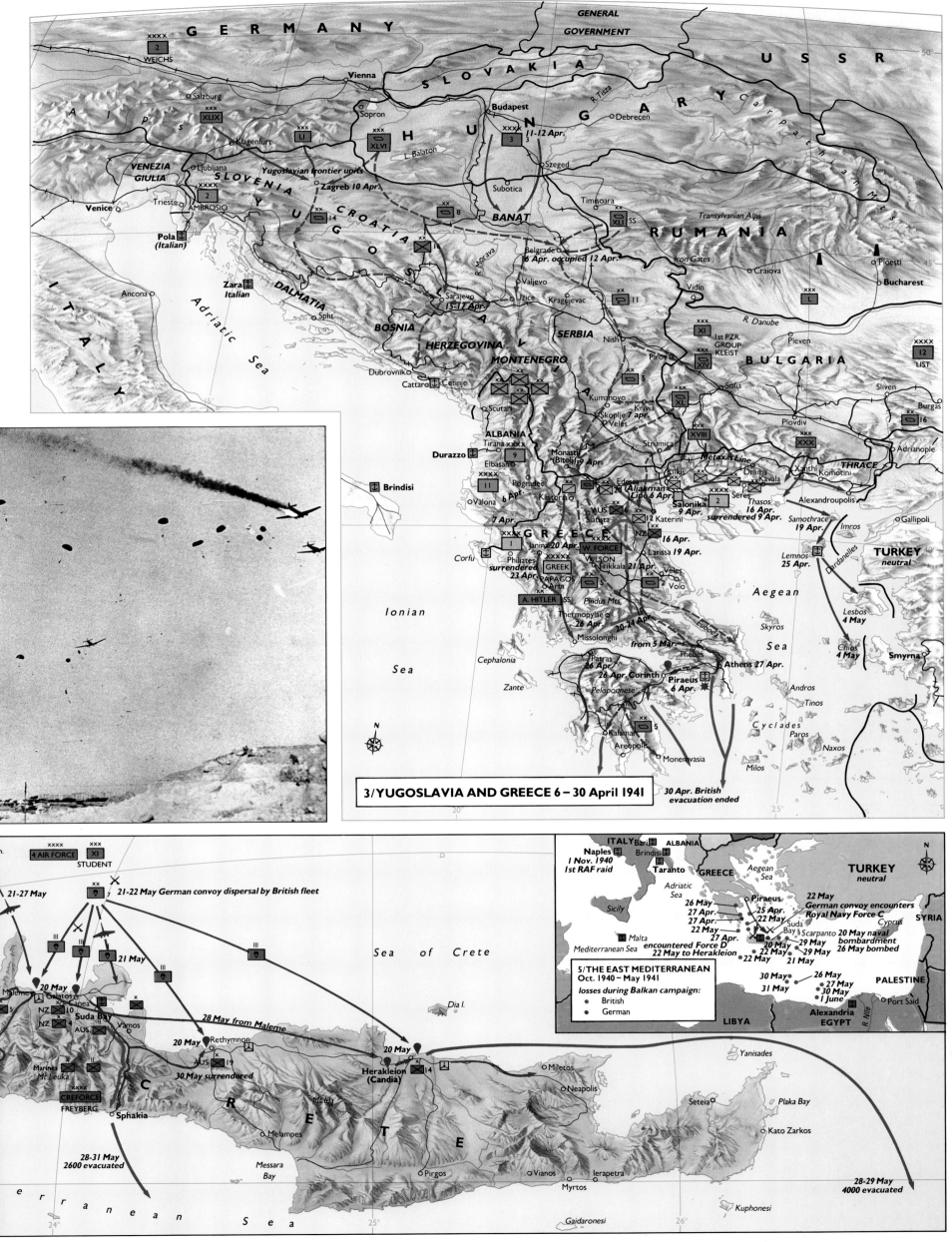

GERMANY

XXXX
2
WEICHS

GENERAL GOVERNMENT

Salzburg
Vienna

XLIX

Sopron

SLOVAKIA

USSR

HUNGARY

Budapest
Debrecen

L. Balaton

LI

XLVI

XXXX
3
11-12 Apr.

Szeged

Subotica

Timisoara

R. Tisza

VENEZIA GIULIA
Klagenfurt
Ljubljana

SLOVENIA

CROATIA

Zagreb 10 Apr.
Yugoslavian frontier units

8

BANAT

Belgrade 6 Apr. occupied 12 Apr.

XLI SS

RUMANIA

Transylvanian Alps

Craiova

Bucharest

Ploesti

Trieste
2
AMBROSIO

Y
14

U

Venice

Pola
(Italian)

ITALY

DALMATIA

Zara
Italian

Ancona

Adriatic Sea

Split

BOSNIA

Sarajevo 15-17 Apr.

Uzice

Kragujevac

11

R. Morava

Valjevo

R. Danube

Vidin

Pleven

L

HERZEGOVINA

SERBIA

Nish

BULGARIA

12
LIST

Dubrovnik

Cattaro Cetinje

MONTENEGRO

5

Pirot

XI 1st PZR. GROUP KLEIST

XIV

Sofia

Scutari

Kumanovo

Skoplje 7 apr.

Krivla

Veles

XL

Plovdiv

Sliven

Burgas

16

ALBANIA

Tirana xxxx

Durazzo

Elbasan

9

Monastir (Bitolj) 9 Apr.

XVIII

XXX

Metaxas Line

Strumica

Edessa

Kilkis

Drama

Xanthi

Kavala

Komotini

THRACE

Adrianople

Brindisi

11

Pogradec

6 Apr.

Valona

Kastoria

1 Apr.

Aliakman Line 6 Apr.

AUS

12 Katerini

Seres

Salonika 9 Apr.

Thasos
16 Apr.
surrendered 9 Apr.

Samothrace
19 Apr.

Alexandroupolis

Imros

Lemnos
25 Apr.

TURKEY
neutral

Corfu

GREECE

Janina 20 Apr.
Philates surrendered 23 Apr.

W. FORCE
WILSON

Trikkala 21 Apr.

Larissa 19 Apr.

16 Apr.

Velestino

Nz

Dardanelles

Gallipoli

Smyrna

GREEK
PAPAGOS
Arta

A. HITLER SS

Pindus Mts.

Thermopylae
26 Apr.

20-24 Apr.

Volo

2

Aegean Sea

Lesbos
4 May

Chios
4 May

Skyros

Ionian Sea

Missolonghi

from 5 Mar.

Euboea

Thebes

Athens 27 Apr.

Patras
26 Apr.

Cephalonia

26 Apr. Corinth

Piraeus
6 Apr.

Peloponnese

Andros

Tinos

Zante

Kalamata

5

Areopolis

Monemvasia

Cyclades

Paros

Naxos

Milos

3/YUGOSLAVIA AND GREECE 6 – 30 April 1941

30 Apr. British
evacuation ended

XXXX
4 AIR FORCE

XXX
XI
STUDENT

21-27 May

21-22 May German convoy dispersal by British fleet

III III III

21 May

III
9

Sea of Crete

III

28 May from Maleme

20 May

20 May

Maleme
Galatos
Canea

NZ
5

NZ
10

Suda Bay

AUS

Vamos

20 May Rethymnon

AUS
19

30 May surrendered

Marines
Mt Leuka

II

CREFORCE
FREYBERG

Sphakia

C R E T E

28-31 May
2600 evacuated

Dia I.

20 May

Herakleion
(Candia)

14

Mt Ida

Melampes

Messara
Bay

Pirgos

Vianos

Myrtos

Miletos

Neapolis

Seteia

Ierapetra

Yanisades

Plaka Bay

Kato Zarkos

28-29 May
4000 evacuated

Gaidaronesi

Kuphonesi

_M e d i t e r r a n e a n   S e a_

ITALY
Naples
1 Nov. 1940
1st RAF raid

Taranto

Bari

ALBANIA

Brindisi

GREECE

Aegean Sea

TURKEY
neutral

Adriatic Sea

Sicily

Malta

Mediterranean Sea

Piraeus

26 May
27 Apr.
27 Apr.
22 May

25 Apr.
22 May

27 Apr.
encountered Force D
22 May to Herakleion

22 May
German convoy encounters
Royal Navy Force C

Cyprus

Suda
Bay

Scarpanto

20 May naval
bombardment
26 May bombed

SYRIA

20 May
22 May

29 May

22 May

21 May

30 May
31 May

26 May

27 May
30 May
1 June

PALESTINE

Port Said

LIBYA

Alexandria
EGYPT

R. Nile

5/THE EAST MEDITERRANEAN
Oct. 1940 – May 1941
losses during Balkan campaign:
● British
● German

55

THE SCALE OF OPERATION *Barbarossa* overwhelms the imagination. On 22 June 1941 armies of three million men on either side, with air and naval support, were aligned along the German/Russian frontier; the potential area of operations covered half of Europe. The German High Command knew that, like earlier invaders, they had to destroy the defending army before it could retreat into the vastness of the Russian interior and prolong the campaign into the Winter. Germany's armoured forces offered the only chance of success. Concentrated on narrow sectors, the four Panzer Groups must trap the first strategic echelon of Soviet armies west of the River Dnieper. The early days of the campaign saw dramatic advances by the armoured forces, averaging 30 or more kilometres a day. Behind them marched the infantry divisions which could not maintain half the Panzers' speed. As the gaps opened armoured forces had to be committed to holding objectives rather than pressing eastwards. The German armoured force was too small for the task and it was further hampered by the inadequate Russian road and rail network. The armoured forces began to run short of fuel and every other sort of supply. The maintenance problems caused by Russian roads exceeded all expectations and the tank strength of German divisions dropped by half in the first month of war.

In the first weeks of the war German forces achieved vast encirclements and hundreds of thousands of prisoners were captured. Despite the shock of the German surprise attack, there was no dramatic collapse of Russian will-power. Whenever German planners had faced the strategic and logistic impossibilities of the invasion of Russia, they had conjured them away by assuming that the Russian soldier was either racially inferior or would not fight to defend the Bolshevik state. They had also over-estimated the effect of the purges of the 1930s on the Soviet officer corps. A third mistake was to underestimate the ability of the Soviet government to generate reserves (page 58). Divisions and whole armies disappeared in the frontier battles but by mid-July the number of Soviet divisions had risen from 170 to 212, although only 90 were at anything like their proper establishment. This reveals the hollowness of much of the western debate about *Barbarossa*. Even had it been possible to start earlier, to agree on Moscow as the main objective and to concentrate armoured forces to reach it, the capital would have been defended as fiercely as Leningrad or Stalingrad were in their turn. What is more, Panzer divisions were hardly ideally suited to street fighting and they would inevitably have become exhausted.

THE *BARBAROSSA* PLAN (2) can be divided into two sectors and three phases. The bulk of the German force was concentrated north of the Pripet Marshes in Army Groups North and Centre. Army Group Centre, with about half the German armour, was to shatter the Soviet force in Byelorussia and then assist Army Group North in clearing the Baltic area and capturing Leningrad. In the southern sector Army Group South was to launch a pinning attack from Rumania while its Panzer Group drove to the River Dnieper and then south to envelop the Soviet force in the Ukraine. It was crucial to the German plan that the Soviet Army should be destroyed in this phase and not permitted to withdraw into the heartland of Russia. In the second phase Moscow would be the objective in the north while Army Group South occupied the Donets Basin and threatened the Caucasus. On 22 June 1941 (1) the bulk of the Soviet forces in European Russia were deployed in the territories occupied since 1939. The border armies were grouped under military districts which would form front headquarters in wartime. Soviet armoured forces were organized into mechanized corps, distributed among the districts. The corps had only recently been formed and were not properly equipped or trained. The Red Army lacked armoured groupings to compare with the German Panzer Groups. Behind the first echelon of armies, four new armies were beginning to form up from the interior military districts, two each in rear of the Kiev and Western Special Military Districts. The Germans had a general idea of the Soviet deployment though they overestimated the strength of the

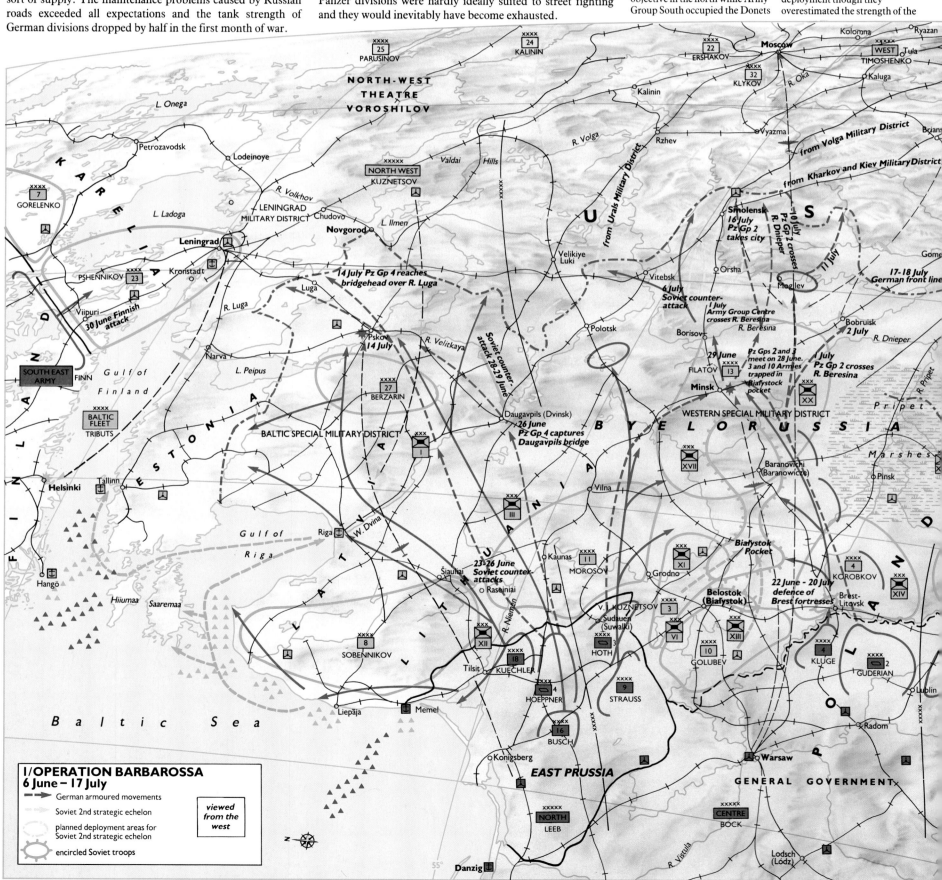

1/OPERATION BARBAROSSA
6 June – 17 July

- → German armoured movements
- Soviet 2nd strategic echelon
- planned deployment areas for Soviet 2nd strategic echelon
- encircled Soviet troops

viewed from the west

infantry armies and seriously underestimated the Soviet armoured strength. The German assault began with a shattering series of air attacks, disrupting headquarters and supply dumps and destroying the bulk of the Soviet air force on the ground. German air superiority was assured, limiting Soviet ability to manoeuvre, particularly in the Pripet and Baltic areas, where tanks soon became bogged down in the swamps if they could not use the roads. Army Group North made excellent progress, capturing the bridges at Daugavpils on 26 June and crossing the River Velikaya on 4 July. However, Panzer Group 4 reached the River Luga on 14 July but was delayed for nearly three weeks to allow the 18th Army to catch up. Army Group Centre also ran to plan initially. Panzer Groups 2 and 3 completed a double envelopment at Minsk on 28 June, leading to the capture of 280,000 men. However, success on this scale brought its own problems; liquidating the pocket took days,

delaying the advance on Smolensk while Soviet reinforcements were concentrated in the area. Most of the city was in German hands by 17 July but Soviet resistance continued. At this point Hitler intervened, over-ruling the Army High Command's desire to press on for Moscow, and insisting that Panzer Group 3 support Army Group North against Leningrad while Panzer Group 2 swung south into the Ukraine where the Germans were falling behind their timetable. The Southwest Front under General Kirponos was the strongest Soviet grouping, particularly in armour, and a series of counter-attacks checked the German onslaught. At the end of the first week in July Panzer Group 1 had not passed the Zhitomir-Berdichev line although Soviet resistance further south was beginning to crumble.

Picture below: Heinz Guderian, commander of Panzer Group 2, and a leading exponent of armoured strategy, surveying opening manoeuvres during Barbarossa.

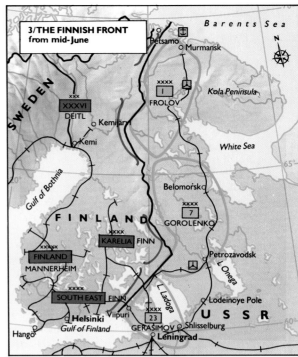

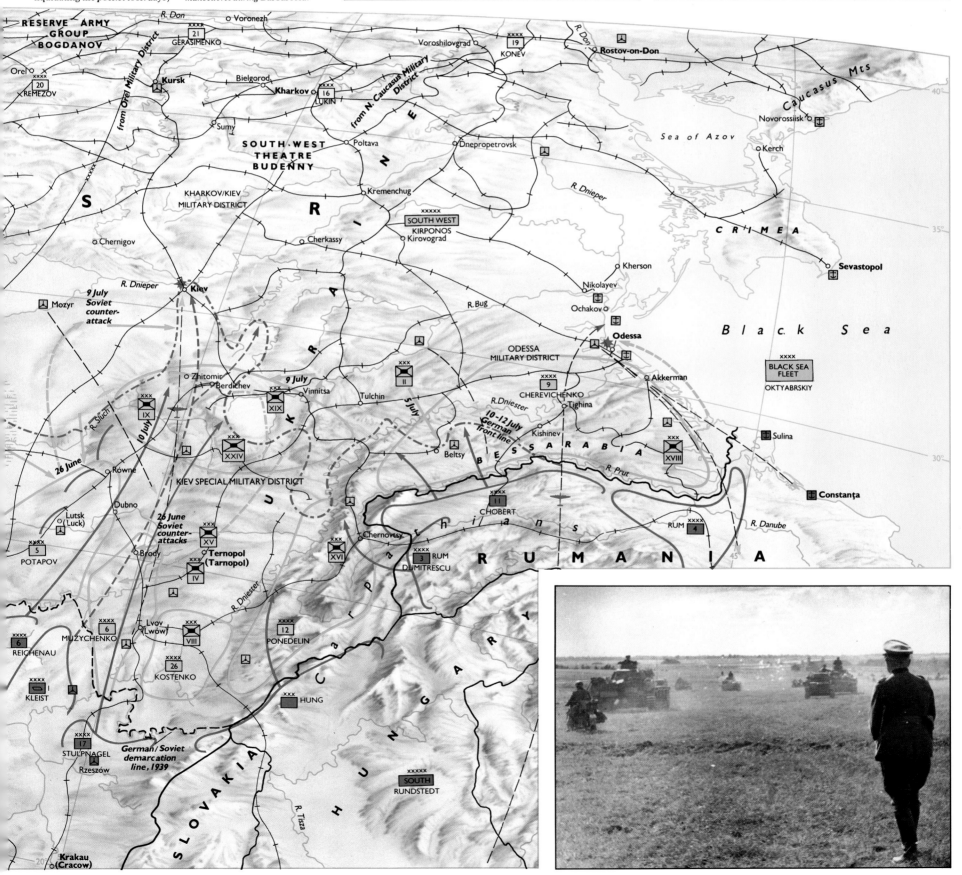

The Soviet Union JULY~SEPTEMBER 1941

BY 17 JULY THE GERMAN ARMY was beginning to confront the problems of its own success. The leading Panzer divisions were 300–400 miles inside Russia, stretching the German supply chain to its absolute limit. Behind those spearheads laboured the infantry and there were many pockets of Soviet troops still capable of resistance. In particular the High Command was concerned by the remnants of several Soviet armies, known to the Germans as the 5th Army, in the Pripet Marshes. Roads were jammed with columns of vehicles and horse wagons. The Russian railways used broad-gauge track, so it was necessary not only to repair combat damage, but to convert the lines to the standard gauge used by Germany. Delay was inevitable while the Army Groups brought their stocks of ammunition and fuel up to the required level. Most of their soldiers' food was expected to be foraged from the country, but the Soviets had used 'scorched earth' tactics as they retreated. As supplies came up, and quartermasters worked miracles of improvisation, new advances became possible until again the armour out-ran its supplies.

This logistic background is vital to an understanding of operations in this period. At its start, for example, XLI Panzer Corps of Panzer Group 4 was within 80 miles of Leningrad, but it had less than half its ammunition establishment. Although General Hoepner, commander of the Panzer Group, suggested trying to seize Leningrad with just this one force, the Army Group could not guarantee to supply it. On the Smolensk-Moscow axis there was hardly any progress at all for over two months. This was partly because Hitler insisted on diverting Army Group Centre's Panzer Groups elsewhere, but also because of the supply problem. As Army Group Centre waited for supplies to come forward, Soviet counter-attacks, such as at Elnya (30 Aug.-8 Sept.) made heavy demands on ammunition stocks, which actually decreased during August and early September. Not until the Soviet offensive was exhausted was it possible to build up the supply base for an attack on Moscow.

The German High Command was also worried by its continually increasing casualty figures. By 13 July the German army had lost 92,120 killed, wounded and missing (3.6% of the field army). A month later the total had risen to 389,924 in all (10% of the field army). By the end of September casualties stood at 551,039 – 16.2% of the field army. Replacements totalled only about half this figure, so that the German army was now more than 200,000 men below strength.

On the Soviet side, although casualties were several times worse, reinforcements continued to arrive. New armies were created and moved to the most threatened sectors of the line, especially in front of Moscow. Equipment was in short supply but by reducing the size of divisions a reserve was created. Divisional artillery strengths were halved which made it possible to form new artillery regiments and divisions as the Reserve of the High Command. These formations played a key role all through the war; they were moved around the front to create vital superiorities at crucial points, both in attack and defence. Similar reserves were created for other arms of the service and the air force.

The Soviet army was gradually learning how to fight. From the catastrophes of 1941 a new generation of soldiers was arising. Among those whose names first came to notice in this period were Koniev, Rokossovsky, Malinovsky, Vlasov and others who would rise to command armies and later fronts. Junior commanders and soldiers were now veterans. There remained a serious shortage of trained staff officers, which would limit the Red Army's capabilities for another year or two. However, the Russians were learning fast and the army was clearly not going to collapse.

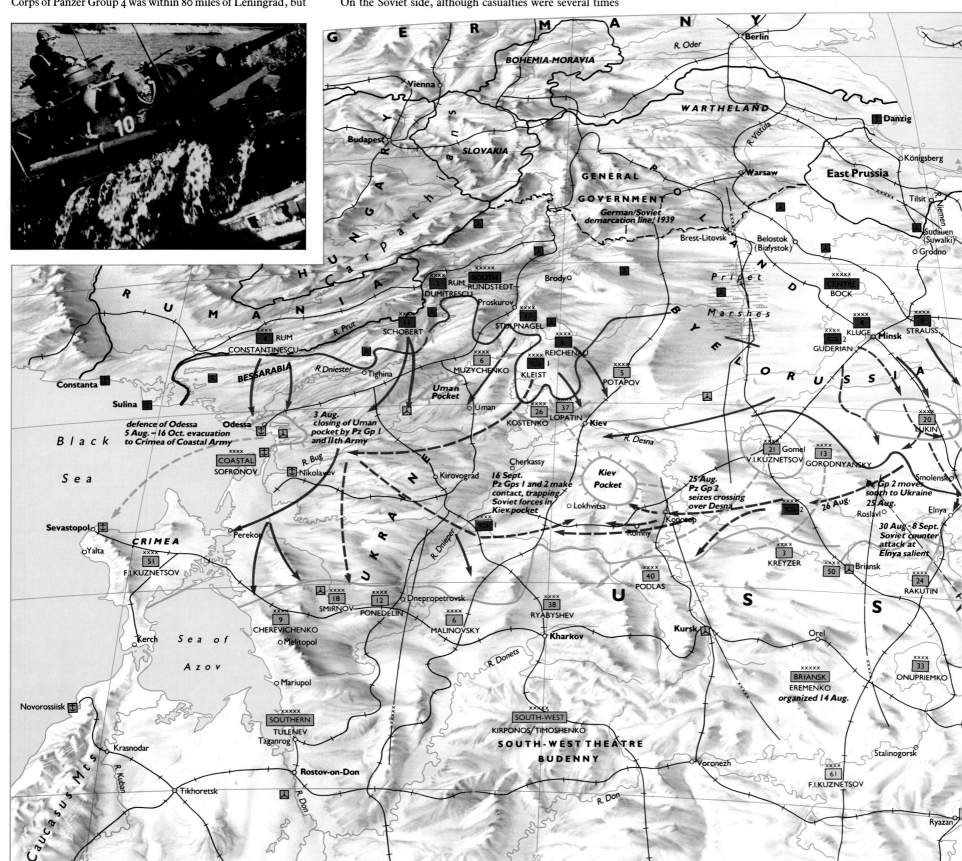

FROM THE MIDDLE of July (1) Army Group South, which had made least progress in the first month of the war, began to break Soviet resistance in the Ukraine. The 11th and 17th Armies began to converge on Uman and a Soviet attempt to withdraw was frustrated when Panzer Group 1 was swung south from the Kiev axis. Between 3-10 Aug. 100,000 Soviet troops were captured in the Uman pocket. Further south the 4th Rumanian Army had advanced to Odessa but the garrison, the Independent Coastal Army, held out from 5 Aug. until evacuated to the Crimea in early October. The defence could not prevent the 11th Army's advance across the Ukraine with support from Panzer Group 2. The 11th Army advanced into the Crimea while the remains of the Southern Front struggled to hold the River Donets. As the battle for Smolensk drew to a close the German High Command debated Army Group Centre's next objective. Hitler would not give priority to Moscow and insisted

that Panzer Group 3 should assist Army Group North with a thrust to cut communications between Moscow and Leningrad, although the area was not suited to armoured operations. Panzer Group 2 was ordered south to meet the main body of Panzer Group 1 near Konotop. The advance on Moscow was to be continued by infantry which needed some weeks to build up the supplies required. Panzer Groups 1 and 2 met south of Romny on 15 Sept., trapping 650,000 troops in the Kiev pocket. The Southwest Front commander, General Kirponos, was killed at this time, completing the collapse of command and control in the area. Only about 150,000 Soviet troops escaped from the Kiev pocket. Army Group North's advance got under way again on 8 Aug. By 21 Aug. Panzer Group 4 had reached Novgorod but a counter-attack in the Staraya Russa area temporarily checked its southern corps. The delay was not long and on 8 Sept. Army Group North reached Lake Ladoga at

Shlisselburg, isolating Leningrad. Hitler decided not to storm the city but to leave it to starve under *Luftwaffe* bombardment. In Karelia the Finns pressed forwards but could not make a final push to link up, thus leaving open a life-line across Lake Ladoga (page 64). Meanwhile, the 18th Army had been clearing the Baltic States, forcing the abandonment of the Baltic Fleet's bases. Success on the flanks, with his objectives apparently almost in German hands, encouraged Hitler to look again at Moscow. Deciding that Soviet resistance must be near its last gasp, on 6 Sept. he authorized the envelopment of Vyazma, to be followed by an advance to Moscow. However, Army Group Centre's supplies had been depleted in beating off Soviet counter-attacks at Elnya and Groups 2, 3 and 4 faced complicated re-organization to create the necessary strike groups. The rest of Sept. was devoted to these preparations and the front remained static, though not

inactive. The movements of General Zhukov (2) during 1941 illustrate the shifting pattern of the campaign and the Red Army's lack of experienced senior commanders. When war broke out Zhukov was in Moscow, as Chief of the General Staff. He was naturally a member of *Stavka*, the Soviet High Command, and was immediately sent south as its representative on the Southwest Front. After 4 days based at Tarnopol, helping to organize counter-attacks in the Brody area, he was recalled to Moscow. Staff

work was not Zhukov's metier and when he quarrelled with Stalin on 29 July over the need to evacuate Kiev, he was replaced as Chief of the General Staff and sent to command the Reserve Front which was created east of Smolensk. There he supervised the Elnya counter-attacks which delayed Army Group Centre. On 9 Sept. he was transferred northwards to command the Leningrad Front, then in some disorder after being cut off as the Germans reached Lake Ladoga. However, once the Germans began Operation

Typhoon (the advance on Moscow) he was recalled on 6 Oct. and by 10 Oct. was commanding the Western Front, defending the capital. There he remained throughout the winter, overseeing the Moscow counter-attack in Dec. (page 60).

*Picture left: a German Panzer Mk.III tank crossing a Russian river. This model formed the spearhead of German armoured thrusts throughout Barbarossa.
Right: Ukrainian peasant evacuees moving east; many destroyed their villages rather than let them fall into German hands.*

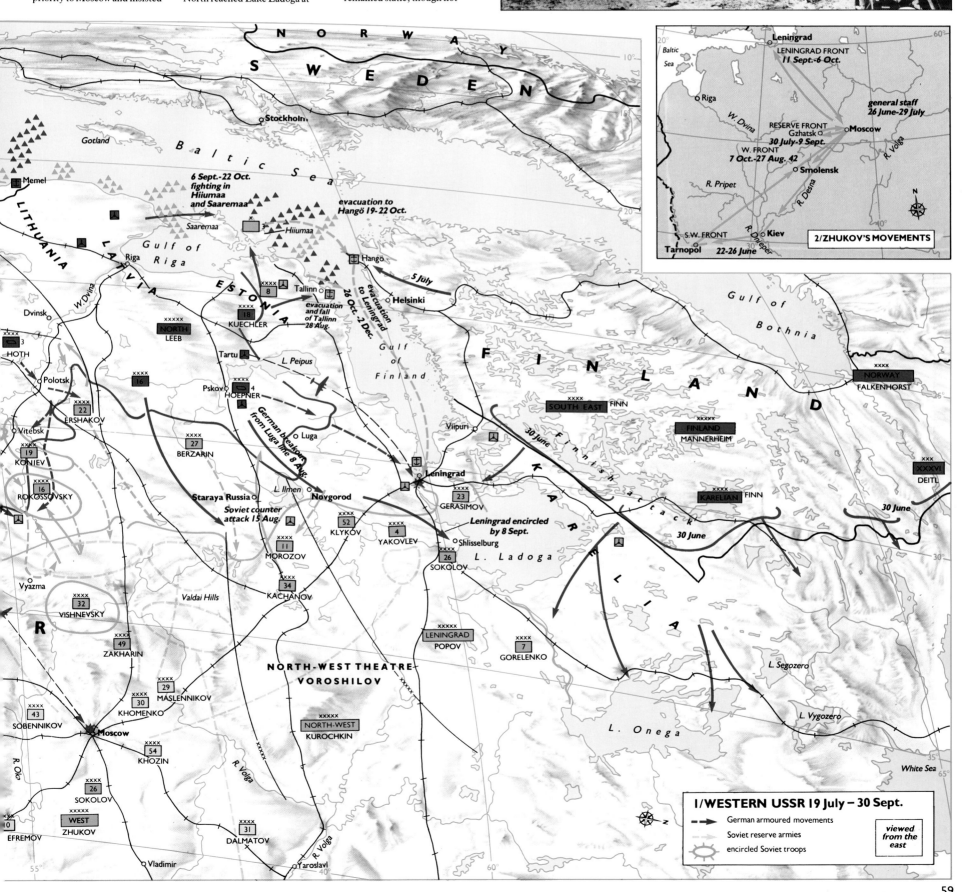

I/WESTERN USSR 19 July – 30 Sept.

➤ German armoured movements
➤ Soviet reserve armies
⊙ encircled Soviet troops

viewed from the east

2/ZHUKOV'S MOVEMENTS

Moscow SEPT. 1941 ~ APRIL 1942

Hitler's Directive No. 35 of 6 September finally made Moscow the objective of the 1941 campaign. Although Army Groups North and South were to continue to advance towards Leningrad and Rostov the bulk of German armour, the 2nd, 3rd and 4th Panzer Groups, were to concentrate under Army Group Centre. Completion of their existing missions and re-grouping would take the rest of September. The German plan for Operation *Typhoon*, the assault on Moscow, followed the standard pattern. Panzer forces would penetrate deeply creating vast encirclements to be annihilated by the infantry armies. However, once again the German High Command was neglecting Russian geography and counting on the collapse of Soviet resistance. October brought the Autumn rains and the *rasputitsa* (the roadless season). Most Russian roads were unmetalled and unusable in Spring and Autumn – the bulk of the German Army would simply stick where it was. November might bring a brief respite before the notorious Russian Winter but pre-war plans had assumed that only a garrison of 60 divisions would be left in Russia by then.

On the Soviet side there was no end to the new divisions which were formed, grouped into armies and brought into the *Stavka* reserve. More significantly, Stalin had been convinced that Japan was about to strike south in the Pacific, so he could afford to move properly trained and combat-tested divisions from the Far East. Zhukov was to take command of the Western Front for the battle of Moscow and around him were now grouped the best of the younger generals. The balance of quality still favoured the Germans but it was far more even than

three months earlier.

At first Operation *Typhoon* seemed to be running to schedule and thousands of prisoners fell into German hands at Vyazma and Briansk. By mid-October there were signs of panic in Moscow, which was put under a state of siege on the 19th. At the front Russian resistance continued, as strong counter-attacks at Kalinin and Mtsensk indicated. Early in November the German High Command finally admitted that the Soviet Union could not be beaten in 1941.

In this final stage of the campaign the Germans continued to attack because to yield the initiative and to go over to the defence entailed a greater risk. New thrusts in mid-November and the first days of December brought their leading elements almost to the Moscow city limits, but each advance was halted more rapidly than the last. However, the German High Command continued to believe that the Red Army must be equally exhausted and that victory would go to the side which hung on to the last battalion. In fact the Russians had concentrated nine reserve armies along the front and were debating when and where to use them. Stalin would not allow this reserve to be sucked into the Moscow battle and during November it was decided that the German army had almost reached exhaustion. The counter-offensive was timed to begin immediately after the arrival of the Winter frosts because German tanks and other equipment would cease to operate in the extreme cold while Soviet equipment had been designed to cope with the conditions.

The first weeks of the Soviet counter-offensive seemed to

justify their calculations. The extreme cold sapped the German soldiers' will to fight and immobilized their equipment. As units were forced to retreat, much of their equipment was left behind. A major command crisis followed on the German side. Hitler was most unwilling to permit withdrawals. The army commanders continued to demand freedom of action as they saw their troops sacrificed to no effect. The Army Group commanders were the middle-men between Hitler and their subordinates. The result was a dramatic change of personnel as Hitler sacked all three army group commanders and several army commanders, including Guderian, in the first month of the Soviet offensive. He then assumed direct command of the German army himself.

In the short term, events justified Hitler. The Red Army began the second phase of its Winter campaign in mid-January, maintaining pressure in the Western Front sector while expanding the offensive on either flank. The aim was to encircle Army Group Centre. The concept was excellent but the Russians lacked the resources to maintain major thrusts into an enemy position. Thanks to the losses of 1941 they were short of tanks and brigades were the largest armoured formations available to them. The 1st Guards Cavalry Corps managed to penetrate the German lines and an airborne corps was dropped in driblets near Vyazma. However, on Hitler's order the German army held 'hedgehogs' around the main centres of communication. However weak the garrison, the Soviet attackers did not possess the artillery, tanks and supplies to break through. The Spring *rasputitsa* only confirmed the stalemate. When Hitler repeated his calls for 'fanatical resistance' in future years, the German Army would be facing an enemy who had grasped the slender opportunity to create strength in depth.

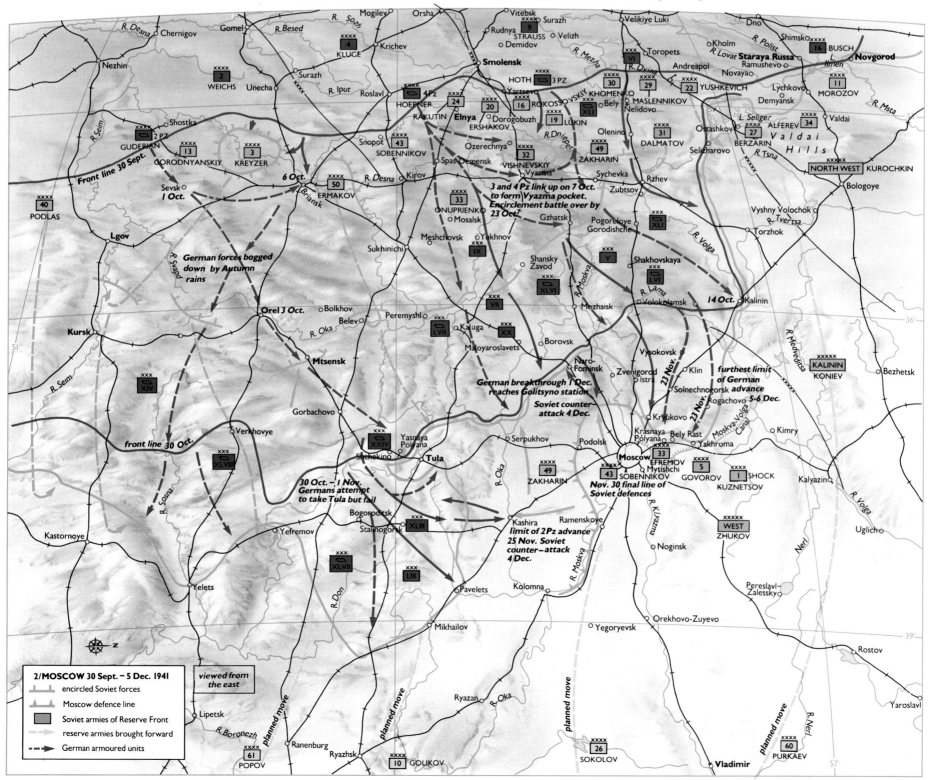

2/MOSCOW 30 Sept. – 5 Dec. 1941

viewed from the east

- encircled Soviet forces
- Moscow defence line
- Soviet armies of Reserve Front
- reserve armies brought forward
- German armoured units

I/THE SOVIET FRONT

reserve armies

IN SPITE OF severe reductions in German combat efficiency as a result of the initial success of *Barbarossa*, Hitler was convinced that a decisive victory in 1941 would finish Soviet resistance for good: Moscow was only 40 miles from the German front line in early November. The assault on Moscow (2) began on 30 Sept. when the 2nd Panzer Group broke through the 13th Army and threatened Orel and Briansk, forcing the 3rd and 50th Armies to attack eastwards to escape encirclement. On 2 Oct. the 3rd and 4th Panzer Groups joined the offensive, splintering the Soviet defences. In the Vyazma pocket large parts of 6 Soviet armies were trapped, bringing the German bag of prisoners to 700,000 in 3 weeks. However, the onset of the Autumn rains and the need to clear up the pockets slowed the German advance and Soviet resistance at Tula, Kalinin and in the Mozhaisk line was stubborn. The second phase of the German offensive began on 15 Nov. It was an attempt to encircle Moscow from the Tula and Kalinin areas but only slow progress was made. At the beginning of Dec. Winter struck; facing 30 or more degrees of frost the exhausted German troops could advance no further. Meanwhile by transferring units

from the Far East and raising new formations the Soviet High Command had conjured up reserves for a decisive counter-offensive (*1*). The Soviets had also created new formations – Shock armies – designed for counter-offensive thrusts. The first phase began on 6 Dec (*3*), when Zhukov unleashed the 1st Shock Army,

and 20th and 10th Armies. The German salients north and south of the city collapsed and with the threat to Moscow removed the Soviet army began to attack all along the front. Although airborne and cavalry corps penetrated the German rear areas there was no general retreat. By the Spring the two sides had fought to a standstill.

Picture above: A battery of Soviet M-39 85mm anti-aircraft guns outside the Exhibition of Economic Achievements in Moscow. German air raids on Moscow began on the first day of the war and reached their greatest intensity during October and November 1941. In all 1200 people were killed and 5400 were wounded during 122 raids.

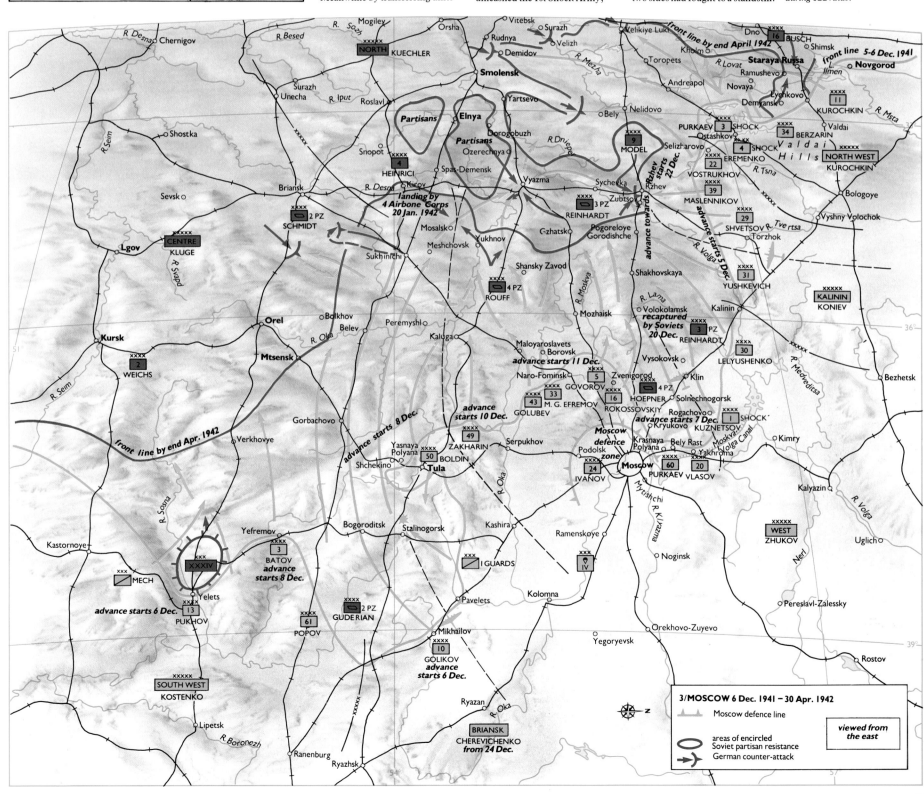

3/MOSCOW 6 Dec. 1941 – 30 Apr. 1942

Moscow defence line

areas of encircled Soviet partisan resistance

German counter-attack

viewed from the east

AT THE END OF 1941, German forces along the whole eastern front from the Baltic to the Black Sea were deployed in a row of defensive areas, nicknamed 'hedgehogs'. Hitler ordered the savagely mauled German forces to stand fast, attempting to construct defensive positions in ground frozen as hard as steel, which could only be excavated with explosives. However, the Germans had made spectacular headway. In the south, they had reached Taganrog, near where the Don flows into the Sea of Azov, and held all the Crimean peninsula except for the fortress of Sevastopol itself, in the west, and (temporarily) the Kerch peninsula in the east. The main hedgehogs in this area were Kharkov, Artemovsk and Taganrog.

On 5 January 1942, *Stavka* met and Stalin outlined his plans. The Germans were in disarray as a result of their defeat at Moscow and were obviously badly kitted out for the Winter. Now was the time to counter-attack, and the plans were cast on a grandiose scale. The Red Army's first significant success had gone to Stalin's head. During November and December, the Russians had launched a counter-offensive north of Rostov-on-Don, symmetrical with that at Tikhvin, near Leningrad (page 64). Stalin planned to attack outwards in every direction, attempting to relieve Leningrad, destroy Army Group Centre and liberate the Donbass and Crimea. Events overtook the planning. On 1 January Southwest Front had launched an attack in the Kursk area against German Army Group South, which lasted 70 days and developed into the *srazheniye* (operational level battle) of Kharkov. From 18 to 22 January, 6th and 57th Armies carved out a 20-mile-deep breakthrough south of Balakleya, German divisions on either side at Balakleya and Slaviansk holding the shoulders of the breakthrough in what would become the text-book German response to the rupture of their front. On 27 January the Russians captured Lozovaya, an important rail junction at the head of the salient they had carved out, the only major shift in the shape of the front lines in the south during the first third of 1942.

Further south, the Germans were in control of most of the Crimea. They had attacked across the Perekop isthmus, devoid of cover, at the end of September 1941, and by 16 November had captured all the peninsula apart from Sevastopol, the great

fortress and naval base. 11th Army, assisted by elements of 3rd Rumanian Army, now began the siege of Sevastopol.

Sevastopol was ringed by forts, with armoured emplacements buried deep in concrete and rock. The garrison, augmented by withdrawing troops, numbered up to 106,000 soldiers and sailors. First attempts to overrun the fortress on 30 October were easily beaten off: the main assault was delayed as the bombardment could not start until 17 December. On 25 December the Russians began Operation *Kerch-Feodosiya* (amphibious assault). The objective was seizure of the Kerch peninsula and the creation of favourable conditions for recapturing the rest of the Crimea. The amphibious assault was carried out by the Transcaucasus Front, part of the Black Sea Fleet, and the Azov flotilla. Over 250 naval and merchant vessels and 660 aircraft helped lift Soviet troops back across the Straits of Kerch, seizing bridgeheads on the north-east littoral of the Kerch peninsula and on 29 December, under cover of superior naval forces, the port of Feodosiya itself. The Germans and Rumanians recaptured Feodosiya by 18 January, but by this time the Straits of Kerch had frozen so the Russians were less dependent on the port for supplying their forces in the bridgehead. Heavy fighting continued through February, and the Russians made several attempts to break out of Sevastopol, but after the beginning of March exhaustion ensued on both sides.

During this time, Soviet forces remained locked in Sevastopol, although only one German corps and one Rumanian · division were there to contain them. Meanwhile, Operation *Bustard*, the German recapture of Kerch, took place between 8 and 18 May. This accomplished, 11th Army faced the hardest task of all, the capture of Sevastopol. The Germans deployed the largest artillery piece ever built, known as *Gustav Gerät* to Krupps, who made it, but nicknamed *Big Dora* by the troops. The bombardment and infantry attack went on from 7 June for 27 days. The Soviet troops, sailors and marines fought on even when the installations were torn open, the Germans using toxic smoke (one of the few occasions in the Second World War when chemical weapons were used) to kill them in

their subterranean strongholds. At the last moment some top officers and officials were taken off, on Stalin's orders, by submarine: the rest fought to the death.

To the north, the bulge around Izyum had held, providing the opportunity for a concentric attack on Kharkov from there to the north-west and from Volchansk to the east. The new head of *Fremde Heere Ost*, Gehlen, predicted such an attack: it materialized between 12 and 29 May. This anticipated a German plan, Operation *Fridericus*, to pinch out the Izyum salient. In some desperation, the southern pincer of Operation *Fridericus* was launched by Army Group Kleist on 17 May, and succeeded in cutting off the salient.

Meanwhile, on 5 April Hitler committed himself to a drive on the flanks, in particular in the south, towards supplies of oil and grain, hoping also to influence Turkey to join the German side and cut western supply lines through Iran. Soviet resistance would first be crushed between the Donets and the Don then German forces would drive down to the Caucasus, between the Black Sea and the Caspian. The operation, first named *Siegfried*, was renamed *Blau* (Blue). Stalin received hard intelligence of the German plans, but was convinced that *Blau* was a massive strategic feint to draw off forces from Moscow. In their attempt to break Russian resistance in the pivotal region of the Don, in order then to drive south, the Germans were drawn inexorably east, towards Stalingrad.

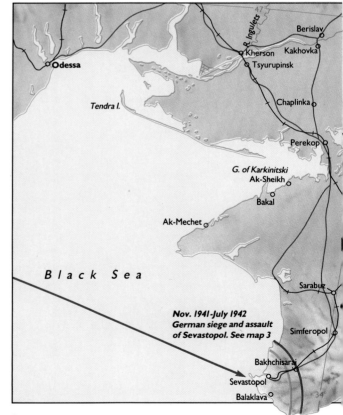

THE OUTER DEFENCES OF SEVASTOPOL *(3)* were entrenchments, covering the second defensive belt with its massive underground forts and gun batteries. The third belt comprised pill-boxes and concrete firing points protecting the city itself. Formidable though the modern forts were, the main problem confronting von Manstein was the extreme difficulty of the terrain and the way the Russians used it. The Germans put down 5 days of heavy fire, combined with air attack, including bombardment by the 31.5-inch *Gustav Gerät*, the largest gun ever built, disabling the 6- to 12-inch guns of Sevastopol. Sevastopol fell on 4 July although Russians held out in the Kherson caves until 9 July. *Gustav Gerät* was later sent to Leningrad, but the Russians raised the siege before it was used.

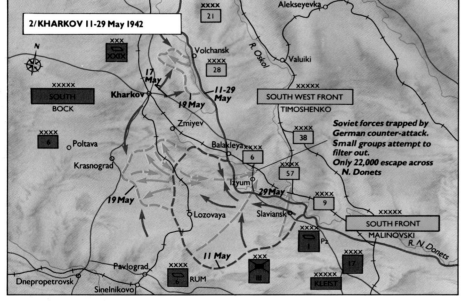

2/KHARKOV 11-29 May 1942

Soviet forces trapped by German counter-attack. Small groups attempt to filter out. Only 22,000 escape across N. Donets

Nov. 1941-July 1942
German siege and assault of Sevastopol. See map 3

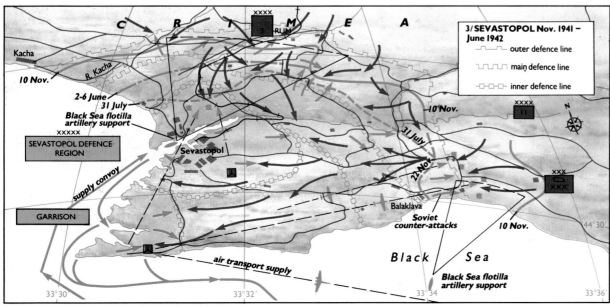

3/SEVASTOPOL Nov. 1941 – June 1942
— outer defence line
⌐⌐⌐ main defence line
⊢⊣⊢⊣ inner defence line

SEVASTOPOL DEFENCE REGION

GARRISON

Soviet counter-attacks

Black Sea flotilla artillery support

air transport supply

BETWEEN THE BATTLE OF MOSCOW at the end of 1941 and May 1942 the front overall remained surprisingly stable, apart from Russian gains round Moscow and the creation of the Izyum salient between Jan. and May 1942 *(4)*. The war in the Ukraine and Crimea *(1)*, began to resemble the First World War: it was characterized by Russian offensives flowing between German 'hedgehogs', which held firm. The highly mobile characteristics of the early German offensives disappeared. The largest Soviet operation was the

attempt to capture Kharkov (12-29 May 1942) *(2)*. In the first 3 days the Russians in the south penetrated up to 30 miles. XXI Tank Corps, however, was committed too late (17 May) to exploit the breakthrough. When the Germans launched Operation *Fridericus*, on the same day, Stalin refused to break off the offensive to defend against the German pincers closing in on the rear. Army Group Kleist and 6th Army met south of Balakleya (23 May). Only 22,000 Russians managed to break out of the salient, back to the north bank of the Northern

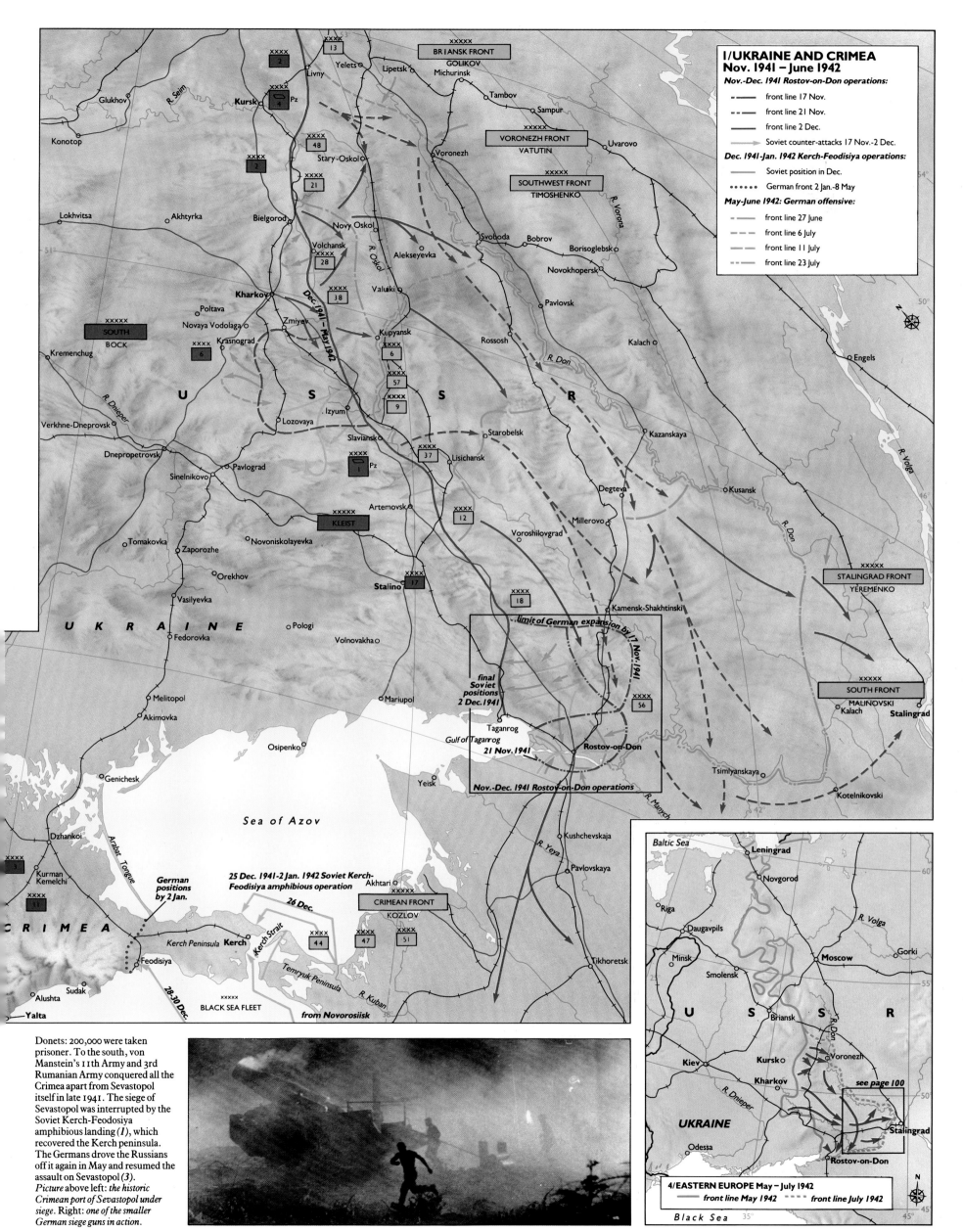

I/UKRAINE AND CRIMEA
Nov. 1941 – June 1942

Nov.-Dec. 1941 Rostov-on-Don operations:

- – – – front line 17 Nov.
- ––––– front line 21 Nov.
- ───── front line 2 Dec.
- ───► Soviet counter-attacks 17 Nov.-2 Dec.

Dec. 1941-Jan. 1942 Kerch-Feodisiya operations:

- ───── Soviet position in Dec.
- • • • • German front 2 Jan.-8 May

May-June 1942: German offensive:

- ─ · ─ · front line 27 June
- – – – front line 6 July
- ─ ─ ─ front line 11 July
- ─ ·· ─ front line 23 July

4/EASTERN EUROPE May – July 1942

- ───── front line May 1942
- – – – front line July 1942

see page 100

Donets: 200,000 were taken prisoner. To the south, von Manstein's 11th Army and 3rd Rumanian Army conquered all the Crimea apart from Sevastopol itself in late 1941. The siege of Sevastopol was interrupted by the Soviet Kerch-Feodosiya amphibious landing (1), which recovered the Kerch peninsula. The Germans drove the Russians off it again in May and resumed the assault on Sevastopol (3).
Picture above left: the historic Crimean port of Sevastopol under siege. Right: one of the smaller German siege guns in action.

Leningrad 1941 ～ 1943

THE TSARIST CAPITAL of St Petersburg, renamed Petrograd in 1914 in an anti-German gesture, and Leningrad from 1924, has always had a unique character, to which the memory of the '900 days' of siege, between September 1941 and 1944, has contributed.

The German Army Group North had Leningrad as its objective when it invaded the USSR on 22 June 1941. Spearheads of German Army Group North (Leeb) reached the Luga river, 60 miles south of Leningrad in mid-July 1941, by which time the Finnish Army had reached the northern shore of Lake Ladoga. The Finns refused to act in direct co-operation with Army Group North, however, and Leeb completed the encirclement of Leningrad on 15 September. A rapid thrust by Army Group North in late July, when its defences were disorganized, could probably have seized the city, but Hitler insisted on diverting forces to help Army Group Centre assault Moscow (page 60).

Leningrad had been under martial law since June; defence was commanded by Lt.Gen. Popov. The first long-range artillery shell fell on the city on 1 September, and by 8 September the city was cut off from land communication with the rest of the Soviet Union. At this time its population was about 2.5 million, plus about 100,000 refugees and the entire Baltic Fleet. On 12 September there remained in the city enough flour for 25 days, cereals for 30, meat for 22, fats for 45

and sugar for 60. Trains that might have been used to bring more into the city in preparation for a siege were being used to evacuate industry (page 172). A small amount of food was brought by barge across Lake Ladoga until the fall of Tikhvin to the Germans (9 Nov.). Any meat and meat substitutes went to the defending troops: the search turned to bread. At first, brewing malt and animal feed were added to bread, but soon artificial substitutes were sought. A method of making cellulose flour from shell packing was developed at the Leningrad Scientific Institute. Wallpaper was stripped and the paste and

size used in artificial bread; dead horses, dogs and cats were processed into food; all of which combined to give a working man about one tenth of the normal calorific intake. The sewage system broke down at the beginning of the siege as a result of bombing and shelling, but soon the excrement froze, reducing the danger of infection. Conditions in the overcrowded hospitals, without sanitation, heating or medicines, were indescribable.

After the fall of Tikhvin a lifeline road was built through the forest, without engineer equipment and under German artillery fire. Thousands died in its construction. The longed-for freeze, which would permit supplies to be dragged over the ice of Lake Ladoga was delayed, but only three days after the road was completed Soviet troops under Gen. Meretskov recaptured

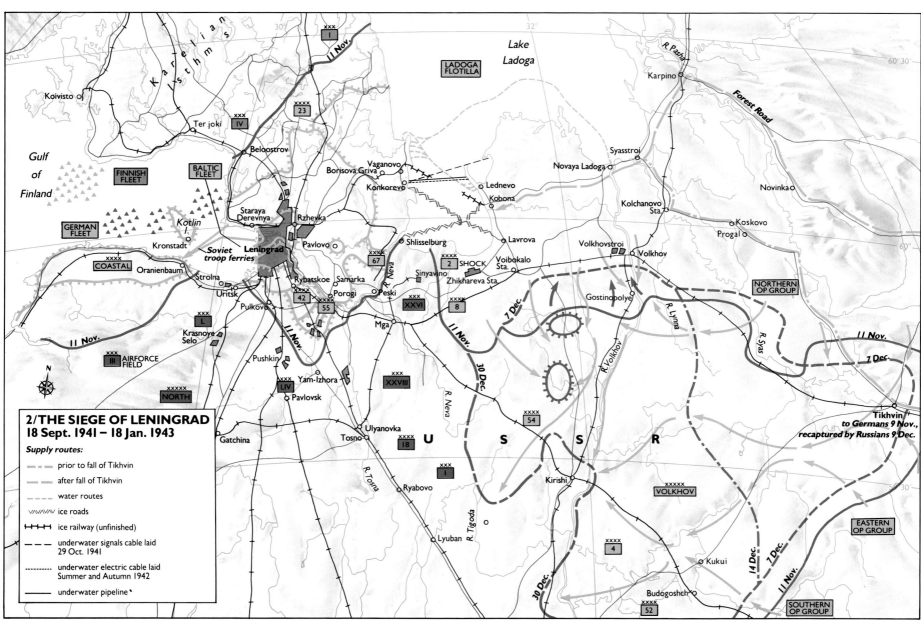

2/THE SIEGE OF LENINGRAD
18 Sept. 1941 – 18 Jan. 1943

Supply routes:

- — — prior to fall of Tikhvin
- – – – after fall of Tikhvin
- - - - water routes
- ∿∿∿ ice roads
- ++++ ice railway (unfinished)
- – – – underwater signals cable laid 29 Oct. 1941
- ········· underwater electric cable laid Summer and Autumn 1942
- —— underwater pipeline

Tikhvin (9 Dec.), promising a more reliable route. But bridges had to be repaired and the last leg into the city had to go over the ice. On 25 December the bread ration was raised slightly. On that day alone 3700 people died of starvation, out of 52,000 recorded deaths in that month. The official death toll for the siege of Leningrad is 632,000 although the victims probably numbered nearer a million.

The German air and artillery offensive was regular rather than intense. During the course of the battle of Leningrad about 150,000 artillery shells, over 100,000 incendiary and over 4600 high explosive bombs fell on the city. The Leningrad Front, pushing outwards, and the Volkhov Front, pushing from the east, attempted to break the blockade from August to October 1941 (Operation *Sinyavino*) and January to April 1942

(Operation *Lyuban*), but without success. The Baltic Fleet covered Soviet moves and attacked the Germans with its aircraft, coastal artillery and naval gunfire from warships. On 12 January 1943, formations of the 67th Army of the Leningrad Front (Govorov) and 2nd Shock Army of the Volkhov Front (Meretskov) began Operation *Iskra* (Spark), to break the blockade. On 18 January 1943 forward units met at workers' housing estate no. 5. The blockade was broken. A corridor 5-7 miles wide was forced open between the northernmost German troops and Lake Ladoga, through which a railway line and a road were built in 17 days. The blockade was broken, but the '900 days' would not be over until the Leningrad-Novgorod operation (page 150) finally dislodged Army Group North in February 1944.

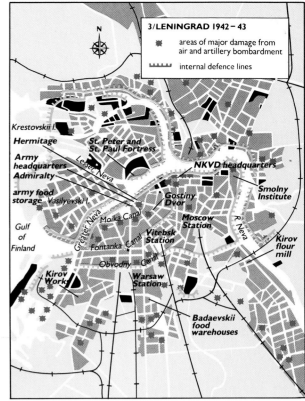

BY 8 SEPT. GERMAN FORCES were within 10 miles of Leningrad (1). With the fall of Tikhvin (9 Nov.) a new 200-mile supply road surfaced with branches of trees, often on top of men who had died building it, had to be constructed. It was finished on 6 Dec. (2). On 9 Dec. Tikhvin was recaptured, with 7000 German casualties, and Meretskov pushed the Germans back, west of the R. Volkhov. The 'Road of Life' across the Lake presented more problems. The ice needed to be a uniform 200mm (8 inches) thick to bear the weight of trucks; this was not reached until the end of Nov. On 26 Nov. a convoy brought in 33 tons of food: 100 tons a day were needed to keep the city alive, but this was only occasionally achieved. The Germans lacked the strength to storm the Soviet city defences (3) or to overcome the seaward protection of the Baltic Fleet and the great fortress of Kronstadt (2). The first attempt to break the blockade occurred in the first *Sinyavino* Operation (Sept. and 20-29 Oct. 1941), and then in the *Lyuban* Operation, (Jan.-Apr. 1942) (5). Other Soviet operations on this front were designed to pin down German forces away from Leningrad (4). Amongst these was 2nd Shock Army's offensive across the R. Volkhov (5). Ill-equipped, it was cut off by German forces; inexplicably Stalin made no great effort to relieve it. By 24 June Vlasov ordered his troops to disperse, and exfiltrate where possible. Later, captured by the Germans, he became leader of the anti-Stalin Russian Liberation Movement. The second *Sinyavino* Operation (6) (19 Aug. to 10 Oct. 1942), failed to break the land blockade but it interrupted German preparations for storming the city and forced the Germans to move 11th Army from the Crimea to help repel Soviet forces. The blockade was finally broken on 18 Jan. 1943, as 67th Army of the Leningrad Front and new 2nd Shock Army of the Volkhov Front met at workers' estate no. 5 (7).

Pictures left: the deprivation endured by the citizens of Leningrad between 1941 and 1944 remains one of the most heroic acts of endurance of the war. Above: lifeline supply routes were built across the frozen Lake Ladoga; in addition to lorry convoys, an uncompleted railway was built across the ice.

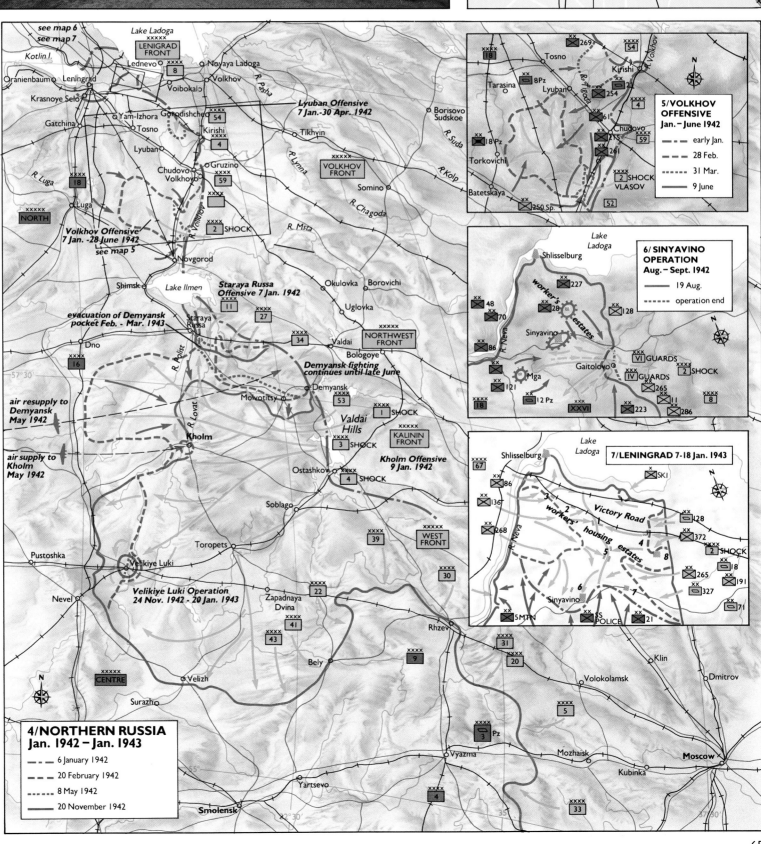

The Pacific SEPTEMBER 1941

THE TREATY OF VERSAILLES had accorded Japan a considerable sphere of influence in the Pacific, countered only by the similar territorial and economic interests of the victorious Allies. The latter were keen to contain any further ambitions Japan may have had. The combination of a commitment to her inconclusive war in China (page 32) and outrage at German behaviour in concluding a pact with the USSR (page 30) led Japan to adopt a waiting policy upon the outbreak of war in Europe, though her ambitions could only be realized in the absence of an Allied

victory. In June 1940 Japan took the opportunity presented by France's defeat: to force the French to close the Hanoi-Nanning railway and the British the Burma Road, thus almost isolating Chiang Kai-shek's regime from the outside world. Japanese demands quickly extended to rights to occupy northern Indo-China in September, when Japan joined Germany and Italy in the Tripartite Pact.

The obvious weakness of the British, Dutch and French in the Far East after June 1940 invited Japan to secure southeast

Asia and with it the resources she needed to maintain herself as a great power, and in December 1940 Japan received from German sources captured British war cabinet reports that indicated that Britain could neither oppose Japan in Indo-China and Siam, nor send a fleet to the Far East and that Malaya was indefensible. This revelation led Japan to seek ever greater concessions from the Allies in southeast Asia, and after February 1941, when the Army began jungle training on Formosa, the Navy displayed a growing desire to secure 'the southern resources area'.

However, in the course of 1941, Japanese ambitions were countered by the United States. Japan's occupation of northern Indo-China provoked the USA to ban trade between the two

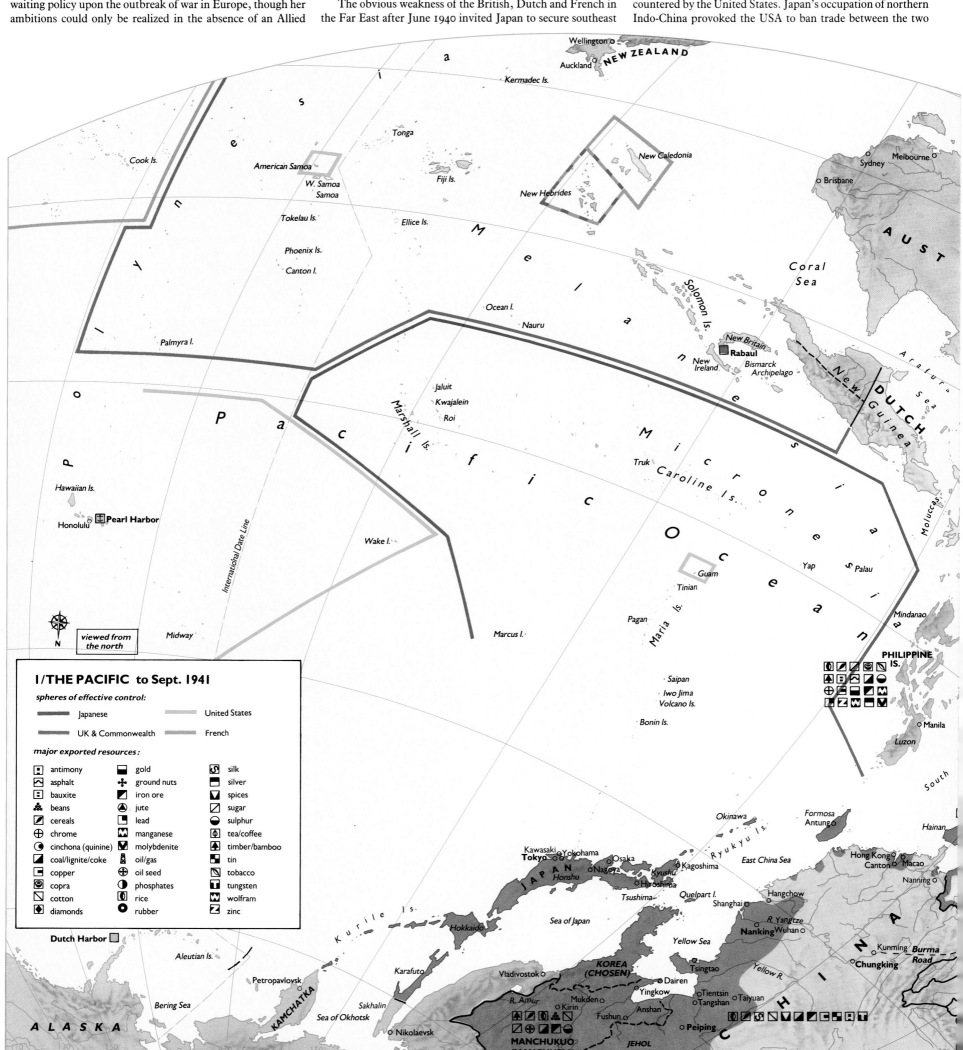

1/THE PACIFIC to Sept. 1941

spheres of effective control:

— Japanese   — United States

— UK & Commonwealth   — French

major exported resources:

antimony	gold	silk
asphalt	ground nuts	silver
bauxite	iron ore	spices
beans	jute	sugar
cereals	lead	sulphur
chrome	manganese	tea/coffee
cinchona (quinine)	molybdenite	timber/bamboo
coal/lignite/coke	oil/gas	tin
copper	oil seed	tobacco
copra	phosphates	tungsten
cotton	rice	wolfram
diamonds	rubber	zinc

Dutch Harbor ▫

countries in certain commodities, but as 1940 gave way to 1941 the most important single factor in Japanese calculations was the Two Ocean Naval Expansion Act passed by Congress in July 1940. By proclaiming her intention to build a fleet greater than those of the next two naval powers combined, the USA in effect served notice on Japan that her fleet, then at 7:10 relative to the US Navy, would be outmatched 3:10 by 1944; by Japanese calculations a 5:10 ratio was the minimum on which their fleet would fight a successful defensive campaign in the western Pacific. Thus the Japanese navy realised that if war with the USA was inevitable it should be induced soon.

The conclusion of a non-aggressive pact with the USSR in April heralded a more assertive Japanese policy in southeast Asia that survived even the start of the German attack on the USSR in June. In that month the Army backed the Navy's insistence on a more forward policy in southeast Asia, and in July the Navy took the decision to occupy southern Indo-China even if this meant war with the USA. This action, and the proclamation of a joint Franco-Japanese protectorate over Indo-China on the 23rd, prompted a total American trade embargo on Japan, which was immediately supported by the British and Dutch. Dependent on the USA for 80% of her oil imports, Japan was presented with the stark choice between war and surrender as the American terms for a resumption of trade was the liquidation of all Japanese mainland gains since 1931. Japan's leadership took the decision in September to

open hostilities with Britain, the Netherlands and the USA if diplomacy failed to lift the sanctions.

Weeks passed with no sign of a compromise on the part of the Americans. An awareness of the disparity between American and Japanese resources precluded any Japanese thought of victory over the USA, the Japanese hoping that the destruction of American will to continue a costly war on the perimeter of the Japanese empire would pave the way to a compromise peace. The Japanese perfected a plan to conquer southeast Asia and thereafter establish a defensive perimeter around their gains on which they would fight the Americans to a standstill. In December this plan suddenly and violently became a reality.

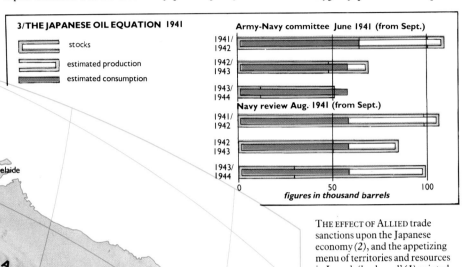

3/THE JAPANESE OIL EQUATION 1941

- stocks
- estimated production
- estimated consumption

Army-Navy committee June 1941 (from Sept.)
1941/1942, 1942/1943, 1943/1944

Navy review Aug. 1941 (from Sept.)
1941/1942, 1942/1943, 1943/1944

0 50 100
figures in thousand barrels

4/THE PACIFIC NAVAL BALANCE Sept. 1941

warships	Japan[1]	US Pacific Fleet	US Asiatic Fleet	UK & Commonwealth[2]	Netherlands	US[3]
capital ships	10	9	?	0	0	15
fleet carriers	10	3	?	0	0	11
cruisers	38	20	2	8	3	54
destroyers	112	50	13	5	7	191
submarines	65	33	17	–	15	73

1. In service or building under 1937 Programme
2. At Singapore and Hong Kong 1 Sept. 1941 and includes three cruisers at Sydney and one at Wellington
3. Building and authorized

THE EFFECT OF ALLIED trade sanctions upon the Japanese economy (2), and the appetizing menu of territories and resources in Japan's 'backyard' (1) pointed Japan down the inevitable road to world war. It was not until June 1941 that the Japanese services conducted a study of oil resources available to Japan in the event of war (3); on the basis of Japanese production meeting 10% of requirements and a slow rehabilitation of Indies oilfields being unable to cover consumption, this study concluded that national reserves would be exhausted in summer 1944. A more sanguine naval report in August suggested that while stocks would decline dramatically in the third year of a war a crisis would be avoided – if Japan did not delay in going to war. In reality both studies were wildly inaccurate: Japan in effect exhausted her reserves in Oct. 1943. Japan's military calculations were more accurate, at least in the short term. British commitments and the smallness of the US Asiatic Fleet meant that the Navy faced no real opposition in southeast Asia (5), whilst the military formations available to potential enemies were understrength, poorly trained and ill-equipped. In the long-term, however, the threat posed to Japanese security by US Navy building programmes (4) was obvious: the numerical disparity would become so great that not even superior ships such as the battleship *Yamato* – 71,659 tons, nine 16.14-in guns, 25.6-in turret armour and 27 knots – could hope to offset sheer American numbers.

Picture above right: The Japanese battleship Yamato *on sea trials.*

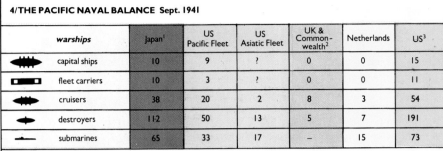

5/THE MILITARY BALANCE Mid-1941

country	effective army units		aircraft	approximate total military manpower
Philippines	3 Luzon	1 Mindanao	120	120,000
Hawaii	1		230	40,000
Dutch East Indies	2 Java		120	40,000
Malaya	3		180	80,000
Burma	1		16	30,000
India	2 Calcutta		40	600,000
Australia	4		not known	250,000
New Zealand	1		230	40,000
Hong Kong	4		0	10,000
China (unoccupied)*	10 Nationalist		not known	2,500,000
Japan	51	59	1500	1,800,000
Home Islands	8		150	160,000
Manchukuo	21		900	660,000
North China	13		250	450,000
Central and Southern China	16		not known	550,000
Korea	2		not known	40,000
French Indo-China	1		not known	18,000
Siam	3		not known	80,000
available for offensive operations	10		1100	200,000

* officially unoccupied China had 95 Armies; in practice this probably meant 60 divisions, of which only half were Nationalist as opposed to warlord irregulars, and in turn only about one third of these were effective.

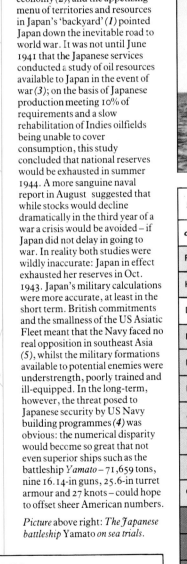

2/JAPANESE FOREIGN TRADE 1940

Imports
- Asia 40.4%
- Africa 3.1%
- Latin America 4%
- N. America 39%
- Europe 10.6%
- Oceania 2.9%

Exports
- Asia 64.2%
- Africa 4.2%
- Latin America 3%
- Oceania 2.6%
- N America 18.4%
- Europe 6.6%

Total value of exports (1940): 3,972,400 million yen
Total value of imports (1940): 3,709,035 million yen
Export surplus: 263,365 million yen

The Pacific DECEMBER 1941

THE PLAN OF CAMPAIGN with which Japan went to war in December 1941 was one of great complexity involving a series of elaborate operations spread across the International Date Line and seven time zones. Its main provisions called for initial attacks designed to eliminate both American naval power in the central Pacific and British power in the Far East; the occupation of the Dutch East Indies; and the creation of a defensive perimeter around conquered south-east Asia.

Japan's first moves involved two operations separated by more than one hundred degrees of longitude – landings in the early hours of 8 December in southern Siam and northern Malaya by formations from Yamashita's 25th Army (page 70) and, some thirty minutes later (but on the morning of the 7th), strikes by carrier aircraft against the US Pacific Fleet at its base at Pearl Harbor in Hawaii.

Thus far in the war no single operation had involved the use of more than a single carrier and a handful of aircraft. For the strike against Pearl Harbor the Japanese committed their entire first-line strength of six fleet carriers (with over 460 aircraft) in a two-wave attack under the command of Admiral Nagumo. The element of surprise was almost total, resulting in the destruction or disablement of 18 US warships although some of these were subsequently refitted.

On 11 December, the Japanese attempt to secure Wake was repulsed without a single man being landed on the atoll, the Japanese losing one transport and two destroyers in the process. This was the only occasion during the Pacific war when an assault landing was prevented, but success proved short-lived. Stung by failure, the Japanese detached two of Nagumo's returning carriers to support a renewed and successful attack on 23 December.

In the western Pacific, Japanese forces very quickly secured an overwhelming advantage over American and Allied forces. On the first day of hostilities Japanese aircraft from Formosa effectively destroyed American air power on Luzon while amphibious forces secured Batan Island on the approaches to the Philippines (page 72). On 10 December Japanese units from 14th Army came ashore on Camiguin Island and on northern Luzon, while on 12 December a formation from the Palaus landed in southern Luzon. By the time of the main landings in Lingayen Gulf on 22 December the defeat of the Philippine garrison was assured. By that time, the Japanese were also in the process of occupying the few places of any importance in Sarawak and British North Borneo. In addition, the 38th Infantry Division had cleared the British from the New Territories on the Chinese mainland and had established itself on Hong Kong Island, which fell on Christmas Day.

To the south the Japanese completed their occupation of Siam, and forced that country into an alliance, at the same time inflicting a series of costly and demoralizing defeats on British forces in northern Malaya (page 70). After having sunk two British capital ships in the Gulf of Siam on 10 December, the Japanese enjoyed an overwhelming superiority both in the air and at sea, not merely in Malaya but throughout south-east Asia: their enemies had been reduced to increasingly ineffective responses to events that were clearly beyond their control.

By the end of December 1941 the Japanese held the initiative throughout the theatre of operations; but the most stunning of their initial victories – at Pearl Harbor – contained within itself the seeds of ultimate defeat. For all its apparent success the attack did not damage a single aircraft carrier or submarine, while the power stations, docks, machine shops and oil-storage facilities of the base were unscathed. Thus the foundations of a reconstituted fleet and the base from which it was to operate remained intact. But perhaps more significantly, by attacking Pearl Harbor at the start of the war, the Japanese sought to demoralize and divide American opinion: instead their attack united American society and provided it with a single aim – total victory. For the moment, however, victory seemed to be a monopoly of the Japanese.

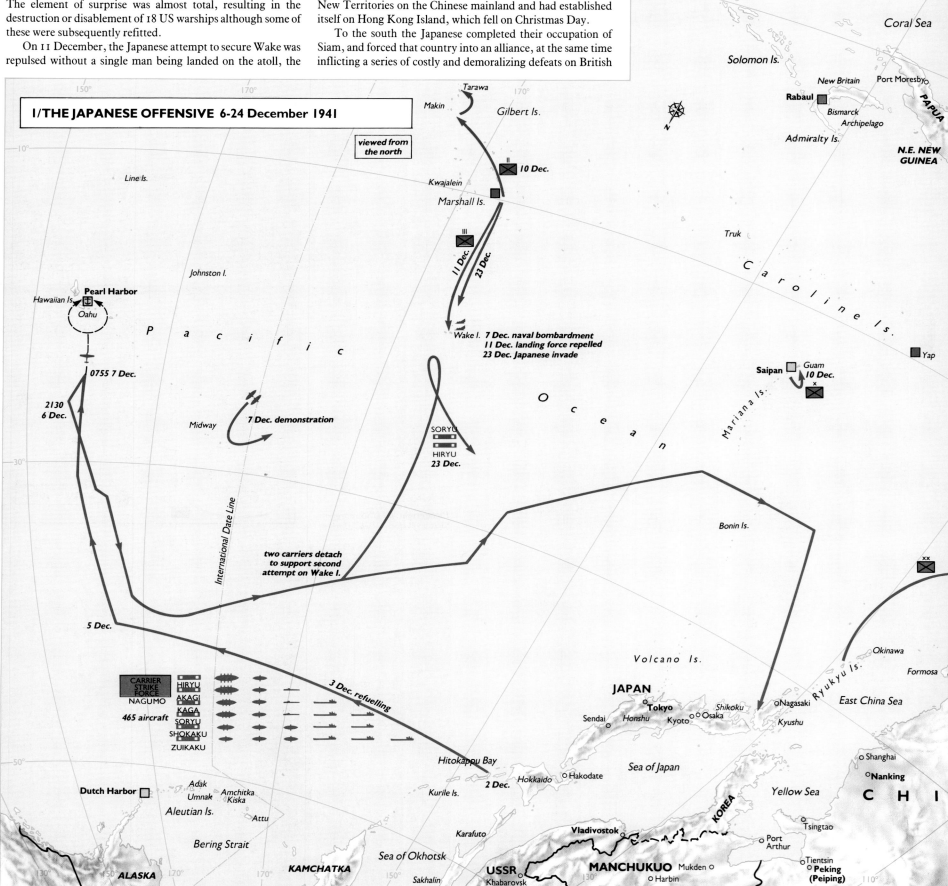

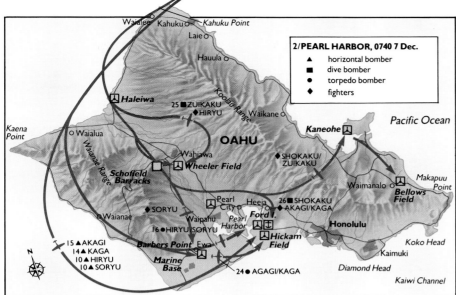

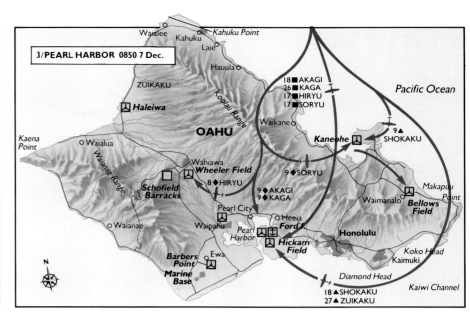

2/PEARL HARBOR, 0740 7 Dec.

▲ horizontal bomber
■ dive bomber
● torpedo bomber
◆ fighters

3/PEARL HARBOR 0850 7 Dec.

THE JAPANESE ASSAULT on Pearl Harbor (7 Dec. 1941) was the most important in a series of moves by the Japanese which opened a war zone of over 6000 miles (*1*). The first attack on Pearl Harbor (*2*), launched at dawn from a point 230 miles north of Oahu, was made by 40 torpedo-bombers, 49 high-level bombers, 51 dive-bombers and 43 fighters. The 30-minute attack began at 0740 and struck the anchorage and outlying air bases. The second attack (*3*), by 54 high-level bombers, 78 dive-bombers and 35 fighters, began at 0850 and lasted 65 minutes, but was hampered by poor visibility and anti-aircraft fire; 20 of the 29 Japanese aircraft lost came from the second-wave force. Of the 94 warships in harbour, 18 were sunk or suffered major damage (*4*). Of these, eight were battleships, but of the five that were sunk, three ultimately saw service again. There were no US carriers in the anchorage. Of the 394 US aircraft on the island, 188 were destroyed and another 159 damaged. On the same day, Guam (*5*) was occupied, after a token resistance on the part of its 365-man garrison, by a 5000-strong force from Saipan. The defence of Hong Kong (*6*) was recognized as hopeless. After having broken through the main line of resistance at its strongest point, the Shing Mun Redoubt, on 10 Dec., the Japanese forced a British retreat to Hong Kong Island by 12 Dec.; a call to surrender was rejected on 17 Dec. and the Japanese crossed the channel the next day, forcing a surrender of colony and garrison on 25 Dec.

Picture right: the USS destroyer Shaw exploding in Pearl Harbor.

4/PEARL HARBOR
Fleet damage:
→ destroyed
→ damaged

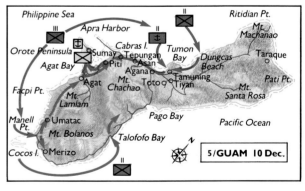

5/GUAM 10 Dec.

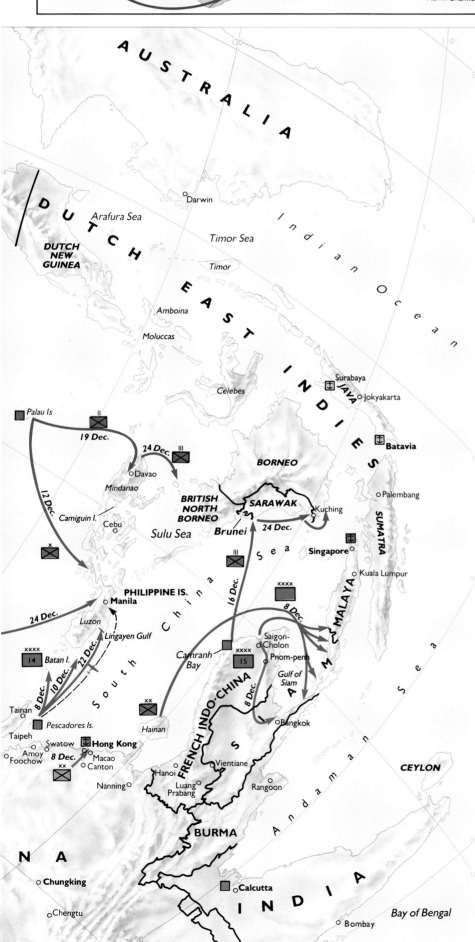

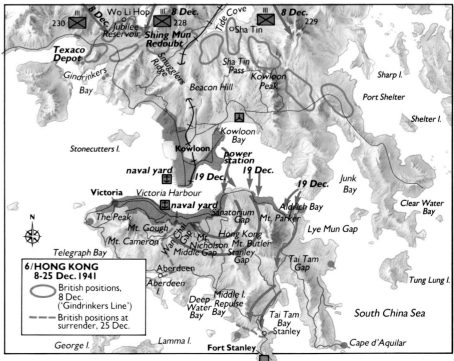

6/HONG KONG 8-25 Dec. 1941
◯ British positions, 8 Dec. ('Gindrinkers Line')
--- British positions at surrender, 25 Dec.

Malaya DECEMBER 1941 ~ FEBRUARY 1942

THE JAPANESE PLAN for breaking British colonial power based in Malaya and Singapore was the most complex of their first-phase operations. It involved formations from two armies in a series of separated landings throughout southern Siam and northern Malaya, plus the movement of forces into Siam from French Indo-China, followed by various moves against British positions in southern Burma, Tenasserim and the movement of formations by rail to northern Malaya. The arrival in Singapore of two British capital ships on 4 December was an additional hazard, threatening Japanese operations in the Gulf of Siam.

The British situation was no less complicated. As early as 1937 the British had realized that the guns of Singapore would prevent a direct seaborne attack on the base, and that as a result any Japanese move against Singapore had to be made from the north through Malaya. The denial of landing beaches in northern Malaya and airfields at Singora and Patani was thus essential to the defence of Malaya. In December 1941, however, when Britain still hoped to avoid providing Japan with a pretext for war, their occupation could not be and was not attempted. But in the absence of a preventive move into southern Siam the

British forces in northern Malaya were saddled with defensive commitments that were beyond their practical resources; at the same time the British command was not prepared to abandon northern and central Malaya in order to concentrate their forces for a defence of Johore. The British military position in Malaya on the eve of war thus was one of dispersal and weakness.

The landings of the 5th Infantry Division at Singora and Patani on 8 December were thus unopposed by the British and whilst the Imperial Guards Division occupied Bangkok and the 18th Infantry Division all but met disaster amidst the surf and

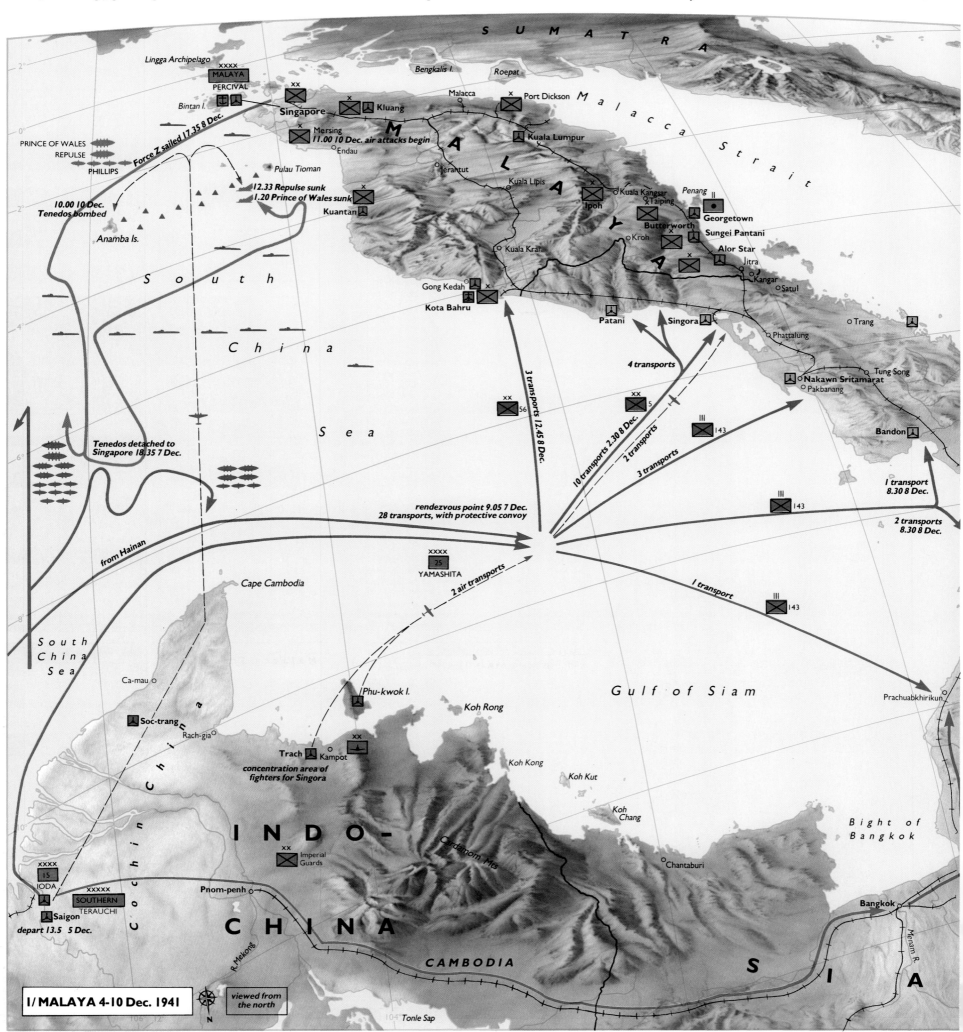

defences of Kota Bharu, the 5th, with armoured support, developed a two-pronged attack into northern Malaya, slashing through the British positions at Betong on 10 December, thereby threatening Kuala Kangsar and to outflank British forces in Kedah and west of the Perak river. By the 21st British formations had been given permission to withdraw behind the river, the intention being to fight a series of delaying actions whilst defensive positions were prepared in central and southern Malaya, but in the event this intention fell apart for two reasons. Firstly, the 11th Indian Division could not fight delaying actions whilst simultaneously preparing defensive positions; its attempt to do both ended in disastrous defeat on the Slim River on 7 January. Secondly, whilst the British had no answer to the Japanese tactic of encirclement through the jungle, the Japanese arrival on the Strait of Malacca with assault boats moved from Singora provided the Japanese with the means to turn British positions on either flank. These two developments rendered northern Johore indefensible, but the evacuation of the mainland – completed on 31 January – and the destruction of the causeway and main water supply between Johore Bahru and Singapore island ensured the fall of Singapore. After fierce initial exchanges the Japanese secured the western part of Singapore island by the 11th. After the surrender four days later, about 130,000 British soldiers were taken prisoner in the greatest single defeat in British history: about the same number of Chinese were killed after the fall of the city by a Japanese army that incurred a mere 3000 casualties in the course of the whole campaign.

CONTROL OF THE GULF OF SIAM was crucial to Japanese success, and with the sinking of the *Repulse* and the *Prince of Wales*, and having secured Singora and Patani airfields, and effected amphibious landings on the north Malayan coast *(1)*, the Japanese were able to advance on two main fronts. The strategic advantage of holding a position on the Ledge (on the Siamese border), was recognised but not realised in practice. Forcing successive British retreats into the interior as they moved down the less populated east coast, the Japanese dealt with a series of defended positions along the west coast by using hook actions *(2)*. Bearing round the defenders by penetrating the dense jungle and, after the fall of Penang, by amphibious hook manoeuvres launched down the coast, the Japanese Army confounded the defenders. Planned delaying actions failed after the capture of Ipoh and Kampar, and the strain of successive withdrawals and rearguard actions culminated in a major British defeat at Slim River *(3)*. Although Johore now seemed indefensible, the 8th Australian Division inflicted a sharp defeat on the Japanese at Gemas (14 Jan.), but again Japanese flanking attacks, simultaneously breaking through British positions on the lower Maw and effecting a landing behind the Batu Pahat (16 Jan.) almost trapped the Australians. The whirlwind advance was temporarily halted at great cost at Parit and Pelandok (20-23 Jan.)*(4)*, but with the capture of Endau (21 Jan.) Johore was lost. Bombing raids over Singapore Island dislocated local services and hampered the civilian evacuation, but failed to stop reinforcements arriving. The Japanese 25th Army concentrated its full strength of three Divisions for the invasion of Singapore on the west of the island (8/9 Feb.) while the British concentrated on the defence of the naval and air installations on the east. The Japanese pushed swiftly to the outskirts of the city itself where, despite vigorous defensive fighting, the British surrendered on 15 Feb *(5)*.

Picture above right: *The advancing Japanese army using great resourcefulness in negotiating a Malayan jungle river. The Japanese, unlike the British, had trained in jungle warfare.*

2/NORTHERN MALAYA 8-28 Dec. 1941

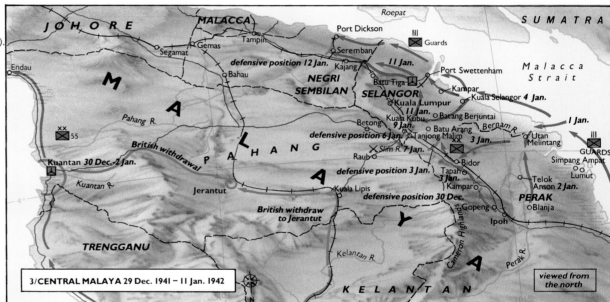

3/CENTRAL MALAYA 29 Dec. 1941 – 11 Jan. 1942

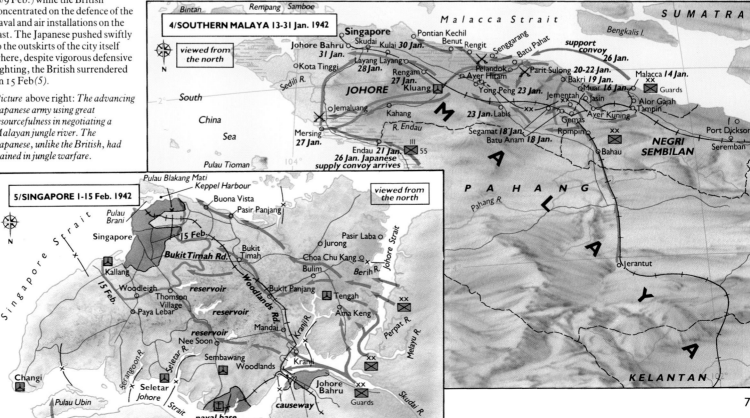

4/SOUTHERN MALAYA 13-31 Jan. 1942

5/SINGAPORE 1-15 Feb. 1942

The Philippines DECEMBER 1941 ~ JUNE 1942

FROM THE START of the Philippines campaign Japanese forces enjoyed advantages bestowed by possession of the initiative and superior geographical position that ensured victory over a garrison that was ill-led, dispersed amongst the eleven main islands of the group, and in effect abandoned to its fate by the United States from the first day of the war.

Pre-war American planning for the defence of the Philippines had been based on the premise that American forces in the islands would be able to withstand a siege until the Pacific Fleet was able to fight its way across the western Pacific to effect their relief. To this very dubious assumption was grafted in 1941 the concentration of heavy bomber forces on Luzon, primarily for deterrence purposes, and the assertion by the US commander in the islands, Lt-Gen Douglas MacArthur, that his forces would be able to prevent Japanese landings anywhere in the Philippines. The unreality of all three aspects of American policy was revealed during the first day of the Pacific war, the crippling of the Pacific Fleet being accompanied by Japanese landings on Batan Island and an attack by Formosa-based naval bombers on Clark and Nichols airfields that caught most of the US planes on the ground and undispersed. With this one strike, some ten hours after the Pearl Harbor attack, the Japanese destroyed 103 American aircraft and ensured themselves air superiority for the remainder of the campaign. The Asiatic Fleet and surviving American bombers were withdrawn from Luzon after the 14th.

The Japanese followed up their occupation of Batan with landings in northern and southern Luzon isolating the main US force around Manila. Meanwhile, Davao was secured in Mindanao. These successes provided the Japanese with a stranglehold on the Philippines even before the main forces landed.

The Luzon landings were executed in the expectation that the Americans would attempt to defend Manila, the dispersal of the Japanese effort being intended to ensure the capital's rapid encirclement. On the 23rd, however, MacArthur took the decision to withdraw his forces into the Bataan peninsula. In its anxiety to secure Manila the 14th Army missed the significance of the American redeployment and by 2 January some 80,000 American and Filipino troops had successfully moved into Bataan, though little effort had been made to stock the rugged peninsula in advance of their arrival.

Before the start of hostilities it had been the Japanese intention to complete the occupation of the Philippines before developing an offensive into the East Indies, but the ease with which its forces secured their objectives on Luzon and Mindanao prompted the Japanese high command to recast its plans, the 14th Army being ordered to release its air support and one division for operations in the Indies on 2 January. The start of these operations had been foreshadowed since Christmas Day when Japanese forces occupied Jolo, on the approaches to Borneo, but this change of plan left the 14th Army outnumbered 3:1 on Bataan and unable to bring the campaign on Luzon to a speedy conclusion. The 14th Army had some initial successes, but lacked the strength to break through the last American line of defence. Forced on to the offensive whilst fresh formations were moved to Luzon, the 14th Army thereafter relied upon a two-month siege to weaken the American garrison. On 22 Feb., when the Dutch East Indies was rapidly falling into Japanese hands, MacArthur was ordered to transfer his headquarters to Australia. On 11 Mar. four torpedo boats evacuated MacArthur, his family and personal staff, and President Quezon with the Philippine gold reserve to Mindanao and thence Australia. The rapid collapse of American resistance on Bataan led to a general surrender on the peninsula on 8 April.

With the fall of Bataan the Americans retained only four island forts in Manila Bay in the north, plus the Visayans and most of Mindanao. Whilst after clearing Bataan the Japanese prepared to assault the American headquarters on Corregidor, two regiments brought from Malaya to Davao set about securing the central and southern Philippines. When Corregidor surrendered on 7 May after a month-long bombardment, and an assault supported by tanks on the previous day, the Japanese refused to accept the surrender of the fortress without a general American surrender throughout the Philippines; an inability to resist this demand and a concern to avoid any massacre of prisoners, wounded and civilians ensured that the Japanese had their way. The result was the only surrender in history to a foreign enemy by an American army in the field. Though many Filipino troops chose to go into the hills rather than into captivity, the surrender of 7 May brought organized resistance in the Philippines to an end, and ensured the largely unopposed occupation by the Japanese of various islands thus far beyond their reach.

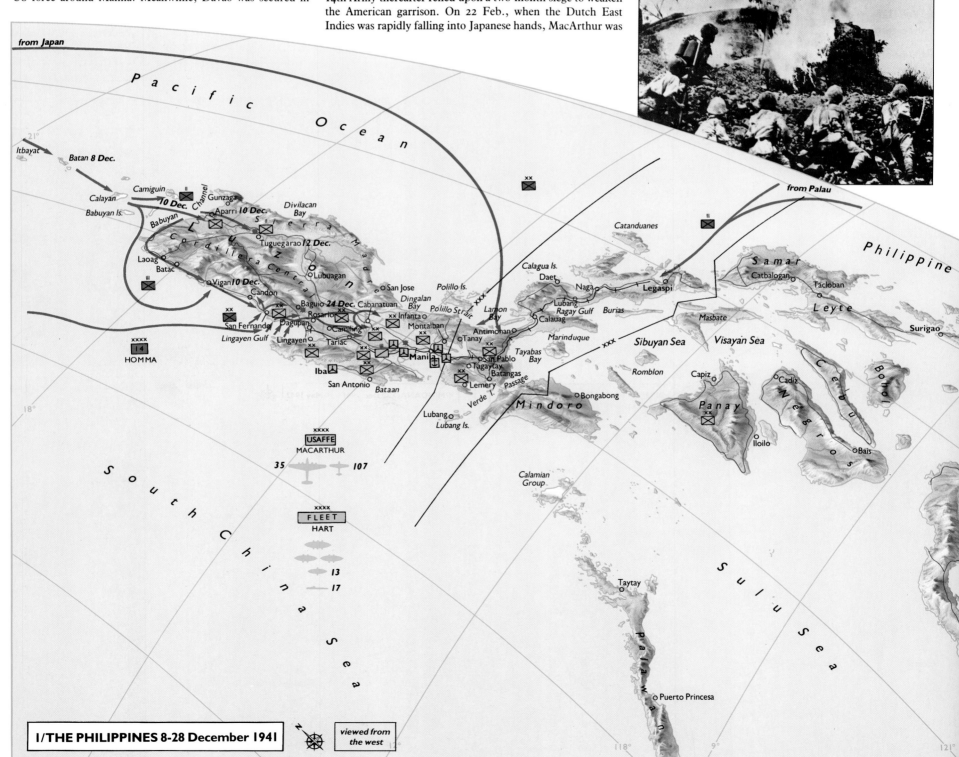

I/THE PHILIPPINES 8-28 December 1941

viewed from the west

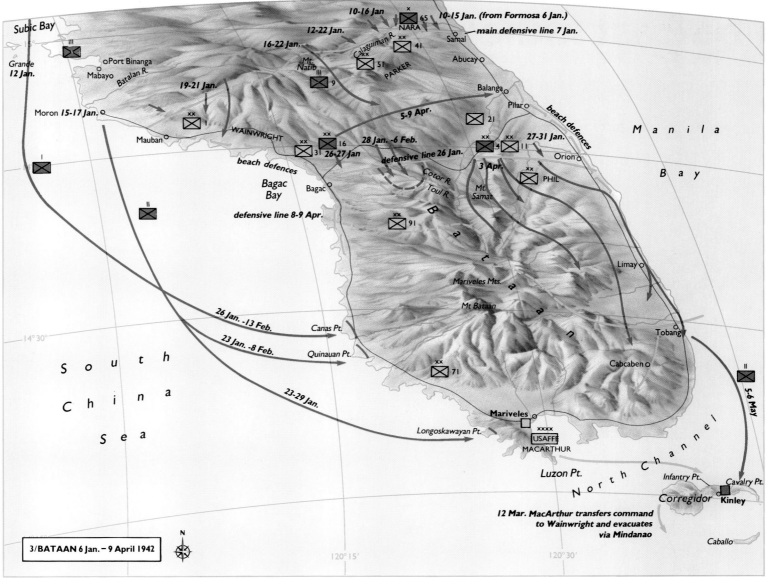

THE JAPANESE ASSAULT on Luzon (1) began on two fronts: in the north the occupation of Batan Island was followed by landings on Camiguin and at Aparri and Vigan (10 Dec.), while Legaspi in southern Luzon was secured on 12 Dec., isolating US forces in central Luzon. While these landings were followed by unopposed advances towards central Luzon, a regiment from the Palaus secured Davao on southern Mindanao (19 Dec.). Following the main force landings at Lingayen Gulf (22 Dec.) and Lamon Bay (24 Dec.), MacArthur began a withdrawal into the Bataan peninsula (2). US formations conducted a phased withdrawal from Lingayen Gulf, while divisions from southern Luzon moved via Manila and San Fernando into the peninsula. Here (3) the main line of US resistance astride Mt. Natib was breached between 10 and 22 Jan., forcing a US withdrawal to the Bagac–Orion line by 26 Jan. Despite major assaults either side of Mt. Samat, and three attempts to land forces behind the US lines between 23 Jan. and 6 Feb., the depleted Japanese army spent two months laying siege to the trapped defenders, only resuming the offensive with fresh formations on 3 Apr. Following the final US withdrawal to Corregidor (3 Apr.) the Japanese turned to the southern Philippines, occupying Cebu city (10 Apr.) and various towns on Panay (16-20 Apr.) which brought them control of the Visayans (5), the same two regiments then moving on to ensure Japanese control of western Mindanao (4) by 7 May.

Picture (left): Japanese troops attack an American fortification on Corregidor using flame-throwers.

3/BATAAN 6 Jan. – 9 April 1942

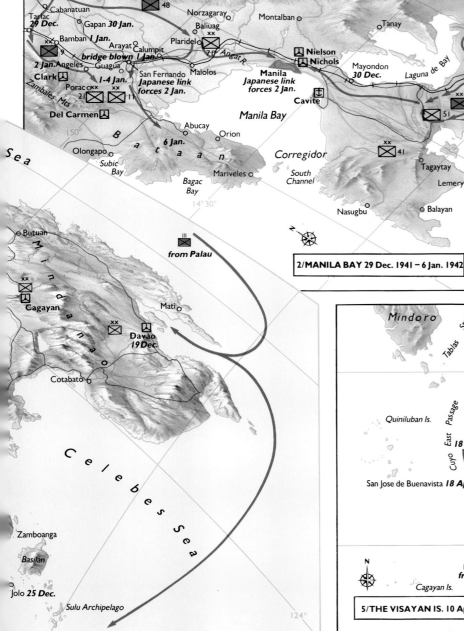

2/MANILA BAY 29 Dec. 1941 – 6 Jan. 1942

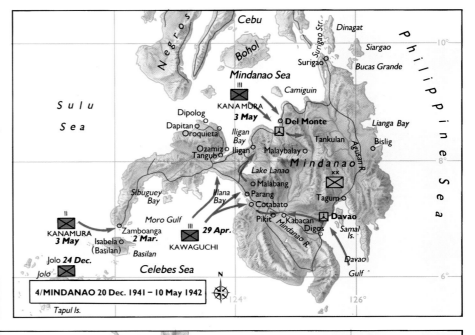

4/MINDANAO 20 Dec. 1941 – 10 May 1942

5/THE VISAYAN IS. 10 April – 9 June 1942

The East Indies JANUARY ~ MAY 1942

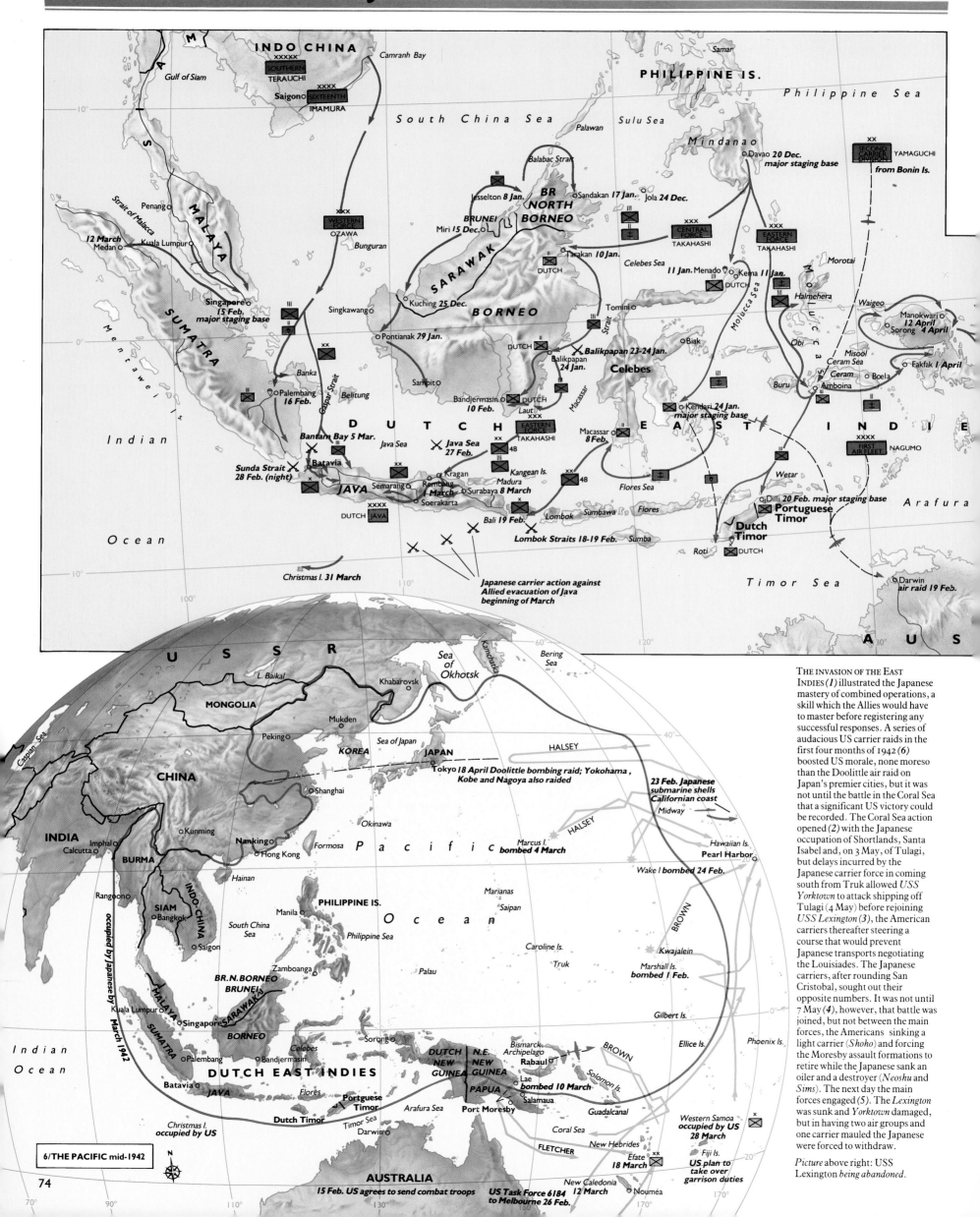

INDO CHINA

XXXXX
SOUTHERN
TERAUCHI

Camranh Bay

Gulf of Siam

Saigon XXXX
SIXTEENTH
IMAMURA

South China Sea

Penang

12 March
Medan

Kuala Lumpur

MALAYA

Strait of Malacca

Singapore 15 Feb. major staging base

WESTERN
FORCE
OZAWA

Singkawang

Bunguran

SARAWAK

Kuching 25 Dec.

Pontianak 29 Jan.

BORNEO

Miri 15 Dec.

Jesselton 8 Jan.

BR NORTH BORNEO

BRUNEI

Balabac Strait

Sandakan 17 Jan.

Palawan

Sulu Sea

Mindanao

Jola 24 Dec.

Davao 20 Dec. major staging base

PHILIPPINE IS.

Philippine Sea

SECOND CARRIER DIVISION YAMAGUCHI
from Bonin Is.

CENTRAL FORCE TAKAHASHI

EASTERN FORCE TAKAHASHI

Tarakan 10 Jan.

DUTCH

Celebes Sea

11 Jan. Menado

Kema 11 Jan. DUTCH

Morotai

Halmehera

Waigeo

Manokwari 12 April
Sorong 4 April

SUMATRA

Palembang 16 Feb.

Banka

Gaspar Strait

Belitung

Sampit

Bandjermasin 10 Feb. DUTCH

Balikpapan 24 Jan. ✕ Balikpapan 23-24 Jan.

Kendari 24 Jan. major staging base

Celebes

Tomini

Biak

Buru

Obi

Misool
Ceram Sea

Ceram

Amboina

Boela

Fakfak 1 April

Macassar Strait

Laut DUTCH

Macassar 8 Feb.

EASTERN FORCE TAKAHASHI

E A S T

I N D I E

FIRST AIR FLEET NAGUMO

D U T C H

Bantam Bay 5 Mar.

Sunda Strait ✕ 28 Feb. (night)

Batavia

Semarang

Rembang

Kragan

Soerakarta

Surabaya 8 March

Madura

Kangean Is.

48

✕ Java Sea 27 Feb.

48

Java Sea

JAVA

XXXX
DUTCH JAVA

Bali 19 Feb.

Lombok

Lombok Straits 18-19 Feb.

Sumbawa

Flores

Flores Sea

Sumba

Roti

Wetar

Dilli 20 Feb. major staging base

Portuguese Timor

Dutch Timor

DUTCH

Timor Sea

Darwin air raid 19 Feb.

Arafura

A U S

Indian Ocean

Christmas I. 31 March

Japanese carrier action against
Allied evacuation of Java
beginning of March

6/THE PACIFIC mid-1942

U S S R

L. Baikal

MONGOLIA

Khabarovsk

Sea of Okhotsk

Kamchatka

Bering Sea

Mukden

Sea of Japan

CHINA

Peking

KOREA

JAPAN

Tokyo 18 April Doolittle bombing raid; Yokohama, Kobe and Nagoya also raided

HALSEY

HALSEY

23 Feb. Japanese submarine shells Californian coast

Midway

Shanghai

Okinawa

INDIA

Imphal

Calcutta

Kunming

BURMA

Rangoono

SIAM

Bangkok

INDO-CHINA

Saigon

Nanking

Hong Kong

Hainan

Formosa

Marcus I. bombed 4 March

Hawaiian Is.

Pearl Harbor

Wake I bombed 24 Feb.

occupied by Japanese March 1942

PHILIPPINE IS.

Manila

South China Sea

Zamboanga

BR. N. BORNEO
BRUNEI

MALAYA

Kuala Lumpur

Singapore

SARAWAK

SUMATRA

BORNEO

Palembang

Bandjermasin

DUTCH EAST INDIES

Batavia

JAVA

Indian Ocean

Christmas I. occupied by US

Flores

Portuguese Timor

Dutch Timor

Timor Sea

Darwino

Pacific Ocean

Marianas

Saipan

Palau

Caroline Is.

Truk

Kwajalein

Marshall Is. bombed 1 Feb.

Gilbert Is.

Sorong

DUTCH N.E. NEW GUINEA

N.E. NEW GUINEA

Bismarck Archipelago

Rabaul

Lae bombed 10 March

Salamaua

PAPUA

Port Moresby

Arafura Sea

BROWN

Solomon Is.

Guadalcanal

Coral Sea

Ellice Is.

Phoenix Is.

Western Samoa occupied by US 28 March

Efate 18 March

Fiji Is. US plan to take over garrison duties

New Hebrides

FLETCHER

AUSTRALIA

15 Feb. US agrees to send combat troops

US Task Force 6184 to Melbourne 26 Feb.

New Caledonia 12 March

Nouméa

THE INVASION OF THE EAST
INDIES *(1)* illustrated the Japanese
mastery of combined operations, a
skill which the Allies would have
to master before registering any
successful responses. A series of
audacious US carrier raids in the
first four months of 1942 *(6)*
boosted US morale, none moreso
than the Doolittle air raid on
Japan's premier cities, but it was
not until the battle in the Coral Sea
that a significant US victory could
be recorded. The Coral Sea action
opened *(2)* with the Japanese
occupation of Shortlands, Santa
Isabel and, on 3 May, of Tulagi,
but delays incurred by the
Japanese carrier force in coming
south from Truk allowed *USS
Yorktown* to attack shipping off
Tulagi *(4 May)* before rejoining
USS Lexington (3), the American
carriers thereafter steering a
course that would prevent
Japanese transports negotiating
the Louisiades. The Japanese
carriers, after rounding San
Cristobal, sought out their
opposite numbers. It was not until
7 May *(4)*, however, that battle was
joined, but not between the main
forces, the Americans sinking a
light carrier *(Shoho)* and forcing
the Moresby assault formation to
retire while the Japanese sank an
oiler and a destroyer *(Neoshu* and
Sims). The next day the main
forces engaged *(5)*. The *Lexington*
was sunk and *Yorktown* damaged,
but in having two air groups and
one carrier mauled the Japanese
were forced to withdraw.

*Picture above right: USS
Lexington being abandoned.*

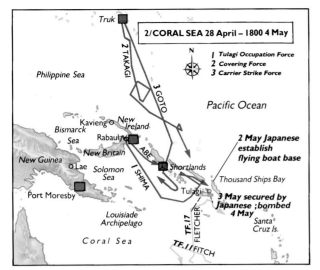

2/CORAL SEA 28 April – 1800 4 May

1 Tulagi Occupation Force
2 Covering Force
3 Carrier Strike Force

2 May Japanese establish flying boat base

3 May secured by Japanese; bombed 4 May

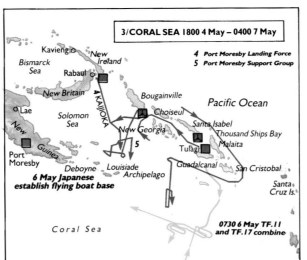

3/CORAL SEA 1800 4 May – 0400 7 May

4 Port Moresby Landing Force
5 Port Moresby Support Group

6 May Japanese establish flying boat base

0730 6 May TF.11 and TF.17 combine

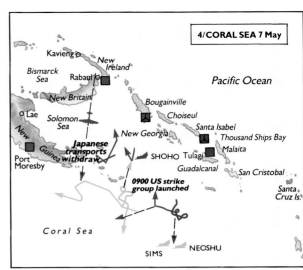

4/CORAL SEA 7 May

Japanese transports withdraw

0900 US strike group launched

SIMS   NEOSHU

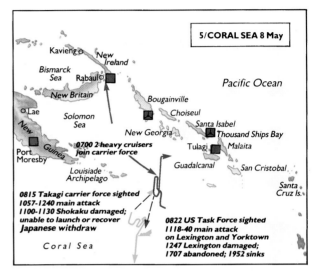

5/CORAL SEA 8 May

0700 2 heavy cruisers join carrier force

0815 Takagi carrier force sighted
1057-1240 main attack
1100-1130 Shokaku damaged; unable to launch or recover Japanese withdraw

0822 US Task Force sighted
1118-40 main attack on Lexington and Yorktown
1247 Lexington damaged; 1707 abandoned; 1952 sinks

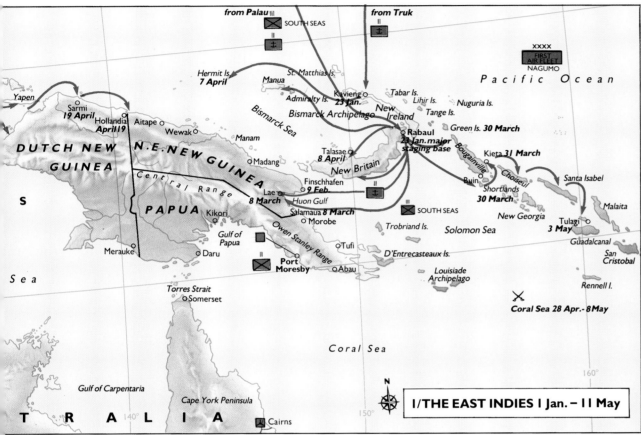

1/THE EAST INDIES 1 Jan. – 11 May

THE NEW YEAR, 1942 found Japan in a position of contrasts. Militarily, the first three weeks of the Pacific war had brought her a series of overwhelming victories in Malaya, the Philippines and the western Pacific, and her general victory throughout southeast Asia was assured. Politically, on New Year's Day 26 nations indicated, in the declaration of the United Nations, that they would wage total war until victory was won over the Axis powers. Thus, while operations then in hand in southeast Asia would go forward to an end that Allies and Japanese alike could foresee, Japan was presented with the problem of how the war was to be prosecuted to a successful conclusion once the initial phase of conquest was complete.

The conquest and consolidation of the East Indies – for the most part in Dutch colonial hands – would be the economic jewel in the crown of the new Japanese empire, but as the defensive perimeter was extended east, became something of an Achilles' heel. Only the British possessions on Borneo played unwilling host to Japanese operations in 1941. Miri was secured by an independent formation from southern Indo-China on 15 December, Kuching being occupied on Christmas Day and the Dutch airfield at Singkawang in late January. From Miri, too, Japanese forces moved to occupy British North Borneo, Sandakan being taken on 17 January. By then, however, the main Japanese offensive into the Indies had opened with landings at Tarakan (10 January) and Menado the next day. From these two ports the Japanese could develop their offensive either side of Macassar, thereby dividing Allied attention and resources, but their next moves, on Balikpapan and Kendari were accompanied by a carrier strike on Rabaul and the occupation of this base and of Kavieng. Possession of the great natural harbour at Rabaul provided the Japanese with the base from which to secure the upper Solomons and eastern New Guinea (page 180), but for the moment Japanese attention centred on Borneo and Macassar where, despite losses incurred off Balikpapan on 24 January, the Japanese moved in strength to secure Macassar city on 8 February after having occupied Amboina, and its airfield, on 31 January. With the occupation

of Bandjermasin on 10 February by a force that advanced overland after first being landed on Laut Island, the Japanese by mid-February dominated the approaches to Java.

The reduction of Singapore was the *sine qua non* for an assault on the East Indies, and with the assault on the island on 8 February (page 170) the Japanese moved to secure Palembang by combined airborne and amphibious assault on the 14th. Palembang and its refineries were occupied on 17 February, when the Allied evacuation of southern Sumatra was complete. Thereafter the main Japanese blows fell in the east, the carrier force, supported by bombers from Kendari and Amboina, reducing much of Darwin to debris on 19 February, while assault forces landed on Bali (also on the 19th) and in both Dutch and Portuguese Timor (20 February). With Japanese forces simultaneously working their way around western Borneo, the Allied defeat on Java was assured even before the Japanese landings on the island on the night of 28 February/1 March.

Various Japanese landings had been disputed, inconclusively, by Allied naval forces, but the assault on Java committed the Allies to a decisive naval action in the eastern Java Sea, two cruisers and three destroyers being lost in a vain attempt to get amongst the transports carrying the 48th Infantry Division to Kragan. After this action, surviving Allied warships in the Java Sea were hunted to destruction by Japanese naval units, while to the south of Java the carrier force dealt with Allied shipping trying to escape from the island. Only at Bantam Bay did Allied cruisers manage to engage Japanese transports, and paid the inevitable price for their fleeting success, the Japanese being able to come ashore in western Java across the wide front and to secure Batavia on 5 March. With the Dutch surrendering throughout the Indies on 9 March and their allies following suit on the 12th, the Japanese were able to proceed with the immediate unopposed occupation of northern Sumatra and of northern New Guinea from Boela to Hollandia between 31 March and 19 April.

By mid-April, however, Japanese policy for the next phase

of operations had been settled. The UN declaration and American carrier operations in early 1942 convinced the Japanese high command that offensive operations would have to be undertaken in order to complete the destruction of the American carrier formations and to force the United States to the compromise peace she so disdained. The plan of campaign that was devised during March, and accepted on 5 April, provided for an attack on the Aleutians and Midway, in the course of which American carrier forces were to be brought to battle and destroyed (page 96). Thereafter Japanese forces were to secure New Caledonia, Fiji and Samoa in July before taking Johnson Island in August, the Hawaiian Islands being the obvious target of subsequent operations. Various American carrier operations against the Marshalls, Rabaul, Wake and Marcus between 1 February and 4 March had achieved negligible results, though they served to underline the Japanese need to bring about the defeat of enemy carrier forces at the earliest possible opportunity, but in Huon Gulf on 10 March American carriers achieved successes against Japanese shipping supporting the landings at Lae and Salamaua; this left Japanese forces in the southwest Pacific without the means to proceed with its next operations, the occupation of Tulagi in the Solomons and Port Moresby in New Guinea. With Japanese intelligence suggesting the continued presence of two American carriers in the southwest Pacific after 10 March, the decision to seek a decisive battle in the central Pacific was followed by the strange decision to detach two fleet carriers to support the operations against Tulagi and Port Moresby, before the central Pacific undertaking began. The result – the battle of the Coral Sea – was not merely the first carrier engagement in history but the first strategic defeat incurred by Japanese forces in the Second World War. Despite sinking the carrier USS Lexington, the Japanese called off their attempt to invade Port Moresby and withdrew. It proved to be the point at which the flow of Japanese successes in the area was finally stemmed, allowing the Allies to gradually consolidate their strengths.

UNTIL 1941, the defense of Burma ranked below that of the West Indies in the list of British strategic priorities. Burma possessed little strategic importance and relatively few natural resources apart from rice. The Japanese occupation of southern Indo-China in July 1941, however, presented Burma with a real external threat, but the higher claim of Malaya and Singapore on military resources meant that in December 1941 the military establishment in Burma consisted of a few combat aircraft and the equivalent of one division.

For Japan, Burma's occupation would sever the Chinese Nationalists' main line of communication with the outside world (via Lashio and Rangoon) and would provide defence in depth to the southern resources area. The Japanese high command thus earmarked the 15th Army for operations in Burma after the occupation of Siam was complete.

The 15th Army, with just one regiment under command, occupied the Kra Isthmus between Prachaub and Nakhorn on 8 December, to secure the rear and the lines of communication of the 25th Army as it advanced into Malaya. Victoria Point airfield was secured on 16 December, but it was not until that the 15th Army began operations in earnest. Airfields at Tavoy and Mergui were secured and from them Japanese fighters were able to escort bomber raids on southern Burma for the first time. By the end of January the port of Rangoon had been brought to a standstill.

The main Japanese effort was made, however, on the Raheng–Moulmein track. The 15th Army had two half-strength divisions under command when it crossed the border on 20 January, but these possessed superiority of numbers over a defence divided between Tenasserim and the Shan States, and which was committed to defending Burma east of the Salween. Despite the arrival at Rangoon of four brigades in the six weeks before the city's fall, the destruction of the 17th Indian Division doomed the capital, and with it any British hope of holding Burma.

It had been the original Japanese intention to secure Rangoon and then to advance into central Burma and with the end of the other campaigns in southeast Asia the Japanese were able to move the equivalent of three divisions by sea to Burma within seven weeks of the capture of Rangoon. The 15th Army quickly developed its offensives in the Irrawaddy Sittang valleys, despite the presence there of Chinese forces (which were dispersed, equivalent to no more than a division and, on the Sittang, were not mutually supporting). The first crucial clash around Toungoo was won by the Japanese. Critically, the Japanese secured the bridge over the Sittang intact and were able to develop an offensive through the mountains which resulted in the capture of Lashio on 28 April. Four days later the Japanese secured Mandalay and with it control of central and northern Burma.

The formal decision to abandon Burma was not taken until 25 April, by which time the withdrawal was threatened as much by the approach of the monsoon as the advancing Japanese. In the first week of May the last British formations in Burma, plus one Chinese division, abandoned the lower Chindwin and began to trek to Imphal, whilst the remainder of the 5th Chinese Army withdrew into northern Burma and thence either to Assam or northern Yunnan. Parts of the 6th Chinese Army contrived to remain in the eastern Shan States, but on the 66th Army's front the Japanese advanced into Yunnan and established themselves on the Salween, where they were to remain until late 1944.

The Japanese presence in most of Burma preoccupied British strategy in the East until 1944 (page 162). Supplies to Nationalist forces in China were disrupted, but the incipient threat to India was never realized, although an assault on Ceylon and other ports signposted disruption of shipping in the Indian Ocean and caused fears of Japanese designs on Madagascar (page 78).

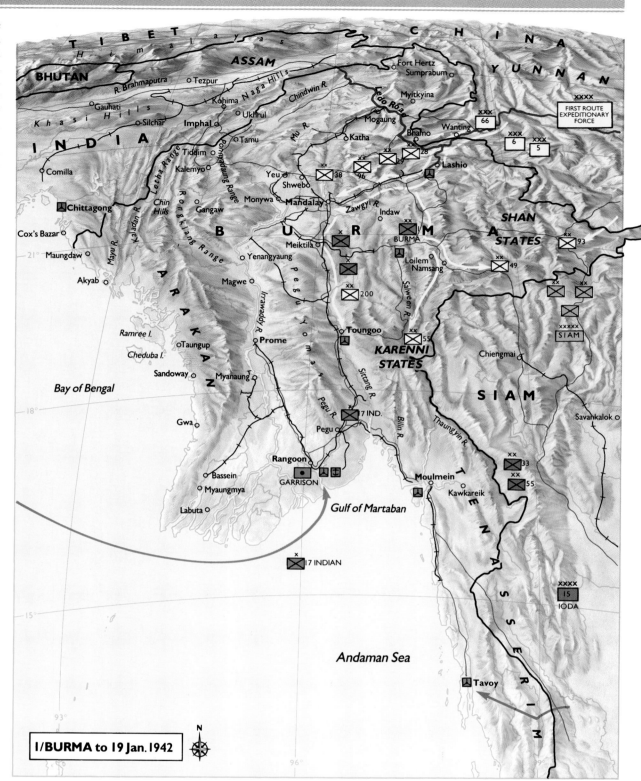

1/BURMA to 19 Jan. 1942

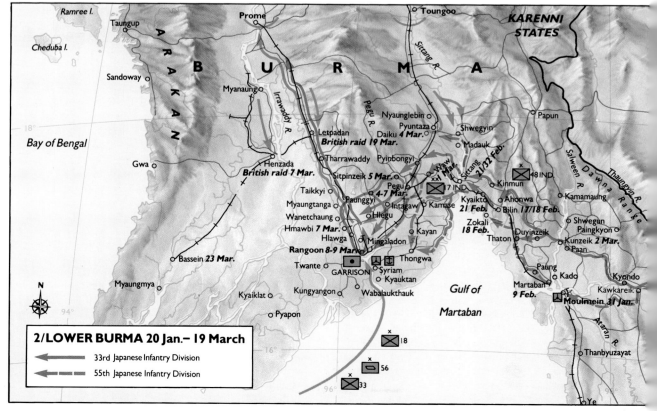

2/LOWER BURMA 20 Jan.– 19 March

→ 33rd Japanese Infantry Division
⇢ 55th Japanese Infantry Division

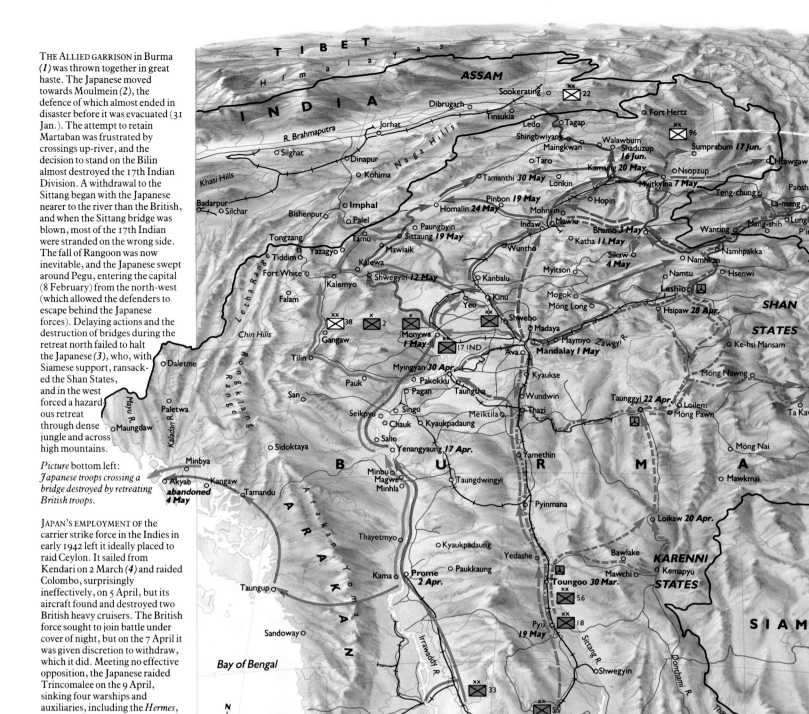

THE ALLIED GARRISON in Burma (1) was thrown together in great haste. The Japanese moved towards Moulmein (2), the defence of which almost ended in disaster before it was evacuated (31 Jan.). The attempt to retain Martaban was frustrated by crossings up-river, and the decision to stand on the Bilin almost destroyed the 17th Indian Division. A withdrawal to the Sittang began with the Japanese nearer to the river than the British, and when the Sittang bridge was blown, most of the 17th Indian were stranded on the wrong side. The fall of Rangoon was now inevitable, and the Japanese swept around Pegu, entering the capital (8 February) from the north-west (which allowed the defenders to escape behind the Japanese forces). Delaying actions and the destruction of bridges during the retreat north failed to halt the Japanese (3), who, with Siamese support, ransacked the Shan States, and in the west forced a hazardous retreat through dense jungle and across high mountains.

Picture bottom left: Japanese troops crossing a bridge destroyed by retreating British troops.

JAPAN'S EMPLOYMENT OF the carrier strike force in the Indies in early 1942 left it ideally placed to raid Ceylon. It sailed from Kendari on 2 March (4) and raided Colombo, surprisingly ineffectively, on 5 April, but its aircraft found and destroyed two British heavy cruisers. The British force sought to join battle under cover of night, but on the 7 April it was given discretion to withdraw, which it did. Meeting no effective opposition, the Japanese raided Trincomalee on the 9 April, sinking four warships and auxiliaries, including the *Hermes*, the first carrier to be sunk by carrier aircraft attack. Supporting operations were conducted by submarines that sank five merchantmen off the west coast of India, and by a carrier-cruiser force that sank 23 merchantmen and raided various cities in eastern India. The blow to British prestige and trade in the Bay of Bengal was considerable, but strategically the Japanese raid achieved little of consequence.

3/UPPER BURMA 20 March – 31 May 1942

- → 33rd Japanese Infantry Division
- → 55th Japanese Infantry Division
- → 18th Japanese Infantry Division
- → 56th Japanese Infantry Division

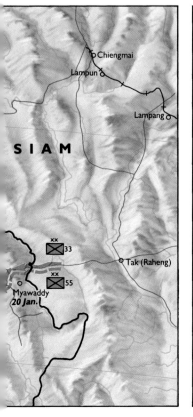

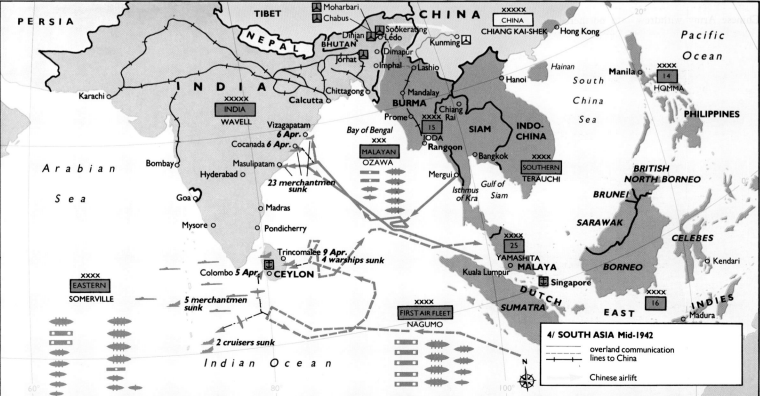

4/ SOUTH ASIA Mid-1942

- ——— overland communication
- ——|—— lines to China
- ——— Chinese airlift

The Middle East 1940~1942

As early as October 1940 Hitler had considered the strategic merit of extending his war against Britain into the Middle East. Mussolini at first resented German involvement in what he regarded as Italy's particular sphere of operations but, after his humiliation in Egypt at the hands of the British (page 50) and in Albania at the hands of the Greeks (page 54), he could no longer sustain the pretence that he did not need German help. Hitler arranged for the despatch of German troops to Libya at a meeting with the Italians on 19-20 January 1941. The *Deutsches Afrika Korps* (DAK), of 5th Motorized and 15th Panzer Divisions, began to arrive at Tripoli on 12 February. It was commanded by Rommel, a tank strategist who had tasted victory in Belgium and France.

The British were keenly aware of the problem posed by the increasing Axis presence in the Mediterranean. New supply lines to the British garrisons in Egypt and East Africa had to be created as alternatives to hazardous Mediterranean routes. The problem was eased by Commonwealth troops from India, Australia, New Zealand and South Africa who were relied upon to shore up the British presence in Africa.

Rommel opened his offensive at El Agheila, lightly held by the British 2nd Armoured Division. Wavell's Western Desert Force had been heavily depleted by transfers to Greece; its air support amounted to only 30 aircraft but fortunately the Axis air forces were not strong. El Agheila fell at once and Mersa Brega, in its immediate rear, on 31 March. Despite orders to the contrary, Rommel continued his advance into Cyrenaica. He organized his mobile forces into three columns, one to follow the coast road, the two others to use desert tracks to cut off the British from the rear. The British withdrew to the Mekili-Wadi Cuff line. Although the Germans found difficulty navigating the desert tracks, and had to be led by Rommel in person on the night of 5 April, the British decided to withdraw again on 6 April, making for Gazala, losing in the process their two leading generals, Neame and O'Connor, captured by an Axis patrol. Mekili was abandoned after a three-day stand (6-8 April). The Australian 9th Division withdrew into Tobruk which was surrounded by 11 April.

Rommel, who could not advance leaving Tobruk to his rear, now decided to make a deliberate assault on the defences. It opened on the night of 30 April/1 May and achieved some

THE PROBLEM OF SUPPLYING British forces in Africa (*1*) was partly overcome by use of supply lines from Commonwealth countries, and by a transcontinental air route from West Africa. But the war in the Western Desert (*2*) developed badly for the Allies after the arrival of German forces in Libya. The success of Rommel's opening offensives was overwhelming, and his response to the British operations *Brevity* (15-26 May) and *Battleaxe* (15-17 June) led to the isolation of Tobruk and counter-offensives at Sollum, Halfaya and Fort Capuzzo which eventually drove the British east of the Egyptian border. The British had problems elsewhere: the Mediterranean (*6*) turned into a major theatre, with a mutual battle for convoy corridors reaching a crisis when the Axis could claim control of the Mediterranean from 10°-25° East, excepting Malta, which was reinforced as an Allied air base and convoy staging post. A campaign to secure Vichy territories in the Middle East (*3*) proved a bitter fight, as did the British invasion of Madagascar (*5*) a year later. Nevertheless, with Vichy and pro-Axis elements west of Egypt eliminated, essential supply routes to the USSR via Persia could be established (*4*), and the vital oil resources of the Gulf guaranteed to the Allies.

Picture below: the arrival of Erwin Rommel and the Deutsches Afrika Korps (DAK) in the Western Desert in Spring 1941 transformed and prolonged the Desert War. A gifted tank strategist, he sustained a remarkable series of campaigns often against overwhelming odds.

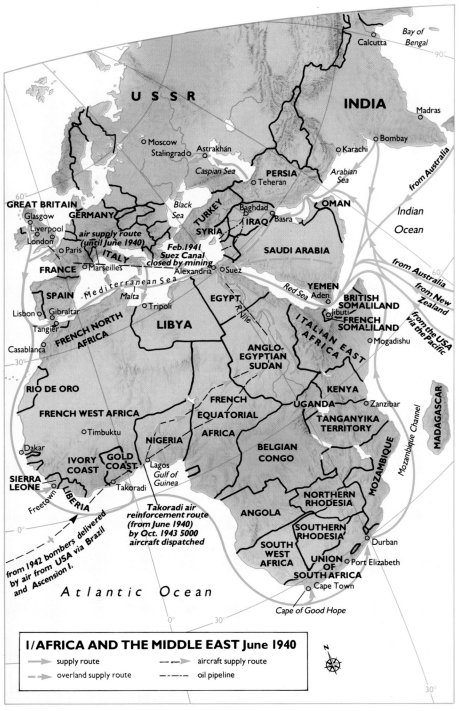

1/AFRICA AND THE MIDDLE EAST June 1940

- → supply route
- ⇢ overland supply route
- ⇠ aircraft supply route
- ─·─ oil pipeline

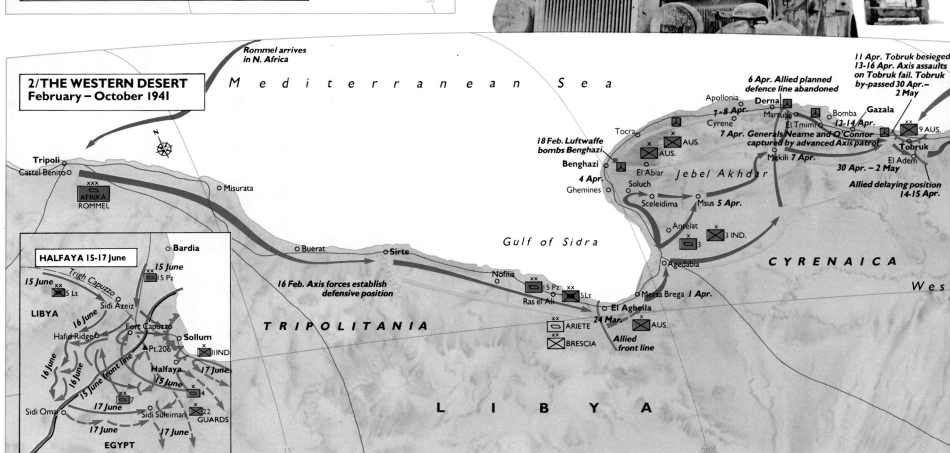

2/THE WESTERN DESERT February – October 1941

success. The Australians, heavily supported by artillery, virtually destroyed half the attacking German tanks, however, and Paulus, who had arrived from Berlin to oversee Rommel's decisions, refused to permit the attack to be renewed. He ordered instead that priority should be given to establishing a defensive line west of Tobruk at Gazala, while reinforcements and supplies were accumulated. His signal to Berlin revealing this change of intention was intercepted by *Ultra* and prompted Churchill to order Wavell, to whom the *Tiger* convoy had brought 240 tanks on 12 May, to undertake a counter-offensive. Codenamed *Brevity*, it was launched by 7th Armoured and 22nd Guards Brigade at Sollum on 15 May, but in too little strength. The British took the outer defences of Sollum, Halfaya and Fort Capuzzo but were counter-attacked and forced to withdraw. On 26 May the Germans recovered the remnants of the ground lost in *Brevity* and there was then a pause until the opening of Wavell's equally unsuccessful *Battleaxe* operation on 15 June which failed to penetrate the forward Axis line near Bardia, and indeed resulted in a British retreat well inside the Egyptian border.

The British had had greater success meanwhile in offsetting indirect German penetration of the Middle East and by June 1941 the Soviet Union had joined the Allied cause. It became essential to ensure supply lines to her, via the Gulf and Persia, and to secure the Middle East in general, not least because of the Gulf oil reserves. On 3 April the pro-British Regent of Iraq, Emir Abdullah, had been overthrown in a coup led by the pro-Axis General Rashid Ali. On 29 April he invested the British air base at Habbaniya, near Baghdad, to forestall the build-up of British troops in the country, where they had the right to use the port of Basra. Fighting broke out at Habbaniya on 2 May and a relief force, Habforce, left Transjordan on 13 May. It was attacked by *Luftwaffe* aircraft operating from Syria and Iraq but forced its way into Baghdad between 27-30 May. Rashid Ali fled to Persia and Abdullah was restored on 30 May. Evidence of German involvement in Syria, where French forces were loyal to Vichy, prompted Churchill to organize a four-pronged assault, beginning on 23 June. From Palestine the Allies advanced on Beirut and Damascus, while the Iraq Habforce and 10th Indian Division advanced to Homs and Aleppo. Most made slow progress, but supported by naval gunfire, the 7th Australians broke through to Beirut on 6 July and in a five-day battle forced Dentz, the Vichy commander, to sue for terms. The armistice, signed on 14 July, allowed French troops to return to France if they chose. Only 5700 out of 38,000 surviving troops opted to join de Gaulle's Free French.

Both British reliance on Commonwealth troops east of Suez and the security of the Indian Ocean shipping lanes were threatened by the Japanese entry to the war in December 1941 (page 68). Fear of Japanese plans to establish submarine bases in Vichy Madagascar prompted, in May 1942, a British invasion and protracted campaign; this completed Allied control between 30° and 90° East, driving a wedge between the Axis powers in Europe and Asia. Now British strategy in the west would centre upon the Western Desert.

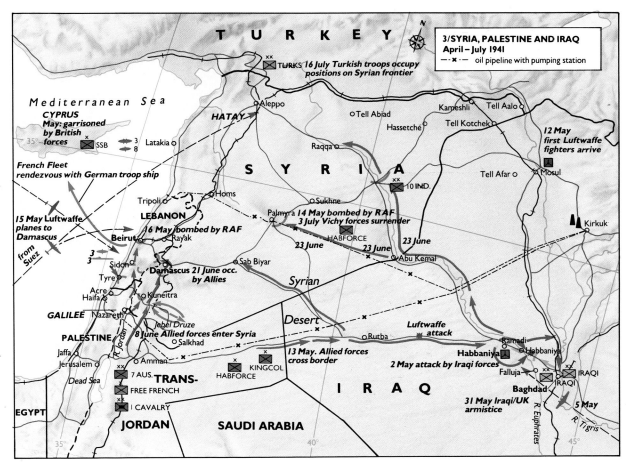

3/SYRIA, PALESTINE AND IRAQ
April – July 1941
—·× — oil pipeline with pumping station

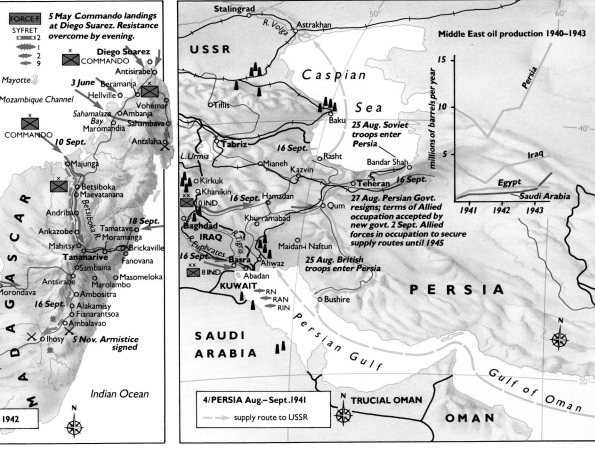

4/PERSIA Aug.–Sept.1941
——→ supply route to USSR

Middle East oil production 1940–1943

5/ MADAGASCAR 5 May – 5 Nov. 1942

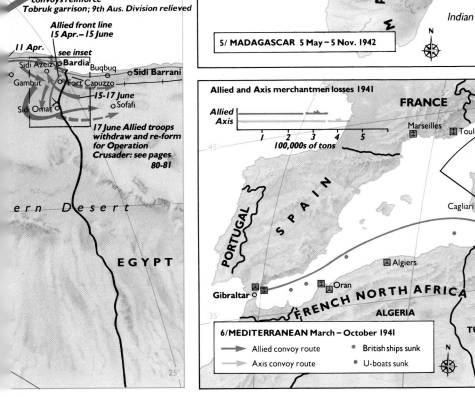

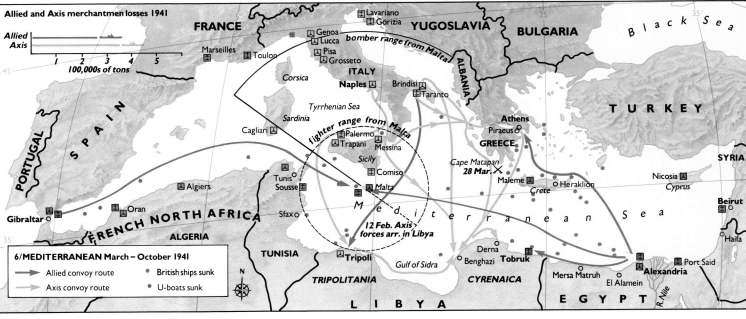

6/MEDITERRANEAN March – October 1941
——→ Allied convoy route   • British ships sunk
——→ Axis convoy route   • U-boats sunk

Allied and Axis merchantmen losses 1941

LEAVING TOBRUK UNDER SIEGE, and advancing to the Egyptian border in March-April 1941 (page 78), Rommel then consolidated his positions near Sollum. Auchinleck, who had succeeded Wavell as Middle East Commander on 5 July, began planning a counterstroke – Operation *Crusader* – with Western Desert Force (redesignated 8th Army on 18 December) in August. The relief of Tobruk and the re-occupation of Cyrenaica were the principal aims of the operation. It was to be commanded by Cunningham, the victor of the East African campaign (page 50). However, the outbreak of war with Japan (pages 68-76) had syphoned off many Far Eastern Commonwealth reinforcements. The importance of maintaining a Mediterranean supply route from Great Britain and her transatlantic allies and of retaining Malta, midway between Gibraltar and Alexandria, was critical. German bombing of the island had begun in late 1940, but RAF units resolutely resisted the almost continuous *Luftwaffe* assault and a series of major

supply convoys began to force a passage through the hazardous narrows south of Sicily and Sardinia.

In the Western Desert, by November 1941, the 8th Army outnumbered the combined Axis force (c.118,000 men to c.113,000), had 680 tanks (with 500 in reserve or in supply) to Rommel's 390 and 1000 British planes confronted 320 Axis aircraft. Thus, *Crusader*, opening on 28 November, and taking Rommel by surprise, should have succeeded. It did not. An initial break-out from Tobruk was contained, as was the major offensive by xxx Corps. Cunningham was replaced with Ritchie, who restored the Allied offensive, causing Rommel to retreat west of Tobruk, abandoning Italian forces at Bardia and Sollum (surrendered 17 December) and reaching Gazala (7 December) then El Aghiela by the end of the year.

The familiar desert warfare phenomenon of over-extension now worked to Rommel's benefit. He had retreated with his main base at Tripoli, where a major supply convoy arrived on 5

January 1942. The 8th Army by contrast having advanced over 300 miles in three weeks was at the extremity of its lines of communication – undersupplied and off-balance. Sensing its weakness, Rommel went over to the counter-offensive on 21 January and quickly drove it back to Gazala, 30 miles west of Tobruk, by 4 February. Both sides stood on this line throughout the Spring, gathering reinforcements.

Rommel attacked again on 26 May. He had 560 tanks, of which 240 were Italian and outclassed; the British had 700, including 200 new American Grants, with powerful 75mm guns. Rommel swung his armour around the southern end of the heavily mined Gazala front, but within three days withdrew into a *kassel* (cauldron) inside British lines. There he resisted heavy attacks, then broke eastwards, driving the British before him. Tobruk garrison was forced to surrender (21 June) and 8th Army retreated 300 miles to the Alam Halfa-Alamein line (7 July). *Crusader* had proved a costly failure.

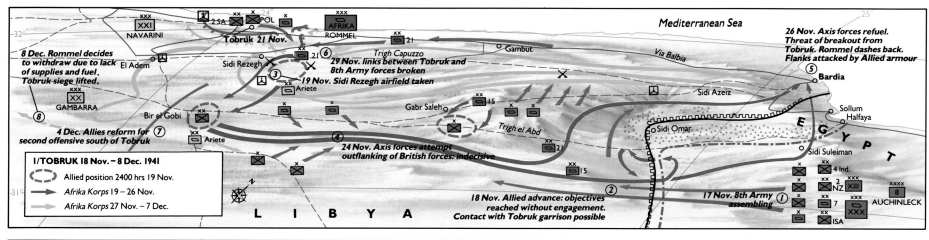

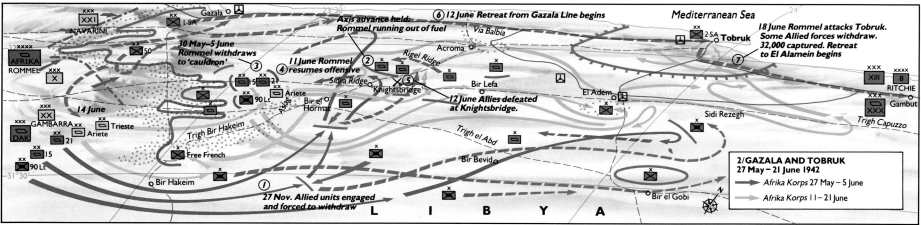

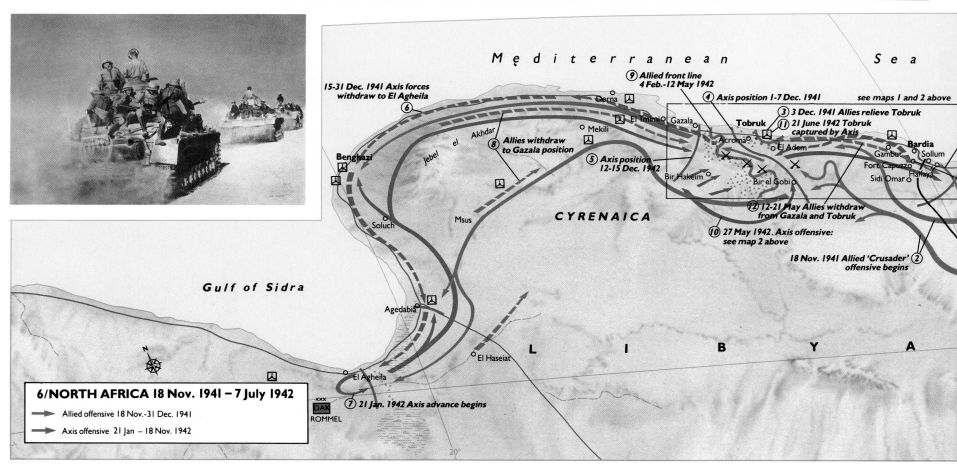

THE PERIOD BETWEEN NOV. 1941 and July 1942 (6) saw the most extended advances and retreats by British and Axis forces of the whole Desert War. The relief of Tobruk and the clearing of Cyrenaica formed the core of the British *Crusader* plan. When Auchinleck attacked the Axis forces besieging Tobruk (1), 70th Division broke out to join XIII Corps which was working westward along the coast. This breakout was held and Rommel counter-attacked towards Sidi Rezegh. Only when faced with the pincers of XIII and XXX Corps did Rommel retire (27 Nov.). On 29 Nov. XIII Corps made contact with the Tobruk garrison but it was broken the next day. After heavy fighting the siege was finally raised, after 240 days (8 Dec.); Rommel began his retreat to El Agheila the day before. Now both sides gathered their strength. Rommel's true strength was in his mobile forces south of the Trigh Capuzzo. With these he attacked (2) south of the heavily mined line engaging the British in heavy tank fighting around 'Knightsbridge'. When his tank losses became too high (30 May) he withdrew to the *kessel* (cauldron) area where he could be supplied through the British minefields. Ritchie was overwhelmed by Rommel's breakout (11 June) and forced to retreat eastward, leaving Bir Hakeim in German hands. Tobruk sustained siege only for 1 week (14-21 June) before surrendering. The Axis position in the Mediterranean was strengthened (5): Malta was effectively neutralized by air attack (4) and 21 German U-boats joined the Italians in harrassing British shipping. Rommel's supply convoys sailed largely unopposed. The Allies lost several major warships to Italian midget submarine attacks at Alexandria, although convoys of submarines supplied Malta. Major convoys, such as *Pedestal* (3, 11-13 Aug.) fought their way to Malta at heavy cost.

Picture below left: German armoured spearheads were supported by mobile mechanized units, allowing considerable freedom of movement in the open desert theatre.

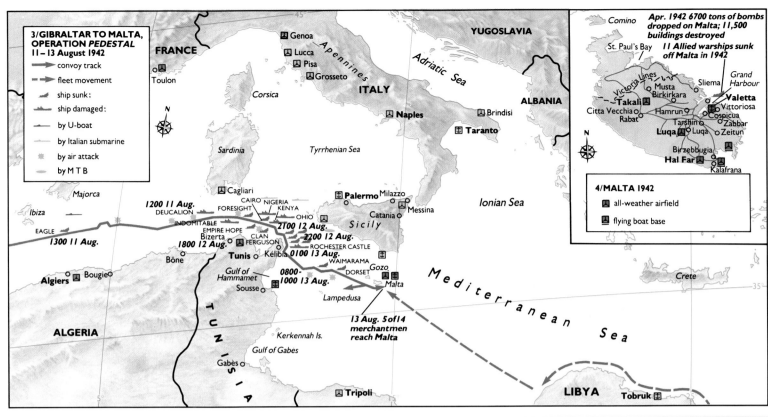

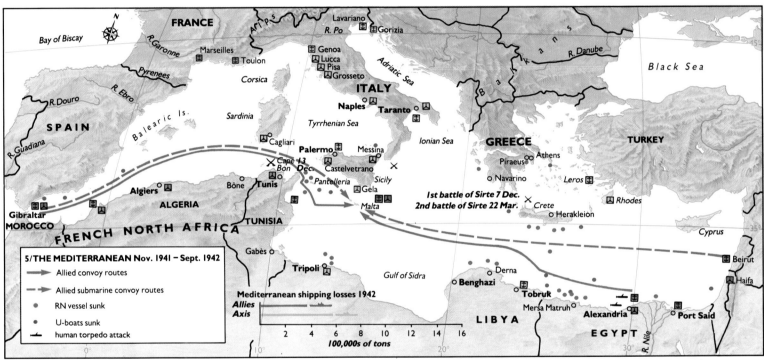

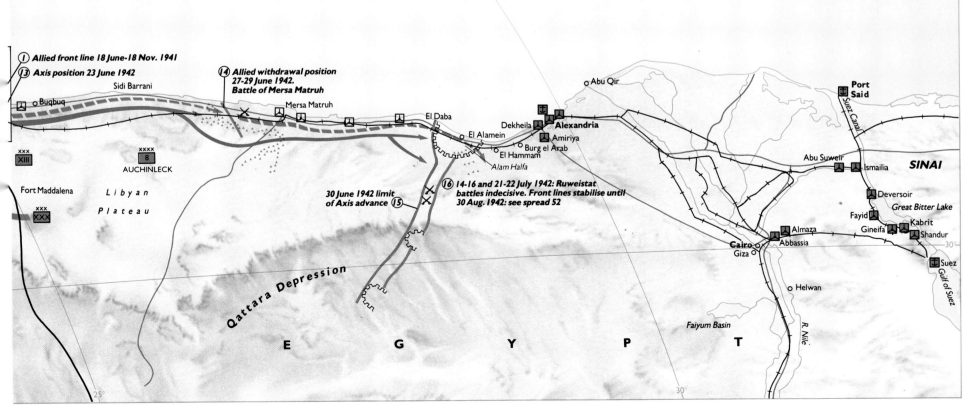

Th Intelligenc War 1939~1945

INTELLIGENCE GATHERING, interpretation and misinformation in the conduct of the war was of immense value to all the belligerents. The most immediate was military intelligence derived from the interrogation of POWs and from surveillance, reconnaissance and aerial photography. More sophisticated information, gained by clandestine means, was broken down, in Allied terminology, into signals intelligence (SIGINT – mainly the penetration and decrypting of enemy radio traffic) and

human intelligence (HUMINT – information collected and passed on by spies, spy rings and resistance organizations).

HUMINT began badly. Officials in foreign embassies regularly relayed information, but only in certain instances was this to prove of major value: the Japanese consulate in Hawaii, for example, regularly fed data on US fleet dispositions in Pearl Harbor back to Tokyo (which was in turn, monitored by the Americans). Germany's blitzkrieg in the west and the rapidity of Japan's advance in the Far East overwhelmed Allied intelligence almost as comprehensively as its armies had been defeated. Networks of agents only intended to operate under peacetime conditions were overrun and destroyed as a blanket of Nazi security descended over Europe. Similarly, in the Far East, the security services of the colonial powers were driven back to bases in India, Ceylon, Australia and Hawaii, thousands of miles from their target areas. A major blow to MI6 came at Venlo, in on the German/Dutch border, in November 1939 when two senior British agents were kidnapped and successfully interrogated by the Germans.

However, modern military operational dependence upon wireless communications offered great opportunities for interception of enemy signals traffic. As far flung armies, ships, diplomats and secret agents endeavoured to communicate with each other SIGINT became of vital importance to all of the combatants. In order to protect their wireless communications, Germany relied totally upon the supposedly unbreakable Enigma encipherment machine. This was used to send

messages at all levels of command. But a combined Polish, French and British intelligence effort, based at Bletchley Park, managed to break the codes and an abundance of German secrets was revealed throughout the war. The information gleaned from decrypting intercepted Enigma traffic was designated Ultra and, passed to senior commanders, made an outstanding contribution to Allied victory, although the sheer volume of material intercepted caused problems, and often decrypts were only belatedly completed. A similar feat was performed by American cryptologists who broke the Japanese Purple code and used the information gathered, Magic, not only in planning their campaigns in the Pacific but also in the spectacular ambush and assassination of Admiral Yamamoto, the Commander-in-Chief of the Japanese Navy, whilst flying to the Western Solomons in April 1943.

Agents operating in enemy territory were also reliant upon the use of clandestine wireless sets and security services developed sophisticated interception, decoding and radio location techniques. The German Abwehr and SD proved to be particularly adept at operating Funkspiele (radio games) such as the Englandspiel, when the German security services in Holland effectively controlled SIS, SOE and Dutch intelligence operations from 1941-42. By capturing an agent and forcing him to 'play back' his radio, 61 Allied agents sent into Holland were arrested. Even more comprehesive was MI5's success in controlling German attempts to infiltrate agents into Great Britain. Captured agents were 'turned', bogus networks

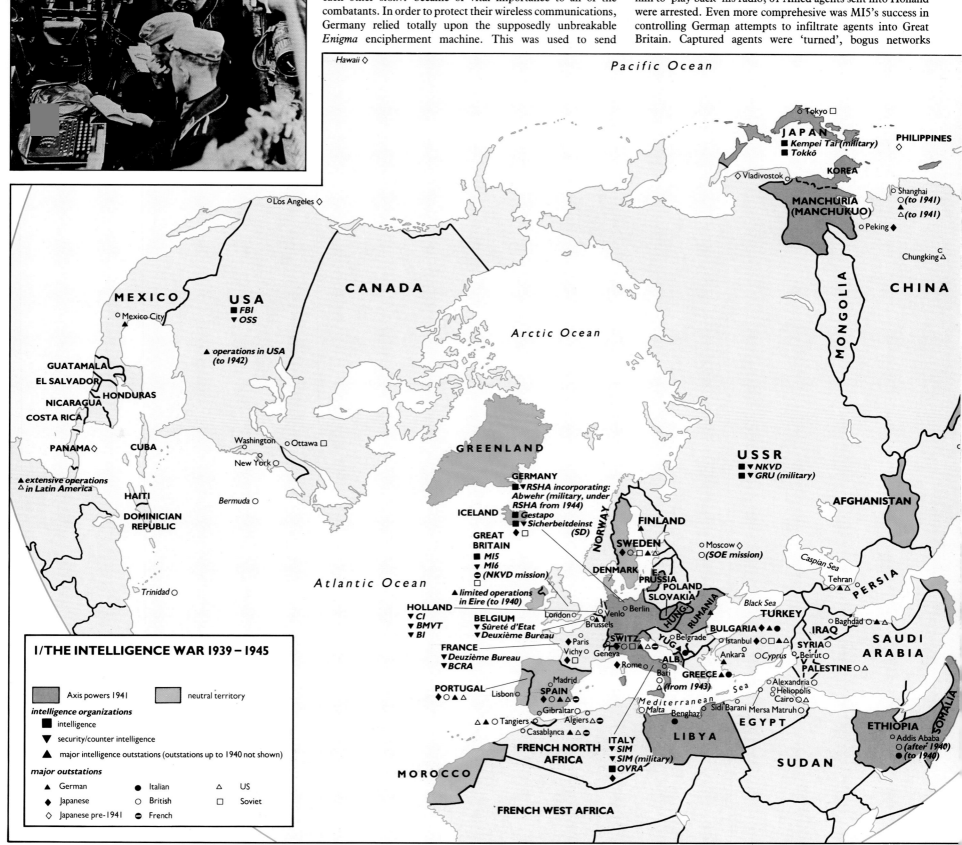

I/THE INTELLIGENCE WAR 1939–1945

- ▨ Axis powers 1941
- ▨ neutral territory

intelligence organizations
- ■ intelligence
- ▼ security/counter intelligence
- ▲ major intelligence outstations (outstations up to 1940 not shown)

major outstations
- ▲ German
- ● Italian
- △ US
- ◆ Japanese
- ○ British
- □ Soviet
- ◇ Japanese pre-1941
- ◒ French

established and false intelligence reports submitted while the efficacy of the scheme was constantly monitored by reading *Abwehr Enigma* traffic. Successful wireless monitoring led the Germans to capture a Soviet spy network, the *Red Orchestra*, based on existing pre-war Communist cells, which extended throughout western Europe.

But the importance of SIGINT should not detract from the continued role of HUMINT. Agents still had to be used for targeting specific areas or to discover special information. Richard Sorge, a Soviet agent operating in Japan, passed crucial information on Japanese and German war plans and Czech intelligence ran their double agent in the *Abwehr*, 'A-54', for several years both before and during the war.

Complementing these key Allied agents was a host of intelligence networks manned by members of the resistance (page 94). With their efforts co-ordinated by Allied intelligence, they produced a wealth of detail on all aspects of enemy military, economic, political and technological activity. Throughout occupied Europe, networks of many political persuasions provided information that not even the Nazi security services could stem. Among these was *Service Clarence*, a Belgian network established in the First World War, and re-activated before the Nazi invasion in 1940.

The role of neutral countries as disinterested territories was of great importance; they became, in effect, conduits for the flow of HUMINT, and although many of the operatives were run as double agents by both sides their value as a means of 'leaking' misinformation to the enemy was considerable. In Switzerland the American, Allan Dulles (later head of CIA), ran an extensive OSS operation, while the Soviet *Lucy* ring gained much information by interviewing dissident German officers on leave.

The nature of intelligence warfare led to rivalry and mistrust, not only between different organizations but even amongst allies. The extraordinary power granted to those who ran security organizations often constituted a security threat in its own right. Further, the sources of *Ultra* were not fully conveyed to the Soviet Union, while Soviet penetration of Western Allied intelligence was maintained throughout the war. But both the Western Allies and the Soviet Union fully appreciated the immense role played by intelligence in the defeat of the Axis powers, and the Western Allies recruited many German agents as the Cold War set in.

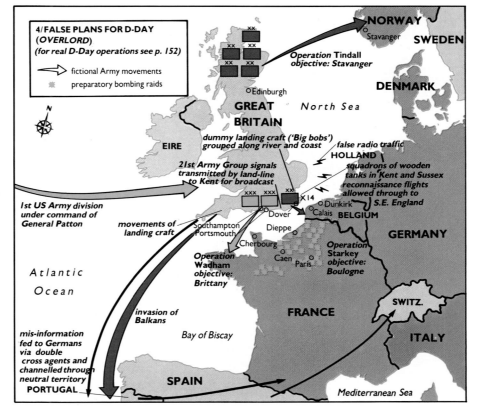

THE UNSTABLE NATURE of international relations and the fragile state of domestic politics in many nations during the inter-war years, led to a marked increase in intelligence gathering and security organizations (*1*). The threat of Communist subversion organized by the Soviet Union was overtaken by the dangerously aggressive policies of Germany, Italy and Japan. Military and diplomatic wireless traffic was intercepted and the encoded messages were attacked by cryptographers of all nations. Mistakenly believing that *Enigma* encoding machine was unbreakable, the Germans failed to comprehend that the Allies had opened a window into many aspects of their war effort (*2*). However, the secret agent still had a vital role to play and the Belgian *Service Clarence* was one of the most successful networks of the war (*3*). From 1939-44 its agents supplied British intelligence with a wealth of information on German activities throughout occupied Europe. Intelligence was not solely concerned with the acquisition of material but also with the protection of secrets and deceiving the enemy. The most elaborate and exhaustive of these deception operations was that surrounding the Allied launching of a Second Front in Europe (*4*). The location, timing and scale of the invasion was meticulously disguised by 'leaking' misinformation concerning Allied plans, and by elaborate feints giving false impressions to both enemy agents and aerial reconnaissance; even when the landings had been made in Normandy on 6 June 1944, the Germans remained uncertain whether this was the major thrust or simply a diversion.

Picture above left: the German tank commander Guderian's field headquarters; mounted on a half-track, he kept an Enigma encoding machine close at hand.

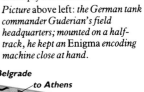

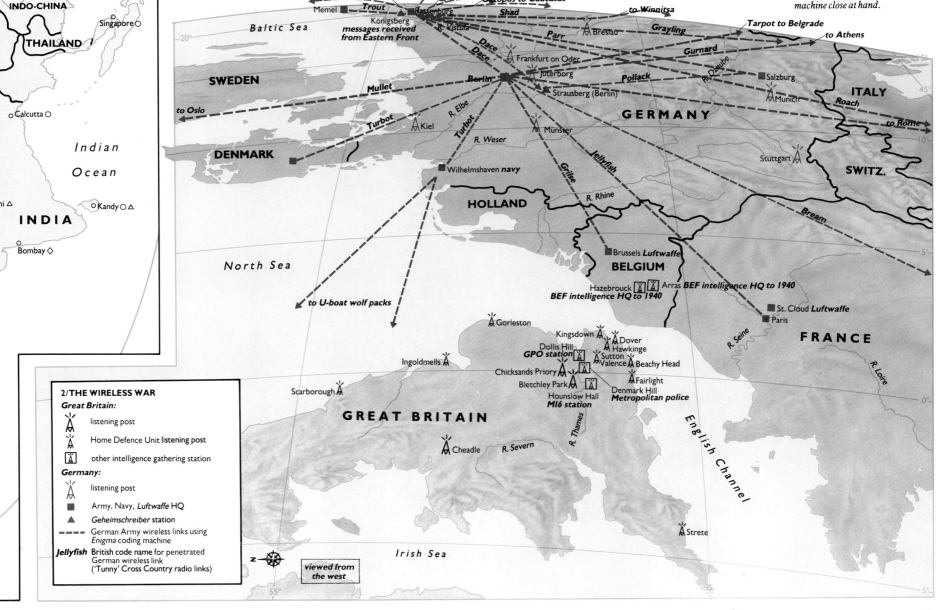

Clandestine war

THE USE OF COVERT techniques to achieve both conventional military objectives and to promote political indoctrination was a particular feature of the Second World War. The development of Special Forces (page 110) was one aspect of this; German Brandenburgers often operated in plain clothes (Danzig 1939, Rotterdam 1940) in advance of conventional forces. The Soviet NKVD operated widely throughout Europe, activating partisans and resistance groups from existing Communist cells (page 170). But the British SOE and American OSS were to become unique.

Fears at Germany's rapid territorial expansion in Europe in the 1930s and the impact of irregular operations witnessed during the Irish and Spanish civil wars encouraged the British War Office and the Secret Intelligence Service (SIS) to establish special departments to study this form of warfare. Military Intelligence Research (MIR) and SIS, Section D had begun their work before the outbreak of the Second World War and some, albeit inadequate, plans had been laid for sabotage, subversion and guerrilla operations in Europe in the event of hostilities breaking out. However, the triumph of Germany's armed forces in the Summer of 1940 and the occupation of most of Continental Europe left Britain desperately seeking to employ virtually any means of striking back. Accordingly, in July, the Special Operations Executive (SOE) was formed to foment resistance and, in Churchill's words, 'to set Europe ablaze'. Section D and MIR were amalgamated and the new organization was placed under the auspices of the Ministry of Economic Warfare.

In spite of Churchill's support, SOE's relations with the Services and other government departments, notably SIS, were not always harmonious. The diversion of ships and aircraft to assist in their operations, together with the secondment of high calibre service personnel to man the new organization brought considerable criticism. Furthermore, SOE's activities were, on occasion, at variance with Foreign Office policy and relations with SIS were frequently acrimonious – intelligence gathering and subversive operations were largely antipathetic, and the two bodies constantly vied for control of spheres of influence, resources and personnel.

Nevertheless, agents were recruited, trained and inserted into all the occupied countries of Western Europe where they helped to organize, supply and instruct resistance groups in clandestine warfare. Special attention was paid to the development of armed groups that could be controlled from London and activated in the event of an Allied invasion. Their task was to attack enemy communications and divert resources away from the main battle front. This achievement, similar to that of the Central Staff of the Partisan Movement on the Eastern Front (page 170), was of great importance. In addition, SOE was called upon to help train members of the armies-in-exile and liaise with their governments in employing them in particular acts of sabotage, assassination and even kidnapping.

The outbreak of the war with Japan resulted in the need for SOE to expand its activities into Asia and, at the same time, provoked the formation of a complementary American organization, the Office of Strategic Services (OSS). Fortunately, American deference for British experience and expertise helped to promote a high degree of Allied co-operation and SOE and OSS worked together in Europe and the Far East.

The often spectacular and controversial nature of clandestine operations and the remarkable post-war revelations about its most celebrated agents and operations have given SOE and OSS a prominence out of all proportion to their overall contribution to the war effort. The expansive claims made for some of the most famous coups – such as the raid on the Norsk-Hydro heavy water plant in Norway (February 1943) and the assassination of Heydrich (May 1942) – have in no small part been a result of self-justification in the face of criticism of irregular operations. However, it may be argued that clandestine warfare was at its most efficacious not necessarily in dramatic, single actions but in its small-scale, attritional effects. Morale in the countries occupied by the Axis forces was undoubtedly lifted by the knowledge of Allied operations within enemy territory and the supply of weapons and explosives transformed the civilian population into an immensely potent force for resistance.

NORWAY
a number of effective sabotage operations including Op. Gunner side sabotage of the Norsk Hydro heavy water plant (27 Feb. 1943)

SWEDEN
limited political activity; Op. Rubble, successful extraction of British freighters from Gothenburg (Mar. 1941)

DENMARK
after a slow start extensive co-operation with MI6 over intelligence gathering and co-ordination of resistance sabotage against railway network 1944-45 (page 54)

HOLLAND
SOE operations foiled by German counter-intelligence operations (Englandspiel, 1941-44) (page 82)

BELGIUM
limited success, undermined by political and organizational rivalry; co-ordination of La Grande Coupure, mass sabotage of Belgium electricity supply (Jan. 1944)

LUXEMBOURG
at least 10 nationals trained by SOE and parachuted back. Limited success

FRANCE
most successful field of operations (see map 3), culminating in co-ordination of rail, road and telephone sabotage campaign by resistance during Normandy invasion, 1944

ITALY
following first liaison mission (Op. Rudder, 1943) supplies and agents sent to partisan groups. Very effective

I/SOE IN EUROPE 1940-1945
- ■ SOE main base
- ● SOE secondary base
- ■ SOE operations

LITHUANIA
limited and unsuccessful attempts to co-ordinate sabotage

POLAND
supplies sent to Polish resistance; SOE political liaison mission, Op. Freston (26 Dec. 1944) unsuccessful

CZECHOSLOVAKIA
limited success in co-ordinating sabotage or political aims; Op. Anthropoid (27 May 1942) assassination of Heydrich, Deputy Protector of Bohemia-Moravia in Prague achieved by SOE-trained Czech agents; provoked heavy reprisals

HUNGARY
continued attempts to encourage anti-Nazi elements in the government; wireless contact maintained 1943-44

RUMANIA
largely ineffective attempts to generate political resistance

BULGARIA
missions contacted partisan groups but success limited by supply problems and Soviet influence

failure – Operation Blunderhead, a one man mission to sabotage shale-oil mines, ended with the agent's arrest soon after landing, 24 Oct. 1942

little effect – Operation Clowder, attempt to make contact with Slovene partisans but ended without significant success in Dec. 1944.

HQ for Balkan operations from 1943

YUGOSLAVIA
continued missions to co-ordinate resistance from Sept. 1941. Hampered by political difficulties (page 128), although eventually maintained supplies and contacts with Tito's partisans

ALBANIA
continued penetration (by Aug. 1943 24 agents and 8 wireless-telegraphy sets in operation) but countered by Communist resistance (page 128)

GREECE
despite severe political difficulties within resistance (page 128), successful co-ordination of sabotage; Op. Harling culminated in destruction of the vital Gorgopotamos railway bridge (25 Nov. 1942) (page 128)

CRETE
small scale sabotage; German general kidnapped (26 Apr. 1944)

FR. NORTH AFRICA ■
small scale sabotage; Op. Falaise destroyed a German infra-red observation station (12 Jan. 1942)

HQ for Balkan operations 1942-43

Clandestine operations in Japanese-occupied territory were limited by obvious problems of racial appearance, and by Japanese anti-imperialist propaganda (page 192). Nevertheless, in South-east Asia (4) British, US and Asian agents were inserted into Japanese-held territory to gather intelligence, co-ordinate guerrilla operations and carry out sabotage attacks against communications and enemy shipping. The most successful action was Operation *Jaywick*, mounted by SOE's India Mission but launched from Australia. After a long and hazardous voyage in a captured fishing boat (the *Krait*), the raiding party transferred to canoes for the attack on Japanese merchant ships at anchor in Singapore harbour. Using limpet mines, the saboteurs sank over 30,000 tons of enemy shipping and made a successful escape. An attempt to repeat the operation in Oct. 1944 proved disastrous – the entire sabotage party was killed or captured and executed in July 1945.

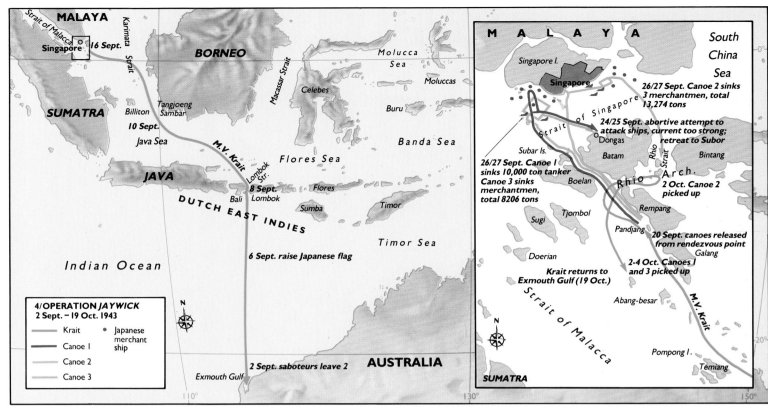

4/OPERATION *JAYWICK*
2 Sept. – 19 Oct. 1943
- Krait
- Canoe 1
- Canoe 2
- Canoe 3
- ● Japanese merchant ship

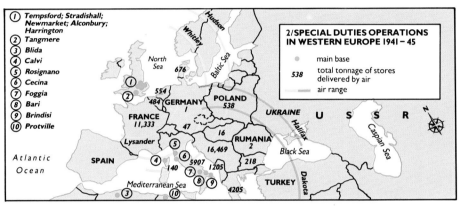

BRITAIN's Special Operations Executive (SOE) was the main Allied organization engaged in clandestine operations in occupied western Europe (1). Divided into 'country' sections, it worked closely with the governments-in-exile, although the harmoniousness of its relations and the nature of its operations varied immensely. In the Balkans and Italy, its operatives were attached to partisan groups to help furnish them with weapons and supplies and to liaise with SOE and Allied headquarters. In north-west Europe its agents generally operated undercover, building up networks to carry out sabotage and preparing the resistance for a concerted effort in support of the Second Front. However, SOE's operations in the Netherlands and France were seriously damaged by the activities of the *SD* and *Abwehr*. Although some agents and supplies were landed by sea, most of this type of work was carried out by RAF Special Duties Squadrons (2). These specialist units operated from bases in Britain, North Africa and Italy and dropped or collected agents as far afield as Poland and Estonia. The weapons, ammunition, explosives, foods, wirelesses and money dropped by the RAF were essential to the growth of armed resistance throughout Europe. France was at the forefront of SOE's plans (3) due to its proximity to Britain, its political and economic importance and its selection as the location of the Second Front. No less than 6 separate SOE sections operated into it, in addition to other British organizations, the American OSS, Free French services and the Soviet NKVD.

Picture above left: SS officers inspecting the bodies of Heydrich's assassins, Prague 1942.

3/FRANCE: INDUSTRIAL SABOTAGE
1942 – 44

targets:
- F fuel
- P power
- A aviation
- M military
- I industrial
- T transport
- E electrical
- C metals and chemicals

date of operation:
- ▲ 1942
- ▲ 1943
- ▲ 1944

IN THE SUMMER OF 1939 Great Britain and France were faced with the likelihood that their guarantee of Poland (page 30) would extend to cover a German attack aimed at rectification of the position of Danzig and the Polish Corridor. It was widely felt that an alliance with the Soviet Union might strengthen that guarantee. In spite of the threat of inviting Communist influence in eastern Europe, such an alliance might contain Hitler's ambitions. By August 1939, Anglo-Soviet discussions had faltered on the question of whether Soviet troops could cross Poland in the event of a German move. The German foreign minister, von Ribbentrop, flew to Moscow on the night of 23-24 August and signed a non-aggression pact with Stalin's government; relations between Nazi Germany and the Soviet Union were surprisingly warm, with substantial economic exchanges and the hand-over of several German exiles back to concentration camps in Germany. But there were strong suspicions on both sides concerning mutual interests – Finland, Turkey and Rumania, where the oil-wells of the Ploeşti region were essential for Germany's war effort. Stalin profited from the German invasion of France in June 1940 to annex much of northern Rumania, and Hitler decided to send a military mission to the country. Before doing so, he resolved to clear up the border disputes which had afflicted this area since 1919. With the Second Vienna Arbitration (30 August 1940) Rumania was required to accept an award of most of northern Transylvania, and the Székely district in its eastern-central part, to Hungary: this satisfied some rankling Hungarian irredentism (though the first Vienna Arbitration had awarded Hungary, in 1938, the southern parts of Slovakia). In October 1940 a German military mission arrived in Rumania, preparing the way for German domination of the Balkans (page 54). In the following months, states in the area agreed to join the Tripartite Pact of Germany, Italy and Japan (27 September 1940). For a brief period, the Soviet Union considered also joining this Pact, and there was a conference in Berlin of Ribbentrop and Molotov, Stalin's Foreign Minister, on 11-12 November 1940. This ended unsatisfactorily, since Molotov demanded a greater role in the Near East than Germany would allow; but by now Hitler was planning his attack on the USSR (page 56).

Between the invasion of France and Hitler's attack on Russia, the British were isolated. However, the attitude of the USA became increasingly benevolent and there were secret naval and military discussions with the British in 1940, as well as economic assistance (Lend Lease, page 98). Roosevelt and Churchill met in August 1941 off Argentia (Placentia Bay, Newfoundland) to discuss future strategy. At this time the British badly wanted United States' help in North Africa, whereas Roosevelt's advisers preferred a 'Europe First' strategy, so as to avoid any danger that Britain might collapse. The meeting produced only a declaration of principles, the Atlantic Charter. This at least enabled the British to resist Soviet demands for recognition of the border changes that had occurred to its advantage since 1939.

When Japan entered the war (pages 66-68) there was a three-week conference in Washington, opening on 22 December 1941, codenamed Arcadia, with Churchill and Roosevelt present with their advisers. 'Europe First' was re-asserted on the American side. Two plans were set up – Sledgehammer, for the build-up of an American force in the British Isles for invasion, and Super-Gymnast, providing for American troops to be landed on the Atlantic coast of Morocco, to help the British (who would also land a force in Algeria, part of Operation Torch, page 116). The conference also set up the machinery of the Combined Chiefs of Staff, and the Declaration of the United Nations was signed, a statement of Allied war aims. However, something had to be done for the Russians, and the US Army Chief of Staff, General George C. Marshall, came to London with Roosevelt's confidant, Harry Hopkins, in April 1942 to sound out the possibility of a cross-Channel landing in 1942. In theory, the British agreed, even though it would mean the end of the North African operation. Churchill visited Roosevelt again in June (at Roosevelt's house, Hyde Park, New York) and argued for this latter – and for a general effort in the Mediterranean. There was a long wrangle, but the facts of the war – the use of great amounts of naval equipment in the Pacific, and the crisis of the British front in North Africa – lent strength to Churchill's argument. In discussions in London 18-25 July 1942 the American delegation finally agreed to a Mediterranean strategy. But the avoidance of Soviet demands for the opening of a Second Front in Europe would constitute a major contention between the Western Allies and their Soviet partner in the year to come.

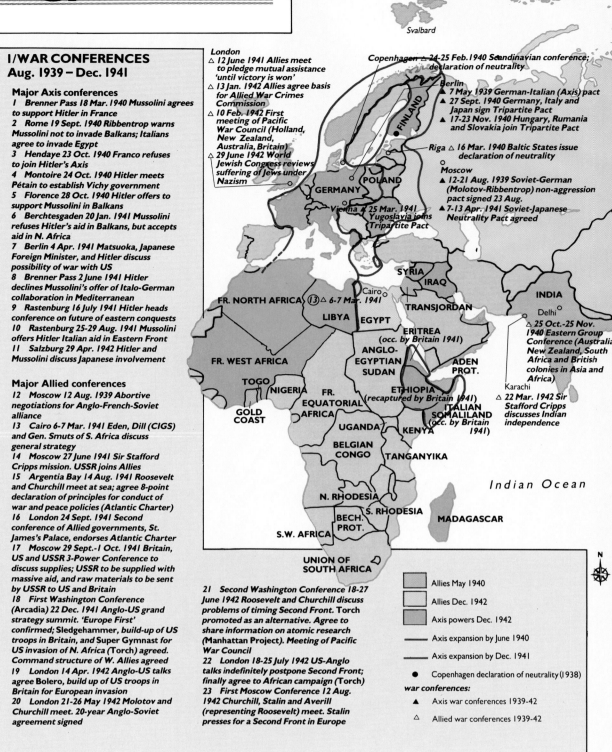

I/WAR CONFERENCES Aug. 1939 – Dec. 1941

Major Axis conferences
1 Brenner Pass 18 Mar. 1940 Mussolini agrees to support Hitler in France
2 Rome 19 Sept. 1940 Ribbentrop warns Mussolini not to invade Balkans; Italians agree to invade Egypt
3 Hendaye 23 Oct. 1940 Franco refuses to join Hitler's Axis
4 Montoire 24 Oct. 1940 Hitler meets Pétain to establish Vichy government
5 Florence 28 Oct. 1940 Hitler offers to support Mussolini in Balkans
6 Berchtesgaden 20 Jan. 1941 Mussolini refuses Hitler's aid in Balkans, but accepts aid in N. Africa
7 Berlin 4 Apr. 1941 Matsuoka, Japanese Foreign Minister, and Hitler discuss possibility of war with US
8 Brenner Pass 2 June 1941 Hitler declines Mussolini's offer of Italo-German collaboration in Mediterranean
9 Rastenburg 16 July 1941 Hitler heads conference on future of eastern conquests
10 Rastenburg 25-29 Aug. 1941 Mussolini offers Hitler Italian aid in Eastern Front
11 Salzburg 29 Apr. 1942 Hitler and Mussolini discuss Japanese involvement

Major Allied conferences
12 Moscow 12 Aug. 1939 Abortive negotiations for Anglo-French-Soviet alliance
13 Cairo 6-7 Mar. 1941 Eden, Dill (CIGS) and Gen. Smuts of S. Africa discuss general strategy
14 Moscow 27 June 1941 Sir Stafford Cripps mission. USSR joins Allies
15 Argentia Bay 14 Aug. 1941 Roosevelt and Churchill meet at sea; agree 8-point declaration of principles for conduct of war and peace policies (Atlantic Charter)
16 London 24 Sept. 1941 Second conference of Allied governments, St. James's Palace, endorses Atlantic Charter
17 Moscow 29 Sept.-1 Oct. 1941 Britain, US and USSR 3-Power Conference to discuss supplies; USSR to be supplied with massive aid, and raw materials to be sent by USSR to US and Britain
18 First Washington Conference (Arcadia) 22 Dec. 1941 Anglo-US grand strategy summit. 'Europe First' confirmed; Sledgehammer, build-up of US troops in Britain, and Super-Gymnast for US invasion of N. Africa (Torch) agreed. Command structure of W. Allies agreed
19 London 14 Apr. 1942 Anglo-US talks agree Bolero, build up of US troops in Britain for European invasion
20 London 21-26 May 1942 Molotov and Churchill meet. 20-year Anglo-Soviet agreement signed

21 Second Washington Conference 18-27 June 1942 Roosevelt and Churchill discuss problems of timing Second Front. Torch promoted as an alternative. Agree to share information on atomic research (Manhattan Project). Meeting of Pacific War Council
22 London 18-25 July 1942 US-Anglo talks indefinitely postpone Second Front; finally agree to African campaign (Torch)
23 First Moscow Conference 12 Aug. 1942 Churchill, Stalin and Averill (representing Roosevelt) meet. Stalin presses for a Second Front in Europe

London
△ 12 June 1941 Allies meet to pledge mutual assistance 'until victory is won'
△ 13 Jan. 1942 Allies agree basis for Allied War Crimes Commission
△ 10 Feb. 1942 First meeting of Pacific War Council (Holland, New Zealand, Australia, Britain)
△ 29 June 1942 World Jewish Congress reviews suffering of Jews under Nazism

Copenhagen
△ 24-25 Feb. 1940 Scandinavian conference; declaration of neutrality

Berlin
▲ 7 May 1939 German-Italian (Axis) pact
▲ 27 Sept. 1940 Germany, Italy and Japan sign Tripartite Pact
▲ 17-23 Nov. 1940 Hungary, Rumania and Slovakia join Tripartite Pact

Riga
△ 16 Mar. 1940 Baltic States issue declaration of neutrality

Moscow
▲ 12-21 Aug. 1939 Soviet-German (Molotov-Ribbentrop) non-aggression pact signed 23 Aug.
▲ 7-13 Apr. 1941 Soviet-Japanese Neutrality Pact agreed

Vienna 4 △ 25 Mar. 1941 Yugoslavia joins Tripartite Pact

FR. NORTH AFRICA (13) △ 6-7 Mar. 1941

Cairo

△ 25 Oct.-25 Nov. 1940 Eastern Group Conference (Australia, New Zealand, South Africa and British colonies in Asia and Africa)

Karachi

△ 22 Mar. 1942 Sir Stafford Cripps discusses Indian independence

ETHIOPIA (recaptured by Britain 1941)

ERITREA (occ. by Britain 1941)

ITALIAN SOMALILAND (occ. by Britain 1941)

Indian Ocean

- Allies May 1940
- Allies Dec. 1942
- Axis powers Dec. 1942
- —— Axis expansion by June 1940
- —— Axis expansion by Dec. 1941
- ● Copenhagen declaration of neutrality (1938)
- war conferences:
- ▲ Axis war conferences 1939-42
- △ Allied war conferences 1939-42

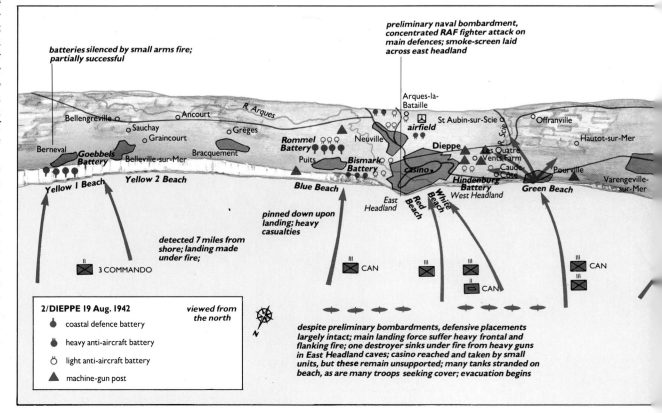

preliminary naval bombardment, concentrated RAF fighter attack on main defences; smoke-screen laid across east headland

batteries silenced by small arms fire; partially successful

pinned down upon landing; heavy casualties

detected 7 miles from shore; landing made under fire;

2/DIEPPE 19 Aug. 1942

viewed from the north

- ◆ coastal defence battery
- ◉ heavy anti-aircraft battery
- ⊙ light anti-aircraft battery
- ▲ machine-gun post

despite preliminary bombardments, defensive placements largely intact; main landing force suffer heavy frontal and flanking fire; one destroyer sinks under fire from heavy guns in East Headland caves; casino reached and taken by small units, but these remain unsupported; many tanks stranded on beach, as are many troops seeking cover; evacuation begins

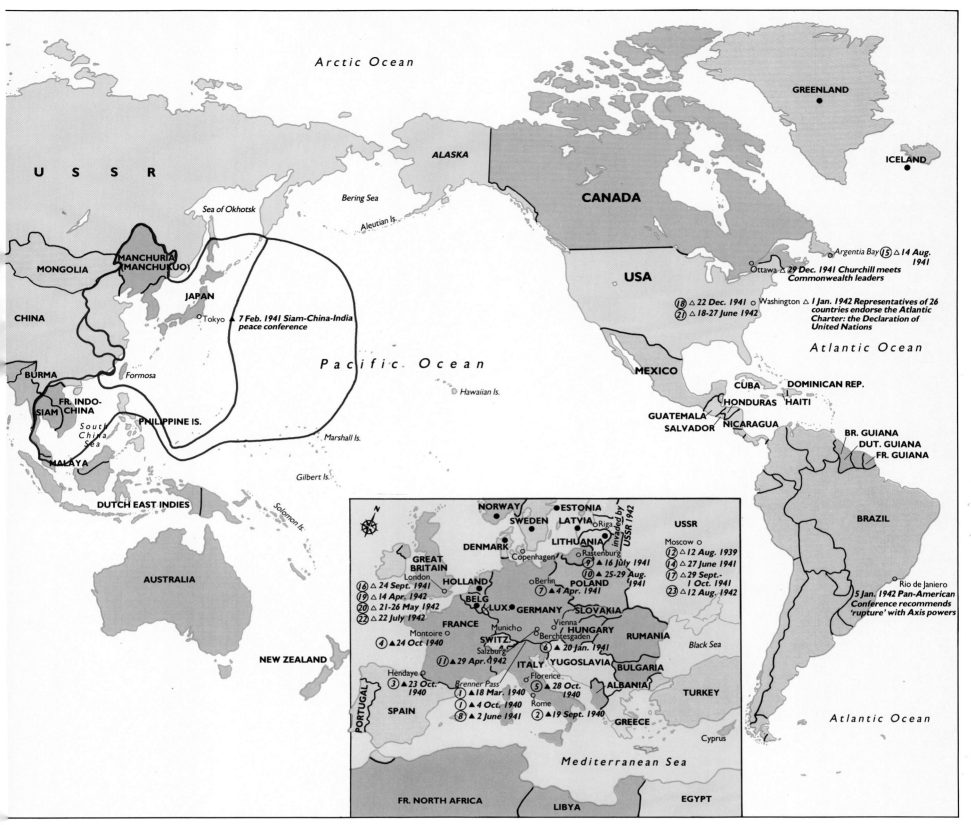

The following map labels and annotations appear on the world map:

Arctic Ocean

GREENLAND

ICELAND

U S S R

ALASKA

CANADA

MONGOLIA

MANCHURIA (MANCHUKUO)

USA

CHINA

JAPAN

○Tokyo ▲ 7 Feb. 1941 Siam-China-India peace conference

Argentia Bay ⑮ △ 14 Aug. 1941

Ottawa △ 29 Dec. 1941 Churchill meets Commonwealth leaders

⑱ △ 22 Dec. 1941 ○ Washington △ 1 Jan. 1942 Representatives of 26 countries endorse the Atlantic Charter: the Declaration of United Nations
㉑ △ 18-27 June 1942

Atlantic Ocean

BURMA

Formosa

FR. INDO-CHINA

SIAM

Pacific Ocean

MEXICO

CUBA   DOMINICAN REP.
HONDURAS   HAITI
GUATEMALA
SALVADOR   NICARAGUA

South China Sea

PHILIPPINE IS.

Hawaiian Is.

BR. GUIANA
DUT. GUIANA
FR. GUIANA

MALAYA

Marshall Is.

DUTCH EAST INDIES

Gilbert Is.

Solomon Is.

BRAZIL

AUSTRALIA

NORWAY   ESTONIA
SWEDEN   LATVIA   ○Riga   USSR
DENMARK   LITHUANIA
GREAT BRITAIN   Copenhagen   ○Rastenburg   Moscow ○
London   ⑨ △ 16 July 1941   ⑫ △ 12 Aug. 1939
⑯ △ 24 Sept. 1941   HOLLAND   ○Berlin   ⑩ △ 25-29 Aug. 1941   ⑭ △ 27 June 1941
⑲ △ 14 Apr. 1942   BELG.   ⑦ ▲ 4 Apr. 1941   ⑰ △ 29 Sept.- 1 Oct. 1941
⑳ △ 21-26 May 1942   LUX.   GERMANY   SLOVAKIA   ㉓ △ 12 Aug. 1942
㉒ △ 22 July 1942   FRANCE   Munich○   Vienna○   HUNGARY
④ ▲ 24 Oct 1940   Berchtesgaden   RUMANIA
Salzburg○   ⑥ △ 20 Jan. 1941   Black Sea
⑪ ▲ 29 Apr. 1942   ITALY   YUGOSLAVIA
Hendaye ○   Florence○   BULGARIA
③ △ 23 Oct. 1940   Brenner Pass   ⑤ ▲ 28 Oct. 1940   ALBANIA
SPAIN   ① ▲ 18 Mar. 1940   TURKEY
① ▲ 4 Oct. 1940   Rome○
⑧ ▲ 2 June 1941   ② ▲ 19 Sept. 1940   GREECE   Cyprus
PORTUGAL   Mediterranean Sea
FR. NORTH AFRICA   LIBYA   EGYPT

New Zealand

Rio de Janeiro ○
5 Jan. 1942 Pan-American Conference recommends 'rupture' with Axis powers

Atlantic Ocean

batteries destroyed; completely successful

St Denis d'Aclon
Ouville-la-Rivière
Longueil
Quiberville
Hess Battery
Vasterival
Orange 1 Beach   Orange 2 Beach

4 COMMANDO

English Channel

THE SECOND WORLD WAR occurred at a time when communications had developed sufficiently to alter the whole nature of diplomacy and decision-making. Air travel made possible personal contact between political leaders at short notice. Both radio and the press enjoyed sufficient resources to make the public accountability of political leaders more important than ever before. Both Hitler and Chamberlain exploited air travel and publicity in the frantic shuttle diplomacy of the months leading up to the outbreak of war. But the unique style of wartime diplomacy – the face-to-face summit conference – was largely Hitler's invention, and reflected his expertise in media manipulation. International diplomacy in the first years of the war (1) was marked by a string of Axis successes: Britain and France had chosen appeasement with Germany at Munich (page 30), giving Hitler the initiative; the Axis pact (7 May 1939) joined the alliance between Germany and Italy, and the Tripartite Pact (27 Sept. 1940) guaranteed mutual support between the European Axis powers and Japan, echoing

the Anti-Communist Pact between the 3 powers of 1936. Hitler succeeded in binding many of the Balkan states to the Tripartite Pact by the end of 1940, but failed to gain Spanish support. But the outstanding German coup was the non-aggression pact with the USSR (23 Aug. 1939), which bought Hitler time to settle his affairs in western Europe before launching Operation Barbarossa (page 56). The USSR agreed a similar pact with Japan 2 months before the German invasion forced her into the Allied camp – an agreement which would be respected until Aug. 1945. Among the Allies in 1939, Britain immediately gained the support of the Commonwealth and by 1940 that of the exiled forces of many occupied European countries. Roosevelt offered support to the British Commonwealth and the USSR in the form of Lend-Lease, prior to the US entry to the war. After Pearl Harbor (Dec. 1941) the two main questions were the division of US effort between the Pacific and European theatres, and the opening of a Second Front in Europe, to relieve pressure on the USSR. In response to Soviet

demands for the latter, a cross-Channel raid was mounted at Dieppe (2). Conceived as a means of gaining intelligence concerning German Channel defences, and as a demonstration of the Western Allies' intention of opening a Second Front in France, the expedition met with disaster. Few of the defensive installations targeted were destroyed and of 6000 British, Canadian, US and Free French troops, 3600 were lost before the landing zone could be evacuated. 106 aircraft, 30 tanks, 33 landing craft and a destroyer were also lost, at a cost of 600 German troops and c. 50 planes. However, the experience proved important in Allied planning for the Normandy invasion (page 152).

Picture right: technological prowess was identified by most of the combatants as of prime importance. A major British advantage over the Germans in the first 2 years of the war was the radar detection system, a key tool in both the Battle of Britain and the Battle of the Atlantic. The Germans quickly developed a similar system, although their early installations (shown here) were enormously clumsy.

AT VARIOUS TIMES BETWEEN APRIL 1941 and March 1943, the initiative in the campaign against Allied shipping changed hands. In general terms, at least superficially, events seemed to favour the Axis cause. As the British Admiralty subsequently noted, the German U-boats never came as close to severing Allied communications across the North Atlantic as in the first twenty days of March 1943. In that month U-boats sank 108 of a total Allied merchantman loss of 120 vessels, not the heaviest monthly loss of the war, but potentially much more serious than previous losses because of the heavy concentration of sinkings amongst escorted merchantmen – 72 in all.

In retrospect, however, the German success of March 1943 can be seen as exceptional, at very best a partial and flawed success achieved against the general trend of the battle of the Atlantic. In this one month the German U-boats achieved their highest monthly return at the expense of convoyed shipping in the course of a campaign that saw a toll of 30 escorted merchantmen sunk by U-boats exceeded in only five months: after March 1943, German monthly returns fell dramatically as the battle turned against the U-boats (page 108).

The long-term trends of the battle of the Atlantic in this phase of the war were such that, by Spring 1942, the German Navy could predict ultimate defeat, even in the midst of a period of unprecedented success. It could do this as a result of its recognition of the coming together of various unfavourable conditions. Outstanding among these was the fact that, after May 1941, the U-boats had been left to carry the burden of the war against shipping without effective support from surface forces, raiders and the *Luftwaffe*. Moreover, after mid-year, an increasing number of U-boats were diverted to the Mediterranean. This reassignment was partly an attempt to prop up a faltering Italy and partly a result of Hitler's determination to avoid a clash with the United States. The latter, despite its neutral status, was intent upon an increasingly belligerent, forward strategy in the North Atlantic.

Thus the second half of 1941 saw the main U-boat effort made in the eastern Atlantic, where British escorts were most heavily concentrated; by the end of the year the U-boats, for the first time, incurred significant losses in attacks on convoys. The American entry into the war in December 1941, however, necessarily provided the Germans with the opportunity to sink merchantmen with little risk off the US eastern seaboard, rather than face the uncertainties of battle in the eastern Atlantic. As a result of first an American, unwillingness and then American difficulties in organizing convoy along the eastern seaboard and in the Caribbean, the U-boats enjoyed massive success in these waters in the first six months of 1942. Thereafter the main combat zone switched back to mid-ocean as the American introduction of convoy forced the U-boats away from the western Atlantic. The field of operations available to the U-boats was already becoming limited.

For nine months after this change the battle between escort and submarine was evenly balanced, at least in terms of losses. Growing submarine numbers, both in commission and operational, ensured that Allied losses remained uncomfortably high. Moreover, the second half of 1942 saw the introduction, on a large scale, of extended U-boat scouting lines; further, German naval intelligence held distinct advantages as a result of its ability to read British naval and maritime signals. But in terms of sinkings per operational boat per

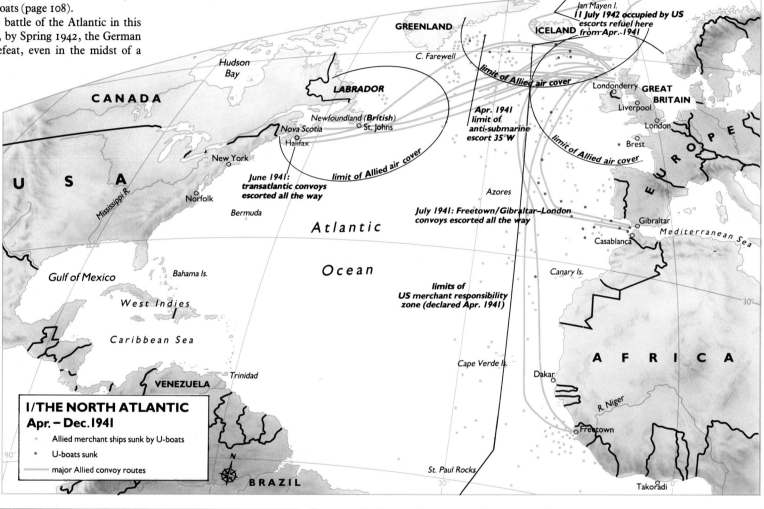

WITH THE UNITED STATES STILL NEUTRAL the burden of convoying ships remained until Dec. 1941 with British and Canadian forces (*1*). As more ships sailed, the organization of convoy operations became ever more complex. 4 separate escort groups had to be co-ordinated for each convoy. U-boat production was rising (*5*), as were operational losses helped by the bombing of U-boat bases on the west coast of France (page 112). Whilst Allied air cover was better than in 1940, there was still a severe shortage of aircraft, and none that could close the air gap: delivery of long-range US Liberators was still 18 months away. Coastal Command (*4*) began to take deliveries of Hudsons and Catalina flying boats in Dec., but detection of U-boats leaving their major operating bases in the Bay of Biscay remained poor: more were detected by sight than radar. However, the use of bases in neutral Iceland, first by the British, then by the Americans (after 11 July 1942) increased the area of the North Atlantic which could be covered by air patrols.

1/THE NORTH ATLANTIC
Apr. – Dec. 1941
- Allied merchant ships sunk by U-boats
- U-boats sunk
— major Allied convoy routes

3/ALLIED MERCHANT SHIPPING LOSSES Apr. 1941 – Mar. 1943 *tonnages (nos. of ships)*

date	U-boat	aircraft	mine	warship raider	merchant raider	E-boat	unknown and other causes	quarterly totals
Apr.-June 1941	885,010 (162)	531,170 (222)	63,408 (25)	none	76,401 (13)	4299 (3)	70,680 (34)	1,630,968 (443)
July-Sept. 1941	377,341 (98)	73,949 (45)	24,931 (19)	7500 (1)	35,904 (6)	10,195 (5)	7798 (7)	537,616 (168)
Oct.-Dec. 1941	342,820 (71)	131,087 (45)	85,304 (28)	6661 (2)	none	21,020 (9)	319,743 (216)	906,635 (371)
Jan.-Mar. 1942	1,341,788 (242)	246,538 (58)	34,183 (18)	19,347 (9)	8591 (2)	951 (1)	202,305 (203)	1,933,703 (533)
Apr.-June 1942	1,739,146 (343)	196,707 (42)	53,730 (23)	100,001 (20)	99,024 (15)	none	13,092 (13)	2,213,703 (456)
July-Sept. 1942	1,505,880 (302)	192,371 (36)	8905 (2)	3188 (1)	76,312 (11)	49,762 (9)	10,147 (4)	1,846,573 (365)
Oct.-Dec. 1942	1,679,393 (272)	63,707 (9)	7767 (8)	7925 (1)	10,698 (2)	20,443 (13)	4556 (2)	1,794,489 (308)
Jan.-Mar. 1943	1,189,833 (208)	90,706 (19)	53,782 (14)	none	7040 (1)	4858 (1)	11,591 (3)	1,357,810 (243)

totals by theatre Apr. 1941-Mar. 1943

Atlantic Ocean	Mediterranean	Indian Ocean	Pacific Ocean
8,631,521 (1727)	1,032,733 (271)	838,511 (231)	1,043,328 (467)

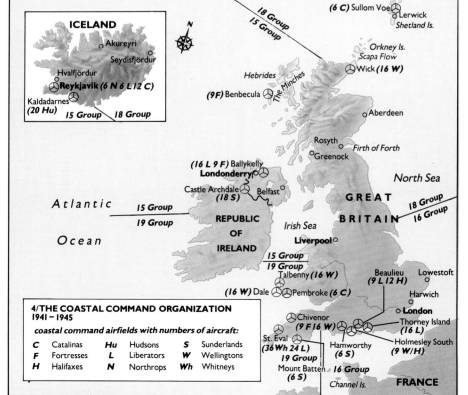

4/THE COASTAL COMMAND ORGANIZATION
1941 – 1945
coastal command airfields with numbers of aircraft:

C Catalinas	Hu Hudsons	S Sunderlands	
F Fortresses	L Liberators	W Wellingtons	
H Halifaxes	N Northrops	Wh Whitneys	

month, the German effort was in decline, and returns after August 1942 would have been very low but for German successes in the Arctic (page 180). There the combination of U-boats, air attack and the presence of major German warships in the Norwegian fjords led to the temporary suspension of Allied convoys to the USSR in late Summer 1942.

This decline of German returns stemmed from the fact that just as U-boat numbers had increased since the start of the war so had British escort strengths. By late 1942, the number of escorts per convoy hovered around the five mark, but the presence of ever more convoys denied German submarines the easy pickings on which they depended for success. In 1942, 962 merchantmen sailing independently were sunk, 840 by German submarines, but as the convoy system was extended, so the U-boats were forced to turn their attention to convoys and battle with escorts that were both individually and collectively far more formidable than in 1940 and 1941. Compounding German difficulties after 1942, moreover, was the fact that British naval intelligence both penetrated German signals security and took steps to ensure the security of its own signals. After January 1943, and with the exception of a brief period when a German procedural change denied the British access to German signals, Ultra intercepts meant the balance of advantage in intelligence matters increasingly favoured the British. The period of temporary British blindness was March 1943, which was in effect the swansong of the U-boats in the Second World War.

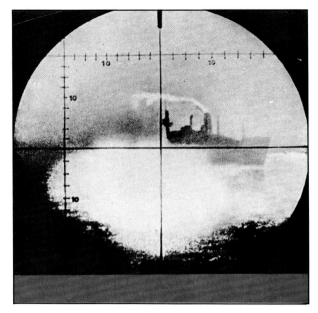

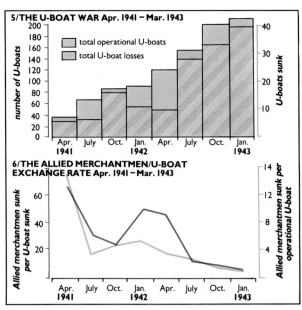

THE ENTRY OF THE US into the war led to an extension of U-boat warfare to the Eastern seaboard of the USA (2). Still unconvinced by the effectiveness of the convoy system, the Americans were later to be persuaded by the huge numbers of losses they suffered. By Feb., however, a reduction in losses from submarine attacks (3) led to growing British confidence that the threat could be mastered. Mar. was to reverse the trend: U-boats sank more than twice as many escorted merchantmen than in any other single month of the war. The passage of convoys HX229 and SC122 (7) saw the hardest fought actions: 40 U-boats sank 141,000 tons of Allied shipping, illustrating the effectiveness of wolf-pack tactics which relied upon an absence of air cover, and upon dense radio traffic with their command in Germany. Radio interception and Ultra decrypts, and continuous air cover, introduced by the Allies in Spring 1943, dramatically increased the security of Allied convoys in the North Atlantic.

Picture above right: an Allied merchantman under attack, viewed through the periscope of a U-boat.

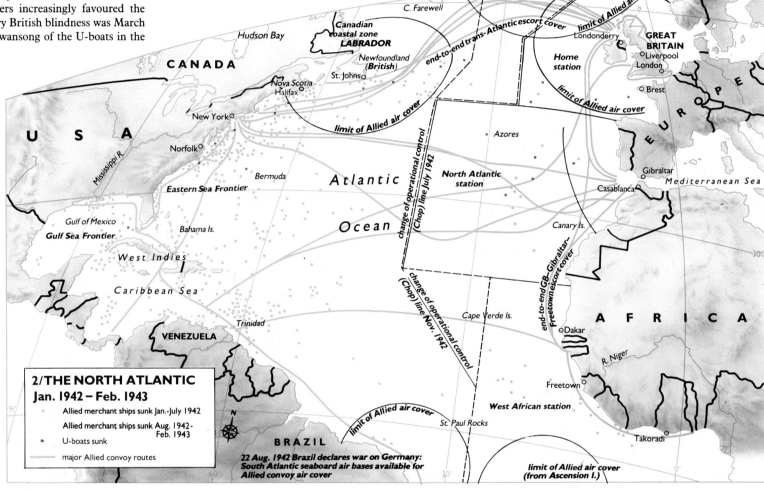

2/THE NORTH ATLANTIC Jan. 1942 – Feb. 1943

— Allied merchant ships sunk Jan.–July 1942
— Allied merchant ships sunk Aug. 1942–Feb. 1943
• U-boats sunk
— major Allied convoy routes

22 Aug. 1942 Brazil declares war on Germany: South Atlantic seaboard air bases available for Allied convoy air cover

5/THE U-BOAT WAR Apr. 1941 – Mar. 1943
total operational U-boats
total U-boat losses

6/THE ALLIED MERCHANTMEN/U-BOAT EXCHANGE RATE Apr. 1941 – Mar. 1943

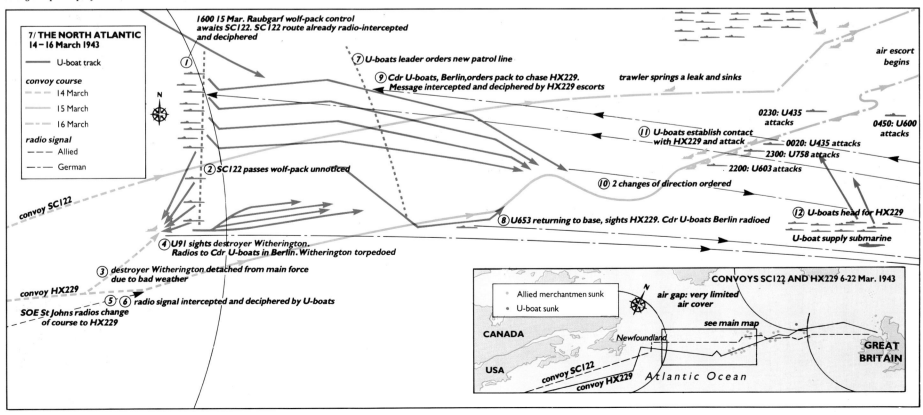

7/THE NORTH ATLANTIC 14 – 16 March 1943

— U-boat track
convoy course
— 14 March
— 15 March
— 16 March
radio signal
— — Allied
— · — German

1600 15 Mar. Raubgarf wolf-pack control awaits SC122. SC122 route already radio-intercepted and deciphered

⑦ U-boats leader orders new patrol line
⑨ Cdr U-boats, Berlin, orders pack to chase HX229. Message intercepted and deciphered by HX229 escorts

trawler springs a leak and sinks

air escort begins

0230: U435 attacks
0450: U600 attacks
0020: U435 attacks
2300: U758 attacks
2200: U603 attacks

⑪ U-boats establish contact with HX229 and attack

② SC122 passes wolf-pack unnoticed

⑩ 2 changes of direction ordered

⑧ U653 returning to base, sights HX229. Cdr U-boats Berlin radioed

⑫ U-boats head for HX229

U-boat supply submarine

④ U91 sights destroyer Witherington. Radios to Cdr U-boats in Berlin. Witherington torpedoed

③ destroyer Witherington detached from main force due to bad weather

convoy SC122

convoy HX229

⑤ ⑥ radio signal intercepted and deciphered by U-boats

SOE St Johns radios change of course to HX229

CONVOYS SC122 AND HX229 6-22 Mar. 1943

• Allied merchantmen sunk
• U-boat sunk

air gap: very limited air cover

see main map

CANADA
USA
convoy SC122
convoy HX229
Atlantic Ocean
GREAT BRITAIN

THE EARLY SUCCESSES IN WAR IN EUROPE gave Nazi leaders the opportunity to begin the building of what they called the 'New Order' – a redrawing of the boundaries of Europe to establish a European states system with Germany as the dominant imperial power. Germany was to become the new Rome, ruling Europe from the ethnic heartland, either through direct annexation (Austria, Bohemia-Moravia and Western Poland), or through satellite states (Ukraine, Slovakia, Croatia, Norway, Holland) with their own governments and Nazi commissioners in residence. The other major states, either through alliance or defeat, would retain a restricted autonomy in a German-dominated Europe. The wartime administration of Europe already reflected these distinctions, though the requirements of war left much of the continent under formal military control. The New Order was to be constructed with the peace.

This order was effectively an economic as well as a political one. The economic resources of the whole continent were to be regulated or influenced from Berlin; Germany would become the major industrial state, selling its goods to the more agrarian, primary resource producing states on its borders. A large, new central-eastern industrial region stretching from Silesia to the Black Sea would provide Germany with high living standards, and change the balance of the European industrial economy. The German domination and exploitation of the European economy became accomplished fact by the middle of the war

(page 202). Conquered Europe gave 90 billion marks to the German war effort; a stream of vital materials, food and labour flowed into the Reich. German businesses, state and private, organized the takeover of much of European industry.

It was Hitler's view that the war was a final war for the future, not only of Germany, but of European culture, and that it should be fought to the bitter end. For this reason he ordered the full use of economic resources in Germany from the start of the conflict. By mid-1941, almost two-thirds of the industrial workforce was engaged in filling war orders – more than in Britain. Living standards were reduced sharply from the very start, with rationing being introduced for almost all major consumer goods and food. The rationing system worked well and black-marketeering was controlled through draconian punishments for both seller and receiver of illicit goods. Consumption levels in Germany dropped much lower than in Britain or the USA. By the end of the war, over half the German workforce was made up of women, and economic life was dominated by war production and the impact of strategic bombing. The German arms industries performed poorly in the early years of the war, but the rationalization of industry enforced by Albert Speer (from 1942 onwards) trebled arms output in two years. In 1943, Goebbels called for all-out war.

By this time the practical reality of Hitler's cultural and racial vision was being fully felt by the victims of Nazi

repression. The ethos of the 'Final Solution' to the European 'Jewish problem' (page 92) had been extended to the populations of the conquered eastern territories: large numbers of Poles, Balts, Ukrainians and other peoples of the western Soviet Union were ruthlessly wiped out. Those who survived would be used as slave labour or exiled to Siberia, and their lands colonized by German settlers.

As the war progressed, Hitler drew more of its conduct under his direct control. In 1942, he took over command of his armies; in the same year, he began to direct war production and weapons development more closely. No decision could be taken without direct reference to Hitler, or, more often, to one of his immediate subordinates, Bormann, Keitel and Lammers – the 'Committee of Three'. Popular enthusiasm for the Party began to wane as the war went sour, but ordinary Germans kept their belief in the *Führer*, in Hitler's ability to save them from disaster, for much longer. The myth of the *Führer* only began to pall after Stalingrad (page 104) and Hamburg (page 112). By then it was fear of the Russians that kept many Germans fighting, as well as fear of the SS, which used the war crisis to increase its power in Germany with savage policing methods. The more brutal the Nazi movement became, the less attractive many Germans found it. As the German New Order collapsed around them, the German people became resigned and apathetic. They called the moment of defeat 'Hour Zero'.

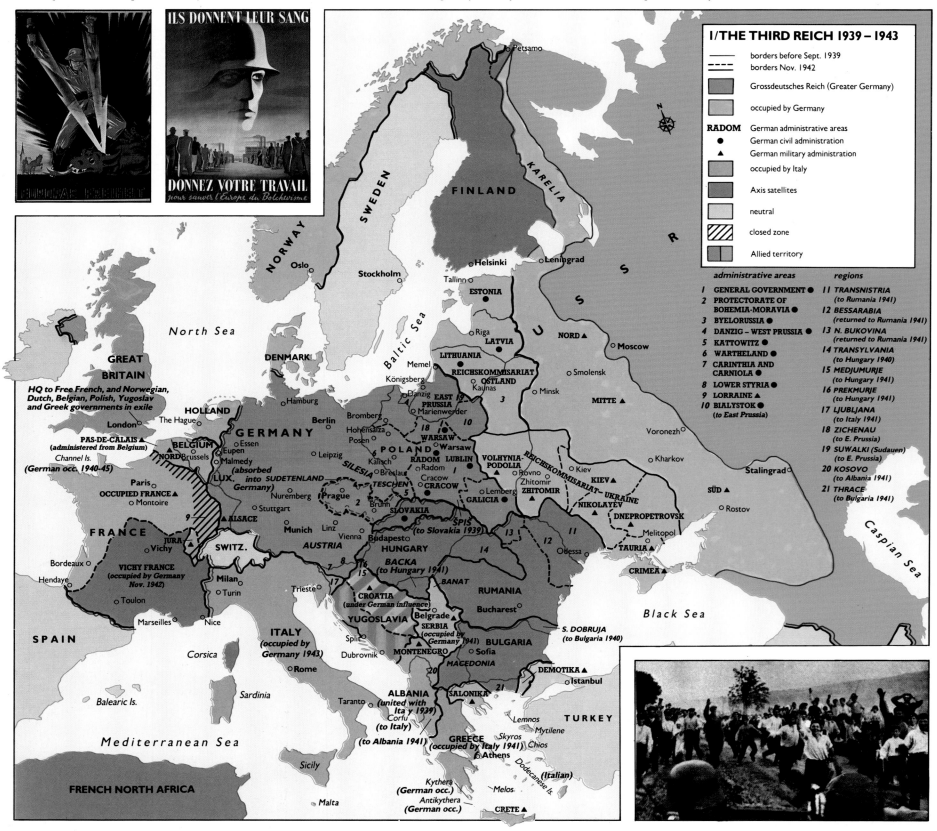

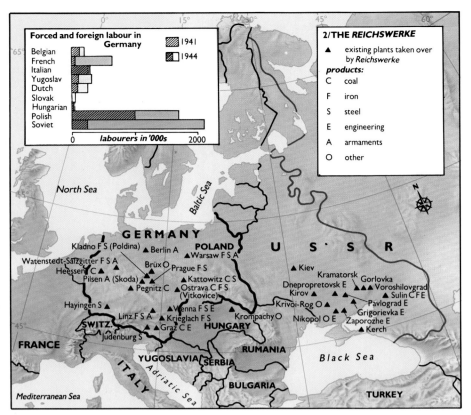

Forced and foreign labour in Germany
☐ 1941 ▨ 1944

- Belgian
- French
- Italian
- Yugoslav
- Dutch
- Slovak
- Hungarian
- Polish
- Soviet

0 — labourers in '000s — 2000

2/THE REICHSWERKE

▲ existing plants taken over by Reichswerke

products:
- C coal
- F iron
- S steel
- E engineering
- A armaments
- O other

(Map labels:) North Sea · GERMANY · POLAND · U S S R · Baltic Sea · Kladno F S (Poldina) · Berlin A · Warsaw F S A · Watenstedt-Salzgitter F S A · Heessen · Brüx F S · Prague F S · Kiev · Kramatorsk · Gorlovka · Pilsen A (Skoda) · Pegnitz C · Kattowitz C S · Ostrava C F S (Vitkovice) · Dnepropetrovsk E · Voroshilovgrad · Sulin C F E · Kirov · Krivoi-Rog O · Pavlograd E · Hayingen S · Vienna F S E · Linz F S A · Krieglach F S · Graz C E · Krompachy O · Nikopol O E · Grigorievka E · Zaporozhe E · Kerch · Judenburg S · SWITZ. · FRANCE · HUNGARY · YUGOSLAVIA · SERBIA · RUMANIA · ITALY · Black Sea · Mediterranean Sea · Adriatic Sea · BULGARIA · TURKEY

1 Weser-Ems
2 East Hannover
3 North Westphalia
4 South Hannover-Brunswick
5 Essen
6 Düsseldorf
7 South Westphalia
8 Kurhassen
9 Thuringia
10 Cologne-Aachen
11 Moselland
12 Hesse-Nassau
13 Main-Franconia
14 Bayreuth
15 Westmark
16 Baden
17 Wuttemberg-Hohenzollern
18 Franconia
19 Swabia
20 Munich-Upper Bavaria
21 Schleswig-Holstein
22 Hamburg
23 Mecklenburg
24 Pomerania
25 Berlin
26 Magdeburg-Anhalt
27 Mark Brandenburg
28 Halle-Mersaburg
29 Saxony
30 Lower Silesia
31 Sudetenland
32 Upper Danube
33 Lower Danube
34 Tyrol-Vorarlberg
35 Salzburg
36 Carinthia
37 Styria
38 Vienna
39 Danzig-W. Prussia
40 East Prussia
41 Wartheland
42 Upper Silesia

(Map labels:) Baltic Sea · DENMARK · North Sea · NORDSEE · NORDOST · Neuengamme A G · Hamburg · OSTSEE · WEICHSEL · Danzig · MITTE · Ravensbrück A · Warsaw · Sachsenhausen A G · WARTHE · POLAND · SPREE · Berlin · WEST · GERMANY · ELBE · Buchenwald A G · Gross-Rosen G · Lublin A · Essen · FULDA-WERRA · SÜDOST · RHEIN-WESTMARK · MAIN · Flossenbürg G · BÖHMEN-MÄHREN · Auschwitz A G · SÜDWEST · SÜD · DONAU · Natzweiler G · Dachau · Munich · Mauthausen A · ALPENLAND · Vienna

3/THE NAZI PARTY AT WAR

— SS regions/military regions (Wehrkreise)
— Gaue (listed above)
● sites of divisions 81-125 of general SS

major SS enterprises:
▲ concentration camp
A armaments production
G gravel and stone-working

By 1941, GERMAN RULE extended into fifteen European countries; only neutral governments in Sweden, Spain, Switzerland and Portugal retained any real independence (1). German officials and leaders began to plan the New Order in Europe from early on in the war. Conquered Russia was to be organized as a series of provinces of the German empire, with a rump Siberian state for the Russian population, kept out of Europe by a series of large German garrisons. Conquered populations would be resettled, Germanized or exterminated. Europe was to be linked by a network of new motorways spreading from Paris to the Crimea (4). The organization of the Party, divided into regions (Gaue) was extended into the occupied territories on Germany's borders. Greater Germany had its own SS organization and was also incorporated into the German economic administration (3). All the heavy industry of the occupied areas was taken over, the bulk of it by the state-run Reichswerke Hermann Goering, a giant holding-company employing one million people, with assets all over Europe, from the iron-ore fields of Lorraine to the steel mills of the Ukraine (2). Europe was exploited as a source of raw materials and labour. Some workers came willingly, lured by higher wages and regular employment, but most were compelled to work in Germany (2). By 1944, 6 million foreign workers helped to treble German war production (5).

Pictures below left: Nazi propaganda showed peoples such as the Ukrainians greeting their Nazi liberators. Above left: Bolshevism was identified as the reason for the war, the Germans presented as heroic freedom fighters.

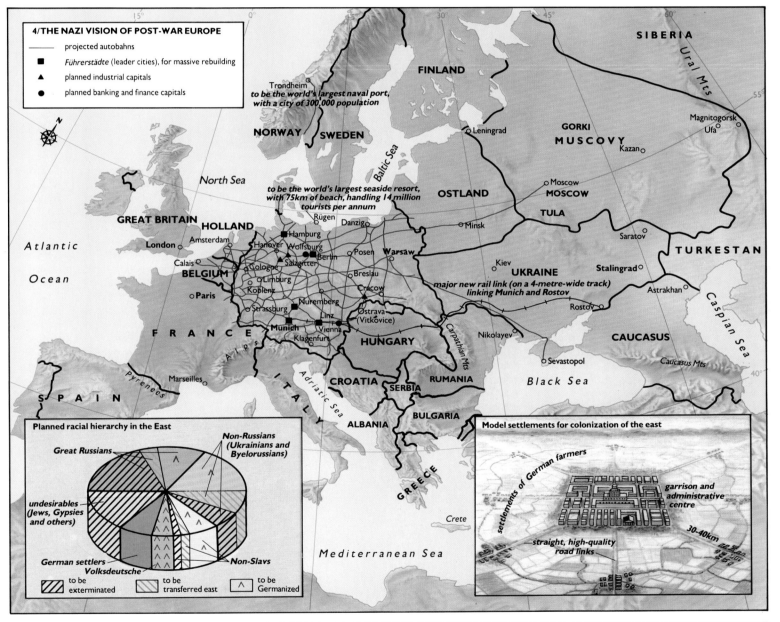

4/THE NAZI VISION OF POST-WAR EUROPE

— projected autobahns
■ Führerstädte (leader cities), for massive rebuilding
▲ planned industrial capitals
● planned banking and finance capitals

(Map labels:) SIBERIA · Ural Mts · FINLAND · NORWAY · SWEDEN · Trondheim *to be the world's largest naval port, with a city of 300,000 population* · Leningrad · GORKI · MUSCOVY · Magnitogorsk · Ufa · Kazan · North Sea · Baltic Sea · Moscow · MOSCOW · OSTLAND · TULA · Rügen *to be the world's largest seaside resort, with 75km of beach, handling 14 million tourists per annum* · Danzig · Minsk · Saratov · GREAT BRITAIN · HOLLAND · London · Amsterdam · Hamburg · Wolfsburg · Salzgitter · Berlin · Posen · Warsaw · Hanover · Calais · Cologne · Limburg · Koblenz · Breslau · Kiev · UKRAINE · Stalingrad · TURKESTAN · Paris · Nuremberg · Cracow · *major new rail link (on a 4-metre-wide track) linking Munich and Rostov* · Astrakhan · BELGIUM · Strassburg · Ostrava (Vitkovice) · Linz · Vienna · Rostov · Caspian Sea · FRANCE · Munich · Klagenfurt · HUNGARY · Nikolayev · CAUCASUS · Alps · Pyrenees · Marseilles · Adriatic Sea · CROATIA · SERBIA · RUMANIA · Sevastopol · Caucasus Mts · Black Sea · SPAIN · ITALY · BULGARIA · ALBANIA · GREECE · Crete · Mediterranean Sea

Planned racial hierarchy in the East

Great Russians · Non-Russians (Ukrainians and Byelorussians) · undesirables (Jews, Gypsies and others) · German settlers · Volksdeutsche · Non-Slavs

▨ to be exterminated
▨ to be transferred east
∧ to be Germanized

Model settlements for colonization of the east

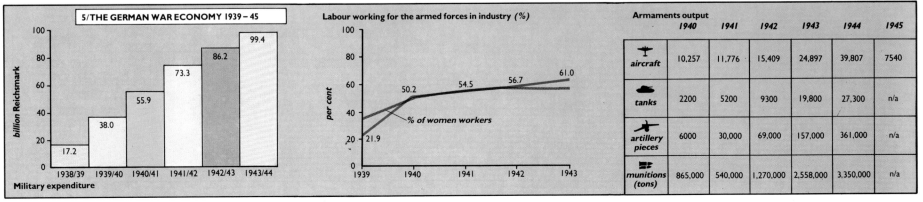

settlements of German farmers · garrison and administrative centre · straight, high-quality road links · 30-40km

---

5/THE GERMAN WAR ECONOMY 1939–45

billion Reichsmark

Year	Value
1938/39	17.2
1939/40	38.0
1940/41	55.9
1941/42	73.3
1942/43	86.2
1943/44	99.4

Military expenditure

Labour working for the armed forces in industry (%)

per cent
21.9 · 50.2 · 54.5 · 56.7 · 61.0
% of women workers

1939 · 1940 · 1941 · 1942 · 1943

Armaments output

	1940	1941	1942	1943	1944	1945
aircraft	10,257	11,776	15,409	24,897	39,807	7540
tanks	2200	5200	9300	19,800	27,300	n/a
artillery pieces	6000	30,000	69,000	157,000	361,000	n/a
munitions (tons)	865,000	540,000	1,270,000	2,558,000	3,350,000	n/a

German persecutions 1933~1945

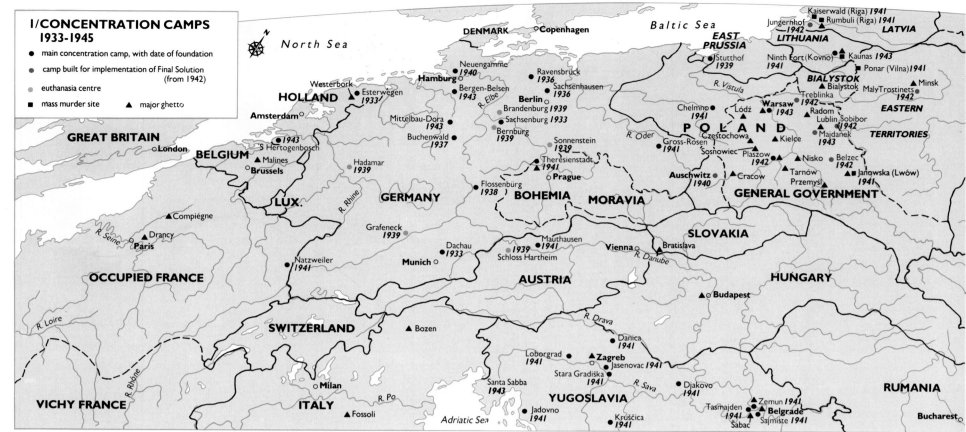

1/CONCENTRATION CAMPS 1933-1945

- ● main concentration camp, with date of foundation
- ● camp built for implementation of Final Solution (from 1942)
- ○ euthanasia centre
- ■ mass murder site ▲ major ghetto

FROM HIS VERY FIRST DAYS as German Chancellor in 1933, Adolf Hitler introduced laws which victimized and persecuted political opponents, the socially 'undesirable' and various racial groups. Outstanding among his victims were the Jews. Within two years, Germany's half million Jews had been isolated from German life, and driven out of their professions. As many as 250,000 found refuge abroad, including 50,000 who were given a haven in Britain. But for those who remained, the future was one of continuing persecution. In November 1938, (Kristallnacht), a hundred Jews were killed, and many synagogues burned down, in co-ordinated attacks on Jews and Jewish property throughout Germany and Austria. The German occupation of Bohemia and Moravia in March 1939 brought a further half million Jews under German rule. But as they too were severely discriminated against, and sought to flee, fewer and fewer governments were willing to take in Jewish refugees.

With the German conquest of Poland (September 1939), a further two million Jews came under German rule. Suddenly, the circumstances of war enabled the Germans to move from persecution to murder. Hundreds of Polish Jews were killed in the streets. In several towns, men, women and children were locked into local synagogues, which were then set on fire. Following this mass murder of several thousand Polish Jews (September–October 1939), the Germans forced the survivors to live in deliberately sealed-off quarters of the towns, which they called ghettos, a reference to mediaeval Jewish life. The

last European ghettos had been abolished by Napoleon. Now they were re-imposed, with added torments: barbed wire, cruelly low rations, and the death penalty for any Jew who tried to leave, or for any non-Jew who tried to bring food to those inside. By mid-1940, thousands were dying of starvation every month in ghettos throughout German-occupied Poland.

From the Summer of 1940, following the German conquest of France, Belgium, Holland, Norway, Denmark and, in the Spring of 1941, Yugoslavia and Greece, hundreds of thousands more Jews came under German rule, and were discriminated against. Then, in June 1941, with the German invasion of the Soviet Union, the mass murder began, on Russian soil, of more than a million Jews. They were killed by specially-trained German murder squads (Einsatszgruppen), often helped by local militia and collaborators. Beginning in June 1941, and continuing for more than a year, Jews were taken to mass murder sites just outside the large cities. Hundreds of thousands of Jews were machine-gunned at these sites, of which the largest and most notorious were Ponar (outside Vilna), Rumbuli (outside Riga), the Ninth Fort (outside Kovno) and Babi Yar (outside Kiev).

At the end of 1941 Hitler and the SS decided to destroy Jewish life throughout Europe – Endloesung or the 'Final Solution'. They set up death camps, most located on Polish soil, to which every Jew in the region would be deported, as well as Jews from western Europe, and then killed on arrival in

specially-designed gas vans and gas chambers. The first death camp was opened at Chelmno (December 1941), followed within a few months by further death camps at Belzec, Sobibor, Treblinka and Maly Trostinets. By 1945, more than 2.5 million Jews had been murdered in these five camps.

For non-Jewish victims of Nazi persecution – Communists and homosexuals among them – terrible tortures had been devised since 1933 in a series of concentration camps, of which Sachsenhausen, Buchenwald and Dachau, in Germany itself, were among the first. Jews were also sent to these camps, and many were murdered there. Mauthausen, in Austria, Natzweiler in Alsace, and Stutthof in Poland, were particularly notorious. In the Summer of 1940 the Germans set up a punishment camp specifically for Poles, at Auschwitz. In the Summer of 1942 this camp was extended, and gas chambers built, so that Jews could be brought there from all over Europe. Hundreds of thousands of Jews were sent to the barracks at Auschwitz, and became slave labourers. But as many as two million, mostly women and children, old people and the sick, were gassed within a few hours of their arrival at the camp. Several hundred thousand gypsies were also murdered at Auschwitz, and at some of the other death camps.

By the end of 1943, most of the death camps had completed their horrific work and been closed down. The gas chambers at Auschwitz, and at another camp in Poland, Majdanek, continued almost until the arrival of the Soviet Army. Those

3/THE PERSECUTION OF THE GYPSIES 1939-1945

- ● concentration camp with gypsy prisoners
- ● extermination camp with gypsy prisoners
- 4000 estimated gypsy deaths 1939–45

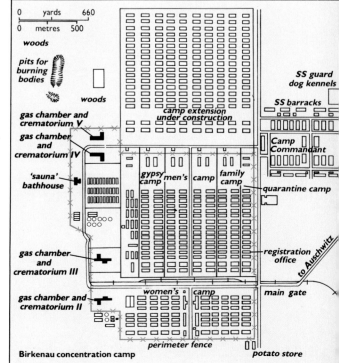

Birkenau concentration camp

THE CONCENTRATION CAMP SYSTEM (*1*) was established in Germany in 1933. With each German conquest it was extended, first to Austria, then to Poland, France, Yugoslavia, western Russia, the Baltic and the Ukraine. The camps were often operated by local collaborators. As well as death camps, the concentration camp system, controlled centrally from Berlin, included camps into which Jews were rounded up from their homes prior to deportation. Drancy in Paris, Malines north of Brussels, and Westerbork in Holland were the largest such holding camps in western Europe; Jews were sent from them to their deaths in Auschwitz and elsewhere. At Theresienstadt, a 'model' ghetto set up by the Germans within Bohemia, hundreds of thousands of German, Austrian and Czechoslovak Jews were confined for as long as two years, before being sent to Auschwitz and Maly Trostinets. The number of Jews whom the Nazis planned to kill (*2*) was set out at a secret conference held in Jan. 1942 at the Wannsee in Berlin. This conference also marked out those Jews not yet under German rule – in Britain and Spain – whom it was hoped would eventually be deported to the death camps. The French total included the Sephardic Jews of French North Africa.

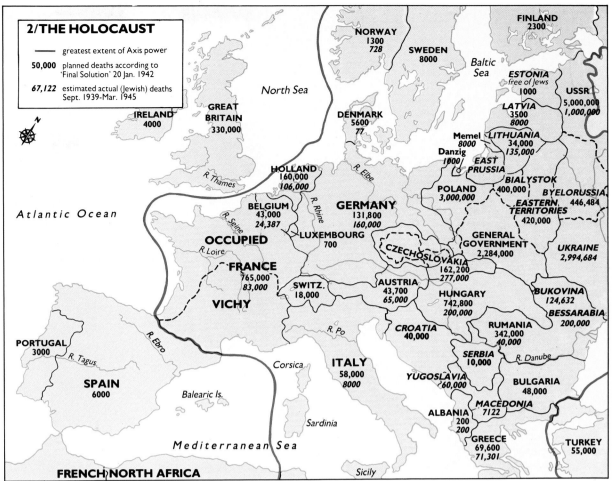

2/THE HOLOCAUST

- —— greatest extent of Axis power
- **50,000** planned deaths according to 'Final Solution' 20 Jan. 1942
- **67,122** estimated actual (Jewish) deaths Sept. 1939-Mar. 1945

FINLAND 2300
NORWAY 1300 / 728
SWEDEN 8000
ESTONIA free of Jews 1000
USSR 5,000,000 / 1,000,000
LATVIA 3500 / 8000
Memel 8000
LITHUANIA 34,000 / 135,000
Danzig 1000
EAST PRUSSIA
GREAT BRITAIN 330,000
IRELAND 4000
DENMARK 5600 / 77
HOLLAND 160,000 / 106,000
BELGIUM 43,000 / 24,387
GERMANY 131,800 / 160,000
LUXEMBOURG 700
OCCUPIED FRANCE 765,000 / 83,000
POLAND 3,000,000 / 400,000
BIALYSTOK 400,000
BYELORUSSIA
EASTERN TERRITORIES 446,484 / 420,000
GENERAL GOVERNMENT
CZECHOSLOVAKIA 162,200 / 277,000
UKRAINE 2,284,000 / 2,994,684
SWITZ. 18,000
AUSTRIA 43,700 / 65,000
HUNGARY 742,800 / 200,000
BUKOVINA 124,632
BESSARABIA 200,000
VICHY
PORTUGAL 3000
SPAIN 6000
ITALY 58,000 / 8000
CROATIA 40,000
SERBIA 10,000
RUMANIA 342,000 / 40,000
YUGOSLAVIA 60,000
BULGARIA 48,000
MACEDONIA 7122
ALBANIA 200 / 200
GREECE 69,600 / 71,301
TURKEY 55,000
FRENCH NORTH AFRICA

still alive in the slave labour barracks at Auschwitz and elsewhere as the Soviets approached, were sent by the Germans on marches westwards. Tens of thousands, emaciated and starving, died or were shot down on these death marches. Those who survived were brought to concentration camps in Germany, among them Dachau and Belsen. By the time the British and US forces reached these camps, tens of thousands more had died of starvation.

The total number of Jews who were murdered between 1939 and 1945 was in the region of 6 million. Hundreds of thousands of gypsies were also murdered, as were more than a hundred thousand Germans and Poles who had been judged by the German euthanasia programme to be too mentally ill or physically retarded to be allowed to live. Three million non-Jewish Polish civilians and a million Serbs, as well as hundreds of thousands of slave labourers from western Europe and the Balkans, were also killed by the Germans, or died of hunger and ill-treatment during the war years. As many as 4 million Soviet prisoners of war were murdered by the Germans; some were killed at Auschwitz, but most were left to die, confined in camps without food or medical help.

More than any other single factor, the Nazi policies of persecution and extermination of Jews and other groups provoked global condemnation, which found expression during the war in the establishment of the War Crimes Commission.

Picture below: suitcases belonging to Jewish deportees, who were sent to Auschwitz or Birkenau death camps under the pretext of resettlement. The systematic Jewish extermination *programme had industrial benefits for Germany: the victims' clothes, glasses, shoes, hair and gold fillings were all collected for resale or reuse in Germany.*

SEVERAL COUNTRIES under German influence refused to deport their Jews, despite German pressure: Finland, Italy (before German occupation in 1943), and Hungary (until German occupation in 1944). In Bulgaria, the King, the Church and the Parliament saved 48,000 Jews from death by not allowing them to be taken away. Gypsies (*3*) were another ethnic group singled out by the Nazis for deportation, slave labour, and death by gassing. Many were sent to the Jewish ghettos. Others were sent direct to the death camps. Yet more were shot in German-occupied Russia by *Einsatzgruppen* (*5*), Special Task Forces whose principal victims were more than a million Jews living in this region. *Einsatzgruppen* operated continually from the first day (22 June 1941) of the German invasion of Russia until well into 1942. Divided into 4 main groups, they followed behind the German Army, killing all the Jews, Bolshevik 'Commissars' and other 'undesirables' they could find in

every city, town, village and hamlet throughout western Russia and the Ukraine. At Babi Yar, near Kiev, their meticulous records listed 33,771 Jews killed within three days. The largest number of Jews to be killed in a single camp, over 2 million, were murdered at Auschwitz (*4*, operating from mid-1942 to end-1944). The camp also housed hundreds of thousands of Jewish slave labourers, and gypsies. Four gas chambers operated continuously to kill the deportees, who came from as far away as France, Norway, Italy, Greece, and the Aegean islands of Kos and Rhodes. Hundreds of thousands of those selected on arrival for slave labour died at their severe work, or were gassed when too ill to work. In the Auschwitz region, vast factory installations, including the synthetic oil factory at Monowitz-Buna, employed slave labourers from Auschwitz as well as Allied prisoners of war. In Jan. 1945, the slave labourers in the region were evacuated westward in a series of death marches.

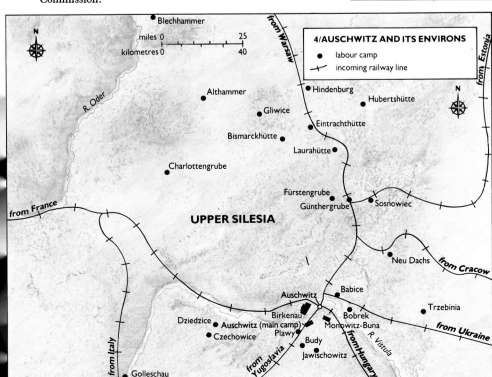

4/AUSCHWITZ AND ITS ENVIRONS

- • labour camp
- ┼┼ incoming railway line

miles 0 — 25
kilometres 0 — 40

Blechhammer
Althammer
Gliwice
Hindenburg
Hubertshütte
Mezhno
Eintrachthütte
Bismarckhütte
Laurahütte
Charlottengrube
R. Oder
Fürstengrube
Günthergrube
Sosnowiec
from France
UPPER SILESIA
Neu Dachs
Babice
from Cracow
Auschwitz
Birkenau
Dziedzice
Auschwitz (main camp)
Monowitz-Buna
Czechowice
Plawy
Bobrek
Budy
Trzebinia
from Ukraine
R. Vistula
Jawischowitz
from Hungary
from Yugoslavia
from Italy
Golleschau

5/THE *EINSATZGRUPPEN* IN EASTERN EUROPE

- ▨ area of *Einsatzgruppe* activity
- ■ location of *Einsatzgruppe*
- • location of *Einsatz* commando group
- **91,721** total number of deaths reported during Spring 1942

Krasnogvardeisk
Mezhno
Kikerino
Pesye
Novoselye
Pskov
USSR
Smolensk
R. Don
Starobielsk
EINSATZGRUPPE A **248,468**
Riga
R. Dvina
EINSATZGRUPPE B **71,555**
Minsk
EINSATZGRUPPE C **105,988**
Poltava
Taganrog
Baltic Sea
Kiev
Dnieper
Zhitomir
Novo-Ukrainka
Sea of Azov
U K R A I N E
Zwiabel
EINSATZGRUPPE D **91,721**
Pervomaisk
Nikolayev
Warsaw
Ananyev
POLAND
Lwów (Lemberg)
R. Dniester
Jassy
R. Prut
Piatra Neamt
Black Sea
CZECHOSLOVAKIA
RUMANIA
HUNGARY
R. Danube
TURKEY

furthest line of German advance

BYELORUSSIA
R. Dvina
Smolensk ▲
UKRAINE
Babi Yar (Kiev) 1941
Shitomir ▲
Drobitsky Yar (Kharkov) 1941
Bar 1941
R. Bug
Bałanovka 1942
R. Dniester
Edineţi 1941
R. Prut
Black Sea

Resistance in western Europe 1940 ~ 1945

THE SPEED AND COMPLETENESS of the German victory in western Europe in 1940 resulted in the absence of any significant plans for resistance to occupation. Shocked by military defeat and cowed by the full weight of the Nazis' well-honed forces of repression, opposition to German rule was initially unco-ordinated and small scale. Instead, large sections of the population sought to conform to the new status quo and endeavoured to recreate a form of pre-war normality. In contrast, the Nazi parties of the newly conquered countries anticipated that the new conditions would enable them to seize power. But even trusted leaders such as Quisling in Norway and Mussert in Holland were allowed by the German occupiers to exercise only limited political control. Nevertheless, the rewards of outright collaboration proved too strong for many to resist, with hundreds of thousands volunteering to work for the occupying forces. Consciences were salved to a great extent by Germany's attack upon the Soviet Union in 1941, and for those who enlisted in the Waffen-SS collaboration became less of a betrayal of nationalist ideals and was elevated to the level of a 'crusade' against Communism.

Arguably the first acts of resistance were offered by those who fled from occupation in order to maintain the struggle from exile. The heads of state of Holland, Norway, Yugoslavia, Greece and Luxembourg and the Belgian, Czechoslovak and Polish governments-in-exile became the figureheads behind which their nations' resistance could develop. The need to secure a widely accepted leadership was highlighted by the problems encountered by General de Gaulle, the Free French leader, whose most senior governmental position had been a brief term as Under-Secretary of State for War.

However, the impact of the exiled forces on the war constituted far more than just a moral stimulant to resisters who had stayed at home. Polish armies in exile fought in Norway, the Soviet Union, North Africa, Italy and the Low Countries

(page 95). Polish, Czech, French and Belgian pilots played an important role during the Battle of Britain, while the adherence of the Norwegian, Danish and Dutch merchant marine to the Allied cause helped offset British losses sustained as a result of U-boat attacks. Similarly, substantial French and Czech forces made significant contributions to Allied campaigns in the Mediterranean and north-west Europe.

Meanwhile, the initial acts of resistance in occupied Europe were of necessity primarily passive. Members of the occupying forces were 'cold-shouldered' by the civilian population, who further expressed their sentiments with a proliferation of anti-German graffiti. More overt acts soon followed and, in spite of the apparent omnipotence and omniscience of the German security forces, public demonstrations were made. In Holland in 1941 a general strike was called to protest against anti-semitic and anti-labour legislation. A year later, Norwegian teachers refused *en masse* to sign a declaration of allegiance to the new regime. Ideological and cultural resistance was also maintained by a clandestine press that flourished in all of the occupied countries. France, Poland and Holland each produced over a thousand illegal newspaper titles and tens of millions of books, pamphlets and newsheets combated Nazi propaganda throughout occupied Europe. Much of the news was acquired from BBC radio broadcasts which were banned by the German authorities; listening to these was, in itself, a punishable act of resistance.

Increased self-confidence amongst resisters within the occupied countries and the establishment of Allied organizations such as the Special Operations Executive (SOE) to assist them (page 84) resulted in increased subversive activity. SOE and, later, the Soviet NKVD and the American OSS, provided trained agents to co-ordinate groups and instruct them in the use of explosives and firearms. More importantly, complex wireless and courier links were forged with the 'free' world,

enabling resistance to be integrated into Allied strategy. Invaluable work was carried out on escape lines that helped fugitive Allied servicemen and refugees to the safety of neutral Spain, Switzerland and Sweden. While this made a useful contribution to the Allied war effort by allowing highly trained aircrew to return to active service, the resistance played an even more important role in the Second Front. Widespread attacks were made on French road, rail and telephone communications in support of the Normandy invasion and sabotage was carried out as far afield as Scandinavia to prevent German reinforcements reaching the front. Furthermore, their efforts forced significant German resources to be diverted to internal security tasks at a time when they were badly needed elsewhere.

Less successful were over-ambitious attempts made by resistance groups to engage German forces in open conflict rather than hit-and-run guerrilla warfare. The crushing of the Vercors and Warsaw uprisings in 1944 (page 170) contrasted with the achievements attained in France, Belgium and Italy when the resistance acted in close concert with advancing Allied ground units.

But the resistance's greatest triumphs were not in moonlight raids on enemy communications nor the highly emotional scenes of liberation in Paris, Brussels or Genoa, but in the consistent flow of vital intelligence to the Allies throughout the war. One network alone, the Belgian *Service Clarence* (page 82), had 1500 agents and supplied SIS with a range of information from bomb damage in Berlin to concentration camps in Poland, and from daily troop movements to railway traffic. Similarly, Danish and Polish cells secured important details of German V-weapons; the Poles also relayed intelligence from agents operating behind the German front as far east as the Caucasus, while French agents passed crucial intelligence to Allied planners on German defences and troop movements in Normandy.

I/RESISTANCE IN WESTERN EUROPE 1940–1945

post-war trials of collaborators:

+   executed   ▪   imprisoned

△   strike or industrial action

▽   mass demonstration

▪   SS/SD base

●   detention centre

✸   major reprisal

resistance organizations listed below

BELGIUM
Front de l'Indépendence *(Communist)*; L'Armée Secréte; Légion Belge; Groupe Mobile des Partisans, **+ 230 ▪ c. 50,000**

FRANCE
Maquis *(originally forced-labour evaders, later a general term for partisan secret armies; in occupied France)* OCM *(former Army officers)*, Libération-Nord *(trade unions)*, Front National *(Communist)*; in March 1943 all merged to form MUR. In unoccupied France, Combat, Libération *(trade unions)*, Francs-Tireurs. After Feb. 1944 French Forces of the Interior (FFI) formed, amalgamating MUR, ORA *(disaffected Army resisters)* and FTP *(Communist partisans)*. By 1944 c. 400,000 resisters, *(only c. 116,000 armed)*. **+ 2093 ▪ 39,000** *(excluding c. 10,000 court-martial executions)*

ITALY *(after Sept. 1943)*
National Liberation Committee (CLN); National Liberation Council for Northern Italy; 'Garibaldi' *(Communist partisans)*. By 1944 c. 200,000 partisans behind German lines

NORWAY
MILORG *(1944: 35,000 resisters)*; HL; Arbejdstjeneste-Komite; Kretsen **+ 25 ▪ 18,000**

DENMARK
Prinserne; Danmarks Frihedsraad; BOPA *(Communist)*; Holger Danske. By 1944 25,000 resisters **+ 46 ▪ 14,495**

HOLLAND
Resistance Council (RvZ); Geuzen; Knokploegen; Ordedienst; BS; LO. By 1944 c. 2000 resisters **+ 36 ▪ c. 50,000**

30 April 1942 village destroyed, male population deported, women and children interned for sheltering Allied agents

19 Sept. 1944 all Danish police and border guards arrested following general uprising in Copenhagen (June 1944); 97 civilians killed

△ ▽ **HOLLAND**
✸ **797 anti-terrorist murders 1943-45**

BELGIUM 32 men executed 24 Dec. 1944

21 Sept. 1942 116 hostages executed following attack on German cinema

GERMANY
organized resistance within Germany limited; Communist sabotage; some illegal press (The White Rose, 1942); ideological resistance to Hitler focussed on small groups such as the Kreisau Circle, largely among aristocracy and Army (page 188)

OCCUPIED FRANCE
Oradour-sur-Glane 10 June 1944 entire village (642 people) massacred

Beyssenac Feb. 1944 SS destroy Maquis base

Ossola Partisan republic declared Summer 1944; 4000 partisans destroyed by 12,000 security police

VICHY FRANCE

Vercors resistance stronghold destroyed July 1944 (see map 3)

30 March 1944, 335 hostages executed following bomb attack on German troops

IN CONTRAST TO eastern Europe, the task facing the German occupying forces in western Europe was eased by the absence of any substantial political or military focus for resistance. Consequently, the onus of maintaining control of the conquered territories lay less with the *Wehrmacht* than with the Nazi security services and paramilitary collaborationist units such as the *Milice* in France and the *Schalburg Korps* in Denmark. Wholesale arrests of likely dissidents neutralized potential sources of resistance while the captives provided useful hostages should the need arise for reprisals to be exacted against the civilian population. In spite of such measures, myriad resistance organizations gradually formed from a wide range of political, religious, professional and ethnic groupings. Their activities varied almost as much as their make-up and included strikes and demonstrations together with more violent measures such as sabotage and assassination *(1)*. But the resistance was not merely concerned with its own, internal affairs; it also made a significant contribution to the Allied victory in Europe. This particularly took the form of intelligence gathering, sabotage against industry and communications, the running of escape lines and, after D-Day, close tactical co-operation with the Allied armies *(2)*. One example of such activity was the Danish underground's attacks on German rail communications *(4)* that escalated from 6 operations in 1942 to 1301 in 1945. Not only did this inhibit the movement of German forces from Norway to France in the Summer of 1944 but also necessitated the employment of some 40,000 men to guard the rail networks in Jutland. While the resistance was effective in mounting sabotage attacks, hit-and-run raids and guerrilla warfare, it was ill-equipped to confront the German armed forces in open conflict or to defend areas that it had 'liberated' without the close support of Allied units. In June 1944 the mountainous redoubt of the Vercors plateau in south-east France, long a safe rallying point for French resisters, declared itself free from German rule (3). Anticipating substantial Allied air-drops of supplies, and only a brief period of armed resistance prior to Allied landings in Provence (Operation *Anvil*) and Normandy (Operation *Overlord*), the French conducted a vigorous defence of the plateau, exploiting the crevassed terrain to their advantage. But the next month its *maquis* forces were faced by determined German counter-insurgency operations. As was to be witnessed again in Warsaw in August, over-confidence and a

misconception of Allied plans led to precipitate action, compounded by an incorrect assessment of German determination to contest the issue. In the ensuing clashes the inadequately armed *maquis* proved to be no match for more numerous, well-equipped and trained troops, supported by artillery, tanks and aircraft, culminating in an airborne (glider) attack following which most of the defenders were massacred.

Pictures below: A poster eliciting American support for the Free French (left). A German poster for Holland attacking the Allied liberation forces (right). Danish workers repairing sabotaged railway track under German guard (bottom).

Areas of co-ordination between Allies and European resistance:

NORWAY
local raiding including major sabotage such as destruction of the heavy water facility at Rjukan (28 Feb. 1943); intelligence from coastwatchers relayed to Britain; kept substantial German forces occupied

SWEDEN
neutral status; important exchange conduit for intelligence and escapees

DENMARK
high quality intelligence including details of V-weapon development and locations; fomenting of industrial action; strikes and sabotage to interrupt military traffic preceding D-Day; maintained escape lines to Sweden

HOLLAND
maintained escape lines; low quality intelligence

BELGIUM
high quality intelligence throughout war; maintained escape lines; co-operation with Allied ground forces after D-Day

LUXEMBOURG
escape lines

FRANCE
wide range of high and low quality intelligence, especially concerning V-weapons, German coastal defences and strengths; extensive sabotage programme, especially of road, rail and telephone preceding D-Day landings; escape lines to Spain and Switzerland; open attacks on German formations and co-operation with Allied armies following D-Day

ITALY
escape lines after Spring 1943; also open attacks on German formations and co-operation with Allied ground forces; liberation of towns and cities ahead of Allied advance

POLAND
high-quality intelligence, especially on V-weapon sites, testing and development sent to London. Also F2 intelligence service run from France

CZECHOSLOVAKIA
intelligence of varying quality; 1940-42 over 20,000 radio messages from Bohemia-Moravia alone

2/RESISTANCE AND THE WESTERN ALLIES 1940 – 45

→ main courier routes
→ main escape routes
□ collecting centre

maritime links operated by fishing fleets in Baltic and North Seas to exchange arms, escapees and intelligence

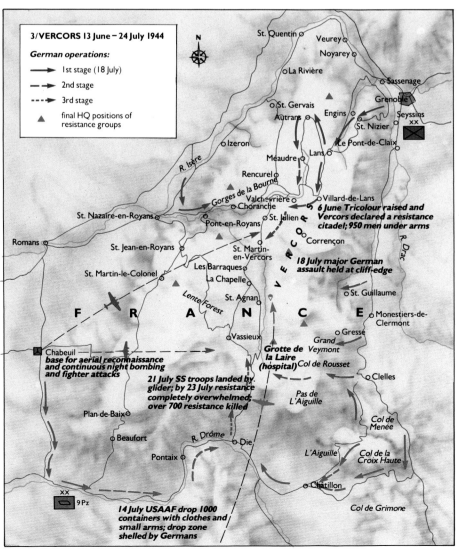

3/VERCORS 13 June – 24 July 1944

German operations:

→ 1st stage (18 July)
--→ 2nd stage
····→ 3rd stage
▲ final HQ positions of resistance groups

6 June Tricolour raised and Vercors declared a resistance citadel; 950 men under arms

18 July major German assault held at cliff-edge

Chabeuil base for aerial reconnaissance and continuous night bombing and fighter attacks

21 July SS troops landed by glider; by 23 July resistance completely overwhelmed; over 700 resistance killed

Grotte de la Laire (hospital)

14 July USAAF drop 1000 containers with clothes and small arms; drop zone shelled by Germans

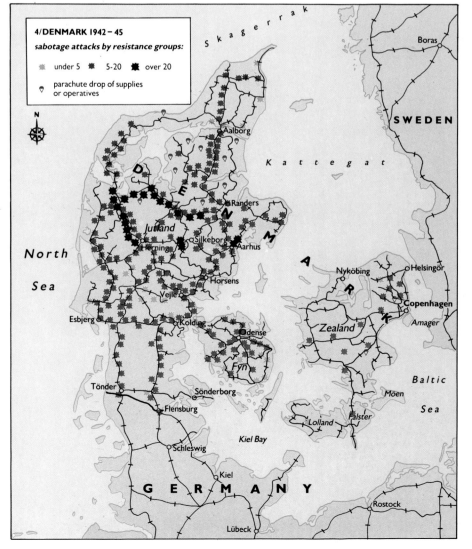

4/DENMARK 1942 – 45

sabotage attacks by resistance groups:

✳ under 5
✳ 5-20
✳ over 20

○ parachute drop of supplies or operatives

Midway MAY ~ JUNE 1942

THE JAPANESE had no opportunity either to evaluate the lessons of the battle of the Coral Sea (page 32) or to recast their plans: they were committed to establishing a Central Pacific perimeter, upon which any American offensive actions would be met. The failure off the Louisiades was dismissed as a local setback; the absence of two fleet carriers from the forthcoming operation was recognized to be serious, but with virtually the entire Combined Fleet committed to the offensive the Japanese remained supremely confident.

With eight carriers deployed for the offensive the Japanese had good reason for confidence, but the pattern of deployment that had almost led to disaster in the Coral Sea – a disperal of strength amongst widely separated formations that were not mutually supporting – was to be repeated. Their plan called for a diversionary attack on, and occupation of, certain islands in the Aleutians, the neutralization and occupation of Kure and Midway, and the annihilation of any enemy carrier force that gave battle. Against an ill-prepared or surprised foe such a plan might have succeeded, but by May 1942 the Americans were neither. Their ability to read Japanese operational signals enabled the Americans to identify the critical weaknesses of the Japanese plan – the broad dispersal of force, the relative smallness of Nagumo's carrier force and its vulnerability in the opening phase. With the Japanese able to use only four carriers for this task, the Americans appreciated that if they could deploy three carriers on the enemy's disengaged beam there was a reasonable chance of turning the tables on Nagumo.

From the outset Japanese plans miscarried. Firstly, submarines tasked to scout the Hawaiian Islands arrived late and failed to detect the US carrier Task Forces, which were moving to attacking positions north of Midway. Secondly, a planned reconnaissance of Pearl Harbor by flying boats from the Marshalls had to be cancelled; Nagumo was not informed of either development. Thus, as he bore down on Midway, at a time when Kakuta's carriers began a desultory attack on the Dutch Harbor (3 June), Nagumo had no reason to assume that US carrier forces were at sea.

The battle which unfolded on 4 June was settled for the Japanese by an unfortunate sequence of events. Nagumo's air groups struck Midway at dawn, and were ineffectually counter-attacked thereon by planes from the base. But during these exchanges Nagumo's seaplanes discovered the US carrier Task Force 17 which, with Task Force 16, attacked the Japanese carrier force after it had recovered the Midway attack groups but before it was able to launch its own attack. Three of Nagumo's carriers were crippled. When finally Nagumo's dive-bombers struck the USS carrier *Yorktown*, the Americans were already preparing a *coup de grâce*. Nagumo's flagship, the carrier *Hiryu*, was in flames before dusk. The operation was

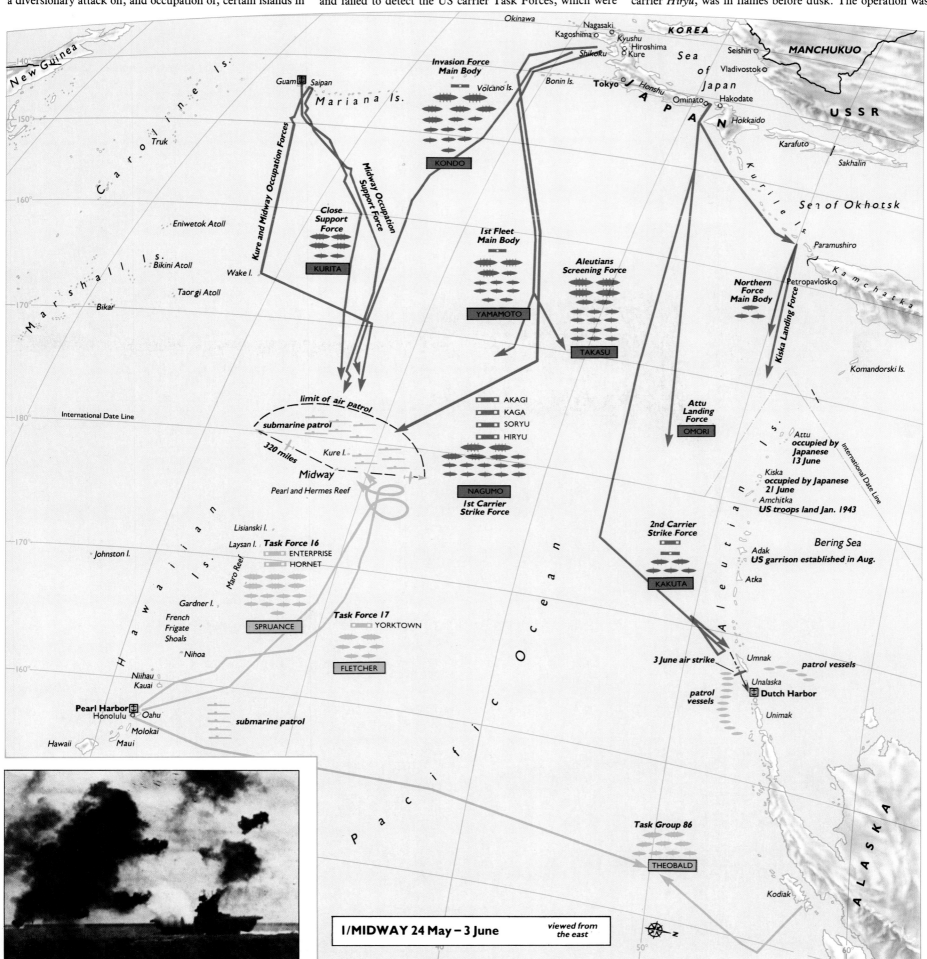

1/MIDWAY 24 May – 3 June   *viewed from the east*

doomed before the main body forces under Yamamoto, Kurita or Kondo had even reached the battlefield. The Americans declined to be drawn into a surface action, and conducted a limited pursuit only when it was clear that the Japanese were withdrawing; by reversing the element of surprise and securing overwhelming superiority in the air, American control of the Central Pacific remained intact.

At Midway the Americans won a crushing victory – the first irreversible Allied victory of the war; it was marred only by the loss of the *Yorktown* and the destroyer *Hammann*, and by the Japanese occupation of Attu and Kiska in the Aleutians. The two warships were lost as a result of an attack by the submarine *I-168* at 1336 on 6 June, the *Hammann* sinking immediately while the *Yorktown* succumbed finally on the 7th. The capture of Attu and Kiska had no strategic significance, the Japanese took the islands for political and propagandist reasons. Nothing could disguise, within the Imperial Navy's High Command, the enormity of its defeat. It marked the end of the period of seemingly overwhelming Japanese advantage; the next phase of the naval war was to be fought by more evenly matched antagonists.

THE SCALE OF THE JAPANESE offensive in the Central Pacific was ambitious (*1*). Following an opening air strike by Kakuta on Dutch Harbor (3 June), Nagumo's first carrier strike force closed for battle. At 0430 on the 4th, at the very time that the *Yorktown* flew off search aircraft and some fifteen minutes after Midway had begun to do the same, Nagumo committed just under half his strike aircraft against Midway from a position some 250 miles north-west of the atoll (*2*). Thereafter Nagumo retained the balance of his force in readiness for operations against any enemy task force that might be encountered, but not until the Midway strike force had left did he complete the launch of reconnaissance patrols. At 0545 a Midway-based Catalina found Nagumo's force, and on receipt of sighting reports the US carriers turned towards an enemy that had to hold his course for Midway in order to recover his strike force. The *Yorktown*, obliged to recover her aircraft, became separated from TF16, but from 0600 Midway, and from 0702 TF16 began to launch their attack formations against Nagumo's carriers; the *Yorktown* was not able to begin to launch her strike aircraft until 0838. The Japanese strike against Midway, therefore, was the first to be delivered, but this attack, between 0635 and 0645, was against a largely empty base, and the Japanese began to re-arm their second-strike aircraft accordingly. From 0705 onwards, attacks by Midway-based formations materialized, though these were beaten off with ease. As the Japanese emerged from these attacks, however, they became aware of the presence of a US Task Force off their port beam, though for the moment they were unaware of the presence of any carriers. Confirmation that US carriers were at sea was provided after 0810 when Nagumo's force came under attack by aircraft operating in numbers that indicated the presence of more than one carrier (*3*). The US carriers had hoped that their air groups could attack *en masse*, but in the event the various squadrons became widely separated and those that found Nagumo's force mounted uncoordinated attacks against an enemy in the process of recovering his strike aircraft. The first of the attacks, by Devastator torpedo-bombers, incurred very heavy losses without recording a

single hit on any Japanese warship, but they served to disorganize Nagumo's formation and pulled the Japanese combat air patrol down to sea level by the time that the final attacks materialized. These, by Dauntless dive-bombers from the *Enterprise* and *Yorktown*, accounted for the *Akagi*, *Kaga* and *Soryu* between 1025 and 1030, just as the Japanese prepared to launch a strike against the US carriers. The *Hiryu* was not attacked, however, and in the course of the afternoon (*4*) her aircraft twice found and attacked the *Yorktown*, leaving her dead in the water. After the second attack the *Yorktown* was abandoned. Unfortunately for the Japanese, however, the *Hiryu* was reduced to a mere handful of strike aircraft as a result of these operations, whilst her command came to the conclusion that two US carriers had been knocked out of the fight. The reality, of course, was that two US carriers were intact, and in the last carrier operation of 4 June, Dauntlesses flown from the *Enterprise* and *Hornet* caught the *Hiryu* just before sunset, reducing her to the same sinking condition of her three companions, the Americans recovered their Dauntlesses by 1907 and thereafter set course to the east and away from the area of the day's battle (*5*). The Japanese response to the disasters of the morning of the 4th was to try to reach Midway and detect and destroy the US carrier formations during the hours of darkness using their surface forces, which now included Yamamoto's 1st Fleet. But by turning away after dusk, TF16 denied the Japanese any chance of forcing a night action. Soon after midnight the Japanese abandoned the attempt; further, two of Kurita's heavy cruisers were crippled in a collision off Kure while attempting to avoid a US submarine. With the four wrecked Japanese carriers either sinking or being scuttled during the night and their escorts pulling back for a rendezvous with Yamamoto's main force, dawn of 5 June found the main Japanese formations well within range of Midway-based aircraft. Throughout the day, however, the two crippled cruisers were undisturbed while US carrier groups searched to the north for other Japanese formations. In the course of these searches the Americans found a detached destroyer, the *Tanikaze*, which was attacked unsuccessfully. On 6 June, the US carriers turned their attention to the cruisers and sank the *Mikuma*, the *Mogami* managing to stay afloat and escaping from the scene of the battle. In the early hours of 7 June TF16 turned for home.

Picture left: the USS Yorktown under attack during the afternoon of 4 June. Although taking avoiding action, she has just been hit by a torpedo on the port side

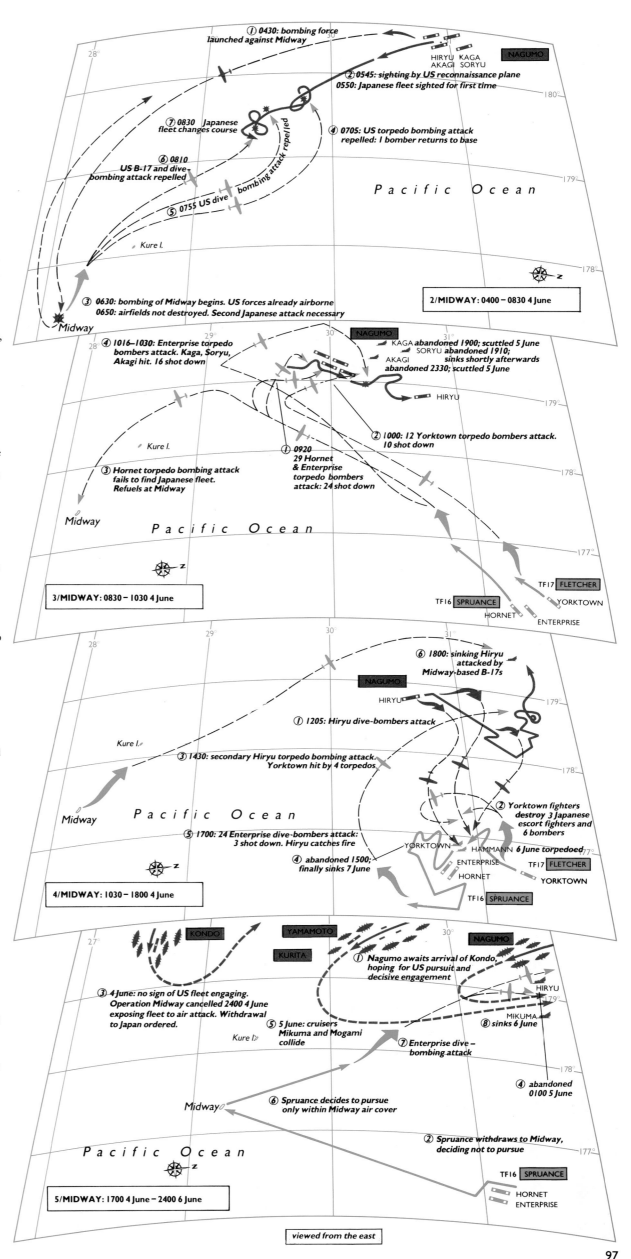

The United States 1941 ~ 1945

THE ECONOMY OF THE USA was vital to the Allied war effort. Without the resources and productive strength of America the Allied cause would have been difficult, if not impossible, to sustain. These resources were already being mobilized for the Allies before America entered the war. From 1939 onwards Britain and France bought large supplies from America and when, in 1941, Britain exhausted her ability to pay any more, Lend-Lease Aid was introduced, a scheme through which military supplies, food and industrial equipment was sent to the British empire, and the Soviet Union too, without payment.

Economic assistance reflected the central part that material strength played in the American view of warfare. From as early as 1938, President Roosevelt recognized that if America were to play any part in the unfolding international crisis, it would have rapidly to mobilize and harness the economy for war. In many ways the war solved the problems underlying Roosevelt's 'New Deal' economic measures of the 1930s (page 30), by providing a motivation for economic growth, government spending and private investment. In 1939 Congress approved a great increase in military spending, much of it directed at new armaments plants, aircraft factories and labour retraining programmes. A War Resources Board was set up in 1939 to prepare industry for conversion to war, and to speed up war investment. Roosevelt insisted on drafting in major businessmen with experience of mass-production for the task, including William Knudsen,

head of General Motors, who became chief of the Office of Production Management set up in January 1941. Much of the American success in mobilizing for war came from the fact that war production was kept in the hands of civilians with managerial and engineering experience. The American motor industry was brought in from 1941 to produce tanks, trucks, aero-engines and aircraft. The experience of mass-production, built up in earlier years, proved invaluable.

The US production record was remarkable. In five years America produced 86,000 tanks (against Germany's 61,000), 8800 naval vessels and 87,000 landing craft. From 1942 to 1945 the Army was supplied with 193,000 artillery pieces and 2.1 million trucks. The aircraft industry produced only 5800 aircraft in 1939, but 96,000 in 1944. In all, the USA produced 297,000 aircraft during the conflict, almost double the output of all the enemy powers together, and treble the Axis output of aero-engines. The most famous production success was the 'Liberty ship', a mass-produced cargo vessel. The average production time per ship fell from approximately 260 days, in early 1942, to 40 days at the end of 1943. This massive production performance meant that the United States could also supply all her allies on a generous scale.

There were a number of serious issues that had to be solved before this production record could be achieved. In 1941 government expenditure was only $12 billion and taxes were

low. Between 1941 and 1945 government spending totalled $317 billion, 88% of this on the war effort. The money came from raising taxes sharply and from borrowing through seven widely-publicized War Loans, and a final Victory Loan. Price controls and rationing, and control on credit, prevented serious inflation, while rising earnings during the war were siphoned off into savings and war bonds. Domestic living standards were maintained well during the war and consumer spending stayed about the same. But all the additional economic growth and industrial development after 1941 was diverted to the war effort. Industrial production more than doubled between 1939 and 1943, and farm production increased by more than a third. The only problem was labour mobilization. The nine million unemployed in 1941 were brought back into the workforce, and five million more women were working by 1945. The size of the workforce increased by almost a fifth, despite twelve million being taken into the armed forces, and the War Labor Board moved workers from the poorer Southern and Midwestern states to the Northeast and the West Coast, where war production was concentrated.

The problem of supplying raw materials for the war effort was solved by extending domestic supply – for example, the massive production of synthetic rubber to compensate for the loss of Far Eastern supplies – and by an increase in trade. Imports, mainly of food and raw materials, grew by $2.6 billion between 1940 and 1945; exports grew even faster, rising from $4 to $14 billion. The balance of payments surplus for the war years totalled $34 billion. The USA was a major beneficiary of the world at war, with a solid foundation of new industrial capacity and export markets for the great post-war boom.

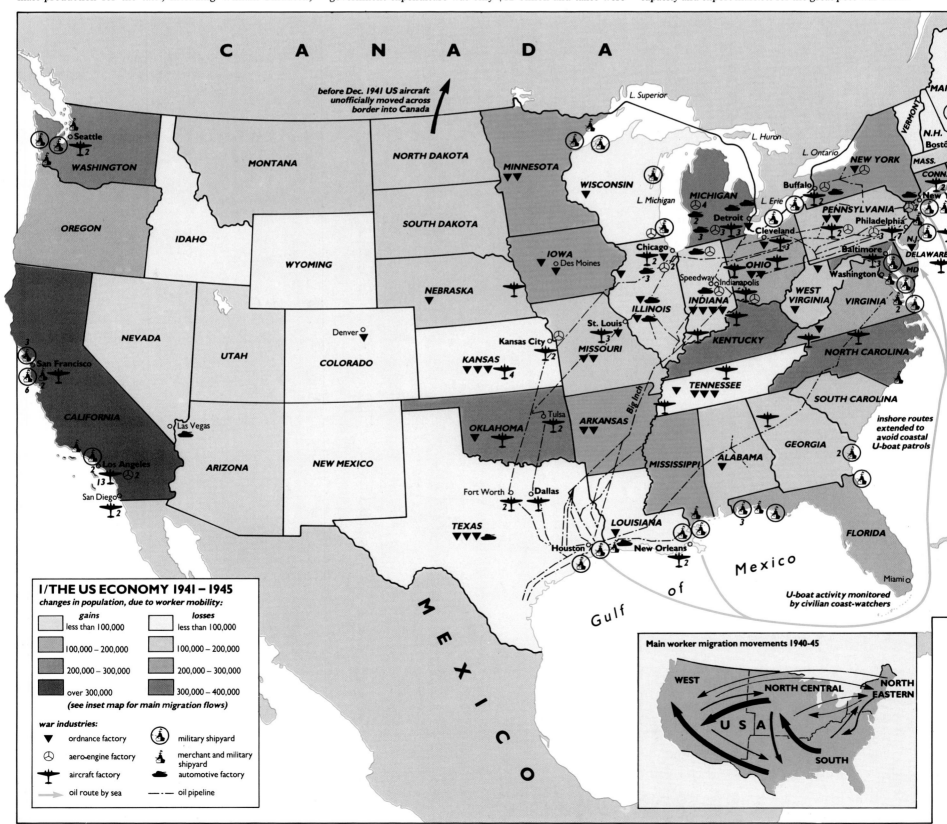

I/THE US ECONOMY 1941–1945

changes in population, due to worker mobility:

gains
- less than 100,000
- 100,000 – 200,000
- 200,000 – 300,000
- over 300,000

losses
- less than 100,000
- 100,000 – 200,000
- 200,000 – 300,000
- 300,000 – 400,000

(see inset map for main migration flows)

war industries:
- ▼ ordnance factory
- aero-engine factory
- aircraft factory
- military shipyard
- merchant and military shipyard
- automotive factory
- oil route by sea
- oil pipeline

Main worker migration movements 1940-45

U-boat activity monitored by civilian coast-watchers

inshore routes extended to avoid coastal U-boat patrols

before Dec. 1941 US aircraft unofficially moved across border into Canada

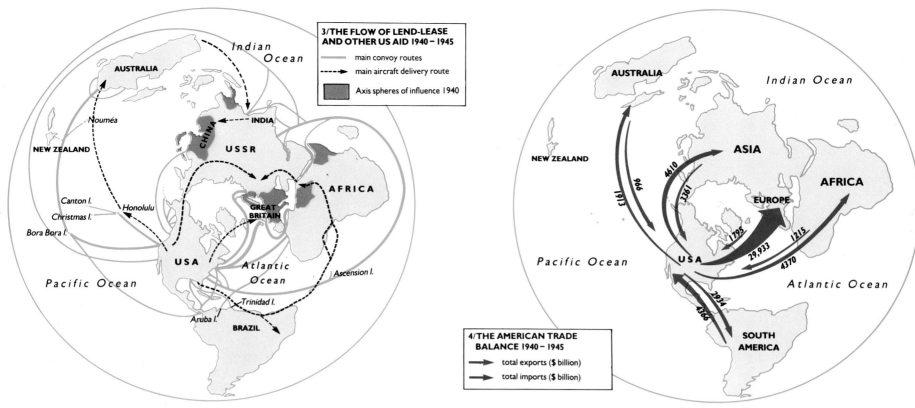

3/THE FLOW OF LEND-LEASE AND OTHER US AID 1940 – 1945

- main convoy routes
- → main aircraft delivery route
- Axis spheres of influence 1940

Indian Ocean

AUSTRALIA

Nouméa

NEW ZEALAND

INDIA

CHINA

USSR

AFRICA

GREAT BRITAIN

Canton I.
Christmas I.
Bora Bora I.
Honolulu

USA

Atlantic Ocean

Ascension I.

Pacific Ocean

Trinidad I.

Aruba I.

BRAZIL

Indian Ocean

AUSTRALIA

NEW ZEALAND

ASIA

AFRICA

EUROPE

Pacific Ocean

USA

Atlantic Ocean

SOUTH AMERICA

1913
996
4610
3367
1795
29,933
1215
4370
2934
4366

4/THE AMERICAN TRADE BALANCE 1940 – 1945

- → total exports ($ billion)
- → total imports ($ billion)

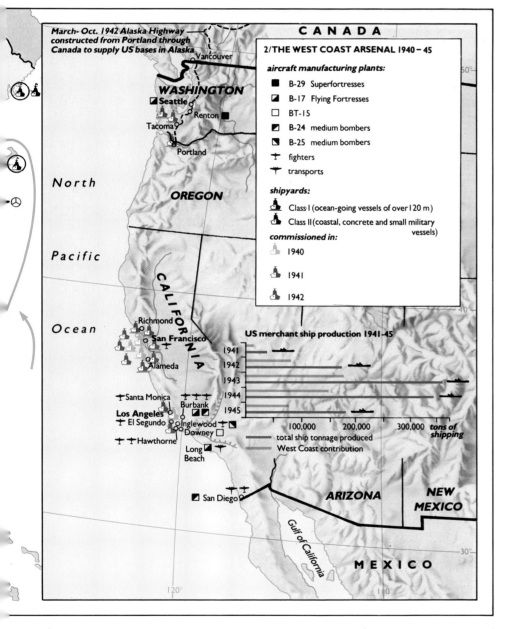

2/THE WEST COAST ARSENAL 1940 – 45

March- Oct. 1942 Alaska Highway constructed from Portland through Canada to supply US bases in Alaska

CANADA

Vancouver

WASHINGTON

Seattle
Renton
Tacoma
Portland

OREGON

CALIFORNIA

Richmond
San Francisco
Alameda

Santa Monica
Burbank
Los Angeles
El Segundo
Inglewood
Downey
Hawthorne
Long Beach

San Diego

North Pacific Ocean

ARIZONA

NEW MEXICO

MEXICO

Gulf of California

aircraft manufacturing plants:
- ■ B-29 Superfortresses
- ◪ B-17 Flying Fortresses
- □ BT-15
- ◩ B-24 medium bombers
- ◪ B-25 medium bombers
- ✛ fighters
- ✈ transports

shipyards:
- ⚓ Class I (ocean-going vessels of over 120 m)
- ⚓ Class II (coastal, concrete and small military vessels)

commissioned in:
- ⚓ 1940
- ⚓ 1941
- ⚓ 1942

US merchant ship production 1941-45

| 1941 |
| 1942 |
| 1943 |
| 1944 |
| 1945 |

100,000   200,000   300,000   *tons of shipping*

- total ship tonnage produced
- West Coast contribution

IN THE 1930s the USA championed disarmament, yet by 1938 it was clear that US security could only be guaranteed by massive rearmament. In the space of only two years, from 1939 to 1941, America transformed its economy for defence and war supply (*1, 5*). Workers moved away from rural areas to the new factories in California and the dockyards of the South and Northeast, creating a new pattern of population distribution. Overland oil supply lines were built from the Texas oilfields to the industrial centres of the north-east to avoid risk of attacks on shipping, including the famous 'Big Inch' line from Houston to New York. During the war US industry produced $186 billion of munitions. The greatest transformation occurred in the Western states (*2*), where the bulk of America's aircraft and shipping was produced. By 1943 shipyards in California and Washington State provided 50% of all ships built and Californian aviation firms produced 24,000 heavy bombers. From 1941 the USA provided a stream of military supplies, raw materials and food for the powers fighting the Axis in Europe and the Far East (*3*). The main routes were through Siberia, through Persia and across the Atlantic to Britain and northern Russia (page 180). Two-thirds of these supplies went to the British empire and 22% to the Soviet Union, including a total of 14,018 aircraft. US trade changed dramatically during the war (*4*). Imports from Europe fell by two-thirds, while exports there increased seven-fold. Trade expanded all over the world as America filled the gaps left by all the belligerent nations. America's world exports were, by 1944, three times greater than in 1940, despite the demands of war production. The war had solved the lingering problems from the Depression, and had geared the American economy and society for the explosion of wealth and unrestrained consumer spending which characterized the post-war years.

Pictures far left: US Government poster stressing the link between heavy industry and the war effort; it clearly demonstrates the American understanding that the war would be decided by industrial power.
Left: A mass-production line in the Boeing factory in Seattle, with a high proportion of women workers.

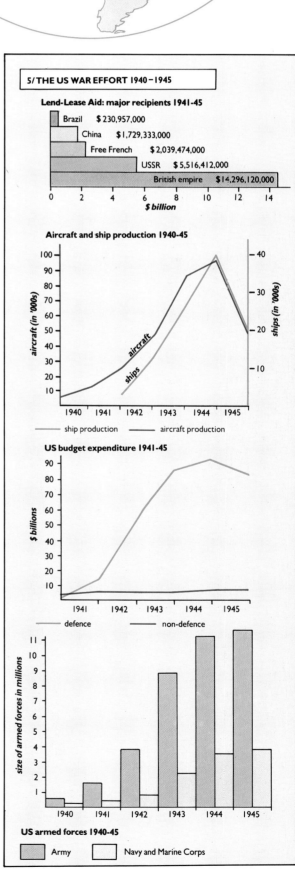

5/ THE US WAR EFFORT 1940 – 1945

Lend-Lease Aid: major recipients 1941-45

Brazil	$ 230,957,000
China	$ 1,729,333,000
Free French	$ 2,039,474,000
USSR	$ 5,516,412,000
British empire	$ 14,296,120,000

0   2   4   6   8   10   12   14
$ billion

Aircraft and ship production 1940-45

aircraft (in '000s) / ships (in '000s)

1940   1941   1942   1943   1944   1945

— ship production   — aircraft production

US budget expenditure 1941-45

$ billions

1941   1942   1943   1944   1945

— defence   — non-defence

US armed forces 1940-45

size of armed forces in millions

1940   1941   1942   1943   1944   1945

- Army
- Navy and Marine Corps

POUR IT ON!

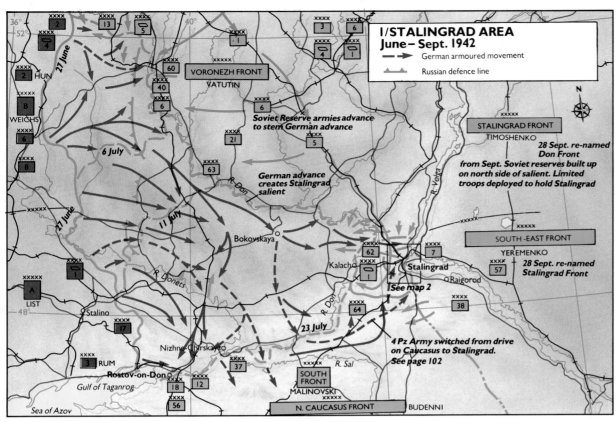

**I/STALINGRAD AREA
June – Sept. 1942**

- - -➤ German armoured movement
 ⊢⊢⊢ Russian defence line

STALINGRAD, FORMERLY TSARITSYN, now modern Volgograd, was the site of the most titanic and terrible battle of the Second World War, the first really significant defeat inflicted on Nazi Germany's land forces. Stalin's association with the city went back to the Civil War, when he had been instrumental in its defence. It was also symbolic, and strategically important, for Hitler. By 1942 Stalingrad was a sprawling conurbation stretching for 30 miles in all, along the high west bank of the Volga, the central part of the city straggling for 12 miles, but nowhere more than 2½ miles wide. It was a crucial industrial and communications centre, dominating the north-eastern approaches to the Caucasus.

By July 1942 it was obvious that the main German thrust had turned south-east; Army Group A to the south and the Caucasus, Army Group B to the Don. On 23 July German units broke through to the western bank of the Don near Kamensk and in the first week of August the Russians suffered disaster in the Don bend. Defence of Stalingrad was now in the hands of two fronts: Stalingrad (Gordov) to the north, and the new South East (Yeremenko) to the south. By the night of 23 August Rostov-on-Don had fallen to the Germans and the Russians were fast running out of space into which to retreat. The Volga was the final defensive line. Evacuation of industry and planting demolition charges in the Stalingrad factories were forbidden. Stalin had committed the Russians to a terrible battle of attrition. From 23 August, when the Germans reached the Volga to the north, Stalingrad was under constant air attack, and as German and other Axis troops closed on the city,

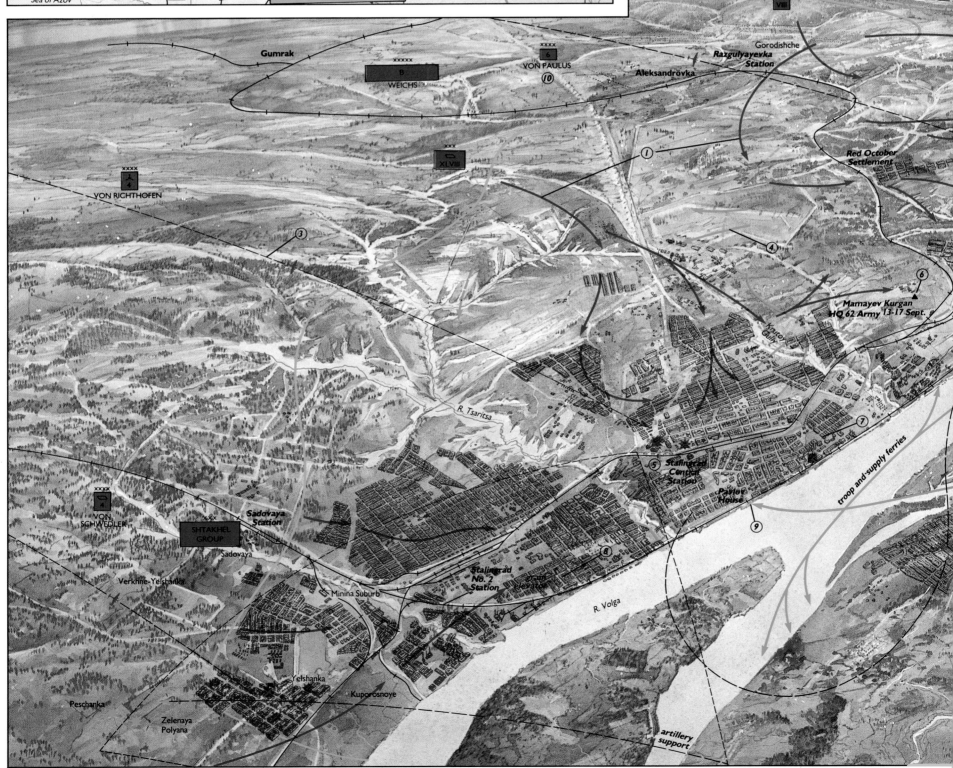

Soviet Russia had reached perhaps the critical point of the war.

On 10 September Lopatin was dismissed from command of 62nd Army, now on the defence in Stalingrad, and replaced by Chuikov. His arrival coincided with the ferocious German assault against the central sector of Stalingrad itself, on 13 September. By this time 62nd Army had been bombed and shelled to pieces, divisions numbering a couple of hundred rather than the regulation 10,000. 7000 workers had been formed into people's militia units to defend their factories, and women and children evacuated to the east bank.

Chuikov's HQ on Mamayev Kurgan, a Scythian tumulus on Hill 102 commanding the central and northern suburbs, became the centre of an inferno as German troops, fighting with unequalled savagery and determination, hacked their way through the city. On 14 September, they occupied engineers' houses near Stalingrad Central Station and brought the main landing stage on the river under accurate machine gun fire, proceeding to fight their way into the area of the grain elevator. 62nd Army, reinforced by 13th Division, moved into the city centre during the night and managed to claw a foothold on the west bank despite murderous German gunfire. Stalingrad Central Station changed hands four times during the 14th: the whole city became a blazing furnace of burned out buildings and small, savage actions. On the 17th Chuikov moved his HQ near the Red October factory. The fighting continued without let up amidst the lurid glow of blazing buildings and illuminating shell, whilst small boats ferried ammunition and brought the wounded back across the river alight with burning

oil. There were renewed German surges on 27 September, when 80 tanks moved on the Red October factory. During the night the Soviet 193rd Rifle Division was ferried across the Volga to retake it. By 5 October the Germans occupied the northern landing stages, and Stalin ordered them to be prised away from the river. A huge bombardment, lasting 40 minutes, by 300 guns and five regiments of *katyusha* multiple rocket launchers smashed German units preparing to break into the Tractor factory and the Barricades gun factory. The Germans then launched an attack of even greater ferocity and by the 16th had taken the Tractor plant and appeared about to take Barricades, but the Russians held on in parts of the factory until the 23rd.

Meanwhile, the German command was receiving reports of Soviet redeployment north of the Don. The only way out was to take Stalingrad, and soon, and in a desperate attempt to do this they piled in more resources. On 11 November the last great German attempt to break through to the Volga split Chuikov's bridgehead for the third time. The Red October factory was in German hands; Soviet units and formations were, at best, down to about a tenth of regulation strength, and running out of ammunition and food. By 17 November the Russian situation was desperate and to make things worse the Volga was beginning to freeze. So far the battle of Stalingrad had cost the Germans 700,000 men killed, wounded, prisoners and missing, 1000 tanks, over 2000 guns and 1400 aircraft.

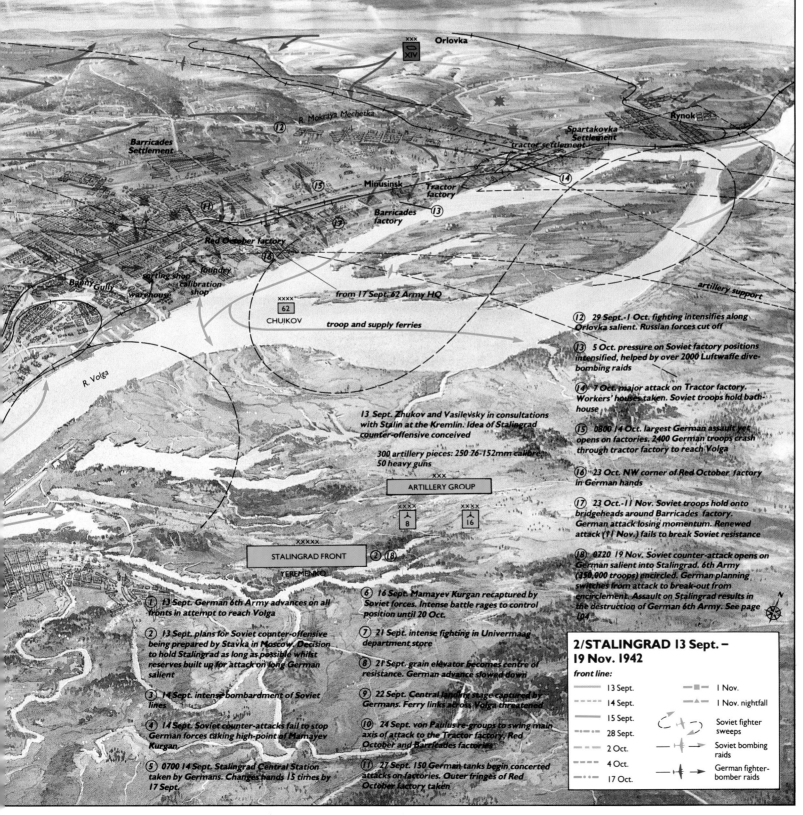

IN 1942 STALINGRAD straggled along 12 miles of the River Volga. In the centre lay Mamayev Kurgan on Hill 102, a key point for which the struggle never slackened. Soviet positions on the eastern bank were relatively safe, except from air attack, and here most of the artillery was concentrated. In mid-Aug., German forces crossed the narrow strip of land which separates the Don and Volga to close in on Stalingrad. By 12 Sept. the city proper was completely surrounded on the west bank, so that the Russians could only get in and out over the river. Mamayev Kurgan, Chuikov's 62nd Army HQ, the Barricades, Red October and Tractor factories, were all key objectives, taken and re-taken many times. German air superiority made the daytime particularly dangerous for the Russians, but they frequently recovered lost ground during the night. The Central Station and the engineers' houses nearby were also an important objective, the latter giving a field of fire over the main Volga jetty. A 4-storeyed house near the ruined grain elevator was turned into a small fortress, covering all the approaches. Its defender, Pavlov, beat off every assault for 58 days. Soviet artillery was concentrated on the east bank, firing across the river. In mid-Oct. extra heavy, 203mm and 208mm long-range guns arrived to intensify the artillery battle. Some of 62nd Army's artillery, however, remained on the west bank, including the very short-range *katyusha* rocket launchers, which by 14 Oct. had to back right into the water of the Volga to get the necessary angle of fire. Russian attempts to distract German efforts at Stalingrad by attacking from the north and south became secondary to the meticulous planning of a major counter-offensive (page 104). For 2 months, until 19 Nov., the inner city area was defended against German attacks. The battle was a perfect illustration of the huge numbers of troops a large city like Stalingrad could absorb. The German assault, designed to overrun the factory districts (14 Oct.) failed despite the use of 3 Infantry divisions and over 300 tanks. Such forces were simply lost, sucked into the blazing maelstrom of Stalingrad.

Picture above: *Soviet troops moving forward in the shattered remains of central Stalingrad.*

Orlovka
XXX
G
XIV

R. Mokraya Mechetka

Barricades Settlement

Spartakovka Settlement

Rynok

tractor settlement

Minusinsk

Tractor factory

Barricades factory

Red October factory

sorting shop
foundry
calibration shop
warehouse

Banny Gully

from 17 Sept. 62 Army HQ

XXXX
62
CHUIKOV

troop and supply ferries

artillery support

R. Volga

12 29 Sept.-1 Oct. fighting intensifies along Orlovka salient. Russian forces cut off

13 5 Oct. pressure on Soviet factory positions intensified, helped by over 2000 Luftwaffe dive-bombing raids

14 7 Oct. major attack on Tractor factory. Workers' houses taken. Soviet troops hold bath-house

15 0800 14 Oct. largest German assault yet opens on factories. 2400 German troops crash through tractor factory to reach Volga

16 23 Oct. NW corner of Red October factory in German hands

17 23 Oct.-11 Nov. Soviet troops hold onto bridgeheads around Barricades factory. German attack losing momentum. Renewed attack (11 Nov.) fails to break Soviet resistance

18 0720 19 Nov. Soviet counter-attack opens on German salient into Stalingrad. 6th Army (250,000 troops) encircled. German planning switches from attack to break-out from encirclement. Assault on Stalingrad results in the destruction of German 6th Army. See page 104

13 Sept. Zhukov and Vasilevsky in consultations with Stalin at the Kremlin. Idea of Stalingrad counter-offensive conceived

300 artillery pieces: 250 76-152mm calibre 50 heavy guns

XXX
ARTILLERY GROUP

XXXX   XXXX
↑   ↑
8   16

XXXXX
STALINGRAD FRONT
YEREMENKO

2 18

1 13 Sept. German 6th Army advances on all fronts in attempt to reach Volga

2 13 Sept. plans for Soviet counter-offensive being prepared by Stavka in Moscow. Decision to hold Stalingrad as long as possible whilst reserves built up for attack on long German salient

3 14 Sept. intense bombardment of Soviet lines

4 14 Sept. Soviet counter-attacks fail to stop German forces taking high-point of Mamayev Kurgan

5 0700 14 Sept. Stalingrad Central Station taken by Germans. Changes hands 15 times by 17 Sept.

6 16 Sept. Mamayev Kurgan recaptured by Soviet forces. Intense battle rages to control position until 20 Oct.

7 21 Sept. intense fighting in Univermaag department store

8 21 Sept. grain elevator becomes centre of resistance. German advance slowed down

9 22 Sept. Central landing stage captured by Germans. Ferry links across Volga threatened

10 24 Sept. von Paulus re-groups to swing main axis of attack to the Tractor factory, Red October and Barricades factories

11 27 Sept. 150 German tanks begin concerted attacks on factories. Outer fringes of Red October factory taken

2/STALINGRAD 13 Sept. – 19 Nov. 1942

front line:
——— 13 Sept.
- - - 14 Sept.
——— 15 Sept.
- - - 28 Sept.
——— 2 Oct.
- - - 4 Oct.
——— 17 Oct.
-■-■- 1 Nov.
-▲-▲- 1 Nov. nightfall

↻ Soviet fighter sweeps
✈ Soviet bombing raids
✈ German fighter-bomber raids

N

The Caucasus 1942~1943

THE FIRST PHASE of the German Summer Offensive of 1942 had brought them to the River Don (page 62). In the second phase, Army Group A was tasked with Operation *Edelweiss*, the capture of the Caucasus oilfields at Maikop, Grozny and Baku. These would be a considerable prize for the German war economy in themselves, but in terms of grand strategy the arrival of German troops in the Caucasus offered even more dazzling rewards. Turkey might be coerced to join the Axis powers, and the *Deutsches Afrika Korps'* success in North Africa might mean a joint encirclement of British possessions in the Middle East – and the Mediterranean become an Axis lake. But dreaming over a map and fighting over the ground were entirely different. From Rostov to Baku was the same distance as from the Polish/Soviet frontier to Rostov – and the terrain grew increasingly difficult. The eastern half of the land between the Caspian Sea and the Black Sea is a roadless desert. In the western half the German armies were restricted to two narrow axes, either along the Black Sea coast, and then inland from Sukhumi to Tiflis, or north of the Caucasus via Armavir, Grozny and Makhach Kala to Baku. Soviet reinforcements faced a long haul round to the front, but they could at least use the Caspian route from Astrakhan to Makhach Kala whilst also bringing some forces up from the Turkish border.

Operation *Edelweiss* began on 25 July and for the first two or three weeks Army Group A swept forwards, advancing up to 30 miles in a day. The Soviet forces defending the Caucasus had not yet recovered from their earlier defeats. But by the middle of August German daily progress was averaging only a mile or two. As the terrain became more difficult Army Group A also found its forces being drained away for the Stalingrad front. In particular the *Luftwaffe's* 4th Air Fleet, planned to provide essential tactical air support, was ordered to concentrate its resources against Stalingrad. At the same time new commanders and fresh troops arrived on the Soviet side. Among them was Lavrenti Beria with internal security troops of the NKVD; these would ensure that German hopes of an anti-Soviet rising by the non-Russian people of the Caucasus would be dashed by the harsh repression of any possible discontent.

German and Rumanian mountain troops were committed to the battle but the Red Army held on. Within the mountain passes the fighting turned into a series of platoon-level battles for individual positions. Hitler refused to consider the evidence of difficult terrain, adverse weather and diminishing resources and continued to press General List, commanding Army Group A, to continue his advance. List was forced to resign on 10 September and for some time Army Group A was left without a commander, while 17th Army and 1st Panzer Army dealt directly with Hitler's headquarters.

On the Soviet side the Supreme Commander was equally intrusive. In considering plans for the 1942 Winter Offensive Stalin rejected the Transcaucasus Front's proposal to put the main axis north of the Caucasus, against 1st Panzer Army, aiming at Maikop. In Moscow a more ambitious plan had been developed which hoped to encircle Army Group A and destroy it totally. This was to be achieved by Southern Front thrusting down through Salsk to Tikhoretsk while the Black Sea Group struck north from Tuapse to Krasnodar to link up with Southern Front at Tikhoretsk. It was another plan which offered a dramatic victory on the map but which ignored the reality of the ground. There was no reason why Soviet troops should find it any easier to conquer the ground and the weather than the Germans had.

The final plan involved two attacks. The first, Operation *Mountains*, was to be launched at Goryachi Klyuch and on to Tikhoretsk; the second, Operation *Sea*, was an amphibious assault to clear Novorossiisk and threaten the Taman Peninsula. However, foul weather delayed preparations and grew worse as Operation *Mountains* got under way. The landing at Novorossiisk failed to capture the city but did leave a small bridgehead (Malaya Zemlya) to the south which remained in Soviet hands through the Summer. The numerous small landings along the coast in this campaign were typical of the Soviet approach to amphibious assault during the Second World War, which was very different to the experience of the Western Allies. There were no major overseas assaults; instead amphibious forces were used for outflanking moves over short distances. Such assaults were often rapidly improvised; it it thus easy to see why the Russians became impatient with Western delays in mounting Operation *Overlord*.

The clearing of the Caucasus was only part of the Soviet Winter Offensive of 1942/43 which turned the tide of German success in the east. It denied Germany the oilfields at Baku, upon which Hitler had pinned substantial hopes.

THE GERMAN ADVANCE into the Caucasus began on 25 July 1942 when Army Group A (*1*) advanced rapidly from the R. Don. By 9 Aug. it had reached the Krasnodar/Stavropol/Maikop line. However, the foothills of the Caucasus began to slow the advance down and the mass of the mountains themselves forced each side to split its forces. German 17th Army, supported by Rumanian 3rd Army fought the 4 Soviet armies of what became known as the Transcaucasus Front's Black Sea Group for control of the coastal road from Novorossiisk to Sukhumi. With the aid of Operation *Blücher II* (2

Sept., an amphibious assault across the Kerch Strait to clear the Taman Peninsula), 17th Army reached Novorossiisk on 6 Sept., but by 11 Sept. the front line stuck at a cement factory on the outskirts: it remained there for 360 days. Attempts to thrust through the mountains to the coast made only slightly faster progress before the arrival of Winter made any advance impossible. In the east 1st Panzer Army had the apparently easier task of skirting the Caucasus to the north against the opposition forces of the Northern Group. LII Corps crossed the R. Terek at Mozdok on 2 Sept. but was then held in its bridgehead by Soviet counter-attacks. Hopes were raised by two more bursts of progress, along the line of the Terek in late Sept. and to Nalchik in late Oct. but Winter rain and snow brought operations to an end on 9 Nov. The Soviet counter-offensive in the Caucasus was to exploit the over-extension of the German forces and the Winter conditions. It formed only part of a general counter-offensive all along the front. In the overall plan for the Soviet 1942 Winter Offensive (page 106) the Transcaucasus Front was to cooperate with the Southern Front in trapping Army Group A before it could withdraw through Rostov (*2*). But the Black Sea Group made only slow

2/NORTH CAUCASUS Jan. – April 1943
- ——— German position at beginning of January
- - - - - - Soviet Front Line 16 January
- ————— Soviet Front Line 24 January
- – – – – German position 4 February
- ——— Soviet Front Line 4 April

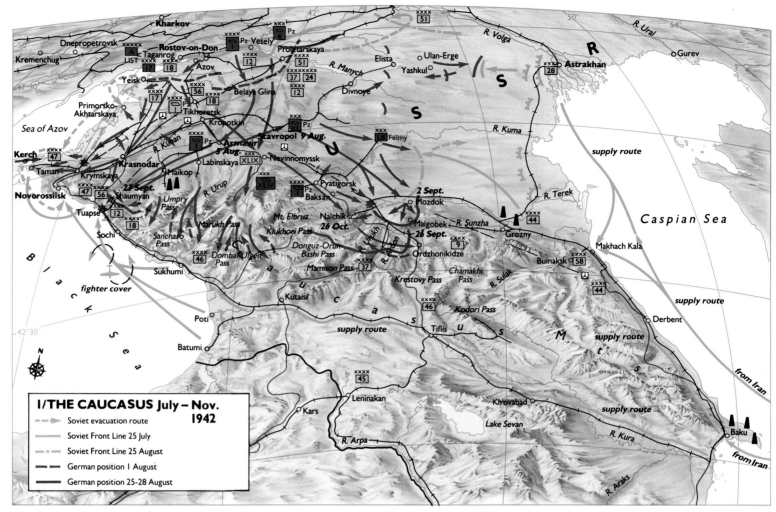

progress in appalling weather along the Tuapse-Krasnodar-Tikhoretsk axis. In the north, 1st Panzer Army was allowed to withdraw steadily from river to river, despite *Stavka*'s attempts to speed up the movement of the Northern Group. A greater threat to 1st Panzer Army was the Southern Front's progress to the R. Manych, but the line held long enough for 1st Panzer to escape and join Manstein's counter-offensive at Kharkov. 17th Army was left holding a large bridgehead on the Taman Peninsula, the *Gotenkopf* position. But during the Summer attention was focussed in the north and the front remained static in the Caucasus. On 9 Sept. the Taman offensive opened with an amphibious assault directly into the harbour of Novorossiisk (3). In the next month frontal pressure, combined with small-scale amphibious outflanking moves along the coast (4), cleared the Taman Peninsula, although the bulk of 17th Army was able to cross the Kerch Strait back into the Crimea.

Picture above left: Soviet cavalry (substantial formations existed in the Soviet Army throughout the war) came into their own in the difficult Caucasus terrain; Gen. Kirichenko's 'Cavalry-Mechanized Group' was given several key tasks in the 1942/43 Winter Offensive. Left: German troops advance into the Caucasus foothills.

1/THE CAUCASUS July – Nov. 1942

- Soviet evacuation route
- Soviet Front Line 25 July
- Soviet Front Line 25 August
- German position 1 August
- German position 25-28 August

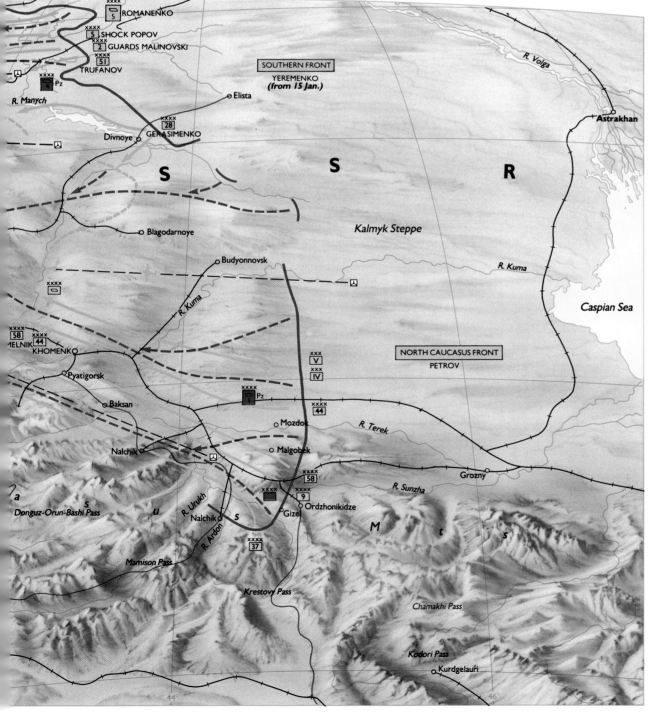

3/THE TAMAN OFFENSIVE 9 Sept. – 9 Oct. 1943
German rear defence line

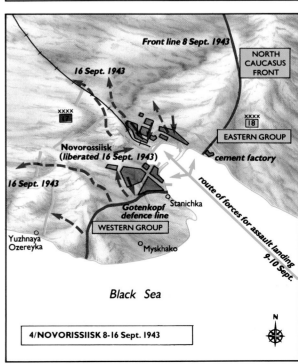

4/NOVORISSIISK 8-16 Sept. 1943

Stalingrad NOVEMBER 1942 ~ FEBRUARY 1943

AT MIDNIGHT ON Wednesday 18 November Chuikov, commanding 62nd Army in Stalingrad was told to stand by for new orders. The next morning an eighty-minute artillery preparation would herald Operation *Uranus*, a counter-offensive by over a million Russian soldiers with over 13,000 guns, 894 tanks and 1150 aircraft, slicing from north and east far behind the forward German troops still assailing Chuikov's ragged perimeter. During the night of the 18/19th, snow clouds brought freezing fog and thicker snow, swathing the tortured terrain in a white mantle and reducing visibility to zero. At 0720 the guns were loaded; at 0730 they fired on what was to be named, from 1944, 'Artillery Day', and at 0850 the infantry attack went in.

Plans for the counter-offensive, the second phase of the Stalingrad *bitva*, were first presented to Stalin on 13 September. There were two main tasks: first, the encirclement of the force operating within the Stalingrad area and, second, its annihilation. To capitalize on the relative ineffectiveness of Rumanian forces, the blows had to be struck far back on the flanks; until then, Stalingrad itself had to hold. In *Operationsbefehl nr. 1* of 14 October, Hitler brought the German Summer offensive to a close, believing that defence of the present positions would suffice until a final annihilating blow could be struck in 1943. On 23 October, Zeitzler, Chief of the General

Staff, reiterated this, stressing that the Russians were in 'no position to mount a major offensive with any far-reaching objective'. In fact, Soviet preparations were well advanced. Only Gehlen, head of the intelligence organization *Fremde Heere Ost*, appears to have had the knowledge or imagination to predict either limited operations against 3rd Hungarian Army or operations over the Don on a larger scale against the Italian and Hungarian armies, on 12 November.

In retrospect, the German position looks terribly vulnerable. Von Manstein, appointed to command new Don Army

Group on 20 November, said that the attempt to gain the Volga by taking Stalingrad as a set-piece battle was only admissible on a very short term basis. To have such a major force bogged down at Stalingrad for weeks with inadequately protected flanks was 'a cardinal error'. The German command structure was 'utterly grotesque'. Army Group A, to the south, was commanded by Hitler on a part-time basis; Army Group B had no less than seven armies, including four allied, an impossible span of control. Uncertainties and divided loyalties as to the chain of command would hamper German response to the well

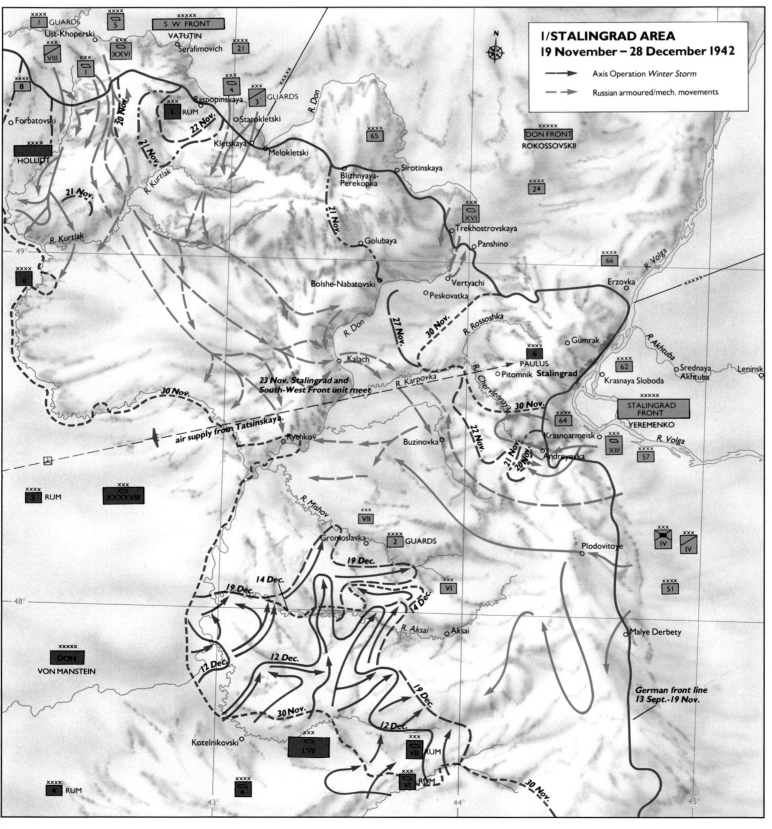

THE MAIN THRUST of Operation *Uranus*, to encircle Axis forces in the Stalingrad area and then annihilate them was launched on 19 Nov. *(1)*. As Soviet units of the Southwest Front ripped an eight-mile gap in the defences, Rumanian divisions began to disintegrate and fell back, pursued by tank columns across the Don steppe. The assault of the Stalingrad Front (20 Nov.) was delayed 2 hours (0800 to 1000) because weather conditions made it impossible to observe fire. During the following night a 20-mile-wide gash was torn in 4th Panzer Army's eastern flank and the HQ had to withdraw. On the morning of 23 Nov. forward brigades (Southwest Front) and Stalingrad Front met in the vicinity of Kalach trapping what they believed to be 90,000 enemy troops in an encirclement 200 miles in circumference. It was at least 2½ times that number. First German transport aircraft flew into the ring on 25 Nov., where the beleaguered 62nd Soviet Army still held its precarious positions on the west bank. The German attempt to relieve the pocket, Operation *Winter Tempest*, was launched on 12 Dec. from the area of Kotelnikovski *(1)*. 57th Panzer was across the Aksai and reached the River Mishov, within 30 miles of the siege front (19 Dec.). The attempt to relieve 6th Army had failed. 5 Soviet armies now surrounded Paulus's 6th Army and units of 4th Panzer. The Don Front was charged with liquidating the encircled force, after the Germans rejected an ultimatum (10 Jan.) *(2)*. By 9 Jan. the western edge of the pocket was 25 to 30 miles from the Volga. By 16 Jan. the Russians were 7 miles from Stalingrad, by the 25th German positions were reduced to two pockets in the city itself, opposite Krasnaya Sloboda and Zaytsev Island. On the 26th the Russians reached the slopes of Mamayev Kurgan, on which the snow had never settled: the heat of constant shell and bomb bursts had melted it off. The southern group, including Paulus, now a Field Marshal, surrendered on 31 Jan., the northern on 2 Feb.

Pictures above left: a German supply plane arriving in a snowstorm. Above right: Soviet artillery on the outskirts of Stalingrad.

organized and meticulously planned Soviet blow.

The Russian counter-offensive opened on 19 November as Southwest Front and 65th Army of the Don Front struck from the north, pushing the breakthrough to 20 miles by the end of day one. The next day the Southern pincer (Stalingrad Front) attacked. On 23 November mobile units of the two fronts met on target in the Kalach area blocking 6th Army's resupply and exit routes. In a giant Cannae that would have appealed to the Prussian General Staff, the Russians had trapped a major enemy force in a pocket extending about 30 miles from west to east and 25 from north to south. There seem to be no definitive figures as to the number of troops in the pocket: von Manstein reckoned that estimates over 300,000 (the official Russian estimate is 330,000) were exaggerated: 200,000 to 220,000 was probably a reliable estimate. It was the first time in the Second World War that the Germans had been caught in anything like this.

Von Manstein considered it imperative to get 6th Army out. The Russians would obviously do everything in their power to destroy 6th Army and might also push mechanized forces across the large Don bend towards Rostov, threatening to cut off Army Group A as well. The force in the pocket needed 550 tons of supplies a day, but might make do with 400 until the ration dumps already in the pocket could be supplied by air: Goering boasting that it could. Hitler remained determined to leave 6th Army in 'Fortress Stalingrad', perhaps supplying it through a land corridor.

The Russians, having completed their encirclement and bolstered up the inner and outer fronts, launched their first attack on 6th Army on 2 December. By this time, the Germans had made plans for the relief attempt, Operation *Winter Tempest*, launched on 12 December. The grotesque command relationships hampered attempts to get 6th Army out of the pocket: Paulus seemed determined to obey Hitler's order to hold, while on 19 December von Manstein, as his immediate superior, ordered 6th Army to begin breaking out to the south west. The German dilemma was insoluble. Leaving 6th Army and a large part of 4th Panzer tied down around Stalingrad placed the Army Group as a whole in a very vulnerable position. But 6th Army was too weak to attempt to make contact with relief forces by breaking out and at the same time to hold its perimeter. Should Paulus obey Hitler or von Manstein?

Meanwhile the Soviet Operation *Kol'tso* (Ring), to destroy the encircled garrison, proceeded. By 26 December Paulus was radioing that he could not hold out for long and that he had only received 70 tons of supplies that day. In a last, almost comic, gesture to induce 6th Army to hold on, Hitler promoted Paulus with indecent rapidity, first to Colonel General, then, by the end of January, to Field Marshal. By 24 January 30,000 wounded had been flown out and the garrison was ordered to break up into small groups. On 31 January the southern group of German forces, including Paulus, surrendered; on 2nd February, the northern surrendered. 91,000 officers and men were taken prisoner; about 140,000 had died in the pocket in

January. The Battle of Stalingrad had destroyed 6th Field and 4th Panzer Armies, 3rd and 4th Rumanian and 8th Italian. In all the Battle of Stalingrad may have cost the Germans as many as one and a half million men killed, wounded, missing and prisoner, nearly a quarter of their strength on the eastern front.

German handling of the encirclement was poor. However, von Manstein believed that 6th Army was a necessary sacrifice: other sectors of Army Group B's front were weakly held and had 6th Army not put up fierce and prolonged resistance, in spite of cold, hunger and shortage of ammunition, the Russians might have surged to the German eastern front as a whole. Germany might have lost the land war almost there and then.

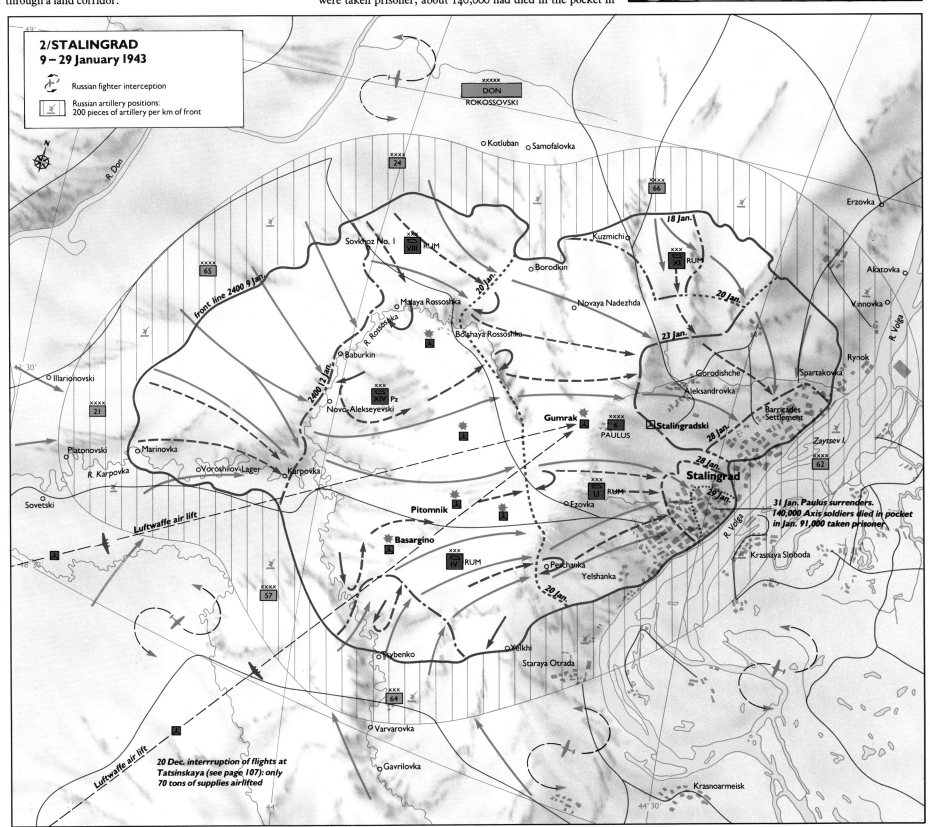

2/STALINGRAD
9 – 29 January 1943

Russian fighter interception

Russian artillery positions: 200 pieces of artillery per km of front

DON ROKOSSOVSKI

Kotluban
Samofalovka

Erzovka

24

66

Sovkhoz No. 1

RUM

18 Jan.

Kuzmichi

RUM

Akatovka

Vinnovka

65

Borodkin

Novaya Nadezhda

20 Jan.

front line 2400 9 Jan.

Malaya Rossoshka

R. Rossoshka

Bolshaya Rossoshka

23 Jan.

Rynok

R. Volga

Baburkin

2400 12 Jan.

Pz

Novo-Alekseyevski

Gorodishche

Spartakovka

Aleksandrovka

Illarionovski

21

Barricades Settlement

Gumrak

6
PAULUS

Stalingradski

28 Jan.

Zaytsev

62

Platonovski

Marinovka

Karpovka

Stalingrad

28 Jan.

R. Karpovka

Voroshilov-Lager

RUM

29 Jan.

Ezovka

Sovetski

31 Jan. Paulus surrenders.
140,000 Axis soldiers died in pocket
in Jan. 91,000 taken prisoner

Pitomnik

Krasnaya Sloboda

Luftwaffe air lift

57

R. Volga

Basargino

RUM

Peschanka
Yelshanka

20 Jan.

Tsybenko

Yelkhi

Staraya Otrada

64

Varvarovka

20 Dec. interrruption of flights at
Tatsinskaya (see page 107): only
70 tons of supplies airlifted

Gavrilovka

Krasnoarmeisk

Luftwaffe air lift

Southern Russia FEBRUARY ~ JUNE 1943

THE FINAL DESTRUCTION of 6th Army at Stalingrad (page 105) on 2 February made a renewed Soviet surge possible beyond the outer front of the Stalingrad encirclement. By 2 February the Russians had advanced beyond the outer front established by *Little Saturn* – the Middle Don Operation – at the end of December, to the Don in the south, the Northern Donets and then a line running north some 50 miles east of Bielgorod and Kursk. The Russians now planned a renewed surge. Exactly as had happened a year before (page 62), Winter victory made Stalin and *Stavka* over-ambitious. Three fronts, Voronezh, South-west and Southern, would liberate the second largest political entity in the USSR: the Ukraine. As well as over-ambitious, it seemed that Stalin could not choose between occupation of territory and control of its resources on the one hand, and destruction of enemy forces, as objectives on the other. The *Stavka* directive of 6 February ordered Southwest Front to cut off the Donets group of German forces and drive it into isolation in the Crimea. To the north, Soviet forces would strike into the rear of Army Group Centre through Briansk and Smolensk, and, further north still would wipe out the Demyansk Pocket and open the way to the relief of Leningrad (page 64).

Soviet Southwest Front attacked on 29 January and the Voronezh on 2 February. German Army Group Don still occupied the 'balcony' between the Don and Donets rivers, placing it in danger of immediate encirclement. On 6 February Von Manstein met Hitler to elicit approval to withdraw from the eastern part of the area. Characteristically Hitler at first refused, then agreed. By 9 February the Russians had taken Bielgorod and Kursk, north of Kharkov. Army Group B now faced a superiority of (in German estimation) up to 8:1. By mid-February, the danger of encirclement of the entire German southern wing from the north had become acute, but these very dispositions created the potential for a counter-stroke.

Kharkov, the fourth largest city in the Soviet Union, was a prestigious prize and on 13 February Hitler ordered it to be held at all costs. The SS Panzer Corps there had no intention of being encircled, however, and pulled out on the 15th. Kharkov fell to the Russians the next day, opening a hundred mile breach between German Army Group B and Don, the latter renamed South. The Germans now shelved plans for expansion in the Caucasus: Army Group A became a reservoir of forces for Army Group South. On 19 February 4th Panzer Army executed a counter-stroke, hitting the Soviet forces trying to

drive a wedge down to the Dnieper, in the flank. The battle between the Donets and the Dnieper raged until 2 March, by which time Army Detachment Hollidt had held the River Mius and 1st and 4th Panzer Armies had severely mauled Soviet forces in the area, counting 23,000 dead, 615 tanks captured, but only 9000 Russian prisoners, most Russians able to escape across the frozen Donets.

The next German counter-attack came on 7 March. 4th Panzer Army hoped to break into the rear of the Voronezh and Central Fronts, cutting them off in the Kharkov area and thus creating what Stalin subsequently called a 'German Stalingrad'. Voronezh Front withdrew 60 to 100 miles, forming the southern face of the huge Kursk salient, about half the size of England. The muddy season gave an advantage to the Germans now going onto the defence, but it provided a menacing springboard for Russian attacks to south and north into the flanks of Army Groups South and Centre. The sooner the Germans attacked, the less prepared the defence of the salient would be. This was the rationale behind Operation *Zitadelle* (page 124), originally timed to start in early May. Had it been launched then, it might have worked, but it was delayed to June, and then the beginning of July.

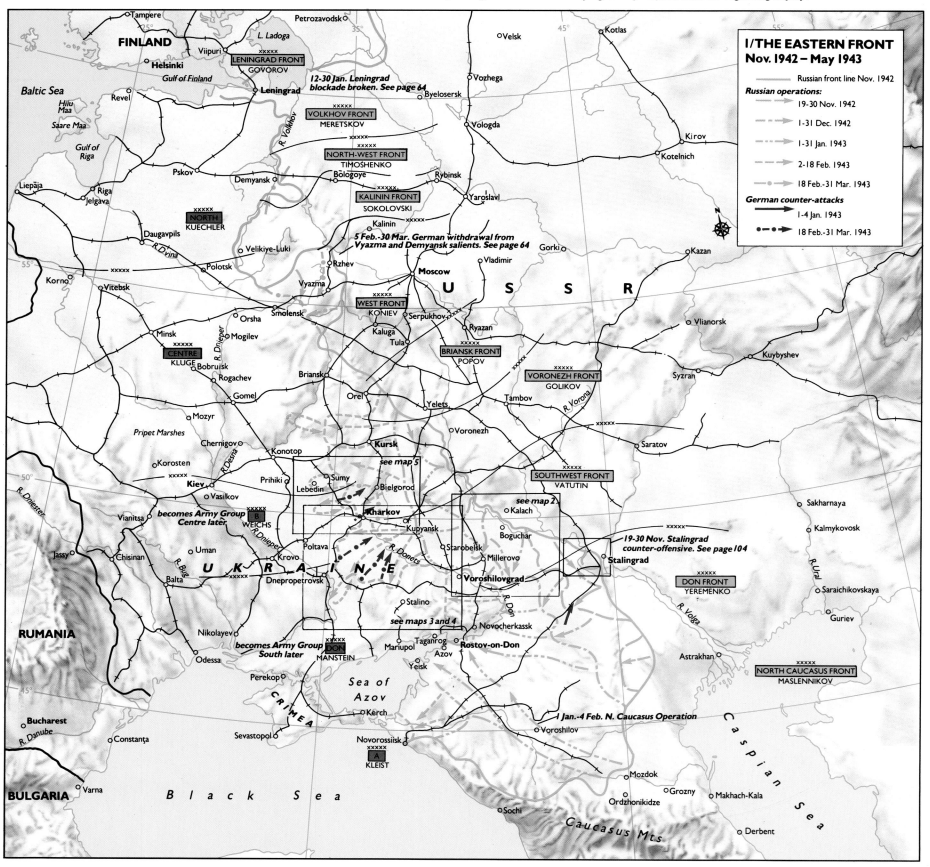

THE STALINGRAD COUNTER-OFFENSIVE (19-30 Nov.) (*1*), and Operation *Little Saturn* (16-30 Dec.) (*2*) had brought Soviet forces to the Middle reaches of the Don. During Jan. 1943, Voronezh, Southwest, Don, Stalingrad and Southern Fronts pushed German forces back to the Lower Don, and a line east of Bielgorod and Kursk. The Russian advance continued (2-28 Feb.), into the western Donets area, which Von Manstein had eventually persuaded Hitler to relinquish. A further penetration took the Russians almost to Dnepropetrovsk. The battles for Kharkov fell into two phases. During the Soviet offensive phase (2 Feb. to 3 Mar. 1943), forces of Voronezh Front and 6th Army of the Southwest Front attacked with the aim of destroying the main forces of Army Group B south of Kharkov, although the city itself, which fell on 16 Feb., was a prestigious bonus (*3*). This very success invited (19 Feb.) a German counter-stroke (*4*), masterminded by Von Manstein commanding

Army Group Don (renamed South from 13 Feb.). To the north (15-28 Feb.) Soviet Northwest Front (Timoshenko) was ordered to liquidate the pocket of German troops around Demyansk (*1*), facilitating thrusts into the rear of German forces besieging Leningrad (page 65). On 7 Mar. 4th Panzer Army attacked towards Kharkov (*5*), aiming not so much to retake the city as to destroy Soviet forces located there. Whilst protected by the thawing Donets from an attack in Voronezh Front's rear, the Russians lost Kharkov on 14 Mar. The result of operations in the southern theatre was the formation of the southern face of the great Kursk salient, which would be the objective of Germany's last major offensive in the east: Operation *Zitadelle* (page 124).

Pictures below: a Soviet K V 2 tank (foreground) and a T 34 Tank move forward, Nov. 1942 (top). Soviet troops advancing in Winter camouflage (bottom).

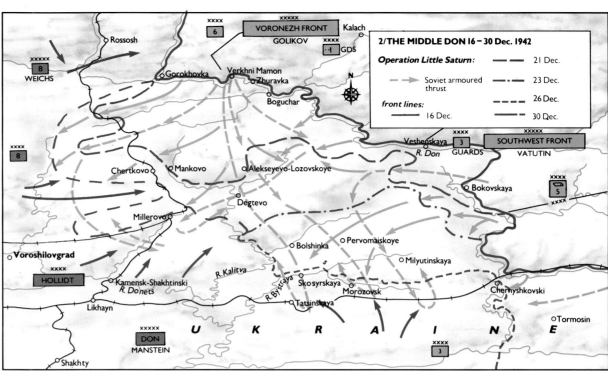

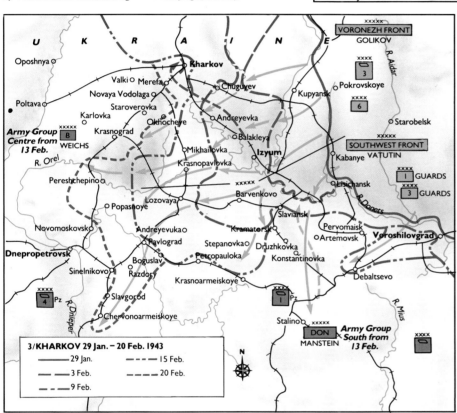

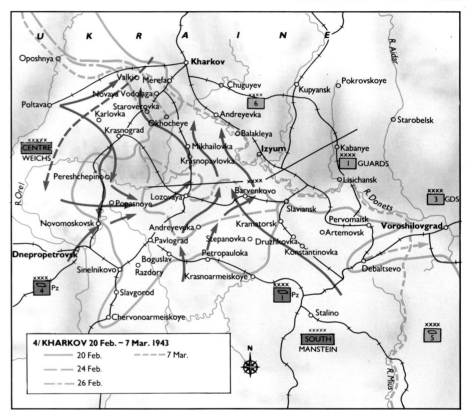

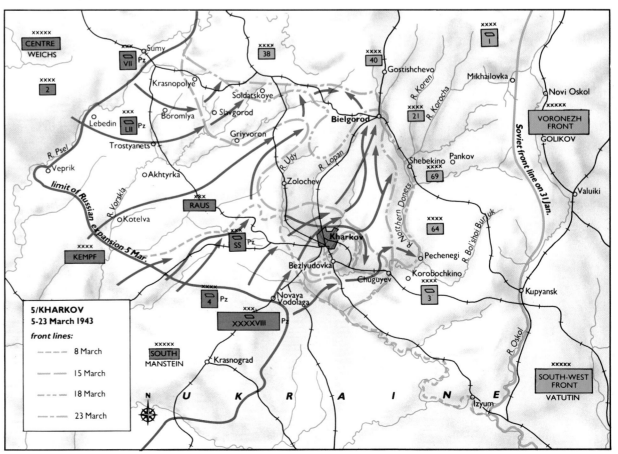

GIVEN THE DEPENDENCE of their future operations – especially the build-up and supply for Operation *Overlord* – upon the defeat of the U-boats, the Americans and British agreed at the Casablanca conference (January 1943) that priority had to be placed upon winning the battle of the Atlantic. By March 1943 the increased U-boat losses indicated that a major new aspect of the struggle was developing: additional very long-range aircraft were allocated to the battle, and their intervention is generally considered to have been crucial to the defeat of the U-boats in May 1943.

In reality, the losses sustained by the U-boats in May 1943 were the result not of any single cause, however important, but of a combination of factors. The defeat of the U-boat campaign against Allied shipping lay not simply in the reverses sustained in May 1943 – when 41 U-boats were destroyed – but in the fact that in July and August 1943 the U-boat arm sustained defeats of similar severity. Though losses in these months – 37 and 25 respectively – were less than in May they were sustained by a force that had regrouped and reorganized after the May debacle, and had intended to mount a sustained, massed offensive to regain the initiative. Thus the losses in July and August were more profound than those of May, and August 1943 marked the real Allied victory in the battle of the Atlantic; thereafter, the U-boat arm was never again able to mount a sustained threat to Allied communications in the North Atlantic. After August 1943 the primary role of the U-boats was to tie down and distract disproportionately large Allied naval forces whilst a new generation of submarines was developed.

The Allied victory in the North Atlantic between May and August 1943 was the product of four related developments: the organizational, tactical and technical superiority of convoy escorts over the U-boats became apparent for the first time; Allied air power became increasingly effective; better intelligence concerning U-boat movements became available to the Allies via *Ultra* intercepts; and finally German errors in the conduct of operations. Possibly the Allied victory might have been won before Spring 1943 had it not been for Operation *Torch* (page 116), which tied down substantial escort forces until this time, but in this period various technical develop-ments – ship-borne radar and direction-finding equipment, improved asdic detection equipment, more powerful depth-charges and new and more accurate firing patterns – allowed convoys to be accorded an adequate scale of escort protection. In its conventional form, the submarine was incapable of the tactical or technological development required to counter the increases in escort numbers and advances of anti-submarine technology: further, in its conventional form the submarine could not withstand the introduction of Allied air power to the battle of the Atlantic in Spring 1943.

The latter took three forms – the escort carrier, very long range (VLR) patrol aircraft operating in direct support of convoys, and standard patrols over transit areas. All three forms were small-scale at this time. In March 1943 the Allies deployed just eighteen VLR aircraft, nine of which were assigned patrol duties, but by May 1943 total strength had risen to 49 aircraft, and this total allowed between twelve and fifteen

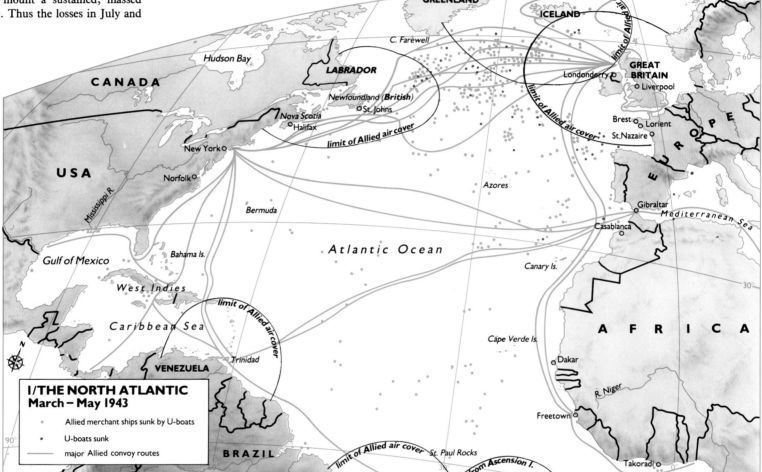

MARCH 1943 WAS A DECISIVE MONTH in the battle of the Atlantic *(1)*. German operational U-boat strengths had reached a peak *(5)*. This was reflected in the fierceness of the convoy battles in previous months (page 89). Changes in the Allied convoy organization, however, began to reap results. Most ships sailing off the US and Caribbean coast were now convoyed with a dramatic fall in sinkings. Further reductions in sinkings in Apr. and May *(6)* were achieved by more effective air cover: escort carriers appeared on some Atlantic convoys, and many more aircraft were made available for convoy duties. As German losses mounted and exchange rates fell, much of the attention of the battle turned upon operations in the Bay of Biscay *(4)*. More aircraft became available for patrols, and in Apr. were provided with 10cm radar sets, undetectable by U-boats. In July, of 86 U-boats that crossed the Bay, 55 were sighted, 16 sunk by aircraft (one by surface ship), and 6 forced to turn back. The cost was 14 aircraft. By Aug., however, better German air-cover, the use of Spanish coastal waters to gain access to the Atlantic and a return to single, submerged sailings, reduced U-boats losses in the Bay.

I/THE NORTH ATLANTIC March – May 1943

- Allied merchant ships sunk by U-boats
- U-boats sunk
- major Allied convoy routes

3/ALLIED MERCHANT SHIPPING LOSSES Apr. – Sept. 1943 *tonnages (nos. of ships)*								
date	U-boat	aircraft	mine	warship raider	merchant raider	E-boat	unknown and other causes	monthly totals
April	327,943 (56)	3034 (2)	11,961 (5)	none	none	1742 (1)	none	344,680 (64)
May	264,852 (50)	20,942 (5)	1568 (1)	none	none	none	12,066 (2)	299,428 (58)
June	95,753 (20)	6083 (3)	4334 (3)	none	17,655 (2)	none	none	123,825 (28)
July	252,145 (46)	106,005 (13)	72 (1)	none	7176 (1)	none	none	365,398 (61)
August	86,579 (16)	14,133 (5)	19 (1)	none	none	none	19,070 (3)	119,801 (25)
September	118,841 (20)	22,905 (4)	4396 (3)	none	9977 (1)	none	300 (1)	156,419 (29)

totals by theatre Apr.-Sept. 1943

Atlantic Ocean	Mediterranean	Indian Ocean	Pacific Ocean
744,507 (130)	246,889 (55)	322,080 (54)	84,341 (16)

4/BAY OF BISCAY Jan. 1942 – Aug. 1943

U-boats sunk:
- Jan. 1942 – Feb. 1943
- Mar. 1943 – Aug. 1943
- U-boat routes to Atlantic under air escort
- Coastal Command airfields employed on Bay patrols

of their number to spend an average of three hours with convoys beyond 650 miles from land on every day of May 1943; thus, with a small number of escort convoys, the Allies acquired the ability both to harry U-boats gathering around convoys and to attack in mid-ocean where U-boats had to run on the surface in order to recharge their batteries. The Spring months witnessed a German attempt to counter the Allied ability to find surfaced submarines as they crossed the Bay of Biscay at night, by sailing in daylight and fighting the aircraft in the process: this error provided the patrols with their only period of substantial success in the entire war.

The combination of air power and increased escort effectiveness was, in technical terms, decisive in bringing about the defeat of the U-boat arm. Nevertheless, that U-boat arm was anyway at that time in qualitative decline because of enforced dilution arising from its rapid expansion in previous years. In any event, even had the successes of 1942 (page 88) been sustained throughout 1943, this could not have secured a German victory, for the extension of convoy struck at the very effectiveness of a U-boat service that achieved its greatest returns at the expense of merchantmen sailing independently. More importantly, by March 1943, US shipyard production (page 98) had outstripped Allied shipping losses. It was with this complex of factors that the critical point of the battle of the Atlantic was passed in 1943, ensuring the Allies against defeat.

JUNE 1943 WAS THE QUIETEST MONTH in the North Atlantic: U-boats concentrated on soft targets off the west coast of Africa and Brazil (2). The combination of increased patrols in the Bay of Biscay (4), rising numbers of escorts and difficulties in deciphering the new Allied codes introduced in May led Dönitz to recall U-boats for the fitting of new anti-aircraft and *schnorkel* devices, and to attempt to persuade Hitler to encourage more Navy/*Luftwaffe* co-operation. In July 1943 Allied ship production exceeded, for the first time, losses from enemy action. Thereafter, the Allies produced an average of 5000 gross tons more per month than they lost. Convoy SC130 was typical of this period (7), reflecting the effectiveness of the combination of escort, support groups and aircraft. By Sept., however, U-boats returned to the North Atlantic in numbers with new tactics: the use of *schnorkel* to re-charge batteries while submerged, the Spanish coast route to the North Atlantic and increased use of mid-Atlantic refuelling led to an increase in sinkings (3). The U-boats had by no means given up the fight.

Picture above: *a surfaced German U-boat under attack from the air.*

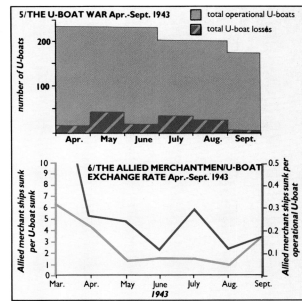

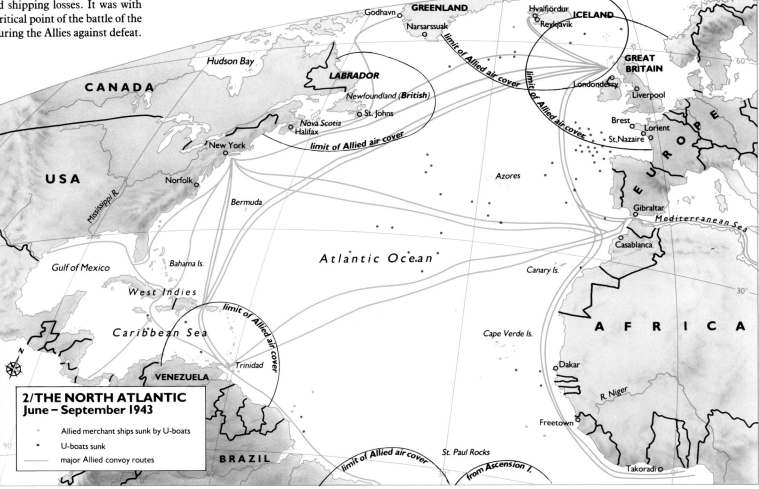

2/THE NORTH ATLANTIC
June – September 1943

· Allied merchant ships sunk by U-boats
● U-boats sunk
— major Allied convoy routes

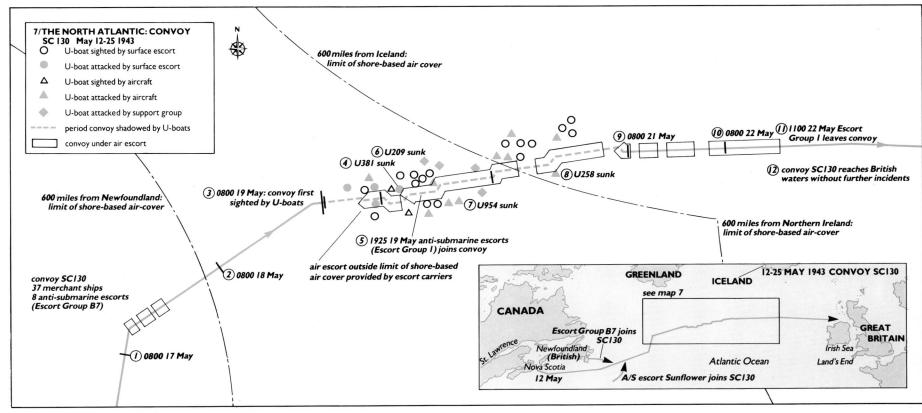

7/THE NORTH ATLANTIC: CONVOY
SC130 May 12-25 1943
○ U-boat sighted by surface escort
● U-boat attacked by surface escort
△ U-boat sighted by aircraft
▲ U-boat attacked by aircraft
◆ U-boat attacked by support group
--- period convoy shadowed by U-boats
▭ convoy under air escort

Special Forces

THE CREATION OF SPECIAL FORCES – military formations comprising teams of specially trained soldiers for unconventional combat missions – was a particular feature of the Second World War. All the major combatant nations developed Special Forces, most usually as a supporting arm of conventional forces, but it was the British who made the most use of them.

The Germans set up the first Special Forces of the war, Construction Battalion 800, organized by the *Abwehr* in 1939 and made up of small parties in civilian clothes who operated ahead of conventional forces to seize or demolish key points. They first went into action on 1 September 1939 against Poland, later expanding to regimental strength under the name *Brandenburg* and serving in every theatre of Germany's war.

On 3 June 1940 Winston Churchill addressed a minute to the Chiefs of Staff calling for raiding forces to keep the German forces on the coasts of occupied Europe tied down. Within two months eleven Commando units had been formed, each of 500 volunteers. One of these, No. 2 Commando, eventually became the Parachute Regiment. The first Commando raid (night 24/25 June) was carried out by No. 11 Independent Company, part of a unit raised for special operations in the Norwegian campaign since the Commandos were still forming, but that against Guernsey a month later did include No. 3 Commando.

Three Commandos were raised in late Summer 1940 from volunteers in the Middle East. At the same time, the Long Range Desert Group (LRDG) came into being. It was to provide invaluable intelligence through infiltration of the Axis lines via the open desert flank (page 78). In early 1941 three UK-raised Commandos combined with a Middle East Commando to form Layforce. This carried out Commando operations on the North African and Syrian coasts, but much of it was lost on Crete in May. This put the future of the Commandos in the Middle East in jeopardy, but Auchinleck backed a new unit, the Special Air Service (SAS), designed to infiltrate enemy lines to destroy aircraft on the ground. By the end of the war the SAS had grown into a brigade-sized unit and was active in behind-the-lines operations in both North-west Europe and Italy. The Middle East, however, soon became swollen by 'private armies' – among them the Special Boat Squadron, which specialized in landing on enemy-held coasts, Popski's Private Army (Libyan Arab Force Commando) and the 1st Special Service Regiment. However, coordinating their activities became increasingly difficult.

During 1941 the Commandos in Britain began to make a name for themselves, especially as a result of the Lofoten Islands and Vaagsö raids. With RAF Bomber Command, they were seen as the only means of striking directly at the Germans. Increasingly, however, it was realized (especially after the disastrous Dieppe raid, August 1942, page 86) that the war in western Europe and the Mediterranean could only be won through successful major landings on hostile coasts. Consequently, Special Forces organizations came to be raised for this purpose. The Combined Operations Pilotage Parties (COPPs) specialized in examining potential landing beaches and No. 30 Commando mirrored the German *Abwehrkommando*, whose purpose was to accompany assaulting troops and seize enemy papers and equipment. The Commandos themselves came to play a major role in spearheading amphibious assaults from the Madagascar landings in May 1942 (page 78) onwards.

In Burma there was further scope for Special Forces, such as the long-range penetration groups, the Chindits, their US equivalent, Merrill's Marauders (page 162) and V-Force, an information-gathering and sabotage group, indigenous tribesmen led by British officers. The Pacific theatre also spawned the US equivalents to the Commandos, the Rangers (Army), who also fought in Europe, Raider (Marine) battalions, the Seabees, the US Navy's Construction Battalions, which cleared beach, harbour and airfield obstacles and the Australian Coastwatchers, who reported on Japanese movements. In the final months of the war, the Japanese instituted suicide *kamikaze* (page 166) wings to combat the US Navy, while the Nazi Party used its organization to field special units: the *Volkssturm* – German Home Army – and *Wehrwolf* – German partisans which attacked Allied armies invading Germany.

While sometimes unpopular and regarded with suspicion by conventional forces, there is no doubt that Special Forces, when properly handled, made an important contribution to raiding, intelligence-gathering and Combined Operations.

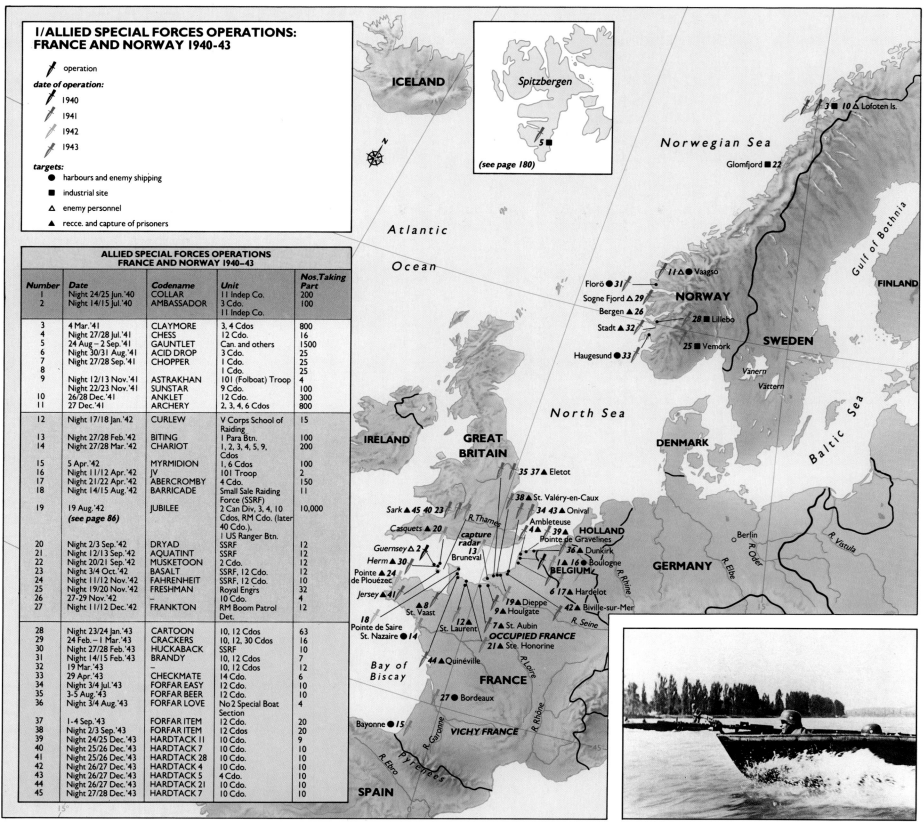

1/ALLIED SPECIAL FORCES OPERATIONS: FRANCE AND NORWAY 1940-43

- operation

date of operation:
- 1940
- 1941
- 1942
- 1943

targets:
- ● harbours and enemy shipping
- ■ industrial site
- △ enemy personnel
- ▲ recce. and capture of prisoners

ALLIED SPECIAL FORCES OPERATIONS FRANCE AND NORWAY 1940–43

Number	Date	Codename	Unit	Nos. Taking Part
1	Night 24/25 Jun.'40	COLLAR	11 Indep Co.	200
2	Night 14/15 Jul.'40	AMBASSADOR	3 Cdo. 11 Indep Co.	100
3	4 Mar.'41	CLAYMORE	3, 4 Cdos	800
4	Night 27/28 Jul.'41	CHESS	12 Cdo.	16
5	24 Aug – 2 Sep.'41	GAUNTLET	Can. and others	1500
6	Night 30/31 Aug.'41	ACID DROP	3 Cdo.	25
7	Night 27/28 Sep.'41	CHOPPER	1 Cdo.	25
8			1 Cdo.	25
9	Night 12/13 Nov.'41	ASTRAKHAN	101 (Folboat) Troop	4
10	Night 22/23 Nov.'41	SUNSTAR	9 Cdo.	100
11	26/28 Dec.'41	ANKLET	12 Cdo.	300
	27 Dec.'41	ARCHERY	2, 3, 4, 6 Cdos	800
12	Night 17/18 Jan.'42	CURLEW	V Corps School of Raiding	15
13	Night 27/28 Feb.'42	BITING	1 Para Btn.	100
14	Night 27/28 Mar.'42	CHARIOT	1, 2, 3, 4, 5, 9, Cdos	200
15	5 Apr.'42	MYRMIDION	1, 6 Cdos	100
16	Night 11/12 Apr.'42	JV	101 Troop	2
17	Night 21/22 Apr.'42	ABERCROMBY	4 Cdo.	150
18	Night 14/15 Aug.'42	BARRICADE	Small Sale Raiding Force (SSRF)	11
19	19 Aug.'42 (see page 86)	JUBILEE	2 Can Div, 3, 4, 10 Cdos, RM Cdo. (later 40 Cdo.), 1 US Ranger Btn.	10,000
20	Night 2/3 Sep.'42	DRYAD	SSRF	12
21	Night 12/13 Sep.'42	AQUATINT	SSRF	12
22	Night 20/21 Sep.'42	MUSKETOON	2 Cdo.	12
23	Night 3/4 Oct.'42	BASALT	SSRF, 12 Cdo.	12
24	Night 11/12 Nov.'42	FAHRENHEIT	SSRF, 12 Cdo.	10
25	Night 19/20 Nov.'42	FRESHMAN	Royal Engrs	32
26	27-29 Nov.'42		10 Cdo.	4
27	Night 11/12 Dec.'42	FRANKTON	RM Boom Patrol Det.	12
28	Night 23/24 Jan.'43	CARTOON	10, 12 Cdos	63
29	24 Feb. – 1 Mar.'43	CRACKERS	10, 12, 30 Cdos	16
30	Night 27/28 Feb.'43	HUCKABACK	SSRF	10
31	Night 14/15 Feb.'43	BRANDY	10, 12 Cdos	7
32	19 Mar.'43	–	10, 12 Cdos	12
33	29 Apr.'43	CHECKMATE	14 Cdo.	6
34	Night 3/4 Jul.'43	FORFAR EASY	12 Cdo.	10
35	3-5 Aug.'43	FORFAR BEER	12 Cdo.	10
36	Night 3/4 Aug.'43	FORFAR LOVE	No 2 Special Boat Section	4
37	1-4 Sep.'43	FORFAR ITEM	12 Cdo.	20
38	Night 2/3 Sep.'43	FORFAR ITEM	12 Cdos	20
39	Night 24/25 Dec.'43	HARDTACK 11	10 Cdo.	9
40	Night 25/26 Dec.'43	HARDTACK 7	10 Cdo.	10
41	Night 25/26 Dec.'43	HARDTACK 28	10 Cdo.	10
42	Night 26/27 Dec.'43	HARDTACK 4	10 Cdo.	10
43	Night 26/27 Dec.'43	HARDTACK 5	4 Cdo.	10
44	Night 26/27 Dec.'43	HARDTACK 21	10 Cdo.	10
45	Night 27/28 Dec.'43	HARDTACK 7	10 Cdo.	10

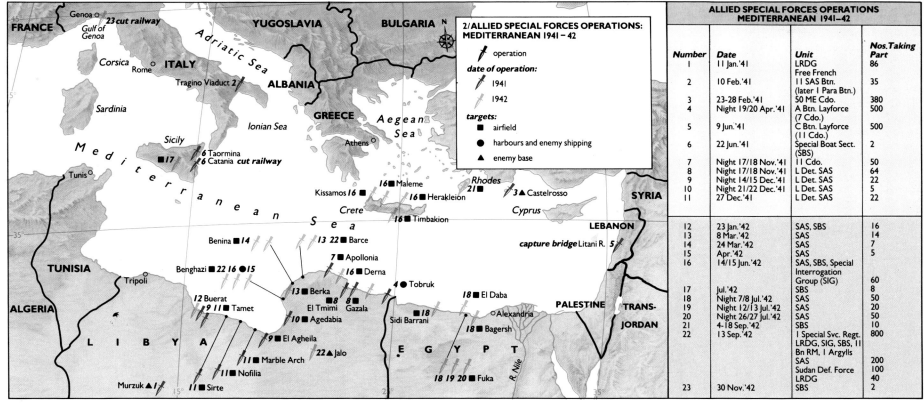

2/ALLIED SPECIAL FORCES OPERATIONS: MEDITERRANEAN 1941–42

operation

date of operation:
- 1941
- 1942

targets:
- ■ airfield
- ● harbours and enemy shipping
- ▲ enemy base

ALLIED SPECIAL FORCES OPERATIONS MEDITERRANEAN 1941–42

Number	Date	Unit	Nos. Taking Part
1	11 Jan. '41	LRDG Free French	86
2	10 Feb. '41	11 SAS Btn. (later 1 Para Btn.)	35
3	23–28 Feb. '41	50 ME Cdo.	380
4	Night 19/20 Apr. '41	A Btn. Layforce (7 Cdo.)	500
5	9 Jun. '41	C Btn. Layforce (11 Cdo.)	500
6	22 Jun. '41	Special Boat Sect. (SBS)	2
7	Night 17/18 Nov. '41	11 Cdo.	50
8	Night 17/18 Nov. '41	L Det. SAS	64
9	Night 14/15 Dec. '41	L Det. SAS	22
10	Night 21/22 Dec. '41	L Det. SAS	5
11	27 Dec. '41	L Det. SAS	22
12	23 Jan. '42	SAS, SBS	16
13	8 Mar. '42	SAS	14
14	24 Mar. '42	SAS	7
15	Apr.'42	SAS	5
16	14/15 Jun. '42	SAS, SBS, Special Interrogation Group (SIG)	60
17	Jul.'42	SBS	8
18	Night 7/8 Jul. '42	SAS	50
19	Night 12/13 Jul. '42	SAS	20
20	Night 26/27 Jul. '42	SAS	50
21	4–18 Sep. '42	SBS	10
22	13 Sep. '42	1 Special Svc. Regt. LRDG, SIG, SBS, 11 Bn RM, 1 Argylls SAS Sudan Def. Force LRDG	800 200 100 40
23	30 Nov.'42	SBS	2

SPECIAL OPERATIONS in Norway (1) were a vital means of keeping up the pretence that the Allies intended to invade it. Cross-Channel raids ceased at the end of 1943 for fear that they would encourage the Germans to strengthen their coastal defences, although there was another flurry in May 1944 to make final checks on beach obstacles. Many more operations were planned than those shown on the map. The Vaagsö raid in Dec. 1941 (4) was an early Commando operation. Destroy German military installations. The Commandos were split into 5 groups – one to prevent German reinforcements being sent to the town of South Vaagsö from the north, one to attack the town itself, another to deal with Maalöy, one to attack a strongpoint at Hollevik, and a floating reserve. The force arrived off Vaagsö at dawn on the 27 Dec. RAF Blenheims and Hampdens laid a smokescreen and the Royal Navy bombarded German batteries on Maalöy prior to the Commando attack using landing craft. Resistance was fierce in South Vaagsö, but all objectives were achieved at a cost of 19 killed. The Commandos destroyed port and military installations, brought back nearly 100 German prisoners and some volunteers for the Norwegian Free Forces. North Africa and the Mediterranean provided much scope for special operations (2) and many demolition raids were carried out. Numerous SAS and SBS reconnaissances are also not shown. From the invasion of Sicily onwards Special Forces remained active in the Aegean, Balkans, Adriatic and Italy. German Special Forces (3) fought in Scandinavia and in the German campaign in the West during May 1940. From Apr. 1941, its agents were active in the Balkans and, later, in Africa and Russia. By 1943, the special military units had expanded to include a Special Boat Service, an SS and a Brandenburg parachute battalion as well as anti-partisan (Jagdverbände) formations. The German Navy introduced human torpedoes, one-man submarines, explosive motor boats and frogmen. The Luftwaffe had a suicide wing and a special squadron, KG 200, which dropped or recovered agents from enemy territory.

Pictures left: Brandenburgers training, 1940.
Right: the Vaagsö raid, Dec. 1941.

GERMAN SPECIAL FORCES OPERATIONS

Number	Date	Objective
1	August 1939	Brandenburg attacks on Polish border at: (i) radio station at Gleiwitz (ii) customs post at Hochhinden (iii) Gamekeeper's house at Pitschen
2	May 1940	Brandenburgers take control of Gennep bridge
3	May 1940	Brandenburgers capture Nieuport bridge
4	April 1941	Brandenburgers capture Iron Gate on R. Danube
5	June–Aug. 1941	Brandenburg operations on eastern front
6	April 1942	Brandenburg operations in North Africa
7	Summer/Autumn 1942	Anti-partisan operations in Yugoslavia
8	Summer 1942	Brandenburg agents operate with Army Group South (USSR)
9	November 1942	Detachment dropped to destroy railway bridges at Sidi Bou Bakir, Tunisia
10	August 1943	Brandenburgers move in against US forces on Kasserine pass
11	May 1944	Combined special forces attack on Tito's headquarters
12	November 1944	Brandenburg groups involved in operations on Leros
13	December 1944	Skorzeny infiltrates commando groups behind enemy lines in Ardennes, Belgium
14	1945	*Jagdverbänd* in operations on eastern front until end of war
15	1944–1945	German naval commandos (K Units) attack enemy shipping at Anzio, Normandy coast and Rotterdam

3/GERMAN SPECIAL FORCES 1939-45

- ⛨ location of operation (special forces)
- location of operation (naval commandos)
- 1939
- 1940
- 1941
- 1942
- 1943
- 1944
- 1945

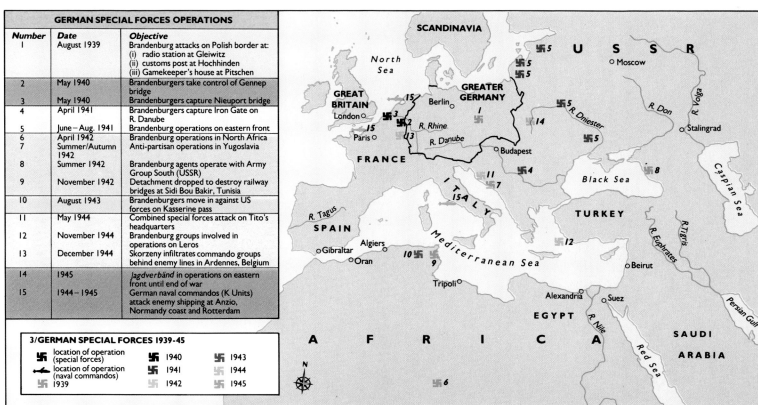

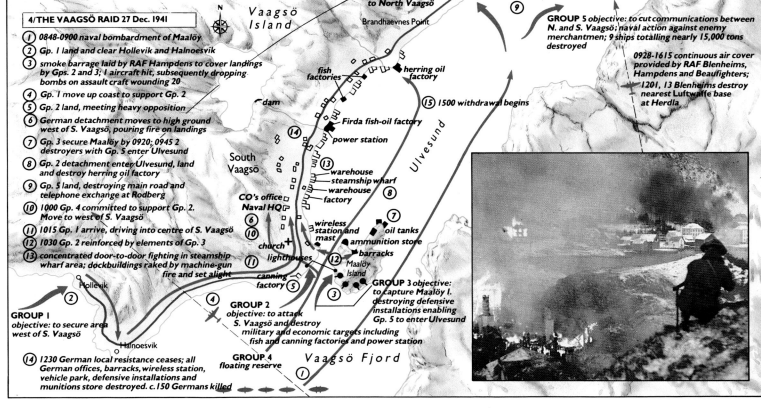

4/THE VAAGSÖ RAID 27 Dec. 1941

1. 0848-0900 naval bombardment of Maalöy
2. Gp. 1 land and clear Hollevik and Halnoesvik
3. smoke barrage laid by RAF Hampdens to cover landings by Gps. 2 and 3; 1 aircraft hit, subsequently dropping bombs on assault craft wounding 20
4. Gp. 1 move up coast to support Gp. 2
5. Gp. 2 land, meeting heavy opposition
6. German detachment moves to high ground west of S. Vaagsö, pouring fire on landings
7. Gp. 3 secure Maalöy by 0920; 0945 2 destroyers with Gp. 5 enter Ulvesund
8. Gp. 2 detachment enter Ulvesund, land and destroy herring oil factory
9. Gp. 5 land, destroying main road and telephone exchange at Rodberg
10. 1000 Gp. 4 committed to support Gp. 2. Move to west of S. Vaagsö
11. 1015 Gp. 1 arrive, driving into centre of S. Vaagsö
12. 1030 Gp. 2 reinforced by elements of Gp. 3
13. concentrated door-to-door fighting in steamship wharf area; dockbuildings raked by machine-gun fire and set alight
14. 1230 German local resistance ceases; all German offices, barracks, wireless station, vehicle park, defensive installations and munitions store destroyed. c.150 Germans killed
15. 1500 withdrawal begins

GROUP 5 objective: to cut communications between N. and S. Vaagsö; naval action against enemy merchantmen; 9 ships totalling nearly 15,000 tons destroyed

0928-1615 continuous air cover provided by RAF Blenheims, Hampdens and Beaufighters; 1201, 13 Blenheims destroy nearest Luftwaffe base at Herdla

GROUP 1 objective: to secure area west of S. Vaagsö

GROUP 2 objective: to attack S. Vaagsö and destroy military and economic targets including fish and canning factories and power station

GROUP 3 objective: to capture Maalöy I. destroying defensive installations enabling Gp. 5 to enter Ulvesund

GROUP 4 floating reserve

Air War in Europe II 1941~1943

BEFORE THE OUTBREAK OF WAR only two air forces, the RAF and the US Army Air Corps, were committed to strategic bombing as a central part of air strategy. Air leaders in both countries believed that it was possible to destroy the war-willingness of enemy countries by attacking their industries and civilian workforces from the air, cutting off supplies to the armed forces, and increasing popular demands for peace. It was evident, however, from early in the war that the RAF lacked the technical means to carry this strategy out (page 52). Not until large numbers of heavy four-engined bombers were available with sufficient trained air-crews could a bombing offensive be launched with any chance of success. Only from 1942, with the larger Lancaster and Stirling bombers coming into service, and with the arrival in Britain of the US 8th Air Force – built around the high-performance four-engined B-17 'Flying Fortress' and the B-24 Liberator – was an offensive possible that could bring real strategic results.

RAF Bomber Command never deviated from the view that the bombing campaign was worth the effort. Even in the difficult early years of the war, plans were drawn up for a systematic attack on German industrial target-systems. Priority was given to oil and power, with transport and the aircraft industry high on the list. But the RAF lacked good navigational aids or escort fighters and was compelled to fly only at night under clear skies, and to aim at whole cities rather than

particular factories. As a result, Bomber Command, led from February 1942 by Air·Marshal Arthur Harris, moved by default to a strategy of 'area bombing'. It was argued that even attacks of an indiscriminate type would disrupt the local economy and undermine war-willingness.

The USAAF took a different view. American planners believed in precision bombing by day, using large, well-armed bombers which could fight their way to the target and back. The Air Corps, under General 'Hap' Arnold, drew up detailed bombardment plans even before American entry into the war. American airmen favoured oil, electric power, the aviation industry, transportation, chemicals and machinery as major targets, but unlike the RAF insisted that it was also necessary to attack the *Luftwaffe* as an 'intermediate target'. Without destroying German air defence, it was argued, the strategic offensive would be blunted as the *Luftwaffe* had been in 1940. When US bombers arrived in Britain in 1942, in small numbers and poorly prepared, they were sent in precision daylight attacks to bomb industrial and air force targets.

The Allied campaign in 1942 was very limited. This was a period of apprenticeship as bomber commanders learned tactics, trained crews and built up a satisfactory ground organization. In May a '1000 Bomber Raid' was launched against Cologne, but this was not typical of the offensive. It was a spectacular demonstration to the Germans of the growing

power and confidence of the RAF, and a reply to critics at home. The bombing offensive only became a major campaign following the Casablanca meeting between Roosevelt and Churchill in January 1943 (page 134) from which came the directive for a 'Combined Bombing Offensive'. By then very large numbers of bombers were in the pipeline, and both Western Allies were under pressure from Stalin to relieve the pressure on Soviet forces in the east. The bombing offensive was a kind of second front, forcing the Germans to divert aircraft and resources to combating the threat from the air. Both Bomber Command and the 8th Air Force began systematically to bomb German targets deeper and deeper within German territory, the Americans hitting specific industrial targets, the RAF attacking cities with devastating effects. In Hamburg in late July bomber forces created the first 'firestorm' destroying 70% of the city and killing over 30,000 people.

During 1943 the German defences began to organize more effectively to counter the bombing. General Kammhuber built a defensive line of anti-aircraft and searchlight batteries in northern Germany, Holland and Denmark, supplemented by an expanded home fighter force for day and night combat. By the late Autumn the balance was swinging in favour of the defence: during the intensive raids on Berlin (1943) RAF Bomber Command sustained losses which forced major attacks

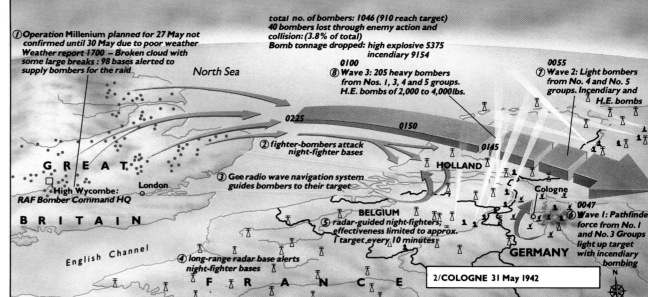

FROM MAY 1940 RAF Bomber Command undertook a strategic bombing campaign against individual cities and military targets in Germany and occupied Europe from the Baltic to western France (*1*), but their effect was limited by poor accuracy, limited range and growing German defences. On the night of 30 May 1942, 1046 bombers took off from Britain for the largest air raid yet mounted (*2*). The target was Cologne on the River Rhine. A carefully orchestrated piece of morale-boosting, the '1000 Bomber Raid' was formed by three waves of aircraft carrying over 2000 tons of high-explosive and incendiary bombs. The bombing caused widespread destruction, but killed only 469 people. In 1942 the US 8th Air Force joined the campaign and began a series of precision daylight raids on specific industrial targets. Bomber Command also struck regularly against Italian cities from 1940 onwards (*3*). The raids were carried out either from Mediterranean bases or on a shuttle run from Britain to North Africa. In 1942 the US 15th Air Force joined the campaign. By 1943 60% of Italian industrial production had been destroyed. Italy lost more civilians to air attack than Britain. In 1942 and 1943 in return for attacks on Germany's historic cities Hitler ordered the *Luftwaffe* to bomb cities like Bath, York and Exeter (*6*). These became known as 'Baedeker' raids, attacks on tourist cities. They petered out with demands from the eastern front for aircraft. Not until the Winter of 1943/1944 was the *Luftwaffe* ordered to attack Britain again. The main target in Operation *Steinbock* (the 'Baby Blitz') was London, but the *Luftwaffe* now encountered strong defences and lacked sufficient aircraft to do much damage. In 1943 the *Luftwaffe* dropped only 2298 tons on Britain (*5*), a fraction of the amount carried by the RAF in a single raid. The air war now turned upon the economics of production and supply (*4*), and the Allies gained the upper hand.

Picture below: USAAF B-17 'Flying Fortress' heavy bombers, flying in high-level, box formation during a daylight raid on Bremen.

to cease. In the 8th Air Force attack on the ball-bearing plants at Schweinfurt in October the bomber streams were harried on the outward and homeward journey, losing 65 bombers out of a force of 291. These rates of attrition were unacceptable. Not until long-range fighters were available to escort the bombers to their targets, and not until heavy damage was inflicted on the *Luftwaffe*, could the offensive hope for greater success. The failure to break down the German defences echoed the German defeat over Britain in 1940, and raised the powerful argument that bombers might be better employed helping the ground forces. By the end of 1943 the bombing campaign was yet to prove its worth.

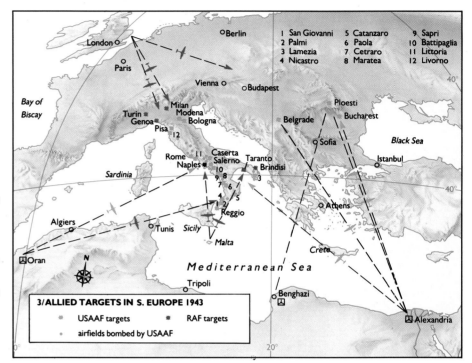

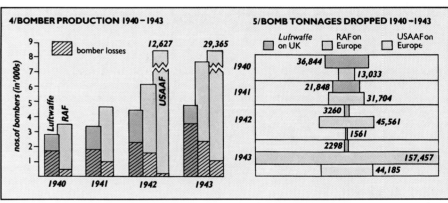

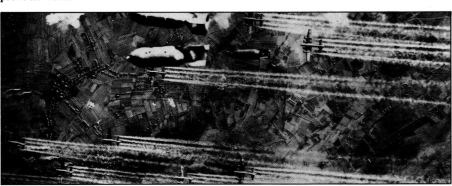

El Alamein AUG. ~ NOV. 1942

DESPITE AUCHINLECK'S SUCCESS in holding Rommel at the Gazala-Bir Hakeim line in July (a battle sometimes called First Alamein, page 80), Churchill decided to replace him following the Cairo conference, 4-10 August 1942 (page 86). On 15 August Alexander was appointed in his place as Commander-in-Chief, Middle East; two days earlier Montgomery had been given command of the 8th Army. Churchill's directive to Alexander was to destroy, as soon as possible, the Axis army in North Africa commanded by Rommel (who had been promoted field marshal on 22 June). Montgomery's first order to 8th Army was that it would retreat no further: it would hold any German offensive on its present, Alam Halfa, line.

Rommel, who had been preparing to attack with his four German and six Italian divisions (two of each nationality being armoured), opened the offensive on 31 August. By evening of 2 September he had made little progress and his armour was short of fuel. Next day he ordered a retreat. Montgomery did not pursue, fearing losses to his armour from German anti-tank defences, but staged heavy air attacks on the retreating Germans. By 7 September fighting had ended.

Montgomery now continued the reorganization of the 8th Army he had begun on assuming command. During September and October reinforcements and new equipment reached Egypt, including 300 American Sherman tanks. By 23 October, the date chosen for the opening of his offensive on Rommel, Montgomery commanded 230,000 men and 1030 tanks; Rommel commanded 100,000 men and 500 tanks (of which 218 were German). The British now had an air superiority of about 5:3. Montgomery resisted pressure from his superiors to open the offensive until he had sufficient troops and firepower to ensure success.

Rommel had fortified his position after Alam Halfa and intermingled his German troops among their Italian allies. Montgomery's plan for the battle, which would be called (El) Alamein, was to attack along the coast with the infantry of XXX Corps and to mount a simultaneous diversionary offensive with XIII Corps in the south. When XXX Corps had opened a corridor, the armour of X Corps was to attack through it, and drive Rommel's Panzer Armee Afrika back along the coast.

The attack opened on the night of 23 October with a hurricane of artillery bombardment, behind which four infantry divisions moved to the assault. Heavy fighting broke out, as the Germans committed 15th Panzer Division to hold the break-in. In the south the Germans resisted strongly and on 25 October Montgomery decided to transfer forces from that sector to the developing dogfight on the coast. Rommel, who had been absent sick in Italy, returned the same day.

The battle which ensued concentrated upon the key features of the coastal corridor, along which most lines of communication ran, and the commanding Kidney Hill position midway between the coast and the Qattara Depression. Despite Rommel's resourceful use of his Panzer divisions, Kidney Hill was gained, and from there Montgomery launched his decisive stroke. Following a heavy artillery barrage, a bitter tank battle ensued, reducing the German armour by the evening of 2 November to 35 serviceable tanks. Rommel decided to withdraw. Hitler countermanded the order but Allied troops broke the German line and armoured units poured through. Next day Rommel was forced to order a full retreat and the remnants of his army set off westwards along the coast road towards Tobruk.

Montgomery paused to regroup before launching a pursuit. When it began on 5 November he at first hoped to trap Rommel by encirclement on the coast. Frustrated by German elusiveness and bad weather, he accepted by 7 November that it would be a long chase but resolved to give Rommel no rest. Over the next three months, with two long pauses at El Agheila and Wadi Zemzem, he sustained his harassment of Rommel, hampered by innumerable booby traps and by an increasing number of prisoners. Rommel's retreat did not end until he reached the temporary safety of the Mareth line in Tunisia (page 116). The 8th Army suffered 13,500 casualties in the battle of Alamein. Rommel, though he preserved the manpower of his German divisions, lost almost all his tanks; his Italian formations effectively ceased to exist. But now he had some time to prepare for a vigorous defence of Tunisia.

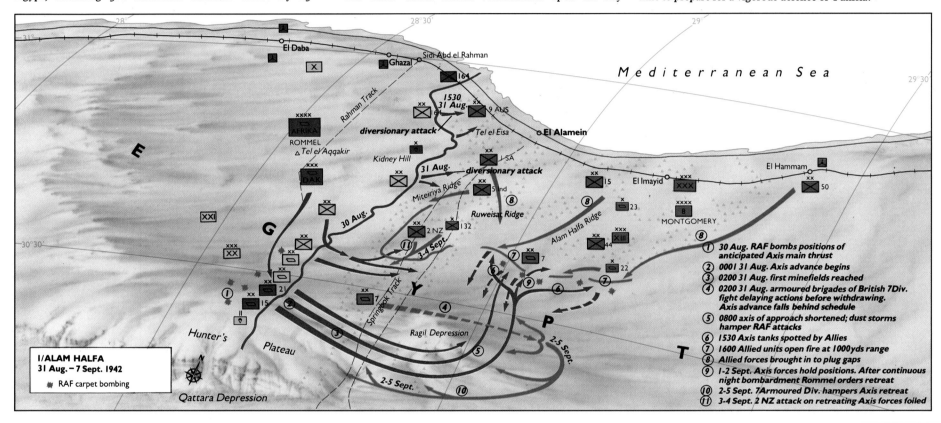

I/ALAM HALFA
31 Aug. – 7 Sept. 1942
✳ RAF carpet bombing

① 30 Aug. RAF bombs positions of anticipated Axis main thrust
② 0001 31 Aug. Axis advance begins
③ 0200 31 Aug. first minefields reached
④ 0200 31 Aug. armoured brigades of British 7Div. fight delaying actions before withdrawing. Axis advance falls behind schedule
⑤ 0800 axis of approach shortened; dust storms hamper RAF attacks
⑥ 1530 Axis tanks spotted by Allies
⑦ 1600 Allied units open fire at 1000yds range
⑧ Allied forces brought in to plug gaps
⑨ 1-2 Sept. Axis forces hold positions. After continuous night bombardment Rommel orders retreat
⑩ 2-5 Sept. 7Armoured Div. hampers Axis retreat
⑪ 3-4 Sept. 2 NZ attack on retreating Axis forces foiled

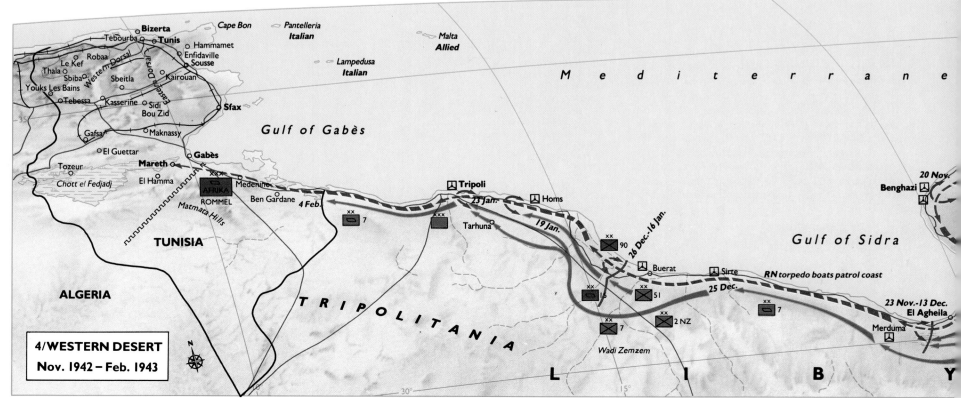

4/WESTERN DESERT
Nov. 1942 – Feb. 1943

THE CONFLICT IN THE WESTERN DESERT reached a climax with a series of actions (1-3), in the second half of 1942. Both sides intended these as knock-out blows and carefully planned both tactics and supply accordingly. Rommel began an attack on Montgomery's Alam Halfa (1) position on the night of 30/31 Aug. The British line ran forty miles from the sea to the Qattara Depression and was least strongly held in the south: it was there that Rommel made his initial effort. Montgomery anticipated this and garrisoned the blocking position of the Alam Halfa ridge with three armoured brigades and an infantry division. When Rommel's 15th and 21st Panzer Divisions, supported by the Italian Trieste Division, breached the minefields, drove 7th Armoured Division back and reached the ridge, they were repelled and forced to withdraw. By 2 Sept. the battle for the ridge was over and Rommel's forces had retired almost to their start line. The only heavy British casualties were suffered by 2nd New Zealand Division in a costly flank attack (3 Sept). Montgomery prepared a major counter-offensive which began with an attack at 2200 on 23 Oct. (2). XIII Corps' diversionary attack held 21st Panzer but 15th Panzer struck at the corridor opened near the coast. There was bitter positional fighting on 24-25 Oct. Montgomery, in order to accelerate progress, put his main effort into fighting for the coast and, by 1st Armoured Division, for Kidney Hill during 26-29 Oct. Rommel continually counter-attacked with 21st Panzer Division and (29 Oct.) brought 90th forward to support 164th on the coast. Montgomery therefore withdrew 1st Armoured and 2nd New Zealand into reserve as a preliminary to breaking out in the

Kidney Hill area. The Alamein breakthrough (3) began on 2 Nov. at 0100 at and north of Kidney Hill, selected by Montgomery because the earlier fighting had drawn the Germans into the corridor and near the coast. The attack was led by 2nd New Zealand Division, supported by 1st Armoured which, during the day, fought a violent tank battle with 15th Panzer, supported by 21st and some Italian armour. Rommel's tank losses were so heavy that he decided to withdraw that night but was forced by Hitler to continue the struggle. Counter-orders sowed confusion from which Montgomery profited. On 3 Nov. he sent 51st and 4th Indian Divisions in a night attack against Kidney Hill and, when they broke through, launched 7th and 10th Armoured Divisions into open country; 1st Armoured and the New Zealanders joined in. The Italian Ariete Division was almost destroyed in the battle as Rommel now withdrew along the coast. In the south, XIII Corps overran the Italian divisions. Montgomery's forces then began a pursuit of their quarry (4). Montgomery attempted to block Rommel's retreat at Fuka (5 Nov.) and to encircle 21st Panzer's remaining armour at Mersa Matruh on 6 Nov. But thereafter Rommel kept ahead of him, reaching the Tunisian border 4 Feb. The 7th Armoured Division led Montgomery's pursuit for most of the 1600 miles, and although the Germans had not been decisively defeated as planned, the Western Desert was now cleared.

Picture below: a British troop convoy in the Western Desert. Negotiating artillery fire and extensive minefields were characteristic features of the campaigns here.

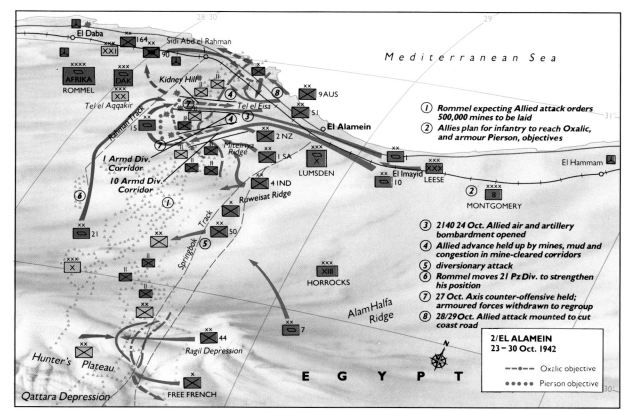

1. Rommel expecting Allied attack orders 500,000 mines to be laid
2. Allies plan for infantry to reach Oxalic, and armour Pierson, objectives
3. 2140 24 Oct. Allied air and artillery bombardment opened
4. Allied advance held up by mines, mud and congestion in mine-cleared corridors
5. diversionary attack
6. Rommel moves 21 Pz Div. to strengthen his position
7. 27 Oct. Axis counter-offensive held; armoured forces withdrawn to regroup
8. 28/29 Oct. Allied attack mounted to cut coast road

2/EL ALAMEIN
23 – 30 Oct. 1942

— · — · — Oxalic objective
· · · · · · Pierson objective

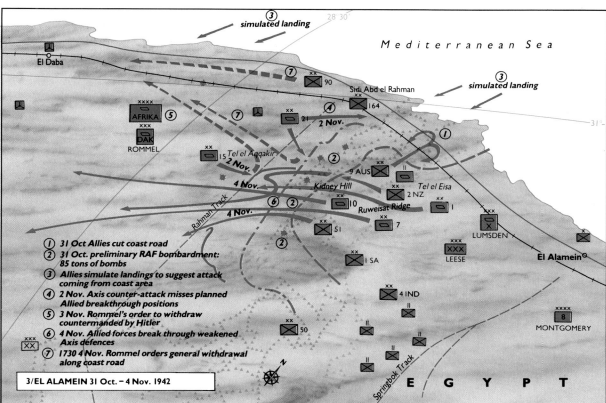

1. 31 Oct Allies cut coast road
2. 31 Oct. preliminary RAF bombardment: 85 tons of bombs
3. Allies simulate landings to suggest attack coming from coast area
4. 2 Nov. Axis counter-attack misses planned Allied breakthrough positions
5. 3 Nov. Rommel's order to withdraw countermanded by Hitler
6. 4 Nov. Allied forces break through weakened Axis defences
7. 1730 4 Nov. Rommel orders general withdrawal along coast road

3/EL ALAMEIN 31 Oct. – 4 Nov. 1942

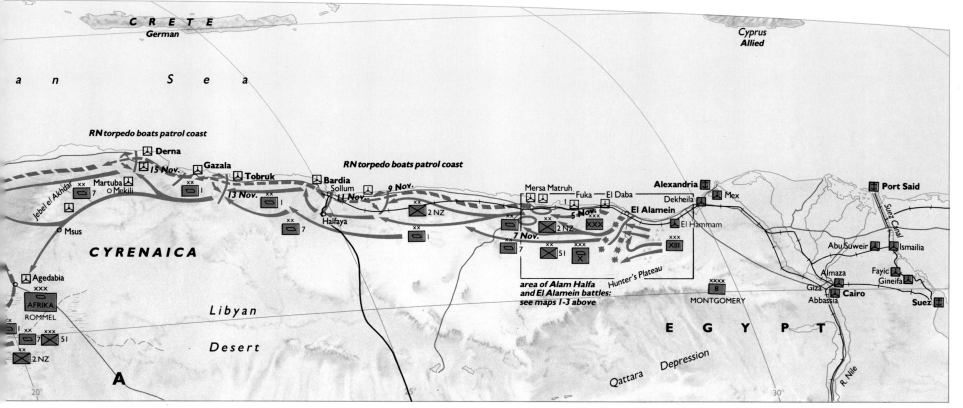

THE ANGLO-AMERICAN conferences of 1942 (page 86) failed to concert a strategy for an early invasion of German-occupied Western Europe, which the British persuaded their Allies was too strong to be attacked with the forces available that year. At a London meeting, 20-22 July, Marshall therefore drafted a plan to use the American forces which had reached Britain, together with the British 1st Army, in an invasion of French North Africa. A headquarters for *Torch*, as the operation was codenamed, was set up under Eisenhower in London on 14 August and the date of the landings fixed for 8 November.

French North Africa – Morocco, Algeria and Tunisia (the Maghreb) – was not occupied by Germàn forces, but remained under the control of the Vichy Government. Since the conclusion of the battle of Alamein (page 114) however, Rommel's *Panzer Armee Afrika* had been in retreat to Tunisia from Egypt and Admiral Darlan, Vichy's commander in North Africa, was under orders to resist an Allied invasion. Of the three Allied Task Forces, Western, commanded by Patton, which had sailed directly from the United States, met the fiercest resistance in Morocco. Eastern, landing at Algiers, found the port in the hands of friendly forces and was opposed only when Vichy officers reasserted control late in the morning

of 8 November.

The Germans had wrongly estimated that the Allied convoys were bound for Malta or Egypt and had therefore not heavily attacked them. On 10 November, however, on receipt of news that Darlan had been taken into protective custody and had negotiated a ceasefire with the Allies, Hitler ordered his troops into the unoccupied (Vichy) zone of France and extracted consent from Laval, Pétain's Prime Minister, to airlift and convoy troops to Tunisia. Italy meanwhile, occupied Corsica. Confusion reigned among the French North African garrison, with some units welcoming the Allies, others seeking

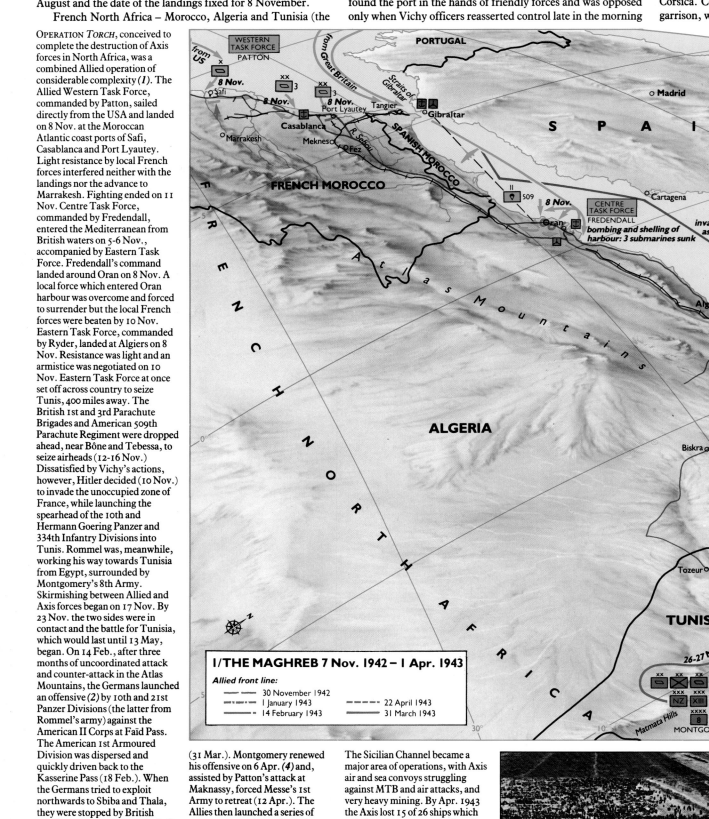

OPERATION *TORCH*, conceived to complete the destruction of Axis forces in North Africa, was a combined Allied operation of considerable complexity (*1*). The Allied Western Task Force, commanded by Patton, sailed directly from the USA and landed on 8 Nov. at the Moroccan Atlantic coast ports of Safi, Casablanca and Port Lyautey. Light resistance by local French forces interfered neither with the landings nor the advance to Marrakesh. Fighting ended on 11 Nov. Centre Task Force, commanded by Fredendall, entered the Mediterranean from British waters on 5-6 Nov., accompanied by Eastern Task Force. Fredendall's command landed around Oran on 8 Nov. A local force which entered Oran harbour was overcome and forced to surrender but the local French forces were beaten by 10 Nov. Eastern Task Force, commanded by Ryder, landed at Algiers on 8 Nov. Resistance was light and an armistice was negotiated on 10 Nov. Eastern Task Force at once set off across country to seize Tunis, 400 miles away. The British 1st and 3rd Parachute Brigades and American 509th Parachute Regiment were dropped ahead, near Bône and Tebessa, to seize airheads (12-16 Nov.) Dissatisfied by Vichy's actions, however, Hitler decided (10 Nov.) to invade the unoccupied zone of France, while launching the spearhead of the 10th and Hermann Goering Panzer and 334th Infantry Divisions into Tunis. Rommel was, meanwhile, working his way towards Tunisia from Egypt, surrounded by Montgomery's 8th Army. Skirmishing between Allied and Axis forces began on 17 Nov. By 23 Nov. the two sides were in contact and the battle for Tunisia, which would last until 13 May, began. On 14 Feb., after three months of uncoordinated attack and counter-attack in the Atlas Mountains, the Germans launched an offensive (*2*) by 10th and 21st Panzer Divisions (the latter from Rommel's army) against the American II Corps at Faïd Pass. The American 1st Armoured Division was dispersed and quickly driven back to the Kasserine Pass (18 Feb.). When the Germans tried to exploit northwards to Sbiba and Thala, they were stopped by British reinforcements and the arrival of the US 9th Division. On 23 Feb. Rommel, now appointed as commander in Tunisia, began to withdraw. He then decided to attack Montgomery's 8th Army (*3*), assembling outside the French fortified line of Mareth on 3 Mar. The attack failed and on 6 Mar. Rommel was invalided to Germany. While Patton mounted a diversionary attack at Gafsa, Montgomery went on to the offensive (20 Mar.). His main thrust was held by 15th Panzer Division, but a flanking movement by the New Zealanders (22 Mar.) turned the Mareth line and forced its German-Italian defenders to retreat to El Alamein

I/THE MAGHREB 7 Nov. 1942 – 1 Apr. 1943

Allied front line:
- 30 November 1942
- 1 January 1943
- 14 February 1943
- 22 April 1943
- 31 March 1943

(31 Mar.). Montgomery renewed his offensive on 6 Apr. (*4*) and, assisted by Patton's attack at Maknassy, forced Messe's 1st Army to retreat (12 Apr.). The Allies then launched a series of concentric attacks on the Axis fortification around Tunis: Montgomery on 19 Apr., British 1st Army (22 Apr.), Bradley's II Corps (23 Apr.). After regrouping, the attacks were resumed on 3 May and Bizerta fell to II Corps and Tunis to 1st Army on 7 May: on 13 May Messe's 1st Army surrendered to Montgomery. Critical to the success of *Torch* and the clearing of Tunisia was control of the Mediterranean (*5*) where strategic questions revolved around supply. Rommel's retreating forces were supplied by air. The capture of ports and airfields along the North African coast allowed the Allies to supply their advancing forces rapidly.

The Sicilian Channel became a major area of operations, with Axis air and sea convoys struggling against MTB and air attacks, and very heavy mining. By Apr. 1943 the Axis lost 15 of 26 ships which sailed, and 117 transport aircraft. Allied success in sealing the area was reflected in the failure of Axis troops to escape. Surface action was limited, the Germans failing to capture the remnants of the French fleet at Toulon intact, whilst the Italian navy was confined in port due to a shortage of fuel. The battle of the Mediterranean (*6*) now passed its crisis point, as the number of Axis convoys declined to a minimum.

Picture right: some of the 275,000 Axis prisoners taken during the Allied conquest of Tunisia. This camp was at Mateur, west of Tunis.

direction from Darlan and some obeying Pétain's original order to resist. The French fleet at Toulon, which Darlan summoned to North Africa on 11 November (by which time he had made its ceasefire effective) was scuttled at its moorings.

The focus of action now transferred to Tunisia, where the Germans were building up a garrison and whither the Allies were sending troops by air and sea from Algiers. The German forces were subjected to heavy aerial and artillery bombardment but the Allied overland advance on Tunis was halted by German counter-attack at Madjez-el Bab, outside the city, on 11 December. Elements of three German divisions had arrived from Italy, which were shortly to form the 5th Panzer Army. To oppose them the Allies had two of their own and were supported by French units, led by Giraud, who assumed

overall command after the assassination of Darlan by a dissident Frenchman on 24 December.

During January the fighting in eastern Tunisia was sporadic, although the Allied bombardment continued, and increasing pressure was exerted on Axis supply routes from Italy. But on 14 February, while Rommel was strengthening the defences of the Mareth line (to which he had retreated from Egypt earlier that month), 5th Panzer Army attacked the American II Corps between Faïd Pass and Gafsa and drove it back fifty miles. This offensive was not halted until 22 February. Eisenhower, who then had three divisions in line, counter-attacked on 26 February and by 3 March had regained his original positions.

Alexander had now arrived to act as Eisenhower's deputy in

command of operations. He reorganized the Allied front to place the American II Corps opposite Bizerta, the British 1st Army opposite Tunis and the French XIX Corps to its south, with Montgomery's 8th Army, which had broken the Mareth line between 26 February and 31 March, in the south. On 4 May he unleashed a general offensive against the Axis forces and by concentric advances forced their total surrender on 13 May. Bizerta and Tunis, both held by German forces, surrendered on 7 May. The Italian 1st Army, remnants of Mussolini's garrison of Libya, was surrounded by Montgomery's 8th Army and surrendered on 13 May. Some 125,000 Germans, and 115,000 Italians became prisoners, including the German commander, Arnim (Rommel had been invalided on 9 March). The Axis presence in North Africa was at an end.

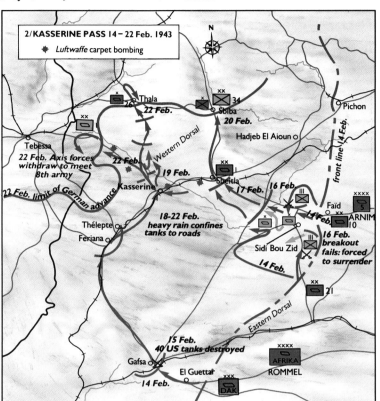

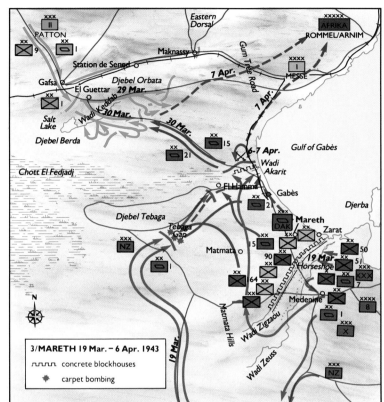

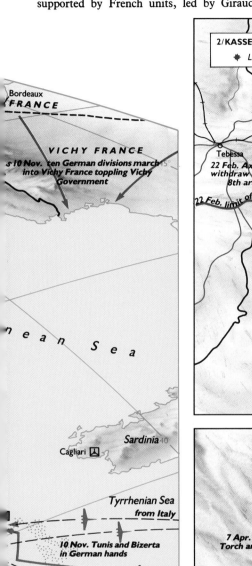

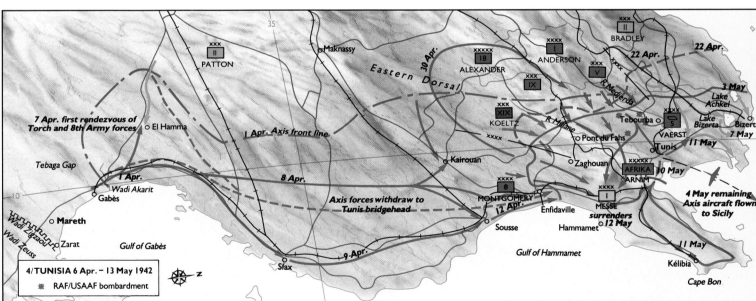

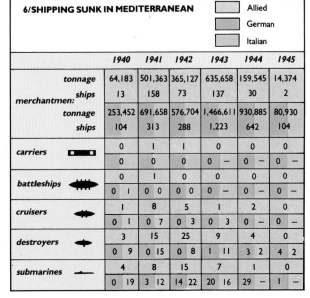

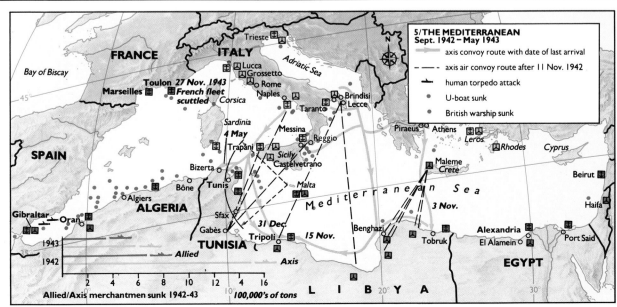

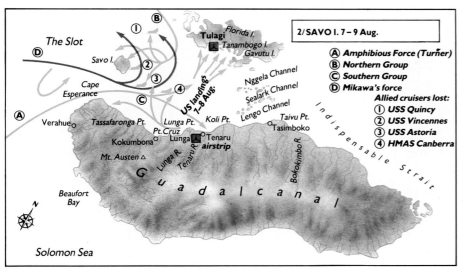

2/SAVO I. 7-9 Aug.

A Amphibious Force (Turner)
B Northern Group
C Southern Group
D Mikawa's force

Allied cruisers lost:
① USS Quincy
② USS Vincennes
③ USS Astoria
④ HMAS Canberra

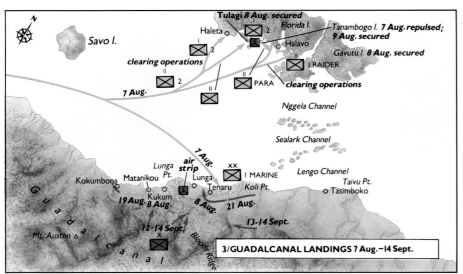

3/GUADALCANAL LANDINGS 7 Aug.-14 Sept.

THE FIRST JAPANESE LANDING on Guadalcanal after the US invasion and resultant battle of Savo Island (2, 3) was on 18 Aug. when some 2000 men were put ashore at Taivu Point. This force attempted to rush the Lunga position and was destroyed around Tenaru in the early hours of the 21st. The Japanese failure in the battle of the Eastern Solomons resulted in the force bringing troops to Guadalcanal being badly mauled by aircraft from Henderson Field on the 25th, but over the next ten days some 4700 troops were put ashore around Kokumbona and Tasimboko under cover of darkness. Problems of movement through dense jungle and of trying to co-ordinate various attacks ensured that the first major attempt to overrun Henderson Field collapsed in a series of costly defeats, most notably on Bloody Ridge (12-14 Sept.) (3). A further effort in October (4), made in greater strength, also failed. A diversionary attack across the Matanikou on 23 Oct. proved premature because the 2nd Infantry Division was constantly delayed as it struggled along jungle trails to its start lines south of Bloody Ridge. Without proper artillery support, the 2nd Infantry Division was forced to attack on the night of the 24th/25th and again the following night at less than half strength. Piecemeal commitment left the formation too weak to make another effort.

Picture below: a Japanese Val dive-bomber attacking the USS Hornet at Santa Cruz, 26 Oct. 1942.

IN THE SPRING OF 1942 the Japanese planned operations throughout the south-west and central Pacific: following the Midway operation (page 96), the Japanese meant to proceed with the occupation of Port Moresby on New Guinea, New Caledonia, Fiji, Samoa, and Johnston Island. The unexpected defeat at Midway cost the Imperial Navy the carrier force needed for the more distant of these operations, but did not lessen the Japanese determination to secure Port Moresby and to consolidate positions in the Solomons. Assuming that no US counter-attack in the south-west Pacific could materialize before the second quarter of 1943, the Japanese sought to complete a network of bases in the area as soon as possible. For the Americans, victory at Midway provided the opportunity to dispute Japanese gains beyond Rabaul on New Britain. Determined not to allow the Japanese to recover from their defeat, the US High Command decided upon a step-by-step advance on Rabaul. In the south-west reaches of the Solomons, the Americans would seize Tulagi harbour and the airstrip that the Japanese were preparing on Guadalcanal; in eastern New Guinea, the Allies were to secure the Dobodura area by an overland advance to Gona and Buna. These two efforts were to begin in early and mid-August respectively.

Before the Allies had a chance to move in either theatre, however, Japanese forces were put ashore at Gona with the intention of advancing to Port Moresby along what was believed to be a motor track over the Owen Stanley Range. In reality, the Kokoda Trail was no more than a jungle track, the full length of which no white man had travelled in two decades. Neither the state of this trail nor the area's forbidding terrain and climate deterred the Japanese, who swept aside feeble Australian resistance around the beachhead, pressed rapidly inland and secured Kokoda on 27 July.

Thereafter the Japanese advance slowed as lack of numbers and supply problems took their toll; further, the second part of their effort – the seizure of Milne Bay at the south-east tip of New Guinea – miscarried on 25 August. Nevertheless, by 16 September the Japanese had fought their way from Kokoda to within 25 miles of Port Moresby, but exhaustion and the need

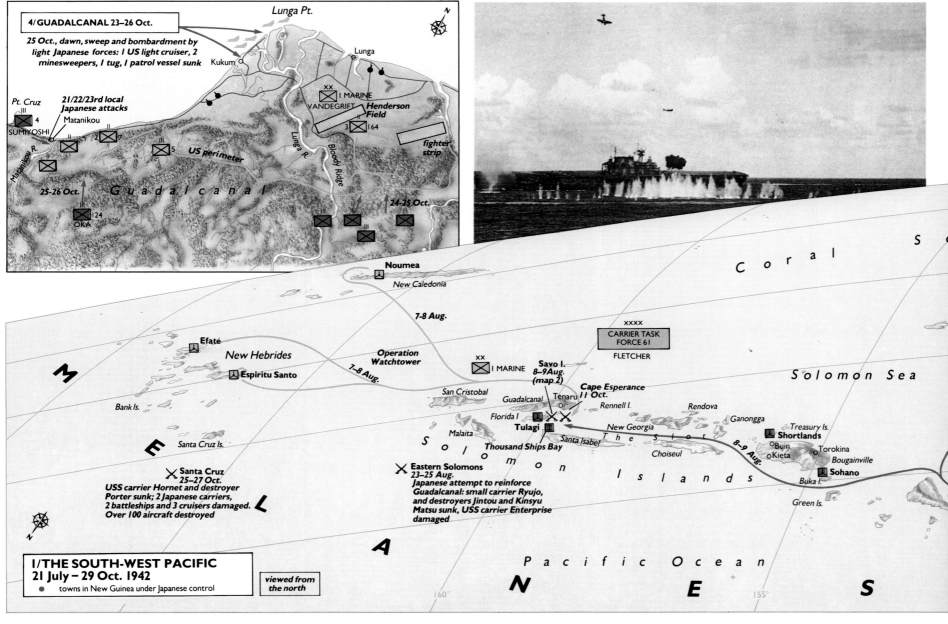

4/GUADALCANAL 23-26 Oct.

25 Oct., dawn, sweep and bombardment by light Japanese forces: 1 US light cruiser, 2 minesweepers, 1 tug, 1 patrol vessel sunk

1/THE SOUTH-WEST PACIFIC 21 July – 29 Oct. 1942

● towns in New Guinea under Japanese control

viewed from the north

Santa Cruz 25-27 Oct.
USS carrier Hornet and destroyer Porter sunk; 2 Japanese carriers, 2 battleships and 3 cruisers damaged. Over 100 aircraft destroyed

Eastern Solomons 23-25 Aug.
Japanese attempt to reinforce Guadalcanal: small carrier Ryujo, and destroyers Jintou and Kinsyu Matsu sunk, USS carrier Enterprise damaged

CARRIER TASK FORCE 61
FLETCHER

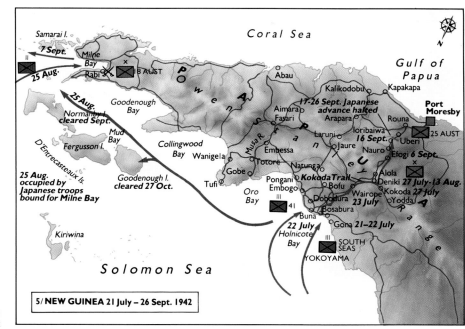

BEFORE THEIR VICTORIES at the Coral Sea and Midway, the Allies failed to strengthen effectively their forces in New Guinea; the Japanese, however, were keen to establish bases there, to extend their control. But the reinforcement of Port Moresby after July 1942 and the occupation of Milne Bay provided the Australians with the means to retain eastern New Guinea in the face of a Japanese attack following landings at Gona and Buna (5) that was made without effective air and naval support. Indeed, such was the slenderness of Japanese resources that the forces stranded in the D'Entrecasteaux Islands during their passage to Milne Bay by Allied air attacks could only be withdrawn with great difficulty. It was with equal difficulty, however, that the Japanese were denied Milne Bay, the Japanese evacuating their surviving forces on 5-6 Sept. The Japanese advance to the Ioribaiwa Ridge and attempt to secure Milne Bay represented the high water mark of the Japanese effort in eastern New Guinea; thereafter the Allied advantage in numbers and ability to move forces by sea and air proved decisive in ensuring the Japanese defeat throughout the theatre. Australian forces from Milne Bay cleared Normanby in September and Goodenough in October, then securing the airstrip at Wanigela (6) as a base for future operations against Buna. With Allied forces also advancing overland to the Solomon Sea, the Japanese position in eastern New Guinea was beyond recall, though November came with Japanese forces still occupying Kokoda.

Picture left: Australian forces negotiating the Kokoda Trail.

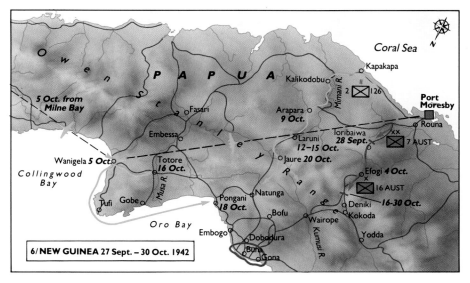

to deal with the situation that had developed on Guadalcanal (see text below) led the Japanese to halt operations on the Kokoda Trail and to settle for the consolidation of the Gona beachhead until the position in the Solomons was resolved. In the face of the threat posed by a massively reinforced garrison, however, the Japanese had to begin to withdraw along the Kokoda Trail on the 24th, and thereafter the Allies developed an outflanking attack and began to airlift forces to the Wanigela-Pongani area – directly threatening the Japanese beachhead around Buna and Gona. By mid-October, without proper reinforcement and supply, the Japanese forces on the Kokoda Trail had been reduced to cannibalism.

In the Solomons, the Americans secured Tulagi harbour in the face of desperate resistance and had occupied Lunga airstrip – renamed Henderson Field – on 7-8 August. The Japanese response was immediate: a cruiser force hurried south from Rabaul, and inflicted a crushing defeat upon the Allied covering force off Savo Island on the night of 8/9 August. However, the Japanese failed to follow up this victory with an attack on the US transports in Tulagi harbour and, without the ground forces to dispute US control of Lunga, the Japanese were unable to prevent the Americans completing Henderson Field and bringing it into service on the 21st.

American possession of Henderson Field proved decisive in settling the Guadalcanal campaign in the Allies' favour. With no large air bases in the northern and central Solomons, Japanese land-based aircraft could operate over Guadalcanal only at extreme range from Rabaul. Unless American air power could be neutralized, both landing troops on Guadalcanal and the naval bombardment of US positions there were fraught with hazards. Further, from the outset the Japanese had no

clear idea of the size of the US forces on the island and the usual lack of co-ordination between the Imperial Army and the Japanese Navy fatally undermined Japanese plans. After the Savo Island action, battle was joined in a piecemeal manner, the Japanese gradually increasing their commitment but always at a pace behind the American build-up. In addition to control of Henderson Field, the support provided by the US carrier force operating to the south of Guadalcanal (despite the loss of the carrier *Wasp* on 15 September), provided the Americans with a power over and around the island that the Japanese could not

overcome even on the two occasions when they committed the fleet to the campaign. At the battle of the Eastern Solomons (23-25 August) two carrier forces fought a cautious and inconclusive action. At the battle of Santa Cruz (25-27 October) the losses sustained by their air groups left the Japanese unable to exploit the tactical advantage that they gained by sinking the *Hornet* and damaging the *Enterprise*. Thereafter, with both Japanese and US carrier forces neutralized, the adversaries were compelled to commit their capital ships to the waters of Guadalcanal as the struggle entered a more urgent phase.

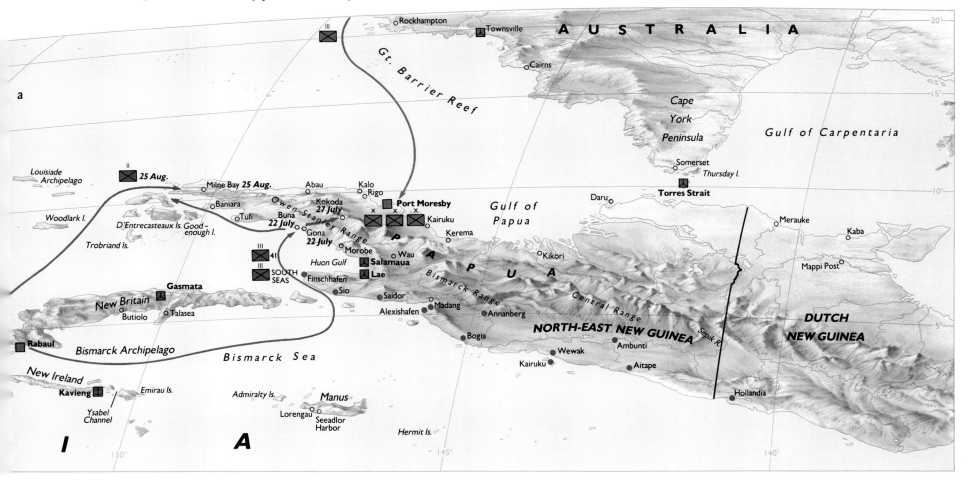

South-west Pacific NOV. 1942 ~ FEB. 1943

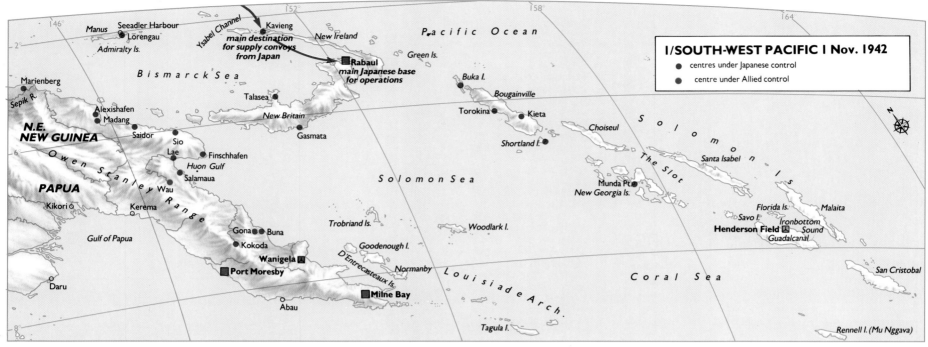

I/SOUTH-WEST PACIFIC | Nov. 1942
- centres under Japanese control
- centre under Allied control

2/NEW GUINEA | Nov. 1942 – 22 Jan. 1943

9 Dec. Gona captured (Aus.)
18 Dec. Gona area cleared (Aus.)

SOUTH SEAS c. 5500 troops by 15 Nov.
Buna area cleared from 3 Jan.

8 Nov. airlift US troops arrive

11-16 Jan. attempt to secure Mobu abandoned
21 Jan. Japanese attack on Wau begins (maps 3a, 3b)

BY NOVEMBER 1942 the Japanese still controlled many key positions in the South-west Pacific (1), despite the loss of Henderson Field on Guadalcanal (page 118). In New Guinea, the Japanese withdrawal along the Kokoda Trail quickly degenerated into a precipitate flight (2). By 30 Nov. the Japanese were confined to beachheads under a mile deep at Gona and Buna. The Gona beachhead was eliminated on 9 Dec., but the remaining Japanese positions, sited behind extensive swamps, were invulnerable to available artillery and could only be attacked by infantry. Disease and battle casualties reduced the Allied force considerably by the time Buna was secured (1 Jan.), and the area finally cleared (22 Jan.). Further north, in mid-Jan. the Japanese attempted to secure an Australian outpost at the mining settlement of Wau with an advance through dense jungle by some 3000 men (3a). A defence force of only 700 Australians was divided into advance scout groups and defensive formations behind the Bulolo R. While the Japanese reached Wau airstrip (28 Jan.) a break in the seasonal rains allowed the Allies to airlift, under fire, enough troops to double their strength. By the beginning of Feb. (3b) the Japanese, having failed to penetrate the defence formations, and subject to a hook movement to their rear, withdrew. Japanese advances in New Guinea had now been decisively checked.

Picture left: *Australian infantry clearing the fiercely defended Japanese positions at Buna.*

OCTOBER 1942 saw the Allies come within measurable distance of defeat in the struggle for control of the South-west Pacific. The Japanese had almost reached Port Moresby, and even now their beachheads at Gona and Buna in eastern New Guinea were still strong although under increasing pressure. In the Solomons Japanese air attacks also led to the partial neutralization of the newly completed American air base at Henderson Field on Guadalcanal Island. November, however, saw the Japanese defeated decisively both on Gaudalcanal and in eastern New Guinea, though both campaigns were to continue well into 1943.

Their inability to continue air attacks on Henderson Field throughout October and then either to secure the airfield or to defeat the US naval force off Santa Cruz (page 118) left the Japanese with no alternative, if they were to continue the battle, but to persist in their attempt to reinforce and resupply their formations on Guadalcanal despite enemy air superiority. A series of convoys (nicknamed the 'Tokyo Express') down the Slot (a relatively sheltered sea lane running through the Solomon Islands) produced a Japanese numerical superiority on Guadalcanal for the first time on 12 November, but in an attempt to ensure a potentially decisive reinforcement of their garrison the Japanese decided upon a major convoy in mid-November, involving eleven fast transports and some 10,000 troops, after surface forces had pounded Henderson Field into passivity. This operation coincided, however, with American command changes in the South Pacific Area; as a result of these the reinforcement of both Guadalcanal and the theatre in general were decided upon when the US High Command identified winning the campaign in the Solomons as of sufficient priority to justify the transfer of naval forces from the Atlantic. However, this American resolve was tempered after the battle of Santa Cruz (page 118) by a refusal to risk a carrier in or north of the Solomons; thus the American reinforcement of the garrison on Guadalcanal on 12 November, in the face of heavy but ineffective air attack, was covered rather than supported by a task group, with the *Enterprise* and two battleships stationed well to the south of the island.

This situation resulted in a series of naval actions between 12 and 16 November which effectively decided the outcome of the Guadalcanal campaign; at the same time Allied forces began to close around the Japanese beachheads at Gona in eastern New Guinea. Two ferocious night actions off the north coast of Guadalcanal in Ironbottom Sound (12th/13th and 14th/15th), the mauling of a Japanese bombardment force as it withdrew on the 14th, and the annihilation of the transport convoy on the 14th and 15th as it tried to fight its way to Guadalcanal resulted in the Japanese loss of two battleships, one heavy cruiser, four destroyers and ten transports; only 2000 Japanese troops – and virtually no equipment and supplies – reached Guadalcanal on 16 November. Though the Japanese garrison was able to withstand the first major American offensive on the island in mid-November and a Japanese naval task group scored a notable tactical success off Tassafaronga (30 November) when it outfought a much superior American formation, the Imperial Navy recognized that its mid-November losses were prohibitive. Concerned as it was with the preservation of its strength in readiness for 'the decisive battle', the Imperial Navy on 12

3a/WAU-MOBU 21 Jan. – 2 Feb. 1943

① Japanese advance down valley observed by Australian forward scouts on hilltops

② Australian forward scouts withdraw

③ Australian platoon move down under jungle cover to monitor enemy moves

④ Australian defence forms into company groups

⑤ Japanese formation splits: northern force engages main war defences, centre force to take airstrip, southern force to destroy defensive flank

⑥ Australian forward defence withdraws

3b/WAU-MOBU 3-9 Feb. 1943

⑥ Australian forward scout positions consolidated

⑤ Japanese withdraw under fire

④ Australians move up on southern flank

③ Japanese withdraw to defensive position

② Australian force moves up towards The Gap to attack Japanese rear

① battle reaches deadlock with companies attempting to out-manoeuvre in jungle

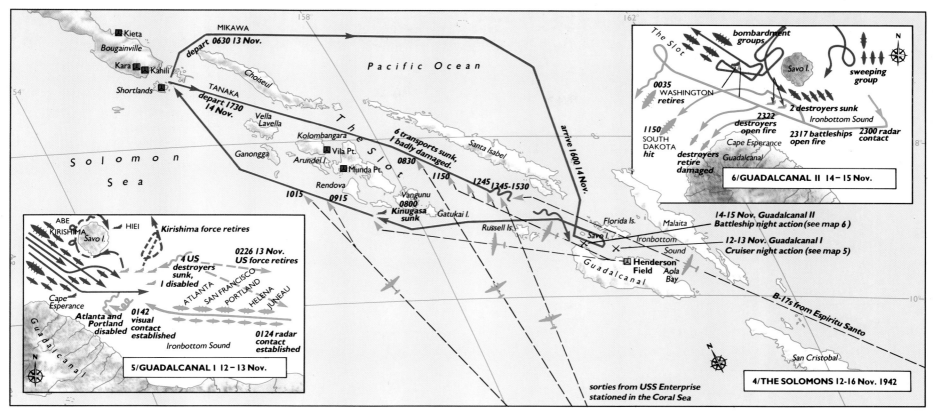

The Slot · MIKAWA · Kieta · Bougainville · Kara · Kahili · Shortlands · *depart 0630 13 Nov.* · TANAKA *depart 1730 14 Nov.* · Choiseul · Vella Lavella · Kolombangara · Vila Pt. · Ganongga · Munda Pt. · Rendova · Arundel I. · Vangunu · *0800 Kinugasa sunk* · Gatukai I. · Russell Is. · Pacific Ocean · *arrive 1600 14 Nov.* · Santa Isabel · 6 transports sunk, 1 badly damaged · 0830 · 1150 · 1245 · 1345-1530 · 1015 · 0915 · Florida Is. · Malaita · Savo I. · Ironbottom Sound · Henderson Field · Aola Bay · Guadalcanal · San Cristobal · B-17s from Espiritu Santo · *sorties from USS Enterprise stationed in the Coral Sea*

6/GUADALCANAL II 14–15 Nov. · The Slot · bombardment groups · sweeping group · Savo I. · 0035 WASHINGTON retires · 1150 SOUTH DAKOTA hit · 2322 destroyers open fire · 2 destroyers sunk · Ironbottom Sound · 2317 battleships open fire · 2300 radar contact · destroyers retire damaged · Cape Esperance · Guadalcanal

14–15 Nov. Guadalcanal II Battleship night action (see map 6) · 12–13 Nov. Guadalcanal I Cruiser night action (see map 5)

5/GUADALCANAL I 12–13 Nov. · ABE · KIRISHIMA · HIEI · Savo I. · *Kirishima force retires* · 4 US destroyers sunk, 1 disabled · 0226 13 Nov. US force retires · ATLANTA · SAN FRANCISCO · PORTLAND · HELENA · JUNEAU · Cape Esperance · Atlanta and Portland disabled · 0142 visual contact established · Ironbottom Sound · 0124 radar contact established · Guadalcanal

4/THE SOLOMONS 12-16 Nov. 1942

December proposed that the Guadalcanal campaign be abandoned. This was agreed by Imperial General Headquarters on 31 December.

This decision came at the time when the Americans had replaced their forces on Guadalcanal with fresh troops, and the battles around Gona in New Guinea had clearly entered their final phase. Here the Allies had applied persistent pressure on the Japanese beachheads, the Australians pressing forward from the Kokoda Trail to Gona, whilst increasing numbers of American troops were airlifted from Port Moresby to the area south of Buna. Japanese resistance was bitter, but without any prospect of reinforcing or resupplying their forces around Gona, the Japanese abandoned their beachheads to their fate whilst concentrating their resources for the clearing of Australian forces further north, behind Lae and Salamaua.

The forces on Guadalcanal, however, could not be similarly written off and, under the cover of preparations to reinforce their garrison, the Japanese completed the evacuation of 10,652 troops from Guadalcanal on three nights between 2/3 and 7/8 February without the Americans being aware of what was afoot. This achievement, during which only one Japanese destroyer was lost, did not alter the fact that Guadalcanal had been lost at the cost of some 20,000 troops, 860 aircraft and 15 warships; with the concurrent collapse of resistance around Gona and the failure of a Japanese attempt to secure a forward position further north at Wau the truth became apparent. The failure of both the Guadalcanal and the eastern New Guinea campaigns revealed that the defensive perimeter which Japan had cast around her conquests could not be maintained. Further, whilst the Americans could not prevent the Japanese evacuation of Guadalcanal, they moved immediately to secure the nearby Russell Islands, thereby serving notice of their intention to continue the campaign – and to inflict further defeats on the Japanese – in the Solomons.

THE JAPANESE ATTEMPT to win the Guadalcanal campaign reached a turning point by mid-Nov. 1942. Two crucial naval actions were fought in Ironbottom Sound, both at night. The first (5) was fought on 12/13 Nov. at ranges at which torpedoes would not arm: 1 Japanese battleship and 1 destroyer, and 1 US cruiser and 4 destroyers, were sunk or left sinking. Two nights later, after the Americans committed 2 battleships to the defence of the Henderson Field lodgement, a further Japanese battleship and single destroyer were sunk at the cost of 2 US destroyers (6); here the ranges were so close that large guns could not be lowered sufficiently to engage. Thereafter, the Japanese attempt to sail a convoy to Guadalcanal (4) faltered when it was attacked by US aircraft from USS Enterprise, Henderson Field and Espiritu Santo; after turning back late on 14 Dec., 4 surviving transports were beached and later destroyed on Cape Esperance. A fortnight later, in a battle off Tassafaronga (7), 1 US cruiser was sunk, and 3 more crippled, but the Japanese could not consolidate this partial success. In Dec. fresh US forces on Guadalcanal began a concerted push to clear the island (8): following steady American success the Japanese withdrew their garrison in early Feb., and converging US forces met (9) around Tenaro (9 Feb.); the Guadalcanal campaign was over.

Picture right: US forces working through the dense jungle foliage on Guadalcanal.

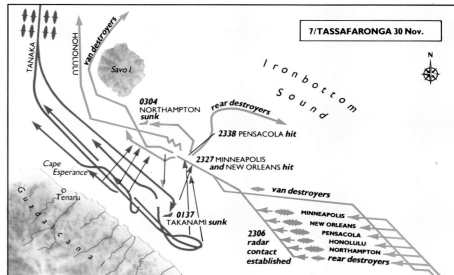

7/TASSAFARONGA 30 Nov. · TANAKA · HONOLULU · van destroyers · Savo I. · Ironbottom Sound · 0304 NORTHAMPTON sunk · rear destroyers · 2338 PENSACOLA hit · 2327 MINNEAPOLIS and NEW ORLEANS hit · Cape Esperance · Tenaru · van destroyers · 0137 TAKANAMI sunk · MINNEAPOLIS · NEW ORLEANS · PENSACOLA · HONOLULU · NORTHAMPTON · 2306 radar contact established · rear destroyers · Guadalcanal

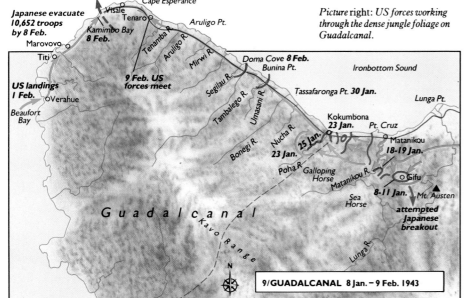

Japanese evacuate 10,652 troops by 8 Feb. · Cape Esperance · Visale · Tenaro · Aruligo Pt. · Kamimbo Bay 8 Feb. · Marovovo · Titi · Tenamba · Aruligo R. · Doma Cove 8 Feb. · Bunina Pt. · Mirwi R. · Ironbottom Sound · 9 Feb. US forces meet · US landings 1 Feb. · Verahue · Beaufort Bay · Segilau R. · Tambalego R. · Umasani R. · Tassafaronga Pt. 30 Jan. · Lunga Pt. · Bonegi R. · Nucha R. · 23 Jan. · 25 Jan. · Kokumbona 23 Jan. · Pt. Cruz · Matanikau 18-19 Jan. · Poha R. · Galloping Horse · Matanikau R. · Gifu · 8-11 Jan. Mt. Austen · Sea Horse · attempted Japanese breakout · Guadalcanal · Kavo Range · Lunga R.

9/GUADALCANAL 8 Jan. – 9 Feb. 1943

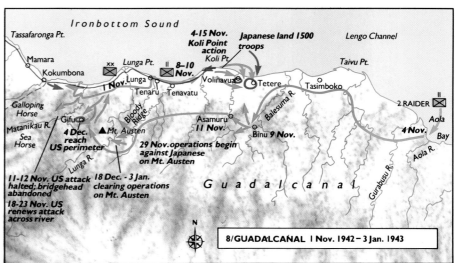

Ironbottom Sound · Tassafaronga Pt. · Mamara · Kokumbona · 4-15 Nov. Koli Point action · Lunga Pt. · Koli Pt. · Japanese land 1500 troops · Lengo Channel · xx · Lunga · 8-10 Nov. · 1 Nov. · Lunga · Tenaru · Tenavatu · Volinavua · Tetere · Taivu Pt. · Tasimboko · Galloping Horse · Matanikau R. · Gifu · 4 Dec. reach US perimeter · Mt. Austen · Bloody Ridge · Balesuma R. · Asamuru 11 Nov. · Binu 9 Nov. · 2 RAIDER · Sea Horse · Aola · 11-12 Nov. US attack halted; bridgehead abandoned · 18-23 Nov. US renews attack across river · 18 Dec. - 3 Jan. clearing operations on Mt. Austen · 29 Nov. operations begin against Japanese on Mt. Austen · Guadalcanal · Gurabusu R. · Aola R. · 4 Nov.

8/GUADALCANAL 1 Nov. 1942–3 Jan. 1943

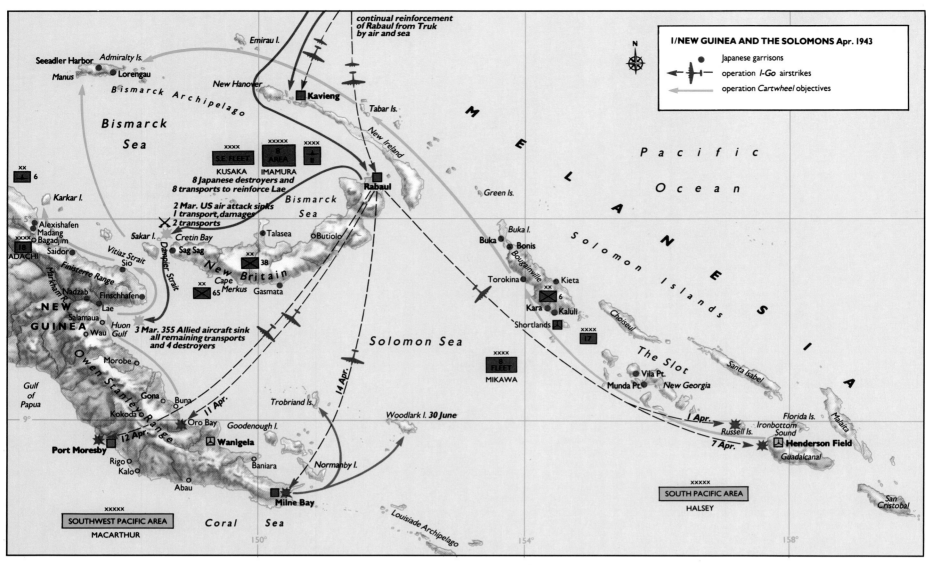

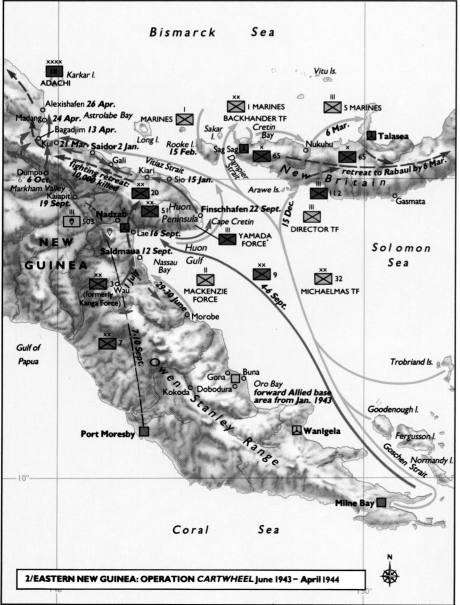

THE ELIMINATION of the Gona beachhead in Jan. (page 122) and the destruction of a reinforcement convoy bound for Lae in Mar. (*1*), confirmed the Allied possession of the initiative in the South-west Pacific theatre. Despite clearing operations in the Woodlark and Trobriand Is. it was not until Sept. that Allied forces effected amphibious landings in Huon Gulf (*2*), (4 Sept.) and one of the very few airborne operations of the Pacific war at Nadzab (6 Sept.) which brought the Allies control of Salamaua (12 Sept.) and Lae (16 Sept.); however, Japanese forces on the Gulf were able to avoid encirclement and fought for the Markham Valley. The Japanese were unable to prevent Allied landings on Cape Cretin, however, and at Finschhafen the Australians routed the numerically-superior Japanese – unique in the Pacific war. Thereafter, and with the start of the US offensive in the Central Pacific (page 140), the Allies moved against western New Britain to begin to isolate Rabaul, though 1943 ended with Allied forces in New Guinea still checked around Nadzab and Saidor.

Picture below: US napalm bombing of Japanese installations on Rabaul.

1943 PROVED TO BE A YEAR of consolidation in the Pacific as both the Americans and Japanese alike sought to strengthen their forces and positions in readiness for the battles that lay ahead. Notwithstanding their defeat in the campaign for Guadalcanal, the Japanese could draw comfort from the fact that securing the island had cost the United States six months sustained effort and that after 14 months of war the Americans still remained thousands of miles from the Southern Resources Area. In the event, however, the Japanese attempt to consolidate their holdings in the South-west Pacific in the course of 1943 was flawed on three counts: first, their shipyards could not match the output of American yards that in this year alone put into service a warship tonnage equivalent to that of the total Imperial Navy at the outbreak of war; second, the air losses sustained over Guadalcanal could not be made good by Japanese naval air service and aircrew – the Americans could do both; third, the Guadalcanal campaign saw the strategic initiative pass to the Americans.

The underlying weakness of Japanese strategic policy was that without the means to defeat the Americans in the air and at sea, any Japanese island garrison could be either subjected to overwhelming attack, piecemeal reduction or simply bypassed by an enemy with the choice of when, where and in what strength to mount operations. The Americans developed a parallel strategy – a drive across the small islands of the Central Pacific (page 140) and a concerted drive to advance in the Solomons and New Guinea (Operation *Cartwheel*).

The American occupation of the Russell Is. within two weeks of the end of the Guadalcanal campaign made clear their

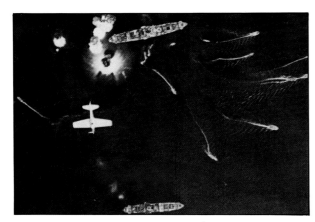

OPERATION *CARTWHEEL* (1) was intended both to give the Japanese no respite after their defeat on Guadalcanal (page 122) and to co-ordinate the southern flank of a broad US advance into the western Pacific. The Japanese made no attempt to dispute the US occupation of the Russell Is. (21 Feb., page 120) as they set about strengthening their garrisons and positions in the New Georgia group, but over the next 4 months battle was joined in the air as both sides sought to secure superiority over the central Solomons. Though the Japanese committed carrier air groups to Rabaul in Apr. in an attempt to halt or slow the US build-up in the southern Solomons, the Japanese decisively lost this struggle. Even Operation *I-Go* amounted to only 4 raids, none by more than 200 aircraft, against different targets. Having secured air superiority, the Americans moved (3) against New Georgia and Rendova (30 June), but despite subsidiary landings the chaotic conduct of this enterprise prevented the capture of Munda Point airfield until 5 Aug. On the 15th US forces landed on Vella Lavella. The clearing of the island

was left to the New Zealanders after mid-Sept. These various landings were punctuated by a series of naval clashes between light forces. The landings in the Treasury Is. (Oct.) and Empress Augusta Bay on Bougainville (1 Nov.) brought the Allies within fighter range of Rabaul. Also, by landing on a difficult coast and opposite a swamp the Americans gained total strategic surprise; by the time Japanese forces on Bougainville came against the beachhead, the swamp had been drained, an airfield was operational and a secure perimeter established. Beaten in battles on these defences, Japanese forces remained on Bougainville until the end of the war, and were then hunted by tracking animals: but for practical purposes the island was in Allied hands. Meanwhile, US forces swept round New Ireland to the Admiralty Is., thereby completing the isolation of Rabaul.

Pictures above: a Japanese seaplane tender under US air attack in the Solomons. Below: US troops negotiating difficult swamp conditions on Bougainville.

determination to carry the war into the central and northern Solomons; but even as the Americans adopted the island-hopping technique for the first time, with the landings on Vella Lavella and the bypassing of Japanese garrisons on New Georgia and Kolombangara, so American policy was in the process of change. Rather than aiming to recover Rabaul, the Americans decided to isolate and bypass what should have been the keystone of the Japanese defence in the area. Despite this decision, the neutralization of Japanese garrisons in the northern Solomons would be a long and bloody struggle.

On the other side of the Coral Sea, a complementary effort began after the annihilation of a Japanese reinforcement convoy in the battle of the Bismarck Sea (2/4 March). After this the Japanese never attempted to reinforce their garrisons in eastern New Guinea. The slow but progressive reduction of Japanese positions around Huon Gulf continued throughout the year, though the main focus of US strategy attention remained the Solomons. It was primarily in the Solomons in April that the Japanese made their last offensive effort of the war (Operation *I-Go*), and it was in order to counter American moves into the northern Solomons that Rabaul was reinforced in October by carrier air groups and cruisers detached from the fleet at Truk. Both were to be savaged in raids on 5 and 11 November by US carrier formations. These were so successful that the Japanese fleet was thereafter left unable to meet the American moves into the Gilberts and around Rabaul. The isolation of the latter remained to be completed, but after November 1943 Rabaul's effectiveness was at an end – though it remained in Japanese hands until the general capitulation on 6 September 1945.

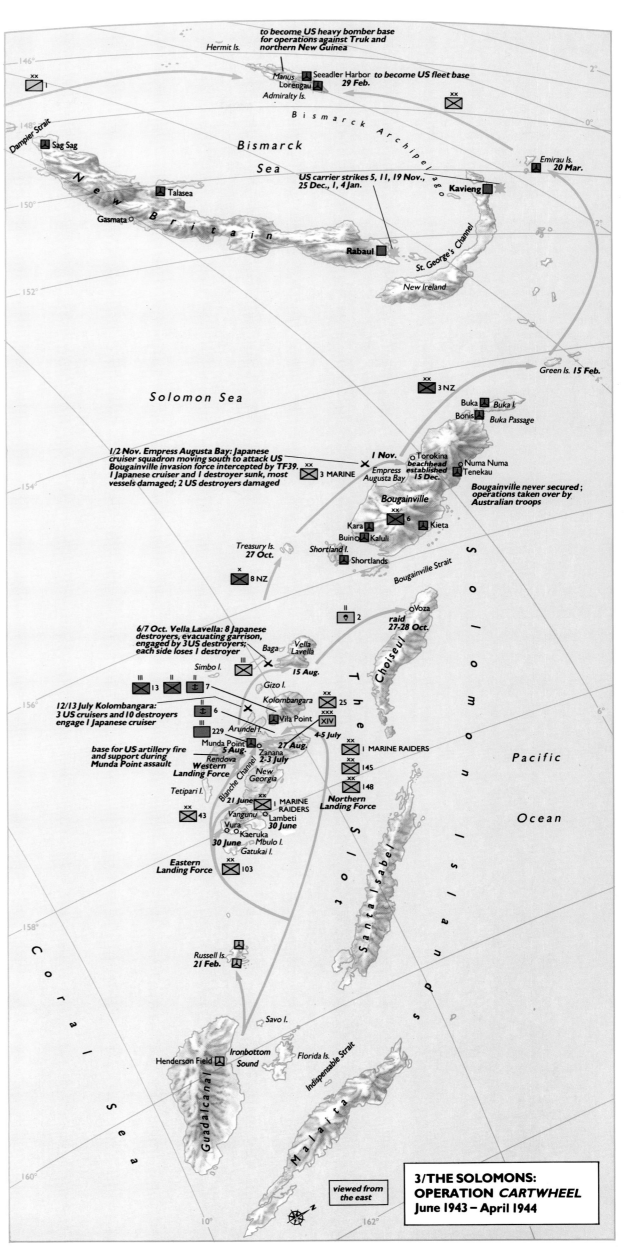

3/THE SOLOMONS: OPERATION *CARTWHEEL* June 1943 – April 1944

Kursk JULY~AUGUST 1943

SOVIET SUCCESSES in early 1943 and German counter-attacks had left a great bulge or salient round Kursk between Orel and Kharkov. Hitler had once postponed Operation *Citadel*, as the plan to pinch out the Kursk salient was known, and had considered a proposal by OKW to build up a strong reserve instead, but on 18 June he decided to proceed: *Citadel* would demonstrate German superiority by reversing the disasters at Stalingrad, and the stalemate on the front. The plan did indeed demonstrate German strength, with 900,000 men, 2700 tanks and assault guns and 1800 aircraft massed for the attack, although this was achieved by concentrating 70 percent of German tanks and 65 percent of the aircraft from the entire Eastern Front. Kursk would also demonstate the pros and cons of new German technology. Since the battle of Moscow, where they encountered the terrifying new T-34, the Germans had tried to develop a comparable tank. The answer was the Panther, which first appeared in May 1943. It had a 75mm gun and 70mm of frontal armour, but was beset by teething troubles. The Germans also used the heavy Tiger tank, with an 88mm gun and up to 100mm of armour, and the Ferdinand assault gun based on the Tiger chassis. The Red Army, meanwhile, had upgunned the T-34 from 76mm to 85mm.

Although often thought of as a tank battle, Kursk as a whole arguably demonstrated the triumph of artillery, infantry and engineers over armour. The Soviet plan was to soak up the German assault in a colossal web of defensive positions, and only then launch their armoured counter-attack. It was also an important air battle, in which the balance now shifted in the favour of the Soviets.

The Soviet *Lucy* spy ring gave Stalin the approximate time of the German attack – between 3 and 6 July. The Soviets were waiting. Battlefield intelligence on 4 July fixed H-Hour at 0200 hrs. European time, on 5 July. Soviet artillery fired the biggest 'counter-preparation' – smashing enemy forces as they prepared to attack – in the history of war. 600 guns and mortars in the 6th and 7th Guards Army areas (on the left of the planned breakthrough to the south) opened fire on the evening of 4 July, and each front (Rokossovski's Centre and Vatutin's Voronezh) fired once more during the night.

At 0500 Hoth's 4th Panzer Army, already shaken, attacked in the south in a wedge formation: motorized infantry at the base, Panthers and Mk. IV tanks on the flanks, heavy Tigers and Ferdinands at the front. They drove into a merciless arc of fire, a 'ring of flame'. Many of the Panthers broke down. The heavy Ferdinands and Tigers ploughed on, to be met by *Pakfronts* – batteries of anti-tank guns all of which engaged one tank at a time in strict co-ordination. By 10 July the attack in the south had stalled, having covered barely 20 miles.

In the north, where Model's 9th Army attacked at 0530, the Soviet 13th Army put up fierce resistance, especially in the area of Ponyri (7-8 July) and by 10 July the Germans had only penetrated eight miles.

Only now that the assault was blunted were Soviet tank armies committed. In the south, Hoth's 4th Panzer Army was used in a final bid to smash the Soviet defences by striking near Prokhorovka. They collided with Rotmistrov's 5th Guards Tank Army, in the largest tank battle of the war. The hot, dry weather had ended on 7 July and Prokhorovka was fought in rain under a sky piled high with thunderclouds. Guderian recalled that he had never received 'such an overwhelming impression of Soviet strength and numbers as on that day'. Soon, T-34s were streaming 'like rats' over the battlefield. In this engagement alone the Germans lost 400 tanks and 10,000 men: Soviet casualties were greater, but they could afford them. At the end of this stage of the battle of Kursk, the Soviet defensive phase, the Soviets claim to have killed 70,000 and destroyed nearly 3000 tanks. The Germans claim to have destroyed or crippled 1800 Soviet tanks on the south face alone. After Prokhorovka, Soviet tank strength was half what it had been eight days before.

The Soviet counter-attack had begun on 12 July. By 2 August the Red Army had recovered the ground lost in the German assault and on 3 August the full counter-offensive, the Bielgorod-Kharkov operation which forms part of the battle of Kursk, began. The counter-offensive was launched after massive artillery and air preparation. Bielgorod was liberated on 6 August and Kharkov on 23 August. The operation was launched in concert with partisan forces behind the German line. On the night of 2/3 August alone they fired over 600 demolitions. Whereas destruction of German communications before the counter-offensive might have made the Germans fight harder by impeding withdrawal, this hit them when they were most vulnerable – in flight. The Soviet use of partisans in close co-ordination with main forces in this way was more effective than the Western Allies' use of resistance movements.

Kursk marked the end of major German initiatives in the east. From now on, Germany and her allies would be on the defensive here, as everywhere else. At the end of the counter-offensive on 27 August, the Soviets were poised to move into the Ukraine.

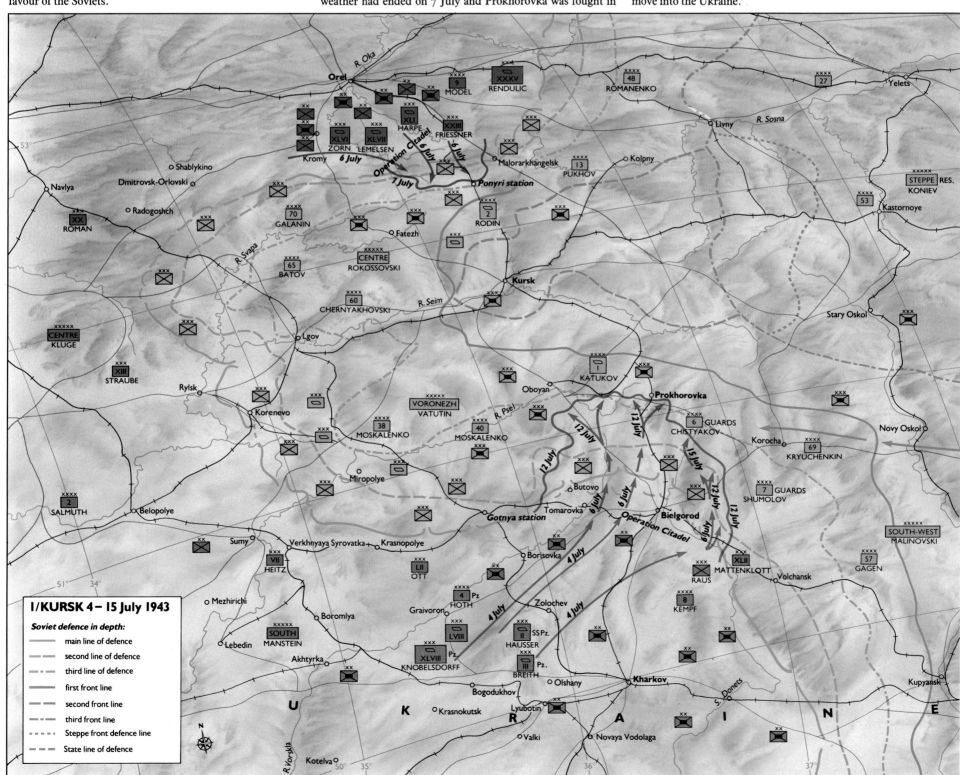

I/KURSK 4 – 15 July 1943

Soviet defence in depth:

- main line of defence
- second line of defence
- third line of defence
- first front line
- second front line
- third front line
- Steppe front defence line
- State line of defence

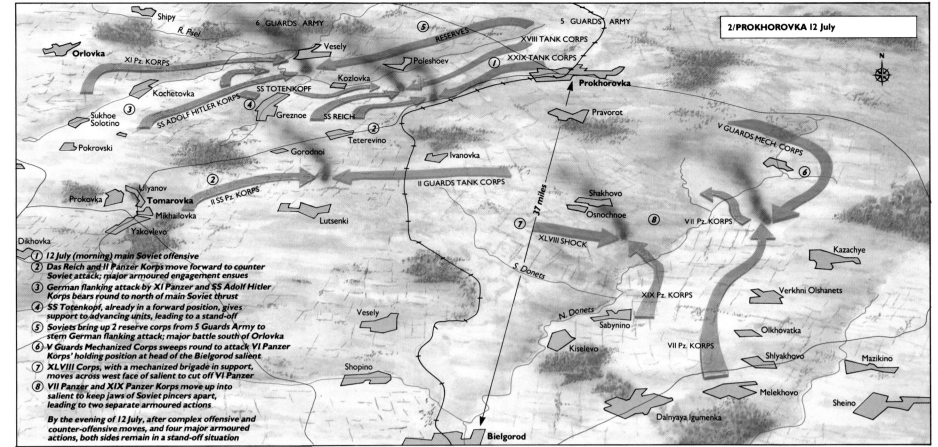

2/PROKHOROVKA 12 July

Shipy
R. Psel
6 GUARDS ARMY
5 GUARDS ARMY
RESERVES
XVIII TANK CORPS
XXIX TANK CORPS
Orlovka
XI Pz. KORPS
Vesely
Poleshoev
Prokhorovka
SS TOTENKOPF
Kozlovka
Pravorot
Kochetovka
SS ADOLF HITLER KORPS
Greznoe
SS REICH
Sukhoe Solotino
Teterevino
V GUARDS MECH. CORPS
Pokrovski
Gorodnoi
Ivanovka
Shakhovo
Ulyanov
Tomarovka
II SS Pz. KORPS
II GUARDS TANK CORPS
Osnochnoe
VII Pz. KORPS
Prokovka
Mikhailovka
Lutsenki
Kazachye
Yakovlevo
Dikhovka
37 miles
XLVIII SHOCK
XIX Pz. KORPS
Verkhni Olshanets
Vesely
N. Donets
Sabynino
Olkhovatka
S. Donets
VII Pz. KORPS
Shlyakhovo
Kiselevo
Mazikino
Shopino
Melekhovo
Sheino
Dalnyaya Igumenka
Bielgorod

(1) 12 July (morning) main Soviet offensive
(2) Das Reich and II Panzer Korps move forward to counter Soviet attack; major armoured engagement ensues
(3) German flanking attack by XI Panzer and SS Adolf Hitler Korps bears round to north of main Soviet thrust
(4) SS Totenkopf, already in a forward position, gives support to advancing units, leading to a stand-off
(5) Soviets bring up 2 reserve corps from 5 Guards Army to stem German flanking attack; major battle south of Orlovka
(6) V Guards Mechanized Corps sweeps round to attack VI Panzer Korps' holding position at head of the Bielgorod salient
(7) XLVIII Corps, with a mechanized brigade in support, moves across west face of salient to cut off VI Panzer
(8) VII Panzer and XIX Panzer Korps move up into salient to keep jaws of Soviet pincers apart, leading to two separate armoured actions

By the evening of 12 July, after complex offensive and counter-offensive moves, and four major armoured actions, both sides remain in a stand-off situation

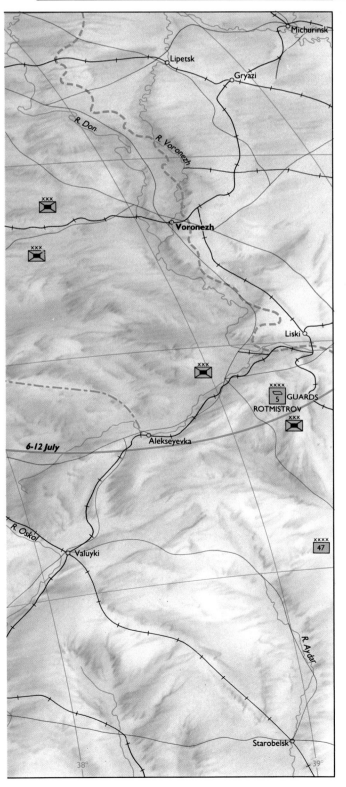

THE RED ARMY built defensive works in the Kursk salient (1) and to the east to a total depth of 150-200 miles. On the Centre and Voronezh fronts there were 5-6 successive defence 'belts', 2 in the 'tactical' (divisional) zone which formed the first 10-12 miles, one in the army rear area and 3 in the front rear areas. Behind this was a defensive perimeter of the Steppe Military District (later Front) and finally a national defence zone on the east bank of the Don. Most of the Engineer effort (field fortifications, mines) was in the tactical zone. Each belt comprised 2-3 positions, each about a mile deep. Each position in turn comprised 2-3 lines of trenches linked by communication trenches. Anti-tank defences were deployed to a depth of over 20 miles. The German plan envisaged Model's 9th Army comprising XX and XXIII Corps, XLI, XLVI and XLVII Panzer Corps striking from the north. Hoth's 4th Panzer Army, comprising LII Corps, XLVIII Panzer Corps and II SS Panzer Corps together with *Armee-Abteilung Kempf*, comprising III Panzer Corps, Corps *Raus* and XLII Corps, would assault from the south. But these assaults barely penetrated the Soviet 'tactical zone' (the first two defensive belts), before reaching the limit of their advance at Prokhorovka and Ponyri. At Prokhorovka (2), the Germans began their drive on 11 July. By dawn on 12 July they threatened to close on Prokhorovka and Rotmistrov's 5th Guards Tank Army was ordered to prevent this. Rotmistrov had about 900 tanks; the Germans 600 tanks west of Prokhorovka and 300 to the south. There was thus rough parity, except that the Germans fielded about 100 Tigers. Over 1000 tanks actually clashed. By nightfall on 12 July the Germans had lost over 300 tanks, but fighting continued far into the night and resumed the next day. This marked the beginning of the Soviet counter-attack, which, with the commencement of the Bielgorod-Kharkov operation on 3 Aug. (3) became a full counter-offensive.

Picture above right: Soviet T-34 tanks advancing under fire, with infantry support.

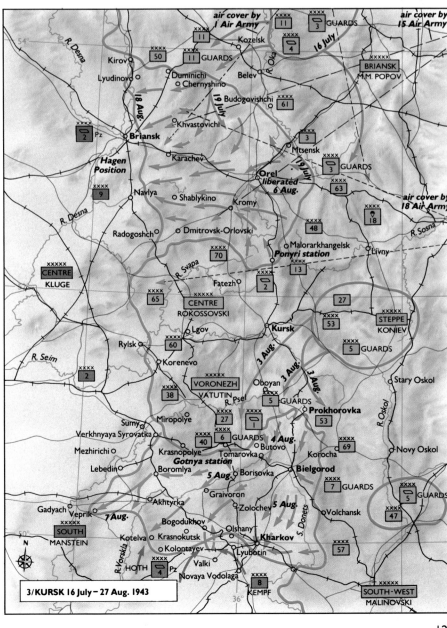

3/KURSK 16 July – 27 Aug. 1943

air cover by 1 Air Army
air cover by 15 Air Army
R. Desna
Kirov
Kozelsk
GUARDS
Lyudinovo
Duminichi
Belev
R. Oka
BRIANSK
Chernyshino
M.M. POPOV
18 Aug.
19 July
Budogovishchi
Khvastovichi
Br. Pz
Briansk
Karachev
Mtsensk
GUARDS
Hagen Position
Orel liberated 6 Aug.
GUARDS
air cover by 18 Air Army
Navlya
Shablykino
Kromy
R. Desna
Maloarkhangelsk
R. Sosna
Radogoshch
Dmitrovsk-Orlovski
Ponyri station
Livny
CENTRE KLUGE
R. Svapa
Fatezh
CENTRE ROKOSSOVSKI
Lgov
STEPPE KONIEV
Kursk
GUARDS
Rylsk
R. Seim
Korenevo
Stary Oskol
VORONEZH VATUTIN
Oboyan
3 Aug.
R. Psel
GUARDS
Sumy
Miropolye
Prokhorovka
R. Oskol
Verkhnyaya Syrovatka
4 Aug.
GUARDS
Novy Oskol
Mezhirichi
Butovo
Korocha
Krasnopolye
Tomarovka
Lebedin
Gotnya station
Borisovka
Bielgorod
Boromlya
Graivoron
GUARDS
Akhtyrka
Zolochev
5 Aug.
GUARDS
Gadyach
Veprik
Bogodukhov
Olshany
Volchansk
7 Aug.
SOUTH MANSTEIN
Kotelva
Krasnokutsk
Kharkov
S. Donets
Valki
Lyubotin
HOTH Pz
Kolontayev
SOUTH-WEST MALINOVSKI
KEMPF
Novaya Vodolaga
Starobelsk

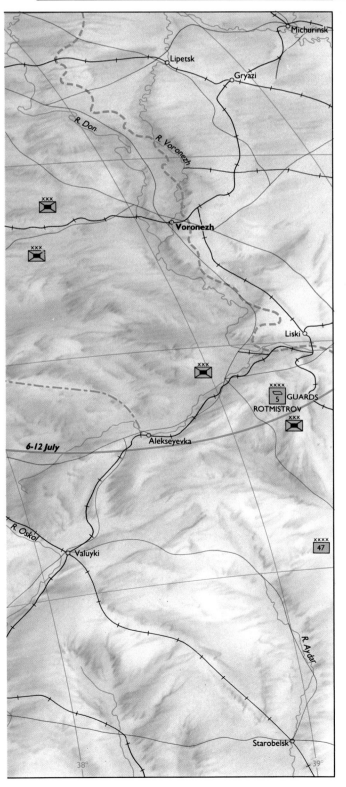

Michurinsk
Lipetsk
Gryazi
R. Don
R. Voronezh
Voronezh
Liski
5 GUARDS ROTMISTROV
6-12 July
Alekseyevka
R. Oskol
Valuyki
47
R. Aydar
Starobelsk

The Ukraine AUGUST ~ DECEMBER 1943

THE BATTLE OF THE RIVER DNIEPER is one of the historic great battles (*bitva*) of the Soviet war. It was fought on an immense scale. Soviet forces comprised five fronts: Centre (Rokossovski), Voronezh (Vatutin), Steppe (Koniev), Southwest (Malinovski) and South (from 21 September, Tolbukhin). On 20 October these were renamed the Byelorussian and 1st to 4th Ukrainian Fronts respectively. The Soviet grouping comprised 2,633,000 men, over 51,000 guns and mortars, 2400 tanks and assault guns and 2850 combat aircraft. German forces comprised 2nd Army from Army Group Centre (Kluge), 4th Panzer, 8th, 1st and 6th Armies from Army Group South (Manstein): in all, 1,240,000 men, 12,600 guns and mortars, 2100 tanks and assault guns and 2100 combat aircraft. The Russians, therefore, had about four times as much artillery as the enemy and twice as many men, but not much more armour or air power.

Russian planning for the Dnieper battle began as the battle of Kursk unfolded (page 124). The aim of the first phase was the liberation of 'Left Bank Ukraine' (east of the Dnieper), the industrial area of the Donbass, and Kiev. Several component operations, whose most distinctive feature was the need for assault river crossings, would take place along a front over 400 miles long. The second phase would see the Russians establishing strategic bridgeheads on the west bank of the Dnieper and the recapture of Kiev. German forces withdraw-

ing towards the Dnieper after the Russian capture of Kharkov (page 124), believed that the river line, though unfortified, would be enough of an obstacle to allow them to stabilize their eastern front for some time.

The right wing of the Steppe Front began its attack towards Krasnograd on 13 August, and on 16 August attacked from a bridgehead on the Northern Donets, as part of the Donbass offensive operation (13 August-22 September). The Southwest Front and 17th Air Army, Southern Front and 8th Air Army launched attacks against German Army Group South and *Luftflotte 4*: by 22 September they had reached the Dnieper south of Dnepropetrovsk. To the north, Centre Front forces attacked on 26 August. 60th Army enjoyed the greatest success, creating a breakthrough south of Sevsk: by 31 August it was 60 miles wide and nearly 50 miles deep.

At the beginning of September, Front commanders were ordered to seize bridgeheads by attacking straight from the line of march. By this time, the Centre and Voronezh Fronts were driving for Kiev, Steppe Front for Poltava and Kremenchug, and Southwest Front for Dnepropetrovsk. During the second half of September the Soviet Centre Front advanced westward towards the river north of Kiev, the Voronezh Front south of it. Voronezh Front deployed a mobile group (a classic Soviet device to keep the enemy off balance); racing ahead of the slower main forces on a 45-mile front, this reached the Dnieper

on the night of 21/22 September. On the next day, forward units established small bridgeheads at Rzhishchev and Veliki Bukrin. During the night of 24/25 September the Russians tried an airborne assault to expand the bridgeheads, but with disastrous results. While the survivors fought behind German lines, main forces approached the river on a front of nearly 500 miles between 22 and 30 September.

The second phase of the great battle, from October to December, revolved around the 23 bridgeheads now established across the Dnieper. On 12 October Voronezh Front (renamed 1st Ukrainian) attacked towards Kiev which was finally recaptured after fierce fighting on 6 November. Soviet forces pushed on nearly 100 miles establishing a strategic bridgehead west of the Dnieper.

By now the idea of liberating Soviet territory, rather than just destroying German forces, was becoming important. Further, the seizure of the strategic bridgehead across the Dnieper created the jumping-off point for the Byelorussian offensive (page 148). In the battle for the Dnieper, 38,000 settlements including 160 towns and cities were recaptured. By the end of December most of the difficult river obstacles were behind Soviet forward troops. The end of 1943 marked the end, from the Soviet viewpoint, of the 'second period of the war' – seeing the fundamental shift in the balance of forces. The third period would see Germany finally and decisively defeated.

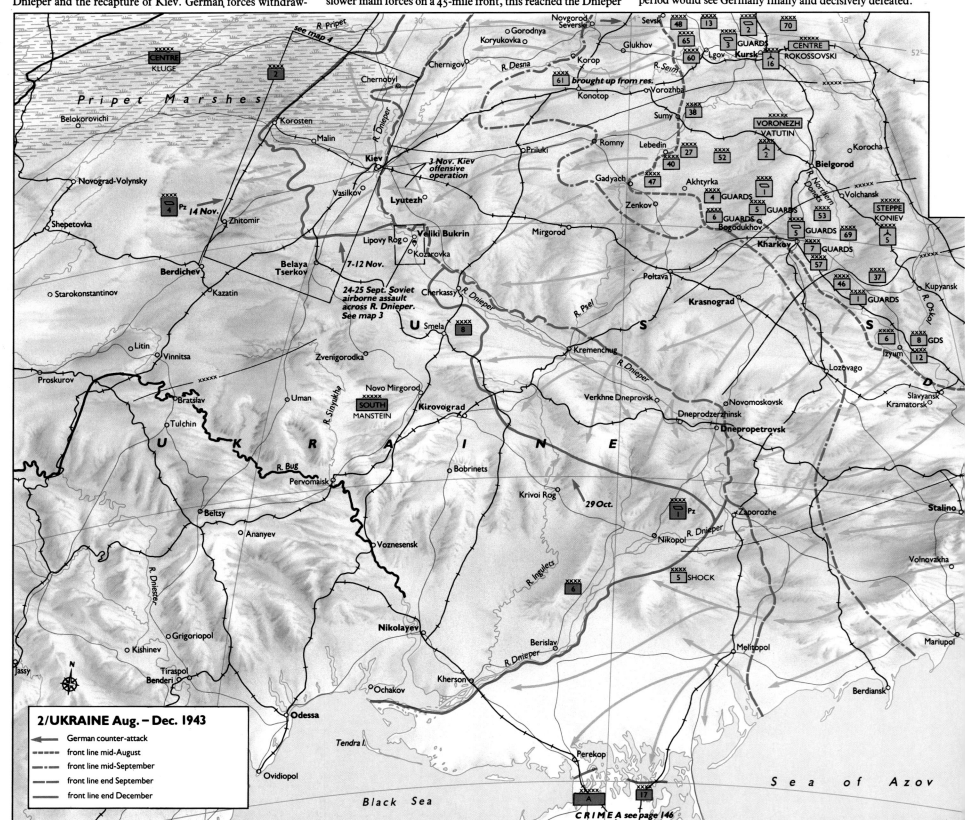

2/UKRAINE Aug. – Dec. 1943

←	German counter-attack
--------	front line mid-August
–·–·–	front line mid-September
– – –	front line end September
———	front line end December

THE BATTLE OF THE DNIEPER took place on a huge front between the Sea of Azov in the south, and the vast Pripet Marshes in the north (1). Operations began (13 Aug.) in the southern sector with the Donbass operation, while the battle of Kursk (page 124) was still underway. Operations to the north began at the end of Aug. (2). Hitler opposed plans to shorten Kluge's Centre Army Group's front and withdraw it to the Dnieper line (14 Sept.), but agreed to von Manstein's Army Group South's withdrawal to the line of Melitopol and the R. Dnieper, and its reinforcement with four of Army Group Centre's divisions. The withdrawal was probably the most difficult operation performed by Army Group South during the 1943-44 campaign undertaken, according to von Manstein, 'in the face of unremitting pressure from a far superior opponent'. From a 440-mile-wide front, 3 armies had to converge on a maximum of five Dnieper crossing points. Once across, they had to fan out again on an equally wide front without letting the Russians get a foothold. It was successfully completed by 30 September.

Picture above: Russian troops crossing a temporary railway bridge across the Dnieper.

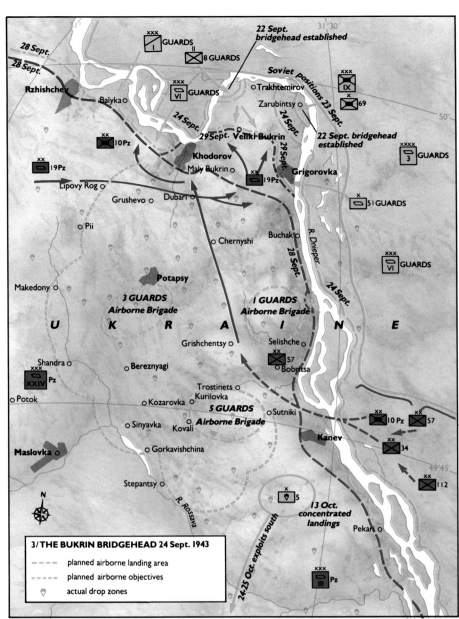

AS THE SOVIET OFFENSIVE proceeded, *Stavka* allocated 3 airborne brigades to the Voronezh Front for an assault across the Dnieper (3). Lead elements of Soviet forces crossed the river on 21/22 Sept. On 24/25 Sept. 3rd Guards was ordered to drop southeast of Rzhishchev to secure a line Lipovy Rog-Kozarovka and hold it until the arrival of 40th Army. 5th Guards would block off German forces advancing from the south. The airborne operation was badly conceived and executed: the paratroopers were scattered, many into enemy positions, and only half of the 4575 paratroops survived to continue offensive operations. Finally, on the night of 13/14 Nov. 254th Division of 52nd Army seized a foothold on the western bank; the following day 52nd Army was over the river. This was to be the last Soviet attempt at a major airborne operation in Europe. For the Kiev operation, the main Soviet attack was around the Bukrin bridgehead (3). The Germans, however, concentrated 10 divisions here, and *Stavka* switched plans: a subsidiary attack was made from the Bukrin bridgehead (1 Nov.) whilst the main attack came from Lyutezh (3 Nov.). Fearing encirclement, the German command began to withdraw from Kiev but on 8 Nov. (4) launched a strong counter-attack on the Soviet main grouping from south of Fastov. Soviet forces were forced onto the defensive from Zhitomir to the Dnieper, but managed to hold the Germans west of Kiev. To the north (2) the Soviet right flank continued its advance to establish a strategic bridgehead across the Dnieper.

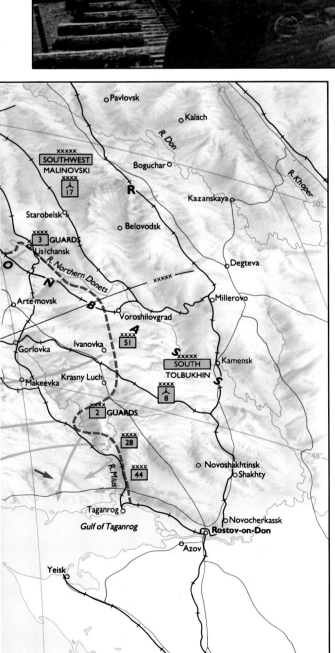

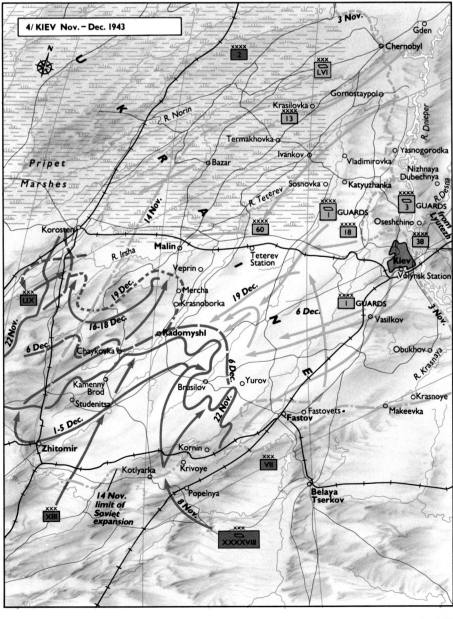

The Balkans 1941~1945

HITLER'S LIGHTNING CONQUEST of Yugoslavia and Greece in April 1941 (page 54), and his hastily improvised division of the spoils, created the conditions for anti-Axis resistance, civil wars, and Communist revolutions in the western Balkans. Wishing to exploit the area with the minimum commitment of troops, he relied on his allies for much of its garrisoning and governance. The punitive and exploitative 'New Order' offered nothing positive to the bulk of the region's inhabitants.

Even before the German invasion of the USSR impelled the Comintern to summon the underground Balkan Communist parties to launch a partisan struggle in defence of 'mother Russia', remnants of the Royal Yugoslav Army had taken to the woods. Known as Chetniks, this movement of Serb officers came gradually under the titular command of Col. Draga Mihailovitch. His aim was to organize a secret army which would be mobilized to restore the Serb-dominated monarchy and to punish the Serbs' enemies as and when the western Allies returned to the Balkans. He had not counted, however, either on competition from the Communists or on the spontaneous

risings among the Serbs of the 'Independent State of Croatia' who were subjected (from May) to a campaign of genocide by their new Ustashi (from *ustaša*, rebel) rulers. In September 1941 the leader of the Communists, Josip Broz Tito, took to the field in western Serbia, where the units they had raised (now dubbed Partisans) were contesting with Mihailovitch for primacy in what had become a veritable insurgent republic.

Mihailovitch was appalled both by the Partisans' disregard for the costs of the unremitting warfare they proclaimed and by the revolutionary means they used to propagate it. Hitler's orders that the rebellion be crushed, and that 100 civilian hostages be executed for every German killed, underscored Mihailovitch's fears. In November he sought arms from the Germans with which to quash the Communists. They refused but neither the authorities they had installed in Serbia nor their Italian allies proved so punctilious. Meanwhile the Germans ejected the Partisans from Serbia and reduced Mihailovitch to a headquarters without an army.

The civil war which broke out in Serbia in November was

soon replicated in much of the rest of the country. 1943 brought the Partisans the assurance of eventual victory. Their survival of two great Axis offensives (*Weiss* and *Schwarz*) in the first half of the year, their reception of missions and aid from the British after April, and the Italian surrender in September permitted them to claim recognition as the future rulers of a federated Yugoslavia. By 1944 Tito claimed to have 300,000 men and women at arms, and to be containing as many Axis troops as were the Allies in Italy. He worked to secure international recognition by making nominal concessions to the exiled King Peter while pressing on with the destruction of the royalist Chetniks in Serbia. He appealed successfully to Stalin to divert the Red Army to help in the latter enterprise. Belgrade fell on 20 October and the Soviets departed for Hungary. The Partisans were left to pursue the Germans and to make good their claims on Slovene and Croat irredenta. The Yugoslavs entered Trieste hours before the Western Allies (1 May).

In Albania, the Communist Party established their National Liberation Movement in September 1942. The Communists' bid for control under Yugoslav influence led to the formation of a republican movement (*Balli Kombëtar*) which found anti-Communist collaboration with the Axis easy to rationalize. The Communists were able to destroy their rivals and supplant the Germans as they withdrew in Autumn 1944.

The Greek Communists were first in their country to gear up for resistance. They set up a National Liberation Front (EAM) in September and a National Popular Liberation Army (ELAS) in December 1941, although guerrilla bands did not form in the mountains until Summer 1942. By then non-Communist officers were also organizing. The Communists concentrated on liquidating the officers' movements while levering their way into the councils of the exile government. Successful in both respects by Summer 1944, they failed to capitalize on their effective control of the country (established as the Germans withdrew) and allowed the government and its British guarantors to return to Athens in October. Realizing their error, they launched a confused struggle to recoup their position in December and failed to eject the desperately reinforcing British – unaware that Stalin had already consigned their country to a British sphere of influence (page 158).

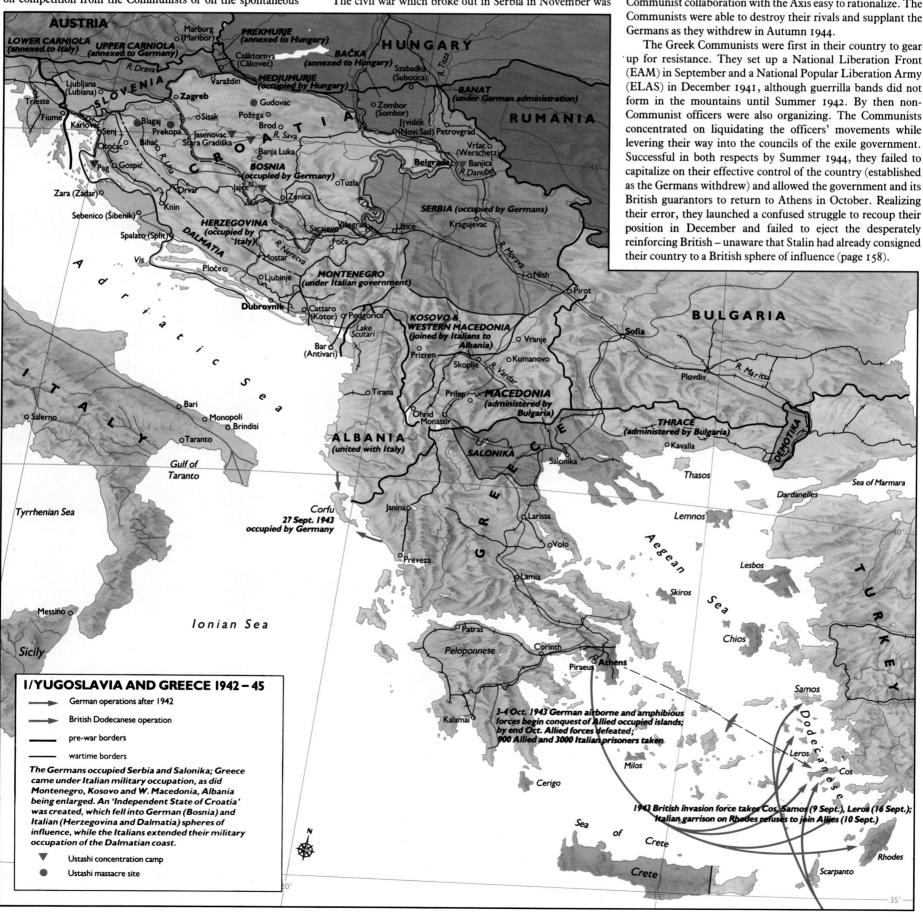

I/YUGOSLAVIA AND GREECE 1942–45

→ German operations after 1942

→ British Dodecanese operation

— pre-war borders

— wartime borders

The Germans occupied Serbia and Salonika; Greece came under Italian military occupation, as did Montenegro, Kosovo and W. Macedonia, Albania being enlarged. An 'Independent State of Croatia' was created, which fell into German (Bosnia) and Italian (Herzegovina and Dalmatia) spheres of influence, while the Italians extended their military occupation of the Dalmatian coast.

▼ Ustashi concentration camp

● Ustashi massacre site

Corfu 27 Sept. 1943 occupied by Germany

3-4 Oct. 1943 German airborne and amphibious forces begin conquest of Allied occupied islands; by end Oct. Allied forces defeated; 900 Allied and 3000 Italian prisoners taken

1943 British invasion force takes Cos, Samos (9 Sept.), Leros (16 Sept.); Italian garrison on Rhodes refuses to join Allies (10 Sept.)

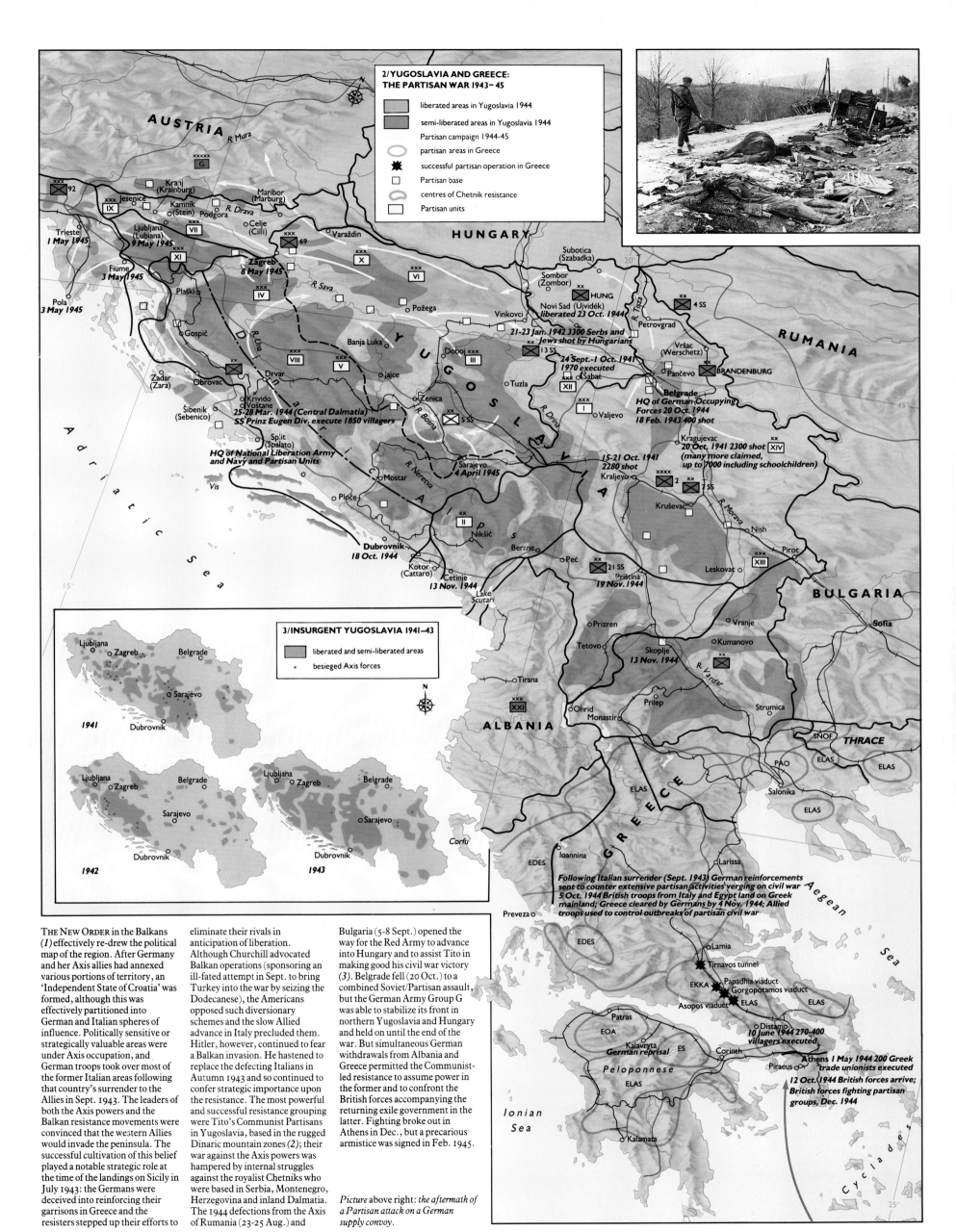

2/YUGOSLAVIA AND GREECE: THE PARTISAN WAR 1943–45

- liberated areas in Yugoslavia 1944
- semi-liberated areas in Yugoslavia 1944
- Partisan campaign 1944-45
- partisan areas in Greece
- successful partisan operation in Greece
- Partisan base
- centres of Chetnik resistance
- Partisan units

3/INSURGENT YUGOSLAVIA 1941–43

- liberated and semi-liberated areas
- besieged Axis forces

1941
1942
1943

THE NEW ORDER in the Balkans (1) effectively re-drew the political map of the region. After Germany and her Axis allies had annexed various portions of territory, an 'Independent State of Croatia' was formed, although this was effectively partitioned into German and Italian spheres of influence. Politically sensitive or strategically valuable areas were under Axis occupation, and German troops took over most of the former Italian areas following that country's surrender to the Allies in Sept. 1943. The leaders of both the Axis powers and the Balkan resistance movements were convinced that the western Allies would invade the peninsula. The successful cultivation of this belief played a notable strategic role at the time of the landings on Sicily in July 1943: the Germans were deceived into reinforcing their garrisons in Greece and the resisters stepped up their efforts to

eliminate their rivals in anticipation of liberation. Although Churchill advocated Balkan operations (sponsoring an ill-fated attempt in Sept. to bring Turkey into the war by seizing the Dodecanese), the Americans opposed such diversionary schemes and the slow Allied advance in Italy precluded them. Hitler, however, continued to fear a Balkan invasion. He hastened to replace the defecting Italians in Autumn 1943 and so continued to confer strategic importance upon the resistance. The most powerful and successful resistance grouping were Tito's Communist Partisans in Yugoslavia, based in the rugged Dinaric mountain zones (2); their war against the Axis powers was hampered by internal struggles against the royalist Chetniks who were based in Serbia, Montenegro, Herzegovina and inland Dalmatia. The 1944 defections from the Axis of Rumania (23-25 Aug.) and

Bulgaria (5-8 Sept.) opened the way for the Red Army to advance into Hungary and to assist Tito in making good his civil war victory (3). Belgrade fell (20 Oct.) to a combined Soviet/Partisan assault, but the German Army Group G was able to stabilize its front in northern Yugoslavia and Hungary and held on until the end of the war. But simultaneous German withdrawals from Albania and Greece permitted the Communist-led resistance to assume power in the former and to confront the British forces accompanying the returning exile government in the latter. Fighting broke out in Athens in Dec., but a precarious armistice was signed in Feb. 1945.

Picture above right: the aftermath of a Partisan attack on a German supply convoy.

Italy JULY 1943 ~ JANUARY 1944

THE DECISION TO INVADE SICILY, rather than transfer the bulk of the Allied armies out of the Mediterranean for an assault on North-west Europe, once Tunisia had been cleared of Axis forces, was taken by Churchill and Roosevelt at the Casablanca Conference (14-24 January 1943, page 134). The Americans remained suspicious, however, that *Husky*, as the operation was codenamed, might become an open-ended commitment which would set back a North-west Europe landing beyond early 1944 and therefore insisted that its aims be limited to securing the Mediterranean line of communications, diverting German divisions from the Soviet Union, detaching Italy from Germany and bringing Turkey into the war on the Allied side. It was only at the *Trident* Conference (Washington, 12-25 May, page 134) that Churchill extracted Roosevelt's consent for Eisenhower, Allied Supreme Commander, to plan for Italy's elimination from the war by the exploitation of *Husky*'s results.

D-Day for *Husky* was set for 10 July and the force allocated consisted of the US 7th (Patton) and British 8th (Montgomery) Armies, comprising divisions drawn from Britain and the United States as well as Tunisia and the Middle East. The Axis defence plan led to the reinforcement of Sardinia and Greece. The Allied assault, preceded by air attacks and airborne landings, was hampered by bad weather but was not seriously opposed. Landing respectively west and east of Cape Passero, the Americans and British each put four divisions ashore without serious difficulty. By 15 July the Allies had advanced to the Agrigento-Augusta line and were landing reinforcements. While Montgomery advanced along the eastern coast towards Catania and Messina, Patton exploited westward to Palermo. On 20 July, however, Alexander ordered Patton to swing his troops east to outflank Axis forces who were impeding Montgomery's advance beyond Mt. Etna.

While the Germans were being reinforced, the Italians began to withdraw their troops from Sicily on 25 July: Mussolini had been removed from power by an internal parliamentary coup, and the Italians began seriously to question their allegiance to the Axis. Against weakening opposition, and aided by amphibious hooks, Patton reached the approaches to Messina on 15 August. Montgomery, who had pressed his divisions westward of Etna, arrived a day later. By then, however, the Germans were in full retreat across the Straits of Messina and when the city fell on 17 August, all 100,000 Axis troops had reached Italy.

In the light of Mussolini's overthrow, Eisenhower received permission to plan a landing on the Italian mainland. He decided to launch diversionary British attacks into the toe of Italy on 3 September and follow these with a major Anglo-American landing, commanded by Mark Clark, in the Gulf of Salerno on 9 September. Badoglio, who had succeeded Mussolini as head of the Italian government, was meanwhile negotiating an armistice with the Allies, which was signed on 3 September and made public on 8 September. Hitler, however, reinforced his troops in Italy. The *Luftwaffe* attacked and damaged the Italian fleet on its way to Malta (9-11 September) and German forces heavily opposed the US 5th Army landings at Salerno. Counter-attacks were particularly heavy on 13 September and by 16 September, when Montgomery's 8th Army (reinforced by 1st Airborne Division which had landed at Taranto on 9 September) joined forces.

Naples was occupied on 1 October and by 12 October 5th and 8th Armies had established a line 120 miles long across the peninsula, from the River Volturno to Termoli on the Adriatic. Axis forces had, meanwhile, evacuated Sardinia (18 September) and Corsica (by 3 October). On 13 October, when Italy now entered the war on the Allied side, 5th Army crossed the River Volturno and began an advance to the River Garigliano on 15 November. Between 20 November and 2 December the 8th Army fought its way across the Sangro. Difficult terrain and Winter weather, bringing torrential rain, then allowed the Germans to hold the Allies, despite bitter hand fighting (especially at Ortona on the Adriatic coast) on the Gustav (Winter) Line, which ran between Minturno on the Mediterranean to Pescara on the Adriatic, from 15 January 1944. Numbers on both sides were about level, 13 German opposing 18 Allied divisions under Alexander, who had assumed command of the Mediterranean theatre upon Eisenhower's departure to prepare the Normandy invasion on 31 December; Montgomery, who had left on 30 December to act as his deputy, handed over command of 8th Army to Leese.

Despite the reasonably rapid success of Allied operations in capturing Sicily and southern Italy, few German forces had been captured or destroyed, and the Allies now faced a protracted struggle north to the Alps.

PLANS FOR THE ALLIED INVASION of Sicily and Italy (1) in Operation *Husky* took some time to be agreed. The Germans, however, began to reinforce the Italian peninsula and develop contingency plans to deal with any invasion. Patton's 7th Army landed on Sicily west of Cape Passero. Montgomery's 8th Army landed to the east. Both US and British airborne drops suffered heavy loss, but the seaborne landings were lightly opposed and by 15 July the Agrigento-Augusta line was reached. A German tank counter-attack towards Gela (11 July) failed. The Allies made steady progress until Montgomery encountered the Hermann Goering Division (15–19 July) south of Catania, where his paratroopers had taken, but lost, the Primasole bridge (13-14 July). Alexander, in overall command, decided to switch Patton, whose troops had subdued western Sicily, to a new axis (20 July) to approach Messina. Montgomery also changed axis, attacking west of Mt. Etna on 31 July. Assisted by seaborne 'hooks' (US on 8, 11 and 15 Aug., British on 16 Aug.), 7th and 8th Armies reached Messina (17 Aug.) to find the enemy gone. The Allied offensive now continued onto the Italian mainland. The Salerno landing (3, inset) (9 Sept.) achieved surprise and the Germans reacted by shifting the weight of their local forces north to guard communications with Naples. When reinforcements arrived they staged heavy counter-attacks (11-13 Sept.), but these were broken up by sea and air bombardment (14 Sept.). By 14 Sept. the perimeter of the bridgehead was secure. Montgomery's landings, at Reggio di Calabria on 3 Sept., and Taranto on 9 Sept., failed to trap German forces in the south. By 16 Sept. Montgomery's advanced guard had made contact with Clark's 5th Army 40 miles south of Salerno. On 18 Sept. Kesselring disengaged and retreated to the Naples-Bari line (25 Sept.); 3 days later his Adriatic flank was at Termoli. Naples fell on 1 Oct. Kesselring now fought a retreat to the Winter Position (the Gustav Line) during the Autumn where Allied offensives were mounted by the 5th Army in the Liri Valley (1 Oct.) and by the 8th Army on the R. Sangro (20 Nov.).

Picture below: bridge-building at Battipaglia near Salerno, Sept. 1943. Allied success relied greatly upon support services.

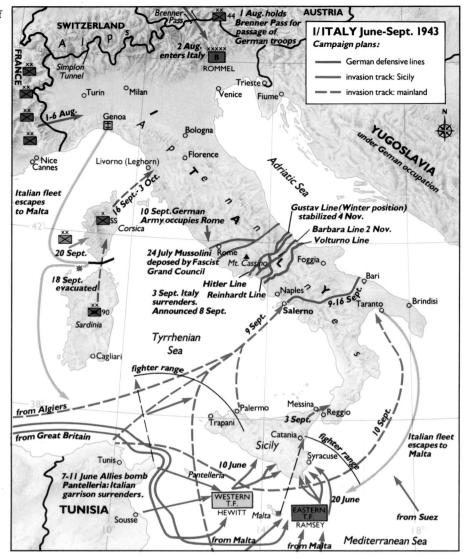

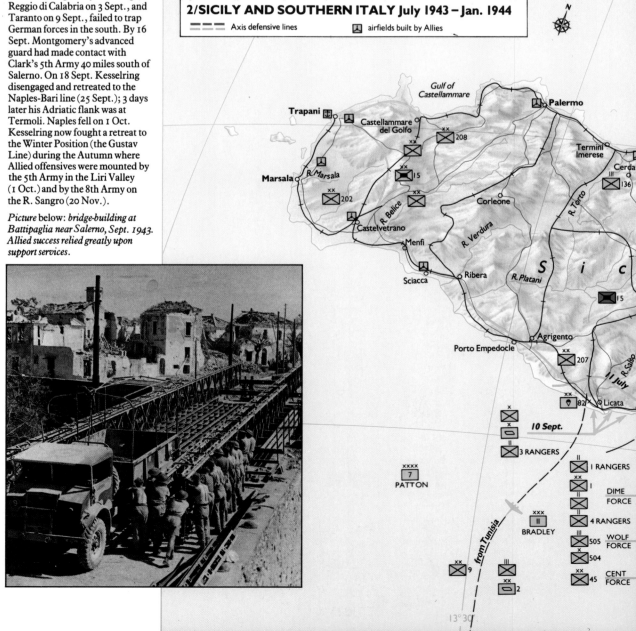

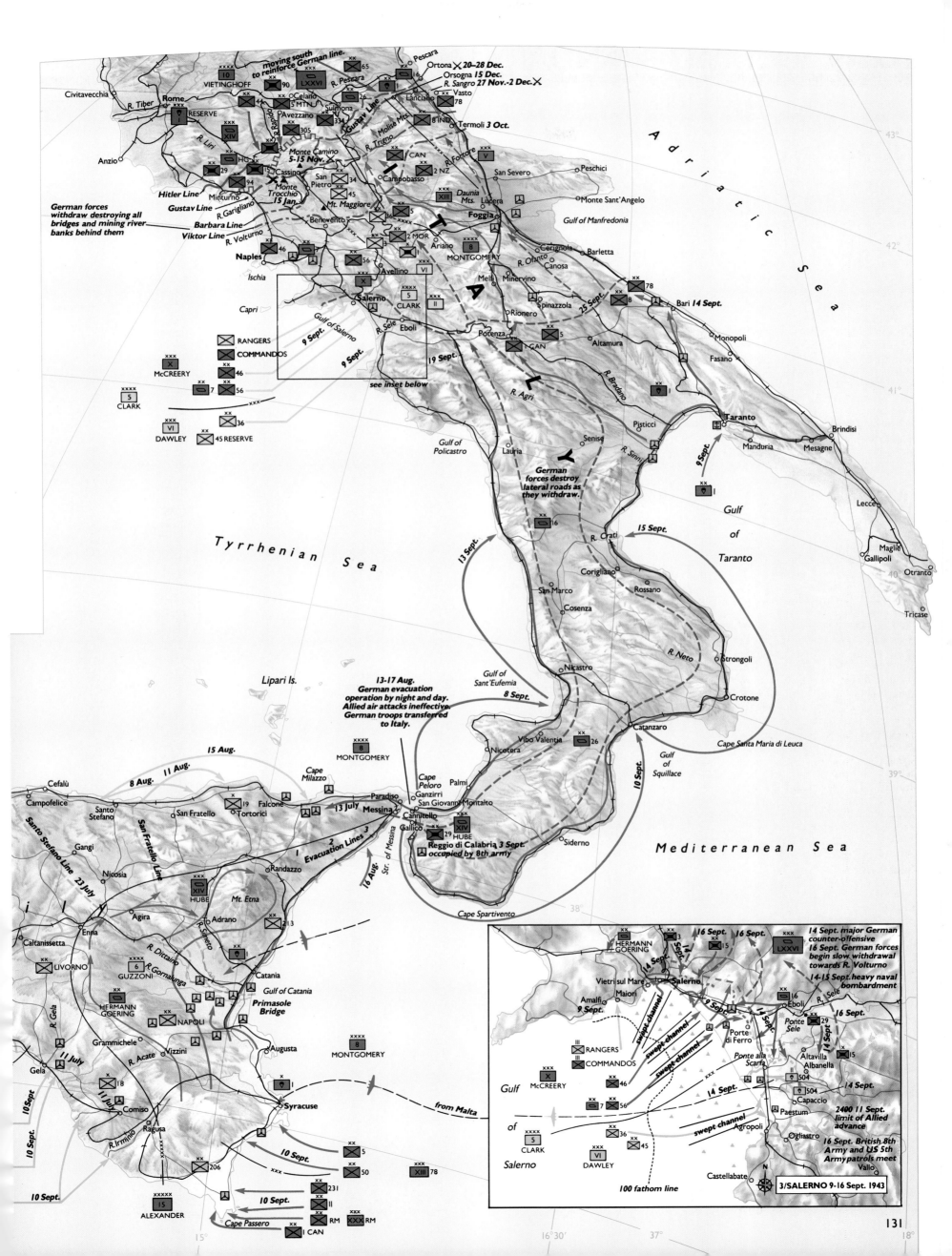

Civitavecchia
R. Tiber
Rome
RESERVE
R. Liri
XIV
Anzio
Monte Camino 5-15 Nov.
Cassino
Minturno
94
Monte Trocchio 15 Jan.
San Pietro
Mt. Maggiore
Hitler Line
Gustav Line
R. Garigliano
Barbara Line
R. Volturno
Viktor Line

moving south to reinforce German line.
VIETINGHOFF
90
5 MTN
Sulmona
334
305
HG
29
15
Benevento
Naples
46
Ischia
Capri

Pescara
Ortona ✕ 20–28 Dec.
Orsogna 15 Dec.
R. Sangro 27 Nov.-2 Dec. ✕
Vasto
78
Lanciano
8 IND
Termoli 3 Oct.
V
San Severo
Peschici
Monte Sant'Angelo
Gulf of Manfredonia

German forces withdraw destroying all bridges and mining river banks behind them

Avellino
VI
X
Salerno
CLARK 5
II
Eboli
19 Sept.

RANGERS
COMMANDOS
McCREERY
46
56
CLARK 5
DAWLEY VI
45 RESERVE
36

Gulf of Salerno
R. Sele
9 Sept.
9 Sept.
see inset below

2 MOR
3
Ariano
56
MONTGOMERY 8

Foggia
Daunia Mts.
Lucera
XIII

2 NZ
Campobasso
CAN
R. Fortore
R. Trigno
Molise Mts.

Cerignola
Canosa
Barletta
Melfi
Minervino
Rionero
Potenza
25 Sept.
78
8
Bari 14 Sept.
Spinazzola
Altamura
Monopoli
Fasano
CAN 5

Gulf of Policastro
Lauria
Senise
R. Agri
R. Sinni
R. Bradano
Pisticci
1
Taranto
9 Sept.
Manduria
Mesagne
Brindisi
Lecce
1

German forces destroy lateral roads as they withdraw.
16
R. Crati
15 Sept.
Corigliano
Rossano
Cosenza
San Marco
R. Neto
Strongoli
13 Sept.
Crotone

T y r r h e n i a n   S e a

A d r i a t i c   S e a

Gulf of Taranto
Cape Santa Maria di Leuca
Maglie
Gallipoli
Otranto
Tricase

Lipari Is.

13-17 Aug. German evacuation operation by night and day. Allied air attacks ineffective. German troops transferred to Italy.
MONTGOMERY 8
Gulf of Sant'Eufanio
8 Sept.
Nicastro
Vibo Valentia
26
Nicotera
Cape Peloro
Palmi
Ganzirri
San Giovanni Montalto
Catanzaro
Gulf of Squillace
10 Sept.

15 Aug.
11 Aug.
8 Aug.
Cefalù
Campofelice
Santo Stefano
San Fratello
19
Falcone
Tortorici
Cape Milazzo
13 July
Paradiso
Messina
Cannitello
Gallico
XIV HUBE 29
Reggio di Calabria 3 Sept. occupied by 8th army

M e d i t e r r a n e a n   S e a

Santo Stefano Line
San Fratello Line 23 July
Gangi
Nicosia
Agira
XIV HUBE
Mt. Etna
Adrano
R. Simeto
213
Evacuation Lines 1 2 3
16 Aug.
Str. of Messina
Cape Spartivento
Siderno

Caltanissetta
Enna
R. Dittaino
R. Gornalunga
LIVORNO
GUZZONI 6
Catania
Gulf of Catania
Primasole Bridge
HERMANN GOERING
NAPOLI
Grammichele
Vizzini
R. Acate
Augusta
MONTGOMERY 8
R. Gela
Comiso
Syracuse
from Malta
11 July
Gela
18
1
10 Sept.
R. Irmino
Ragusa
10 Sept.
10 Sept.
206
50
231
II
RM
RM
CAN
10 Sept.
10 Sept.
XIII 78
5
ALEXANDER 15
Cape Passero

Inset: 3/SALERNO 9–16 Sept. 1943

HERMANN GOERING 3
16 Sept.
16 Sept.
LXXVI
14 Sept. major German counter-offensive
16 Sept. German forces begin slow withdrawal towards R. Volturno
14-15 Sept. heavy naval bombardment

Vietri sul Mare
Salerno
15
Amalfi
Maiori
9 Sept.
swept channel
9 Sept.
Porte di Ferro
Eboli
16
R. Sele
16 Sept.
29
14 Sept.

RANGERS
COMMANDOS
McCREERY
46
7
56
Ponte alla Scarfa
14 Sept.
swept channel
swept channel
15
II
504
504
Albanella
Altavilla
Capaccio
14 Sept.

Gulf of Salerno
CLARK 5
DAWLEY VI
36
45
swept channel
14 Sept.
Agropoli
100 fathom line
Ogliastro
Paestum
2400 11 Sept. limit of Allied advance
16 Sept. British 8th Army and US 5th Army patrols meet Vallo
Castellabate
N

131

AT THE BEGINNING OF JANUARY 1944 the Allied armies in Italy had driven the German 10th Army from the approaches to Kesselring's Winter Position in a series of hard-fought operations (page 130). Now, in accordance with a directive issued by Alexander on 8 November, 5th Army undertook a succession of offensives, designed to open up a passage north to Rome through the Liri Valley. Alexander's conception was that the city should eventually be taken by an offensive up the Liri, supported by an amphibious assault nearer the city, at Anzio. During December, 5th Army had fought battles for Monte Cassino (1-10 December) and San Pietro (20-21 December) which barred the way into the Liri Valley. Between 5-15 January 1944, 5th Army moved forward to the line of the Rapido River, which flows into the Liri near its confluence with the Garigliano, and on which the strongest point of the Winter Position, the Gustav Line, was established.

On 17 January the British X Corps, of 5th Army, stormed and crossed the Garigliano. When the 36th (Texan) Division assaulted the Rapido, however, on 20 January, it was bloodily repulsed. Next day the Anzio landing (Operation *Shingle*) began. Four British and US divisions, with supporting Commandos and Rangers, got ashore without loss, having taken Kesselring by surprise. But Lucas, the VI Corps commander, then concentrated on building up force within the bridgehead rather than driving on Rome. An immediate drive might have been defeated; but Lucas's inaction allowed Kesselring to rush emergency units to Anzio. While forward

reserves were transferred from other sectors of the Winter Position, by 15 February he had assembled sufficient force to mount a deliberate counter-offensive (Operation *Fischgang*) which nearly bisected the bridgehead: it was checked only by heavy Allied air, artillery and naval bombardment.

The initial failure of the Anzio landing cast responsibility for rescuing the Italian campaign from stalemate back upon the troops of US 5th Army, opposite the Gustav Line, despite a continuing depletion of Allied forces as troops and equipment were withdrawn to mount operations *Overlord* (page 152) and *Anvil* (page 156). The key to the Gustav Line was Monte Cassino, the fortress monastery which commanded the approaches to the Liri Valley. Clark, commanding 5th Army, made four attempts to capture it, employing in the process two of the reinforcing contingents – the Free French Expeditionary Force and the Polish II Corps – which had joined the Allied Army in Italy since the start of the battle for the Winter Position. Clark's US 34th Division attacked first on 24 January but was eventually defeated (12 February) by the German 1st Parachute Division, which defended the monastery heights. The New Zealand Corps attacked in the second battle, 16-18 February, but, despite the heavy bombardment of the monastery by B-17s on 16 February, was also defeated. The New Zealand Corps tried once more, 15-23 March, again supported by bombers, but, after winning more ground, was forced to desist.

Alexander's Chief of Staff, Harding, now devised a plan

(*Diadem*) to unlock the stalemate on the front south of Rome. VI Corps at Anzio had been reinforced. The final battle for Monte Cassino began on 11 May. The mountaineers of the Free French Expeditionary Corps bypassed the monastery to the west; after an initial and costly surprise the Polish II Corps took the monastery on 18 May; the British XIII Corps breached the coastal line west of Cassino on 23 May. On the same day VI Corps began to break out from Anzio and II Corps advanced to join it on 25 May. Harding's plan – which was to trap the German 10th Army between the Anzio-Cassino pincers – now seemed on the point of fruition. Next day, however, Mark Clark, who was determined that the Americans should be the first to enter Rome, shifted the axis of 5th Army's advance to the north-west. German rearguards were then able to check VI Corps at Velletri and Valmontone until 2 June, allowing 10th Army to join 14th (formed the previous November and used to contain the Anzio bridgehead) in a retreat towards the Pisa-Rimini (Gothic) Line, 150 miles north of Rome.

American troops entered Rome on 4 June, in the forefront of a general Allied advance. While 8th Army cleared the Adriatic coast between Pescara and Ancona, 5th Army moved along the Mediterranean. Livorno fell on 19 July. Florence on 11 August. Both 5th and 8th Armies were by then in contact with the Gothic Line and, because of the withdrawal of the French Expeditionary and US VI Corps to mount the southern France landing (Operation *Anvil/Dragoon*, page 156) were forced to pause temporarily before launching an assault upon it.

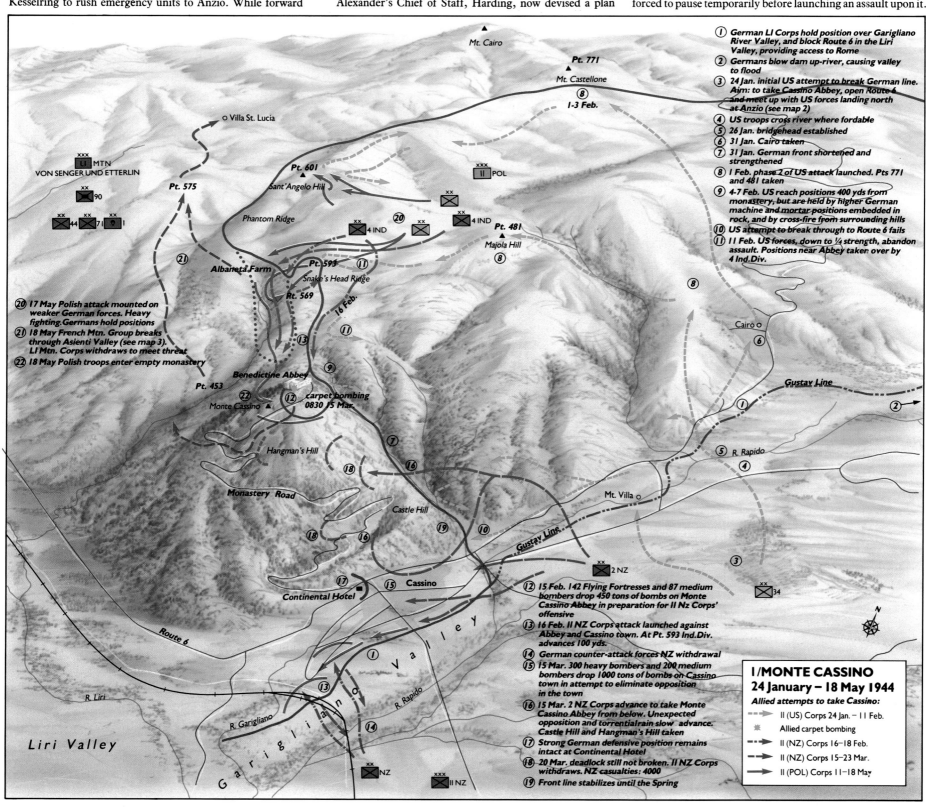

① German LI Corps hold position over Garigliano River Valley, and block Route 6 in the Liri Valley, providing access to Rome
② Germans blow dam up-river, causing valley to flood
③ 24 Jan. initial US attempt to break German line. Aim: to take Cassino Abbey, open Route 6 and meet up with US forces landing north at Anzio (see map 2)
④ US troops cross river where fordable
⑤ 26 Jan. bridgehead established
⑥ 31 Jan. Cairo taken
⑦ 31 Jan. German front shortened and strengthened
⑧ 1 Feb. phase 2 of US attack launched. Pts 771 and 481 taken
⑨ 4-7 Feb. US reach positions 400 yds from monastery, but are held by higher German machine and mortar positions embedded in rock, and by cross-fire from surrounding hills
⑩ US attempt to break through to Route 6 fails
⑪ 11 Feb. US forces, down to ¼ strength, abandon assault. Positions near Abbey taken over by 4 Ind.Div.

⑳ 17 May Polish attack mounted on weaker German forces. Heavy fighting. Germans hold positions
㉑ 18 May French Mtn. Group breaks through Asienti Valley (see map 3). LI Mtn. Corps withdraws to meet threat
㉒ 18 May Polish troops enter empty monastery

⑫ 15 Feb. 142 Flying Fortresses and 87 medium bombers drop 450 tons of bombs on Monte Cassino Abbey in preparation for II Nz Corps' offensive
⑬ 16 Feb. II NZ Corps attack launched against Abbey and Cassino town. At Pt. 593 Ind.Div. advances 100 yds
⑭ German counter-attack forces NZ withdrawal
⑮ 15 Mar. 300 heavy bombers and 200 medium bombers drop 1000 tons of bombs on Cassino town in attempt to eliminate opposition in the town
⑯ 15 Mar. 2 NZ Corps advance to take Monte Cassino Abbey from below. Unexpected opposition and torrential rain slow advance. Castle Hill and Hangman's Hill taken
⑰ Strong German defensive position remains intact at Continental Hotel
⑱ 20 Mar. deadlock still not broken. II NZ Corps withdraws. NZ casualties: 4000
⑲ Front line stabilizes until the Spring

I/MONTE CASSINO
24 January – 18 May 1944
Allied attempts to take Cassino:

------> II (US) Corps 24 Jan. – 11 Feb.
✳ Allied carpet bombing
--▶ II (NZ) Corps 16–18 Feb.
--▶ II (NZ) Corps 15–23 Mar.
——▶ II (POL) Corps 11–18 May

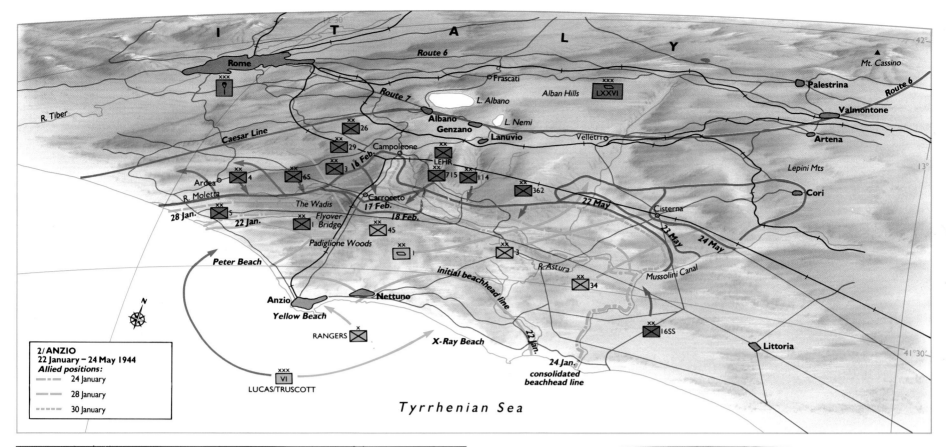

2/ANZIO
22 January – 24 May 1944
Allied positions:
- — 24 January
- – – 28 January
- ···· 30 January

LUCAS/TRUSCOTT

Tyrrhenian Sea

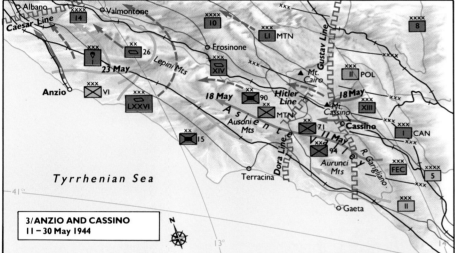

3/ANZIO AND CASSINO
11 – 30 May 1944

Tyrrhenian Sea

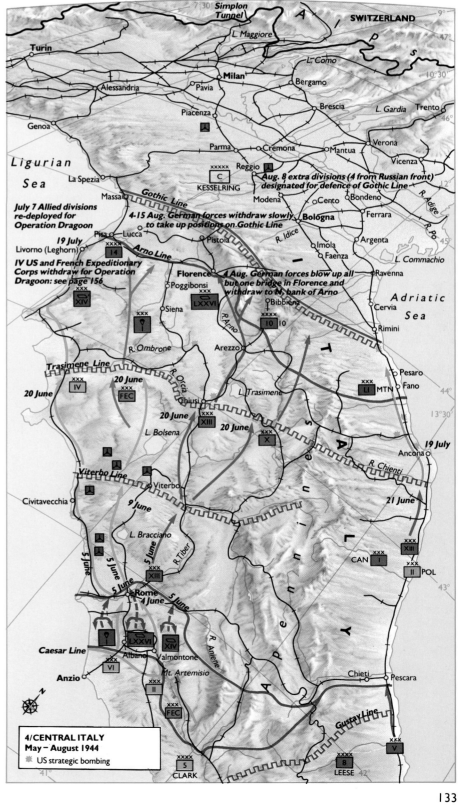

4/CENTRAL ITALY
May – August 1944
✴ US strategic bombing

Picture left: German machine-gunners on the north bank of the River Arno in Florence. Although Rome was declared an open city (10 Aug. 1943, having been bombed by USAAF on 19 July) many other Italian towns and cities were severely damaged.

THE BATTLES FOR Monte Cassino (1), a monastery perched on towering heights which commanded access to the Liri Valley, proved enormously costly for the Allies, but also provided acts of extraordinary bravery and endurance among all participants. The first battle was staged on 24 Jan. 1944 by the US 34th Division, which succeeded at heavy cost in capturing high ground to the north-east of the monastery by 11 Feb. The German 1st Parachute Division was not occupying the monastery buildings, at the order of the LI Corps commander, von Senger und Etterlin. The monastery was nevertheless destroyed by Allied heavy bombing (16 Feb.), to prepare the assault of the New Zealand Corps (2nd NZ and 4th Indian Divisions) that day. Their attack, though it took more high ground, was terminated on 18 Feb. The NZ Corps attacked again on 15 Mar., when Allied medium bombers

saturated the German parachutist positions with carpet bombing, but on 23 Mar. was forced to call the attack off, having seized most of the southern approaches to the monastery and north of Cassino town. Finally on 11 May, as part of the Operation *Diadem*, the Polish II Corps opened the fourth battle. Repulsed at first, they eventually captured the ruins of the monastery on 18 May. Further north, at Anzio, VI Corps landed by surprise (2, 21 Jan.), having sailed from Naples. Lucas, the Corps commander, did not press on to Rome, but consolidated his bridgehead, only 6 miles deep. Kesselring surrounded it with 'emergency units' and brought up reinforcements. He attacked (15 Feb.) and almost broke through to the coast but was halted by heavy Allied firepower. The battle then resolved itself with a bloody siege but by 23 May VI Corps (commanded by Truscott after 23 Feb.) had been built up to 7

divisions and it easily broke out on that date to play its part in Operation *Diadem*. This was launched on 11 May (3) as a means of breaking the Gustav Line and encircling the German 10th Army south of Rome. While Polish II Corps attacked north of Cassino, the British XIII, French Expeditionary and US II Corps all attacked between it and the coast. XIII and II Corps drove along the coast towards the Anzio bridgehead, out of which VI Corps broke on 23 May. This threatened 10th Army with envelopment but, on 26 Mar., the day after the Anzio force had linked with the rest of 5th Army, Mark Clark shifted its axis of advance directly towards Rome, allowing 10th Army to cover its retreat and escape. Kesselring recognized that, once the Winter Position (Gustav Line) was broken, his next and last line of defence in Italy ran between Pisa and Rimini, the Gothic Line. He had prepared intermediate positions (4), to which he fell back as soon as Rome was taken (4 June) and with reinforcements was to stand on the Viterbo and Trasimene Lines, before retiring to the Gothic Line (4 Aug.)

Politics and strategy 1943

AFTER *TORCH* HAD SUCCEEDED (page 116), the question of Allied strategy had to be re-addressed. Should effort be switched to a 'Second Front' in France, or continued into Italy after final victory in North Africa? Roosevelt and Churchill met in Casablanca in mid-January 1943. On the US side, Gen. Marshall spoke for a Second Front, while Admiral King wanted more action against Japan. The British doubted Allied capacity for a French landing before 1944, and they advocated action in the Mediterranean, against Italy and the Balkans; meanwhile, they claimed that their bombing of Germany was weakening Germany's effort on the Eastern Front. Eventually, Roosevelt sided with the British although two large-scale offensives were planned in the Pacific (Operation *Cartwheel*, page 122, 140). Politically, Casablanca was important for the demand, made almost casually by Roosevelt, that the enemy powers would have to accept 'unconditional surrender'.

In May, Roosevelt and Churchill met again, in Washington, for a further conference (*Trident*). There were difficulties in reconciling the various claims made for a build-up of force in the British Isles for invasion of France, for an invasion of Italy, and for offensive action in the Pacific. At *Trident* a Second Front was agreed, for 1 May 1944, and a force of 29 divisions was to be set up for this. However, a landing in Sicily was also agreed, though not an invasion of Italy; in the Pacific, further aims were somewhat reduced, to the opening-up of the Burma Road into China, and the establishment of US air bases in the areas controlled by Chiang Kai-shek.

After the invasion of Sicily (page 130) and the fall of Mussolini (25 July 1943) the American Joint Chiefs of Staff were won round to Churchill's view that the next effort should be launched in Italy. To work out details, and apportion supplies between the Channel, the Mediterranean and the Pacific, a further Anglo-American conference was held at Quebec in mid-August (*Quadrant*). Here, the Americans insisted on a cross-Channel invasion of France (*Overlord*, page 152) but also agreed that it would have to be very strongly backed; that there should be a further effort in Italy (still the chief ambition on the British side) but that part of that effort might be shifted to an invasion of southern France (*Anvil*, page 156), coinciding with *Overlord*. Meanwhile, there were further exchanges concerning the manufacture of the atomic bomb – now heavily concentrated in the USA.

However, the Italian campaign went very slowly (despite Italy's change of side) whereas, on the Eastern Front, the Soviets were rapidly pushing the Germans before them. It was necessary to arrive at agreement on strategy – to reassure Stalin as to the Second Front, but also to cater for Soviet involvement in the war in the Far East. Before meeting Stalin, Roosevelt and Churchill met Chiang Kai-shek at Cairo (*Sextant*). It provided little except the Cairo Declaration of 1 December 1943, which laid down terms for Japan's surrender, and for the restoration of Manchuria to China and independence for Korea.

Roosevelt and Churchill then proceeded to Teheran, for a conference (*Eureka*, 28 November-1 December) with Stalin. The conference was preceded by a meeting of their three foreign ministers (Eden, Cordell Hull and Molotov) at Moscow (19-30 October), where various problems were discussed in an atmosphere of mounting Soviet victory. There Soviet consent was gained to the formula for Italy's surrender and occupation – a tripartite political commission might advise a military commander who otherwise would take orders from the Combined Chiefs of Staff in the West. In addition, the Foreign Ministers agreed upon the restoration of Austria and the establishment of a European Advisory Commission in London to discuss the future of Germany.

At Teheran, Stalin promised that he would eventually intervene against Japan, and was satisfied as to prospects for a Second Front in Europe. However, he wanted assurance concerning Poland. The Soviet Union had annexed a large part of eastern Poland in 1939-40, mainly on the grounds that its population, being Ukrainian or White Russian, 'naturally' belonged to the USSR. The exiled Polish government expected support from London. At Teheran, Churchill and Roosevelt, recognizing the fact of Stalin's power in the area, agreed, though not formally, that Poland should be compensated with industrially-rich German territory for her losses in the east. At the same time, the integrity of Persia, occupied by the Allies (page 78), was guaranteed, and post-war withdrawal promised. Returning to Cairo, Roosevelt and Churchill conferred, and by 7 December they recognized that, the Italian campaign having slowed down, *Overlord* in northern France and *Anvil* in southern France should now take priority.

1/WAR CONFERENCES
Jan. – Dec. 1943

Major Axis conferences

1 Rome 24-28 Feb. Ribbentrop meets Mussolini to review African situation

2 Berchtesgaden 31 Mar.-18 Sept. Hitler receives Axis allied leaders to consolidate military and political support: King Boris of Bulgaria, Antonescu (Rumania), Admiral Horthy (Hungary), Vidkung Quisling (Norway), Tiso (Slovakia), Pavelić (Croatia), Neditch (Serbia)

3 Salzburg 7-10 Apr. Hitler and Mussolini decide to attempt to hold positions in Africa

4 Berchtesgaden 29 Apr. Hitler reviews situation in French North Africa with Laval, now effectively in charge of occupied France

5 Verona 19 July Hitler and Mussolini discuss Africa and defensive measures for Italy

Major Allied conferences

6 Casablanca 14-24 Jan. Roosevelt and Churchill meet to resolve Allied differences and decide future strategy. Resolutions include a cross-Channel invasion of France in 1944; a subsidiary offensive in Italy; U-boat offensive and supplies to USSR to receive top priority; the Combined Bombing Offensive against Germany formally announced; unconditional surrender terms announced

7 Adana 30 Jan. Churchill meets Pres. Inönü of Turkey, who refuses to join war

8 Second Washington Conference (Trident) 11-27 May Roosevelt and Churchill reach compromises on all major issues: cross-Channel offensive date set (1 May 1944); immediate Pacific and Italian offensives approved; British hopes for a Balkan offensive abandoned

9 First Quebec Conference (Quadrant) 17 Aug. US and British military leaders to discuss details of cross-Channel offensive; also support for Italian offensive agreed; aid to China to continue; preliminary discussions for Burma offensive

10 Washington 2 Sept. Churchill and Roosevelt continued planning talks

11 Second Moscow Conference 18 Oct.-1 Nov. Allied foreign ministers devise provisional formulas for joint military/political decision-making in liberated countries

12 Atlantic City 9 Nov.-1 Dec. First United Nations Relief and Rehabilitation Administration (U.N.R.R.A.) meeting

13 First Cairo Conference (Sextant) 22-25 Nov. Roosevelt, Churchill and Chiang Kai-shek discuss Burma–China plans. No resolutions. Failure to discuss joint Western strategy for Teheran Conference (below)

14 Teheran (Eureka) 28 Nov. Stalin, Roosevelt and Churchill meet for first time. Cross-Channel invasion approved, as are plans for invasion of southern France. Stalin promises to join war against Japan

15 Second Cairo Conference 4-6 Dec. Roosevelt and Churchill meet Pres. Inönö of Turkey, who again refuses to join war

☐	Allies Dec. 1943
▨	Axis and Axis satellites Dec. 1943
—	Allied/Axis front lines Dec. 1943
▲	Axis war conference 1943
△	Allied war conference 1943

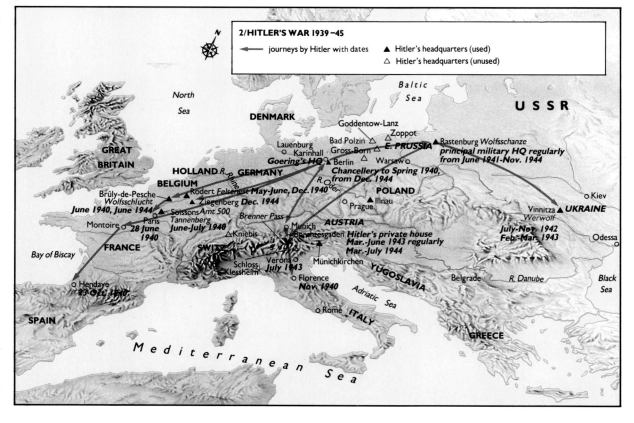

2/HITLER'S WAR 1939–45

⟵ journeys by Hitler with dates
▲ Hitler's headquarters (used)
△ Hitler's headquarters (unused)

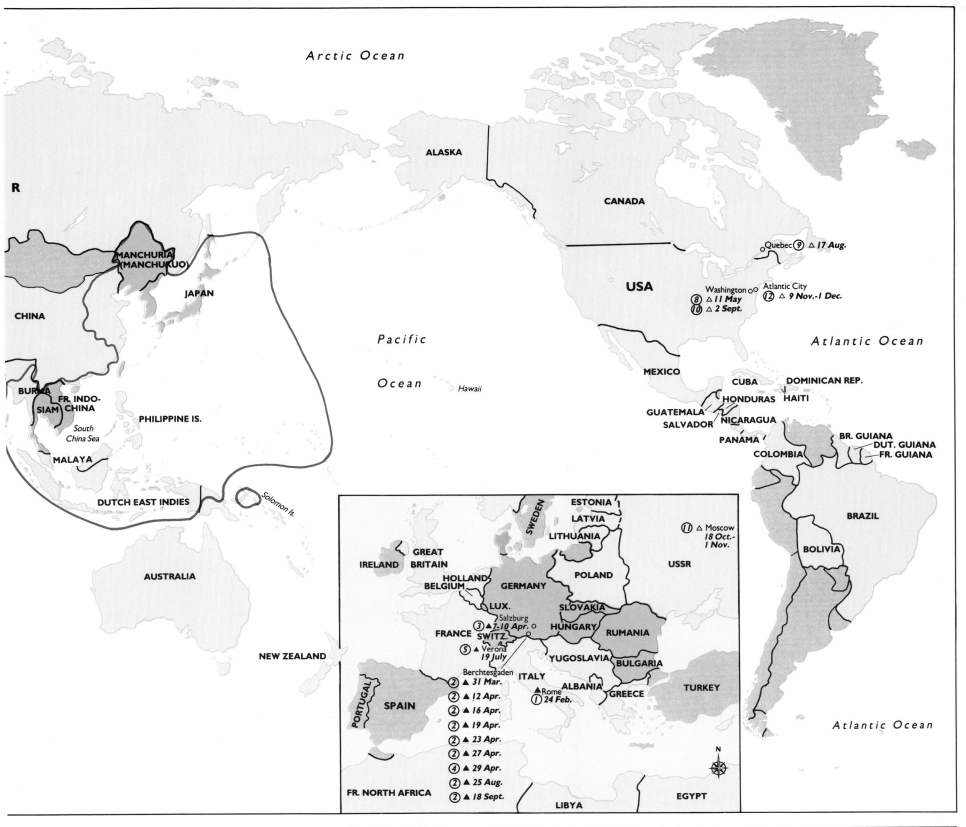

1943 WAS A YEAR of important decisions for the Allies (1). The shape of grand strategy which would bring the war in Europe to an end was decided, and provisional plans laid for the political restructuring of the post-war world. Although the Second Front in Europe was yet to open, the Western Allies had recovered North Africa and were invading Italy. The Red Army had liberated Stalingrad, and won critical battles at Kursk and Kharkov. By Autumn it was beginning its victorious advance west, pushing the Germans and their allies back to the line of the Dnieper. In the South-west Pacific, the Japanese were beating a retreat and preparing for an inevitable US drive into the western Pacific, although they were unaware of when or where it would occur. The Allied cause was still growing: Turkey remained neutral, but Italy changed sides (declaring war on Germany, Sept. 1943); Brazil and Mexico both had formations in the field, and Anders' 1st Polish Army had arrived in the Mediterranean theatre (from the USSR) to see action in Italy. The turning tide of Axis success was

reflected in the conduct of Hitler's affairs (2): the glorious summit meetings of earlier years were abandoned and he now spent his time in military conclave at his eastern HQ at Rastenburg (Vinnitsa was now abandoned) or at his private house at Berchtesgaden, dealing increasingly frantically with each ensuing crisis on the Eastern Front, and with his allies at confrontational personal audiences. He avoided his political responsibilities by avoiding Berlin. Hitler now began vainly to hope that he could win the war with secret weapons – the V-1 flying bomb and V-2 rocket, jet-propelled fighters, very long-range artillery, the XXIII U-boat – all in development but all, except the V-weapons (in use from 1944), became operational far too late, if at all.

Picture above right: Soviet poster celebrating the Allied cause. Below right: *the* Sextant *Conference, Cairo 22-25 Nov. seated (from left) Chiang Kai-shek, Roosevelt, Churchill, Madame Chiang Kai-shek.* Far right: *the German V-2 rocket on a test launch, Peenemünde, 1943.*

NEVER, EVEN AT ITS HEIGHT, had British naval supremacy rested upon the outcome of a single battle; the command of the sea which Britain had exercised in successive wars was secured through successive victories but was never able to prevent substantial mercantile losses at the hands of enemies employing a *guerre de course*. After August 1943 the Allies had to repeat their Summer victories (page 108) over the U-boats in the battle of the Atlantic, albeit on more modest scales, throughout the remaining twenty months of the European war. During this period there were two quite distinct aspects to the Allied application of victorious sea power: a defensive success in continuing to thwart the German campaign against shipping, and an offensive success in carrying the war into northwest Europe, and in completing the destruction of German seaborne commerce.

The last phase of the European war witnessed the effective neutralization of the U-boat menace but not the defeat of the U-boat arm itself. In 1943 as a whole the German Navy commissioned 272 boats, in 1944 another 242, and with losses of 237 and 242 boats in these same years, the U-boat arm was able to maintain, indeed slightly increase its numerical strength until it reached its maximum wartime strength of 444 boats in commission in April 1945. In the whole of 1944, however, German submarines sank 432 merchantmen of 773,327 tons,

fewer ships (but more tonnage) than the Allies lost to all causes in June 1942. However, in this final phase of the struggle at sea, the effectiveness of German submarines lay not in their sinking Allied commerce but in tying down disproportionately large Allied naval forces while awaiting the entry into service of a new generation of submarine (Type XXIII with high-speed underwater performance) that would – it was confidently hoped – wrest the initiative from the Allies. The first operational mission of these new submarines began on 30 April 1945, the day that Hitler committed suicide, coming far too late to have any impact on the war at sea.

In this final phase of the war, the escort re-emerged as the main agency of U-boat destruction: the introduction of the *schnorkel* breathing apparatus (which allowed submarines to recharge their batteries at periscope depth, thus avoiding surfacing, but reduced their mobility) provided German submarines with a degree of immunity from detection (and hence destruction) from the air, albeit at the cost of greatly degraded performance. The various technological develop-

ments of previous years provided the means whereby the Allies could now take the battle to the U-boats. When linked to increases in numerical strength, this meant that escort groups now became larger and capable of operating independently in waters known to be used by U-boats. The German introduction of the acoustic torpedo as the antidote to escort effectiveness proved counter-productive. Forced to operate at low speed in order to nullify these torpedoes, the escorts found themselves obliged, for the first time, to use forward-firing weaponry against submerged U-boats rather than employing high-speed depth-charge attacks. Such weaponry had been introduced in 1941 but had been little used, but from 1944 it emerged as the most formidable means of attacking and destroying U-boats.

The Allied offensive campaign in the war at sea (apart from the movement, support and maintenance of field armies on the continental mainland), was primarily carried by shore-based air power. Eight of the nine major German warship losses in the last year of the war were to direct air attack, and such operations

AFTER THE DEFEAT OF AUG. 1943, when they sank only 2 merchantmen in the North Atlantic (page 108), the U-boats made successive attempts to regain the initiative, but despite the introduction into service of acoustic torpedoes and *schnorkel* breathing apparatus they were forced to withdraw from the Atlantic following severe losses in Nov. 1943 and March 1944 (*1*). Thereafter, the U-boats were concentrated for operations in British home waters (*4*) and against Allied invasion forces, but against the latter they sank only 21 vessels before the evacuation of French ports. Subsequently, as the *schnorkel* entered general service, success for both sides became increasingly rare, the U-boats being conferred with a high degree of immunity from detection and destruction, but at the cost of offensive effectiveness (*3*). The Allied successes registered in the last weeks of the war (*5, 7*) in the Kattegat (*4*) were mainly at the expense of older boats.

Picture above right: British Beaufighters attacking German minesweepers in harbour. Allied air superiority from 1944 seriously hampered German naval activity.

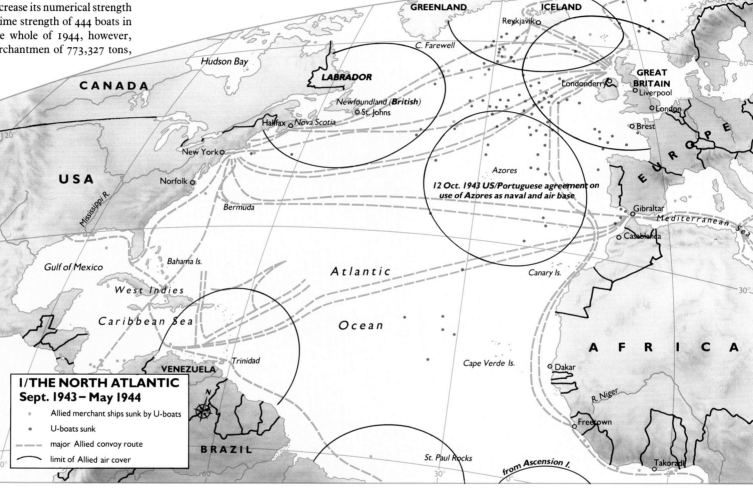

I/THE NORTH ATLANTIC
Sept. 1943 – May 1944

- Allied merchant ships sunk by U-boats
- U-boats sunk
- - - major Allied convoy route
- limit of Allied air cover

12 Oct. 1943 US/Portuguese agreement on use of Azores as naval and air base

3/ALLIED MERCHANT SHIPPING LOSSES Oct. 1943 – May 1945 : tonnages (nos. of ships)

date	U-boat	aircraft	mine	warship raider	merchant raider	E-boat	unknown and other causes	monthly totals
Oct.-Dec. 1943	250,959 (47)	160,603 (28)	32,526 (9)	none	none	8538 (4)	150 (1)	452,776 (89)
Jan.-Mar. 1944	328,145 (54)	45,853 (7)	14,352 (2)	7840 (1)	none	2280 (4)	755 (4)	405,450 (74)
Apr.-June 1944	144,448 (24)	31,636 (6)	24,654 (6)	none	2280	10,735 (4)	213,753 (44)	213,753 (44)
July-Sept. 1944	205,448 (37)	none	16,745 (7)	none	none	14,395 (2)	5277 (2)	241,865 (48)
Oct.-Dec. 1944	95,286 (17)	43,167 (6)	40,104 (13)	none	none	1141 (1)	4863 (2)	184,561 (39)
Jan.-Mar. 1945	187,298 (39)	14,353 (2)	70,508 (18)	none	none	10,222 (5)	7036 (7)	289,417 (71)
Apr.-May 1945	82,979 (16)	29,998 (4)	8733 (6)	none	none	none	none	121,710 (28)
June-Aug. 1945	11,439 (1)	none	14,422 (4)	none	none	none	1833 (3)	25,888 (7)

total by theatre Oct. 1943 - Aug. 1945

Atlantic Ocean	Mediterranean	Indian Ocean	Pacific Ocean
497,895 (88)	371,012 (69)	417,938 (68)	120,023 (16)

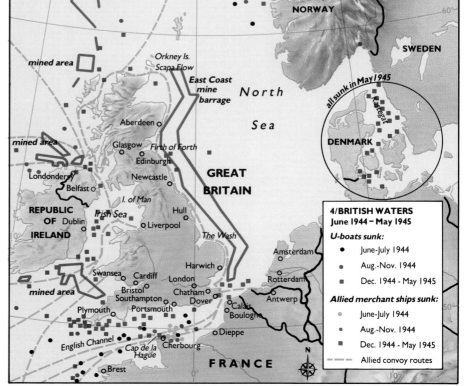

all sunk in May 1945

East Coast mine barrage

4/BRITISH WATERS
June 1944 – May 1945

U-boats sunk:
- • June-July 1944
- ■ Aug.-Nov. 1944
- ■ Dec. 1944 - May 1945

Allied merchant ships sunk:
- June-July 1944
- Aug.-Nov. 1944
- ■ Dec. 1944 - May 1945
- - - Allied convoy routes

and mining brought about the collapse of the German minesweeping fleet and merchant marine in the last five months of the war. Conventional naval power, however, had driven German commerce from the oceans from the start of the war, but as a result of her own resources, requisitions and captures, Germany until 1944 possessed sufficient shipping to meet her modest seaborne requirements. In 1944, however, the withdrawal of Swedish shipping from the iron ore trade left Germany unable to cover the deficiency in this one area. The German navy and marine retained a degree of effectiveness until the end of the war, but by May 1945 the German marine, which had totalled some 4,500,000 tons of shipping in 1939, retained only 1,500,000 tons, and it lost 1,052,000 tons of shipping – 42 per cent of its 1944 strength – in the last 16 months of hostilities.

The Allied victory at sea was thus as comprehensive as the outcome of the struggles on land and in the air. In the course of the war as a whole, all forms of Axis action and natural causes accounted for 22,000,000 tons of Allied and neutral shipping, but Allied construction amounted to 42,000,000 tons of shipping. Further, the access to world-wide resources provided by their command of the sea gave the Allies the upper hand over Germany, which was increasingly obliged to wage war on the basis of her own resources. The German Navy had proved unable to maintain Germany's oceanic trade: also, ultimately, it failed to protect Germany's conquests and allies from invasion.

APART FROM WITHDRAWALS before major invasions, Allied escort strength in the Atlantic increased (7) throughout the war with the exception of the last months, when there was an increasing concentration of strength in British home waters in response to a changing pattern of German operations (2). Even with the *schnorkel*, however, the U-boats were unable to reverse the general trend of the various exchange rates (6) that were the best indicators of the course of the battle; the new coastal Type XXIII submarine claimed its first victim only in Spring 1945. In the last months of the war Allied strategic bomber forces registered their only sustained success of the naval war in destroying 62 submarines and, critically, by imposing a series of delays and losses upon Type XXI and Type XXIII construction. Of the 1162 U-boats that were built, 830 saw service: 784 were lost, and of these 696 were destroyed by Allied action.

Picture below: a Liberty ship under construction in Oregon. Using production-line techniques and prefabricated components, US shipbuilders could manufacture one of these merchant vessels in only 10 days.

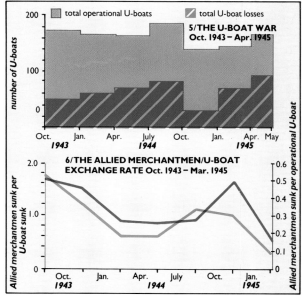

5/THE U-BOAT WAR
Oct. 1943 – Apr. 1945

total operational U-boats   total U-boat losses

number of U-boats

6/THE ALLIED MERCHANTMEN/U-BOAT
EXCHANGE RATE Oct. 1943 – Mar. 1945

Allied merchantmen sunk per U-boat sunk

Allied merchantmen sunk per operational U-boat

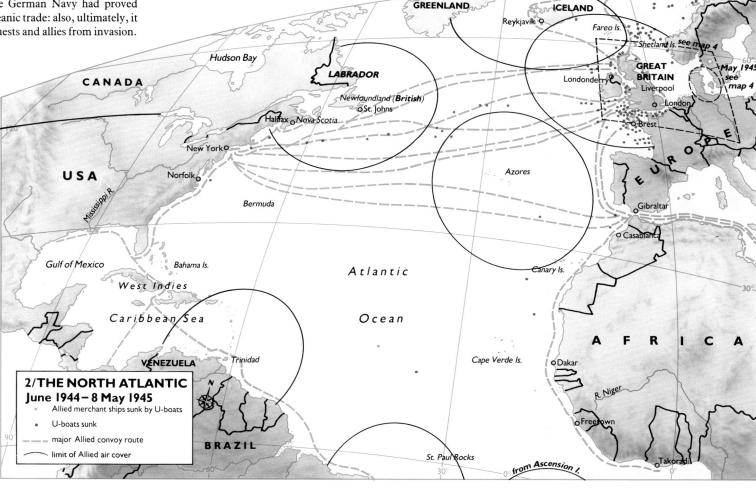

2/THE NORTH ATLANTIC
June 1944 – 8 May 1945
• Allied merchant ships sunk by U-boats
• U-boats sunk
– – – major Allied convoy route
—— limit of Allied air cover

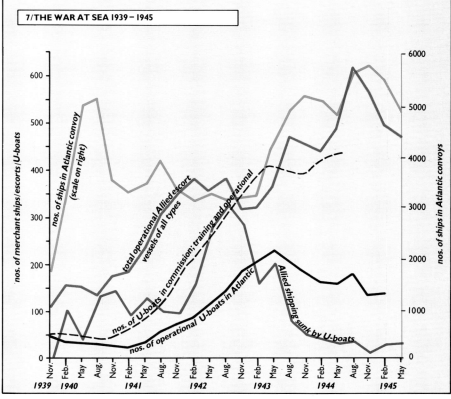

7/THE WAR AT SEA 1939 – 1945

nos. of merchant ships/escorts/U-boats

nos. of ships in Atlantic convoys

nos. of ships in Atlantic convoy (scale on right)

total operational Allied escort vessels of all types

nos. of U-boats in commission: training and operational

nos. of operational U-boats in Atlantic

Allied shipping sunk by U-boats

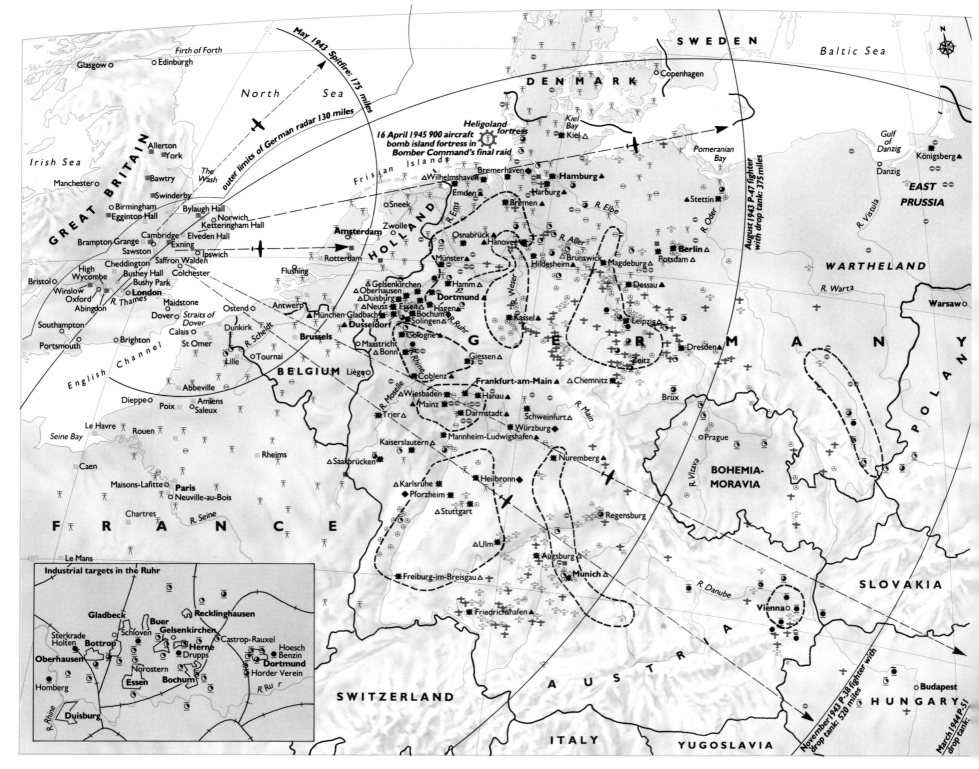

Industrial targets in the Ruhr

THE STRATEGIC BOMBING OFFENSIVE, launched four years before by the RAF, finally came of age in 1944. Not until then did either Bomber Command or the United States 8th Air Force have enough bombers in the front line to inflict serious damage on the German economy; only in 1944 did the use of newly developed radio direction finding become general, and the accuracy of bombing improve; only in 1944 did the Allies develop the long-range escort fighter, the P-51 Mustang with drop fuel-tanks, which could fight the *Luftwaffe* over its own territory and win the air superiority necessary to permit further bombing. The vast numerical superiority enjoyed by the Allies was brought to bear with critical effect. By the Summer of 1944 the *Luftwaffe* was no longer an effective fighting force, and the Allies could finally test the strategic value of the Combined Offensive.

Before that stage was reached the Allied supreme commanders insisted that the bombers, kept from the Reich by the strength of German air defences, should instead be used to help pave the way for the Allied invasion of mainland Europe. This help took two forms: firstly, Operation *Pointblank* aimed at the destruction of the German air force and its sources of supply; secondly, a systematic destruction of tactical targets (bridges, railway lines and storage depots) to prevent the German armed forces from repelling the invasion of Normandy. The bomber commanders objected to the diversion of effort from what they saw as the major objective in the Reich. But in practice the attack on the German air force, most successfully carried out in 'Big Week' in February 1944 which destroyed a great deal of

the German aircraft industry and of aircraft in the supply pipeline, benefited the strategic bombing offensive as well. The air battle preceding *Overlord* finally destroyed the German air force, the 'intermediate target', and from June left Allied bombers free to roam over the German heartland.

Although the two Allied air forces still attacked separately by day and night, both now undertook to attack with greater precision, made possible by new navigational aids. In the second half of 1944, first the oil industry then transportation were systematically attacked. Both proved decisive in undermining the continuation of war production at a high level; although German output expanded into late 1944, the last, now irreplaceable, reserves of raw materials were being used up. Strategic attacks in later 1944 and 1945 brought the German economy to the verge of disintegration. The Combined Offensive fatally weakened the Reich and permitted the armies from east and west to drive into Germany and end the war.

In all, the Combined Offensive dropped 906,000 tons of bombs on German and French targets. Most of this was on industrial targets; 224,000 on oil, 319,000 on transportation, 57,000 on the aircraft industry. In addition, the RAF dropped a further 674,000 tons on targets in Europe, mainly on German and Italian cities both before and during the Combined Offensive. By March 1945 the 8th Air Force had 7100 aircraft on hand, Bomber Command 6900. In total the two forces lost 21,900 aircraft, and 158,000 flying personnel. But the toll on Germany was a great one: the damage or destruction of huge areas of urban Germany, and an estimated 650,000 German

dead, the great bulk women, children and old men. Indeed, the scale of destruction involved in the firestorm raids on Dresden (February 1945) invoked heated post-war debate concerning the ethics of area bombing tactics.

Bombing did not bring the war to an end on its own as some of the bombing strategists had hoped. Yet the impact on Germany was very considerable. The bombing offensive required the diversion of enormous resources. By 1944, over two million Germans worked in anti-aircraft defence forces, more than the entire workforce in the aircraft industry. A third of all artillery production and a fifth of all shells went to anti-aircraft defence, as did half of all electro-technical production and a third of the output of the optical industry. The aluminium used in the anti-aircraft defences would have built an estimated 10–15,000 more fighters. In addition, Allied precision bombing forced the dispersal of much arms production to less efficient and decentralized sites, and left the working population in constant fear of death and disruption. Morale did not collapse, but people reacted with apathy and passivity. Under these circumstances it was impossible for Germany to produce what was needed for the war effort. The German air force planned to produce 80,000 aircraft a year by 1945, but in 1944 could only produce 36,000, many of which were destroyed in transit or at the airfields, or could not be flown for lack of aviation fuel. Without the bombing Germany would have been much more heavily armed with battle-front weapons and the *Luftwaffe* would have proved a much more effective opponent.

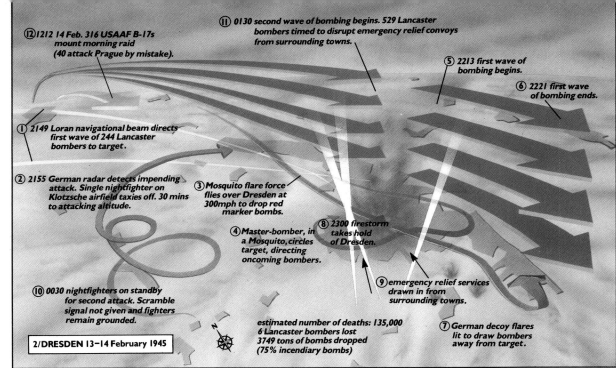

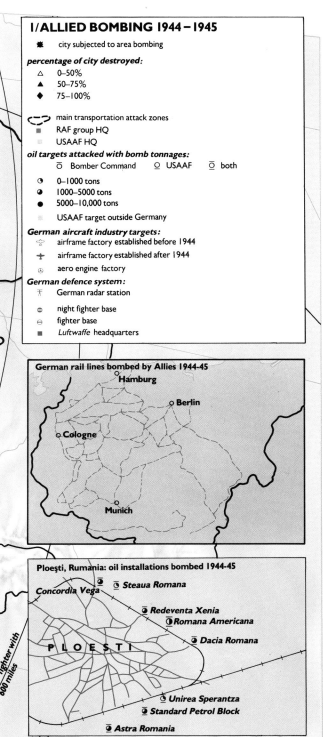

1/ALLIED BOMBING 1944-1945

✳ city subjected to area bombing

percentage of city destroyed:
△ 0-50%
▲ 50-75%
◆ 75-100%

⌒ main transportation attack zones
■ RAF group HQ
□ USAAF HQ

oil targets attacked with bomb tonnages:
Ō Bomber Command   Ō USAAF   Ō both
• 0-1000 tons
• 1000-5000 tons
● 5000-10,000 tons
□ USAAF target outside Germany

German aircraft industry targets:
✧ airframe factory established before 1944
✦ airframe factory established after 1944
⊕ aero engine factory

German defence system:
⊼ German radar station
⊖ night fighter base
⊖ fighter base
■ *Luftwaffe* headquarters

German rail lines bombed by Allies 1944-45
Hamburg
Berlin
Cologne
Munich

Ploeşti, Rumania: oil installations bombed 1944-45
Concordia Vega
Steaua Romana
Redeventa Xenia
Romana Americana
Dacia Romana
P L O E S T I
Unirea Sperantza
Standard Petrol Block
Astra Romania
fighter with 600 miles

In the last two years of the war the Combined Bombing Offensive was directed at Germany's industrial economy (*1*). The RAF bombed major cities and industrial centres, the US 8th Air Force attacked precision industrial targets – mainly fuel oil plants, transportation and the aviation industry (*4*). Technical improvements permitted bombing over most of Germany, escorted by long-range fighter aircraft. By late 1944, despite great increases in air defences, the German economy was brought to the point of collapse. Dresden was a victim of the logic of city-bombing strategy. It was attacked (*2*) between 13-15 Feb. 1945 by 3 waves of bombers which destroyed 70% of the city (*3*). In the Summer of 1944 Hitler ordered attacks on London (*6*) with what he hoped would be war-winning secret weapons, the V-1 flying bomb and later the V-2 rocket. Some 2420 V-1s and 517 V-2s reached London but this represented only a tiny tonnage of explosives. The effectiveness of the campaign was undermined by Allied bombing of the launch sites, and by fighter attack on the missiles. A large defensive zone – the Diver gun belt – was set up to intercept the missiles. However, the attacks did not cease until the launch sites were captured.

Picture right: The aftermath of Allied raids on Dresden.

3/DRESDEN 13-15 Feb.1945
to Berlin
to Breslau and Cracow
River Elbe
■ completely destroyed
▨ badly damaged
▨ partially damaged
□ undamaged
▲ factory
Military Transport Centre
Park
Air Command HQ
to Nuremberg and Munich
to Vienna and Prague

4/1944-1945 RAF/USAAF BOMBING STRATEGY

targets	bomb tonnage	total %	bomb tonnage	total %	USAAF/RAF total
German aircraft industry	51,017	5.2	6024	0.5	57,041
air bases, Germany	46,979	4.8	4353	0.3	51,332
submarine yards	17,108	1.8	16,721	1.3	33,829
ball bearings	6,513	0.7	13,522	1.0	20,035
oil installations	130,979	13.5	93,902	7.1	224,881
chemicals	14,615	1.5	18,212	1.4	32,827
rubber factories	1,032	0.1	771	0.1	1,803
tank factories	16,922	1.7	68	0.01	16,990
land transport (incl. Fr)	307,115	31.6	107,420	8.1	414,535
sub total	592,280	60.9	260,993	19.71	853,273
area bombing	378,780	39.1	1,053,758	80.29	1,432,538
total	971,060	100.0	1,314,751	100.0	2,285,811

5/THE ALLIED BOMBING EFFORT 1940-45

tons of bombs dropped
| 1,461,864 | 1,235,609 |

bomber sorties
| 754,818 | 687,462 |

fighter sorties
| 991,750 | 1,695,049 |

bomber planes lost
9949 ‖ 11,965   □ USAAF

fighter planes lost
8420 ‖ 10,045   ▨ RAF

personnel lost in action
79,265 ‖ 79,281

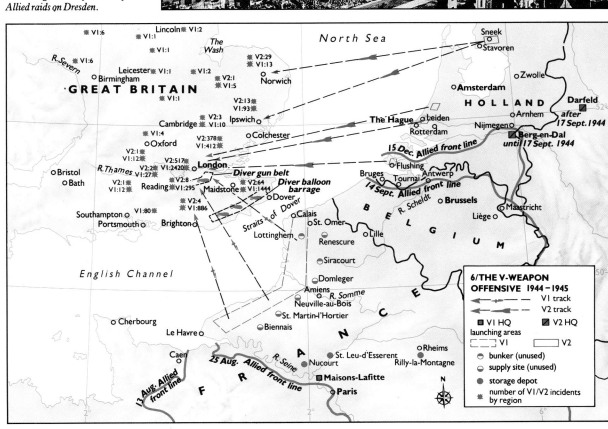

Lincoln ✳ V1:2
R. Severn ✳ V1:6
✳ V1:6   Leicester ✳ V1:1   ✳ V1:2
Birmingham
The Wash
✳ V2:29
✳ V1:13
✳ V2:1
✳ V1:93
Norwich
✳ V1:5
✳ V1:1
GREAT BRITAIN
North Sea
Sneek
Stavoren
Zwolle
Amsterdam
HOLLAND
Darfeld after 17 Sept.1944
✳ V2:13
✳ V1:93
Cambridge ✳ V2:3   Ipswich
✳ V1:10
Arnhem
Nijmegen
Berg-en-Dal until 17 Sept. 1944
✳ V1:4
Oxford
✳ V2:378
✳ V2:412
Colchester
The Hague
Leiden
15 Dec. Allied front line
✳ V2:1
✳ V1:12
✳ V2:517
London
✳ V2:2   ✳ V1:2420
Rotterdam
Flushing
Bristol
✳ V2:8
✳ V1:27
Diver gun belt
Bruges
Tournai
Antwerp
14 Sept. Allied front line
R.Thames
Bath
Reading ✳ V1:295
Maidstone ✳ V1:444
Diver balloon barrage
Dover
Brussels
Liège
Maastricht
✳ V2:1
✳ V1:12
✳ V1:80
✳ V2:4
✳ V1:886
Southampton
Portsmouth
Brighton
Straits of Dover
Calais
St. Omer
Lille
B E L G I U M
R. Scheldt
English Channel
Lottinghem
Renescure
Siracourt
Domleger
Cherbourg
Amiens
R. Somme
Neuville-au-Bois
St. Martin-l'Hortier
Biennais
Le Havre
Rheims
Rilly-la-Montagne
Caen
St. Leu-d'Esserent
Nucourt
25 Aug. Allied front line
Maisons-Lafitte
R. Seine
F R A N C E
Paris
13 Aug. Allied front line

6/THE V-WEAPON OFFENSIVE 1944-1945
◄— V1 track
◄-- V2 track
■ V1 HQ ▨ V2 HQ
launching areas
□ V1 □ V2
⊖ bunker (unused)
⊖ supply site (unused)
● storage depot
✳ number of V1/V2 incidents by region

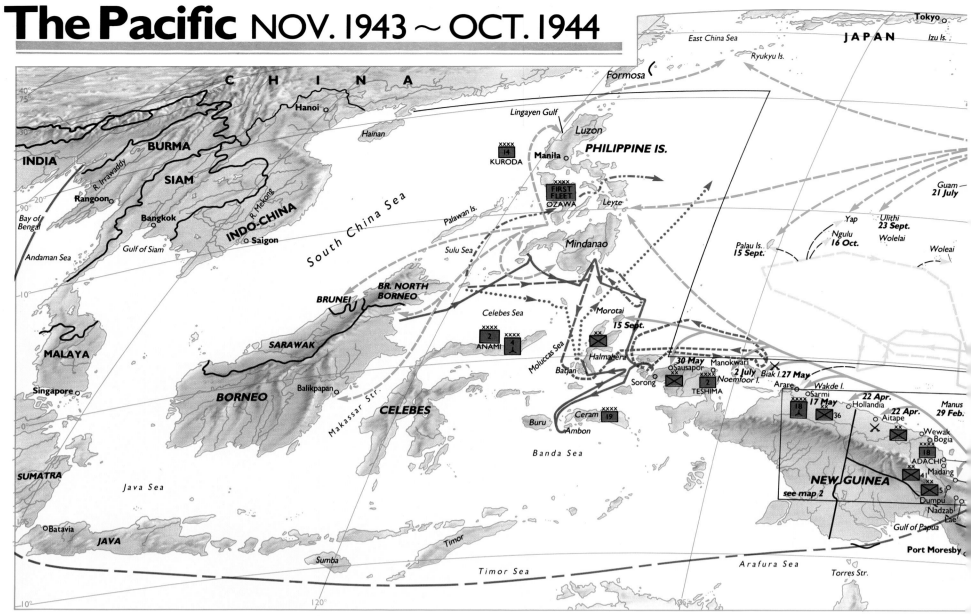

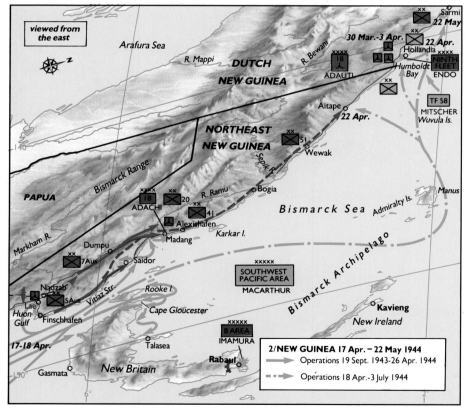

Picture left: US carrier-borne raid on Japanese shipping off Hollandia.

BY THE END OF NOV. 1943 the Allied net around Rabaul had begun to close as a result of landings in Huon Gulf in New Guinea and in the northern Solomons (page 138). Thereafter Rabaul's isolation was to be achieved in two stages (2). The close investment of Rabaul was achieved by Allied landings on western New Britain, at Saidor, and in the Admiralty Is. between 15 Dec. 1943 and 20 Mar. 1944. The distant blockade of Rabaul was completed as a result of landings at Hollandia and Aitape on 22 Apr., which bypassed the Japanese 18th Army in the Markham Valley and around Wewak. Though committed to the support of the Apr. landings, TF58 was largely superfluous to requirements: in six heavy raids between 30 Mar. and 16 Apr. the land-based US 5th Air Force effectively destroyed the 6th Air Division at Hollandia before the landings. The loss of Hollandia forced the Japanese to substitute Biak and Manokwari as their twin centres of resistance in New Guinea but losses at sea led the Japanese to abandon these in favour of Sorong and Halmahera. On 17 May, however, US forces landed on Wakde and in the Arare area, and 10 days later on Biak (1). The latter induced the Japanese to force 'the decisive battle' upon the Americans off the island, but it was not until 10 June that battle forces were committed to action, and by the time that these reached Batjan (11 June) US carrier forces had raided Guam, Tinian and Saipan. No decisive action was fought in the South-west Pacific, but even without one the Allied front had advanced some 500 miles in 2 months.

DESPITE DEFEAT on Guadalcanal and in eastern New Guinea (page 120), until October 1943 the Japanese High Command could console itself with the belief that its policy of waging a defensive war along an extended perimeter, with the aim of wearing down American resolve, was working: after nearly two years Japan's position in the Central and South-west Pacific was barely compromised. The recent reverses in the central Solomons (page 122) were unpromising in their implications, but a recasting of strategic policy in September 1943 would solve the problem. Saipan-Truk-Timor were designated the main line of resistance in the Pacific, with garrisons to the east assigned a delaying role. The Japanese High Command did not now regard future operations with foreboding and despair. By November 1943, these Japanese assumptions concerning their strength and durability were shown to be an illusion.

Between September and November 1943 the Americans executed two parallel operations (Cartwheel) that had the effect of ripping open the Japanese defensive positions in the Central and South-west Pacific, and which simultaneously revealed that Japanese calculations regarding the effectiveness of their fleet based on Truk were flawed. Rather than being able to check American advances in either the Central or the South-west Pacific from Truk, the Imperial Fleet was shown to be unable to concentrate against either offensive. Carrier raids on the Japanese base at Rabaul in November 1943 effectively neutralized it; the base thereafter was bypassed (page 122), whilst in that same month a series of landings in the Gilbert Is. gave the Americans control of the island group and placed them in a position from which operations against the Marshall Is. could be successfully launched.

The prosecution of a two-front war in the Pacific by the Americans was largely the result of a major expansion of the US Pacific Fleet during 1943; for example, they could now afford to deploy eleven fleet and light fleet carriers in support of the Gilbert landings. This greatly increased strength prompted the US Navy to insist upon an advance to Saipan in the Marianas, from which a bombing campaign against the Japanese Home Islands could be mounted. There was no agreement within the American High Command on the crucial questions of which of these offensives – Central or South-west Pacific – was the major effort; further, no decision had yet been reached concerning which targets in the western Pacific would be selected for the next major Allied offensive effort. The heavy losses sustained

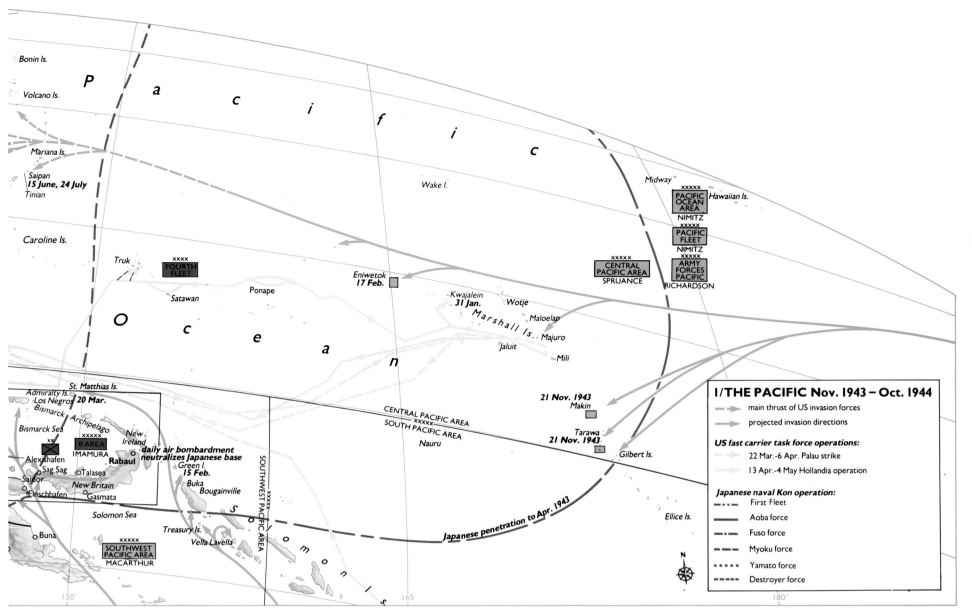

I/THE PACIFIC Nov. 1943 – Oct. 1944

- – – main thrust of US invasion forces
- → projected invasion directions

US fast carrier task force operations:
- 22 Mar.-6 Apr. Palau strike
- 13 Apr.-4 May Hollandia operation

Japanese naval Kon operation:
- – · – First Fleet
- ——— Aoba force
- – · – Fuso force
- – – – Myoku force
- · · · · · Yamato force
- - - - - Destroyer force

during the US invasion of Tarawa in the Gilberts temporarily strengthened the claims of MacArthur's South-west Pacific command for primacy. However, a combination of policy decision and the momentum of events in the Central Pacific were instrumental in redressing the balance: the Marshalls and Eniwetok were cleared between 31 January and 23 April 1944, during which period an American carrier force rampaged through the Central Pacific, penetrating as far west as the Palaus, which forced the Japanese Combined Fleet to withdraw its main forces to Singapore.

With the Japanese base at Truk neutralized, the whole of the Central and South-west Pacific was bared to American arms, despite the Japanese attempt to recast defensive plans around the Saipan-Truk-western New Guinea line. Long before such an intention could be translated into reality, however, the Japanese had been forced to withdraw their southern flank in the face of American coast-hopping advances along the northern shore of New Guinea. The Japanese now hoped that any future American move would be made against a target in defence of which the Japanese could concentrate their land- and carrier-based air power in such strength as to meet and defeat the enemy. The American landings on Biak on 27 May seemingly provided the Japanese with the opportunity to force battle upon the Americans, but even as the Imperial Navy tried to assemble forces for a counter-attack the main American effort was developed in the Marianas (page 142); US carrier forces first neutralized Japanese land-based air power in the island group and then effectively destroyed its carrier-borne air power in the battle of the Philippine Sea.

Thereafter, the US Navy considered their target options in the western Pacific. The Japanese defensive perimeter had been decisively ruptured, and their means of sustaining such an oceanic perimeter – the Combined Fleet – was falling back in disarray. A direct move might be made against Iwo Jima, which would place US bombers with fighter escorts in easy range of the Japanese Home Islands. A successful assault on Okinawa would drive a wedge between the Home Islands and the Southern Resources Area. However, MacArthur's claim that the Philippines be made the American priority received unexpected support in September 1944 when a US carrier raid encountered little resistance over the islands. As a result of this timetable that had scheduled amphibious landings on Leyte in the southern Philippines (page 164) was urgently accelerated.

BETWEEN 20 AND 29 NOV. 1943 American forces successfully occupied 6 atolls in the Gilberts (1), including Makin (3), thereby breaching the Japanese outer defensive perimeter in the Central Pacific. This undoubted success was overshadowed by the 3301 casualties that were sustained on Tarawa (4), a loss unacceptable to the American public. However, these losses were remarkably light relative to overall numbers employed in this operation. The results that flowed from the successful occupation of the islands were enormously significant. From the Gilberts the Americans secured the undefended atoll of Majuro in the Marshalls (31 Jan. 1944), which thus became the first national territory lost by Japan in the course of the war. On the same day, American forces landed on the atoll of Kwajalein, the forward Japanese base for operations in the Central Pacific. Backed by overwhelming fire support, Marines from V Amphibious Corps secured Kwajalein I. by 4 Feb. (5), and backed by aircraft of the 7th Air Force from Tarawa, the Americans secured Eniwetok between 17 and 23 Feb. (1). Thereafter the Americans completed the clearing of the Marshalls but for the Japanese garrisons on Wotje, Maloelap, Jaluit and Mili. Throughout these operations the Imperial Navy was helpless to intervene, and instead collected its forces for the Kon operation, for a decisive action in the Philippine Sea (page 142). The loss of the Gilberts, Majuro and Kwajalein rendered both Truk and Rabaul indefensible, and two massive carrier raids on Truk, on 17/18 Feb. and 29/30 Apr., completed the destruction of Japanese power in the Carolines.

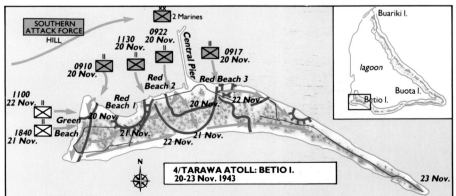

3/MAKIN ATOLL: BUTARITARI I. 20-22 Nov. 1943

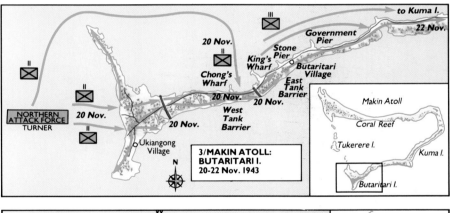

4/TARAWA ATOLL: BETIO I. 20-23 Nov. 1943

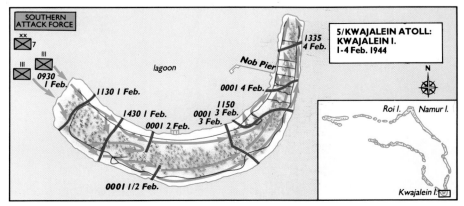

5/KWAJALEIN ATOLL: KWAJALEIN I. 1-4 Feb. 1944

The Marianas JUNE ~ AUG. 1944

AFTER NOVEMBER 1943 the Japanese were presented with the problem of trying to counter a twin American offensive across the Pacific: without the means to meet even one of these thrusts, the Japanese fleet was unable to prevent either the isolation of Rabaul (page 122) or the collapse of the outer defensive perimeter in the central Pacific (page 140). Nevertheless the Japanese could not decline battle as the Americans reached into the western Pacific to positions from which they could menace the Southern Resources Area. By Spring 1944 Japan was intent upon a policy of resistance in the Marianas, the Carolines and in western New Guinea.

In a halting, irresolute manner the Japanese attempted to offer battle when the Americans landed on Biak in May, but the test of Japanese resolve occurred on 11 June when American carrier forces struck Guam, Saipan and Tinian as the prelude to landings in the Marianas. With Saipan as their first and main objective, the Americans sought to secure the Marianas as the base for further operations into the western Pacific and for bombing operations against the Home Islands. The result of this clash of aims was the first carrier battle in the Pacific for twenty months – and the greatest carrier battle of the war. The battle of the Philippine Sea was an overwhelming victory for the United States, though the full extent of their victory was not readily apparent at the time.

By the time American forces came ashore on Saipan, on 15 June, the basis of an American victory had been established by the neutralization of Japanese shore-based air power in the Marianas. The Japanese had planned to combine this with their carrier-borne air power in order that they each might compensate for the weakness of the other, thus allowing the Imperial Navy to give battle on the basis of numerical equality. With nine carriers and 450 aircraft under command, Ozawa's 1st Mobile Fleet was massively inferior in numbers and quality to America's TF58 (Mitscher), which had at its disposal 15 carriers and 902 aircraft. TF58 also had intelligence decrypts of Japanese intentions and plans, but divergent tasks to perform. In addition to the countering of shore-based air power, it had to provide cover for the US amphibious forces committed to the Marianas whilst dealing with the Japanese fleet. Despite numerical and qualitative inferiority, the Japanese possessed two advantages over the Americans: the superior range of their aircraft and an advantageous position. The prevailing trade winds from the east allowed the Japanese to engage at long range an enemy that could not close because of the need to steam away from the wind in order to successfully launch and recover aircraft.

Faced with these tasks Spruance chose to await an attack and to concentrate his fighter strength in defence of his groups. Despite all but running out of sea room, on 19 June these tactics worked. By the morning of 20 June only 100 serviceable aircraft remained to the Japanese carriers, and two of these had been sunk by submarine attacks (including Ozawa's flagship). Meanwhile, the US carriers continued to pound Japanese airfields in the Marianas.

Misled by claims of success by his own pilots and headquarters ashore, Ozawa intended to refuel his ships on the 20th and resume the battle on the 21st. He was out of touch with the battle after his flagship was sunk, and it was not until he reboarded a carrier at midday on the 20th that he became aware of the extent of his previous day's losses: Ozawa then ordered a retirement. But by then it was too late for the Japanese to escape. American carrier aircraft, operating at extreme range and in failing light, sank one fleet carrier and damaged four more carriers, one battleship, one cruiser and two oilers (both of which were scuttled). At the end of this attack the Japanese were left with 35 aircraft: the attack cost the Americans 99 of the 216 aircraft committed to the strike, 82 being lost in trying to return to their carriers.

Having failed to regain contact on 22 June, TF58 struck Pagan on the 23rd and the Jimas on the 24th, its final toll of Japanese shore-based air power between the 17th and 24th being about 200 aircraft. The American victory off the Marianas – popularly known as the 'Great Marianas Turkey Shoot' – ensured the ultimate fall of any island in the group the Americans wished to take; it was also a victory from which the Japanese were not able to recover. Because of the speed with which the Americans were able to develop operations against the Philippines, in the wake of the Marianas battle, the Imperial Navy was never again able to challenge the Americans with a balanced fleet.

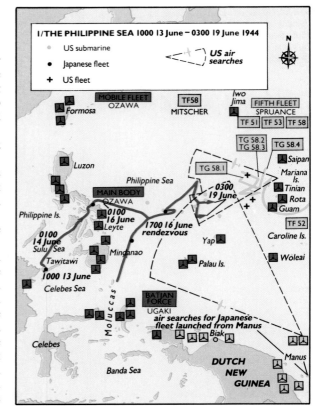

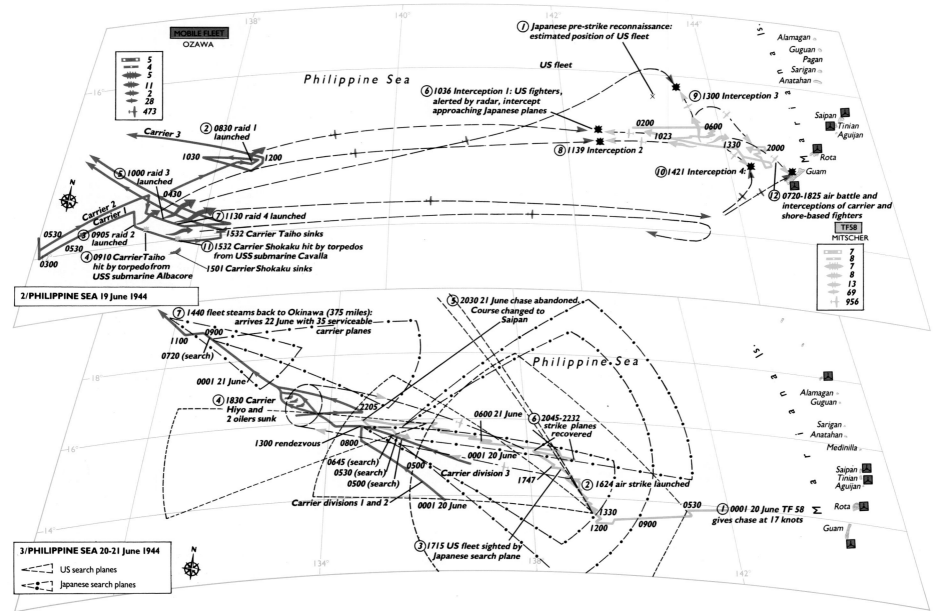

THE US DECISION to land on Saipan saw their fleet entering the Philippine Sea, thus crossing the Japanese perimeter defensive (page 140). Numerous air searches (1), however, failed to detect the Japanese fleet, which held off until the landings were under way; these provide a good example of the efficiency and careful co-ordination of US amphibious assault techniques. Their mastery of ship-to-shore assaults under fire was essential to American success in the central and western Pacific, and also proved invaluable in the North African, Italian and Normandy campaigns. On the morning of 15 June a huge fleet of US transports steamed into their positions off Charan Kanoa beaches (4, 4a). Whilst the landings went according to plan, the island was not secured for 3 weeks; 27,000 Japanese, almost the entire garrison, were killed. The US fleet remained off Saipan providing constant air and naval bombardment until 18 June, when it prepared to meet the advancing Japanese fleet (1). The battle of the Philippine Sea (2) revolved around a series of air strikes which saw c. 280 Japanese planes shot down for the cost of c. 20 US planes. The second half of the action (3), a chase by US forces on the retreating Japanese fleet, was subsequently abandoned to concentrate on providing support for the further landings on Guam and Tinian. The landings on Tinian (5), with its excellent 4700-yd-runway airfield, were far more successful. Undertaken by marines from the Saipan landings, the island was secured in 9 days, a measure of US efficiency in the face of Japanese forces which, although in a helpless position, fought to the last man. Isolated pockets of Japanese resistance remained active on the island for 3 months. Guam was the last of the Marianas to be taken (6). US planning originally envisaged landings there on 18 June, but the need to defeat the Japanese fleet beforehand delayed the landings until 21 July. Unlike on Saipan and Tinian, the Japanese filled any possible landing beaches with obstacles. Landings took place either side of the Orote Peninsula (secured on 29 July). By 30 June US planes were using the Orote airstrip. Despite a last stand by Japanese forces on Mt. Santa Rosa, organized resistance ceased by 10 Aug. Many Japanese officers and men continued sporadic guerrilla warfare on the island although the majority capitulated upon Japan's eventual surrender in Sept. 1945.

Picture above left: the battleship USS Pennsylvania bombarding Guam (20 July 1944) in preparation for the US amphibious assault the following day.

Below: US amphibious landing force assaulting the beachhead, Blue Beach, Guam, 21 July 1944.

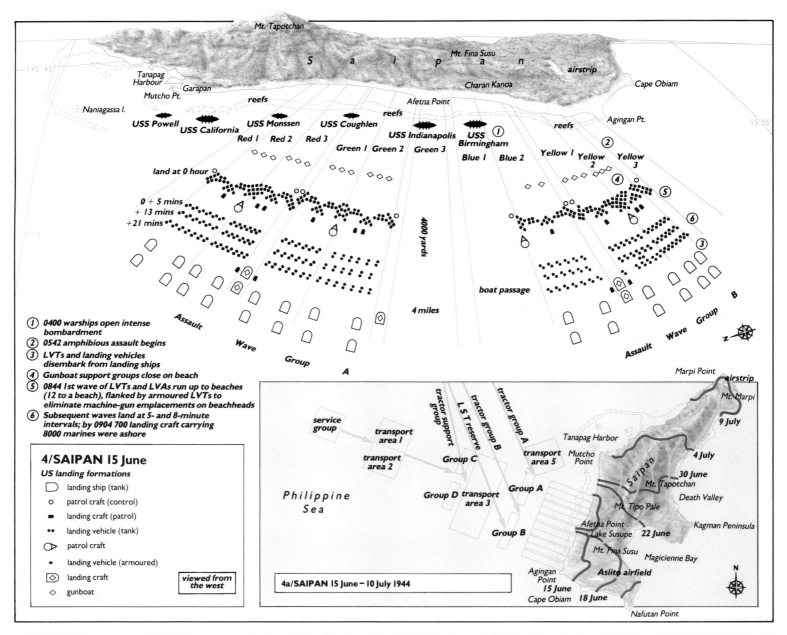

① 0400 warships open intense bombardment
② 0542 amphibious assault begins
③ LVTs and landing vehicles disembark from landing ships
④ Gunboat support groups close on beach
⑤ 0844 1st wave of LVTs and LVAs run up to beaches (12 to a beach), flanked by armoured LVTs to eliminate machine-gun emplacements on beachheads
⑥ Subsequent waves land at 5- and 8-minute intervals; by 0904 700 landing craft carrying 8000 marines were ashore

4/SAIPAN 15 June
US landing formations

⬜	landing ship (tank)
○	patrol craft (control)
➤	landing craft (patrol)
••	landing vehicle (tank)
◗	patrol craft
◆	landing vehicle (armoured)
◈	landing craft
◇	gunboat

viewed from the west

4a/SAIPAN 15 June – 10 July 1944

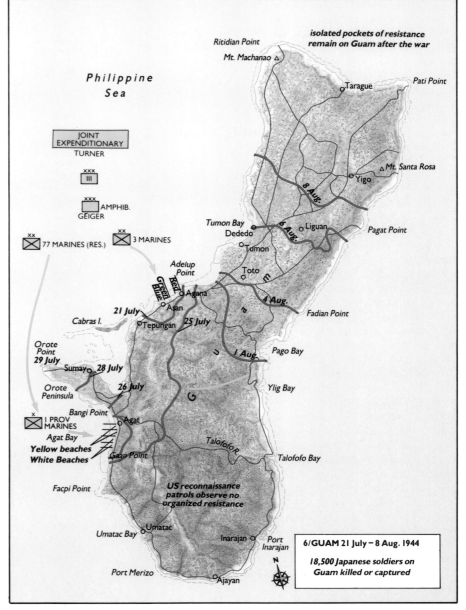

isolated pockets of resistance remain on Guam after the war

JOINT EXPEDITIONARY TURNER

AMPHIB. GEIGER

77 MARINES (RES.) 3 MARINES

I PROV MARINES

Yellow beaches
White Beaches

US reconnaissance patrols observe no organized resistance

6/GUAM 21 July – 8 Aug. 1944

18,500 Japanese soldiers on Guam killed or captured

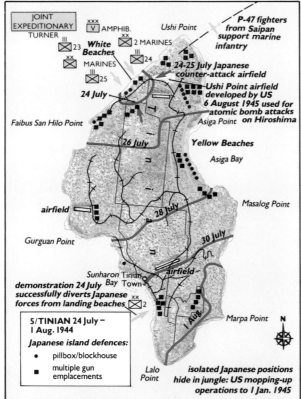

JOINT EXPEDITIONARY TURNER

V AMPHIB.

White Beaches

2 MARINES

MARINES

P-47 fighters from Saipan support marine infantry

24-25 July Japanese counter-attack airfield

Ushi Point airfield developed by US 6 August 1945 used for atomic bomb attacks on Hiroshima

Yellow Beaches

demonstration 24 July successfully diverts Japanese forces from landing beaches

5/TINIAN 24 July – 1 Aug. 1944

Japanese island defences:
• pillbox/blockhouse
■ multiple gun emplacements

isolated Japanese positions hide in jungle: US mopping-up operations to 1 Jan. 1945

China 1941～1945

THE NATURE OF THE CHINA theatre between 1939 and 1945 was dominated by the fact that in 1937 and 1938 the Japanese overran virtually the whole of China that was worth occupying and, apart from a series of coastal operations in the south in 1941, thereafter their basic stance in China was defensive. This left three main parties to struggle for power in China. The Kuomintang (KMT) regime of Chiang Kai-shek, the Communists of Mao Tse-tung and the Japanese. Without the means to bring the Kuomintang regime to the peace table by further military victories, the Japanese were to be led into Indo-China – and thence into the Pacific war – in their attempt to ensure the isolation of Chungking, yet at the same time the Japanese authorities would not invest the puppet regime at Nanking (nor its Peking rival) with power sufficient to allow it to present itself as a credible alternative to the Kuomintang. For its part, the latter increasingly adopted a passive policy towards the Japanese forces of occupation to the extent that American liaison teams coming to China before the outbreak of the Pacific war were shocked to find that 'special undeclared peace' prevailed in much of the country and that a flourishing trade existed across no-man's land: indeed, it was one standing American grievance that throughout the war the Japanese outbid the United States for Kuomintang-supplied tungsten.

Kuomintang acquiescence in Japanese occupation of much of China was primarily the result of Chiang's calculation that Japan's ultimate defeat was assured and that the Japanese would be forced to relinquish their holdings in China by the Allies. Moreover, Kuomintang strength had to be preserved in readiness for a resumption of the struggle with the Communists. Communist policy was no more than a mirror image of that of Chungking. The co-operation between the two factions established as a result of the Sian Incident (page 32) was little more than nominal: the period between 1940 and 1945 was marked by many clashes between the Communists and Kuomintang. These soon badly compromised Communist offensive power and forced the Communists to attempt to reconsolidate their position in Yenan rather than actively pursue operations against either of their enemies.

The limited offensive capacity of all three parties in effect led to the observation of de facto truces between the Japanese and each of the Chinese factions, though these were punctuated by periodic rice raids and by a series of ferocious pacification operations in which the Japanese adopted policies of systematic and widespread slaughter and destruction. But the main threat of these various accommodations was presented by the American determination to develop China as an active theatre of military and air operations as a complement to the US naval and amphibious efforts in the Pacific. A Chinese army of 90 divisions was raised for large-scale offensive operations and air bases developed in south-east China for a bombing campaign of the Japanese Home Islands.

Practical difficulties of supplying China from India on the scale needed to realize these intentions, and Chungking's procrastination in meeting American expectations, ultimately led to the trimming of American aims with the result that the strategic air offensive came to represent the main American undertaking. In the event, however, this policy produced the very situation that the air effort was supposed to forestall: a general Japanese offensive – Operation Ichi-Go – throughout southern China aimed at eliminating the air bases from which the US bombers were to attack Japan.

This Japanese effort, the last major Japanese offensive effort of the war, began in April 1944 with the clearing of that part of Honan that had remained in KMT hands since 1938: the collapse of KMT resistance in the province led to massacres of fleeing nationalist troops by an enraged and deserted peasantry. Thereafter the main Japanese effort across the middle Yangtze began on 27 May and over the next six months various converging Japanese offensives slowly resulted in linking up existing holdings. By late November, the Japanese were able to claim the establishment of uninterrupted overland communications between Singapore and Manchuria: the elimination of US air bases throughout southern China was all but completed at the same time. However, the decision to capture the Marianas (page 142) had freed the Americans of the need for air bases in China, and whatever gains the Japanese had made were illusory. By Spring 1945, the Japanese had begun to withdraw from their recent conquests as a result of belated awareness of over-extension and the need to consolidate their positions in northern China and Manchuria: as they did so they were followed, usually at a respectful distance, by KMT and Communist forces seeking to steal a march on one another in anticipation of the resumption of the 'real' war.

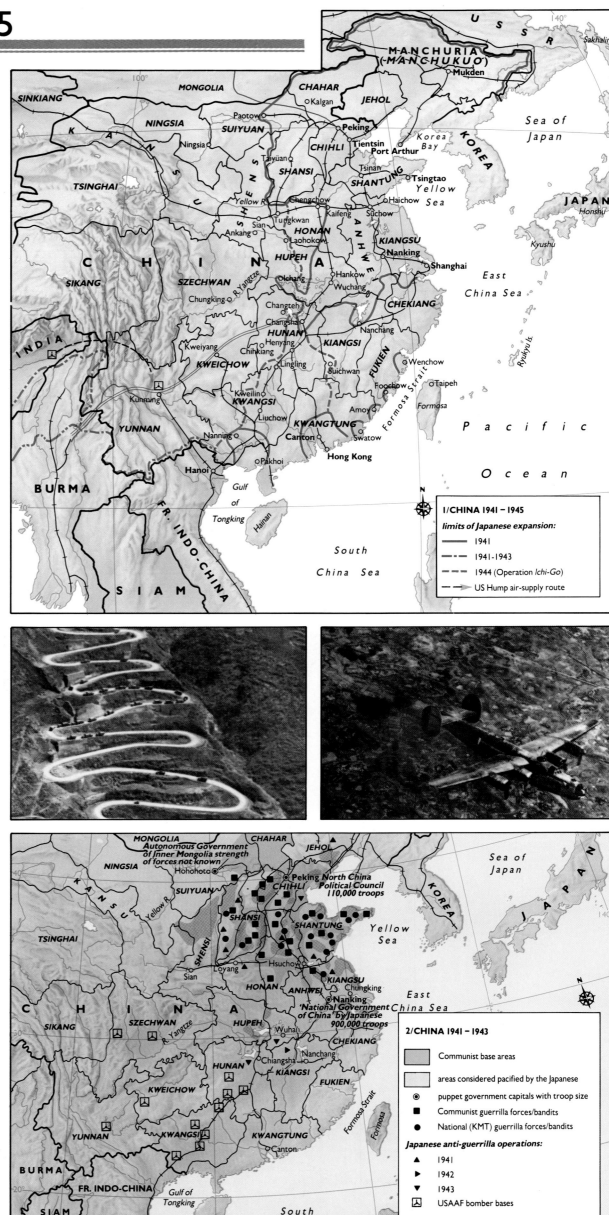

1/CHINA 1941 – 1945
limits of Japanese expansion:
— 1941
—·—·— 1941-1943
— — — 1944 (Operation Ichi-Go)
——→ US Hump air-supply route

2/CHINA 1941 – 1943
Communist base areas
areas considered pacified by the Japanese
⊙ puppet government capitals with troop size
■ Communist guerrilla forces/bandits
● National (KMT) guerrilla forces/bandits
Japanese anti-guerrilla operations:
▲ 1941
▶ 1942
▼ 1943
⌂ USAAF bomber bases

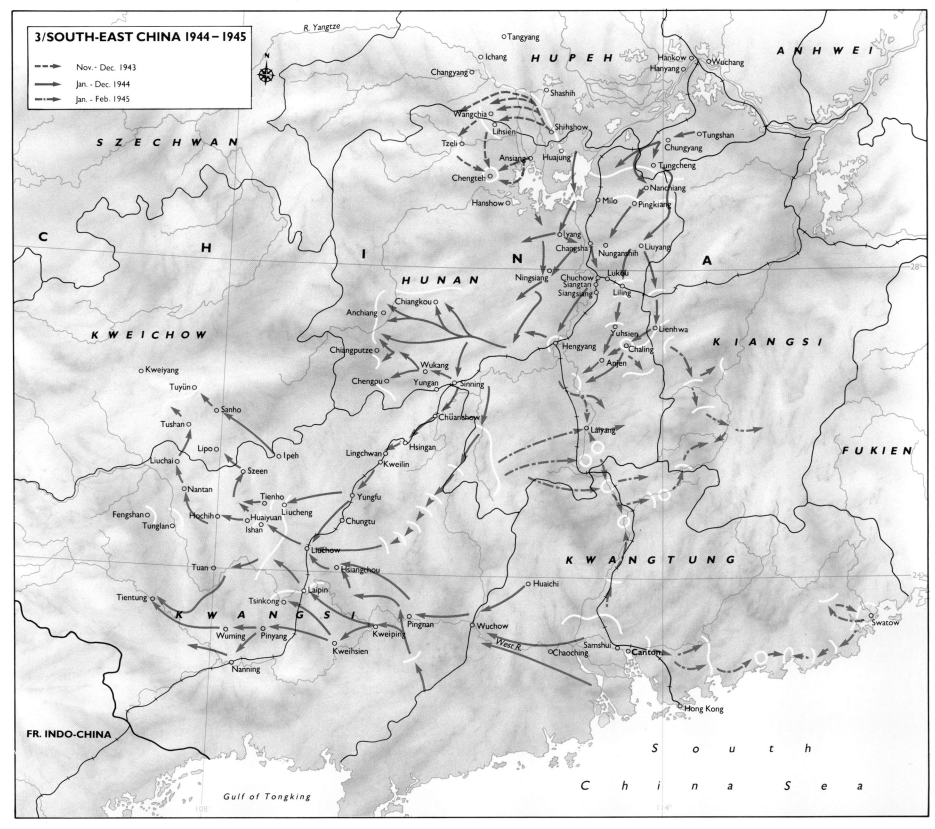

3/SOUTH-EAST CHINA 1944-1945

- – – – Nov. - Dec. 1943
- ——→ Jan. - Dec. 1944
- –·–·→ Jan. - Feb. 1945

FOR MOST OF THE PERIOD BETWEEN 1941 and 1945 China, and especially China north of the Yangtze, represented an untidy patchwork of the limits of power of the various factions contending for control within China. Though nominally all of northern China was under Japanese control (1), in reality Japanese occupation extended primarily over the main centres of population, industrial and mining areas and lines of communication: rural areas were mostly under KMT or Communist control (2) or under no formal control whatsoever. In general terms, however, communist influence prevailed in northern China whereas KMT power extended over 'unoccupied' China, and it was in the latter areas that the Americans had to develop the airfields from which to stage operations against Japan. The main concentration of these airfields lay along the Changsha-Kweilin axis, and it was here that the Japanese made their main effort – the *Ichi-Go* offensive – between May and Dec. 1944 (3). Beginning with the occupation of Leiyang on 26 May, Japanese forces secured Changsha on 10

June and Henyang airfield on the 26th though the town itself withstood assault until 8 Aug. Thereafter failing supplies slowed Japanese operations, but Foochow was secured in Oct. by a combination of overland and amphibious assault and the separate Japanese offensives from Henyang and Canton secured both Kweilin and Liuchow on 11 Nov. Thereafter the Japanese extended their operations to ensure an alternative line of communication to the south: the losses at sea and the American drives into the western Pacific demanded this. At the same time Japanese forces advanced on Kweiyang and secured Tushan and Tuyün in early Dec., but despite a short-lived panic at the prospect of a Japanese advance on Chungking, the Japanese withdrew from Tuyün within a week in recognition of their over-committment on this particular front. The *Ichi-Go* offensive provided the essential background to the final denouement of US policy in China. It brought to a head the rivalry inherent in American plans for both air and military operations. The

predominance of the air plan in 1944 owed much to Chiang Kai-shek's willingness to sanction an offensive requiring minimal KMT involvement. The ranking American officer in China, Stilwell, was opposed to both Chiang because of KMT passivity and to the air plan because of the lack of ground forces needed to ensure the security of the air bases. When the Japanese offensive began to fulfill Stilwell's prediction, Washington demanded of Chiang that Stilwell be given effective control of the whole KMT regime. But without the means to enforce this demand, Washington had to recall Stilwell when Chungking demanded his removal: thereafter the US administration found itself bound to the Chungking regime. The KMT were, however, to eventually lose the struggle for control of those areas formerly in Japanese hands (4), their forces in the south being steadily eroded by the northern-based Communists.

Pictures above far left: a section of the tortuous Kunming Road. Near left: a US B-24 after raiding Japanese supply dumps at Henyang.

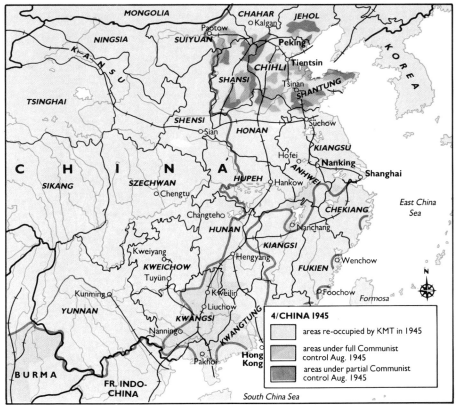

4/CHINA 1945

- ☐ areas re-occupied by KMT in 1945
- ▨ areas under full Communist control Aug. 1945
- ▨ areas under partial Communist control Aug. 1945

The Ukraine and Crimea DEC. 1943 ~ MAY 1944

I/EASTERN EUROPE Dec. 1943 – May 1944

THE END OF 1943 marked the completion of a fundamental shift in the balance of forces on the Eastern Front. The next phase of the war would witness the final expulsion of enemy troops from Soviet soil, and the beginning of Germany's slide towards total military defeat. The Teheran conference in November 1943 had firmly fixed the date of *Overlord* – the opening of the second front in the west – in the late Spring of 1944. This gave Stalin encouragement that a major effort drawing off German forces was not far off, and also kept rival Allied armies away from his southern flank, giving the Russians a free hand.

By 23 December 1943 Soviet forces had reached a line west of Kiev (page 126) and north of the Crimean peninsula. In the Ukraine, the Red Army resumed offensive operations on Christmas Eve 1943. These operations, collectively known as those for the 'Right Bank Ukraine' (west of the Dnieper), lasted from 24 December 1943 to 17 April 1944 and extended over a front of 900 miles. The objectives were the destruction of Germany Army Groups A and South (von Manstein). Simultaneously with the right bank Ukraine operations, Soviet forces also attacked at Leningrad and Novgorod (14 January to 1 March 1944, page 150). In the Ukraine, *Stavka* launched a strategic offensive operation with five Fronts (1st (Vatutin), 2nd (Koniev), 3rd (Malinovski) and 4th (Tolbukhin) Ukrainian and 2nd Byelorussian (Kurochkin)). *Stavka* representatives co-ordinating the actions of the several Fronts were Zhukov (1st and 2nd Ukrainian) and Vasilevski (3rd and 4th Ukrainian). The operations fell into two phases: Winter (to the end of February) and Spring (4 March to 17 April). Right bank Ukraine comprised no less than ten component operations.

In the last days of 1943 1st Ukrainian pushed German armies away from Kiev, clearing Belaya Tserkov and Berdichev by 5 January. On that day 2nd Ukrainian, working in co-operation with 1st, attacked near Kirovograd. The weather helped the ground forces, light snow and frost hardening the ground, but low cloud hindered aircraft. Neither 1st nor 2nd Ukrainian fronts could collapse the German salient jutting out as far as the Dnieper around Korsun-Shevchenkovski, where hilly country aided the defence by 12 German divisions from 1st Panzer and 8th Army from von Manstein's Army Group South. This became the object of a special operation (24 January to 17 February), a classic encirclement battle by both fronts which ended with carnage and debris strewn across the snow. The encircled grouping had comprised about 73,000 officers and men. In addition, fifteen German divisions attacking the outer front of the encirclement suffered severely.

The southern grouping of 1st Ukrainian broke through to Tarnopol and Proskurov, splitting the German 1st and 4th Panzer Armies. 2nd Ukrainian defeated German 8th Army, its

forward detachments reaching the southern Bug and preventing 1st Panzer Army's withdrawal. Mobile Groups also cut off the withdrawal of the Bereznegovatoye-Snigirevka groupings. A huge hole had also been smashed between Army Groups South and A. Between 11 and 13 March, *Stavka* approved Zhukov's plan to carry on over the Dniester and as far as Chernovtsy, on the Prut near the Rumanian border. The effect of this was finally to split German forces in Poland from those in southern Russia, the latter backing nervously onto the Danube.

The Germans had held onto the Crimea for longer than might have been expected. As a result of the Melitopol and Kerch-Eltigen (amphibious) operations of 1943 the Red Army was at last in a position to assault the peninsula with its key naval base at Sevastopol and its ability to command the Black Sea and the Rumanian and Bulgarian littoral. By early 1944 Soviet troops had broken through the 'Turkish Wall' and seized bridgeheads over the wide, salty Sivash lagoon. 4th Ukrainian Front attacked from Sivash-Perekop and the Independent Primorsk Army (Yeremenko) from the Kerch peninsula bridgehead in the east. The Soviet operation was launched on 8 April, reaching the approaches to Sevastopol on 5 May. The speed with which the Russians recaptured the fortress-port was remarkable.

Throughout, German reactions were divided. Hitler constantly expected exhaustion to bring the Red Army to a halt; others expected the *rasputitsa*, or season of mud, to halt them in March. Von Manstein was less optimistic, in February expecting the Red Army to sever the Lwów-Odessa railway behind the northern flank of Army Group South. He did not, however, expect operations of the scale to the second (Spring) phase, with four Fronts attacking from the Pripet Marshes to the Black Sea which aimed to utterly destroy German forces in the south. Gehlen, in charge of German military intelligence, reeled off cold statistics and reported on 30 March that the Soviets could sustain continuous operations; they would undoubtedly move on to the eastern frontier of the Reich.

By 17 April the Russians had been on the unbroken offensive for four months and destroyed the entire southern wing of the German armies, except for 17th Army locked in the Crimea, and by mid-May the Crimea was also recovered. Four million Soviet troops, over 45,000 guns and mortars, over 4000 tanks and assault guns and 4000 aircraft had attacked on a 900 mile wide front in one of the most gigantic operations of the war, penetrating 150 to 300 miles to the Carpathians.

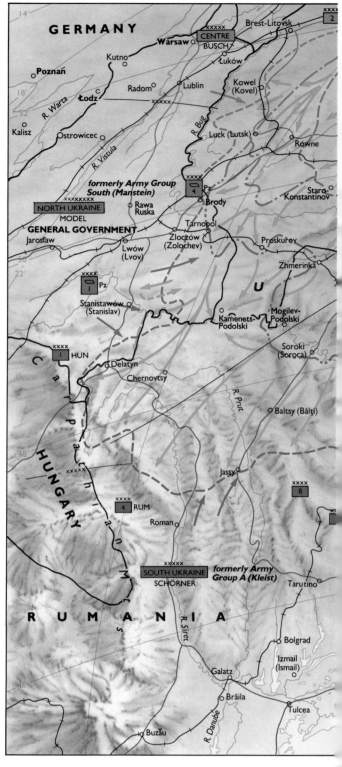

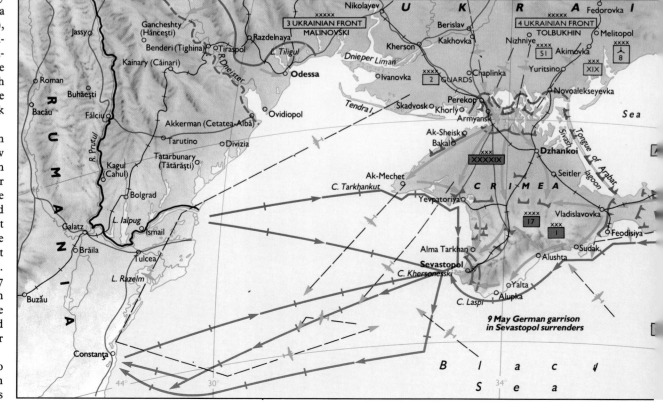

9 May German garrison in Sevastopol surrenders

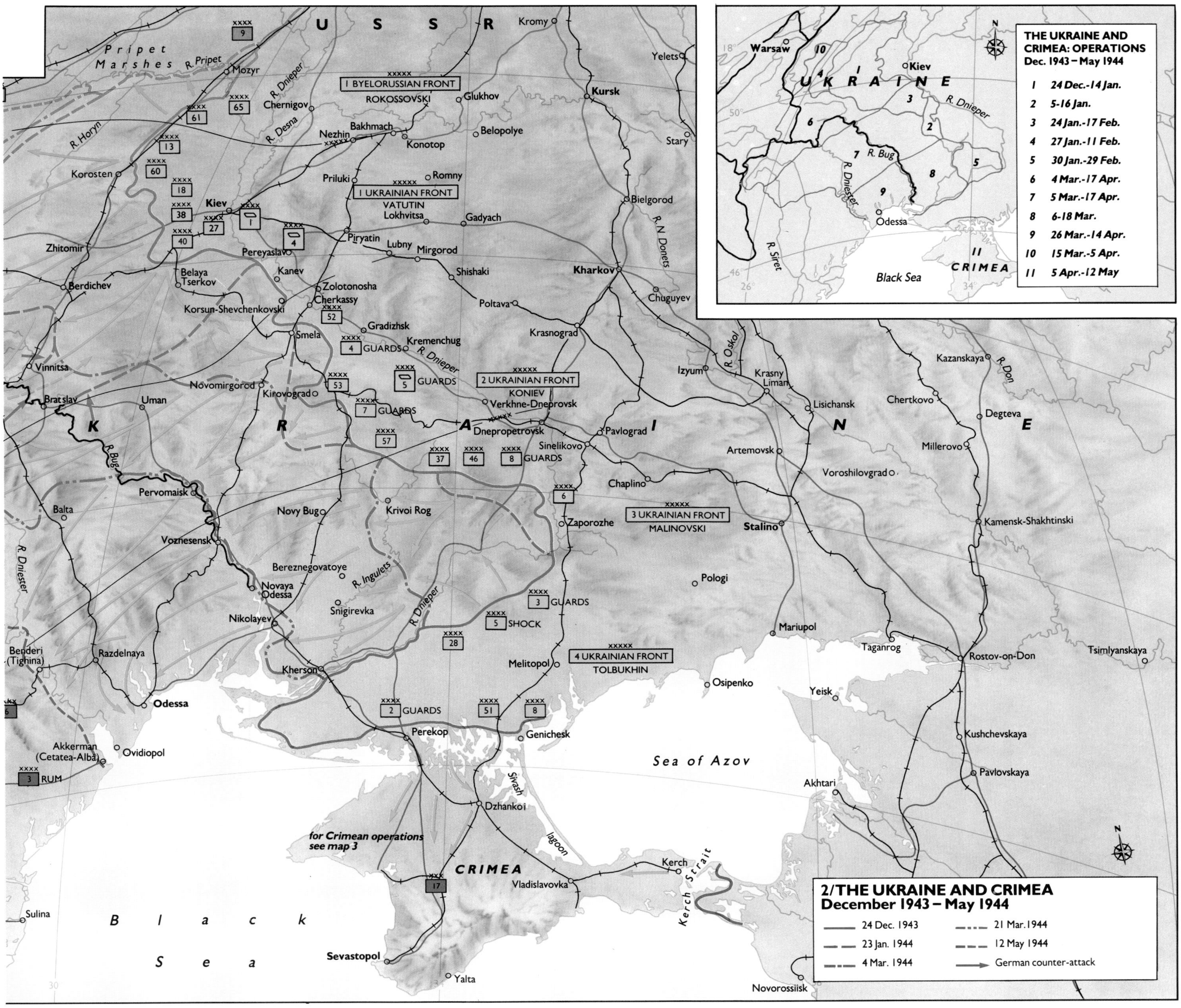
THE UKRAINE AND CRIMEA: OPERATIONS
Dec. 1943 – May 1944
1 24 Dec.-14 Jan.
2 5-16 Jan.
3 24 Jan.-17 Feb.
4 27 Jan.-11 Feb.
5 30 Jan.-29 Feb.
6 4 Mar.-17 Apr.
7 5 Mar.-17 Apr.
8 6-18 Mar.
9 26 Mar.-14 Apr.
10 15 Mar.-5 Apr.
11 5 Apr.-12 May
Warsaw
Kiev
UKRAINE
R. Dnieper
R. Bug
R. Dniester
Odessa
R. Siret
Black Sea
CRIMEA
2/THE UKRAINE AND CRIMEA
December 1943 – May 1944
24 Dec. 1943
23 Jan. 1944
4 Mar. 1944
21 Mar. 1944
12 May 1944
German counter-attack
USSR
UKRAINE
Pripet Marshes
R. Pripet
Mozyr
R. Dnieper
Chernigov
R. Desna
R. Horyn
Korosten
Kiev
Zhitomir
Berdichev
Vinnitsa
Bratslav
Uman
Kromy
Kursk
Yelets
Glukhov
Bakhmach
Nezhin
Konotop
Belopolye
Stary
Romny
Priluki
Gadyach
Lokhvitsa
Piryatin
Lubny
Mirgorod
Shishaki
Bielgorod
R. N. Donets
Kharkov
Chuguyev
Poltava
Pereyaslavl
Kanev
Belaya Tserkov
Zolotonosha
Cherkassy
Korsun-Shevchenkovski
Smela
Gradizhsk
Kremenchug
Krasnograd
Izyum
R. Oskol
Krasny Liman
Lisichansk
Kazanskaya
R. Don
Chertkovo
Degteva
Millerovo
Artemovsk
Voroshilovgrad
Novomirgorod
Kirovograd
Verkhne-Dneprovsk
Dnepropetrovsk
Pavlograd
Sinelikovo
Chaplino
Zaporozhe
Stalino
Kamensk-Shakhtinski
Pervomaisk
R. Bug
Balta
Novy Bug
Krivoi Rog
Voznesensk
R. Dniester
Bereznegovatoye
R. Ingulets
Novaya Odessa
Snigirevka
Nikolayev
Pologi
Mariupol
Taganrog
Rostov-on-Don
Tsimlyanskaya
Bendery (Tighina)
Razdelnaya
Kherson
Melitopol
Osipenko
Yeisk
Odessa
Perekop
Genichesk
Akkerman (Cetatea-Alba)
Ovidiopol
Kushchevskaya
Pavlovskaya
Sea of Azov
Akhtari
Sivash
Dzhankoi
lagoon
for Crimean operations see map 3
CRIMEA
Kerch
Kerch Strait
Vladislavovka
Sulina
Black Sea
Sevastopol
Yalta
Novorossiisk
1 BYELORUSSIAN FRONT
ROKOSSOVSKI
1 UKRAINIAN FRONT
VATUTIN
2 UKRAINIAN FRONT
KONIEV
3 UKRAINIAN FRONT
MALINOVSKI
4 UKRAINIAN FRONT
TOLBUKHIN
3 RUM

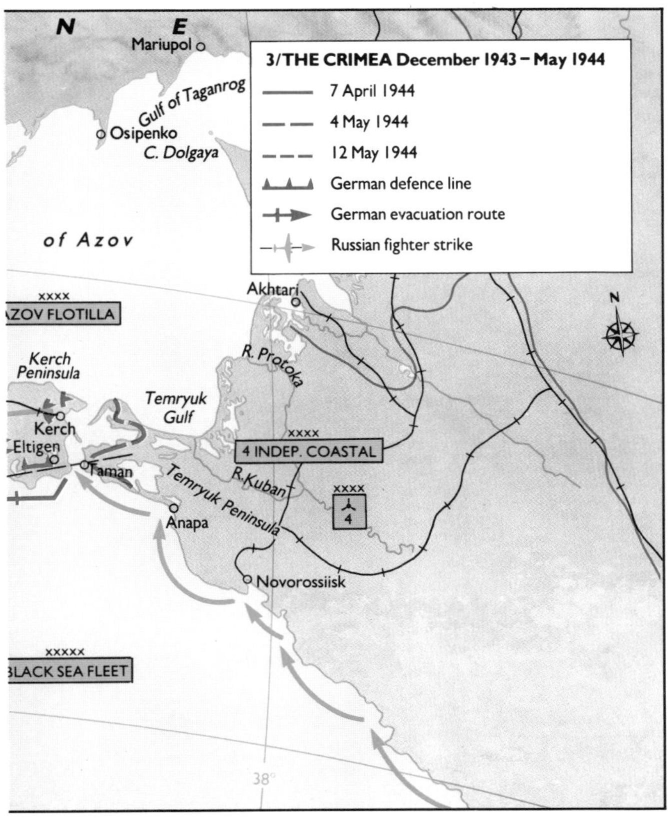
3/THE CRIMEA December 1943 – May 1944
7 April 1944
4 May 1944
12 May 1944
German defence line
German evacuation route
Russian fighter strike
Mariupol
Gulf of Taganrog
Osipenko
C. Dolgaya
of Azov
Akhtari
AZOV FLOTILLA
Kerch Peninsula
Temryuk Gulf
R. Protoka
Kerch
Eltigen
Taman
4 INDEP. COASTAL
R. Kuban
Temryuk Peninsula
Anapa
Novorossiisk
BLACK SEA FLEET

On 23 Dec. 1943 Soviet forces had advanced to a line stretching from Leningrad in the north to Sivash lagoon in the south, the boundary of the Crimean peninsula *(1)*. By May 1944 they had recovered the Crimea and Ukraine; but Axis forces still possessed Byelorussia. Operations to recover the Ukraine west of the Dnieper ('Right bank Ukraine') began on 23 Dec. 1943 *(2)*. This comprised 10 component operations *(2 inset)* which lasted until 17 Apr. In addition, the Crimean Operation *(3)* (8 Apr. to 12 May 1944) constituted an eleventh operation. Soviet forces totalled 470,000 men, 6000 guns and mortars, 560 tanks and assault guns and 1250 aircraft. In addition, the Black Sea Fleet and the Azov Flotilla would support the offensive. German forces comprised 150,000 German and Rumanian troops (11 divisions), and the bulk of the German 17th Army withdrawn from Taman, under General Jänecke. Jänecke's forces could have considerable confidence in their three defensive belts opposite the Sivash bridgehead, two on the Perekop Isthmus and four against the Kerch bridgehead. However, against Soviet superiority they crumpled quickly. The attack from north and east was launched on 8 Apr. By 12 Apr. Soviet forces were pursuing Axis troops withdrawing from the east of the peninsula, initially along the Feodosiya-Sudak-Sevastopol route *(3)*. By 9 May Sevastopol's German garrison had surrendered, the remnants of 17th Army withdrawing along the Kherson head. Massive Soviet air superiority made it possible to massacre troops attempting to withdraw from Sevastopol to Constanța and Varna. The Russians also attacked convoys carrying troops out with aircraft and submarines, major attacks occurring mid-way between the Rumanian coast and the Crimea on 23 Apr., 3 and 12 May, and off Sevastopol on 12 Apr. and 11 May. By noon on 12 May, 25,000 German troops had surrendered at Kherson. Soviet estimates of German losses – the destruction of 17th Army – total 110,000 killed, wounded and prisoners.

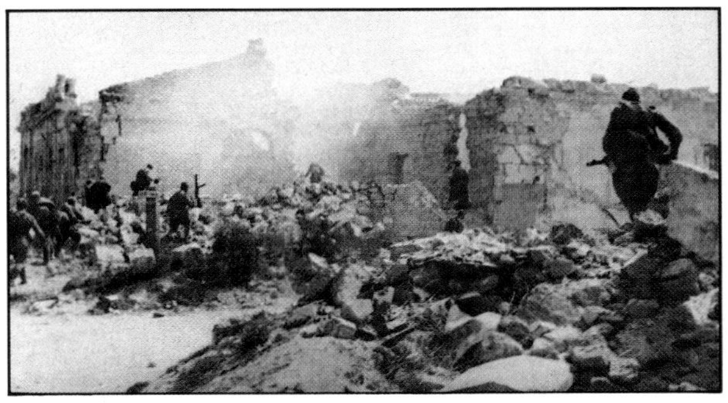

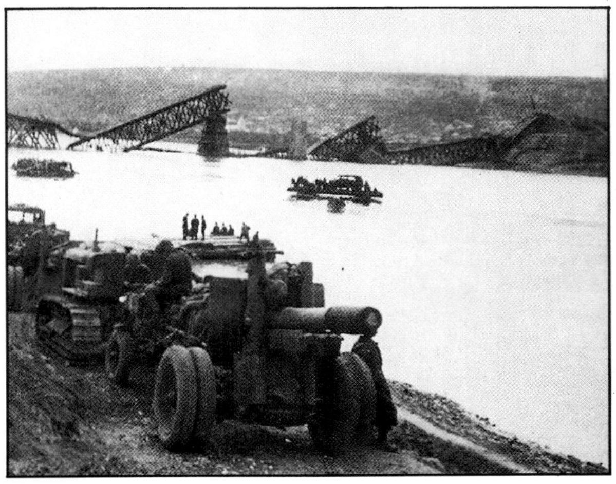

Pictures opposite: *Soviet cavalry near Odessa*. Right top: *Soviet troops in the ruins of Sevastopol*. Bottom: *Soviet ML20 152mm gun-howitzers being ferried across the R. Dniester.*

Byelorussia 1944

SOVIET PLANNING FOR THE Byelorussian operation began in Spring 1944. The Soviet High Command reached the conclusion that White Russia and its capital Minsk was the next priority for liberation, a conclusion anticipated by German Army Group Centre. The latter's large salient still appeared threateningly close to Moscow, and still posed a potential air threat to the northern flank of the three Ukrainian Fronts, preventing any offensive by the latter further west. The Byelorussian salient also represented the shortest route for the Russians to the heart of Germany. The operation was codenamed *Bagration*, after one of the heroes of 1812, and the sense of grand opera was maintained in the timing of the offensive, to begin on 22 June, three years to the day after the German invasion of Russia. In May the scope of the operation was extended, to a depth of 400 miles, in order to take it well clear of the Pripet Marshes and seize the 'land bridge' between the Dvina and Neman rivers. The operation would extend almost as far from north to south. It would also take place after the Allied landing in Normandy, exploiting the Anglo-American challenge to German land power and any confusion arising from German involvement in a two-front land war.

Russian forces comprised 19 all-arms and 2 tank armies, in all 1.4 million men, 31,000 guns and mortars, 5200 tanks and assault guns, supported by over 5000 aircraft. The principal military objective, agreed at a *Stavka* conference on 22-23 May 1944, was destruction of the German Army Group Centre, with a simultaneous breakthrough on six sectors (each forward Soviet division in these sectors thus having a front of one and a half kilometres), and with the three Byelorussian fronts converging on the main forces of Army Group Centre in the Minsk area. German forces had adopted a deeply echeloned defensive position, up to 17 miles deep and comprising in all 1.2 million men, 9500 guns and mortars, 900 tanks and assault guns and 1350 aircraft.

On 10 June, German intercepts picked up an order to partisans behind German lines ordering them to step up the 'rail war' and cripple troop movements from 20 June onwards. Railway lines west of Minsk were attacked on 19-20 June. On the night of 22-23 June, Soviet long-range aircraft attacked, first airfields and railway lines, then artillery positions and reserves and troops on the move. German reports noted new, more skilful infantry tactics and the employment of air forces 'on a scale not previously experienced'.

The first phase, from 23 June to 4 July, comprised the Bobruisk, Vitebsk-Orsha, Mogilev and Polotsk operations and completed the encirclement of the Minsk grouping. By the evening of 26 June 1st Byelorussian Front forces were breaking into Army Group Centre positions in the Bobruisk area and 3rd Byelorussian between Vitebsk and Orsha, two cities which together with Mogilev, Hitler had ordered should be held as 'firm positions' (*Feste Plätze*): to the last round and the last man. By the evening of 3 July, XXVII Panzer Corps, 110th Division and Task Force Muller were on the run and encircled east of Minsk, with the rest of Army Group Centre being pushed back west of Minsk. In the second phase (5 July to 29

August) the Fronts conducted five more offensive operations: Šiauliai, Vilna, Kaunas, Bialystok and Lublin-Brest Litovsk. The grouping encircled east of Minsk was destroyed (5-11 July). By 8 July, Model, who had taken command of Army Group Centre from Busch on 28 June, requested a meeting with Hitler, seeking to extricate the Vilna garrison. Hitler, characteristically, ordered it to be held at all costs. He agreed, at Model's insistence, to some reinforcement of Army Group Centre from Army Group North, but refused to countenance the latter's withdrawal, Admiral Dönitz insisting that the Baltic ports be kept open. Vilna fell on 13 July, Pińsk on the 14th and Grodno on the 16th. On 15 July the Russians gained their first bridgehead over the Neman at Alytus.

Hitler's insistence on holding 'firm positions' and refusal to allow withdrawal had contributed to the entrapment of large German forces. Army Group Centre had been destroyed in a classic *Kesselschlacht* (cauldron battle), with 17 divisions totally annihilated and 50 losing half their strength. On 20 July, the day when the destruction of the Army Group was finally accomplished, German officers, dismayed at Hitler's conduct of the war, made an attempt on his life. It failed. Meanwhile the Russian advance, inevitably, ran out of steam. They had reached a line just west of Bialystok and east of Kaunas. In the next month, to 29 August, they pushed forward, taking Kaunas and just touching the frontier of East Prussia. In the south, they pushed on another 60 miles, to the edge of Warsaw. Whilst the restoration of territory was symbolic and significant in terms of prestige, the Byelorussian Strategic Offensive Operation underscored a classic rule of war: that the enemy's main forces must be the main objective.

1/ THE EASTERN FRONT June – Sept. 1944

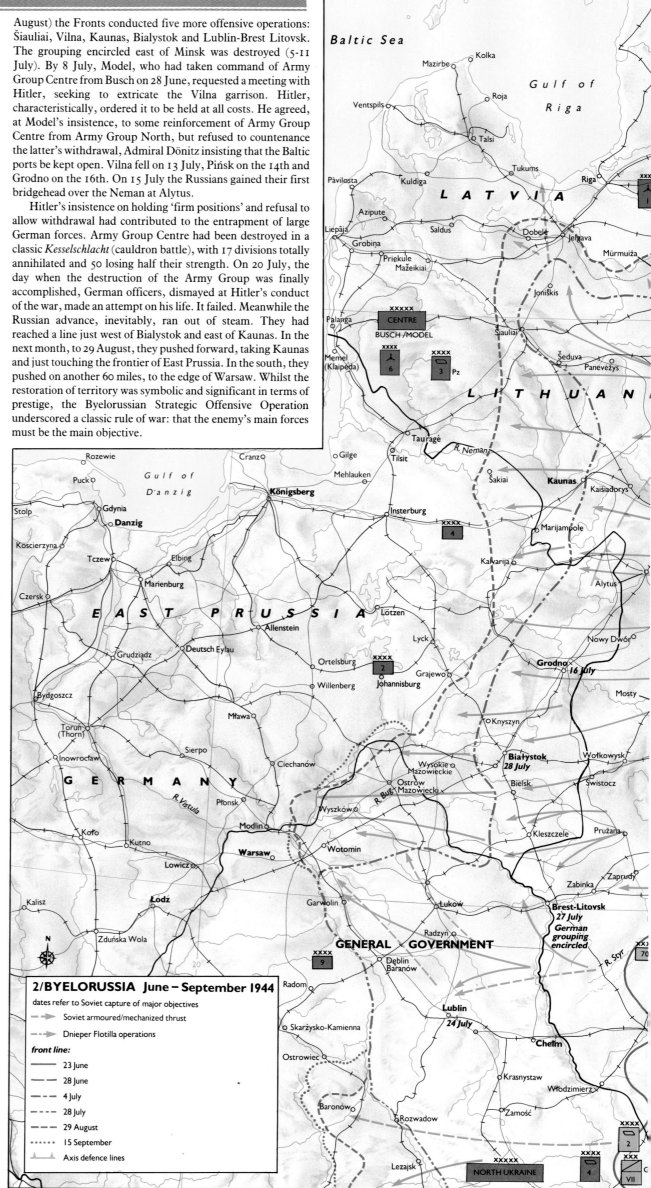

2/BYELORUSSIA June – September 1944

dates refer to Soviet capture of major objectives

- ⟶ Soviet armoured/mechanized thrust
- ⟶ Dnieper Flotilla operations

front line:

- —— 23 June
- —— 28 June
- —·— 4 July
- - - - 28 July
- — — 29 August
- ⋯⋯ 15 September
- ⟱⟱ Axis defence lines

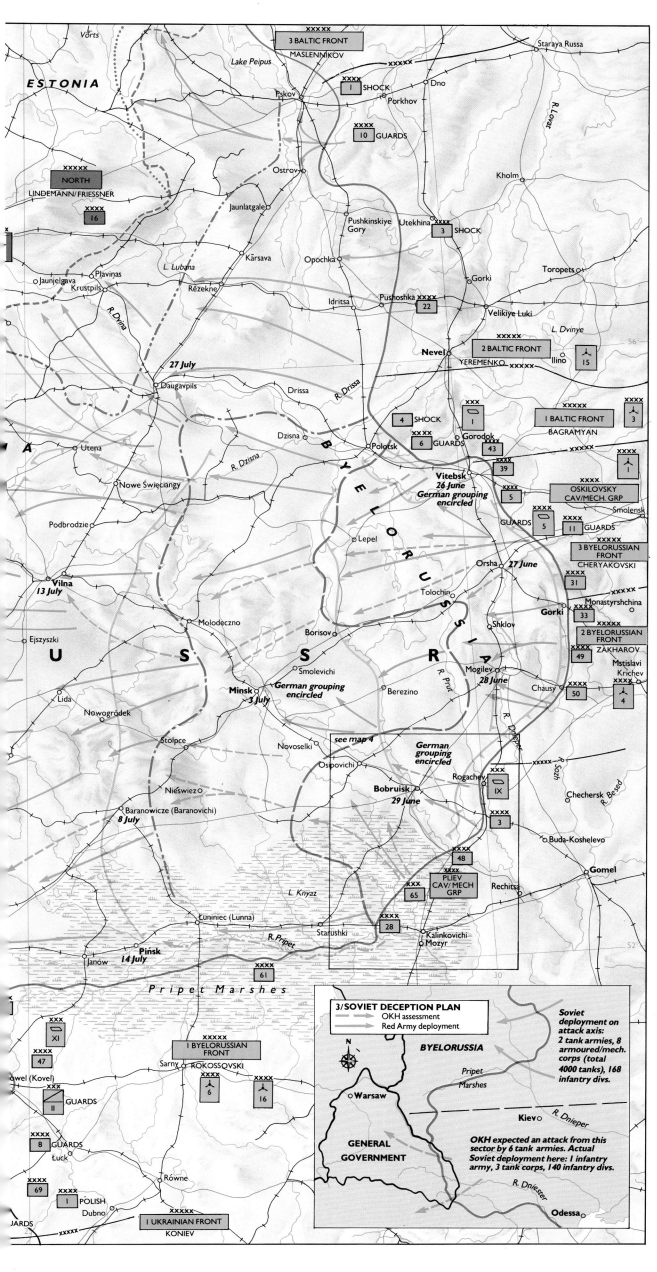

THE BYELORUSSIAN Strategic
Offensive Operation (23 June to 29
Aug.) was one of the largest Soviet
operations of the war (1). The
Russian plan involved a vast
strategic deception (maskirovka)
(3). In the area of 3rd Ukrainian
Front, to the south, the Russians
feigned a major concentration of
forces for the attack, whilst in
Byelorussia the real concentration
was carefully concealed. The
German command was fooled to
some extent. Of 30 Panzer and
mechanized divisions on the Soviet
German front, 24 were
concentrated south of the Pripet
Marshes. Within the context of
German Army Group Centre's
front, north of the Pripet Marshes,
Soviet deception was also
maintained. The order of battle of
Soviet forces was clarified in good
time, and the Germans noted that
air forces in the south remained
markedly stronger than those on
the central and southern sectors.
But the Germans underestimated
the strength of the Soviet forces
facing them. The Germans
assumed all five Soviet Tank
Armies to be on the southern
sector; there were unconfirmed
reports of 5th Guards Tank Army
opposite Army Group Centre: in
fact it was one of 3rd
Byelorussian's 'Mobile Groups'
(along with its 'Cavalry-
Mechanised Group'), opposite 3rd
Panzer. The Bobruisk operation
(24-29 June) (4), on the southern
flank of the attack on Army Group
Centre, formed an important part
of the Byelorussian operation. It
involved 3rd, 48th, 65th and 28th
All-Arms and 16th Air Armies, 9th
and 1st Guards Tank Corps and 1st
Byelorussian Front's Cavalry/
Mechanized Group (KMG). The
Tank Corps formed Army Mobile
Groups and the KMGs, Front

Mobile Groups, to be inserted to
exploit success, ideally after a
'clean break' through the tactical
zone. The area was defended by
German 9th Army and two
divisions of 4th Army. The Soviet
aim was to drive for Bobruisk,
encircling the main Bobruisk
grouping. 'Reconnaissance by
Battle' took place on 23 June and
on the 24th Soviet forces attacked
after a two-hour five-minute
artillery preparation. Soviet forces
penetrated to a depth of three to
five miles and then 1st Guards
Tank Corps was pushed in to
exploit the breakthrough. On the
second day, the KMG which had
been waiting between 65th and
28th Armies was inserted to drive
deeper, by-passing the encircled
force, driving north-west to the
River Ptich and Glusk. Another
important manoeuvre was a
massive regrouping of artillery
forces to strengthen the southern
wing of the Soviet assault, between
5 and 13 July. Once the
breakthrough was accomplished in
the Bobruisk area and the
Germans fell back reaching a line
west of Minsk on 4 July, 3500
artillery pieces were moved
through the wild Pripet Marshes
area from Zhlobin though
Kalinkovichi to new positions east
of Kowel, increasing artillery
strength on 1st Byelorussian's left
flank to 9000 pieces and around
300 pieces per mile of front. As a
result, 1st Byelorussian was able to
push into Poland later in July, just
ahead of the other front clearing
Soviet territory.

*Picture above: Soviet infantry and
armour moving forward near Minsk.*

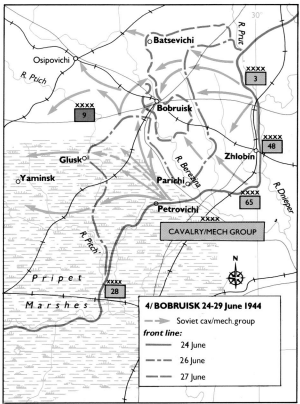

4/ BOBRUISK 24-29 June 1944

→ Soviet cav/mech group

front line:
— 24 June
– – 26 June
– · – 27 June

The Baltic 1944 ~ 1945

IT WAS NOT UNTIL the beginning of 1944, as a result of Soviet victories at Kursk (page 124) and in the Ukraine and Donbass (page 146) that the Russians were able to undertake a general offensive to the north-west to clear German troops right away from the city of Leningrad, under siege since September 1941 (page 64), and restore something approaching wartime normality. The Leningrad-Novgorod operation involved the Leningrad, Volkhov (to 15 February 1944) and 2nd Baltic Fronts, long-range aviation (the nearest Soviet equivalent to British and American strategic bombers, although they were used almost exclusively against battlefield and associated rear-echelon targets) and 35,000 partisans. The offensive began on 14 January 1944. Novgorod was recaptured on the 20th, and by 1 March the Russians had pushed forward to the borders of Latvia. Only now was the 900-day Siege of Leningrad truly over. By the end of Winter Soviet forces had pushed almost as far as Lake Peipus.

Between July and November 1944, Soviet forces advanced through the Baltic States, incorporated into the Soviet Union only in 1940 with the tacit approval of the Germans under the Nazi-Soviet Pact. The 1st Baltic Front (Bagramyan) conducted the Memel (*Klaipeda*) operation from 8-10 October, securing the city on the Lithuanian coast, while 2nd Baltic (Yeremenko) captured Riga, capital of Latvia. This left a pocket of German troops from 16th and 18th Armies of Army Group North, 33 divisions in all, on the Courland peninsula, which was renamed Army Group Courland on 26 January 1945. The *Stavka* of the Russian High Command assessed, correctly, that while the Courland grouping was an annoying anomaly, it was a lesser priority than pressing on into Poland and East Prussia, and the Russians contented themselves with blockading it by land and sea. The Soviet Navy in the Baltic had suffered severely from the purges and many of its sailors had been used for fighting on land. Its ships and submarines had been bottled up by German mining and blockade of the Gulf of Finland for most of the war and the ships had been used principally as heavy firepower to enhance land artillery. Only with the capture of Narva in Estonia in July 1944, and Finnish withdrawal from hostilities on 19 September, which made bases on the northern shore including Hangö available to the Russians, was the Soviet Navy able to break out into the Baltic. The Russians, however, did not have the ships, the men or the skills to take on first-rate German warships like the *Admiral Hipper*, and the Germans

were able to evacuate large numbers of men and much material from Courland. Only 21 divisions and one brigade – 189,000 officers and men plus 42 generals – remained on Soviet territory to surrender on 9 May 1945, the end of the war in Europe.

Meanwhile, Soviet forces skirted the pocket and from 13 January to 25 April 1945, and concurrently with the Vistula-Oder operation, conducted the East Prussian operation using 2nd (Rokossovski) and 3rd (Chernyakovski, then Vasilevski) Byelorussian and part of 1st Baltic Fronts. On 10 February 2nd Byelorussian broke away west to conduct the East Pomeranian operation (until 4 April).

As the Russians broke into German territory, many felt they had scores to settle. Many sources speak of massacre and rape on a large scale. Soviet troops believed that raping German women and girls would go unpunished, and it appears that these events were widely condoned, if not officially encouraged. Stories of atrocities contributed to the panic-stricken flight of civilians and service personnel to the Baltic ports: Gdynia, Danzig, Königsberg and, at the end of an isolated spit, Pillau. The sea route was arguably the safest and certainly the most efficient way of moving large numbers of troops and sailors, refugees, wounded and stores. Admiral Dönitz, who was to succeed Hitler briefly as *Führer*, masterminded the evacuation of a reported 2,022,602 persons from pockets along the Baltic: Courland, East and West Prussia and Pomerania between 23 January and 8 May 1945. The Soviet Baltic Fleet was ordered to step up its activities against German lines of communication. As a result, three large ships, crammed with refugees, were sunk sailing from Danzig-Gdynia: the greatest loss of life in any recorded ship sinking (probably over 7000 people) occurred on 30 January when the *Wilhelm Gustloff* was torpedoed by Soviet submarine S-13 off Stolpebank. Other ships were the hospital ship *Steuben* (9 February) and the *Goya* (16 March). Catastrophic though these losses were, they only represented one per cent of the number evacuated by sea: 99 per cent got out safely. Gdynia fell on 28 March and Danzig on the 30th. The last major port was Pillau, captured by the Russians on 25 April. After this, the Germans continued a Dunkirk-style operation picking people up from the beaches to take them to the west where they would fall into British or American hands, as the Russians closed in. Admiral Dönitz, in a little known but masterly operation, had supervised the greatest seaborne evacuation in history.

I/ THE BALTIC
Jan. 1944 – Feb. 1945

⩕⩕ German defence position

⩕▲ East Prussia defensive system

Russian advances:

——— 12 January-1 March 1944

– – – July-November 1944

– – – January-February 1945

– – – – February-March 1945

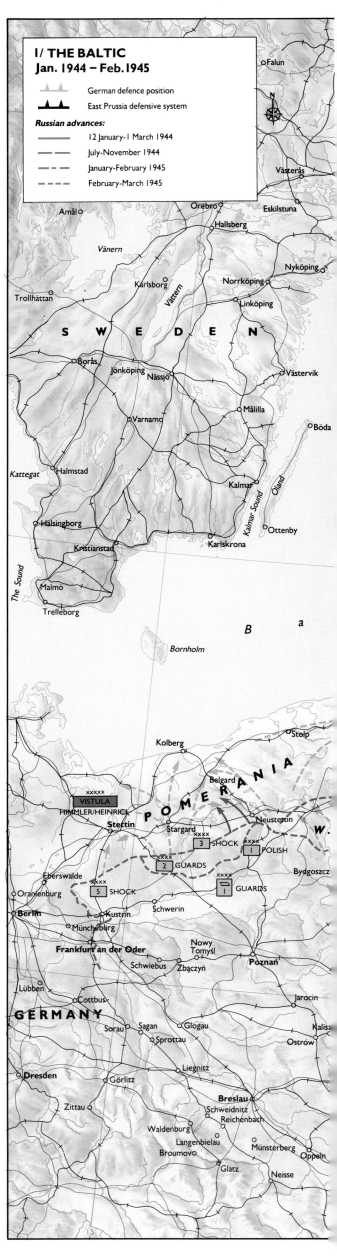

BETWEEN THE BEGINNING OF 1944 and May 1945 Soviet forces advanced along the Baltic coast from Leningrad to Wismar, a distance, as the crow flies, of over 800 miles. The Courland grouping was by-passed in pursuit of more vital strategic objectives, notably the German territory of East Prussia. The Germans had constructed a powerful defensive scheme, with no less than seven defensive perimeters, strengthened with concrete pill-boxes, dragon's teeth, and other permanent fortifications, and six fortified regions. In the East Prussian operation, Soviet forces numbered nearly 1.7 million men, over 25,000 guns and mortars, nearly 3900 tanks and assault guns and over 3000 aircraft. The

Germans had 8200 guns, 700 tanks and 775 aircraft. 3rd Byelorussian Front (Chernyakovski) attacked north of the Masurian Lakes (a significant obstacle) in order to cut Army Group Centre off from the rest of Germany and pin it to the sea, (13 Jan.). 2nd Byelorussian Front (Rokossovski) attacked on the axis Marienburg-Elbing on 14 Jan. By the end of Jan., the Russians had reached the Vistula Lagoon, severing most of East Prussia from the rest of Germany, and on 10 Feb., 2nd Byelorussian was directed west, into East Pomerania, leaving 3rd Byelorussian to liquidate German forces in East Prussia. This involved the reduction of the fortress city of Königsberg (Kaliningrad). This was defended

by three defensive positions: the first four to five miles from the city centre comprised between two and seven interconnected lines of trenches and 15 old forts; the second, on the edge of the city itself, was based around minefields, barricades and strong German stone buildings. The third comprised nine old forts around the old city perimeter. Russian artillery bombarded it for four days before the attack went in on 7 Apr.: the city fell on 9 Apr. The Germans succeeded in evacuating many civilians and military personnel from East Prussia and the Polish corridor by sea, which included Operation *Hannibal*, to evacuate valuable U-boat personnel. One of the ships, the *Wilhelm Gustloff* with over

8000 people left Gdynia on 30 Jan. At 2308 Soviet time the USSR submarine S-13, which had been at sea for three weeks since she left Hangö to attack German lines of communication, fired three torpedoes. One chalked 'for Stalin' failed to fire: one of those that struck was chalked 'for Leningrad'. Over 7000 died in the worst ship sinking in history.

Pictures above left: The Wilhelm Gustloff *whilst serving as a 'Strength through Joy' cruise-liner in peacetime. Above right: the Soviet submarine* S13, *which sank the* Wilhelm Gustloff *in the world's greatest shipping tragedy, loading torpedoes at the Finnish port of Hangö.*

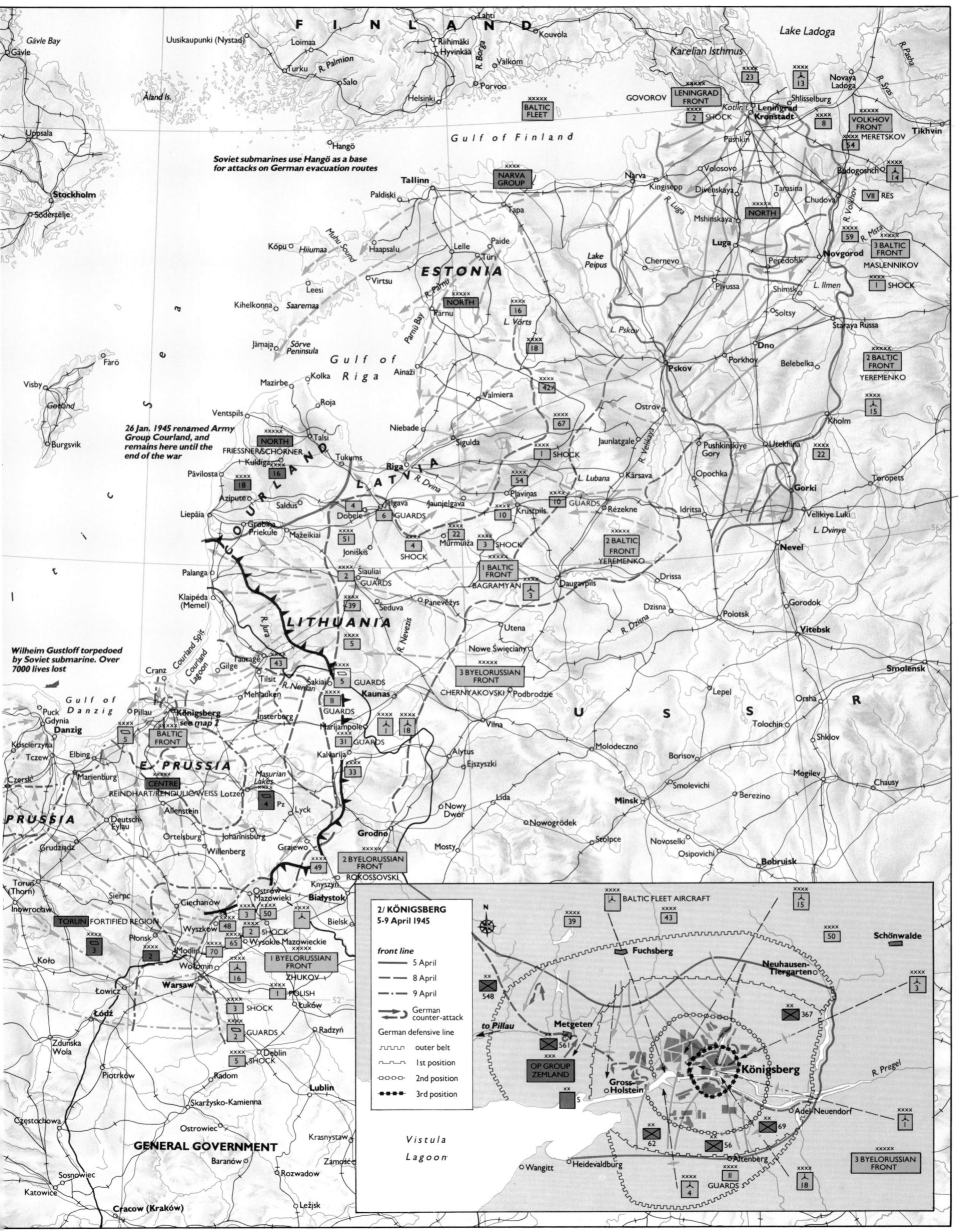

Normandy JUNE ~ JULY 1944

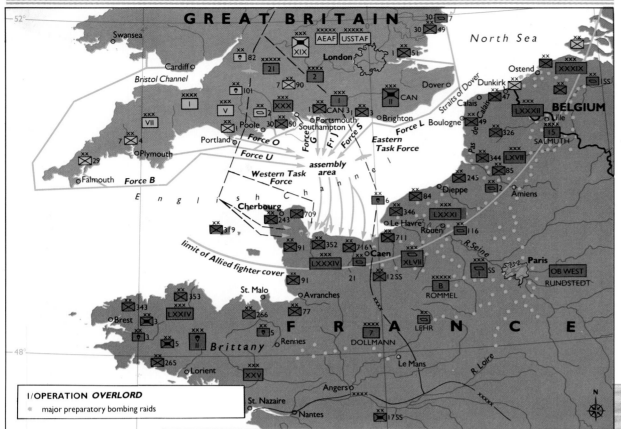

1/OPERATION OVERLORD
* major preparatory bombing raids

PLANS FOR THE INVASION of occupied Europe via northern France had been discussed by the British and Americans since early 1942, but strategic weakness and then strategic disagreement forced a series of postponements in favour of a 'Mediterranean' strategy. At the Quebec Conference (August 1943), the British agreed to name commanders (page 134). In December, Eisenhower was appointed Supreme Allied Commander; he directed Montgomery to prepare detailed invasion plans and act as commander of the invasion ground forces.

Hitler, embroiled on the Eastern Front, delayed preparing plans for the defence of the West until November 1943. Then in Führer Directive 51 he gave it new priority. In December, he appointed Rommel to take charge of defensive preparations as commander of Army Group B (Seventh and Fifteenth Armies); Rundstedt remained Supreme Commander West over Army Groups B and C (First and Nineteenth Armies). In all, Rundstedt disposed some fifty infantry and ten armoured divisions. But German strategy was hampered by the need to defend all coasts, because of the Allies' success in disguising their intentions (page 82). Too many infantry divisions were, therefore, left in the south (Army Group C). Rommel and Rundstedt also disagreed about the deployment of armour, the former wanting it on the beaches, the latter in central reserve. Hitler imposed a compromise, and unwisely took some of the armoured units under his direct control.

THE OPERATIONAL RADIUS of a Spitfire was a crucial factor in the *Overlord* plan, for it determined the area in which landings could be mounted (*1*). Despite a carefully disguised build-up of troops and equipment on the south coast, Allied convoys also had to be brought from Wales and East Anglia to rendezvous off the Isle of Wight in order to reach Normandy in one night. Air cover hid them and bombardment threw the Germans into disarray. Airborne troops landed in darkness, while the convoys reached the Normandy coast at dawn, 6 June (*2*). Rundstedt reacted to the landings by sending 21st Panzer Division against the British beaches that evening. He and Hitler then released their own armoured reserves (1st and 12th SS, Panzer Lehr). Allied power and ground resistance held them at bay. Meanwhile the Allies reinforced the lodgement area, pushed inland and built up strength for a break-out. Mulberry floating harbours (*3*), one British at Arromanches, one American at St Laurent, were assembled directly offshore. The American harbour was wrecked by a gale (19-22 June) but the British harbour remained in use, discharging up to 11,000 tons of supplies daily. At *Utah* beach, where US parachutists had seized much inundated territory (*4*), German resistance was slight. At *Omaha*, on beaches dominated by high cliffs, defended by the best German coastal division in Normandy (352nd), the US infantry, suffered heavily. Following the consolidation of the Allied beachheads into a defensible lodgement, Operation *Epsom* (*5*) was intended to isolate Caen. In heavy fighting (24 June-1 July), German armoured reinforcements halted it. Operation *Goodwood* (18-20 July) was also checked. Its object had been to isolate Caen from the east and secure an opening towards Paris. However, both efforts soaked up German resistance, freeing the US forces to the west for the forthcoming break-out.

Picture above right: *the Allied invasion force disembarking on Juno beach, June 1940*

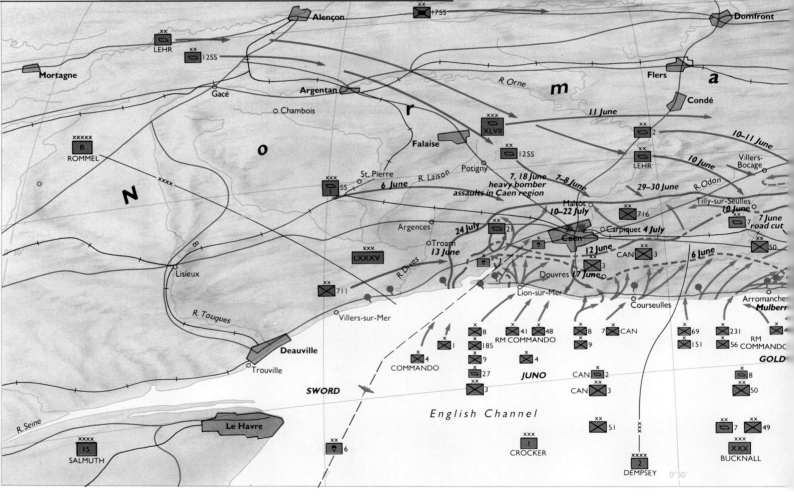

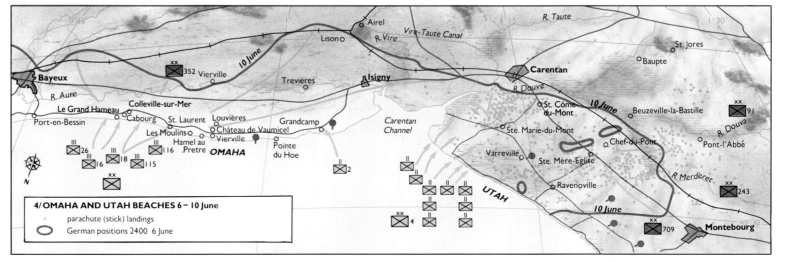

4/OMAHA AND UTAH BEACHES 6 – 10 June
parachute (stick) landings
German positions 2400 6 June

The Allies had decided in March 1943 to invade Normandy. It lay within fighter cover from British airfields and was thought – correctly – to be judged by the Germans a less likely landing point than the Pas de Calais. But Montgomery altered the plan for Operation *Overlord* he inherited so as to land five rather than three seaborne divisions, as well as three airborne. He retained the scheme of using the airborne divisions to secure the flanks of the bridgehead, to build up a strong 'lodgement', to follow-up with seaborne divisions; to secure Caen early and fight a battle to destroy the German armour; and to eventually unleash US divisions from the western end of the bridgehead to break out into mainland France. But the timetable foreseen was a lengthy one. It was not expected that the Franco-German frontier would be reached until 1945.

The cross-Channel passage of some 6500 naval and transport craft, forming 75 convoys, was to be protected or supported by 12,000 aircraft, against which the Germans could deploy only 425 fighters. On the night of June 5/6, the convoy began to cross the Channel, while widespread Allied air raids blinded or distracted the German warning and command systems. Heavy naval and air bombardments covered the disembarkation of the 3rd British, 3rd Canadian, 50th British and 1st and 4th US Divisions on *Sword*, *Juno*, *Gold*, *Omaha* and *Utah* beaches. Meanwhile the 6th British and 82nd and 101st US Airborne Divisions had landed during the night east of *Sword* and west of *Utah* respectively.

The seaborne divisions were accompanied by amphibious armour and got ashore without serious loss or delay, except at *Omaha*, where the armour had been launched too far from shore and swamped. Losses there of 3000 were the heaviest in the toll for D-Day. By nightfall, however, all beachheads were secured, a German armoured counter-attack had failed because of slowness by the High Command to react and reinforcements were coming ashore. By 10 June, the separate beachheads had been consolidated into a single lodgement and the Americans were making ground inland and towards Cherbourg. The British, having beaten off German Panzer attacks, were preparing to take Caen.

Despite heavy bombardment of Caen, and of German positions to the south, an attempt to outflank the city via Villers-Bocage failed on 10-12 June. A second attempt, made in greater strength by 15th Scottish Division (Operation *Epsom*, 24 June to 1 July), was also checked. Meanwhile the Americans were occupying the Cotentin peninsula and forced the surrender of Cherbourg on 27 June. The Germans had begun to withdraw infantry divisions from First and Nineteenth Armies to reinforce Normandy, but Hitler, fearing a follow-up invasion of the Pas de Calais, refused to allow withdrawals from Fifteenth Army until 30 July. The third British attempt to capture Caen (Operation *Goodwood*) was again contained by local forces. *Goodwood* had the effect, nonetheless, of holding and attracting German armour at the eastern end of the lodgement area. When the Americans, who had been creating a reserve to the west, unleashed it in the powerful *Cobra* operation (25 July, page 154), it met little resistance. The breakout had begun.

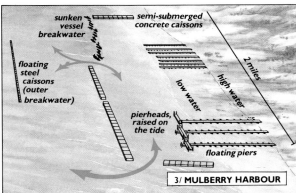

floating steel caissons (outer breakwater)

sunken vessel breakwater

semi-submerged concrete caissons

floating piers

pierheads, raised on the tide

low water   high water   2 miles

3/ MULBERRY HARBOUR

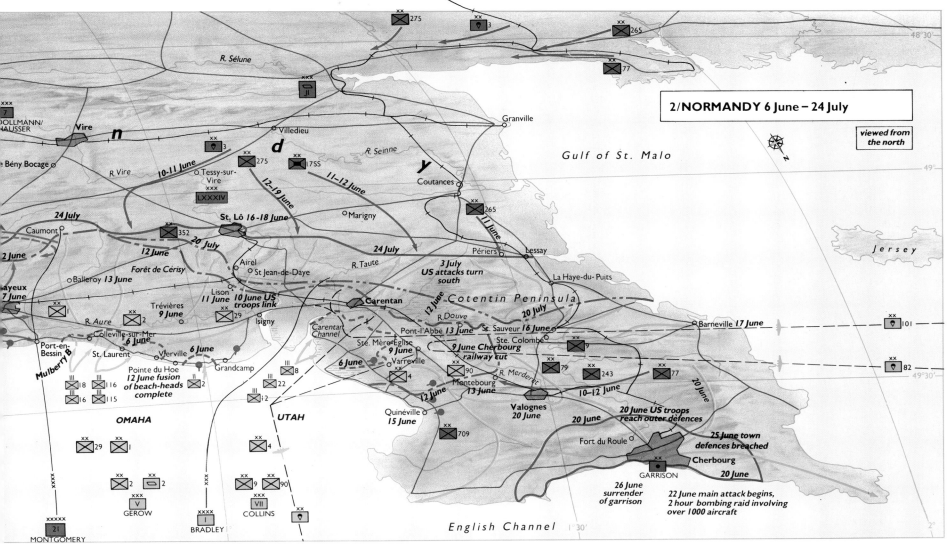

2/ NORMANDY 6 June – 24 July

viewed from the north

Gulf of St. Malo

Jersey

English Channel

OMAHA   UTAH

GEROW   V   VII   COLLINS

MONTGOMERY   BRADLEY

Cotentin Peninsula

Cherbourg   GARRISON

26 June surrender of garrison

22 June main attack begins, 2 hour bombing raid involving over 1000 aircraft

25 June town defences breached

20 June US troops reach outer defences

Fort du Roule

Valognes 20 June

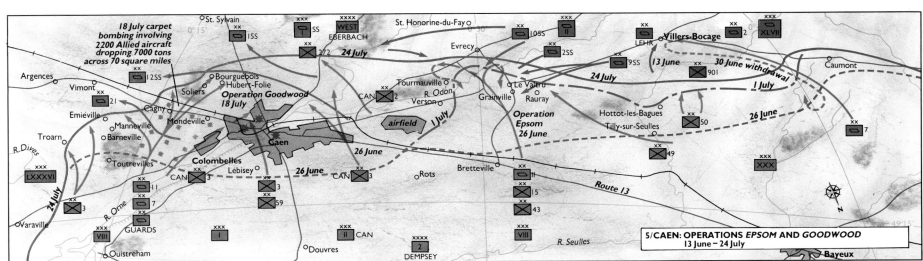

18 July carpet bombing involving 2200 Allied aircraft dropping 7000 tons across 70 square miles

Operation Goodwood 18 July

Operation Epsom 26 June

Caen   Villers-Bocage

Route 13

Bayeux

5/ CAEN: OPERATIONS *EPSOM* AND *GOODWOOD* 13 June – 24 July

Northern France JULY~AUGUST 1944

IN THE SIX WEEKS following the D-Day landings the Allies had consolidated a substantial beachhead, and at considerable cost achieved their secondary objective (page 152). The Germans were not slow to respond and moved up all available units to contain the problem. The size and quality of these reinforcements were somewhat less than the Allies had anticipated, as commitments on other fronts were beginning to reveal the amount to which German manpower was over-extended.

Operation *Cobra*, which opened on 25 July, originally intended to seize ground west of St Lô from which an Allied break-out could be mounted; but the extent of its success was not foreseen. That was the outcome of two factors: the destructive effect of the preparatory aerial bombardment and the absence of German reserves behind the chosen attack sector. The dropping of 4000 tons of bombs – some of which fell short, killing hundreds of Americans on the start line – wrecked the only German Panzer division (*Lehr*) behind the front. Most of the others were still near Caen, drawn thither by the *Goodwood* Operation (page 152).

Finding resistance weaker than expected, the US VII Corps advanced rapidly towards Coutances. East of St Lô, XIX Corps also made ground and acted as flank guard when Kluge (who had replaced Rommel, wounded in an air strike, on 17 July) redeployed two panzer divisions against Bradley's army on 27 July. In heavy fighting around Tessy-sur-Vire, XIX Corps allowed VII and the reinforcing VIII Corps to reach Avranches and open the way into Brittany – but also towards the rear of the German positions in Normandy.

On 1 August Bradley transferred command of First Army to Hodges and became commander of Twelfth Army Group,

THE BREAKOUT FROM NORMANDY (*1*) proved a more effective campaign than the Allies had originally envisaged. Despite British difficulties in isolating Caen, and effecting a breakthrough there, the US build-up in the west soon forced an inevitable logic. The breakthrough would be effected by a push down south, which would then sweep round to encircle German forces in what became known as the 'Falaise Pocket'. Operation *Cobra* (*2*) had a false start when Allied aircraft, bombing short on 24 July, hit troops of US VII Corps. On 25 July the bombing was accurate, destroyed the German defence and led to rapid advances out of Normandy, towards the Atlantic ports (defended as fortresses by Hitler's order and to be besieged by the US Ninth Army, activated in September) and eastward towards the Seine. The *Overlord* plan was amended on 4 August to substitute an encirclement in Normandy for an occupation of western France. The line of the Loire was nevertheless reached (11 August) and the Seine was crossed on 19 August. Brest fell on 19 September, but Lorient and St Nazaire held out until 1945, as did La Rochelle and Bordeaux further south. The US VII Corps moved rapidly to take Coutances, followed by VIII, while XIX blunted an initial German counter-attack east of St Lô (27-30 July). The main German counter-attack from Mortain towards Avranches (6-10 August), was turned back by American armour and airpower which had been alerted by *Ultra* intelligence. The US XV Corps reached Argentan on 13 August and the Canadian First Army Falaise two days later. They were then separated by only fifteen miles but, despite the heroic efforts of the Polish 1st Armoured Division to close the neck of the Falaise Pocket, sheer press of German numbers held it open until 20 August. A popular uprising, in which the resistance (FFI) and the gendarmerie joined forces, broke out on 19 August, as soon as it became clear that the Allied armies were approaching. The response by the occupying Germans was half-hearted, and a plan to destroy the bridges and public services was not fulfilled. Nevertheless, nearly a thousand members of the FFI were killed in the insurrection, although it was left to the advancing armed forces to claim the laurels of Liberation. Eisenhower nominated the French 2nd Armoured Division to liberate the city. Leclerc, its commander, accepted the German surrender on the Ile de la Cité (19 Aug.).

Picture above right: Abandoned German equipment in the Falaise Pocket following Allied bombardment; the narrow, steep-sided lanes in the area proved lethal traps for forces on both sides.

Opposite: General Patton crossing a US pontoon bridge over the river Seine; Allied tactical bombing raids had destroyed nearly all the bridges across the river.

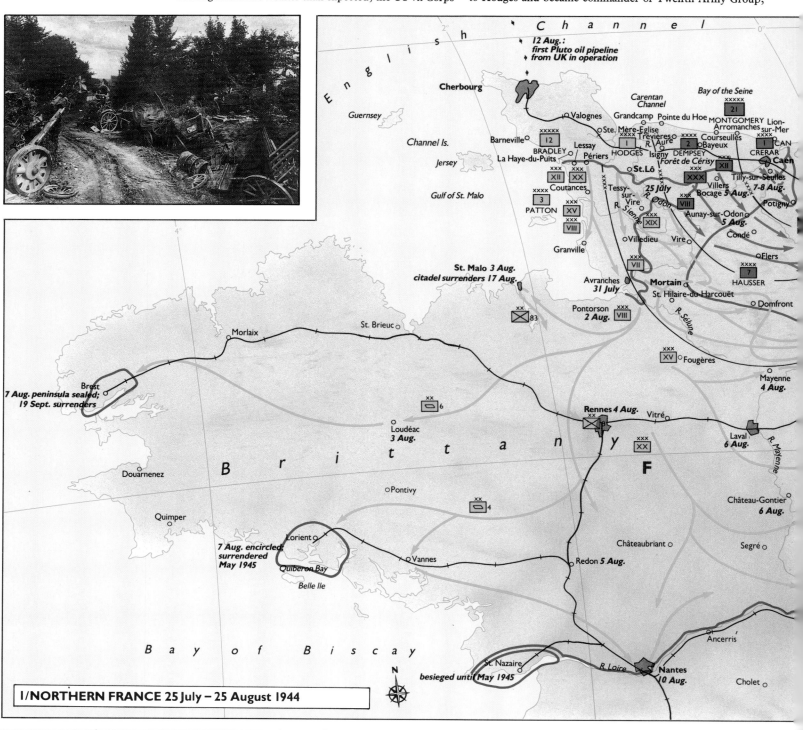

1/NORTHERN FRANCE 25 July – 25 August 1944

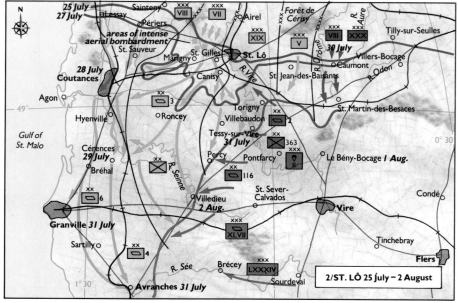

2/ST. LÔ 25 July – 2 August

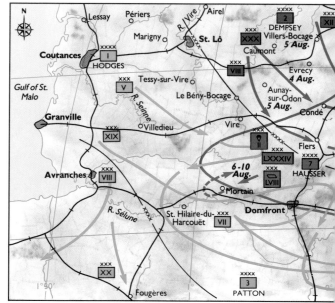

controlling also the newly-formed Third Army under Patton. The latter now assumed direction of the advance from Coutances, exploiting the talent for hard-driving leadership of an armoured offensive he had displayed in Sicily. By 4 August his spearheads had reached Mayenne and on that day Montgomery, still exercising control of ground operations, ordered the first change to the *Overlord* plan. Instead of advancing to occupy Brittany and the Atlantic ports, the Americans were to send only minor units in that direction. First Army was to continue its swing eastwards, thus encircling German positions in Normandy in a wide loop. Patton was to strike directly across the German rear towards Le Mans. The British Second and the new Canadian First Army (activated 23 July) were to continue attacking southwards from Caen.

The Germans were now threatened with a close encirclement in Normandy and a wider encirclement on the line of the Seine. Hitler, however, glimpsed opportunity. On 2 August he ordered Kluge to transfer all available panzer divisions westwards and strike from Mortain towards the sea, with the aim of cutting off the American break-out at its root. This redeployment was detected by *Ultra* intercepts: when the Mortain counter-attack began on 6 August it was promptly halted by American forces which had been hurried to the spot.

The defeat at Mortain, by attracting and then destroying the German panzer divisions from Caen, opened the way for the British and Canadian armies to drive southwards towards Falaise. While they struggled to block the German retreat towards the Seine, the American First and Third Armies were

sweeping westwards and then northwards to Argentan (reached 13 August). Bradley also sent units of xv Corps directly to the Seine, which was crossed at Mantes on 19 August.

The neck of the Falaise Pocket was finally closed on 20 August, trapping 50,000 Germans and all the heavy equipment of Seventh and Fifth Panzer Armies. The bulk of their personnel had, however, escaped and managed to cross the Seine by ferry and pontoon (all bridges downstream of Paris having been destroyed by Allied air attack) in the last week of August. Paris, in which an uprising orchestrated by various resistance factions had begun on 19 August, was liberated on 25 August by the French 2nd Armoured Division. General de Gaulle, who had arrived in France under his own auspices on 20 August, made a triumphal entry into the city next day.

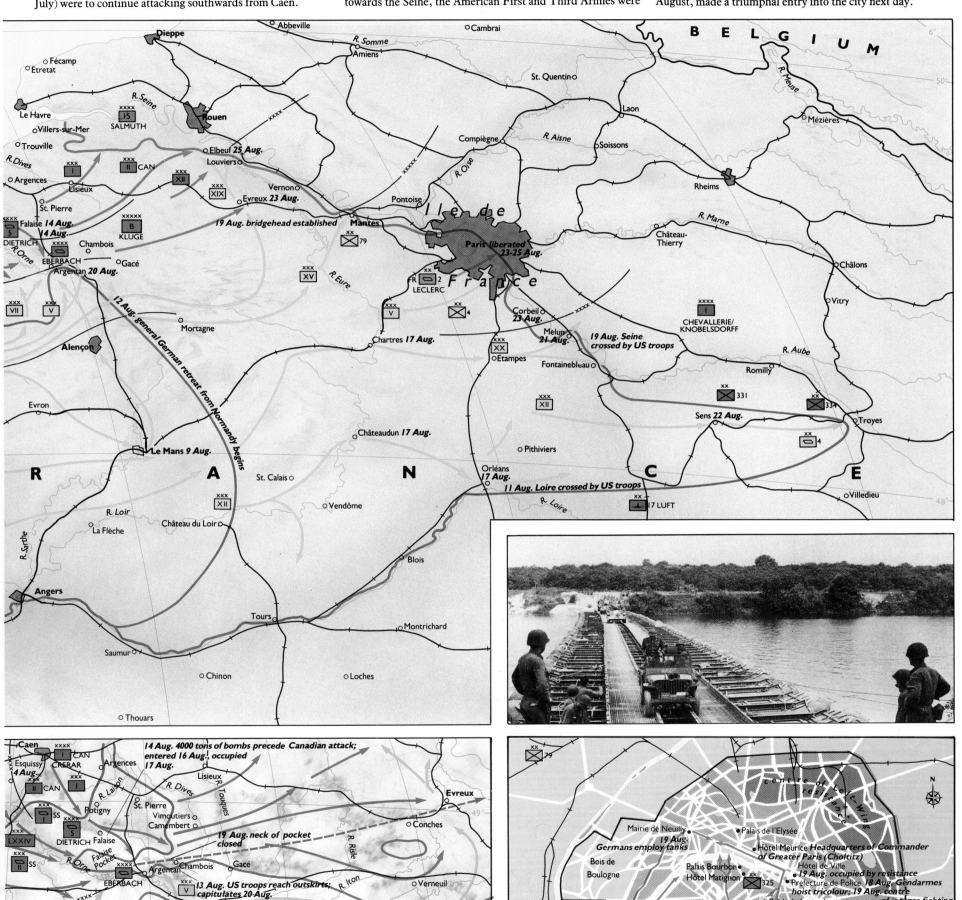

3/THE FALAISE POCKET 10 – 19 August

4/PARIS 10 – 25 August

A LANDING IN THE SOUTH OF FRANCE, timed to complement *Overlord*, had been considered by the Combined Chiefs of Staff as early as August 1943 and was endorsed at the Teheran Conference in November. No date for Operation *Anvil* was fixed, however, because of the difficulty of providing shipping and troops to mount it. In January 1944 Eisenhower secured its postponement beyond the *Overlord* date and as late as 11 June, five days after the Normandy landings, Churchill suggested that it should be cancelled in favour of an attack into the Balkans. Roosevelt, in view of an agreement made with Stalin, rejected this; *Anvil* was finally fixed for 15 August.

The operation had also been opposed by the commanders in the Mediterranean, Wilson, Alexander and Clark, who felt it would rob them of the troops needed to prevent the Germans establishing strong positions on the Pisa-Rimini line. One French division was brought from North Africa; the rest – three US, three French – were indeed withdrawn from Clark's 5th Army in Italy and, with US and Canadian paratroop Rangers, formed the US 7th Army under General Patch. The formations sailed from Taranto, Salerno, Brindisi, Corsica and Oran to rendezvous off Provence on the night of 14/15 August.

There were eight German divisions in 19th Army defending the sector but of these only one, 11th Panzer, was first-class. Under a heavy air and naval bombardment, the landing was completed easily and while the French captured Toulon and Marseilles (28 August), the Americans set off to pursue the Germans, who had orders to retreat, up the Rhône Valley. Patch embarked on a breakneck chase because *Ultra* intelligence reassured him that he was in no danger of being attacked by Germans from northern Italy. 19th Army, however, covered its withdrawal skilfully and although 57,000 of its soldiers were taken prisoner, its formations, including 11th Panzer Division, reached Alsace intact. 7th Army made contact with Patton's 3rd near Dijon on 11 September (page 158).

Meanwhile, the Allied armies in Italy had been sustaining their pursuit of the Germans from the Winter Position towards the Gothic Line. Obliged to halt on 4 August by the transfer of troops for *Anvil*, after an advance of 270 miles in 64 days, Alexander regrouped for a deliberate assault on what Kesselring had identified as the last strong position south of the Po Valley. The 8th Army was repositioned on the Adriatic coast but the British XIII Corps left with the US 5th Army, which was

to launch a breakthrough towards Bologna as soon as 8th Army had drawn the German reserves onto the east flank. After considerable engineering work had been done to repair the roads and bridges destroyed by the retreating Germans, 8th Army attacked on 25 August. This initial assault carried 8th Army through the Gothic Line and by 4 September it was fighting for Rimini. Kesselring transferred troops to hold the sector, weakening his centre, which was assaulted by 5th Army on 1 September. Between 13 and 18 September the US II Corps made a rapid advance towards Bologna. Rimini fell to the British on 21 September and on 1 October 5th Army opened its final assault on Bologna. Kesselring concentrated his reserves to hold the city, which allowed 8th Army to advance beyond Rimini, but on 20 October Clark, though only nine miles from Bologna, was forced to halt.

Winter weather now halted operations. The number of German divisions in Italy (26) actually exceeded the Allied (20),

though the Germans lacked armour and air power. While 8th Army continued to inch forward between Rimini and Ravenna (despite a German counter-attack in the Serchio Valley on 26 December) the battle line hardly moved through the Winter.

The final Allied offensive began in early April towards Spezia (5 April) on the Mediterranean, towards the Argenta Gap in 8th Army sector (9 April) and in the centre, towards Bologna (14 April). By 20 April Bologna was outflanked and all Allied formations (except those at Spezia) had broken out into the plains of the Po. Exploitation was rapid. 8th Army swung north-east to Venice, 5th Army north-west to Milan; the US 92nd Division, which made the Spezia attack, moved along the coast to Genoa and Monaco. On 28 April Italian partisans captured and murdered Mussolini; the remnants of his Fascist army began to surrender the same day. On 29 April Vietinghoff, who had succeeded Kesselring in command in Italy, asked for an armistice. It became effective on 2 May.

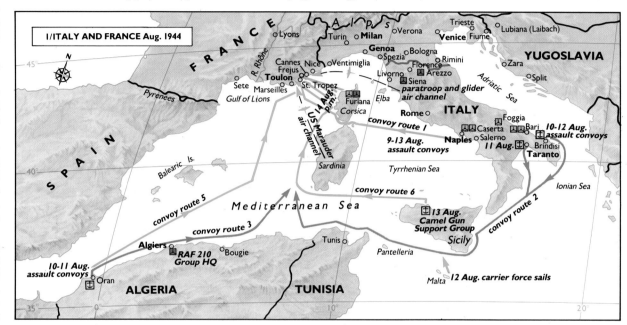

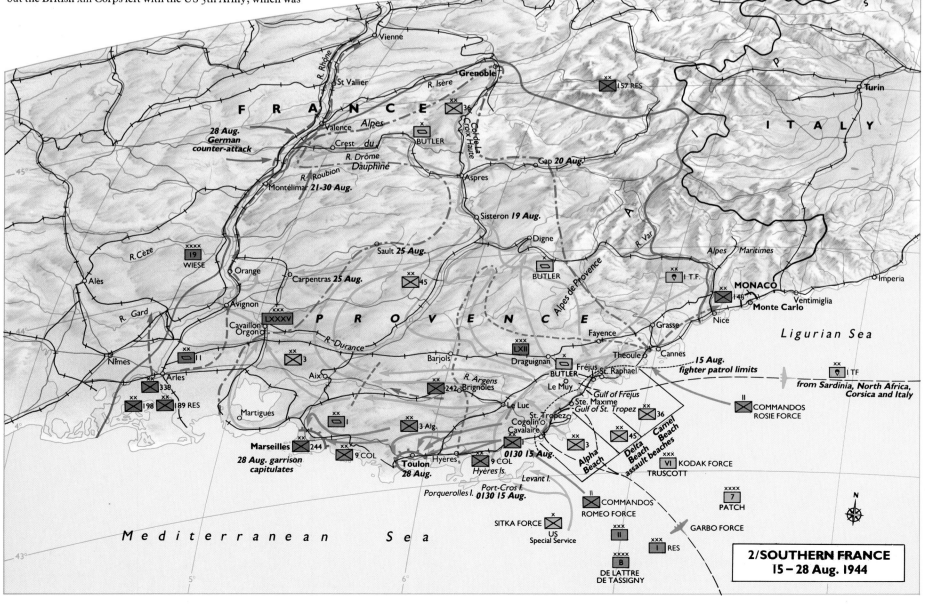

2/SOUTHERN FRANCE 15 – 28 Aug. 1944

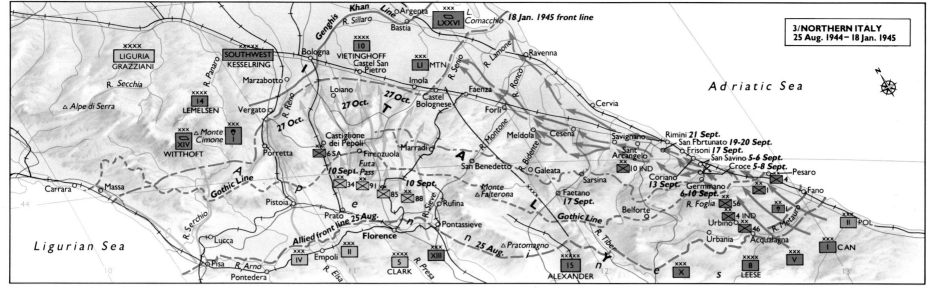

3/NORTHERN ITALY
25 Aug. 1944 – 18 Jan. 1945

LIGURIA
GRAZZIANI
SOUTHWEST KESSELRING
Genghis Khan Line
Argenta
Bastia
L. Comacchio
18 Jan. 1945 front line
LXXVI
R. Sillaro
Adriatic Sea
N
VIETINGHOFF
10
Bologna
Marzabotto
R. Panaro
R. Secchia
△ Alpe di Serra
14 LEMELSEN
Vergato
Loiano
27 Oct.
Castel San Pietro
Imola
LI MTN
R. Senio
R. Lamone
Ravenna
Faenza
R. Montone
R. Ronco
Cervia
R. Reno
27 Oct.
XIV WITTHOFF
△ Monte Cimone
1
Porretta
27 Oct.
Castiglione dei Pepoli
Firenzuola
Futa Pass
10 Sept.
6 SA
Marradi
Castel Bolognese
Forlì
Meldola
Cesena
Savignano
Sant'Arcangelo
Rimini 21 Sept.
San Fortunato 19-20 Sept.
Frisoni 17 Sept.
San Savino 5-6 Sept.
Croce 5-8 Sept.
Fano
Carrara
Massa
R. Serchio
Pistoia
Prato
34 91
85
88
10 Sept.
Rufina
Veve
Monte △ Falterona
San Benedetto
Galeata
Sarsina
10 IND
Coriano
13 Sept.
Germmano 6-10 Sept.
R. Foglia
56
4 IND
46
Urbino
Urbania
Acqualagna
4
1
II POL
R. Metauro
Pesaro
Ligurian Sea
44
Lucca
Pisa
R. Arno
Pontedera
Empoli
IV
II
Florence
25 Aug.
Pontassieve
XIII
Allied front line 25 Aug.
△ Pratomagno
25 Aug.
Gothic Line
R. Tiber
Belforte
Gothic Line
5 CLARK
R. Pesa
15 ALEXANDER
X
V
I CAN
8 LEESE

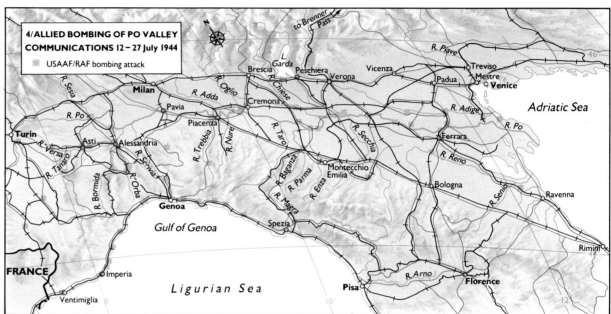

4/ALLIED BOMBING OF PO VALLEY
COMMUNICATIONS 12 – 27 July 1944
✳ USAAF/RAF bombing attack

N
to Brenner Pass
R. Piave
Treviso
Mestre
Venice
46
L. Garda
Brescia
Peschiera
Verona
Vicenza
Padua
Milan
R. Oglio
R. Adda
Chiese
R. Adige
Adriatic Sea
R. Sesia
Pavia
Cremona
R. Po
Turin
R. Po
R. Versa
Asti
Alessandria
Piacenza
R. Trebbia
R. Nure
R. Taro
R. Secchia
Ferrara
R. Tanaro
R. Bormida
R. Orba
R. Scrivia
R. Baganza
R. Parma
R. Enza
Montecchio Emilia
R. Reno
Bologna
Ravenna
Genoa
Spezia
R. Magra
R. Senio
Gulf of Genoa
FRANCE
Imperia
R. Arno
Pisa
Florence
Ventimiglia
Ligurian Sea
Rimini

DURING THE ALLIED invasion of S. France, Operation *Anvil, Delta, Camel* and *Alpha* Forces landed between Toulon and Cannes *(1)* (15 Aug.); only *Camel* Force met serious opposition. 4 French divisions then captured Toulon and Marseilles, essential for their port facilities, while US divisions pursued the Germans up the Rhône Valley *(2)*. Delaying action by the 11th Panzer Div. prevented the US 36th Div. from blocking the German retreat. The US advance eventually reached Dijon (11 Sept.), where 7th and Patton's 3rd Armies linked. The bulk of the German 19th Army escaped into Alsace. In Italy, an Allied bombing campaign destroyed every major bridge in the Po Valley by the end of July *(4)*. The Allies then attacked Kesselring's Gothic Line south of Rimini *(3)* (25 Aug.); US IV Corps penetrated the centre, by-passing the strongly defended Futa Pass *(1 Sept.)*. 8th Army crossed a succession of rivers up to Ravenna during Dec. The US drive on Bologna was halted on 20 Oct. Following a harsh Winter the Allied assault on the Gothic Line was renewed *(5)* (9 and 14 Apr.) supported by air power. The US 10th Mountain Div. breached the mountain positions above Bologna (14-17 Apr.), breaking out into the Po Valley (20 Apr.), by which date 8th Army had passed through the Argenta Gap. German defensive withdrawals collapsed as the US forces exploited east and west of Verona, to cut the German retreat. 8th Army swept east through Venezia, reaching Trieste by May, in advance of Tito's forces.

Picture above: part of the mass Allied airborne assault behind the Provençal coastline, 15 Aug. 1944.

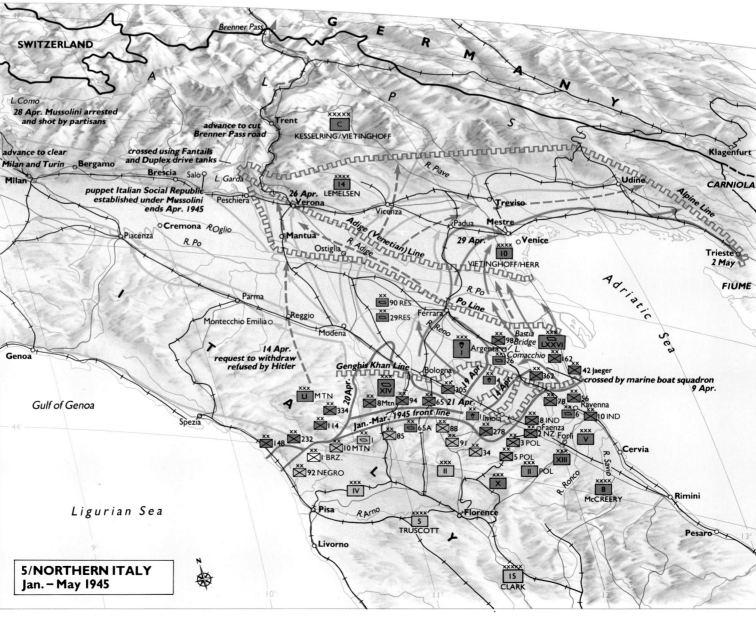

SWITZERLAND
Brenner Pass
GERMANY
A L P S
L. Como
28 Apr. Mussolini arrested and shot by partisans
advance to cut Brenner Pass road
Trent
KESSELRING/VIETINGHOFF
Klagenfurt
CARNIOLA
advance to clear Milan and Turin
Bergamo
crossed using Fantails and Duplex drive tanks
Milan
L. Garda
puppet Italian Social Republic established under Mussolini ends Apr. 1945
Peschiera
14 LEMELSEN
26 Apr.
Verona
R. Piave
Udine
Treviso
Alpine Line
Cremona
R. Oglio
Vicenza
Padua
Mestre
29 Apr.
Venice
Trieste 2 May
FIUME
Piacenza
R. Po
Mantua
Ostiglia
R. Adige
Adige (Venetian) Line
10
VIETINGHOFF/HERR
Adriatic Sea
I
Parma
Reggio
Modena
14 Apr. request to withdraw refused by Hitler
Po Line
90 RES
29 RES
R. Reno
Ferrara
Bastia Bridge
Argenta
L. Comacchio
LXXVI
62
Genoa
Genghis Khan Line
20 Apr.
XIV
Bologna
1
26
42 jaeger
crossed by marine boat squadron 9 Apr.
Spezia
U MTN
8 Mtn
334
94
305
363
78
56
6
Ravenna
10 IND
Gulf of Genoa
114
65
6 SA
85
21 Apr.
Faenza
8 IND
3 NZ
Forlì
Jan.-Mar. 1945 front line
Imola
278
5 POL
V
148
232
10 MTN
1 BRZ
88
91
34
3 POL
II POL
XIII
R. Ronco
R. Savio
Cervia
92 NEGRO
II
IV
X
5 POL
8 McCREERY
Rimini
Ligurian Sea
Pisa
R. Arno
Florence
5 TRUSCOTT
Livorno
15 CLARK
Pesaro

5/NORTHERN ITALY
Jan. – May 1945

N

France and Belgium 1944

THE EXTENT OF THE GERMAN Army's defeat in the Falaise Pocket (page 154) forced the surviving units of Army Group B to retreat at high speed across the Seine and then, since Hitler had earlier refused permission for a line to be prepared on the River Somme, to the next major water obstacle, the Meuse (Maas) and Scheldt in eastern France and central Belgium. The Allies pursued, hampered by shortage of fuel and supplies. Hitler had ordered the ports along the Channel coast to be held as fortresses; of these, Le Havre was besieged until 12 September, and Boulogne and Calais fell on 30 September but Dunkirk held out until the end of the war. This obliged both Montgomery and Patton to draw on shipments landed across the Normandy beaches – necessarily both slowing the Allied advance and limiting the amount of supplies available to them. Each petitioned Eisenhower, as Supreme Allied Commander, to allot him a major share of the supplies available, thus provoking what came to be called the 'Broad versus Narrow' dispute over strategy. Montgomery insisted that he could break into Germany via Holland if given the lion's share; Patton similarly argued that he might rush the Siegfried Line through Lorraine. Eisenhower diplomatically distributed equal shares, with the result – probably inevitable in view of Hitler's mustering of reserves – that the Allied advance came to a halt on the approaches to the German frontier in early September.

In uncharacteristically headstrong mood, Montgomery then persuaded Eisenhower to allot him the Allied Airborne Army (82nd and 101st US, 1st British Airborne Divisions) to mount an air-ground thrust across the Rhine in order to project the Allied advance into the German plain. Advance airborne units would secure certain bridges across the Rhine, paving the way for an armoured thrust by ground forces. The manoeuvre was codenamed Operation *Market Garden* and was launched on 17 September. The operation was conceived in two parts: *Market*, the seizure of the Eindhoven and Nijmegen bridges by the Amercian divisions worked perfectly. *Garden*, in which the British would gain control of the bridges at Arnhem, met with disaster. The airborne forces swiftly came under counter-attack by the 9th and 10th SS Panzer divisions, who were at Arnhem recuperating from the battle in Normandy. Only the northern

section of the main road bridge was taken, and the British were forced, after vicious house-to-house fighting, to relinquish it on 21 September. The British Armoured Division (Guards) meanwhile forcing its way through the airborne corridor on a 'one tank' front was held up by fierce resistance. Despite reinforcement by the Polish Parachute Brigade, 1st Airborne Division could not hold its positions after 25 September and abandoned them that night. Among the survivors, those that evaded capture attempted to make their way across the Rhine and back to Allied lines.

Montgomery's insistence on venturing the airborne crossing of the Rhine had left the Germans in his rear free to strengthen the defences of the Scheldt, with deplorable effect on the supply situation. Although Antwerp had been captured on 4 September, its port facilities, the largest in Europe, could not be used while the estuary remained in German hands. Operations to take it began on 2 October but were not completed until 8 November and were severely hampered by the flooding of certain areas by the Germans. The port was not opened until 20 days later. The '85 days' between the capture of Antwerp and its utilization as a port was a period of logistic famine for the Allied armies on the German frontier. This was also the period in which Hitler developed his plan to isolate the advanced Allied armies in the west with a bold armoured thrust through the Ardennes to the North Sea coast (page 160).

The American generals Hodges, commanding 1st Army, and Patton, commanding 3rd, had meanwhile been fighting with the resources available to capture ground around Aachen and in Lorraine. Hodges, supported by Simpson's 9th Army, painfully broke through the Siegfried Line (West Wall) into the Hürtgen Forest during November. They reached the River Roer in early December. Until the opening of the German Ardennes offensive in mid-December, they devoted their prinicpal efforts to securing the Roer river dams. Patton, supported by the 6th Army Group of American and French troops who had landed in Provence in August, made better progress in Lorraine. By mid-December, he had reached the line of the Rhine and the West Wall along most of his sector. The Allies now stood on the very threshold of the Reich.

THE CHASE from the Seine to the borders of Germany began 10 weeks after the Normandy landings. Patton debouched from his bridgeheads across the river on 26 Aug., Montgomery 3 days later (1). On 3 Sept. the British entered Brussels. Patton had crossed the Meuse near Verdun on 30 Aug. By 15 Sept. Luxembourg had been liberated by Hodges' 1st Army, Patton's 3rd was on the line of the Meuse and the British were at Antwerp and Maastricht in Holland. Mongomery's plan to use the Allied Airborne Army to seize key Rhine bridges ahead of the ground advance was codenamed *Market Garden*. *Market* (4), the seizure of the Eindhoven and Nijmegen bridges by American divisions went according to plan. *Garden* (5) was a partial, and eventually a total failure. Concerted German counter-attack wrested control of the one Arnhem bridge captured by the British within 4 days. The advancing British ground forces were unable to reach Arnhem in time to save the beleaguered British force. General von Zangen, the new commander of 15th Army, energetically gathered remnants and reinforcements to hold the Scheldt banks and islands (6) while Montgomery was mounting *Market Garden* in mid-Sept. The British began a clearing operation from Antwerp on 2 Oct., the Canadians attacking on the south bank. Walcheren, the last German position, was secured in an amphibious operation, 1-8 Nov. Patton's advance from the Moselle was counter-attacked by 5th Panzer Army on 18 Sept. (7) but not long delayed. His 3rd Army resumed its advance into Lorraine, besieged Metz, which fell on 22 Nov., and then fought its way to the River Saar, across which it had secured bridgeheads by 15 Dec. Hodges and Simpson's armies pierced the West Wall in Oct., at heavy cost, and on 16 Nov. entered the difficult terrain of the Hürtgen Forest, through which they reached the River Roer in early Dec.

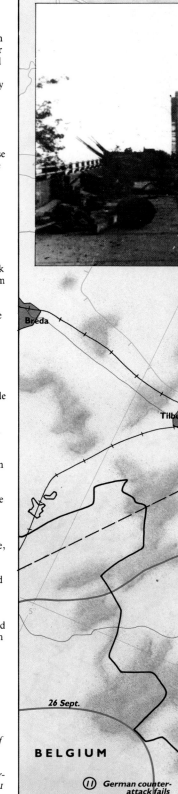

Picture above right: *the bridge across the Rhine at Arnhem. This was one of the principal objectives of Operation* Market Garden, *and quickly became the focal point of British resistance to German counter-attack, which forced the bridge on 21 Sept.*

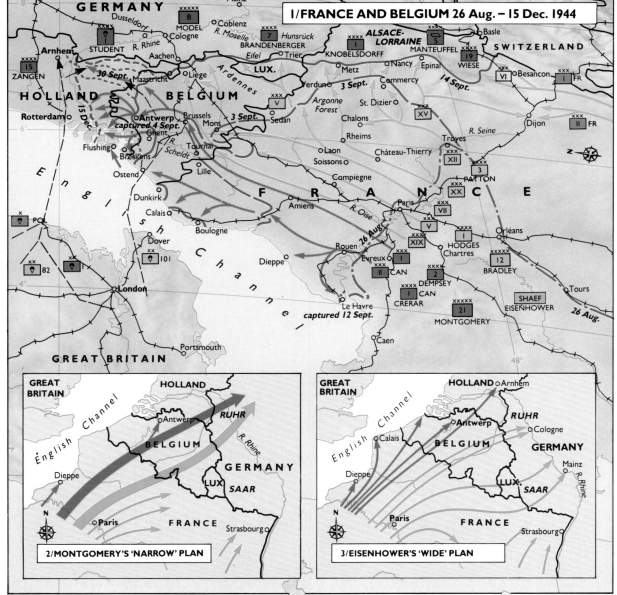

1/FRANCE AND BELGIUM 26 Aug. – 15 Dec. 1944

2/MONTGOMERY'S 'NARROW' PLAN

3/EISENHOWER'S 'WIDE' PLAN

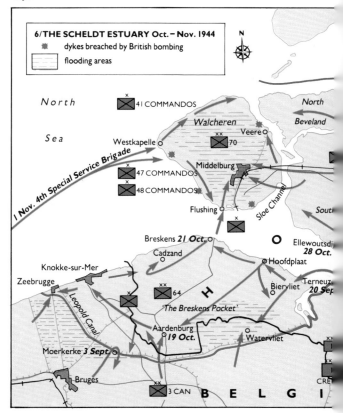

6/THE SCHELDT ESTUARY Oct. – Nov. 1944

- dykes breached by British bombing
- flooding areas

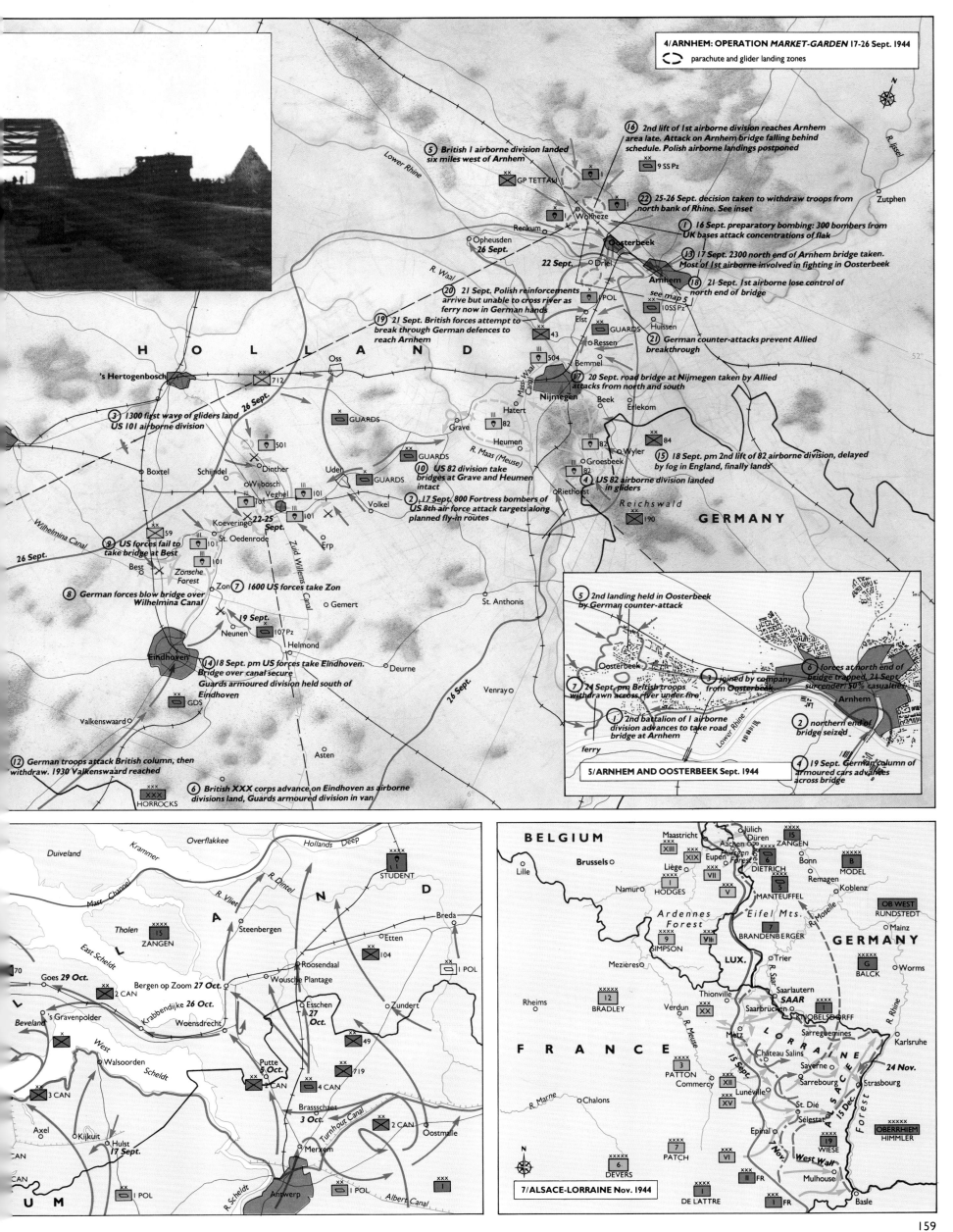

parachute and glider landing zones

⑤ British 1 airborne division landed six miles west of Arnhem

⑯ 2nd lift of 1st airborne division reaches Arnhem area late. Attack on Arnhem bridge falling behind schedule. Polish airborne landings postponed

9 SS Pz

GP TETTAU

Zutphen

R. Ijssel

Wolfheze

Renkum

⑫ 25-26 Sept. decision taken to withdraw troops from north bank of Rhine. See inset

① 16 Sept. preparatory bombing: 300 bombers from UK bases attack concentrations of flak

Opheusden
26 Sept.

Oosterbeek

Driel

22 Sept.

Arnhem

⑬ 17 Sept. 2300 north end of Arnhem bridge taken. Most of 1st airborne involved in fighting in Oosterbeek

see map 5

⑱ 21 Sept. 1st airborne lose control of north end of bridge

R. Waal

⑳ 21 Sept. Polish reinforcements arrive but unable to cross river as ferry now in German hands

POL

10 SS Pz

⑲ 21 Sept. British forces attempt to break through German defences to reach Arnhem

Elst

GUARDS

Huissen

43

Ressen

㉑ German counter-attacks prevent Allied breakthrough

HOLLAND

's Hertogenbosch

712

Oss

504

Bemmel

26 Sept.

⑰ 20 Sept. road bridge at Nijmegen taken by Allied attacks from north and south

GUARDS

Nijmegen

Beek

Erlekom

③ 1300 first wave of gliders land US 101 airborne division

Grave

Hatert

82

Heumen

Wyler

84

501

Boxtel

Schijndel

Dinther

Uden

GUARDS

R. Maas (Meuse)

⑩ US 82 division take bridges at Grave and Heumen intact

82

Groesbeek

82

⑮ 18 Sept. pm 2nd lift of 82 airborne division, delayed by fog in England, finally lands

Wijbosch

Veghel

101

GUARDS

Volkel

② 17 Sept. 800 Fortress bombers of US 8th air force attack targets along planned fly-in routes

Riethorst

④ US 82 airborne division landed in gliders

Reichswald

Koevering

101

22-25 Sept.

59

St. Oedenrode

101

Erp

190

GERMANY

⑨ US forces fail to take bridge at Best

Best

101

26 Sept.

Zonsche Forest

Zon ⑦ 1600 US forces take Zon

St. Anthonis

⑧ German forces blow bridge over Wilhelmina Canal

⑲ 19 Sept.

Neunen

107 Pz

Gemert

Helmond

Eindhoven

⑭ 18 Sept. pm US forces take Eindhoven. Bridge over canal secure. Guards armoured division held south of Eindhoven

Deurne

GDS

Venray

Valkenswaard

26 Sept.

Asten

⑫ German troops attack British column, then withdraw. 1930 Valkenswaard reached

⑥ British XXX corps advance on Eindhoven as airborne divisions land, Guards armoured division in van

XXX
HORROCKS

Inset map 5:

⑤ 2nd landing held in Oosterbeek by German counter-attack

③ joined by company from Oosterbeek

⑥ forces at north end of bridge trapped, 21 Sept surrender. 50% casualties

Oosterbeek

⑦ 24 Sept. pm British troops withdrawn across river under fire

Arnhem

① 2nd battalion of 1 airborne division advances to take road bridge at Arnhem

② northern end of bridge seized

ferry

Lower Rhine

5/ARNHEM AND OOSTERBEEK Sept. 1944

④ 19 Sept. German column of armoured cars advances across bridge

---

Lower left map:

Duiveland

Krammer

Overflakkee

Hollands Deep

R. Dintel

1
STUDENT

R. Vliet

Tholen

15
ZANGEN

Steenbergen

Breda

104

Goes 29 Oct.

East Scheldt

Bergen op Zoom 27 Oct.

Roosendaal

Etten

1 POL

2 CAN

Krabbendijke 26 Oct.

's Gravenpolder

Woensdrecht

Wouwsche Plantage

Zundert

49

Esschen 27 Oct.

Beveland

West Scheldt

Walsoorden

Putte 5 Oct.

719

4 CAN

2 CAN

3 CAN

Brasschaet

3 Oct.

2 CAN

Axel

Kijkuit

Hulst 17 Sept.

Merxem

Oostmalle

1 POL

Antwerp

R. Scheldt

Turnhout Canal

Albert Canal

1

Lower right map:

BELGIUM

Maastricht

Jülich

Düren

15
ZANGEN

XIII

XIX

Eupen

DIETRICH

B
MODEL

Brussels

Lille

Liège

VII

Bonn

Remagen

Koblenz

Namur

1
HODGES

V

MANTEUFFEL

OB WEST
RUNDSTEDT

Ardennes Forest

Eifel Mts.

R. Mosel

Mainz

9
SIMPSON

7
BRANDENBERGER

VII

LUX.

Trier

GERMANY

Mezières

Rheims

12
BRADLEY

Verdun

Thionville

Saarlautern

SAAR

G
BALCK

Worms

FRANCE

Metz

Saarbrücken

KNOBELSDORFF

R. Saar

R. Rhine

Sarreguemines

Karlsruhe

15 Sept.

Château Salins

LORRAINE

24 Nov.

3
PATTON

Commercy

XII

Lunéville

Sarrebourg

Sayerne

R. Marne

R. Meuse

Chalons

XV

St. Dié

Strasbourg

ALSACE

15 Sept.

Epinal

Sélestat

West Wall

7
PATCH

VI

19
WIESE

OBERRHEIM
HIMMLER

6
DEVERS

II FR

Mulhouse

1
DE LATTRE

1 FR

Basle

7/ALSACE-LORRAINE Nov. 1944

The Ardennes 1944

HITLER CONCEIVED THE IDEA of mounting a Winter counter-offensive against the Allies even while his armies were reeling back in defeat from Normandy (page 154). He foresaw that, if they could be held on the line of the West Wall and the Dutch rivers and denied ports of supply along the Channel coast, their long lines of communication would hamper their offensive power and render them vulnerable to a counter-stroke. He therefore ordered Le Havre, Boulogne, Calais and Dunkirk to be held as fortresses, the mouth of the River Scheldt to be garrisoned, so that Antwerp, though lost to the Allies on 4 September, could not be used, and 25 new *Volksgrenadier* divisions to be created behind the West Wall for the coming operation.

Hitler's conception for Operation *Autumn Mist*, as it was eventually codenamed, was of a drive by two Panzer armies from concealed positions in the Eifel Mountains, through the Ardennes forests and across the Meuse, to reach Antwerp a hundred miles distant. The operation would not only recapture the port (which the Allies at last re-opened on 28 November, page 158) but also separate the British and Canadian armies in the north from the Americans in the south. Profiting by the confusion thus caused, and the time won, Hitler then planned to transfer his reserves eastwards to deal a similar blow against the Russians advancing on Berlin.

Rundstedt and Model, respectively Commander-in-Chief

West and Army Group B commander, both thought the plan over-ambitious and during October argued for a 'small solution', designed merely to cast the Allies off balance by a drive to the Meuse. Hitler was adamant and laid down that as soon as a spell of bad weather promised protection from Allied air attack, the tanks were to roll. By early December they were ready. Eight re-equipped Panzer divisions and a Panzer grenadier division were to spearhead 6th SS and 5th Panzer Armies' attack on a sector of front held by four inexperienced and tired American divisions.

Allied intelligence had failed to detect signs of the impending attack, because strict radio silence gave *Ultra* no clues, and had discounted the likelihood of heavy fighting in the remote and difficult Ardennes. When the Germans appeared early in the morning of 16 December, therefore, they quickly overran the defenders, whose brave resistance nevertheless imposed delay. Eisenhower's quick reaction also forestalled German intentions. By sending the US 7th Armoured and 101st Airborne divisions to hold the key junctions of St Vith and Bastogne on 17 December, he ensured that the timetable of advance was further set back. St Vith was abandoned on 23 December but Bastogne was held. It became the focus of the American counter-attack from the south, which Patton began on 22 December. On 20 December, Eisenhower had appointed Montgomery to co-ordinate the attack from the

north, which was greatly assisted by an improvement in the weather, permitting the resumption of air operations, on 23 December. The Germans were also halted on that day by petrol starvation, having failed to capture the fuel dump on which they had counted for re-supply. On 26 December the US 2nd Armoured Division halted 2nd Panzer at Celles, thus terminating the German effort to reach the Meuse. Rundstedt now proposed that the offensive be abandoned, but Hitler refused. During 27-30 December there was heavy fighting around Bastogne, which Patton had relieved on 26 December, while Hitler ordered the opening of a diversionary offensive in Alsace on 1 January (the day on which the *Luftwaffe* mounted its last large-scale operations, destroying 156 aircraft, at heavy cost to itself, on Allied airfields in Belgium).

Montgomery was, meanwhile, gathering his forces on the northern flank of the 'bulge' and unleashed a major counter-attack on 3 January. On 7 January the US VII Corps cut the Laroche-Vielsalm road, leaving German troops in the 'bulge' only the Houffalize road as a line of supply. On 8 January Dietrich, commanding 6th SS Panzer Army, therefore requested and was granted permission to withdraw. The Wehrmacht had suffered 100,000 casualties and lost 600 tanks and 1600 aircraft; the Allies had suffered 76,000 casualties. Hitler had set back the Allied drive into Germany by six weeks, but in the process lost his last armoured reserve. *Autumn Mist* had proved a daring but costly failure.

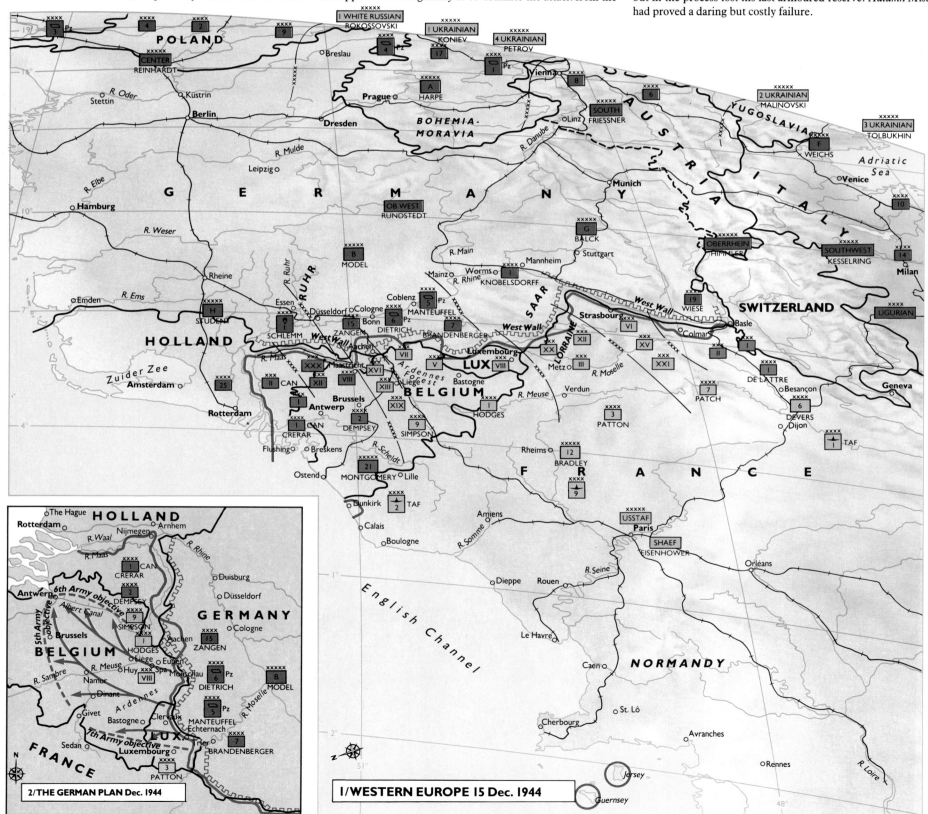

2/THE GERMAN PLAN Dec. 1944

1/WESTERN EUROPE 15 Dec. 1944

In December 1944 the bulk of the Allied forces on the German border were concentrated for offensive operations against the Ruhr and in Lorraine (1). Hitler's plan (2) was for 6th SS (Sepp Dietrich) to drive for Antwerp, while 5th (von Manteuffel) supported it on the left flank. Special forces disguised as US troops were to sow confusion in the army rear, and a parachute drop near Spa was to protect Dietrich's initial break-in. 6th SS Panzer Army's attack began with a drive to seize ground between St Vith and the Meuse, but was checked by the US 2nd and 99th Divisions (3). Dietrich's armour bogged down in the narrow roads of the Ardennes. Best progress was made by 1st SS Panzer, whose tank group commander, Peiper, committed serious atrocities during the advance. Manteuffel, a more experienced tank general, secured quicker gains, but his axis of advance was a subsidiary one. He was only weakly supported by 7th Army (Brandenburger) and so was drawn into a frustrating battle for Bastogne, (4), which had been reinforced by the 101st US Airborne Division on 17 Dec. On 26 Dec. Manteuffel's advance to the Meuse was checked at Celles. Thereafter the concentration of 33 Allied divisions strongly supported by air power, against 29 German, gradually restored the situation. At its deepest the 'bulge' had penetrated 70 miles; by 16 Jan. almost all the ground taken by the Germans had been recaptured.

Picture right: the 'Battle of the Bulge' was dominated by tank manoeuvres. An abandoned US M-10 tank destroyer amid the ruins of Bastogne is inspected by a German armoured car patrol.

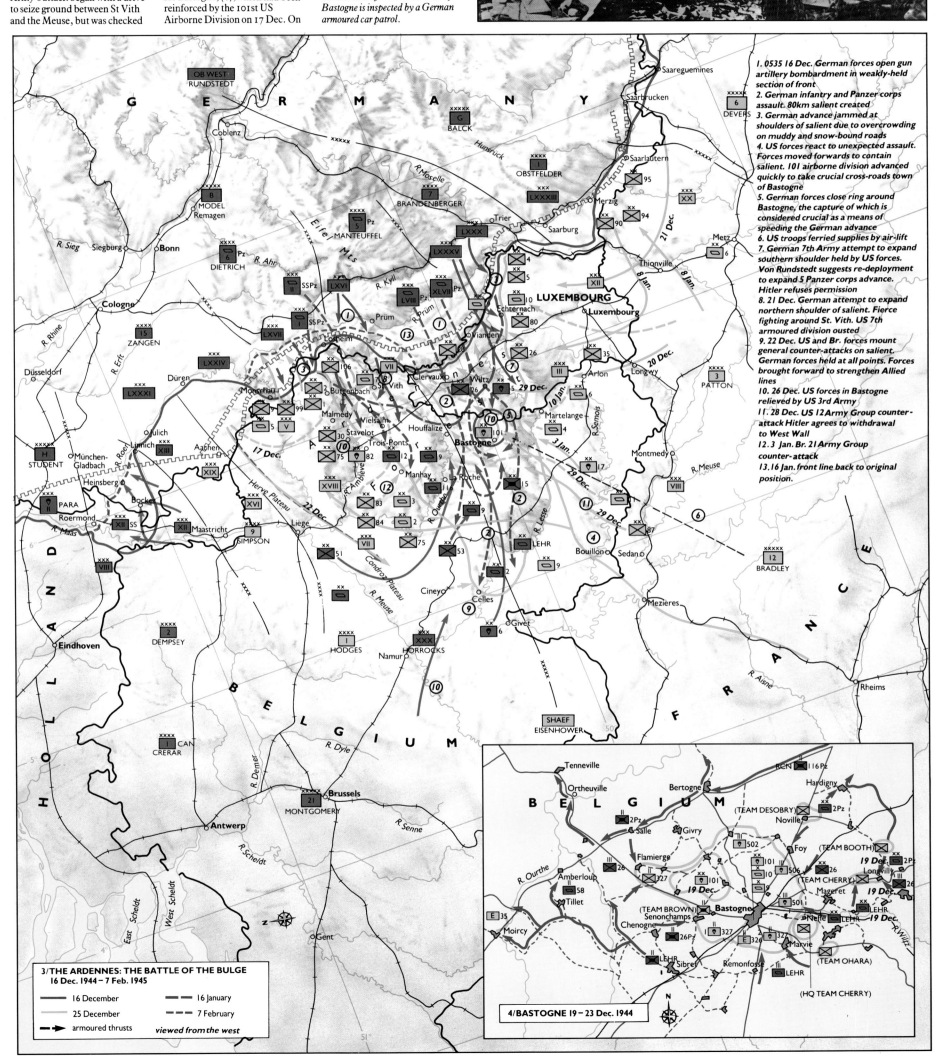

1. 0535 16 Dec. German forces open gun artillery bombardment in weakly-held section of front
2. German infantry and Panzer corps assault. 80km salient created
3. German advance jammed at shoulders of salient due to overcrowding on muddy and snow-bound roads
4. US forces react to unexpected assault. Forces moved forwards to contain salient. 101 airborne division advanced quickly to take crucial cross-roads town of Bastogne
5. German forces close ring around Bastogne, the capture of which is considered crucial as a means of speeding the German advance
6. US troops ferried supplies by air-lift
7. German 7th Army attempt to expand southern shoulder held by US forces. Von Rundstedt suggests re-deployment to expand 5 Panzer corps advance. Hitler refuses permission
8. 21 Dec. German attempt to expand northern shoulder of salient. Fierce fighting around St. Vith. US 7th armoured division ousted
9. 22 Dec. US and Br. forces mount general counter-attacks on salient. German forces held at all points. Forces brought forward to strengthen Allied lines
10. 26 Dec. US forces in Bastogne relieved by US 3rd Army
11. 28 Dec. US 12 Army Group counter-attack Hitler agrees to withdrawal to West Wall
12. 3 Jan. Br. 21 Army Group counter-attack
13. 16 Jan. front line back to original position.

3/THE ARDENNES: THE BATTLE OF THE BULGE
16 Dec. 1944 – 7 Feb. 1945

— 16 December   – – 16 January
— 25 December   - - - 7 February
➤ armoured thrusts   *viewed from the west*

4/BASTOGNE 19 – 23 Dec. 1944

Burma 1942~1945

THE AMERICAN STRATEGIC intention to develop China as an active theatre of military and air operations necessarily involved a campaign to recover Burma because only by re-establishing overland communications with Chiang Kai-shek's regime at Chungking through Burma could China and KMT armies be made ready for offensive operations. The relevance of this intention, and the difficulties presented in attempting an overland reconquest of either Upper Burma or the whole of Burma from northeast India gave rise to a never-ending series of Anglo-American disputes between 1942 and 1944.

At the heart of these disputes was the difficulty of moving forces through the roadless mountains and jungles that divided India and Burma against an enemy that could operate on good, secure lines of communications in the Sittang, Irrawaddy and Chindwin valleys to ensure superiority at the point of contact, Chinese forces in Yunnan being unable to play an effective containing role on the Salween River without first being supplied and equipped by the road that was supposed to be opened by the Allies. The first Allied attempt to undertake even a limited offensive, in the Arakan in the 1942-43 dry season, resulted in the comprehensive defeat of the 14th Indian Division. However, a three-week foray behind Japanese lines by air-supplied columns – the first Chindit operation – proved more significant. In 1942 the Japanese Army had dismissed the suggestion of an overland offensive into northeast India as impractical, but this raid, though it achieved little apart from the temporary disruption of Japanese lines of communication, provoked the Burma Area Army into demanding (and Tokyo into accepting) the need for a pre-emptive offensive. This would secure Imphal and Kohima at the end of the 1943-44 dry season, the calculation being that the onset of the monsoon would preclude any effective Allied counter-attacks.

This Japanese effort began in February 1944 with a diversionary attack in the Arakan that drew into the battle six British divisions, plus transport aircraft from as far afield as the Mediterranean theatre. The offensive began after the American-controlled Northern Combat Area Command, with two Chinese armies raised and maintained from US sources, began an advance in October 1943 with an advance in the Hukawng Valley that was to result in the taking of Myitkyina airfield in May 1944. There Sino-Chinese forces were to link up with forces that remained in Upper Burma from the second Chindit operation that had begun in March, the combined Allied effort resulting in the capture of Myitkyina itself in August. By then, however, the Japanese offensive into northeast India had encountered disaster. Forewarned of Japanese intentions, British forces in front of Imphal were able to avoid encirclement in the first phase of the Japanese offensive and to then establish themselves on the Imphal plain. Here their superiority of numbers and firepower, plus support and supply from the air, resulted in the siege being broken. The Japanese formations, lacking secure lateral lines of communication, could not secure superiority at any single point of the attack. Around Kohima the same first Japanese onrush was checked; the Japanese refusal to admit failure at either Imphal or Kohima, and to withdraw into Burma, resulted in the 15th Army being effectively destroyed in a series of protracted battles, Imphal being relieved by overland advance from Kohima on 22 June. What amounted to the destruction of Japanese power during 1944 in northeast India exposed Burma itself to invasion and conquest from the north in 1945. Whilst Chinese forces attended to the clearing of the northeast, the main Allied effort was undertaken by the British against Japanese forces concentrated in defence of Mandalay. Supported by a series of amphibious landings in the Arakan that secured airfields from which to support an assault on Rangoon, the main British effort was developed through Kalewa and Nyaungu against Meiktila, which was taken on 4 March. Forced to respond because of the threat to its lines of communication, the Burma Area Army committed itself to a major counter-attack that retook Meiktila airfield, but it could neither recover the town nor continue to hold Mandalay; by the end of March Burma Area Army had accepted defeat at both cities. Thereafter the British were to continue their overland advances into Lower Burma securing Rangoon by amphibious assault in May. The war ended with the Japanese attempting to re-form their still numerous forces in Burma in defence of Tenasserim and Siam.

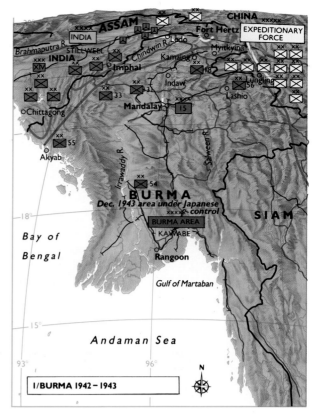

1/BURMA 1942–1943

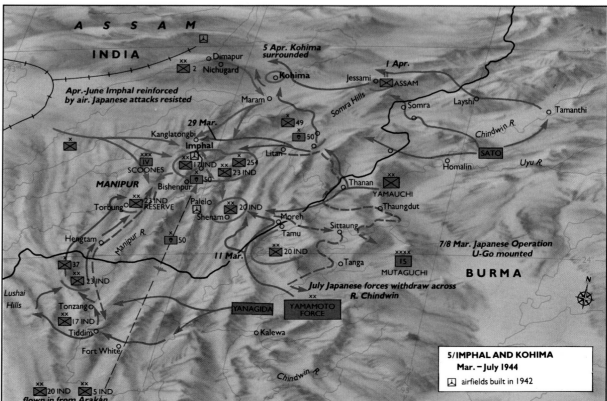

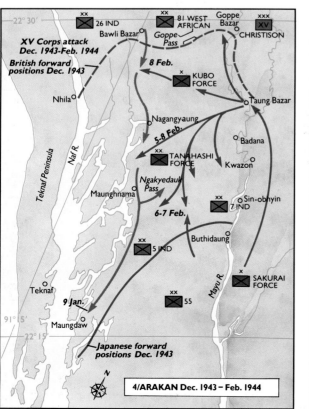

4/ARAKAN Dec. 1943 – Feb. 1944

5/IMPHAL AND KOHIMA
Mar. – July 1944
airfields built in 1942

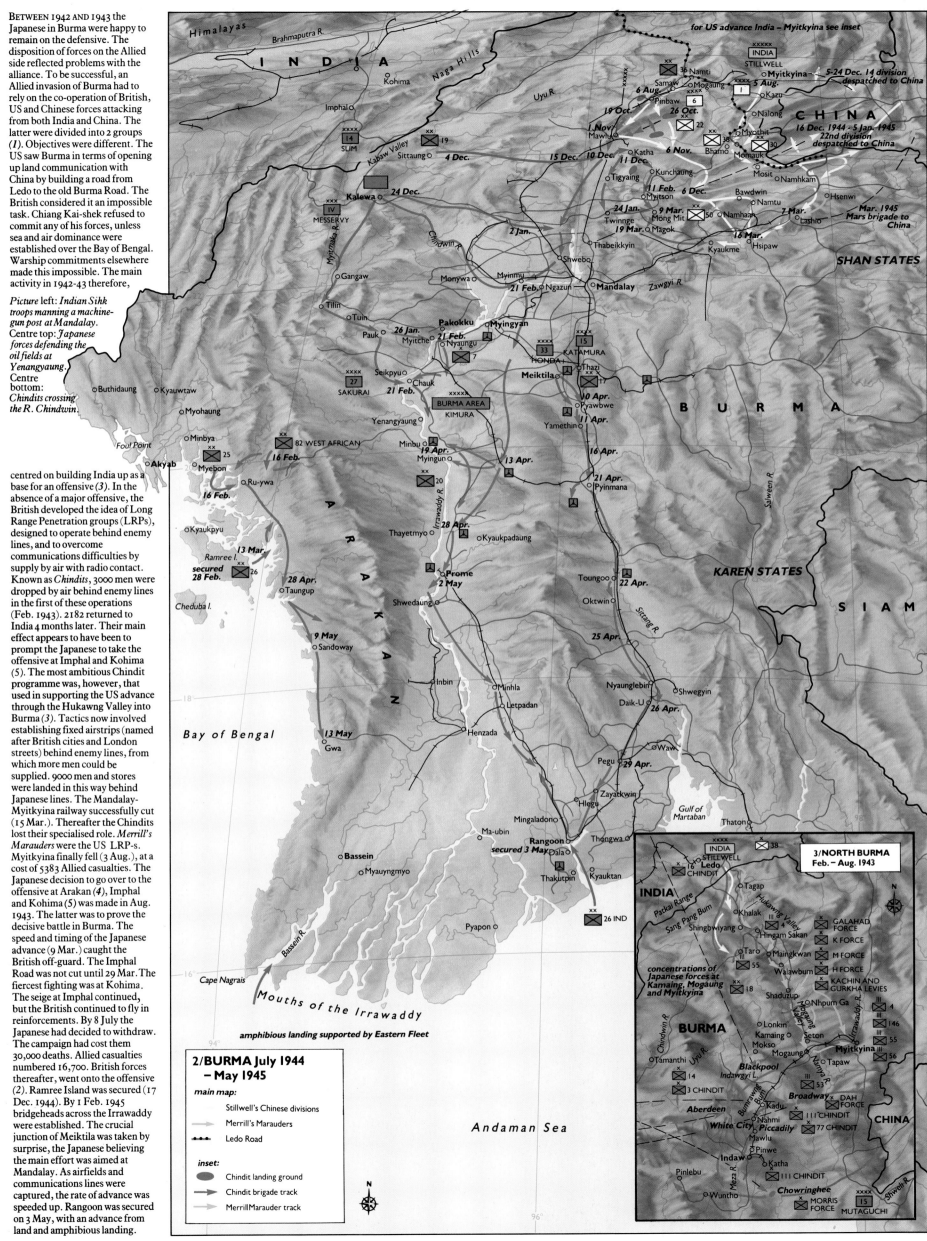

BETWEEN 1942 AND 1943 the Japanese in Burma were happy to remain on the defensive. The disposition of forces on the Allied side reflected problems with the alliance. To be successful, an Allied invasion of Burma had to rely on the co-operation of British, US and Chinese forces attacking from both India and China. The latter were divided into 2 groups (*1*). Objectives were different. The US saw Burma in terms of opening up land communication with China by building a road from Ledo to the old Burma Road. The British considered it an impossible task. Chiang Kai-shek refused to commit any of his forces, unless sea and air dominance were established over the Bay of Bengal. Warship commitments elsewhere made this impossible. The main activity in 1942–43 therefore,

Picture left: Indian Sikh troops manning a machine-gun post at Mandalay. Centre top: Japanese forces defending the oil fields at Yenangyaung. Centre bottom: Chindits crossing the R. Chindwin.

centred on building India up as a base for an offensive (*3*). In the absence of a major offensive, the British developed the idea of Long Range Penetration groups (LRPs), designed to operate behind enemy lines, and to overcome communications difficulties by supply by air with radio contact. Known as *Chindits*, 3000 men were dropped by air behind enemy lines in the first of these operations (Feb. 1943). 2182 returned to India 4 months later. Their main effect appears to have been to prompt the Japanese to take the offensive at Imphal and Kohima (*5*). The most ambitious Chindit programme was, however, that used in supporting the US advance through the Hukawng Valley into Burma (*3*). Tactics now involved establishing fixed airstrips (named after British cities and London streets) behind enemy lines, from which more men could be supplied. 9000 men and stores were landed in this way behind Japanese lines. The Mandalay-Myitkyina railway successfully cut (15 Mar.). Thereafter the Chindits lost their specialised role. *Merrill's Marauders* were the US LRP-s. Myitkyina finally fell (3 Aug.), at a cost of 5383 Allied casualties. The Japanese decision to go over to the offensive at Arakan (*4*), Imphal and Kohima (*5*) was made in Aug. 1943. The latter was to prove the decisive battle in Burma. The speed and timing of the Japanese advance (9 Mar.) caught the British off-guard. The Imphal Road was not cut until 29 Mar. The fiercest fighting was at Kohima. The seige at Imphal continued, but the British continued to fly in reinforcements. By 8 July the Japanese had decided to withdraw. The campaign had cost them 30,000 deaths. Allied casualties numbered 16,700. British forces thereafter, went onto the offensive (*2*). Ramree Island was secured (17 Dec. 1944). By 1 Feb. 1945 bridgeheads across the Irrawaddy were established. The crucial junction of Meiktila was taken by surprise, the Japanese believing the main effort was aimed at Mandalay. As airfields and communications lines were captured, the rate of advance was speeded up. Rangoon was secured on 3 May, with an advance from land and amphibious landing.

2/BURMA July 1944 – May 1945

main map:

Stillwell's Chinese divisions
Merrill's Marauders
Ledo Road

inset:

Chindit landing ground
Chindit brigade track
Merrill Marauder track

3/NORTH BURMA Feb. – Aug. 1943

Leyte Gulf 22 ~ 27 OCTOBER 1944

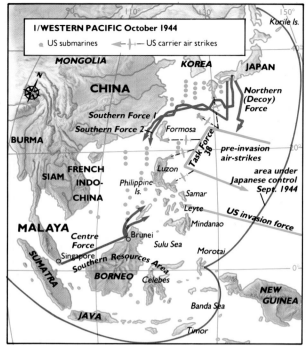

THE JAPANESE DEFEAT off the Marianas in June 1944 (page 142) opened the whole of the western Pacific to an American advance. Whilst American planners debated whether to take or by-pass Luzon in favour of Formosa, the Japanese were facing starker choices. Without an effective carrier force to take the initiative they had to respond to landings which could be made anywhere between Okinawa and Mindanao. American superiority and the threat to the links between the Home Islands and the Southern Resources Area demanded this. Once again the Japanese prepared to fight the 'decisive battle', committing all their effective sea and air power to what was to become the largest naval action ever fought: the Battle of Leyte Gulf.

American carrier raids over the Philippines in September, however, confounded early Japanese planning. Japanese air power was ravaged, and the US took advantage of Japanese weakness to accelerate their timetable to land on the Philippines in October. Further US strikes, using four naval task groups with seventeen carriers and nearly 1100 aircraft left the Japanese with only 200 aircraft on the Philippines. In addition a shortage of fuel oil on the Home Islands forced the Japanese to disperse their naval forces. The need to concentrate naval forces off Brunei in preparation for battle meant a longer reaction time to any US landing.

The final Japanese plan, finalized in the days before the largest convoy in the Pacific war brought the American landings on the Philippines, took account of these operational difficulties. Japanese naval forces were split into three formations: Centre Force, Southern Force (sections 1 and 2) and Northern Force. Ozawa's Northern Force, which included four carriers with just 116 aircraft (depleted to 29 by the 24th), was to act as a decoy to draw the bulk of the US Third Fleet, supporting the landings, away from the landing beaches,

THE AMERICAN CAMPAIGN to recapture the Philippines was prefaced by US Task Force 38 carrier raids on Formosa and Luzon, and intense submarine activity (1). The landings began on 17 Oct. when a Ranger battalion secured the islands of Suluan and Dinagat (2). On 20 Oct. two US corps landed either side of Tanauan on Leyte and thereby opened a campaign that was to continue until May 1945 (page 167). Japanese Southern Army had decided that an American landing would be opposed wherever it took place, and within a matter of hours of these initial landings Japanese naval forces were steaming to rendezvous off Brunei. It was not until 22 Oct., however, that the main forces were to sail for the Philippines. Kurita's Centre Force – with 5 battleships, 10 heavy and 2 light cruisers and 15 destroyers – immediately encountered trouble as it negotiated the difficult Palawan Passage. 2 US submarines sank 2 heavy cruisers and severely damaged a third on the morning of 23 Oct. Despite the setbacks Centre Force entered the Sibuyan Sea on 24 Oct. only to find that whatever air power remained to the Japanese had been committed to attacks on TF38 rather than to providing air cover for its passage. Sustained American carrier attacks sank the battleship *Musashi* and 1 destroyer and damaged 5 other warships of the Centre Force before, at 1500, Kurita reversed course to the west. The Japanese had one notable success on the 24 Oct. when a lone *Judy* bomber sank the light cruiser *Princeton* east of Luzon. On the same day Southern Force 1 – with 2 battleships, 1 heavy cruiser and 4 destroyers – experienced only intermittent attacks as it crossed the Sulu Sea and entered the Mindanao Sea. As it did so, however, the various US support groups off Leyte were organized into successive MTB, destroyer, cruiser and battle forces within and across the Surigao Strait (3). The first clash took place about 2200 but a running fight developed after 0015 on 25 Oct. as the Japanese entered the Strait: by 0319 all but the cruiser *Mogami* and 1 destroyer had been overwhelmed by torpedoes and gunfire. A second Japanese force – with 1 light and 2 heavy cruisers and 7 destroyers – some 40 miles astern, suspected what awaited it and declined to

enter the Strait. As it withdrew, however, one of its number collided with the *Mogami*: the latter, slowed, was to be caught after daybreak by US aircraft and pounded into a wreck (page 96). By dawn on 25 Oct. the Americans, despite the loss of the *Princeton*, had clearly had the better of the exchanges. At 1640 on the previous day, however, a scout plane from TG38.3 located Ozawa's decoy carrier force (2). The US and Japanese carrier forces were now some 140 miles apart, and TF38 was immediately ordered to turn north in order to engage next morning. In so doing TF38 took with it its battleships and made no provision for the guarding of the San Bernardino Strait. It was through this Strait that Centre Force passed soon after midnight on 25 Oct. Coming around Samar, at 0549, the Japanese sighted the first of 3 escort carrier groups standing off the Leyte beachheads, and by 0612 battle was joined with the other two US groups (4). Overall the 3 US groups had some 500 aircraft and these subjected Centre Force to successive waves of attacks until 1136, when the Japanese broke off the battle and retired northwards. To the north (2) battle was joined, off Cape Engaño, between the fast carrier formations of Halsey's Third Fleet and Ozawa's Northern (decoy) Force soon after 0735 on the morning of 25 Oct., the Americans launching 6 attacks during the course of the day which sank 3 carriers and a destroyer. During the initial strikes, however, TF38 received word of developments off Samar, and in response to desperate appeals for support it ordered two TGs to make for Samar and the battle force to turn to the south and close the San Bernardino Strait. Carrier planes from TG38.1 and TG38.2 joined US bombers in attacking retreating Centre Force, which made it back to Brunei with the loss of 1 destroyer. The various naval and air actions known as the Battle of Leyte Gulf effectively extinguished the ability of the Japanese to fight a major naval action. In the face of American superiority they came to rely more on unorthodox methods – kamikaze attacks, first used successfully in the action off Samar Island (4).

Picture above right: US anti-aircraft fire in Leyte Gulf.

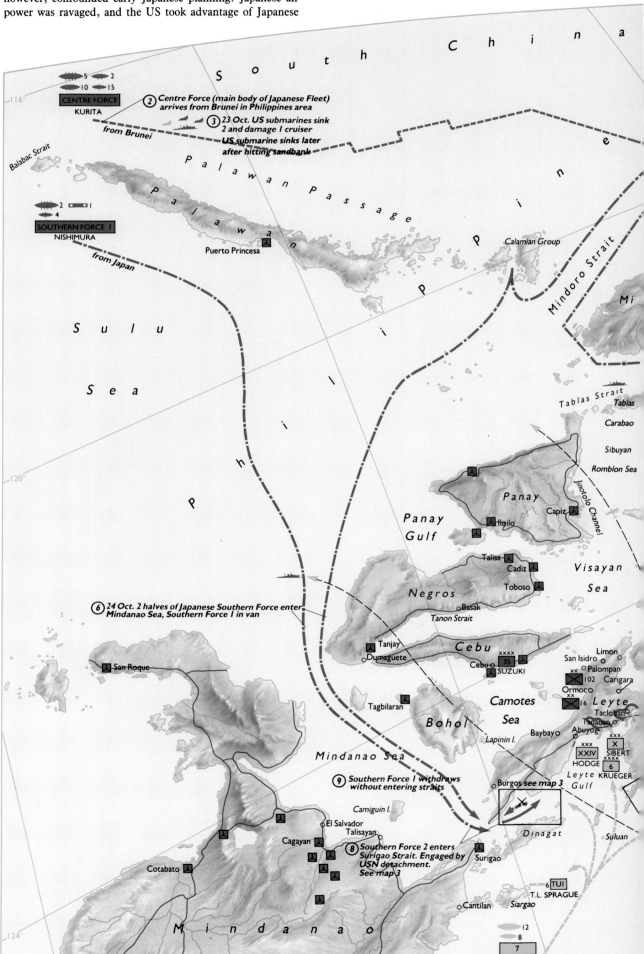

allowing Centre and Southern Forces to advance in a pincer movement north and south of Leyte, and there to destroy the landing forces.

On the 23rd the naval battle was joined. Centre Force lost two cruisers to US submarines in the Palawan passage. As Centre Force advance into the Sibuyan Sea US air strikes sunk a further cruiser. The two sections of Southern Force, however, advanced successfully into the Mindanao Sea. A tightly organized US action with MTBs, destroyers and the last broadside in naval history blocked the passage of this force in the Surigao Strait. On the 25th, Ozawa's Northern Force was finally spotted by a US scout plane. Reading the presence of carriers as the greatest threat to the landings, US Third Fleet commander, Halsey, ordered the bulk of his forces to rendezvous off Catanduanes and to steam north, away from the landing beaches, in pursuit. The Japanese decoy had worked. Kurita's Centre Force was able to pass through the San Bernardino Strait unopposed, to sweep down on the US landing beaches, defended only by three Task Forces of escort carriers. A fierce action ensued, the Americans relying on their air power, the Japanese on fire-power, and towards the end of the action *kamikazes*. Unaccountably the Japanese commander decided to call off the action just as he had the upper hand. The Americans were given crucial time to re-group and the Japanese were forced to withdraw.

Overall, between 23-27 October, when the battle finally died, the Americans sank 4 carriers, 3 battleships, 6 heavy and 4 light cruisers and 11 destroyers from the 64 Japanese warships committed to the battle. Over 10,500 Japanese sailors and airmen were killed. The Americans lost the light cruiser *Princeton*, 2 escort carriers, 2 destroyers and a destroyer escort from a total force of 218 vessels. Leyte Gulf had confirmed the Americans' superiority at sea, and extinguished the ability of the Japanese to fight a major naval action.

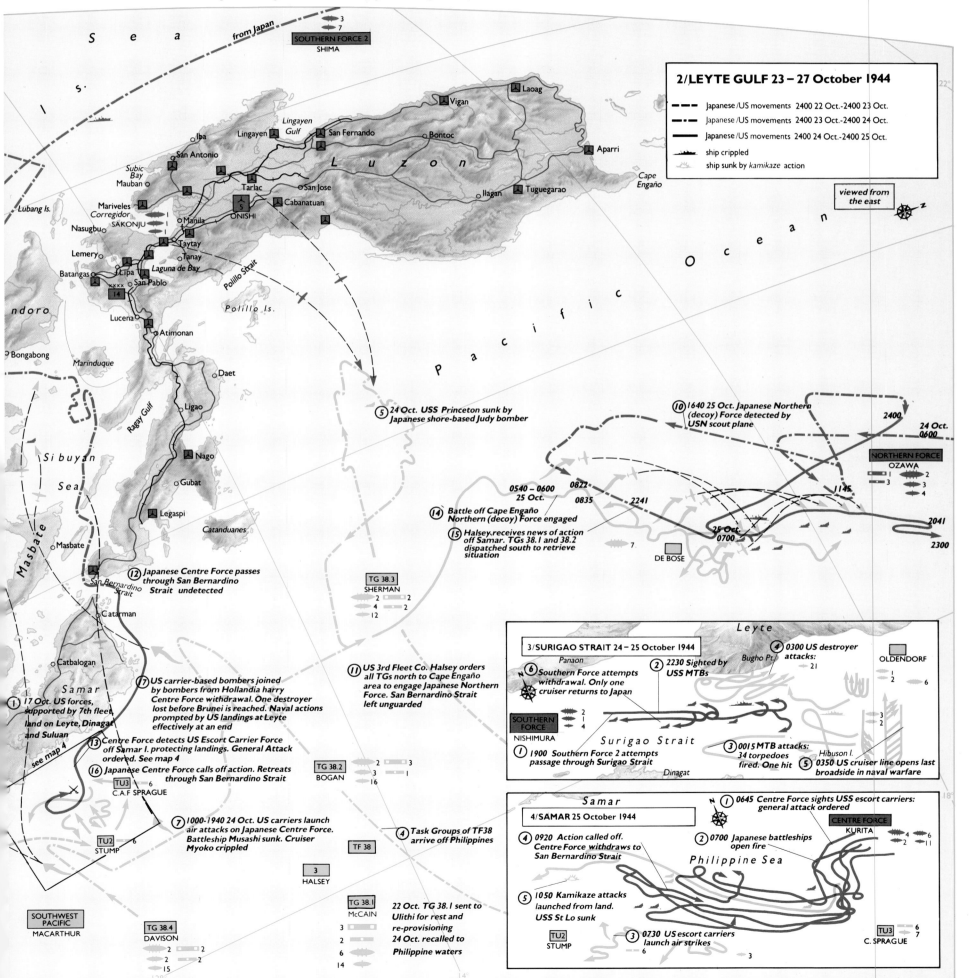

2/LEYTE GULF 23 – 27 October 1944

- – – – Japanese /US movements 2400 22 Oct.–2400 23 Oct.
- – · – Japanese /US movements 2400 23 Oct.–2400 24 Oct.
- ——— Japanese /US movements 2400 24 Oct.–2400 25 Oct.
- ship crippled
- ship sunk by *kamikaze* action

viewed from the east

⑤ 24 Oct. USS *Princeton* sunk by Japanese shore-based Judy bomber

⑩ 1640 25 Oct. Japanese Northern (decoy) Force detected by USN scout plane

⑭ Battle off Cape Engaño Northern (decoy) Force engaged

⑮ Halsey receives news of action off Samar. TGs 38.1 and 38.2 dispatched south to retrieve situation

NORTHERN FORCE
OZAWA

⑫ Japanese Centre Force passes through San Bernardino Strait undetected

TG 38.3
SHERMAN

⑪ US 3rd Fleet Co. Halsey orders all TGs north to Cape Engaño area to engage Japanese Northern Force. San Bernardino Strait left unguarded

⑦ US carrier-based bombers joined by bombers from Hollandia harry Centre Force withdrawal. One destroyer lost before Brunei is reached. Naval actions prompted by US landings at Leyte effectively at an end

① 17 Oct. US forces, supported by 7th fleet land on Leyte, Dinagat and Suluan
see map 4

⑬ Centre Force detects US Escort Carrier Force off Samar I. protecting landings. General Attack ordered. See map 4

⑯ Japanese Centre Force calls off action. Retreats through San Bernardino Strait

TU3
C.A.F SPRAGUE

⑦ 1000-1940 24 Oct. US carriers launch air attacks on Japanese Centre Force. Battleship Musashi sunk. Cruiser Myoko crippled

TG 38.2
BOGAN

TU2
STUMP

④ Task Groups of TF38 arrive off Philippines

TF 38

3
HALSEY

SOUTHWEST PACIFIC
MACARTHUR

TG 38.4
DAVISON

TG 38.1
McCAIN

22 Oct. TG 38.1 sent to Ulithi for rest and re-provisioning
24 Oct. recalled to Philippine waters

3/SURIGAO STRAIT 24 – 25 October 1944

Panaon

④ 0300 US destroyer attacks:

② 2230 Sighted by USS MTBs

⑥ Southern Force attempts withdrawal. Only one cruiser returns to Japan

SOUTHERN FORCE
NISHIMURA

① 1900 Southern Force 2 attempts passage through Surigao Strait

③ 0015 MTB attacks: 34 torpedoes fired. One hit

⑤ 0350 US cruiser line opens last broadside in naval warfare

Leyte
Bugho Pt.
OLDENDORF
Surigao Strait
Hibuson I.
Dinagat

4/SAMAR 25 October 1944

Samar

① 0645 Centre Force sights USS escort carriers: general attack ordered

② 0700 Japanese battleships open fire

④ 0920 Action called off. Centre Force withdraws to San Bernardino Strait

⑤ 1050 Kamikaze attacks launched from land. USS St Lo sunk

③ 0730 US escort carriers launch air strikes

CENTRE FORCE
KURITA

Philippine Sea

TU2
STUMP

TU3
C. SPRAGUE

SOUTHERN FORCE 2
SHIMA

from Japan

S e a

Vigan
Laoag
Lingayen Gulf
Iba
Lingayen
San Fernando
Bontoc
Aparri
L u z o n
San Antonio
Subic Bay
Mauban
Tarlac
San Jose
Ilagan
Tuguegarao
Cape Engaño
Mariveles
Corregidor
SAKONJU
Manila
ONISHI
Cabanatuan
Nasugbu
Lemery
Taytay
Tanay
Lipa
Laguna de Bay
Batangas
San Pablo
Lucena
Atimonan
Polillo Strait
Polillo Is.
Marinduque
Daet
Bongabong
ndoro
Ligao
Nago
Siubuyan Sea
Gubat
Legaspi
Catanduanes
Masbate
Masbate
Ragay Gulf
Lubang Is.
DE BOSE
P a c i f i c O c e a n
San Bernardino Strait
Catarman
Catbalogan
Samar
Philippine Sea

24 Oct. 0600
2400
25 Oct. 0700
2041
2300
0540 – 0600 25 Oct.
0822
0835
2241
1145

The Philippines 1944~1945

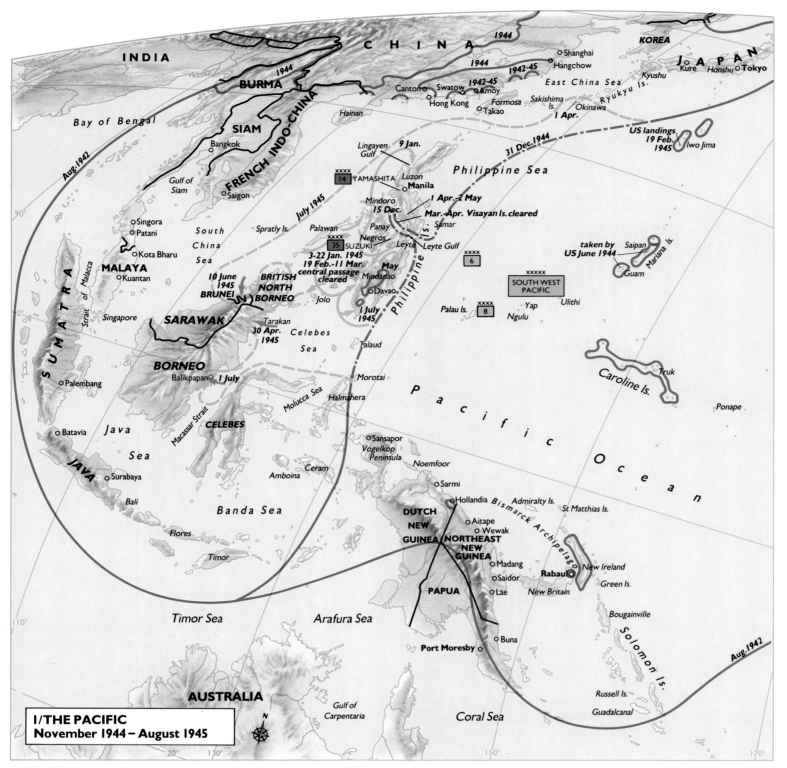

THE ELIMINATION of effective Japanese naval and air power at Leyte Gulf (page 164) left the Americans with the means to separate the Japanese from their southern resources area. The landings and campaign on Leyte (2) secured useful US air and naval bases from which to clear the Visayan Islands in the Philippines (1). In spite of their impossible strategic position, Japanese forces on each island fought to the last man, and stepped up the use of *kamikaze* attacks on American landing forces. The possibility of by-passing Luzon in favour of a campaign against Formosa was abandoned for political, as much as military, reasons. The battle for Luzon (3, 4) was to become the most protracted campaign of the Pacific war. Huge logistical difficulties were overcome to land US forces successfully at Lingayen Gulf, and by 31 Jan. all the major airfields were in US hands. The Japanese adopted a policy of a static defence, and the use of isolated jungle troops. Whilst most of the island was cleared at huge cost, the latter half of the campaign was left to Filipino guerrilla forces (4) marking an acceptance that Japanese troops would continue to occupy pockets of the island until the end of the war. The campaign in Borneo (5) was carried out by Australian forces and was essentially a mopping-up operation with the oilfields at Brunei, Tarakan and Balikpapan as its main objective. The oil, whilst it would prove useful to the US Pacific fleet, had at this point no strategic value to the Japanese who no longer had the means to transport it to the Home Islands. Little effort was made to clear the island of Japanese forces; instead the areas captured were secured. All these campaigns saw American and Australian chiefs of staff concentrating on political and prestige considerations, whilst the war to defeat Japan was carried on to Iwo Jima and Okinawa (page 168).

Picture above right: US 105mm howitzers in Manila, Feb. 1945. Below right: American troops and supplies following the Allied landings on the Lingayen Gulf, Luzon, Jan. 1945.

THE OUTCOME OF THE WAR in the Philippines was determined from the beginning of the campaign by the American advantages of surprise, concentration and position. The overwhelming American victory at Leyte Gulf in October (page 164) served to compound these American advantages in a campaign that thereafter conformed, in basic outline, to those campaigns that had been and remained to be fought in the Pacific; the American ability to isolate Japanese garrisons from outside support ensured their ultimate defeat. The Philippines campaign nevertheless proved protracted and, in different ways, costly to both sides.

Defeat at sea in no way lessened the Japanese determination to dispute the ownership of Leyte, and in seeking to reinforce its single division on the island, the 35th Army enjoyed some measure of protection against air attack because of the seasonal rains, the enforced withdrawal of TF38 after the Leyte Gulf battle and *kamikaze* success. Between 24 October and 12 December some 45,000 troops drawn from five divisions were transferred to Leyte from other islands in the Philippines, but in the process the Japanese inevitably weakened their grip on the central and southern Philippines. Further more, they could not match the American build-up on Leyte. The Japanese sustained growing losses as the scale, intensity and effectiveness of American air operations increased. By December 1944 the Americans had some 200,000 combat troops on Leyte, but it was not until the middle of the month that Japanese resistance was broken in the northwest of the island following landings in Ormoc Bay and at Palompon. On 19 December, the Japanese

abandoned the struggle for Leyte, though resistance on the island continued into May 1945.

What had brought the Americans to the Philippines, however, was the desire to liberate the islands from Japanese rule and the need to secure air and fleet facilities in the island. Control of Leyte provided the Americans with access to San Pedro Bay (first used by US fleet carriers in April) but continued Japanese control of air bases on other islands precluded its being rendered secure. Luzon alone offered the facilities sufficient to meet American requirements. Accordingly, on 15 December, American forces, having passed through the Mindanao Sea, landed on southwest Mindoro, and by the end of the year had two airfields around San Jose in service even though the island itself was not secured for another month. Then, with Task Force 38 pounding various targets between Luzon and Okinawa from 3 January, two corps of the US 6th Army were put ashore in Lingayen Gulf on the 9th and moved rapidly inland – as had the Japanese before them in 1941 – across the central plain towards Manila. Clark Field and Calumpit were both secured on 31 January, the day that landings were made at Nasugbu. These achievements were made possible because the Japanese intention was not to offer serious resistance in front of the capital, but instead to concentrate forces in the mountains in an attempt to draw as many American formations as possible into a protracted struggle. The three Japanese commands on Luzon were thus ordered to withdraw into the mountains, the Zambales and the Sierra Madre, and behind Baguio; meanwhile, naval forces in

Manila denied the Americans control of the capital until 3 March – despite the 6th Army having entered the city on 4 February and completed its encirclement by the 12th. With Corregidor secured on 28 February, however, the clearing of Manila – at the cost of an estimated 100,000 Filipino casualties – provided the Americans with effective control of everything of political and military value on Luzon.

The Japanese had in effect abandoned Luzon on 13 January when the despatch of further air reinforcements to the Philippines was halted. By that time the airfields remaining in Japanese hands had been rendered unviable and Japanese resources had to be preserved for the defence of the Home Islands. American naval losses, which in the month before this decision had totalled 79 warships, merchantmen and amphibious vessels sunk or damaged by *kamikaze* attack, now all but ceased. The Americans set about clearing the central and southern Philippines in order to free shipping routes through the islands. On 19 February, American forces landed on Samar and on 28 February at Puerto Princesa on Palawan. In the following seven weeks, a further 38 landings were conducted throughout the central and southern Philippines. In spite of the fact that they had some 110,000 troops spread across these islands, the Japanese could offer sustained resistance only on Negros and Mindanao; even on Luzon in mid-1945 the presence of 115,000 Japanese troops in the field failed to prevent a steady decline in the Imperial Army's ability to sustain its defensive campaign. This was tacitly recognized by the Americans in June when the 6th Army was withdrawn from

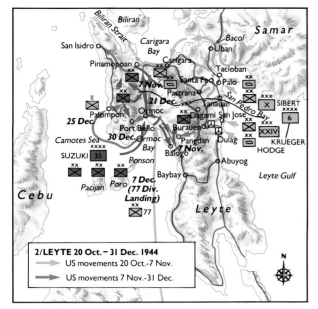

2/LEYTE 20 Oct.–31 Dec. 1944
→ US movements 20 Oct.-7 Nov.
→ US movements 7 Nov.-31 Dec.

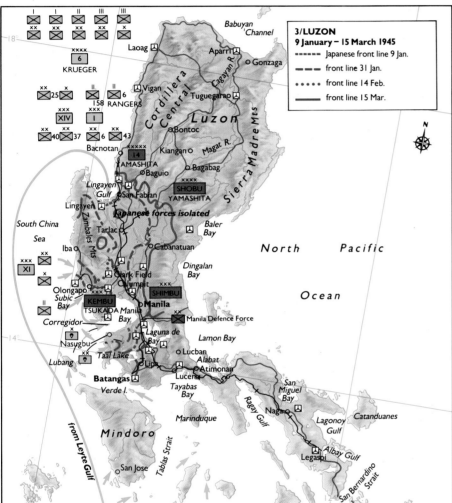

3/LUZON 9 January – 15 March 1945
Japanese front line 9 Jan.
front line 31 Jan.
front line 14 Feb.
front line 15 Mar.

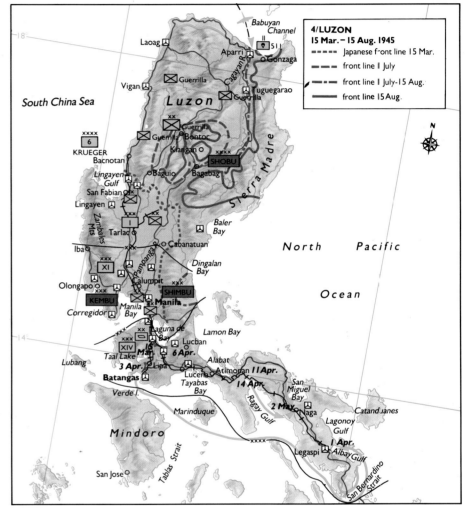

4/LUZON 15 Mar. – 15 Aug. 1945
Japanese front line 15 Mar.
front line 1 July
front line 1 July–15 Aug.
front line 15 Aug.

operations. At the end of the war, four US divisions remained committed to operations in the Philippines, though responsibility for mopping-up Japanese resistance was being passed to Filipino formations, with Australian troops being designated the messy task of clearing and securing the now isolated Japanese garrisons in Borneo and the East Indies. With 16 US divisions having been committed to the Philippines, the securing and partial clearing of the islands cost the US Army nearly 146,000 casualties.

In a broader context, American control of key points in the Philippines by Spring 1945 (Leyte, Manila), provided essential bases from which the approach to the Japanese Home Islands could be made. With the launching of Allied campaigns against Iwo Jima and Okinawa (page 168), the main focus of the war-winning effort shifted north.

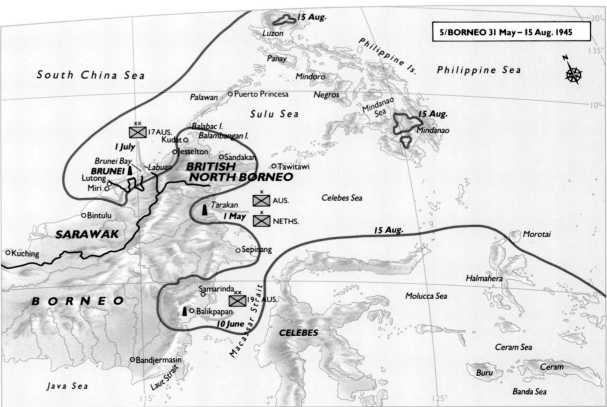

5/BORNEO 31 May – 15 Aug. 1945

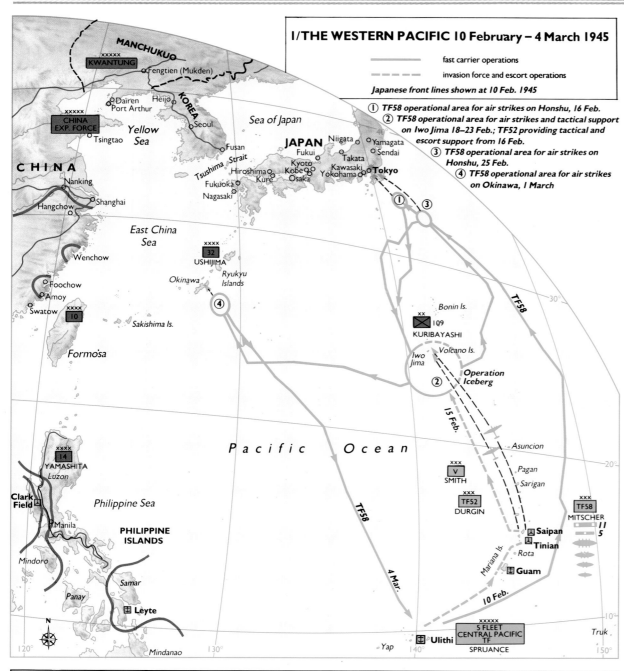

1/THE WESTERN PACIFIC 10 February – 4 March 1945

―― fast carrier operations

---- invasion force and escort operations

Japanese front lines shown at 10 Feb. 1945

① TF58 operational area for air strikes on Honshu, 16 Feb.

② TF58 operational area for air strikes and tactical support on Iwo Jima 18–23 Feb.; TF52 providing tactical and escort support from 16 Feb.

③ TF58 operational area for air strikes on Honshu, 25 Feb.

④ TF58 operational area for air strikes on Okinawa, 1 March

AMERICAN PLANNING FOR THE ADVANCE across the western Pacific (pages 140-142) had paid little attention to the islands of Okinawa and Iwo Jima until mid-1944, being mainly concerned with whether the Philippines were to be invaded or bypassed. When the US Navy's plans for in invasion of Formosa were finally set aside, however, Okinawa assumed a significance previously denied it: air power based on the Philippines would still be too distant to support an invasion of the Japanese Home Islands, but Okinawa could provide an important base for both tactical and strategic air operations over Japan. Iwo Jima, however, was different in that even before June 1944 its importance, in terms of the planned bombing offensive from the Marianas, was recognized. The capture of both islands was thus authorized by the US Joint Chiefs of Staff in October 1944.

The strategic significance of Okinawa and Iwo Jima was obvious to the Japanese long before the Americans fought their way into the southern Marianas (page 142) and the central Philippines (pages 164-166), but the defence of the islands presented the Japanese with considerable problems. Iwo Jima, the largest of the Volcano Islands, was too small to be defended in depth, and Okinawa was only one of several Japanese defensive problems in the southwest approaches to Kyushu. The Japanese recognized that neither island could be denied the Americans, and thus the aim of any defence would be not to meet any invasion on the beaches, but to mount protracted campaigns that might sap the American will to proceed with an invasion of the Japanese Home Islands; such a strategy would also force the Americans to commit heavy naval forces to the beachheads where they could be subjected to concentrated, and hopefully withering, air attack.

The scale of both operations was enormous, involving extensive preliminary carrier bombardments of the Home Islands, huge naval escort forces, and the transport of invasion troops across large distances: combined operations of greater complexity even than *Overlord* in Normandy (page 152). Delays in the campaign on Luzon (page 166) forced the American High Command to postpone the invasion of Iwo Jima until 19 February and of Okinawa until 1 April. This left the

ASTRIDE THE ROUTE of bombers operating against the Tokyo area from bases in the Marianas (*1*), Iwo Jima was assaulted on 19 Feb. (*2*). The Americans successfully landed six regiments on the first day of the assault. By 23 Feb. the Americans had secured the heavily fortified outcrop of Mt Suribachi, which overlooked the invasion beaches, fought their way onto Airfield No. 2 and almost reached the Japanese main line of defence. Thereafter V Amphibious Corps, with three divisions committed, overran remaining Japanese positions by 16 Mar., but whilst the island was declared secure on 26 Mar. some 2409 Japanese soldiers were killed or captured as resistance flickered on into June. Off Okinawa TF 58 found itself committed (*3*) to a protracted campaign in support of the 10th Army because the latter, after considerable initial success, found itself opposed by a Japanese force that displayed a keen appreciation of terrain, a highly-developed sense of self-preservation, and great skill in the conduct of a defence that employed a great diversity and weight of artillery. On 26 Mar. the 77th Infantry Division secured the Keramas and

the Keises (*4*), gaining positions from which southern Okinawa could be brought under fire. On 1 Apr. 4 divisions came ashore around Katena, and within 36 hours had thrust across the narrow waist of Okinawa to reach its eastern coast. The 6th Marine Division then set about securing northern Okinawa, encountering only scattered resistance except on the Motobu peninsula. By securing the latter, the Marines could bring fire down on Ie Shima, secured by the 77th Infantry Division between 16-21 Apr. With units of the 27th Infantry Division securing some of the eastern islands between 8-22 Apr., the main US strength advanced into southern Okinawa (*5*). Japanese resistance did not collapse until 17 June, though the 24th Infantry Division continued to offer organized resistance for a further 4 days. The Japanese Home Islands were now within striking distance.

Pictures above left: US amphibious forces streaming towards Iwo Jima; the natural redoubt of Mt. Suribachi is in the background. Above right: a Japanese A6M Zero kamikaze fighter about to strike the side of battleship USS Missouri.

2/IWO JIMA 19 Feb. – 26 Mar.

Kangoku Rock

Kitano Point

Pacific Ocean

final Japanese position 26 Mar.

16 Mar.

Hiraiwa Bay

Nishi

Kita

Hanare Rock

Orange 1

Kama Rock

Orange 2

1 Mar.

I w o

27 Feb.

airfield no.3 (under construction)

10 Mar.

White 1

24 Feb.

Hill 362

J i m a

White 2

Motoyami

Brown 1

XX 5 MARINES

XX 3 MARINES

airfield no.2

Hill 382

Brown 2

airfield no.1

Purple

quarry

XX 4 MARINES

Minami

Higashi

Tachiiwa Point

east boat basin

19 Feb.

Pacific Ocean

Mt. Suribachi over 200 gun emplacements and 21 blockhouses

Green 1

Red 1

Red 2

Yellow 1

Yellow 2

Blue 1

Blue 2

XX 4 MARINES

Futatsu Rock

XX 5 MARINES

XX 3 MARINES

Tobiishi Point

XXX V MARINES SCHMIDT

US Fast Carrier Force with time for only one raid on Honshu before the assault on Iwo Jima but allowed more time for the preliminary bombardment of the island. Iwo Jima was bombarded both from the sea and by B-24 and B-25 raids from the Marianas for 72 days before the landing, the longest bombardment afforded any island in the Pacific war; heavy US warships joined the effort on 16 February. The assault itself was accompanied by a creeping barrage provided by warships (the first of the Pacific war); but the effectiveness of air and naval bombardment was largely offset by a combination of the soft lava of Iwo Jima – which covered the island in dust – and the Japanese preparation of a dense network of tunnels and defensive positions. The soft lava and the steep shelving of the beaches produced chaos amongst assault shipping on 19 February; after swift initial success, US forces confronted bitter resistance which continued for some five weeks before the island was declared secure on 26 March. The campaign cost the Japanese 23,300 dead and 1000 prisoners; the Americans suffered 24,391 casualties, plus a fleet carrier badly damaged and an escort carrier sunk on 21 February. But the island was rapidly transformed into a base for the bombing campaign over Japan (page 196). By the end of the war, 2251 Superfortresses had made emergency landings on Iwo Jima – the first on 4 March – and fighters operated from the island from 11 March.

Three days later, on 14 March, TF 58 cleared Ulithi to begin operations in support of the landings on Okinawa; she remained at sea for 92 days, reflecting not simply the sheer length of the Okinawa campaign, but the intensity of operations over and off the island. Here support was also provided by a British carrier force. Again resilient Japanese defence led to a protracted and costly month-long campaign which involved both clearing the outlying islands and dislodging the main Japanese force on the island, which seemed committed to a last-ditch defence.

110,000 Japanese died defending Okinawa. The American losses totalled 20,195 dead and 55,162 wounded. For the first time in the war, however, Japanese surrendered in significant numbers – 7400. The Allies lost 38 naval vessels sunk and 368 damaged, but in the course of the struggle for Okinawa, and at the cost of 763 aircraft, Allied naval power destroyed the last remaining Japanese naval force (the *Yamato* left Japan at the head of a relief task force, but was sunk by US bombers) and 691 Japanese aircraft, including some 190 suicide aircraft.

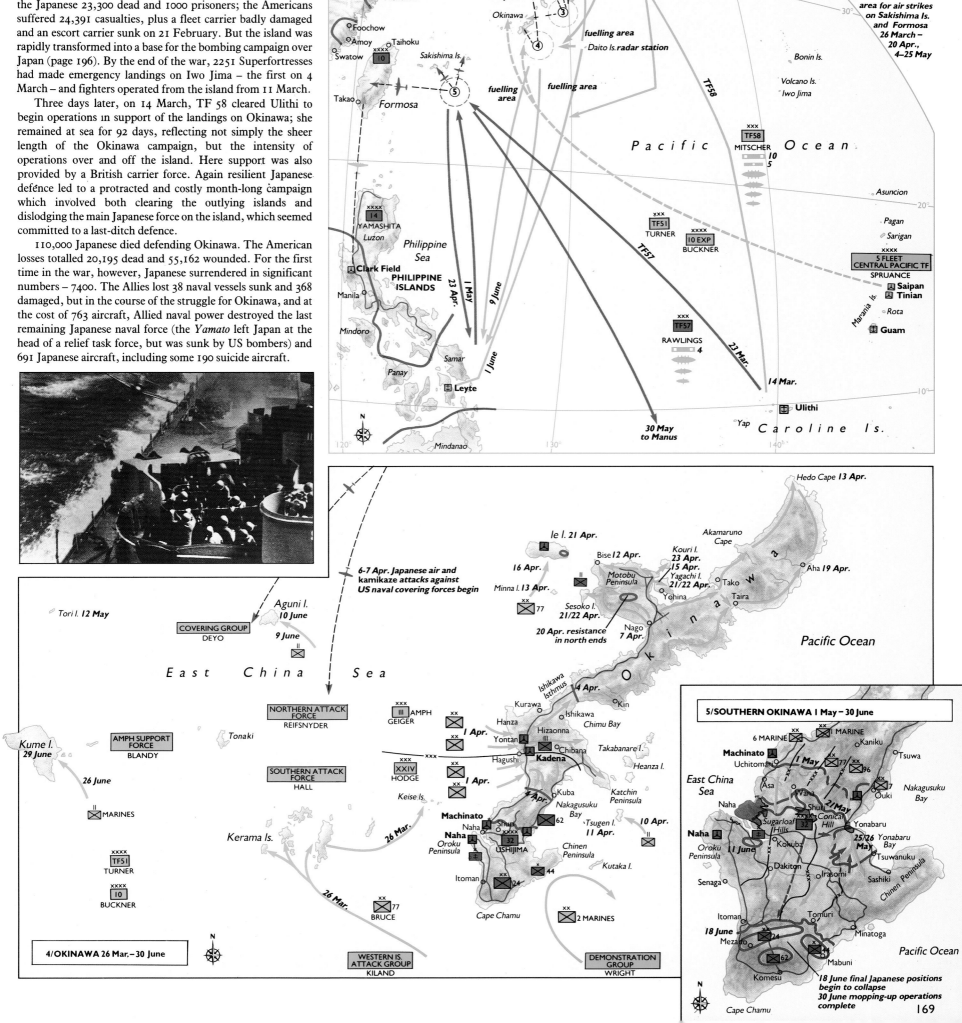

Resistance in Eastern Europe 1941 ~ 1945

WHEREAS HITLER'S 'NEW ORDER' in western Europe conceded a degree of fraternity and even independence to the conquered states, in the east, German rule was absolute and unbending. Nazi racial theories and ideology gave their administrators every justification to pursue ruthless policies of exploitation and repression in Poland, the Baltic states and the occupied areas of the Soviet Union. This attitude naturally led to only limited success in promoting collaboration with the civilian population, although nationalist elements (Byelorussians, Ukrainians) within former Soviet territory were encouraged and, with German manpower shortages becoming an increasingly serious problem, Red Army prisoners were accepted into the *Wehrmacht* (notably Vlasov's Russian Liberation Army).

The harshness of German policies towards the civilian population in the east contributed, in part, to the growth of resistance. For, when Slavs and Jews recognized their ultimate fate as proscribed 'subhumans', many felt that they had little to lose by resisting. In contrast to the occasionally indulgent German reaction to minor acts of resistance in western countries (page 94), in the occupied east there was little opportunity to register opposition with strikes and demonstrations. Anti-fascist demonstrations and industrial action were, however, more widespread in the now occupied Axis satellite countries of central and south-eastern Europe. Schools and

universities were suppressed and systematic attempts were made to eradicate Poland's intelligentsia and professional classes. Nevertheless, a flourishing illegal press was maintained in Warsaw and the other cities. Furthermore, the Polish underground was able to provide the Allies with important intelligence and offered assistance to escaped prisoners-of-war.

But resistance in the east was largely characterized by partisan warfare. The vastness of the area behind the German front lines and a terrain of marshes, forests and mountains lent themselves to guerrilla tactics. The partisan movement had largely stemmed from the presence in German occupied territory of whole Red Army units that had been cut off by the rapidity of the German advance in 1941 (page 58). Although they hardly constituted a serious military threat, they nevertheless offered a base upon which to build effective partisan operations. In much the same way as Britain sought to ease pressure on its conventional forces by promoting resistance on the continent, the Soviet Union was quick to exhort its civilian population to adopt guerrilla tactics against the invader. As early as July 1941 the Central Committee of the Communist Party called upon Soviet citizens to take up arms, and in May 1942 the Soviet High Command took steps to co-ordinate guerrilla activity by establishing a Central Staff of the Partisan Movement. Liaison officers, wireless equipment, weapons and supplies were provided in ever increasing numbers and partisan

operations were fully integrated into Red Army strategy. In addition to widespread attacks on German communications, partisans made specific efforts in support of Soviet offensives, notably in 1943 to assist operations at Kursk. Similarly, guerrilla forces were able to ease the progress of conventional forces by securing bridges and key installations in the path of their advance. Such a role was markedly more effective than partisan attempts to engage German forces in open combat or to liberate or defend territory. For, in spite of diminishing numbers and resources, German units tended to be better and more heavily equipped than the partisans. Popular uprisings were consequently usually short-lived and armed resistance was crushed by determined German counter-insurgency operations in Warsaw and Slovakia in 1944.

The efficacy of partisan operations has been questioned, not least because of exaggerated post-war claims made to promote their activities. Similarly, it should be acknowledged that the large areas held to be under partisan control were often conceded to them by the Germans rather than conquered by guerrilla forces. Nevertheless, these facts should not discount the very real contribution made by partisan forces in eroding German dominance in eastern Europe. Furthermore, Communist partisan groups were a reminder of Soviet intent to recapture the territory it had lost and to extend their influence into the other occupied countries of eastern Europe.

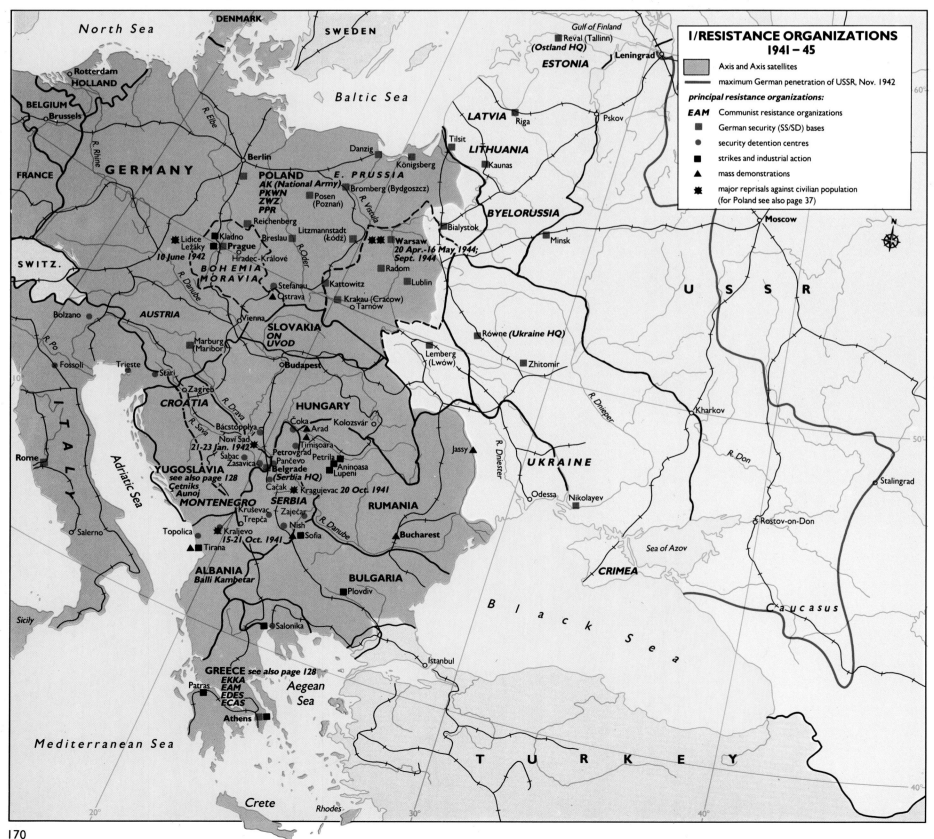

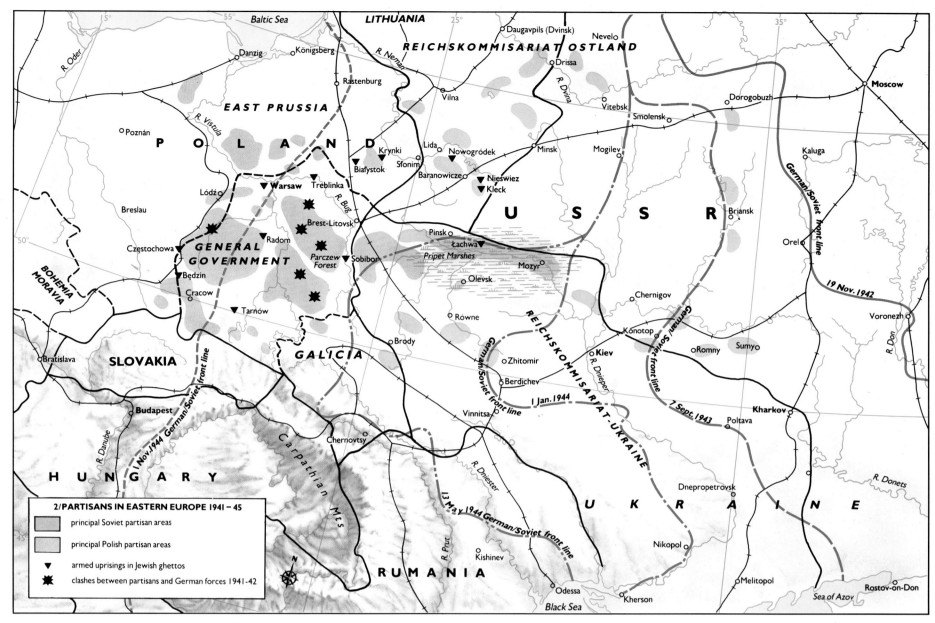

2/PARTISANS IN EASTERN EUROPE 1941–45

principal Soviet partisan areas

principal Polish partisan areas

▼ armed uprisings in Jewish ghettos

✷ clashes between partisans and German forces 1941-42

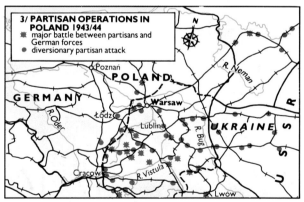

3/ PARTISAN OPERATIONS IN POLAND 1943/44

✷ major battle between partisans and German forces

● diversionary partisan attack

4/ KOVPAK'S RAID July-Aug. 1943

IT WAS IMPOSSIBLE for Germany completely to police all of its conquests in eastern Europe (1). The Germans relied upon the use of constant reprisals against civilian population and major offensives against guerrilla groups. These failed to curtail resistance activity and tied down large numbers of troops – estimates in Soviet territory alone show c. 0.5 million Germans dealing with c. 250,000 partisans (2). Even allowing for exaggeration, partisan activity was substantial, with vast tracts of German-occupied territory being virtually no-go areas, allowing the Soviets to co-ordinate partisan sabotage activities with conventional operations, as in Poland, 1943-44 (3). In response, the *Wehrmacht* and the security forces carried out extensive anti-partisan sweeps, the largest of which, Operation *Cottbus*, took place in Byelorussia in June 1943 and involved nearly 17,000 men who failed to trap their quarry. The Soviets also launched deep-penetration operations. In Summer 1943 S A Kovpak carried out an extended raid into north-west Ukraine but, overreaching himself, his 3000 strong force suffered heavy casualties (4).

Kovpak was able to call upon the assistance of the Red Army to help reorganize his command but such co-operation was singularly lacking a year later when the Polish Home Army (*Armia Krajowa*) embarked upon an uprising in (5) Warsaw. The rebels initially gained control of two-thirds of the city. However, its leaders, under Gen. Bor-Komorowski, underestimated the ferocity of the German response. SS units launched a ferocious campaign which, as supplies of food and ammunition became exhausted, forced the survivors literally underground, into the sewers, where they were gradually reduced. The Poles had also relied upon supplies airlifted from the Allies in the west (which were flown in with great difficulty) and the imminent liberation of the city by combined units of the Polish emigré and Red armies. The latter did not materialize.

Picture below: *Warsaw, 1944. The summary public execution of suspected partisans was a common German security measure in eastern Europe.*

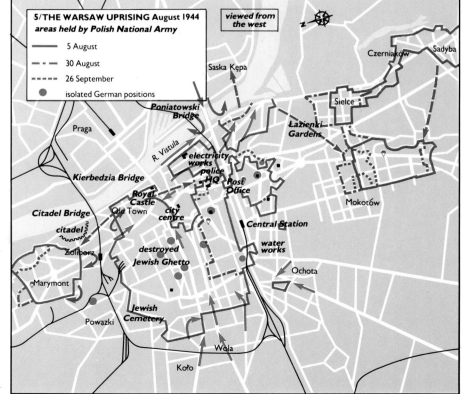

5/THE WARSAW UPRISING August 1944
areas held by Polish National Army

viewed from the west

—— 5 August

—·—·— 30 August

········· 26 September

● isolated German positions

The Soviet Union 1940~1945

IN 1940, GERMANY DEFEATED France with about 3000 tanks. In 1945, Marshal Zhukov launched 6200 tanks and assault guns against Berlin alone. This, despite the loss in the first six months of the war of 63 per cent of the USSR's coal output, 68 per cent of its iron production and 58 per cent of steel, 40 per cent of its population and the same amount of farmland. How did they do it?

The Soviet war economy was not a hasty improvization. Determined to avoid a repeat of Tsarist Russia's weakness in the First World War, Soviet Russia began preparations for total war in the mid-1920s. With the start of the Five Year Plans in 1928 (page 30), much factory and mine construction was diverted to Soviet Asia. This was partly to give some industry to non-Russian nationalities and to be near raw materials, but principally for strategic reasons. When Hitler invaded Russia in June 1941, one-third of Soviet coal, iron and steel output was in or east of the Urals. Asia's share of chemical and non-ferrous metals was greater still. However, this still left some two-thirds of these basic war materials west of the Urals, much of which fell into German hands or was destroyed. Without the pre-war migration of heavy, basic industry, Russia would have lost the war in the first few months.

Most Asiatic production came from a few huge factory complexes. The Gorki auto factory, the Nizhni Tagil railway building plant (which made tanks), the Ural machine-building works at Sverdlovsk, the Chelyabinsk tractor factory and the giant metallurgical combine at Magnitogorsk (literally meaning 'Magnetic Mountain', and larger than any in Europe) were all begun in the early 1930s. Besides being out of range of enemy bombers, the Ural metallurgical industry enjoyed another advantage. To make steel, toughening metals like nickel and chromium have to be added to iron; Ural iron ore comes out of the ground with these metals already in it. Of 13 large nitrate plants, vital to the manufacture of explosives, which existed in 1941, seven were in Asia. This relocation of basic materials of war had not been matched by a migration of light industry, or machine-building. Little more than one-tenth of the machine-building industry was in or behind the Urals when Hitler attacked. This, and some explosives manufacture, formed the main part of a mass industrial migration once war began.

However, the German-occupied area contained two-fifths of the grain and four-fifths of the sugar beet of the USSR, and about a quarter of the nation's farm animals, tractors and combine harvesters were lost. Collectivization of agriculture (also begun in the 1930s) meant that the state could extract the maximum from the remaining agricultural enterprises. Rationing was introduced throughout the country during the first six months of war. Servicemen and industrial workers got most, then office workers, and, last, dependents. Official rations were not always issued in full, and local authorities set aside parks and suburban gardens as allotments for growing food. By Summer 1942 there were five million such garden allotments.

One of the characteristic features of the Soviet war effort was the mobilization and employment of women. A law of February 1942 mobilized all able-bodied urban men from 16 to 55 and all able-bodied city women from 16 to 45. The only exemptions were students and women responsible for children under eight. In September 1942 the upper age limit for women's conscription was raised to 50. Many Russian women joined the services and many were employed as pilots, political officers, military police and snipers.

The Soviet armed forces helped maximize the war effort. Most armament and ammunition production was controlled by the Main Artillery Directorate (GAU) under N D Yakovlev. Innovations such as stamping tank turrets and gun wheels increased output many times. Once the Red Army took the offensive, after Kursk (page 124), captured equipment and supplies also played an important part.

From 1941, the Western Allies committed themselves to aiding the Soviet war effort. As Churchill acknowledged in December, Russia was the principal land theatre and aid to the USSR was the best way to 'weave the mighty Russian effort into the general texture of the war'. However, throughout the war the Red Army and Air Forces relied on Russian production for most categories of weaponry. The British tanks, artillery and aircraft supplied to the USSR were considered to be obsolescent and inferior. However, the Western Allies made a significant contribution where there were gaps in Russian

Во имя Родины
ВПЕРЕД БОГАТЫРИ!

For the Motherland's Sake, Go Forward Heroes

Tannu Tuva People's Republic established under Soviet protection, Aug. 1921, incorporated into Soviet Union 1944

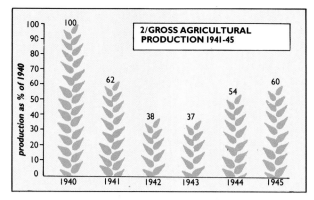

2/GROSS AGRICULTURAL PRODUCTION 1941-45

production as % of 1940

1940	1941	1942	1943	1944	1945
100	62	38	37	54	60

3/MILITARY PRODUCTION

per cent

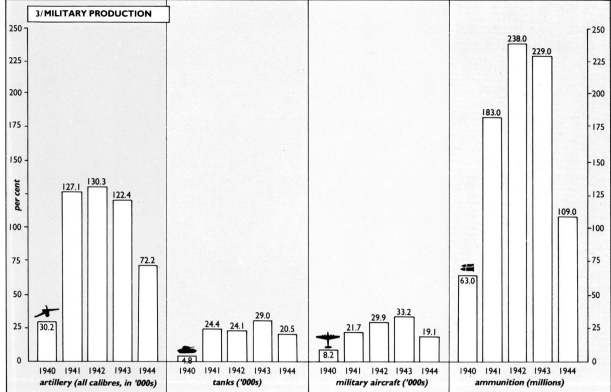

artillery (all calibres, in '000s)

1940	1941	1942	1943	1944
30.2	127.1	130.3	122.4	72.2

tanks ('000s)

1940	1941	1942	1943	1944
4.8	24.4	24.1	29.0	20.5

military aircraft ('000s)

1940	1941	1942	1943	1944
8.2	21.7	29.9	33.2	19.1

ammunition (millions)

1940	1941	1942	1943	1944
63.0	183.0	238.0	229.0	109.0

production – mainly in trucks and jeeps. Of 665,000 motor vehicles in Red Army service at the end of the war, 427,000 were of Western origin – vital to Soviet mobility in the later stages of the war. Other decisive contributions were 250,000 telephones with wire, copper, aluminium, rubber, high octane fuel and food. The USA sent five million tons of food, much of it concentrated battlefield rations – enough to keep an army of twelve million men supplied for every day of the war.

The Soviet home front, however, endured an abysmally low standard of living. Food, clothing, soap – all were in short supply, but the Russian people believed that victory would bring a rapid and remarkable turn for the better. They were to be disappointed. The most developed and populous part of the country had been laid to waste, and gangs of orphans roamed the countryside: the price of victory would not easily be met.

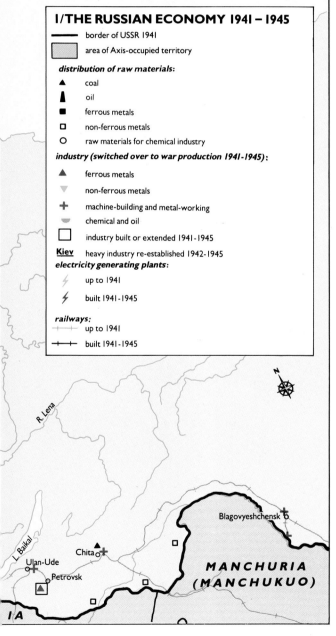

1/THE RUSSIAN ECONOMY 1941 – 1945

— border of USSR 1941

▓ area of Axis-occupied territory

distribution of raw materials:

▲ coal

⬧ oil

■ ferrous metals

□ non-ferrous metals

○ raw materials for chemical industry

industry (switched over to war production 1941-1945):

▲ ferrous metals

▼ non-ferrous metals

✛ machine-building and metal-working

▽ chemical and oil

□ industry built or extended 1941-1945

Kiev heavy industry re-established 1942-1945

electricity generating plants:

⚡ up to 1941

⚡ built 1941-1945

railways:

—⊢— up to 1941

—+—+— built 1941-1945

In 1941, a substantial amount of basic Soviet heavy industry lay in, or west of, the Urals: ferrous and non-ferrous metals, chemicals and oil *(1)*. Machine-building, concentrated in European Russia in areas quickly captured by the Germans, was the main activity moved east after the war began *(5)*. By the late Autumn, Soviet industry was *na kolesakh* (on wheels), the great Asiatic industrial centres established by the pre-war Five Year Plans being the principal destination, the largest concentration being in the Urals. Despite attempts to develop Central Asia as an agricultural region, in 1941 European Russia still provided nearly half of the USSR's food: the loss of the great cereal heartland of Ukraine was a serious blow *(2)*. Soviet armaments manufacture was colossal even before the war *(3)*. A factory might produce a few tanks in parallel with many tractors; when war came, the proportions simply reversed. Thus, although the USA sent some 14,795 aircraft to the Soviet Union *(3)*, this equalled little more than 4 months Soviet wartime production. 12,000 Western tanks similarly equalled only 4 months Soviet output. Much of the Soviet success in the war must be attributed to Stalin's leadership. Like Hitler, he assumed personal responsibility for all major decisions, effected through the command structure of *Stavka* and through the State Defence Committee (GKO), a cabinet of Politburo members formed on 30 June 1941. The war began, however, when the Stalinist terror was still in progress *(4)*. During the 1930s over 30 million people had been killed in the USSR as a result of collectivization and Stalin's purges. The purge of the Red Army was still in progress. Repressions on a massive scale, often targeted against newly-acquired territories in the west, continued throughout the war (and until Stalin's death in 1953).

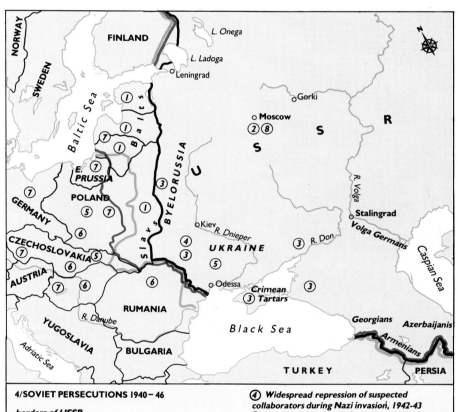

4/SOVIET PERSECUTIONS 1940 – 46

borders of USSR

— 1939

— Sept. 1939-June 1941

— after 1945

① Mass deportations of class enemies from territories annexed 1939-40 (c. 3 million)

② Continued political purges, repressions and deportations throughout USSR of Soviet citizens to the Gulag prison camps, mainly in Siberia (c. 1 million per annum 1939-45)

③ Mass deportation of nationalities accused of conspiring with Nazi invasion, 1942-43

④ Widespread repression of suspected collaborators during Nazi invasion, 1942-43

⑤ Destruction of all independent wartime resistance movements

⑥ Widespread repression of all political opposition during Soviet liberation of eastern Europe, 1944-45

⑦ Mass killing and rape of German civilians during Soviet liberation of eastern Europe, 1944-45

⑧ Mass deportation to the Gulag of all Soviet citizens returning to USSR from German captivity, 1945, including slave labourers, soldiers who served under Nazi command, peoples handed over by the Western Allies and c. 1 million POWs liberated from German camps

Pictures left: an underground armaments factory in Sevastopol 1941/42; the manufacture and assembly of ammunition and weapons by civilians was often performed within the war zones. Far left: Soviet propaganda often appealed to historical precedents as a means of rallying national unity.

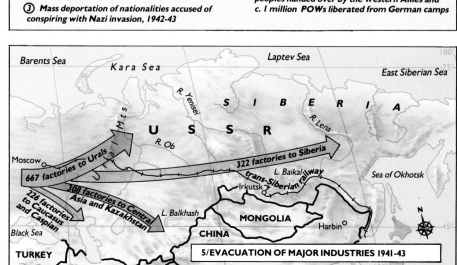

5/EVACUATION OF MAJOR INDUSTRIES 1941-43

667 factories to Urals

322 factories to Siberia

308 factories to Central Asia and Kazakhstan

226 factories to Caucasus and Caspian

Poland JAN. ~ FEB. 1945

THE GERMAN COUNTER-OFFENSIVE in the Ardennes in December 1944 diverted Hitler from the gathering storm in the east. In spite of the attempts of Guderian and Gehlen, in charge of intelligence for the eastern front, to alert him, Hitler refused to believe that the Russians were capable of launching another massive offensive. He remained mesmerized by the possibilities in the west and by illusions that Soviet tank armies lacked tanks – in fact, operations by powerful Soviet tank armies were one of the distinctive features of the campaign. Gehlen predicted the Russian offensive with amazing accuracy, expecting it towards the middle of January. On 9 January Gehlen announced that the Russians would aim to destroy the German will and ability to carry on the war completely, and three days later the attack began. It was probably brought forward to 12 January in response to Western Allied requests for help in the wake of the Ardennes, but possibly also to preempt German attempts to strengthen their defences.

The outline of the Soviet plan had been sketched in November 1944, taking the shortest distance to Berlin: straight through Warsaw. The operation was charged to 1st Byelorussian Front (Zhukov) and 1st Ukrainian Front (Koniev), in co-operation with the left wing of 2nd Byelorussian (Rokossovskiy) and the right of 4th Ukrainian (Petrov). Zhukov aimed for Poznań, Koniev for Breslau. Their two fronts alone comprised 2.2 million men, 33,500 guns and mortars, 7000 tanks and assault guns and 5000 aircraft in 22 armies. Their mission was the destruction of Army Group A (Harpe) (from 26 January renamed Centre) and the conquest of Poland. Harpe's Army Group comprised 400,000 men, 1136 tanks and assault guns and 270 aircraft in three armies: 30 divisions stretched from the Vistula north of Warsaw to the Carpathians. In addition, Reinhardt's Centre Group in East Prussia (580,000 men, 700 tanks and assault guns and 515 aircraft) posed a threat to the flank.

The operation fell into two phases: in the first (to 17 January), Soviet forces attacked from three bridgeheads – 1st Byelorussian from Magnuszów and Puławy, 1st Ukrainian from Sandomierz. Bad weather hampered air support and placed even greater stress on artillery. 1st Ukrainian attacked on 12 January, the Sandomierz-Silesian Operation, after a 107-minute artillery bombardment. 1st Byelorussian attacked two days later, the Warsaw-Poznań Operation, after a 25-minute preparation in which double 'fire lanes' were ploughed into German positions, between which the Russians advanced. The Russians broke through on a 300-mile wide front to a depth of 60–100 miles. The first phase ended on 17 January with the fall of Warsaw. Whereas the Russians had stood back as the Warsaw rising, led by the London-backed *Armija Krajowa* (National Army), had been wiped out, now the Soviet-controlled 1st Polish Army in co-operation with 1st Byelorussian Front fought its way into the city. In spite of Hitler's orders to hold, the German command in Warsaw was determined not to become another Stalingrad and hastily withdrew to avoid encirclement.

During the second phase, to 3 February, the Russians encircled and seized the Silesian industrial region, which Stalin ordered Koniev to capture intact in a typically oblique but unambiguous fashion: he pointed it out on the map and said one word: 'gold'. After advancing over 300 miles in two weeks, between 26 January and 3 February 1st Byelorussian Front established bridgeheads across the Oder, the last major river obstacle, forty miles from Berlin.

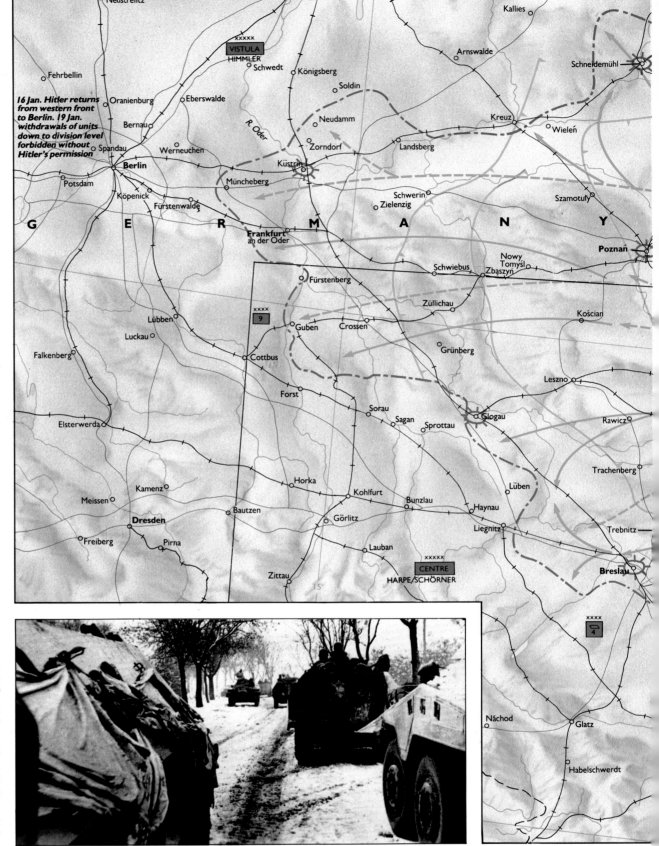

16 Jan. Hitler returns from western front to Berlin. 19 Jan. withdrawals of units down to division level forbidden without Hitler's permission

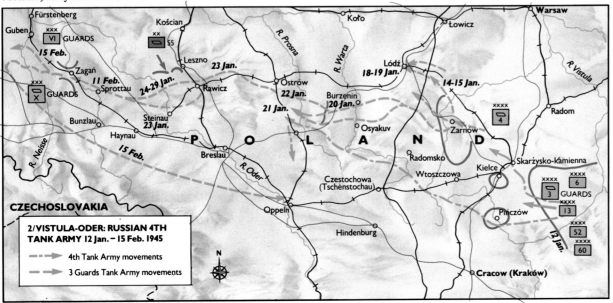

2/VISTULA-ODER: RUSSIAN 4TH TANK ARMY 12 Jan.– 15 Feb. 1945

- - - 4th Tank Army movements
- - - 3 Guards Tank Army movements

THE GERMANS FORTIFIED the territory between the Vistula and the Oder with some seven defensive zones, altogether 300 miles deep (1). Wide use was made of the natural features of the rivers and 'fortress cities'. 1st Ukrainian Front attacked from the Sandomierz bridgehead on 12 Jan: 1st Byelorussian two days later. On 1st Ukrainian's sector, all 4 tank armies broke through into the operational depth and pursuit phase. 200 German tanks, half of them heavy Tigers, were detroyed on the first day. The Russians prevented the Germans occupying prepared defence lines, keeping them constantly off-balance. By 31 Jan. 1st Mechanized Corps had crossed the Oder, seizing a bridgehead round Küstrin which would play a key part in the subsequent offensive against Berlin. 'Armoured spearheads':

tank armies deployed 25-55 miles ahead of the main forces, accelerated and maintained the Russian rate of advance. 3rd Guards and 4th Tank armies were particularly successful. A spectacular circuit by the former isolated a German Silesian grouping, capturing the region realtively intact. The advance by 4th Tank captured Kielce and Lódź (19 Jan.), outmanoeuvering the *Grossdeutschland* Panzer Corps. Substantial cavalry forces also ranged fast and far into the German rear. The Russians experienced some problems supplying their faster-moving forces. They used a prodigious amount of fuel and began to run out as they reached 400 miles from their supply depots.

Picture above: *German armoured troops in retreat, central Poland 1945.*

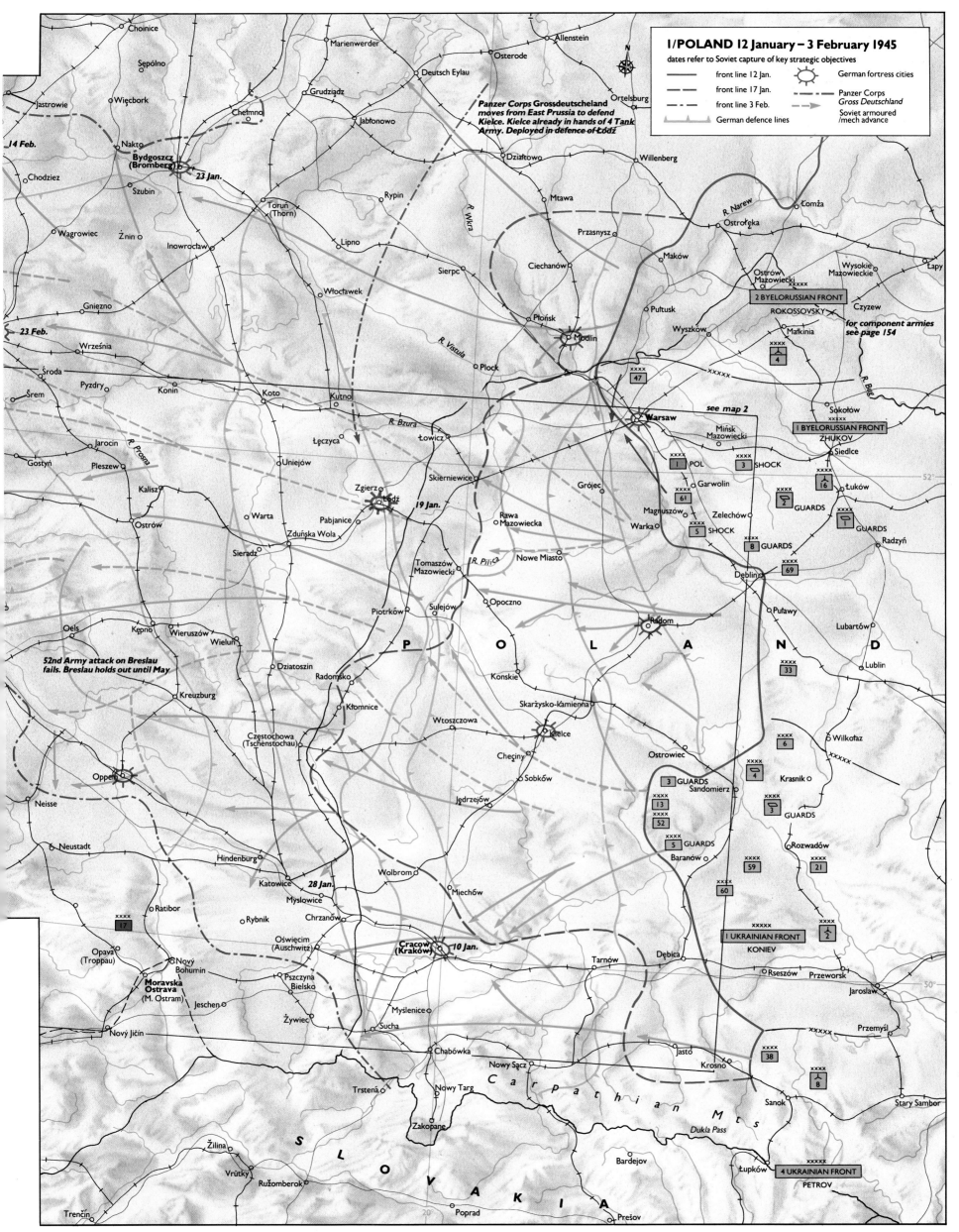

1/POLAND 12 January – 3 February 1945

dates refer to Soviet capture of key strategic objectives

- front line 12 Jan.
- front line 17 Jan.
- front line 3 Feb.
- German defence lines
- German fortress cities
- Panzer Corps *Gross Deutschland*
- Soviet armoured /mech advance

Panzer Corps Grossdeutscheland moves from East Prussia to defend Kielce. Kielce already in hands of 4 Tank Army. Deployed in defence of Łódź

52nd Army attack on Breslau fails. Breslau holds out until May

Choinice
Sępólno
Więcbork
Jastrowie
14 Feb.
Nakło
Bydgoszcz (Bromberg)
23 Jan.
Chodziez
Szubin
Wągrowiec
Żnin
Gniezno
Wrzesnia
23 Feb.
Środa
Śrem
Pyzdry
Konin
Jarocin
Gostyń
Pleszew
Kalisz
Ostrów
Warta
Oels
Kępno
Wieruszów
Wielun
Kreuzburg
Neisse
Oppeln
Neustadt
Ratibor
Opava (Troppau)
Nový Bohumin
Moravska Ostrava (M. Ostram)
Jeschen
Nový Jičín
Žilina
Vrútky
Trenčín
Ružomberok

Choinice
Marienwerder
Osterode
Deutsch Eylau
Grudziądz
Jabłonowo
Chełmno
Rypin
Toruń (Thorn)
Lipno
Inowrocław
Sierpc
Włocławek
Płońsk
Koło
Kutno
R. Bzura
Łowicz
Łęczyca
Uniejów
Skierniewice
Zgierz Łódź
19 Jan.
Pabjanice
Zduńska Wola
Sieradz
Rawa Mazowiecka
R. Pilica
Nowe Miasto
Piotrków
Sulejów
Opoczno
Dziatoszyn
Radomsko
Konskie
Częstochowa (Tschenstochau)
Kłomnice
Wtoszczowa
Kielce
Chęciny
Sobków
Jędrzejów
Hindenburg
Wolbrom
Katowice
28 Jan.
Mysłowice
Miechów
Rybnik
Chrzanów
Oświęcim (Auschwitz)
Cracow (Kraków)
10 Jan.
Pszczyna
Bielsko
Myślenice
Żywiec
Sucha
Chabówka
Nowy Sącz
Trstená
Nowy Targ
Zakopane
Poprad

Allenstein
Ortelsburg
Willenberg
Działdowo
Mława
Ciechanów
Przasnysz
Maków
Pułtusk
Płock
Modlin
Warsaw
see map 2
Grójec
Magnuszew
Warka
Tomaszów Mazowiecki
Radom
Puławy
Ostrowiec
Skarżysko-Kamienna
Sandomierz
Baranów
Dębica
Tarnów
Rzeszów
Jasło
Krosno
Dukla Pass
Sanok
Bardejov

Osterode
Ostrów Mazowiecki
Łomża
Ostrołęka
Wysokie Mazowieckie
Łapy
Czyzew
Sokołów
Malkinia
Wyszków
Mińsk Mazowiecki
Siedlce
Łuków
Zelechów
Radzyń
Dęblin
Lubartów
Lublin
Wilkołaz
Kraśnik
Rozwadów
Przeworsk
Jarosław
Przemyśl
Stary Sambor
Prešov

R. Narew
R. Wkra
R. Vistula
R. Bug
R. Prosna

2 BYELORUSSIAN FRONT
ROKOSSOVSKY
for component armies see page 154

1 BYELORUSSIAN FRONT
ZHUKOV

1 UKRAINIAN FRONT
KONIEV

4 UKRAINIAN FRONT
PETROV

P O L A N D

C a r p a t h i a n   M t s
S L O V A K I A

XXXX 4
XXXX 47
XXXX 1 POL
XXXX 3 SHOCK
XXXX 16
XXXX 61
XXXX 2 GUARDS
XXXX 5 SHOCK
XXXX 9 GUARDS
XXXX 8 GUARDS
XXXX 69
XXXX 33
XXXX 6
XXXX 4
XXXX 3 GUARDS
XXXX 13
XXXX 52
XXXX 3 GUARDS
XXXX 5 GUARDS
XXXX 59
XXXX 21
XXXX 60
XXXX 2
XXXX 17
XXXX 38
XXXX 8

52°
50°
20

175

As ARMY GROUP CENTRE disintegrated under the hammer blows of Operation *Bagration* (page 148) in mid-July 1944, the Soviet command extended their offensive to the area south of the Pripet Marshes, where Army Group North Ukraine (Harpe) held the German front down to the formidable natural barrier of the Carpathian range. Here, in the west Ukraine and south-east Poland, the Germans had expected the blow which in fact fell in Byelorussia. Now, they had to move six divisions to Army Group Centre, leaving 34 infantry and five Panzer, to cover Lwów, the industrial region of Drohobycz-Borislaw, the approaches to southern Poland, and Czechoslovakia and Silesia and their valuable industrial resources.

Stalin had proposed one thrust in the direction of Lwów but Marshal Koniev wanted two, the other towards Rava-Russkaya, which Stalin allowed, on Koniev's 'own head'. This was the import of the *Stavka* directive issued on 24 June, for what would become Operation *Lwów-Sandomierz* (13 July to 29 August). Koniev's 1st Ukrainian Front, already the strongest in the Red Army, was massively reinforced. The plan was to encircle and destroy German forces in the area of Brody and Lwów, then to split Army Group North Ukraine in two, driving one half west, the other half into the Carpathians, and advancing as far as the Vistula.

As the first phase of the operation began, on 13 July, German 4th and 1st Panzer armies withdrew troops from the forward positions, a technique they had learned to mitigate the effect of the massive Soviet preparatory bombardment. Detecting this, the Russians in turn forgot about the bombardment and attacked immediately. For the first two days there was heavy fighting north-west of Brody, but by evening on the 15th KMG Baronov was committed to cut off the escape route for German forces in the area. The attack on the Lwów axis, for which the Germans were ready, fared poorly as mist and rain hampered the artillery bombardment. Soviet troops only made a shallow penetration when they attacked in the afternoon of 14 July, and the Germans immediately committed their tactical reserves. As the German counter-attacks were worn down, Rybalko's 3rd Guards Tank Army was committed on 16 July. The Russians succeeded in encircling up to eight divisions south-west of Brody, passing the two KMGs either side of the encircled force. The three tank armies were committed outside these, two to the south and one to the north. The Russians moved on to take Rawa-Ruska, Przemyśl, Lwów and Stanislawów and reach the River San.

The fall of Lwów on 27 July marked the end of the first phase of the operation, in which the Soviet objectives had been achieved exactly as planned. The axis now shifted from Lwów-Przemyśl to Sandomierz (to the north), where the crucial Vistula crossings were nearer. As early as 30 July units of 3rd Guards Tank Army and KMG Sokolov were over the Vistula, but the bridgeheads were too small and precarious to be enlarged. A ferocious battle developed, Soviet units crossing the river parallel with withdrawing German ones. Like Army Group North Ukraine, 1st Ukrainian Front also found itself split. At the end of July, Koniev recommended that the armies on the left (Carpathian) axis come under separate command, and within a few days (8 August) a new Front command, Petrov's 4th Ukrainian, took control of 1st Guards and 18th Armies, in operations in the Carpathian foothills.

Meanwhile, on 2 August, *Stavka* had issued the order for the attack on Rumania. With Army Group North Ukraine split and shattered, it was now the turn of Army Group South Ukraine (Friessner) to be eliminated. Friessner had a nominal strength of 600,000 German and Rumanian troops, the latter now about to stab the Germans in the back. Much of Army Group South Ukraine's armour had been moved north to cope with other massive Soviet attacks. Against this background *Stavka* framed the plan for the Jassy-Kishinev strategic operation to destroy Army Group South Ukraine and split the German-Rumanian alliance by capturing Moldavia.

2nd Ukrainian launched its main blow north west of Jassy on 20 August. 3rd Ukrainian attacked from the Kitsman (Cozmeni) bridgehead towards Huşi. 23 August was a critical day in the campaign. 18 German divisions were encircled south west of the city, and 3rd Rumanian Army similarly surrounded. Soviet armour reached the Prut at Leovo and 6th Tank Army was racing on towards the Focşani gap, threatening the entire German Army Group. On the same day, Germany's position in south-east Europe collapsed with the Bucharest coup. King Michael of Rumania ordered Rumanian troops to stop firing at the Russians, had Marshal Antonescu (who had seen Hitler as recently as 5 August) arrested, and surrendered unconditionally to the Allies. The Rumanian change of sides

took the Germans completely by surprise, the German ambassador in Bucharest committing suicide. The suggestion that the Russians halt their advance and that the Rumanians deal with the remaining German forces was declined by *Stavka*, and Soviet forces entered Bucharest on 31 August.

After Rumania seceded from the Axis, events in Bulgaria reached a crisis. On 26 August, with the Russians closing in, the Bulgarian government declared neutrality. This was not good enough for the Russians and on 5 September they declared war on Bulgaria. On 8 September Tolbukhin's 3rd Ukrainian Front crossed the Bulgarian frontier. There was no exchange of fire. On the following day the 'Fatherland Front' (Agrarians and Communists) seized power in Bulgaria and Soviet troops were ordered to halt military operations. It had been a bloodless victory.

On 29 August, the Slovak revolt had begun south of the Carpathians. 1st (Koniev) and 4th (Petrov) Ukrainian Fronts launched the East Carpathian operation on 8 September, in order to break Axis forces and seize control of the Carpathian passes, opening communications with the Slovak partisans (page 186). By 28 October, German forces had been driven out of eastern Czechoslovakia and north of the Tisza. With Rumania and Bulgaria now also in Soviet hands, the massive eastern front was being rolled up from the right flank, which, as far as the defence of the Reich was concerned, now lay in Hungary and western Czechoslovakia.

1/SOUTH-EASTERN EUROPE June – December 1944

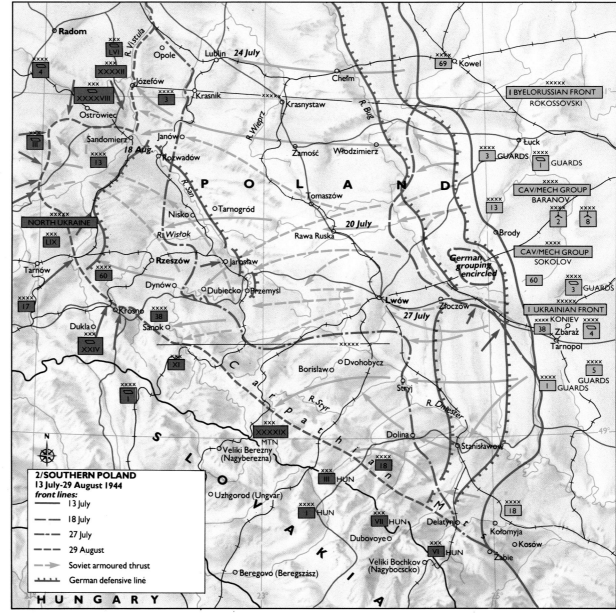

2/SOUTHERN POLAND
13 July-29 August 1944
front lines:

——————— 13 July
— — — — 18 July
– – – – – 27 July
– · – · – · 29 August
——➤ Soviet armoured thrust
╫╫╫╫╫ German defensive line

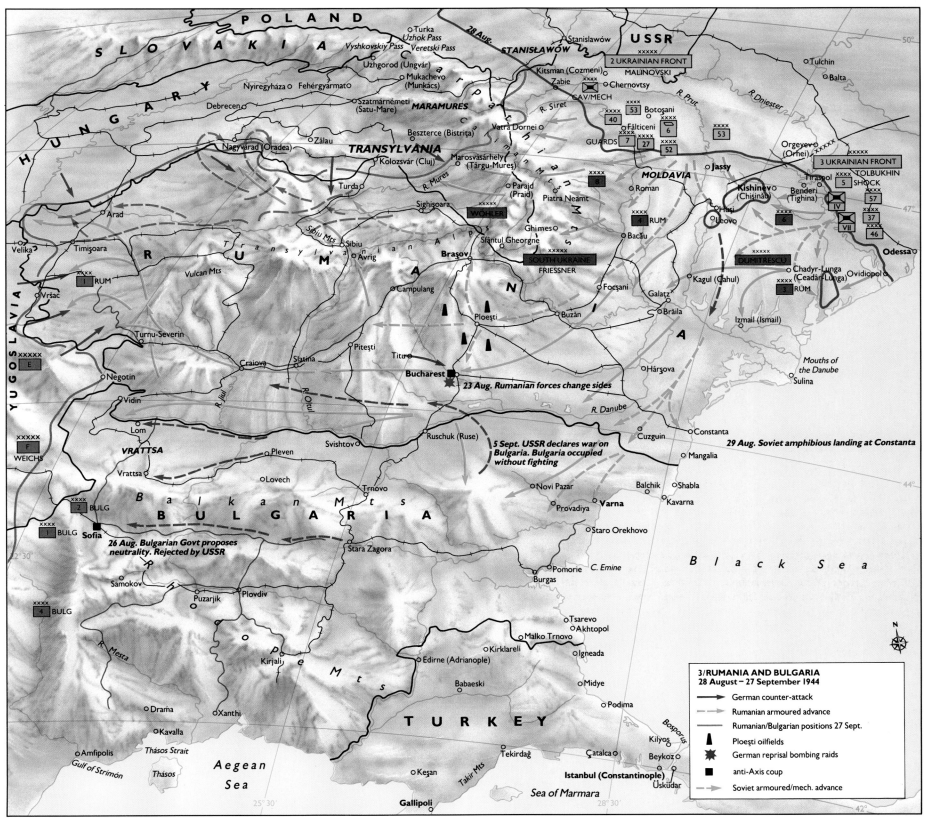

Map labels (clockwise/notable): POLAND, SLOVAKIA, HUNGARY, USSR, Turka, Uzhok Pass, Veretski Pass, Vyshkovskiy Pass, 28 Aug., STANISLAWÓW, Stanislawów, Tulchin, Uzhgorod (Ungvár), Mukachevo (Munkács), Chernovtsy, Balta, 2 UKRAINIAN FRONT, MALINOVSKI, CAV/MECH, Nyíregyháza, Fehérgyarmat, Debrecen, Szatmárnémeti (Satu-Mare), MARAMURES, Vatra Dornei, R. Siret, R. Prut, R. Dniester, Kitsman (Cozmeni), Zabie, Botoşani, 40, 53, 6, GUARDS, 7, 27, 52, 53, Fälticeni, Zălau, Nagyvárad (Oradea), TRANSYLVANIA, Besztercze (Bistriţa), Orgeyev (Orhei), 3 UKRAINIAN FRONT, Kolozsvár (Cluj), Marosvásárhely (Târgu-Mures), 8, MOLDAVIA, Jassy, Roman, Kishinev (Chişinău), TOLBUKHIN, 5, SHOCK, Turda, Sighişoara, Paraid (Praid), Piatra Neamt, Uleovo, Husi, Tiraspol, Benderi (Tighina), 57, IV, 37, VII, 46, Arad, Velika, Timişoara, RUMANIA, Sibiu Mts, Sibiu, Avrig, R. Mures, Sfântul Gheorghe, Brasov, WÖHLER, Bacău, 4 RUM, 6, Chadyr-Lunga (Ceadâr-Lunga), Odessa, Vulcan Mts, Câmpulung, SOUTH UKRAINE, FRIESSNER, Focşani, Galatz (Galati), Kagul (Cahul), DUMITRESCU, 3 RUM, Ovidiopol, Vršac, 1 RUM, E, Turnu-Severin, Ploeşti, Buzău, Brăila, Izmail (Ismail), Mouths of the Danube, Negotin, Craiova, Slatina, Piteşti, Titu, Bucharest, 23 Aug. Rumanian forces change sides, R. Jiul, R. Olt, Hârsova, Sulina, Vidin, Lom, R. Danube, Ruschuk (Ruse), 5 Sept. USSR declares war on Bulgaria. Bulgaria occupied without fighting, Cuzguin, Constanta, 29 Aug. Soviet amphibious landing at Constanta, F, WEICHS, VRATTSA, Pleven, Svishtov, Lovech, Trnovo, Novi Pazar, Provadiya, Varna, Balchik, Shabla, Kavarna, Black Sea, 2 BULG, Vrattsa, Stara Zagora, Staro Orekhovo, Sofia, 1 BULG, 26 Aug. Bulgarian Govt proposes neutrality. Rejected by USSR, Balkan Mts, BULGARIA, Pomorie, C. Emine, Burgas, Samokov, Puzarjik, Plovdiv, 4 BULG, R. Mesta, Tsarevo, Akhtopol, Malko Trnovo, Igneada, Rodopi Mts, Kirjali, Edirne (Adrianople), Kirklareli, Drama, Xanthi, Babaeski, TURKEY, Podima, Amfipolis, Thásos Strait, Kavalla, Thásos, Aegean Sea, Midye, Kilyos, Tekirdağ, Bosporus, Beykoz, Üsküdar, Istanbul (Constantinople), Keşan, Takir Mts, Gallipoli, Çatalca, Sea of Marmara

Map legend

3/RUMANIA AND BULGARIA
28 August – 27 September 1944

→ German counter-attack
--→ Rumanian armoured advance
— Rumanian/Bulgarian positions 27 Sept.
▲ Ploeşti oilfields
✶ German reprisal bombing raids
■ anti-Axis coup
--→ Soviet armoured/mech. advance

BETWEEN JUNE AND DEC. 1944, the front south of the Pripet Marshes, west and south of the great salient thrust into the Ukraine, was pushed almost halfway across Poland, across the east Carpathians and Hungary to Czechoslovakia, and half-way up Yugoslavia (1, also see page 128). In southern Poland, Lwów was a crucial link between German forces defending the approach to the Reich with those in Rumania. The favourable terrain, including the barriers formed by the numerous tributaries of the R. Dniester, was used to establish defence in depth with three defensive belts 25-30 miles wide, enhancing the strength of the San, Dniester and Vistula river lines and using the towns of Wlodzimierz, Brody, Zloczów, Rawa Ruska and Stanislawów as defensive 'hedgehogs'. The main German force held the axis covering Lwów, with infantry holding the first 2 defensive lines and the armour held some 10 miles back. Lwów was one of the axes of the Lwów-Sandomierz operation (13 July to 29 Aug.), the other lay towards Rawa Ruska. The first phase lasted until 27 July; the second, until 29 Aug., and took

Soviet forces to the Carpathians (2). The Jassy-Kishinev operation (20-29 August), brought Soviet troops as far south into Rumania as Bucharest, where there was a popular rising on 23 Aug., and Rumania defected from the Axis (3). The Rumanians tried to persuade the Russians to halt their advance, but Malinovski, commanding 2nd Ukrainian Front, was ordered to continue his advance into Bucharest itself from 31 Aug. On 29 Aug., 2nd Ukrainian only faced the remnants of 7 Axis divisions: the rest of the opposition had disintegrated. The Russians moved on towards Bulgaria, crossing the frontier on 8 Sept. Within 12 hours, after meeting no resistance, they were 40 miles inside. On 28 Sept., the Soviet LXXV Corps (Tolbukhin's 3rd Ukrainian Front) reached the Yugoslav frontier and the gunboats of Gorshkov's Danube flotilla approached Negotin, the first Soviet objective in Yugoslavia, which fell on 30 Sept. (3). Meanwhile, on 8 Sept. the east Carpathian operation had begun, which involved the Jablunkov, Vyshkovskiy, Veretskiy, Uzhok, Russkiy, Lupkovskiy and Dukla passes over the range. The

Carpathian-Dukla operation marked the beginning of the Soviet capture of Czechoslovakia (4). This was carried out by 38th Army with the 1st Czechoslovak Army Corps under command. Capture of the pass would open contact with Slovak partisans, so the choice of the Czechoslovak Army Corps was logical. Dukla town itself was seized on 20 Sept. In keeping with Russian practice for taking mountain passes, airborne brigades were landed on the southern side of the mountains. On 1 Oct. elements of 38th Army reached the border north-west of the Dukla pass; on 6 Oct. units of 1 Czechoslovak Corps in co-operation with Soviet LXVII and XXXI Tank Corps captured the pass. By 28 Oct. Soviet-Czech forces had penetrated 10-15 miles west and south-west of the pass (4).

Pictures above left: a Czech poster (left) part of a concerted effort to turn Germany's eastern European allies against her. Soviet propaganda made much of the Red Army liberation forces (right) Don Cossacks are greeted by Rumanian villagers.

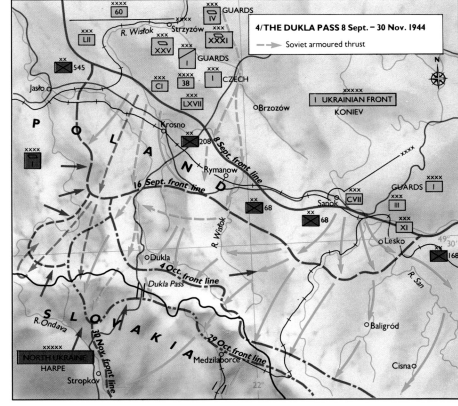

4/THE DUKLA PASS 8 Sept. – 30 Nov. 1944
--→ Soviet armoured thrust

Map labels: 60, GUARDS, IV, LII, R. Wisłok, Strzyzów, XXXI, XXV, GUARDS, 1, 545, CI, 38, CZECH, I, Jasło, 1, LXVII, I UKRAINIAN FRONT, KONIEV, POLAND, Brzozów, Krosno, 208, Rymanow, 8 Sept. front line, 16 Sept. front line, Sanok, GUARDS, I, 68, CVII, III, 68, XI, 168, 1, Lesko, 4 Oct. front line, Dukla, Dukla Pass, R. Wisłok, R. San, R. Ondava, NORTH UKRAINE, HARPE, SLOVAKIA, 29 Nov. front line, 30 Nov. front line, Medzilaborce, Stropkov, Cisna, Baligród, N

Hungary SEPTEMBER 1944 ~ MARCH 1945

BY 24 SEPTEMBER 1944, the Russians had overrun Rumania and part of eastern Hungary as far as Târgu Mureş (page 176). Hungary had been occupied by the Germans in March; now Malinovski's 2nd Ukrainian Front mounted Operation *Debrecen* (6-28 October) to destroy Friessner's Army Group South and three divisions of Army group F in Hungary and northern Transylvania, in order to enable 4th Ukrainian Front (Petrov) to cross the Carpathians. Soviet 2nd Ukrainian Front included two Rumanian armies, 1st and 4th, and two Cavalry-Mechanized Groups (KMG), KMG Pliev and KMG Gorshkov. The offensive began on 6 October and within three days KMG Pliev had penetrated 60 miles into the enemy rear, and by 20 October had reached the River Tisza along with units of KMG Gorshkov, cutting off the withdrawal of 1st and 2nd Hungarian and 8th German armies. By 28 October the Russians and their allies were 50 miles from Budapest.

Stalin wanted Budapest captured immediately. Malinovski asked for five days, but was told to attack tomorrow, and immediately launched the Budapest operation (29 October to 13 February), in co-operation with formations of Tolbukhin's 3rd Ukrainian Front. Friessner's Army Group South and formations of Army Groups F and, to the north, A (renamed Centre on 26 January 1945) had fallen back to the north west. By 10 December the Russians and Rumanians had cut off the Axis retreat northwards from Budapest, which was completely surrounded on 26th. Despite three strong German counter-attacks, Budapest finally fell on 13 February. By refusing Malinovski's request for five days, Stalin may have lost three and a half months. The twin cities of Buda and Pest were terribly ravaged, and it became a sensitive subject with Stalin. Soviet efforts in Hungary had, however, drawn off substantial German forces (Army Group A) from the north, thus weakening the protection for Germany's heartland, to be reached through Poland (page 174). With the fall of Budapest a German-Hungarian force of 188,000 men was knocked out of the war. Meanwhile, a provisional government reached agreement with the Soviet Union on the conclusion of hostilities.

By 5 March Soviet and East European forces had reached a line level with the south-western end of Lake Balaton. Hitler ordered a counter-attack, codenamed *Frühlingserwachen* (*Spring awakening*) north and south of the lake. To the north 6th SS Panzer Army was to strike north to Budapest, re-establishing a defence line along the major obstacle of the Danube. To the south, 2nd Panzer Army would do likewise, striking east. The advance bogged down in the muddy spring conditions, and ploughed into hastily improvised Soviet defences 15 to 30 miles deep, the Russians turning their anti-aircraft guns on German tanks and infantry. Battle with Tolbukhin's 3rd Ukrainian Front raged for ten days, with 800,000 men 12,500 guns and mortars, 1300 tanks and assault guns and 1800 aircraft engaged on both sides. By 15 March *Spring awakening* had ground to a halt and the Russians resumed their advance against Army Group South. By 4 April they had cleared the end of Lake Balaton and were within five miles of Vienna.

BY SEPT. 1944, the Byelorussian Operation had created a Soviet salient threatened by German forces in Poland from the north and Rumania in the south (1). As units of 1st Ukrainian Front reached the eastern boundaries of Czechoslovakia (8 Apr.) Slovaks deserted to join Red Army units. Detailed military plans for a Slovak rising had been worked out with the active interest of London. Moscow was also active, as the creation of a Soviet-controlled partisan movement on Slovak territory would help prevent a London-linked 'bourgeois' government gaining control. After 25 Aug. guerrilla actions intensified and on 27th a German general was captured and shot. Hitler immediately ordered 357th Infantry Division (20,000 men) to enter Slovakia (2). The Germans easily disarmed Slovak regular formations, but some got away to join the partisans. On 2 Sept. *Stavka* ordered 2nd Ukrainian Front to join up with Slovak troops. During Sept. Soviet and Soviet-trained Czech troops fought inside Slovakia, while the Slovak partisan movement came under overt Soviet command. In early Oct. German units, with the Waffen SS particularly prominent, proceeded to crush the rising. These events underlined the importance placed by OKH on Hungary and the Carpathians, the latter a natural defensive obstacle. The Soviet conquest of Hungary fell into two main phases: Operation *Debrecen* (to 28 Oct.) and Operation *Budapest* (29 Oct. to 13 Feb.). In the first phase a particularly prominent role was played by Cavalry-Mechanized Groups. Fighting in Budapest was particularly savage. On 24 Dec. 2nd and 3rd Ukrainian Fronts linked up, encircling the city, trapping 188,000 men with four divisions. IV SS Panzer Corps was shifted to Hungary from Army Group Centre, and participated in the attempt to relieve Budapest mounted on 1 Jan. (3). By 17 Jan. almost all of Pest was in Soviet hands. The German garrison surrendered the following day. Fighting for Buda raged until 13 Feb. the Russians having to take one fortified building at a time. After the fall of Budapest, the Germans mounted a major counter-attack north and south of Lake Balaton (4). 6th Army (Balck), transferred from the west, would attack between Lakes Balaton and Velence, breaking 3rd Ukrainian in two. The Germans cut into Russian 57th Army as far as Kaposvár but were fought to a standstill in a deep defensive battle. Tolbukhin asked permission from *Stavka* to commit 9th Guards Army, but was told to hold it back for the counter-stroke (7 Mar.). After the Germans came to a halt on 15 Mar., 6th Guards Tank Army was ordered to

concentrate in the area of 9th Army, west of Budapest. 4th and 9th Guards Armies attacked, and 6th Guards Tank Army was committed to the breach. By 25 Mar. 2nd Ukrainian had torn a 60-mile gap in the German defences, and the Russians pushed on through the Hron Valley and towards Bratislava.

Picture below: Soviet house-to-house fighting in Budapest.

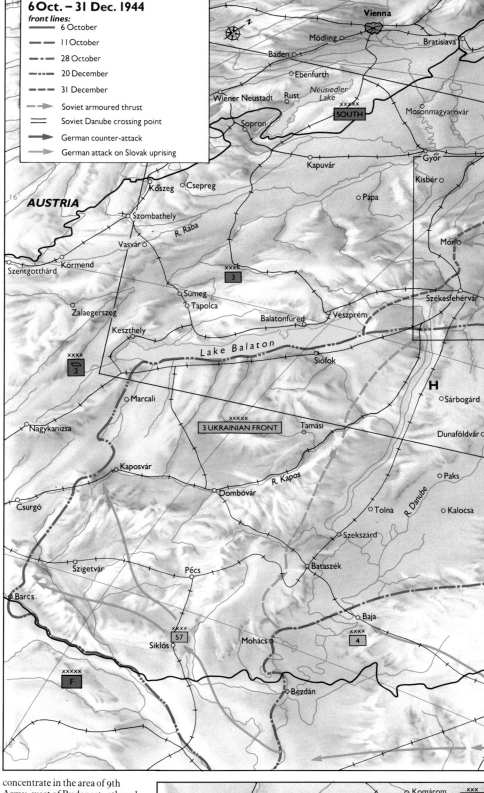

2/HUNGARY 6 Oct. – 31 Dec. 1944
front lines:
— 6 October
--- 11 October
-·-·- 28 October
---- 20 December
---- 31 December
→ Soviet armoured thrust
═ Soviet Danube crossing point
→ German counter-attack
→ German attack on Slovak uprising

see page 150
see page 148
see page 174
see page 176

SWEDEN
Baltic Sea
USSR
POLAND
GERMANY
SLOVAKIA
HUNGARY
RUMANIA
Black Sea
YUGOSLAVIA
ITALY
Adriatic Sea
Mediterranean Sea
GREECE
TURKEY

1/EASTERN EUROPE 15 Sept. – 16 Dec. 1944

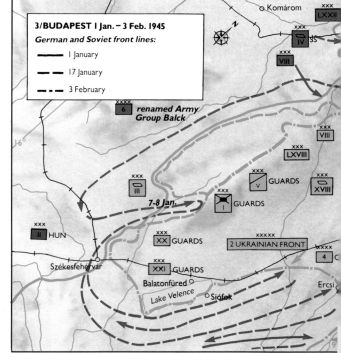

3/BUDAPEST 1 Jan. – 3 Feb. 1945
German and Soviet front lines:
— 1 January
--- 17 January
-·-·- 3 February

renamed Army Group Balck

2 UKRAINIAN FRONT

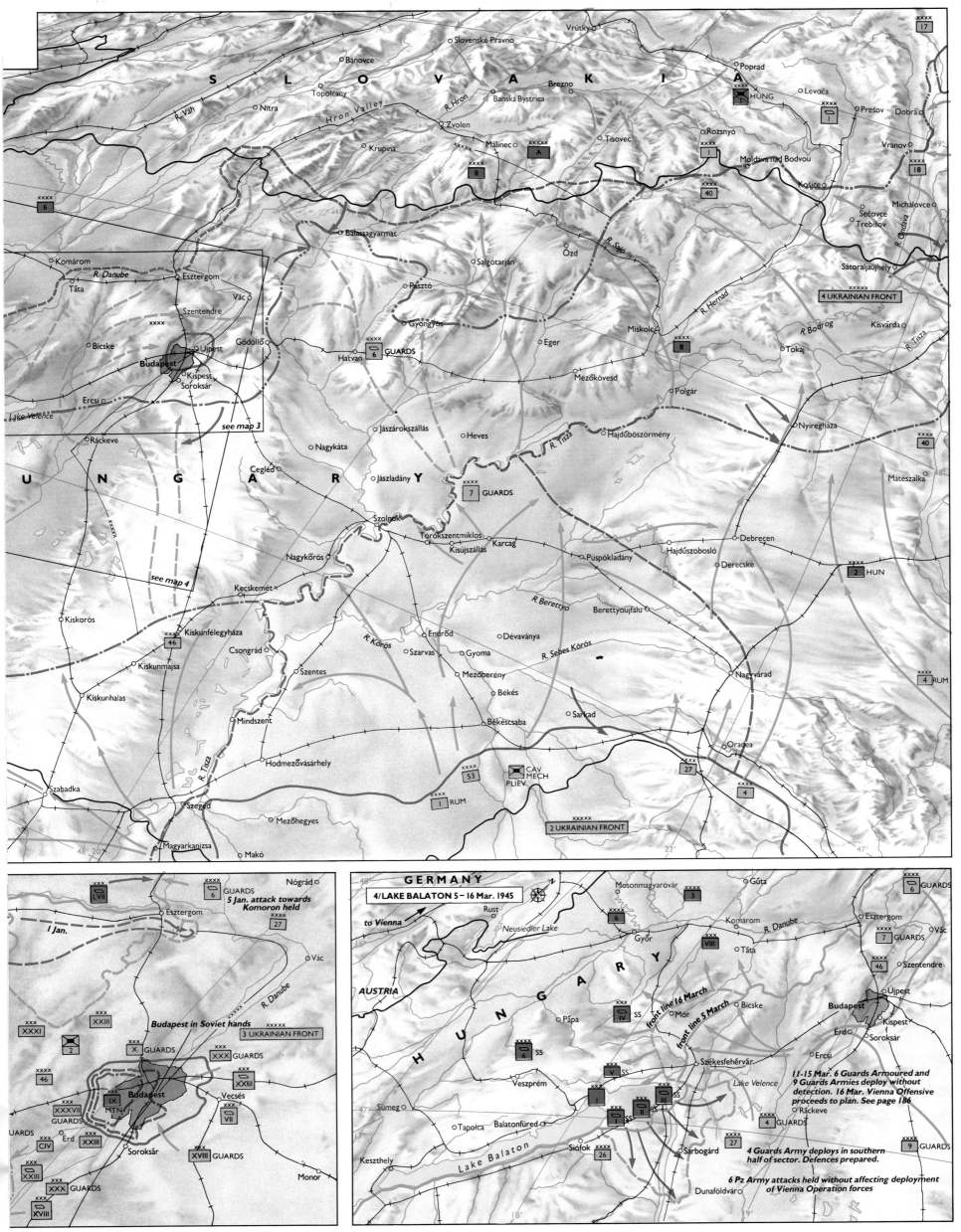

Arctic warfare 1941 ~ 1945

As THE GEOGRAPHICAL EXTENT of the war zones in both Europe and the Pacific expanded, so the Arctic region proved increasingly important to the combatants. There were a number of reasons for this: the Arctic seas were an essential communication route, particularly between British, North American and north Russian ports, for the transfer of war material to the Soviet Union; Arctic territories provided approach routes or land bridges to more populated and strategically significant regions below the Arctic Circle; they also yielded valuable mineral products, and weather stations established in the Arctic gave early warning of meteorological conditions affecting sea and air operations in lower latitudes. German attempts to establish weather stations west of Norway were largely foiled; briefly garrisoned Spitzbergen following a Commando raid (August 1941), and returned in 1943 to destroy the wiring installations on the island.

The Germans used Norwegian coastal waters to ship minerals from the Arctic at the outbreak of the war. Admiral Raeder's fears that the British would interrupt the traffic by mining, and his desire to seize bases for naval operations into the Atlantic, prompted him from October 1939 to urge Hitler to invade Norway. It was only, however, when evidence emerged that Britain and France might intervene in the Russo-Finnish war that Hitler decided to act (page 40).

The north Norwegian fjords then became important bases for the German navy which began to operate against British convoys to Murmansk and Archangel after June 1941; the arrival of the battleship *Tirpitz* at Trondheim in January 1942 greatly increased this threat. But the most important Arctic operations after the opening of *Barbarossa* in June 1941 were fought on land. By 1940 the Finns were in formal alliance with

Germany, seen as a means of securing their relations with the USSR. On 28 June 1941, the Finnish III Corps and the German *Armeeoberkommando Norwegen* attacked towards the Kola peninsula, but this drive was stopped on 1 July. To the south, they made some headway in the Karelian peninsula but stopped before reaching Leningrad. The Germans also attacked towards Kandalaksha on the White Sea, an offensive which the Finns successfully took over (19 August-19 September). When the Germans, who had brought reinforcements from the Balkans, reopened the offensive to cut the Murmansk railway (which remained the principal link to the Soviet heartland for supplies arriving by Arctic convoy), the Finns at first co-operated successfully (3 November onwards) but then declined to cross their 1939 border. From 1942 until September 1944 the German Lapland Army, commanded by Hitler's favourite general, Dietl, made little progress and was chiefly occupied in protecting the Petsamo nickel mines. When Finland changed sides in September 1944, only weeks into a major Soviet offensive, Dietl made a slow and skilful withdrawal into northern Norway, retaining a foothold in

Finland at Kilpisjärvi, which prevented its troops in the far north from being cut off, until April 1945.

On the far side of the Arctic ice cap, the Japanese occupied Kiska and Attu in the Aleutian Islands during the Midway campaign, to open the threat of an offensive towards American Alaska, and were not expelled until two years later. The force deployed there did not, however, constitute a serious strategic threat to the North American continent, although a Japanese presence on US territory continued to constitute a major propaganda coup. The Japanese presence on American soil eventually provoked a heavy-handed response in the form of bombardments and naval demonstrations which culminated in full force amphibious landings in 1943 by which time most of the Japanese garrisons had been evacuated. The important American convoys to Russia via the North Pacific and Bering Sea to Nikolayevsk were sustained.

The combatants' awareness of the potential that the Arctic region possessed as a peripheral but strategically valuable theatre of war was indicative of a major change in strategic thinking which began to emerge after 1941: no longer was warfare limited to a two-dimensional battlefield, located in or near the geographical centre of the dispute. It had now become an exercise in power projection around a global arena.

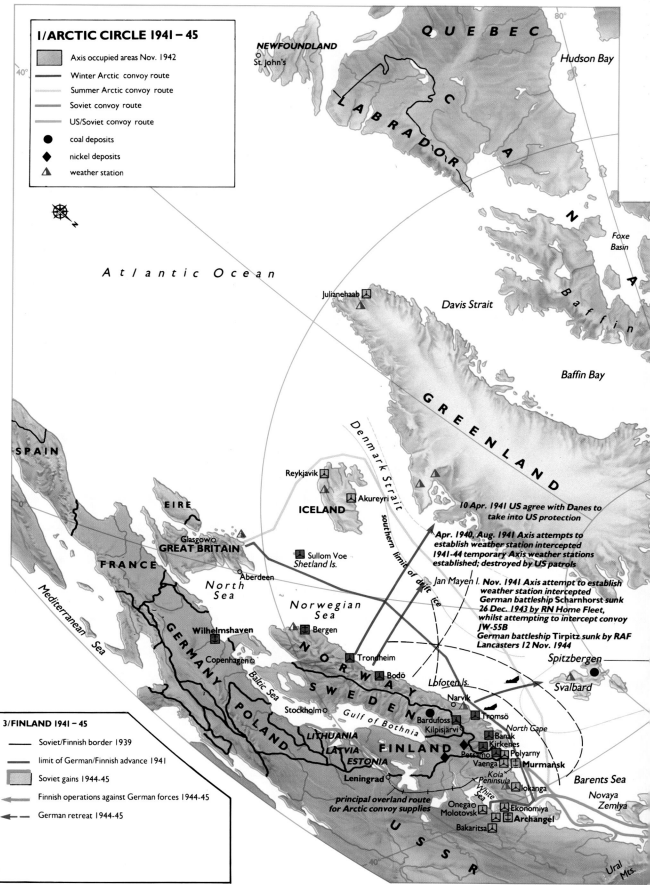

1/ARCTIC CIRCLE 1941 – 45

- Axis occupied areas Nov. 1942
- Winter Arctic convoy route
- Summer Arctic convoy route
- Soviet convoy route
- US/Soviet convoy route
- ● coal deposits
- ◆ nickel deposits
- △ weather station

10 Apr. 1941 US agree with Danes to take into US protection

Apr. 1940, Aug. 1941 Axis attempts to establish weather station intercepted
1941-44 temporary Axis weather stations established; destroyed by US patrols

Jan Mayen I. Nov. 1941 Axis attempt to establish weather station intercepted
German battleship Scharnhorst sunk 26 Dec. 1943 by RN Home Fleet, whilst attempting to intercept convoy JW-55B
German battleship Tirpitz sunk by RAF Lancasters 12 Nov. 1944

principal overland route for Arctic convoy supplies

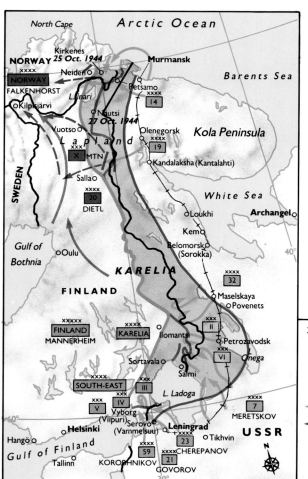

3/FINLAND 1941 – 45

- Soviet/Finnish border 1939
- limit of German/Finnish advance 1941
- Soviet gains 1944-45
- Finnish operations against German forces 1944-45
- German retreat 1944-45

THE MOST IMPORTANT Arctic ports for convoys bringing Lend-Lease war materials to Russia (1) were Murmansk and Archangel in the White Sea and Vladivostok in the Sea of Japan. Iceland, occupied by the British in May 1940 and taken over by the Americans in July 1941, was a vital intermediate base for air escorts to the north Atlantic and Arctic convoys. Iceland was also a major weather-reporting station, as were Greenland, Jan Mayen I. and Spitzbergen. The Germans sent meteorological parties to the last 3 territories, all of which were intercepted or captured by Free Norwegian, Royal Navy or US Coastguard patrols. The route to Vladivostok was threatened by the Japanese invasion of Kiska and Attu in the Aleutian islands (6-7 June 1941). Following a Japanese-American cruiser action off the Komandorski Islands (26 Mar. 1943) Attu (11-30 May), and Kiska (15 Aug.) were recaptured. Out of 39 Allied convoys to north Russian

ports via the Norwegian Sea in 1941-42, 69 ships, of 533 escorted, were lost to U-boat, air or surface attack. Convoy PQ17 (2) was attacked the most heavily. On hearing that the battleship Tirpitz, together with Scheer and Hipper, had sailed from Norway, the convoy commander ordered it to scatter: 23 out of 37 merchantmen were sunk by U-boat or air attack – although the battleship fleet abandoned its mission. Churchill then suspended north Russian convoys for some months. As an adjunct to Operation Barbarossa (page 56) Finnish and German forces opened an offensive (3) towards the Kola peninsula (28 June 1941) which was stopped by fierce Soviet resistance. In Nov., a new attempt was made to cut the Murmansk railway but the Finns refused to cross their 1939 frontier. In Sept. 1944, after the Finns changed sides, they and the Russians gradually forced the Germans back into northern Norway by Apr. 1945.

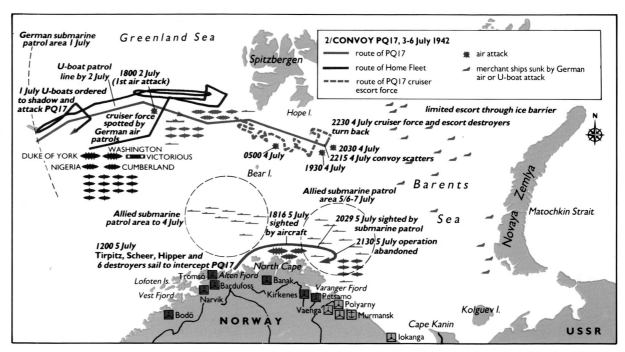

2/CONVOY PQ17, 3-6 July 1942
— route of PQ17
— route of Home Fleet
--- route of PQ17 cruiser escort force
★ air attack
⚓ merchant ships sunk by German air or U-boat attack

German submarine patrol area 1 July
U-boat patrol line by 2 July
1800 2 July (1st air attack)
1 July U-boats ordered to shadow and attack PQ17
cruiser force spotted by German air patrols
DUKE OF YORK
NIGERIA CUMBERLAND
WASHINGTON VICTORIOUS
limited escort through ice barrier
2230 4 July cruiser force and escort destroyers turn back
0500 4 July
2030 4 July
2215 4 July convoy scatters
1930 4 July
Allied submarine patrol area 5/6-7 July
Allied submarine patrol area to 4 July
1816 5 July sighted by aircraft
2029 5 July sighted by submarine patrol
2130 5 July operation abandoned
1200 5 July Tirpitz, Scheer, Hipper and 6 destroyers sail to intercept PQ17
North Cape
Tromsø Alten Fjord Banak
Lofoten Is. Bardufoss Kirkenes Varanger Fjord
Vest Fjord Narvik Petsamo
NORWAY Vaenga Polyarny Murmansk
Bodö Kolguev I. Cape Kanin
Greenland Sea
Spitzbergen
Hope I.
Bear I.
Barents Sea
Novaya Zemlya
Matochkin Strait
Iokanga
USSR

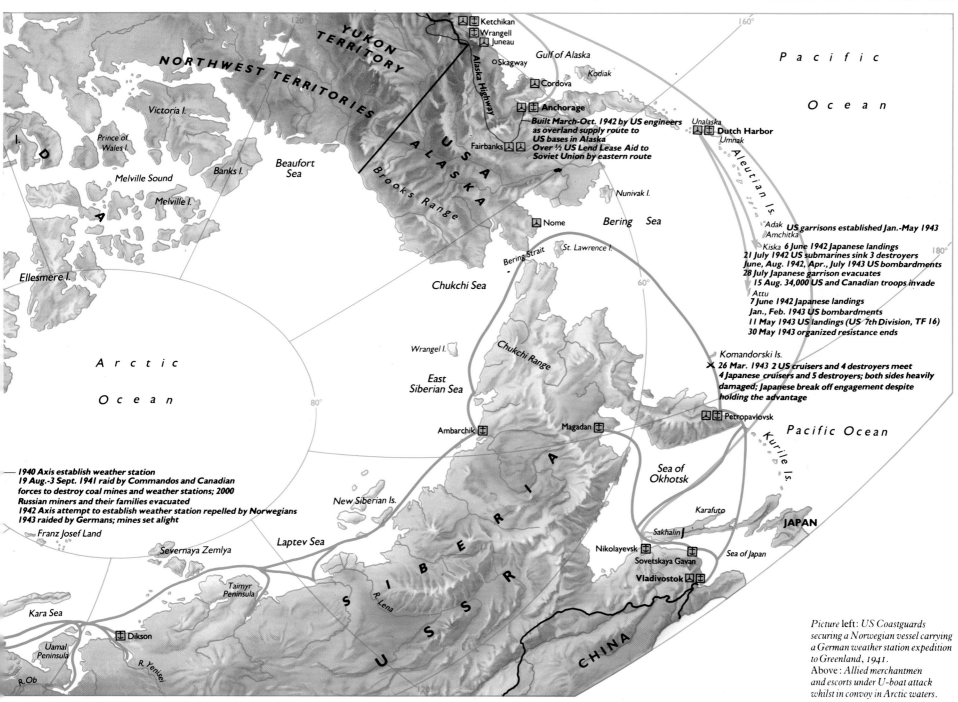

Ketchikan
Wrangell
Juneau
Skagway
YUKON TERRITORY
NORTHWEST TERRITORIES
Gulf of Alaska
Kodiak
Pacific Ocean
Cordova
Alaska Highway
Anchorage
Built March-Oct. 1942 by US engineers as overland supply route to US bases in Alaska
Over ½ US Lend Lease Aid to Soviet Union by eastern route
Unalaska
Dutch Harbor
Umnak
Fairbanks
ALASKA
Brooks Range
Aleutian Is.
Victoria I.
Prince of Wales I.
Beaufort Sea
Banks I.
Melville Sound
Melville I.
Nunivak I.
Nome
Bering Sea
Adak US garrisons established Jan.-May 1943
Amchitka
Kiska 6 June 1942 Japanese landings
21 July 1942 US submarines sink 3 destroyers
June, Aug. 1942, Apr., July 1943 US bombardments
28 July Japanese garrison evacuates
15 Aug. 34,000 US and Canadian troops invade
Attu
7 June 1942 Japanese landings
Jan., Feb. 1943 US bombardments
11 May 1943 US landings (US 7th Division, TF 16)
30 May 1943 organized resistance ends
Ellesmere I.
Bering Strait
St. Lawrence I.
Chukchi Sea
Arctic Ocean
Wrangel I.
East Siberian Sea
Chukchi Range
Komandorski Is.
26 Mar. 1943 2 US cruisers and 4 destroyers meet 4 Japanese cruisers and 5 destroyers; both sides heavily damaged; Japanese break off engagement despite holding the advantage
Petropavlovsk
Pacific Ocean
Ambarchik
Magadan
Sea of Okhotsk
Kurile Is.
1940 Axis establish weather station
19 Aug.-3 Sept. 1941 raid by Commandos and Canadian forces to destroy coal mines and weather stations; 2000 Russian miners and their families evacuated
1942 Axis attempt to establish weather station repelled by Norwegians
1943 raided by Germans; mines set alight
Franz Josef Land
New Siberian Is.
SIBERIA
Karafuto
Laptev Sea
Severnaya Zemlya
R. Lena
Nikolayevsk
Sakhalin
JAPAN
Taimyr Peninsula
Sovetskaya Gavan
Sea of Japan
Kara Sea
Dikson
USSR
Vladivostok
Yamal Peninsula
R. Yenisei
R. Ob
CHINA

Picture left: US Coastguards securing a Norwegian vessel carrying a German weather station expedition to Greenland, 1941.
Above: Allied merchantmen and escorts under U-boat attack whilst in convoy in Arctic waters.

Germany 1945

THE FAILURE OF the Ardennes offensive destroyed the counter-offensive potential of the German Army in the west and greatly reduced its defensive capabilities. In February it consisted of only three army groups, H (Student), defending Holland and the northern Rhineland, B (Model), defending the Ruhr, and G (Blaskowitz), in south Germany; all were under strength and lacked heavy equipment, particularly tanks.

Eisenhower, by contrast, deployed 85 full-strength divisions, of which 23 were armoured and five airborne, and enjoyed overwhelming airpower. His plan for the crossing of the Rhine and the advance into Germany fell into three phases. In the first, Montgomery's 21st Army Group was to clear the approaches to the lower Rhine, supported by Bradley's 9th Army. In the second, Bradley's 1st and 3rd Armies were to drive the Germans out of the Eifel and secure the middle reaches of the Rhine. In the third 7th and 3rd Armies were to clear the banks of the Moselle, while Montgomery launched a deliberate assault across the lower Rhine, together with 9th Army. In the exploitation phase, 9th and 1st Armies, once they had crossed the Rhine, were to encircle Army Group B in the Ruhr, while the others advanced to the Elbe-Czech/Austrian border, where they would make contact with the Red Army advancing from the East.

Eisenhower's plan unrolled as anticipated, with two exceptions: the Canadians, under Montgomery's command, met heavier opposition than expected on the lower Rhine, while US 1st Army surprised the German defenders of the Rhine bridge at Remagen, between Bonn and Coblenz, on 7 March and thus secured an unopposed landing on the far bank. 1st Army used this bridge to establish a lodgement from which it began its drive into Germany on 25 March. By then the British and Canadians, together with US 9th Army, had crossed the lower Rhine (23 March) and the US 7th and French 1st Armies were to do so shortly afterwards.

The German Army in the west had been reduced to a strength of 26 divisions in the fighting west of the Rhine and could offer only patchy resistance to the Allied assault and advance. Most forces, as before, were concentrated against the Russians; estimates of the latter in mid-April are as high as 214 divisions, including 34 Panzer and 15 motorized. Hitler had replaced Rundstedt with Kesselring on 10 March, but the successful defender of Italy altogether lacked the resources to organize a coherent defence of the Reich. The Ruhr was encircled by US 1st and 9th Armies on 1 April and the remnants of Army Group B within the pocket surrendered on 18 April; Model, its commander, committed suicide. The other Allied armies were meanwhile advancing, at up to 50 miles a day, towards the agreed border of their occupation zones on the Elbe, where their patrols met the Russians on 25 April.

Berlin was by then under siege and Hitler was directing the movement of phantom armies from his bunker. He refused his

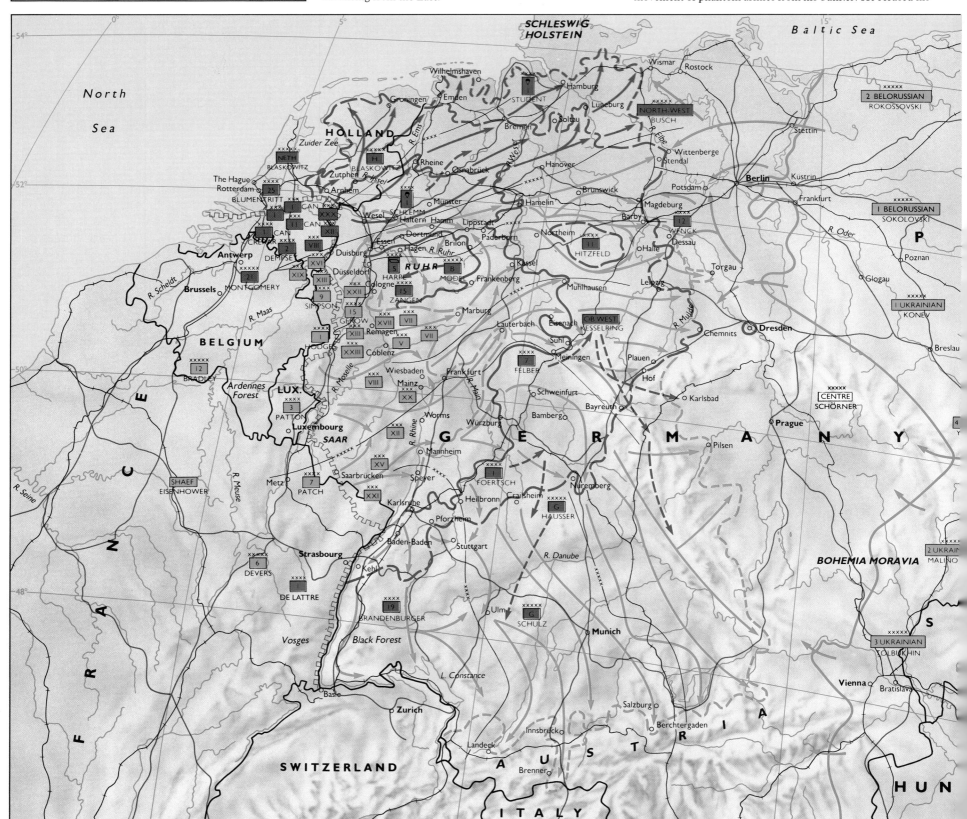

last chance to escape on 22 April, allowing his OKW staff to join OKH and Admiral Dönitz in a flight to the north. They eventually set up headquarters at Mürwik in Schleswig-Holstein which, after Hitler's suicide on 30 April, became the last seat of the government of the Third Reich.

By this time Soviet troops were in the suburbs of Berlin and by 27 April only a strip ten miles long and three and a half wide remained (page 184). Ringed by Russian guns and troops, the *Führer* reacted angrily on the 28th when he learned of Himmler's treachery in approaching Britain and the United States about a separate peace. That evening Artillery General Weidling, commander of Berlin, reported on the state of the collapsing city to Hitler, whom he later described to a Soviet interrogator as a 'sick, broken man'. The final battle conference was held on 29 April in the *Führerbunker*, Hitler sounding tired but forbidding the surrender of Berlin. At 0100 hours on 30 April, Keitel reported that all the German forces attempting to relieve Berlin had stalled, been encircled and forced onto the defensive. Hitler then, apparently, decided to kill himself. At 1530, about an hour after the Soviet victory banner was hoisted from the second floor of the Reichstag, Hitler and his bride Eva Braun retired to his study and committed suicide by biting ampoules of cyanide. That evening Weidling was summoned to the *Führerbunker* and told by Bormann, Himmler and Krebs that Hitler was dead and his body burned. At 2330 a German delegation informed Soviet officers that they had important news: at 0350 on 1 May General Chuikov, commanding 8th Guards Army, was told of Hitler's suicide.

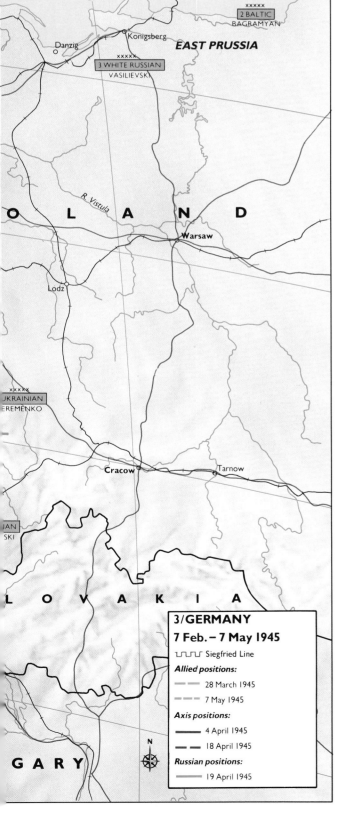

THE RHINELAND CAMPAIGN (*2*). After the containment (*1*) of the Ardennes offensive, the Canadian 1st Army moved to the attack. Operation *Veritable* (8 Feb.), designed to win ground west of the Rhine, encountered heavy resistance by 1st Parachute and 25th Armies. The US 9th Army, delayed by German inundation in the Rur Valley, could not join in (Operation *Grenade*) until 23 Feb., when it advanced northward to meet the Canadians (and the British who had moved forward in between). The US 1st Army, meanwhile, kept pace with 9th (Operation *Lumberjack*) and captured Cologne on the Rhine (5 Mar.). In the southern Rhineland the most dramatic event of the campaign was the capture of the Remagen bridge (7 Mar.), which fell to a surprise attack of 1st Army, after its German defenders had failed to set off demolition charges. Meanwhile, 3rd Army captured Trier (1 Mar.) and cleared the region south of the Moselle by 11 Mar. Between then and 25 Mar., 3rd and 7th Armies together occupied the Palatinate and the Saar and on 22 Mar. 3rd seized a bridgehead across the Rhine at Oppenheim. Operation *Plunder*, 21st Army Group's Rhine crossing, opened on 23 Mar. between Xanten and Rees. 9th Army crossed at Wesel next day, when the US 17th and British 6th Airborne Divisions were dropped across the Rhine to seize an airhead. By nightfall both were in contact with British 2nd and US 9th Armies which had established a bridgehead 6 miles deep. The US 3rd Army expanded its bridgehead on 25 Mar., entered Frankfurt the next day and linked bridgeheads with 1st Army (29 Mar.). The US 7th Army crossed at Worms (26 Mar.) and the French 1st Army at Speyer (31 Mar.). All armies then began their exploitation into Germany. (*3*) The US 9th and 1st Armies moved to encircle the Ruhr and met at Lippstadt, near Paderborn, on 1 Apr. The German defenders surrendered on 18 Apr. The British 2nd Army crossed the Weser on 5 Apr., reached the Elbe on 24 Apr. and took Hamburg on 3 May. When German emissaries arrived at Montgomery's headquarters to negotiate a surrender, the Canadian 1st Army was meanwhile clearing Holland. Spearheads of the US 9th Army reached the Elbe on 11 Apr. and 1st Army took Leipzig on 18 Apr. Both armies made contact with the Red Army near Togau on 25 Apr. 3rd Army, advancing through southern Germany, entered Austria and Czechoslovakia on 4 May. The US 7th and French 1st Armies both crossed the Danube on 22 Apr., to seize Munich on 30 Apr. and Salzburg on 4 May.

Pictures below left: *US Lt. Gen. Simpson and Field Marshal Montgomery inspect the Siegfried Line (West Wall) tank traps.* Below right: *US troops crossing the Rhine by boat.*

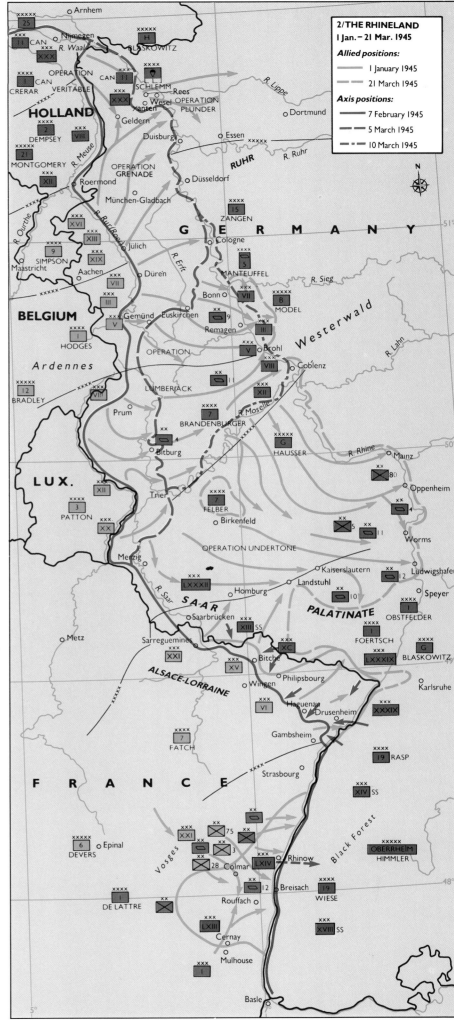

Berlin 1945

At the start of the Berlin operation (16 Apr.-18 May), the army groups defending Berlin could, on paper, muster a million men. The German command had constructed five defence lines in the Oder-Neisse Defence Zone, some 12 to 25 miles deep, in three 'belts'. Behind this lay the Berlin defence zone. The urban setting and the numerous rivers and canals made Berlin a very tough nut to crack. On 26 Apr. half a million Soviet troops supported by 12,700 guns and mortars and 21,000 multiple rocket launchers attacked the city centre. In the centre of the city (2), the high *Flak* towers with anti-aircraft guns on their roofs, which could fire down on Soviet tanks, presented a major hazard. Inside, and in cellars throughout the city, civilians sheltered, some driven insane by the intensity of shellfire. On 28 Apr., the bridge on the *Potsdamerstrasse* was seized. In the face of ferocious SS opposition, the storming of the *Tiergarten* (Zoo) began. That evening forces of 1st Byelorussian Front seized the Moltke bridge over the Spree and the Ministry of Internal Affairs (Himmler's House) (3). The Germans tried to blow the Moltke bridge but failed. The Reichstag was a formidable defensive position and could not be taken until Soviet forces were across the Spree in strength. Soviet artillery (including heavy 6- and 8-inch guns firing over open sights) fired a barrage at the Interior Ministry at 0700 on 29 Apr., and Soviet infantry broke into the Zoo whence they could fire up at the *Flak* towers (from the Hippopotamus House, one of whose residents survived). At midday on 30 Apr. regiments of 150th and 171st Rifle Divisions took up final assault positions, and at 1300 under a swathe of covering fire from heavy guns, *Katyusha* rocket launchers and even captured *Panzerfausts*, the Russians careered across the open ground before the Reichstag and up the central staircase. Soviet troops raised the victory banner on the roof at 2250, but the building was not entirely cleared until 2 May, the day the Berlin garrison ceased resistance.

Picture below right: the Reichstag, May 1945.

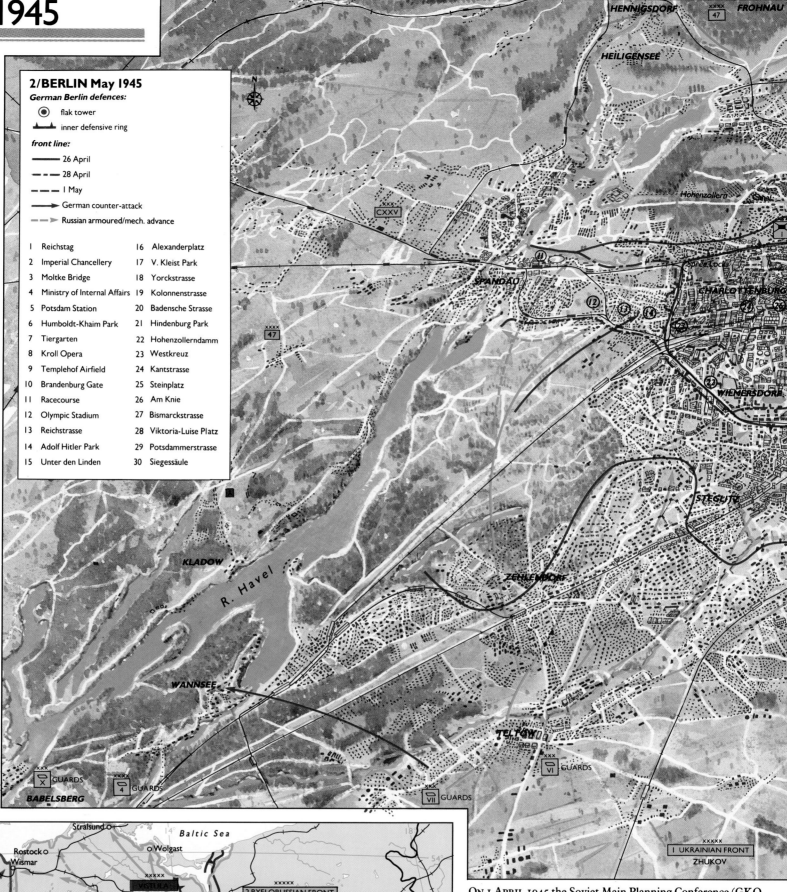

2/BERLIN May 1945

German Berlin defences:
- flak tower
- inner defensive ring

front line:
- —— 26 April
- — · — 28 April
- — — 1 May
- →→ German counter-attack
- ⇢⇢ Russian armoured/mech. advance

1	Reichstag	16	Alexanderplatz
2	Imperial Chancellery	17	V. Kleist Park
3	Moltke Bridge	18	Yorckstrasse
4	Ministry of Internal Affairs	19	Kolonnenstrasse
5	Potsdam Station	20	Badensche Strasse
6	Humboldt-Khaim Park	21	Hindenburg Park
7	Tiergarten	22	Hohenzollerndamm
8	Kroll Opera	23	Westkreuz
9	Templehof Airfield	24	Kantstrasse
10	Brandenburg Gate	25	Steinplatz
11	Racecourse	26	Am Knie
12	Olympic Stadium	27	Bismarckstrasse
13	Reichstrasse	28	Viktoria-Luise Platz
14	Adolf Hitler Park	29	Potsdammerstrasse
15	Unter den Linden	30	Siegessäule

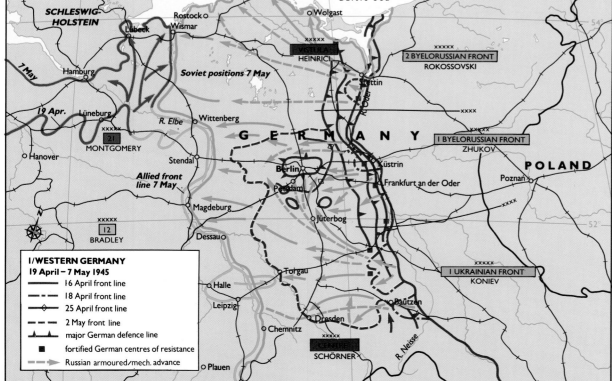

1/WESTERN GERMANY
19 April – 7 May 1945
- —— 16 April front line
- — — 18 April front line
- —◇— 25 April front line
- — · — 2 May front line
- ▲▲ major German defence line
- ■ fortified German centres of resistance
- ⇢⇢ Russian armoured/mech. advance

On 1 April 1945 the Soviet Main Planning Conference (GKO, plus Zhukov commanding 1st Byelorussian Front, Koniev commanding 1st Ukrainian, Antonov of the General Staff and Shtemenko of the Main Operations Directorate) met in Stalin's office. Stalin asked who was going to take Berlin: they or the Allies. Believing that the Western Allies were about to mount an operation to capture Berlin, there was no time to lose. Berlin lay in the path of Zhukov's 1st Byelorussian, with 1st Ukrainian to the south, but as an extra incentive Stalin scrubbed out the fixed operational Front boundary lines from 40 miles east of the Nazi capital. From there on in, Zhukov and Koniev would race. Rokossovski, whose 2nd Byelorussian was still heavily engaged in East Prussia, was ordered to stand by to swing from east to west, across devastated country, and attack north of Berlin.

The two fronts vying for first place in Berlin approached the task in distinctive ways. Zhukov already had a bridgehead across the Oder, around Küstrin, into which he poured over 8000 guns across 25 bridges. Zhukov would use over 140 searchlights to blind and confuse the defenders, but a short artillery barrage: only 30 minutes. Koniev, in contrast, opted for *Nacht und Nebel*: an attack under cover of darkness and smokescreens, but for a 145-minute barrage. Concealment was a real problem, especially for Zhukov's tightly-packed bridge-

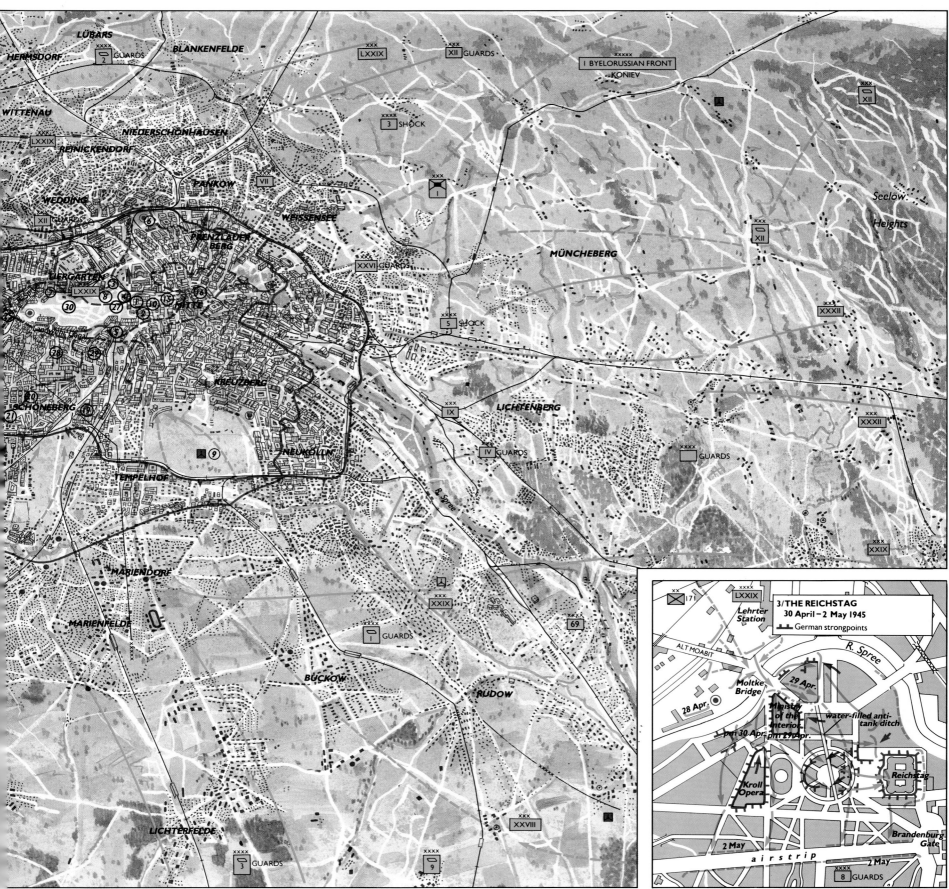

head. Spring came late that year and the leafless trees and sodden ground made camouflage and digging difficult. Soviet troops, many still wearing their winter fur hats, dug in their guns and brought seven million rounds of artillery ammunition to Zhukov's front line dumps.

The bombardment and assault were targeted with ruthless precision. Zhukov used a huge, elaborate scale model of Berlin for briefing and both fronts used air photographs of the German defences to a depth of 60 miles, with Soviet aircraft overflying some sectors eight times. Artillery fire-plans used the combined results of ground and air observation, and the engineers built their own model to study problems of street fighting.

Reconnaissance in force began on 14 April, but Zhukov failed to identify the main line of resistance further back. Zhukov's Front attacked at 0500 on the 16th, Koniev's at 0615. Koniev's attack across the Neisse went well, but Zhukov's troops stalled in the face of stiff resistance and the difficult obstacle of the Seelöw Heights. Stalin was furious at the delay, and that in his attempt to overcome it, Zhukov had launched both his tank armies (1st and 2nd Guards Tank) early, against *Stavka*'s instructions. Although behind schedule, by 19 April Zhukov had cracked all three defence belts in the Oder-Neisse zone and seized the Seelöw Heights and Müncheberg, west of Küstrin. On that night, Rokossovski's 2nd Byelorussian also

began its attack. Koniev and Zhukov raced on, Koniev ordering his two tank armies (3rd and 4th Guards) to break into Berlin on the night of 20th. By now, Russian artillery was pounding the city itself, already largely reduced to rubble by Anglo-American air bombardment. However, as the Russians knew, rubble makes a formidable fortress, even for boys and old men armed with *Panzerfausts*. On 23 April Stalin decreed that Zhukov had won the race: the front boundary line would run just 150 metres west of the Reichstag, the outstanding prize, placing it in 1st Byelorussian's sector. Berlin was completely encircled by 25 April, and next day nearly half a million Russian troops broke into the city centre. Late on the 28th, 79th Rifle Corps began to prepare its attack on the Reichstag. By the 30th, the 150th Division stood on the threshold of the symbolic seat of Nazi power, to the Red Army, 'target No. 105'. At 1425 hours two sergeants, Yegorov and Kantariya, flew the Red Victory Banner from the second floor, and at 2250 it was finally raised above the roof, although many German troops were still inside. For once, precious ammunition was fired off in a brief salute. That night, the Russians learned of Hitler's suicide. Negotiations continued until the middle of the next day, when Chuikov, commanding 8th Guards Army, exasperated at the unproductive talks, ordered artillery fire to be resumed. The Russians also learned of

Goebbels' death and improvised cremation on 1 May. Early in the morning of 2 May, Weidling commanding the Berlin garrison, drafted an order for Berlin to surrender, which the Russians approved. Germans hiding in the basement of the Reichstag began to surrender. At 1500 hours Soviet guns ceased fire in Berlin. The Third Reich lay in ruins.

Vienna and Prague 1945

As a result of the operations around Lake Balaton (page 178), Soviet forces had gained the southern shore of the lake by 15 March 1945. To the north, the forward edge of the advance ran west of Budapest and along a fold of the Carpathians behind the River Hron. The Vienna operation would complete the destruction of German forces in Hungary, capture the Austrian capital Vienna, and carry Soviet forces over the Lesser Carpathians, the western limit of the Carpathian range and a natural phase line.

Stavka's aim was to launch two splintering blows, one towards Pápa, one towards Gyor. 3rd Ukrainian attacked on 16 March after a heavy artillery and air preparation. On 19 March weakened tank armies were committed. The Germans made good use of the numerous defiles, narrow mountain passes and rivers to hold off the Soviet armour. The grouping from 2nd Ukrainian attacked on 17 March and successfully broke through German defences south of the Danube. On 2 April Soviet forces reached the Neusiedler Lake and the frontier between Austria and Hungary. Hungary was completely cleared of German occupation by 4 April.

From 5 to 8 April, the Soviet 46th Army was embarked on vessels of the Danube flotilla and landed on the north bank of the Danube to encircle Vienna from the north. 4th Guards Army attacked from the south east. Between 5 and 9 April

fierce street fighting raged in the suburbs of the city. On 6 April the Russians appealed to the remaining citizens of Vienna not to allow the Germans to demolish what remained of the city, and on 9 April the Soviet Government announced that they would fulfil the Moscow Declaration on the independence of Austria. Savage fighting for the city continued, however, until 13 April when Soviet forces took firm control of the city; 130,000 German troops were taken prisoner. The advance halted at Stockerau, as attention turned to the last battle being fought for Berlin (page 184).

Immediately after the fall of Berlin at the beginning of May, attention moved south again, to the last major concentration of Nazi forces in Europe: Schörner's Army Group Centre, now effectively encircled east of Prague by Soviet, and, more distantly, American forces. The Germans still hoped for a separate peace with the Western Allies: that was never on the cards, although Churchill and Eisenhower were agreed on the need to establish the demarcation line between the Russians and the Western Allies as far east as possible. This possibility encouraged the Russians to eliminate the last German groupings swiftly. Eisenhower proposed to the Russians that the Americans might now advance on Prague, but was sharply told that Western Allied forces should keep west of the demarcation line and out of Prague.

At the beginning of May nationalist risings broke out all over Czechoslovakia and on 5 May there was a rising in Prague itself, following news of the US advance into Bohemia. The situation was further complicated by the presence of Vlasov's KONR divisions, Russians in German employ. Vlasov himself urged his men to stand by the Germans; the Prague insurgents called on them as 'Russian and Soviet citizens' to desert the Germans and help them, while most of the Vlasov troops wanted nothing more than to surrender to the Americans and not be taken by the Red Army. Initially, Bunyachenko's 1st KONR division helped the insurgents, but as German forces from Army Group Centre moved in to crush the rising, they were trapped and forced to fight alongside the Waffen SS.

The Germans had surrendered unconditionally at Rheims on 7 May, but there was no guarantee that German forces would obey their own High Command and Schörner's troops were still fighting. Marshal Koniev transmitted details of the capitulation to all German units in western Czechoslovakia at 20.00 hours on 8 May, giving them three hours to respond. When they did not, the Russians fired a huge artillery barrage and resumed operations. Lelyushenko's 4th Guards Tank Army raced into Prague in the small hours of 9 May to report: 'Remaining fascist resistance destroyed. Many prisoners. … there are no American forces'. Prague had fallen, but Soviet forces raced on to accomplish the tight encirclement of Army Group Centre. On 11 May, three days after the Western Allies celebrated victory in Europe, and two days after the Russians did so, the last major German force surrendered.

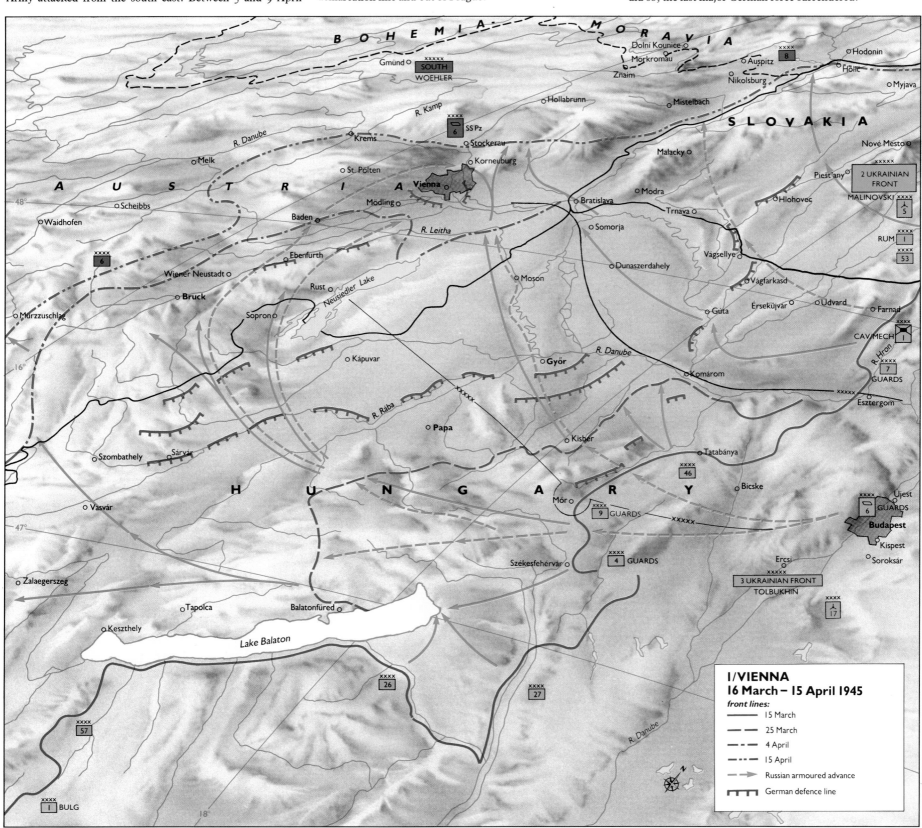

I/VIENNA
16 March – 15 April 1945

front lines:

———— 15 March

– – – – 25 March

–·–·– 4 April

–··–··– 15 April

⟶ Russian armoured advance

⊢⊢⊢⊢ German defence line

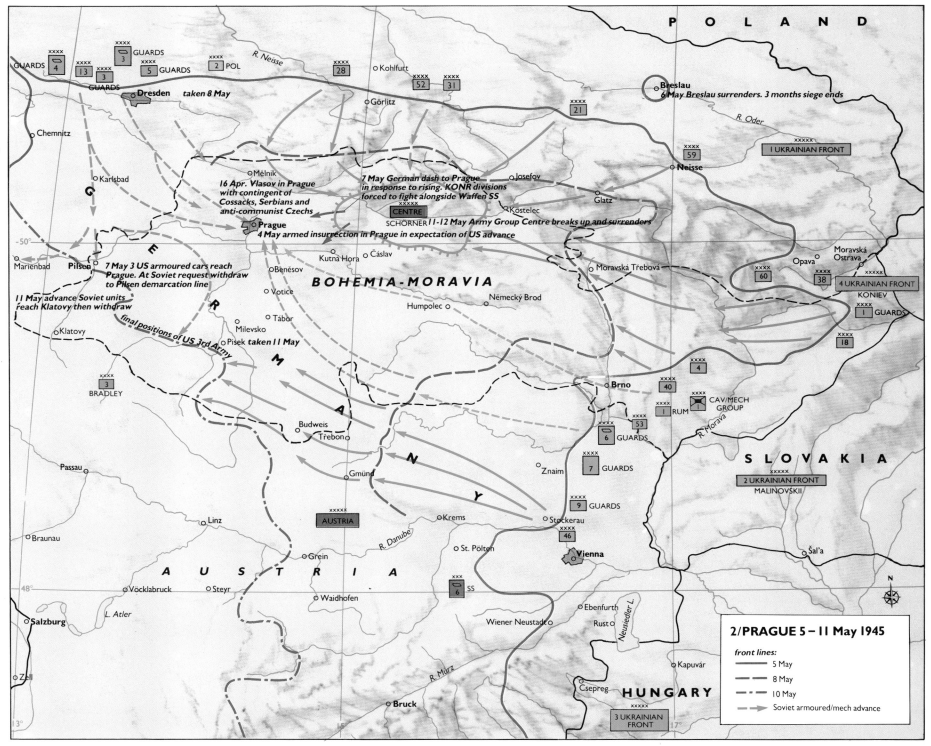

GUARDS **GUARDS** **GUARDS**
XXXX 4 | XXXX 13 | 3 | 3 GUARDS | XXXX 5 GUARDS | XXXX 2 POL | XXXX 28 | R. Neisse

POLAND

Kohlfurt ○
Görlitz ○
XXXX 52 | XXXX 31
XXXX 21

Breslau ○
6 May Breslau surrenders. 3 months siege ends

GUARDS **Dresden** *taken 8 May*
Chemnitz ○

Karlsbad ○

R. Oder

XXXX 59
○ **Neisse**

Glatz ○

I UKRAINIAN FRONT

Mělník ○
16 Apr. Vlasov in Prague with contingent of Cossacks, Serbians and anti-communist Czechs

7 May German dash to Prague in response to rising. KONR divisions forced to fight alongside Waffen SS

Josefov ○
Kostelec ○

Moravská Ostrava ○
Opava ○

XXXX 60 | XXXX 38 | 4 UKRAINIAN FRONT KONIEV

CENTRE
SCHÖRNER *11–12 May Army Group Centre breaks up and surrenders*
Prague ○
4 May armed insurrection in Prague in expectation of US advance

G E R M A N Y

Kutná Hora ○ Čáslav ○

Moravská Třebová ○

XXXX 1 GUARDS | XXXX 18

Pilsen
7 May 3 US armoured cars reach Prague. At Soviet request withdraw to Pilsen demarcation line
Mariembad ○

Benešov ○
Votice ○

Humpolec ○
Německý Brod ○

B O H E M I A - M O R A V I A

XXXX 4 | XXXX 40

11 May advance Soviet units reach Klatovy then withdraw
Klatovy ○
final positions of US 3rd Army
Milevsko ○
Tábor ○
Pisek taken 11 May ○

Brno ○
XXXX 1 RUM | CAV/MECH GROUP

XXXX 3 BRADLEY

XXXX 6 GUARDS | XXXX 53

R. Morava

Budweis ○
Třebon ○

XXXX 7 GUARDS

S L O V A K I A

Passau ○

Gmünd ○

Znaim ○
Stockerau ○

XXXX 9 GUARDS

2 UKRAINIAN FRONT MALINOVSKII

Šal'a ○

Linz ○
Braunau ○
Vöcklabruck ○
Steyr ○

R. Danube
Krems ○

XXXX 46
Vienna ○

AUSTRIA

St. Pölten ○
Grein ○

Salzburg ○
Zell ○
L. Atler

Waidhofen ○

XXX 6 SS

A U S T R I A

Ebenfurth ○
Rust ○
Neusiedler L.

Wiener Neustadt ○

N

2/PRAGUE 5–11 May 1945

front lines:
——— 5 May
– – – 8 May
–·–·– 10 May
⇒ Soviet armoured/mech advance

R. Mürz

Kapuvár ○
C.se preg ○

HUNGARY

Bruck ○

3 UKRAINIAN FRONT

DENMARK
Baltic Sea

3/THE EASTERN FRONT
16 Feb. – 11 May 1945

–·–·– agreed US/USSR demarcation line

16 Feb. front line

N

Berlin ○
7 May

POLAND

R. Mulde
R. Oder

25 Apr. front line

GERMANY

Breslau ○

16 Apr. - 7 May front line

Pilsen ○
R. Elbe
Prague ○

BOHEMIA-MORAVIA
7 May

R. Danube
Slavkov (Austerlitz) ○
Soviet front line

16 Apr Soviet front line

SLOVAKIA

US positions 7 May
Vienna ○

AUSTRIA

see map 2

Budapest ○
7 May
L. Balaton

see map 1

ITALY

HUNGARY

7 May

Adriatic Sea

YUGOSLAVIA

IN THE VIENNA OPERATION (16 Mar. to 15 Apr., 1945) (*1*), the Soviet 3rd Ukrainian Front comprised 18 Rifle Divisions, 3900 guns and mortars, 800 aircraft but only 197 tanks and assault guns. 2nd Ukrainian comprised 12 rifle divisions, 2686 guns and mortars and just 165 tanks and assault guns. The low density of armour was in part due to the terrain. Despite the German defensive positions at Gyor, by 4th Apr. Soviet forces were 5 miles to the south of Vienna, defended by 1 mechanized and 8 Panzer divisions and 15 independent battalions. Soviet progress into the city itself was slow, and Vienna did not fall until 13 Apr. Soviet advances in this region stalled for the rest of the month. After the fall of Berlin, German Army Groups Centre and Austria (total of 900,000 men, 9700 guns and mortars, 1900 tanks and assault guns and 1000 aircraft) remained the last centres of German resistance in Europe. Allied advances from the west and the uprisings in Czechoslovakia from 1 May added to the urgency, and the Russians mounted the Prague operation (6-11 May 1945) (*2*). Three Russian fronts closed for the kill, 1st, 2nd and 4th Ukrainian; 1st Guards Cavalry-Mechanized Group (KMG), and various independent corps, including 2nd Polish, 1st and 4th Rumanian Armies and 1st Czech Army Corps. These forces totalled

two million men, 30,500 guns and mortars, 2000 tanks and assault guns and over 3000 aircraft. The Prague uprising, in which some 30,000 insurgents fought behind 1600 barricades, occurred on 5 May; on 6 May, the Soviet operation was launched, eliminating the German grouping at Breslau. On 8 May, Dresden was captured and on 9 May, after German forces in Czechoslovakia ignored the surrender signed at Rheims on 7 May, Soviet armoured formations raced into Prague. The possibility of US forces from the west reaching Prague ahead of the Russians had arisen in late Apr. (*3*), but the Americans agreed to respect the agreed demarcation line in Czechoslovakia, since the Russians had deliberately halted their advance in Germany at the lower Elbe. The Russians fulfilled their undertaking to restore an independent Austria, although the last two Soviet divisions were not withdrawn from Austria until 1955. US forces vacated Czechoslovakia almost immediately. Excepting the Soviet gain of Ruthenia, in this area, unlike Germany and Poland to the north, the 1938 national boundaries were restored.

Picture right: Soviet T-34 tanks line a Prague thoroughfare following the expulsion of German forces.

Politics and strategy 1944~1945

THE MAIN LINES of Allied agreement had been established by the end of 1943: there would be a great concentration of force for the invasion of western Europe, whereas Stalin would be free to occupy such areas as his army conquered. Churchill continued to hope for an Allied thrust beyond Italy into northern Yugoslavia, Hungary and Austria, at the expense of Operation *Anvil* in southern France. However, *Anvil* went ahead (page 156) slowing the Allied front in Italy after the capture of Rome in June 1944 (pages 130-132).

Following the success of *Overlord* Churchill and Roosevelt met again at Quebec (*Octagon*, 11-16 September 1944) where Eisenhower's plan for a thrust into north-central Germany was approved, and Roosevelt supported plans to parachute British troops into Greece, with a suggestion for landing an Anglo-US force in northern Yugoslavia and to relieve Chiang Kai-shek (under pressure, by now even in Chungking, page 144), by an attack on Rangoon and clearing of the Burma Road. Further, a division of post-war Germany into British, American and Soviet zones was adopted, and the Morgenthau Plan for turning the German economy into a pastoral one was accepted.

Churchill then flew to Moscow to confer with Stalin (9-20 October) and the US ambassador, W. Averell Harriman. Churchill proposed a division of eastern Europe into zones of influence – the Soviets being preponderant in Bulgaria and Rumania, the British in Greece, with rough equality in Yugoslavia and Hungary. There was a lengthy wrangle about Poland's future. Stalin remained adamant concerning those territories annexed in 1939/40 – the more so as his troops now occupied the entire area in question – Churchill believed that the Polish exile government's only hope of retaining independence from the Soviet Union after the war was to accept this, with territorial compensation at Germany's expense. The spheres of influence did, however, work tolerably well as far as immediate British interests were concerned: Stalin strongly discouraged the Greek Communists from seizing power in the Winter of 1944-45 (page 128), and the Italian Communists from disrupting the multi-party system in Italy. Western political influence in Yugoslavia appeared, also, to be secured through an agreement with the Communist leader, Tito (page 128).

The final meeting of Roosevelt, Stalin and Churchill was at Yalta between 4 and 11 February 1945. Here the Western Powers finally withdrew their recognition of the Polish exile government in London. The proposed compensation of Poland at Germany's expense was agreed in principle. In Germany, the Morgenthau Plan had already been dropped; instead, a conference in Moscow would determine how Germany should pay reparations for the damage that she had done. A fourth zone of occupation, for the French, was agreed, at British insistence; there would be trials of major war criminals; and, as part of a general hand-over of each Allies' nationals, the Western Powers agreed that they would repatriate Soviet citizens found in German control (page 190). Stalin also promised that he would intervene against Japan. In return for this promise Stalin secured territorial gains in Sakhalin and the Kurile Is. (page 200).

Arrangements for the post-war world had been discussed during the War. In San Francisco, on 25 April 1945, the basis of the United Nations was agreed, the Charter of which, as drafted at Dumbarton Oaks, had been considered at Yalta. In 1943 the United States created a United Nations Relief and Rehabilitation Agency (UNRRA) which did most, after the war, to resolve the stricken circumstances of most of Europe. But these arrangements did not prevent the development of rival power blocs and an arms race (the Cold War). However, a new Council of Foreign Ministers continued to hold meetings for some years to come. The final conference of the war (*Terminal*, 17 July-2 August 1945) was held at Potsdam. The late President Roosevelt was replaced by Harry S. Truman who came with the new Secretary of State, James F. Byrnes; Stalin was present, as were Churchill and Eden, and the future Prime Minister, Clement Attlee. On 26 July, Japan was summoned to surrender by the Declaration of Potsdam which, through a still-neutral Moscow, she accepted, but with such qualification as amounted to a refusal in Allied eyes. The US now had atom bombs to use against Japan and Stalin was informed, in general terms, of this fact; he was also set to intervene in the Pacific War, although it was recognized that this would extend Soviet power over parts of China. Various other questions proved too difficult for Potsdam to resolve, and these were handed over to the new Council of Foreign Ministers. These questions included the drafting of peace treaties, but arriving at an agreement over the details of these would prove a long and arduous task.

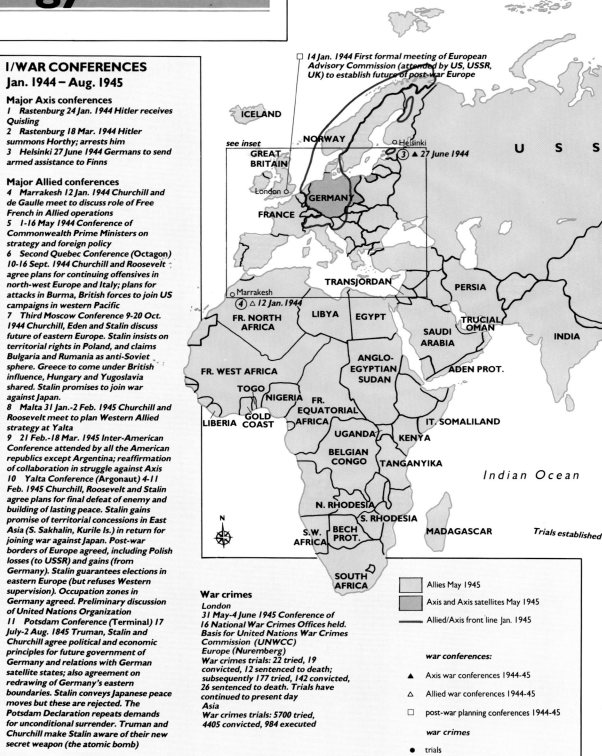

1/WAR CONFERENCES
Jan. 1944 – Aug. 1945

Major Axis conferences
1 *Rastenburg 24 Jan. 1944 Hitler receives Quisling*
2 *Rastenburg 18 Mar. 1944 Hitler summons Horthy; arrests him*
3 *Helsinki 27 June 1944 Germans to send armed assistance to Finns*

Major Allied conferences
4 *Marrakesh 12 Jan. 1944 Churchill and de Gaulle meet to discuss role of Free French in Allied operations*
5 *1-16 May 1944 Conference of Commonwealth Prime Ministers on strategy and foreign policy*
6 *Second Quebec Conference (Octagon) 10-16 Sept. 1944 Churchill and Roosevelt agree plans for continuing offensives in north-west Europe and Italy; plans for attacks in Burma, British forces to join US campaigns in western Pacific*
7 *Third Moscow Conference 9-20 Oct. 1944 Churchill, Eden and Stalin discuss future of eastern Europe. Stalin insists on territorial rights in Poland, and claims Bulgaria and Rumania as anti-Soviet sphere. Greece to come under British influence, Hungary and Yugoslavia shared. Stalin promises to join war against Japan.*
8 *Malta 31 Jan.-2 Feb. 1945 Churchill and Roosevelt meet to plan Western Allied strategy at Yalta*
9 *21 Feb.-18 Mar. 1945 Inter-American Conference attended by all the American republics except Argentina; reaffirmation of collaboration in struggle against Axis*
10 *Yalta Conference (Argonaut) 4-11 Feb. 1945 Churchill, Roosevelt and Stalin agree plans for final defeat of enemy and building of lasting peace. Stalin gains promise of territorial concessions in East Asia (S. Sakhalin, Kurile Is.) in return for joining war against Japan. Post-war borders of Europe agreed, including Polish losses (to USSR) and gains (from Germany). Stalin guarantees elections in eastern Europe (but refuses Western supervision). Occupation zones in Germany agreed. Preliminary discussion of United Nations Organization*
11 *Potsdam Conference (Terminal) 17 July-2 Aug. 1845 Truman, Stalin and Churchill agree political and economic principles for future government of Germany and relations with German satellite states; also agreement on redrawing of Germany's eastern boundaries. Stalin conveys Japanese peace moves but these are rejected. The Potsdam Declaration repeats demands for unconditional surrender. Truman and Churchill make Stalin aware of their new secret weapon (the atomic bomb)*

□ *14 Jan. 1944 First formal meeting of European Advisory Commission (attended by US, USSR, UK) to establish future of post-war Europe*

War crimes
London
31 May-4 June 1945 Conference of 16 National War Crimes Offices held. Basis for United Nations War Crimes Commission (UNWCC)
Europe (Nuremberg)
War crimes trials: 22 tried, 19 convicted, 12 sentenced to death; subsequently 177 tried, 142 convicted, 26 sentenced to death. Trials have continued to present day
Asia
War crimes trials: 5700 tried, 4405 convicted, 984 executed

	Allies May 1945
	Axis and Axis satellites May 1945
▬	Allied/Axis front line Jan. 1945

war conferences:
▲ Axis war conferences 1944-45
△ Allied war conferences 1944-45
□ post-war planning conferences 1944-45

war crimes
● trials

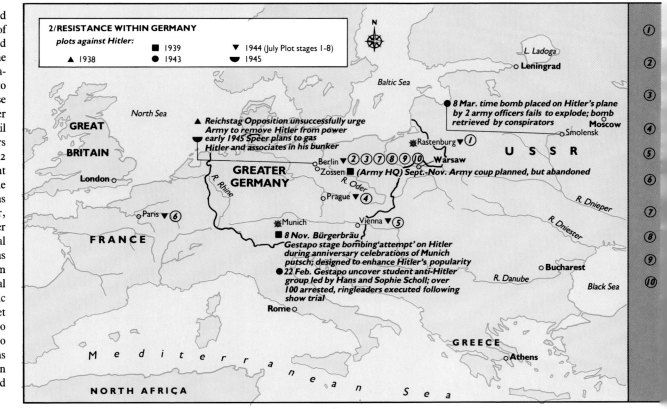

2/RESISTANCE WITHIN GERMANY
plots against Hitler:
▲ 1938   ■ 1939   ● 1943   ▼ 1944 (July Plot stages 1-8)   ▼ 1945

▲ *Reichstag Opposition unsuccessfully urge Army to remove Hitler from power*
▼ *early 1945 Speer plans to gas Hitler and associates in his bunker*

● *8 Mar. time bomb placed on Hitler's plane by 2 army officers fails to explode; bomb retrieved by conspirators*

■ *(Army HQ) Sept.-Nov. Army coup planned, but abandoned*

■ *8 Nov. Bürgerbräu*
Gestapo stage bombing 'attempt' on Hitler during anniversary celebrations of Munich putsch; designed to enhance Hitler's popularity
● *22 Feb. Gestapo uncover student anti-Hitler group led by Hans and Sophie Scholl; over 100 arrested, ringleaders executed following show trial*

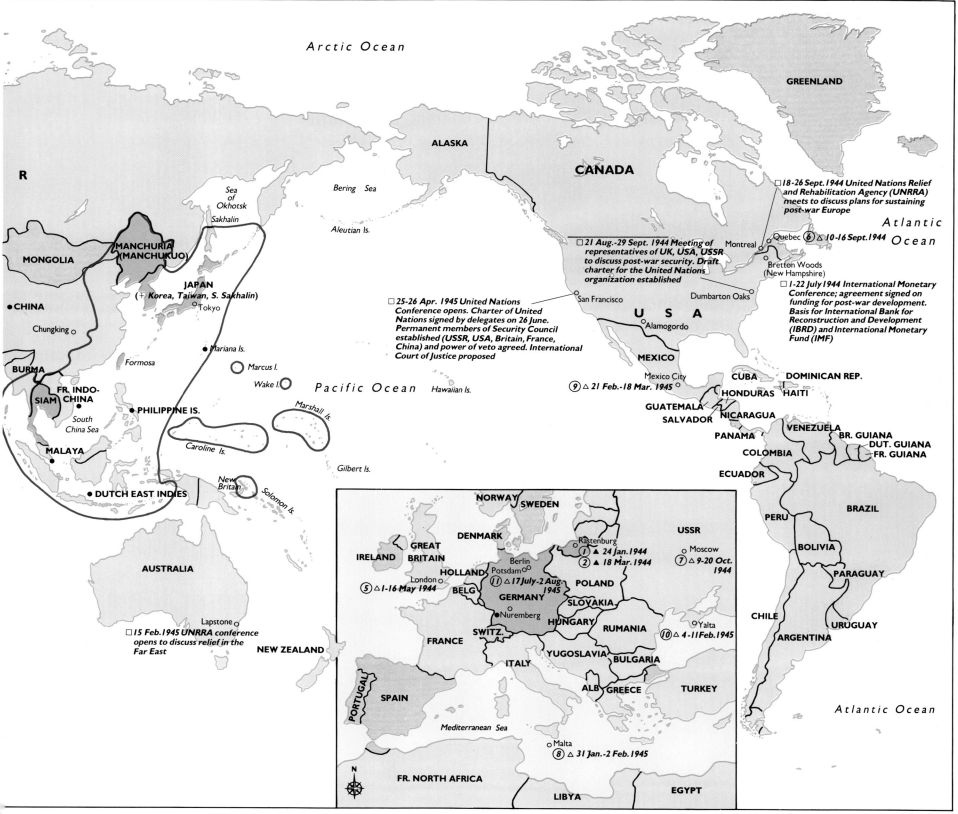

Arctic Ocean

GREENLAND

ALASKA

CANADA

□ 18-26 Sept. 1944 United Nations Relief and Rehabilitation Agency (UNRRA) meets to discuss plans for sustaining post-war Europe

Atlantic Ocean

R

Sea of Okhotsk

Sakhalin

Bering Sea

Aleutian Is.

Montreal

Quebec ⑥ △ 10-16 Sept. 1944

MONGOLIA

MANCHURIA (MANCHUKUO)

CHINA

JAPAN (+ Korea, Taiwan, S. Sakhalin)

Tokyo

□ 21 Aug.-29 Sept. 1944 Meeting of representatives of UK, USA, USSR to discuss post-war security. Draft charter for the United Nations organization established

Bretton Woods (New Hampshire)

Dumbarton Oaks

□ 1-22 July 1944 International Monetary Conference; agreement signed on funding for post-war development. Basis for International Bank for Reconstruction and Development (IBRD) and International Monetary Fund (IMF)

Chungking

Formosa

Mariana Is.

Marcus I.

□ 25-26 Apr. 1945 United Nations Conference opens. Charter of United Nations signed by delegates on 26 June. Permanent members of Security Council established (USSR, USA, Britain, France, China) and power of veto agreed. International Court of Justice proposed

San Francisco

U S A

Alamogordo

MEXICO

BURMA

FR. INDO-CHINA

SIAM

Wake I.

Pacific Ocean

Hawaiian Is.

Mexico City

⑨ △ 21 Feb.-18 Mar. 1945

CUBA

DOMINICAN REP.

HONDURAS HAITI

PHILIPPINE IS.

South China Sea

Marshall Is.

GUATEMALA

SALVADOR

NICARAGUA

VENEZUELA

BR. GUIANA

DUT. GUIANA

MALAYA

Caroline Is.

Gilbert Is.

PANAMA

COLOMBIA

FR. GUIANA

ECUADOR

New Britain

Solomon Is.

NORWAY

SWEDEN

PERU

BRAZIL

DUTCH EAST INDIES

DENMARK

USSR

IRELAND

GREAT BRITAIN

Rastenburg

① ▲ 24 Jan. 1944

Moscow

⑦ △ 9-20 Oct. 1944

BOLIVIA

AUSTRALIA

HOLLAND

London

② ▲ 18 Mar. 1944

BELG

⑤ △ 1-16 May 1944

Berlin

Potsdam

⑪ △ 17 July-2 Aug. 1945

POLAND

PARAGUAY

GERMANY

SLOVAKIA

CHILE

Lapstone

□ 15 Feb. 1945 UNRRA conference opens to discuss relief in the Far East

NEW ZEALAND

FRANCE

Nuremberg

SWITZ.

HUNGARY

RUMANIA

ITALY

YUGOSLAVIA

BULGARIA

Yalta

⑩ △ 4-11 Feb. 1945

URUGUAY

ARGENTINA

PORTUGAL

SPAIN

ALB

GREECE

TURKEY

Atlantic Ocean

Mediterranean Sea

Malta

⑧ △ 31 Jan.-2 Feb. 1945

N

FR. NORTH AFRICA

LIBYA

EGYPT

189

July Bomb Plot

20 July Bomb placed by Stauffenburg explodes at conference; 1 officer killed, Hitler injured

20 July Stauffenburg flies to Berlin, activates coup (1545) with Beck, Goerdeler, Witzleben, Olbricht

20 July Army fails to secure SS and government quarter upon hearing of Hitler's survival

20 July Army coup activated from Berlin, fails

20 July Army coup activated from Berlin, fails

20 July Gen Stülpnagel activates army coup, arrests 1200 SS and SD; Army control collapses 21 July

Olbricht and Stauffenburg shot by SS; Beck allowed to commit suicide

0300 Hitler broadcasts his survival from all German radio stations

7 Aug. Witzleben, Höppner, Hase, Stieff tried and (8 Aug.) executed

Over next 5 months c.5000 'suspected' conspirators tried and executed; many more sent to concentration camps, Rommel invited to commit suicide

THE LAST 2 YEARS OF THE WAR saw Allied diplomacy reach a peak as successful large-scale offensives in western, eastern and southern Europe opened the way for detailed discussions over the future of Europe and indeed the post-war world as a whole. In the Pacific, the Western Allies' offensives met such determined opposition that the decision to deploy the newly-developed atom bomb against Japan became inevitable. The Soviet Union declared war on Japan 2 days after the first nuclear attack, on Hiroshima (8 Aug. 1945). Despite the turning tide of the war, support for Hitler in Germany remained strong. Active resistance (2) had always been limited and largely focussed on the left-wing, the aristocracy and the Army. Drawn from the latter groups, the Kreisau Circle had abandoned several attempts on the *Führer's* life; the only serious plot, on 20 July 1944, failed when Hitler survived a bomb explosion at his HQ at Rastenburg. A lack of resolve among many of the senior officers who stood ready to take control of the Reich upon the announcement of Hitler's death, led the coup to misfire, and

brought extensive and horrific recriminations. Nine months later Hitler committed suicide as the Russians entered Berlin. Goebbels and Himmler also took their lives, and Bormann was killed in the ruins of Berlin; Mussolini was executed by Italian partisans. With these exceptions, the majority of the Axis war leaders eventually stood trial before the International War Crimes Commission which convened at Nuremberg and at Tokyo, and which defined the moral and ideological nature of the Allied victory.

Picture below: a poster redirecting the Allied war effort against Japan following the German surrender in Europe. Right: the first atomic (plutonium fission) bomb was detonated in a test explosion at Alamogordo, New Mexico on 16 July 1945. On 24 July President Truman decided to use the weapon against Japan if peace terms were not forthcoming. On 6 Aug. a uranium isotope bomb was dropped on Hiroshima, and on 8 Aug. a plutonium fission bomb was dropped on Nagasaki. Approximately 120,000 people were killed by the bombs outright.

THE ALLIED LEADERS, Roosevelt, Churchill and Stalin had agreed at Teheran in November 1943 to set up a European Advisory Commission which, sitting in London, would draw up plans for the eventual occupation of Germany. These, which anticipated the advance of the Allied armies from the east and from Normandy, allotted eastern Germany to the Russians, north Germany to the British and south Germany to the Americans. Berlin was to be under tripartite control; a proposal of Roosevelt's for a corridor linking Berlin to the western zones was overlooked. The Commission completed its plan in March 1944 and it was adopted at Yalta in February 1945; there, at Britain's suggestion, British and American areas were reduced to allot France an occupation zone in the Palatinate, Baden and Württemberg, and a sector of Berlin.

Knowledge that the boundary between the Russian and western zones of occupation was to follow the line of the River Elbe reached the Germans before their collapse; this prompted Admiral Dönitz, who assumed German leadership following Hitler's suicide, to prolong resistance against the Russians while seeking to persuade the British and Americans to hold open a line of retreat for the millions of Germans fleeing from the east. Dönitz sent Admiral von Friedeburg to negotiate a local surrender in north Germany with Montgomery on 3 May, but he was obliged to sign a capitulation which became effective on 4 May. Jodl was similarly treated at Eisenhower's

headquarters at Rheims on 6 May. His delegates were forced to surrender unconditionally on 7 May. The terms became effective on 8 May and were ratified at Berlin on 9 May. The Western Allies did not, however, complete their withdrawals from east of the Elbe until 7 July, two days before they took possession, against marked Russian reluctance, of their sectors of Berlin. The Allied Control Commission for Germany came into operation on 22 June, one month after Dönitz and his 'government' had been confined at Flensburg.

The first heads of administration in the four zones were military commanders: Clay (American), Montgomery (British), Zhukov (Russian) and Koenig (French). The Western commanders imposed policies of 'non-fraternization' while 'denazification' began; the Soviets were more interested in stripping their zone of industrial plunder for war reparation. In all zones, however, the powers quickly permitted the revival of the pre-Nazi parties; local elections were permitted in the American zone in January 1946 and the revival of political life in the British and French zones resulted in the formation of a German Federal Republic, embracing all three, on 21 September 1949. Its creation, however, stemmed from the failure of the Western powers to agree terms for a general German peace settlement with the Russians, who quickly extinguished the non-Communist parties in their zone (through which they denied the Western powers land access to Berlin

during the blockade of 1948-49) and sponsored its transformation into the German Democratic Republic, under Communist government, on 7 October 1949. The United States, Britain and France terminated their state of war with the Federal Republic in 1951 and the Soviet Union followed suit in 1955.

Zones of occupation in Austria were not agreed until Yalta, where Vienna was also placed under quadripartite status, with the centre as an international zone. On 29 April 1945, however, the *Anschluss* with Germany was renounced and the pre-1938 republic declared restored by a Russian-sponsored government. The Western powers reluctantly recognized this government on 20 October but elections held in November returned a democratic majority. As Austria was deemed a 'liberated' state, its new government progressively assumed authority from the occupation powers and all foreign troops left Austria on the signing of the Austrian draft Treaty of Independence (1955).

The war left Europe in 1945, not only politically disorganized but also in a state of economic prostration, greatly exacerbated by large-scale population movements. Agriculture and industry in the war zone countries had been seriously impaired; the communications network (especially railways) crippled. Until 1949 the outlook was bleak, and political uncertainty, fostered by the growing antagonism between the USA and the USSR, hampered recovery. For Western Europe an injection of massive American aid (the Marshall Plan,

1 3 May US and Soviet forces in contact

2 30 April Seyss-Inquart, Nazi commissioner for Holland, agrees to truce on Dutch front, to supply food to starving civilians and to stem flooding

3 30 April Hitler commits suicide.
2 May City surrenders to 1st White Russian and 1st Ukrainian Armies

4 1 May Radio announces Hitler's death and Admiral Dönitz's nomination as successor

5 1 May Contact between New Zealand troops of 8th Army and Tito's forces

6 4 May Admiral Hans von Friedeburg surrenders German forces in Holland, North-west Germany, Schleswig-Holstein, Denmark, Heligoland and the Frisian Is. to General Montgomery. Effective from 5 May

7 4 May German 9th and 12th Armies liquidated by US 9th Army

8 6 May General Blaskowitz surrenders German forces in Holland

9 9 May Army Group Weichsel surrenders to Russians

10 14 May Austrian Republic under provisional government announced; Anschluss declared null and void

I/THE GERMAN SURRENDER May 1945

areas occupied by the German Army at time of surrender

1948-52) helped to lay the foundations for a new prosperity.

As a result of the 'cold war' Europe became divided into three blocs: Western, Communist and neutral. The first of these groups of countries were bound by a defensive alliance with the United States and Canada in the North Atlantic Treaty Organization (1949), and by the emergence in stages of the European Economic Community. These developments were mirrored in Eastern Europe in the Warsaw Pact Organization and Comecon. But it was not until the Helsinki Conference on Security and Co-operation in Europe in 1975 that frontiers in Europe were finally recognized by both factions, and accepted as inviolable.

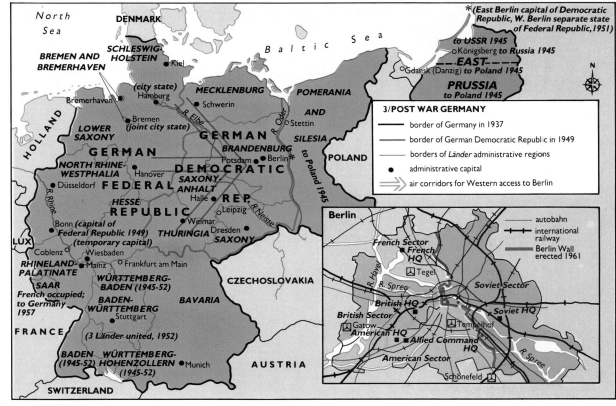

3/POST WAR GERMANY

* (East Berlin capital of Democratic Republic, W. Berlin separate state of Federal Republic, 1951)

—— border of Germany in 1937
—— border of German Democratic Republic in 1949
—— borders of *Länder* administrative regions
● administrative capital
⇒ air corridors for Western access to Berlin

Berlin

┼┼┼ autobahn
┼┼ international railway
━━ Berlin Wall erected 1961

FOLLOWING HITLER'S SUICIDE on 30 April 1945, political authority in Germany was transferred to Grand Admiral Dönitz. The only German forces still operational (1) were then confined into pockets on the Baltic coast, around Berlin, on the east-west zonal boundary on the Elbe, and in the putative 'Alpine Redoubt' in south Germany. German forces in Italy had signed a local surrender on 29 April, effective from 2 May. Army Group G, in Austria, capitulated on 5 May. General surrender became effective on 8 May. Europe's new frontiers (2, 3) were negotiated at the Potsdam conference (July 1945). The Soviet-sponsored Polish government took over the administration of eastern Germany up to the Oder-Neisse line. East Prussia was absorbed into Poland and the USSR. Poland was reconstituted, though much shrunken, Czechoslovakia reunited and Yugoslavia restored. Germany's western frontiers returned to the line of 1939. The western and eastern zones became separate republics in 1949. The erasure of the Nazi map of Europe involved vast movements of population (2). Germans were expelled from Czechoslovakia and Poland, while 'ethnic' Germans fled from Yugoslavia, Hungary, Rumania, the Baltic States and the USSR. Some 10 million Germans reached the Western zones of occupation, but as many as 3 million may have died en route. Several million Russians who had made their way westward during the war were sent back, many to certain death. This had been agreed at Yalta; many thousands of Yugoslavs who had chosen the wrong side during the partisan war were also returned to Tito's government. About a million 'displaced persons' of many nationalities were resettled in Western countries from the Western occupation zones and many Jewish survivors of the Holocaust made their way to Palestine (Israel after May 1948). Some 400,000 Finns were displaced by the Russian annexation of Karelia; the Soviet government forcibly uprooted 200,000 Balts (an equal number had fled to Germany), and compulsorily resettled or exiled minorities suspected of collaborating with the Germans.

Picture above: US armoured troops entering Munich, May 1945.

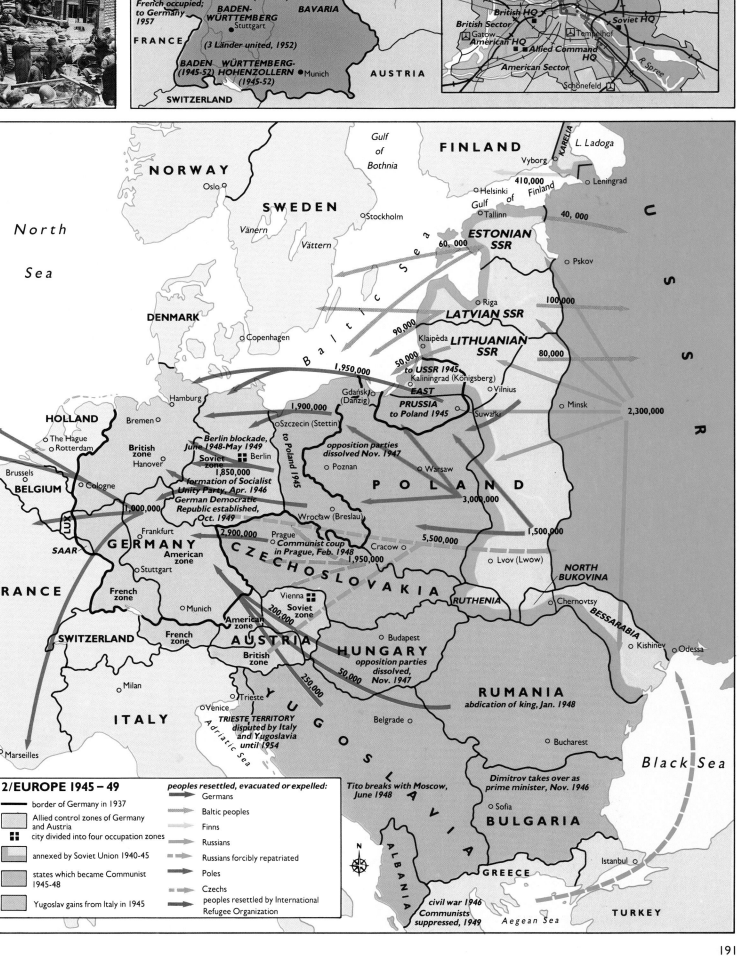

2/EUROPE 1945–49

—— border of Germany in 1937
▨ Allied control zones of Germany and Austria
■■ city divided into four occupation zones
▨ annexed by Soviet Union 1940-45
▨ states which became Communist 1945-48
▨ Yugoslav gains from Italy in 1945

peoples resettled, evacuated or expelled:
→ Germans
→ Baltic peoples
→ Finns
→ Russians
⇢ Russians forcibly repatriated
→ Poles
⇢ Czechs
→ peoples resettled by International Refugee Organization

The Japanese empire 1941~45

A BRITISH WAR CABINET paper of the Second World War stated that Germany would lose the war because she had factories and no raw materials, whilst Japan would lose because she had raw materials and no factories. Allowing for the element of hyperbole in this statement, its sense was accurate enough with respect to Japan: despite securing the Southern Resources Area, Japan lacked the means and time to develop her conquered territories and to turn their resources into military assets.

In large measure this failure was political. Assumptions of their own racial superiority precluded the Japanese offering the various peoples which they conquered between 1931 and 1942 any basis for genuine co-operation and partnership. Despite the installation of various puppet regimes and the ceding of nominal independence to such countries as Burma and the Philippines, the Japanese retained the power of decision in all their conquered territories. Although the Japanese were able to raise quite substantial local armed forces in some areas, they were never able to secure a general political endorsement of their rule; they ruled only what they could command by force.

Nevertheless, in emulation of Hitler's 'New Order' in Europe, the Japanese introduced the notion of a Greater East Asia Co-Prosperity Sphere (1938). This was to be the lynch-pin of a Japanese propaganda effort to bind together its conquests into an ideological, political and economic whole. Despite a handful of conferences attended by politicians from puppet governments, which attempted to outline its *raison d'être* and future development: the Co-Prosperity Sphere remained a hollow sham, never acquiring the economic power of, say, Goering's *Reichswerke* in Europe. The sheer size and complexity of Japan's colonial empire confounded any attempt to impose cohesion or collaborative co-operation. The Japanese launched an ambitious media campaign, based around press and radio broadcasting in an attempt to win the hearts and minds of their conquered peoples. The results of Japan's political warfare were mixed: in the Philippines alone they would have had to broadcast in over 70 languages and dialects to reach the total population. In Malaya, however, their anti-British propaganda brought them an army raised from the

Tamil population of the peninsula (1943); organized under the leading Indian nationalist Subhas Chandra Bose, the Indian National Army was destined to fight in Burma and was intended to liberate the subcontinent itself.

Economically, the Japanese secured for themselves certain, often substantial, short-term advantages but only at the cost of dissipating whatever goodwill they enjoyed. By ruthless exploitation, and by the manipulation of exchange rates to her advantage, Japan funded her trade deficits with the outside world before 1941 by surpluses secured in dealings with Manchuria; further, after 1938, Japan secured coal and other raw materials from northern China at prices between 10 per cent and 25 per cent of real cost. But however rapacious and self-defeating was Japanese rule in these and other territories, the root cause of Japan's economic defeat in the Second World War lay in the fact that she lacked the industrial muscle to meet the challenge of the United States in the western Pacific.

Japan's outstanding failure related to scale and finance capital, but there were others that related to the lack of structure and economic planning; but the most obvious single part of Japan's economic defeat was the annihilation of her seaborne commerce (page 194). Much of Japanese production was geared to capital goods and not to the developed end-product market that enabled the American and British economies to be switched to war production with comparative ease. In Japan, the task of the orderly direction of the national economy was beset by a lack of effective central planning, a dissipation of production resources through the proliferation of design specifications, and chronic inter-service rivalries that extended – in the case of the air forces – to a failure to standardize guns, radar and voltage systems. Moreover, whilst certain aspects of Japanese war production was very impressive on paper, results were often offset by qualitative decline. For example, while carrier numbers were maintained at very respectable levels into 1944, the converted light carriers that were used could not handle the heavier, more modern aircraft that were then coming into service. Some had to be completed with concrete because of steel shortages. By 1944 few of Japan's military products were a match for their US counterparts.

SINCE THE BEGINNING of Japan's industrial revolution, following the Meiji Restoration in 1867, her industries had depended upon imports of raw materials and upon export to foreign markets (1). Given that these considerations were primary factors in Japan's decision to go to war, her inability either to maintain trading flows with the Southern Resources Area or to effectively develop her conquests nearer home – in China and Manchuria – signalled her inevitable defeat. The Allied assault on her merchant fleet (page 194) followed by a devastating aerial bombardment of the Home Islands (page 196), struck at the very weakness of Japan's economic structure. Although Japanese war production (3) continued to sustain a high output until 1944, the products themselves suffered clear qualitative decline. Politically, for all her claims to be fighting to free East Asia from the control of western imperialists, Japan's military and propaganda effort between 1937 and 1945 was concentrated against China. China's refusal to come to terms with Japan, and the savagery of Japanese occupation policy in northern China, gave the lie to

Japanese claims to leadership of an Asian confederation of peoples (promulgated in the creation of the Greater East Asia Co-Prosperity Sphere, 1938, 2). Nevertheless, in virtually all the other territories she occupied, Japan was able to secure some measure of co-operation on the part of nationalists or traditional hierarchies, though in the long term the aims of all proved to be mutually exclusive. In various parts of South-east Asia the Japanese harnessed local anti-imperialist sentiments, but failed to recognize that these could be as easily directed against themselves. Even Siam, which between 1940 and 1943 secured parts of French Indo-China, Burma and Malaya as a result of Japanese patronage, was no more than a prisoner of increasingly severe Japanese economic demands.

Pictures above: Emperor Hirohito inspects Tokyo's air-raid warning system. Huge sonic horns were designed to detect the noise of approaching aircraft. Below: a Japanese poster (1943) in which a Japanese soldier tramples westerners: the chain-links A, B and D stand for American, British and Dutch.

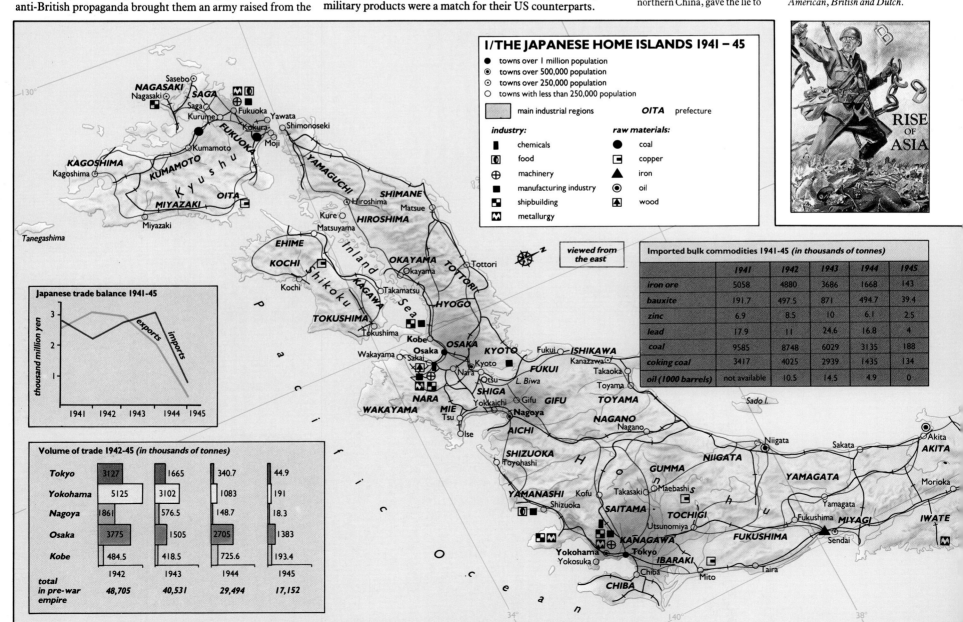

I/THE JAPANESE HOME ISLANDS 1941 – 45

- ● towns over 1 million population
- ◉ towns over 500,000 population
- ⊙ towns over 250,000 population
- ○ towns with less than 250,000 population

▢ main industrial regions   **OITA**   prefecture

industry:
- ■ chemicals
- ◨ food
- ⊕ machinery
- ◼ manufacturing industry
- ▣ shipbuilding
- ◲ metallurgy

raw materials:
- ● coal
- ⊡ copper
- ▲ iron
- ◉ oil
- ◮ wood

RISE OF ASIA

Japanese trade balance 1941-45

(line graph, exports and imports, thousand million yen, 1941–1945)

Imported bulk commodities 1941-45 (in thousands of tonnes)

	1941	1942	1943	1944	1945
iron ore	5058	4880	3686	1668	143
bauxite	191.7	497.5	871	494.7	39.4
zinc	6.9	8.5	10	6.1	2.5
lead	17.9	11	24.6	16.8	4
coal	9585	8748	6029	3135	188
coking coal	3417	4025	2939	1435	134
oil (1000 barrels)	not available	10.5	14.5	4.9	0

Volume of trade 1942-45 (in thousands of tonnes)

	1942	1943	1944	1945
Tokyo	3127	1665	340.7	44.9
Yokohama	5125	3102	1083	191
Nagoya	1861	576.5	148.7	18.3
Osaka	3775	1505	2705	1383
Kobe	484.5	418.5	725.6	193.4
total in pre-war empire	**48,705**	**40,531**	**29,494**	**17,152**

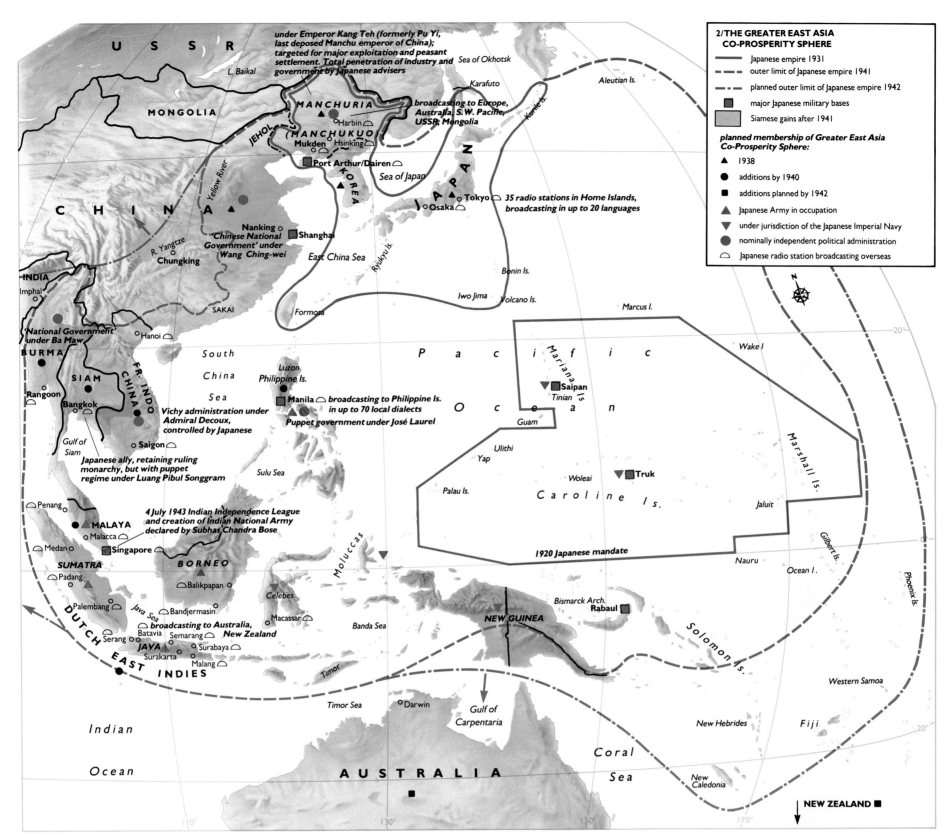

2/THE GREATER EAST ASIA CO-PROSPERITY SPHERE

— Japanese empire 1931
-- outer limit of Japanese empire 1941
-·- planned outer limit of Japanese empire 1942
■ major Japanese military bases
▨ Siamese gains after 1941

planned membership of Greater East Asia Co-Prosperity Sphere:

▲ 1938
● additions by 1940
■ additions planned by 1942
▲ Japanese Army in occupation
▼ under jurisdiction of the Japanese Imperial Navy
● nominally independent political administration
⌂ Japanese radio station broadcasting overseas

USSR

under Emperor Kang Teh (formerly Pu Yi, last deposed Manchu emperor of China); targeted for major exploitation and peasant settlement. Total penetration of industry and government by Japanese advisers

L. Baikal
Sea of Okhotsk
MONGOLIA
Karafuto
Aleutian Is.
MANCHURIA
Harbin
JEHOL
MANCHUKUO
Mukden
Hsinking
broadcasting to Europe, Australia, S.W. Pacific, USSR, Mongolia
Port Arthur/Dairen
KOREA
Sea of Japan
Yellow River
CHINA
Tokyo   35 radio stations in Home Islands, broadcasting in up to 20 languages
R. Yangtze
Nanking 'Chinese National Government' under Wang Ching-wei
Osaka
Chungking
Shanghai
East China Sea
Ryukyu Is.
INDIA
Imphal
SAKAI
Iwo Jima
Bonin Is.
Volcano Is.
Marcus I.
Formosa
Wake I.
'National Government' under Ba Maw
Hanoi
South China Sea
Luzon
Philippine Is.
Pacific Ocean
Mariana Is.
BURMA
SIAM
FR. INDO CHINA
Manila   broadcasting to Philippine Is. in up to 70 local dialects
Saipan
Tinian
Rangoon
Bangkok
Vichy administration under Admiral Decoux, controlled by Japanese
Puppet government under José Laurel
Guam
Gulf of Siam
Saigon
Japanese ally, retaining ruling monarchy, but with puppet regime under Luang Pibul Songgram
Yap
Ulithi
Woleai
Marshall Is.
Penang
Malacca
4 July 1943 Indian Independence League and creation of Indian National Army declared by Subhas Chandra Bose
Sulu Sea
Palau Is.
Truk
Caroline Is.
Jaluit
Gilbert Is.
MALAYA
Medan
Singapore
SUMATRA
BORNEO
1920 Japanese mandate
Nauru
Ocean I.
Phoenix Is.
Padang
Balikpapan
Celebes
Moluccas
Palembang
Java Sea
Bandjermasin
Macassar
Banda Sea
Bismarck Arch.
Rabaul
Solomon Is.
DUTCH
Serang
Batavia
Semarang
Surabaya
broadcasting to Australia, New Zealand
NEW GUINEA
EAST
JAVA
Surakarta
Malang
Western Samoa
INDIES
Timor
Fiji
Timor Sea
Darwin
Gulf of Carpentaria
New Hebrides
New Caledonia
Indian Ocean
AUSTRALIA
Coral Sea
New Caledonia
NEW ZEALAND ■

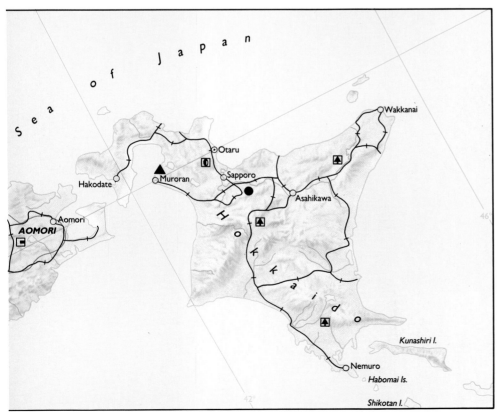

Sea of Japan
Wakkanai
Otaru
Hakodate
Muroran
Sapporo
Asahikawa
Aomori
AOMORI
HOKKAIDO
Kunashiri I.
Nemuro
Habomai Is.
Shikotan I.

3/JAPANESE WAR PRODUCTION 1940–45

Aircraft production 1941-45	1941	1942	1943	1944	1945*
airframes	5088	8861	16,693	28,180	11,066
aero-engines	12,151	16,999	29,541	46,526	12,360
fighters	1080	2935	7147	13,811	5474
bombers	1461	2433	4189	5100	1934
others	2547	3493	5357	9269	3658

Automotive production 1940-45	1940	1941	1942	1943	1944	1945*
tanks	1023	1024	1165	876	342	94
military tractors	708	529	634	232	48	5
armoured cars	0	0	88	505	385	126
trucks	33,218	42,125	35,386	24,000	20,446	1758
other military vehicles	272	503	468	629	784	153
passenger cars	1547	1707	947	522	0	0
total	36,768	45,888	38,688	26,764	22,005	2136

Warship production 1941-45	1941	1942	1943	1944	1945†
battleships	1	1	0	0	0
aircraft carriers	5	6	3	4	0
cruisers	1	2	2	1	0
destroyers	9	9	15	31	6
submarines	11	22	40	37	22

* Jan.-Aug. 1945   † April-July 1945 (see also page 66)

Japanese merchant shipping 1941~45

THE CREATION of an extended empire – an enlarged resource area – was the essential reason for Japan's commitment to a war against the Western powers in 1941. It was also a precondition of victory (page 66). The demolition of the infrastructure of that empire – especially the Japanese merchant shipping fleet – was recognized by the US High Command as a vital requirement for eventual victory.

In 1941 Japan imported 20 million tons of bulk commodities (excluding oil) and to meet her various commitments required some 9.3 million tons of merchant shipping, one-third of which had hitherto been supplied by nations with which she went to war in December. Of the 6 million tons of shipping under the Japanese flag at the outbreak of war, 600,000 tons were tankers. In December 1941 10 per cent of the merchant fleet was laid up awaiting routine maintenance. The Naval staff expected to lose no more than 600,000 tons in any year of a war, which was anyway expected to be a short one.

With the outbreak of war the Japanese merchant navy was divided into three separate fleets: one of 2 million tons and another of 1.5 million tons to meet the respective demands of the Army and the Navy, and a third of 2 million tons allocated to meet civilian and industrial requirements. Without any means of effective co-ordination between these three fleets, and with each one working routes independently of the other two, this inefficient arrangement ensured that the Japanese merchant service worked well below capacity. In this it was further hindered by two other factors. Firstly, the Japanese failed to introduce a triangular sailing pattern between the resources area, the Home Islands and the Pacific combat zones, with the result that – apart from oil shipments from the Indies to the

Pacific – there were no direct sailings between the resources and the operational areas. Secondly, Japanese shipyards proved unable to complete the routine maintenance programmes of the merchant service in addition to meeting the other demands placed upon them. Thus, the amount of Japanese shipping laid up progressively increased, until by August 1945 some 44% of what little shipping remained to Japan was immobilized.

In the first seven months of the war three-quarters of Japan's modest shipping losses were sustained by the Army and Navy fleets, and until the end of 1942 losses, though much heavier than anticipated, were largely offset by new construction and by capturing foreign vessels – though the losses incurred in October and November during the struggle for Guadalcanal (page 118, 120) were a major factor in the decision to abandon the island. Thereafter, despite a rise in new construction, Japan's capacity to replace her ships rapidly declined, because of the increasing rate of sinkings of her merchantmen. The growing effectiveness of American submarines after September 1943 was partly responsible for this; at the same time the US carrier and amphibious operations had brought the war into the western Pacific forcing Japanese merchantmen to enter waters controlled by US aircraft. In November 1943, despite the recently introduced general convoy system, Japanese monthly merchantmen losses passed 200,000 tons for the first time; in only two of the following fourteen months did Japanese losses fall below this figure. As American offensive actions in the East Indies and the Philippines escalated, so did Japanese losses. With the collapse of the Japanese oceanic convoy system by the end of 1944, Japan entered 1945 with just 2.75 million tons of shipping and by August had little more than 1.5 million tons – barely enough to weather a further 3 to 4 months. In effect the American forces had succeeded in achieving, in the Pacific, what the U-boats had failed to do in the Atlantic. A major industrial nation had been strangled, its native industry and populace rapidly deprived of their means of survival and Japan's empire lay dismembered.

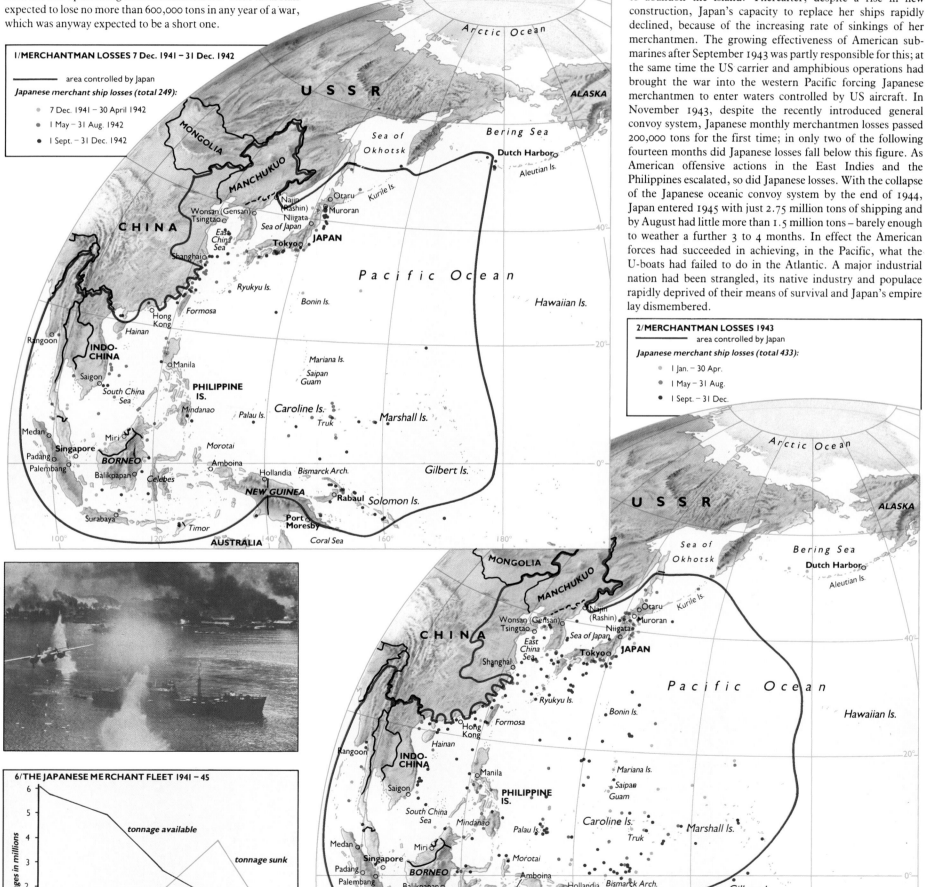

1/MERCHANTMAN LOSSES 7 Dec. 1941 – 31 Dec. 1942

— area controlled by Japan

Japanese merchant ship losses (total 249):

- 7 Dec. 1941 – 30 April 1942
- 1 May – 31 Aug. 1942
- 1 Sept. – 31 Dec. 1942

2/MERCHANTMAN LOSSES 1943

— area controlled by Japan

Japanese merchant ship losses (total 433):

- 1 Jan. – 30 Apr.
- 1 May – 31 Aug.
- 1 Sept. – 31 Dec.

6/THE JAPANESE MERCHANT FLEET 1941 – 45

tonnages in millions

tonnage available
tonnage sunk
tonnage built

1941 1942 1943 1944 1945
period of operations

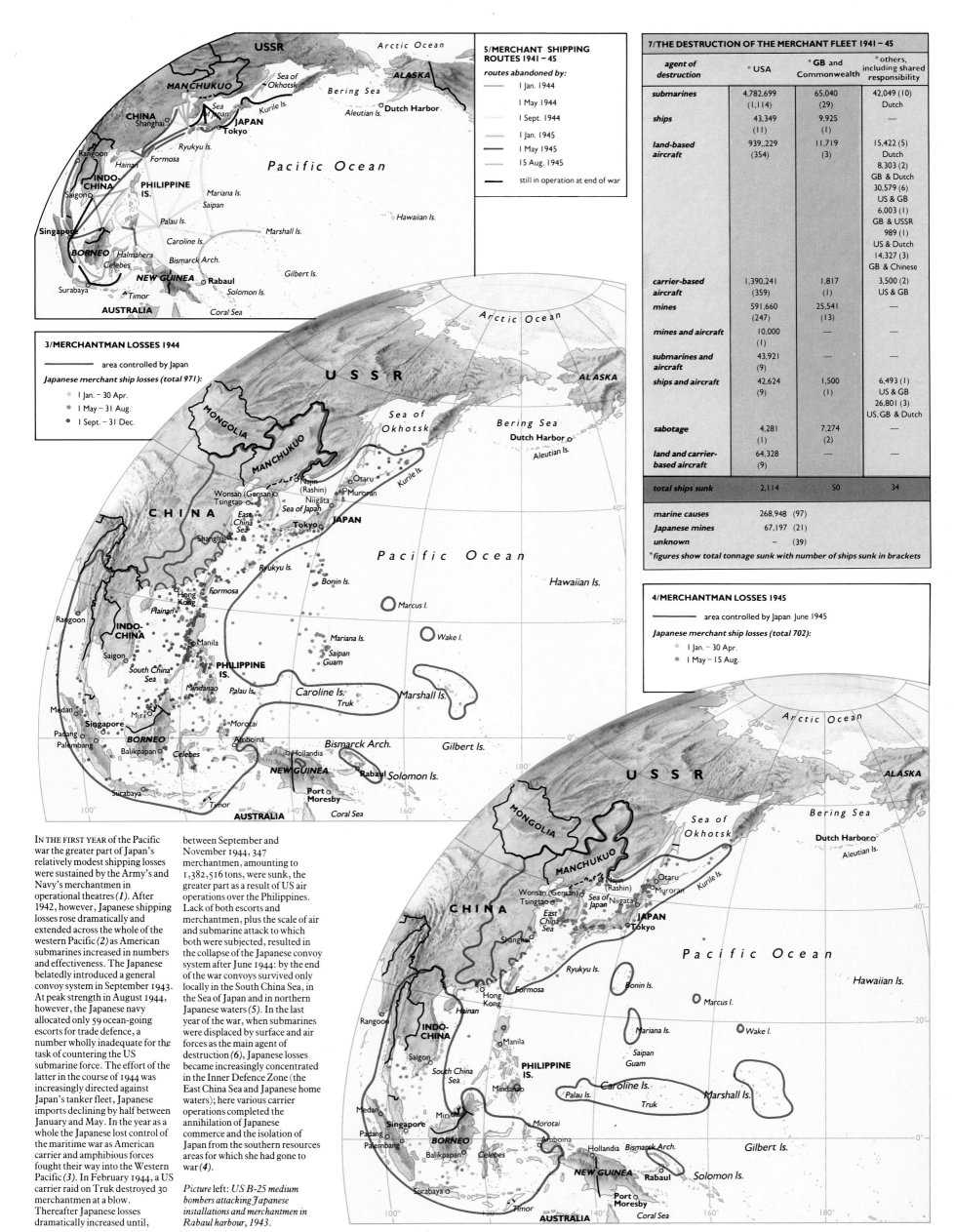

5/MERCHANT SHIPPING ROUTES 1941–45

routes abandoned by:

- 1 Jan. 1944
- 1 May 1944
- 1 Sept. 1944
- 1 Jan. 1945
- 1 May 1945
- 15 Aug. 1945
- still in operation at end of war

7/THE DESTRUCTION OF THE MERCHANT FLEET 1941–45

agent of destruction	*USA	*GB and Commonwealth	*others, including shared responsibility
submarines	4,782,699 (1,114)	65,040 (29)	42,049 (10) Dutch
ships	43,349 (11)	9,925 (1)	—
land-based aircraft	939,229 (354)	11,719 (3)	15,422 (5) Dutch 8,303 (2) GB & Dutch 30,579 (6) US & GB 6,003 (1) GB & USSR 989 (1) US & Dutch 14,327 (3) GB & Chinese
carrier-based aircraft	1,390,241 (359)	1,817 (1)	3,500 (2) US & GB
mines	591,660 (247)	25,541 (13)	
mines and aircraft	10,000 (1)	—	
submarines and aircraft	43,921 (9)	—	
ships and aircraft	42,624 (9)	1,500 (1)	6,493 (1) US & GB 26,801 (3) US, GB & Dutch
sabotage	4,281 (1)	7,274 (2)	—
land and carrier-based aircraft	64,328 (9)	—	—
total ships sunk	**2,114**	**50**	**34**
marine causes	268,948 (97)		
Japanese mines	67,197 (21)		
unknown		(39)	

*figures show total tonnage sunk with number of ships sunk in brackets

3/MERCHANTMAN LOSSES 1944

— area controlled by Japan

Japanese merchant ship losses (total 971):

- 1 Jan. – 30 Apr.
- 1 May – 31 Aug.
- 1 Sept. – 31 Dec.

4/MERCHANTMAN LOSSES 1945

— area controlled by Japan June 1945

Japanese merchant ship losses (total 702):

- 1 Jan. – 30 Apr.
- 1 May – 15 Aug.

IN THE FIRST YEAR of the Pacific war the greater part of Japan's relatively modest shipping losses were sustained by the Army's and Navy's merchantmen in operational theatres (*1*). After 1942, however, Japanese shipping losses rose dramatically and extended across the whole of the western Pacific (*2*) as American submarines increased in numbers and effectiveness. The Japanese belatedly introduced a general convoy system in September 1943. At peak strength in August 1944, however, the Japanese navy allocated only 59 ocean-going escorts for trade defence, a number wholly inadequate for the task of countering the US submarine force. The effort of the latter in the course of 1944 was increasingly directed against Japan's tanker fleet, Japanese imports declining by half between January and May. In the year as a whole the Japanese lost control of the maritime war as American carrier and amphibious forces fought their way into the Western Pacific (*3*). In February 1944, a US carrier raid on Truk destroyed 30 merchantmen at a blow. Thereafter Japanese losses dramatically increased until, between September and November 1944, 347 merchantmen, amounting to 1,382,516 tons, were sunk, the greater part as a result of US air operations over the Philippines. Lack of both escorts and merchantmen, plus the scale of air and submarine attack to which both were subjected, resulted in the collapse of the Japanese convoy system after June 1944: by the end of the war convoys survived only locally in the South China Sea, in the Sea of Japan and in northern Japanese waters (*5*). In the last year of the war, when submarines were displaced by surface and air forces as the main agent of destruction (*6*), Japanese losses became increasingly concentrated in the Inner Defence Zone (the East China Sea and Japanese home waters); here various carrier operations completed the annihilation of Japanese commerce and the isolation of Japan from the southern resources areas for which she had gone to war (*4*).

Picture left: US B-25 medium bombers attacking Japanese installations and merchantmen in Rabaul harbour, 1943.

The Bombardment of Japan 1945

A MOUNTAINOUS EMPIRE, with few natural resources and many densely-populated cities, Japan was all but wholly dependent upon seaborne trade for the maintenance of both her civilian population and her war effort. She was hopelessly vulnerable to campaigns against that trade and her major population centres. Until June 1944 American planning for the Pacific war was based on the premise that an invasion of Japan might not prove necessary to enforce her surrender: thereafter planning proceeded on the basis that such an invasion was unavoidable. This switch of emphasis, nevertheless, coincided with the start of the strategic air offensive against Japan.

The first raid on Yawata (15 June 1944) by B-29 Superfortresses based in China, came as part of a bombing effort that had begun in March 1943 and which, over the next fourteen months, extended across Indo-China, southern China and Formosa. By June 1944, however, the Americans had decided to switch the base of their bombing effort from China to the Marianas, which were attacked that month (page 147). American raids on Japan from China thus ended in November 1944, the same month as XXI Bomber Command carried out its first raids on Japan from Saipan. For four months, however,

this offensive failed to achieve any significant result; only a small number of Superfortresses were available at this time, and a lack of fighter cover over Japan forced the B-29s to bomb from high altitude, thereby decreasing accuracy.

In February 1945 the decision was taken to commit XXI Bomber Command to area bombing at night from low altitude. The effect was devastating against cities that were densely inhabited and largely built with timber and paper. In six months, in 1945, Japan sustained damage from air attack equivalent to that sustained by Germany in the last three years of the European War.

Operations by XXI Bomber Command against Japanese cities were underpinned by two other efforts: firstly, an escalating series of bombardments around the Home Islands by carrier forces and bombers, now based on Okinawa; secondly, by its own mining operations, supported in the mining of Korean waters by naval aircraft, also operating from Okinawa. Operation *Starvation* was designed to reduce, to an impractical minimum, the flow of Japanese merchant shipping and, in the months between April and July 1945, it was largely successful. In 1945, the five great Pacific ports handled less than

one-eighth of their 1941 trade. With the collapse of coastal trade, the Japanese were forced to transfer most of their Honshu trade to railways, which were, in turn, reduced by bombing to 25% of their carrying capacity. Further, three-quarters of the Japanese fishing fleet was destroyed.

The scale of American mining overwhelmed the Japanese minesweeping force, though such ports as Yawata and Wakamatsu remained open to the last weeks of the war. After April 1945, however, what little shipping remained was largely directed to the import of coal and food, and with carrier and surface forces joining the bombardment, the war neared its end with Japan, not simply unable to defend herself, but realizing that she could not feed herself into the next Spring.

The bombardment of Japan was yet to reach its climax. The fanatical resistance with which the Japanese had met the Allies at every stage of the Pacific war led a special commission to recommend to President Truman, in July 1945, that the newly-developed nuclear weapon (page 188) be used against the Home Islands. With the explosion of atomic bombs over Hiroshima and Nagasaki (6, 9 August), the world entered the nuclear age. On 8 August the USSR declared war on Japan.

APART FROM the Doolittle Raid of April 1942 (page 74) and operations against the Kurile Islands, the war did not come directly to Japan until 15 June 1944, when B-29 Superfortresses based in China bombed Yawata on Kyushu. From bases in China, however, Superfortresses could not reach the whole of the Japanese Home Islands, but the capture of the southern Marianas in mid-1944 provided bases from which to attack Japan's main islands and to mine her waters. By the end of the war these raids were complemented by operations based on Okinawa (2). Strategic bombing operations between June 1944 and February 1945 were conducted at high altitude against precision targets, with minimal results and at great cost in terms of engine life. In March 1945, the Americans adopted low-level area bombardment techniques: the first great raid, on Tokyo on 10 March, destroyed about 40% of the city (3) and killed more people than either of the atomic bomb attacks at Hiroshima or Nagasaki. With the five great cities of Japan singled out for similar treatment (4) and American bombers ultimately raiding over 50 other cities (5), over 30% of all buildings in Japan were destroyed, 13 million people made homeless and a further 8 million evacuated. The economy, too, heavily dependent upon small-scale enterprises and imported raw materials, was in ruins. An enormous mine-laying operation was directed against Japan's ports. Over 12,000 mines were laid, 2100 in the crucial Shimonoseki Strait (6) through which the bulk of surviving Japanese shipping had to pass in order to reach the major ports of the Inland Sea. In March, 796,200 tons of shipping passed through the Straits without loss; by July this shrank to 165,300 tons, 126 merchantmen being sunk in this four-month period. From April until the end of the war, mines destroyed 223 ships of 512,656 tons, all other causes – mostly aircraft – sinking a further 255 ships of 518,263 tons. The mining and air campaign between them caused Nagoya to be closed in April, Tokyo and Yokohama in May; virtually every one of Japan's 22 ports were closed at various times in Spring and Summer 1945 as a result of Allied operations.

Pictures above right: Atomic bomb damage at Hiroshima; this clearly shows how brick or concrete structures resisted the force of the blast.
right: Carrier-based US planes pass Mt. Fujiyama during an air strike on Tokyo, Feb. 1945.

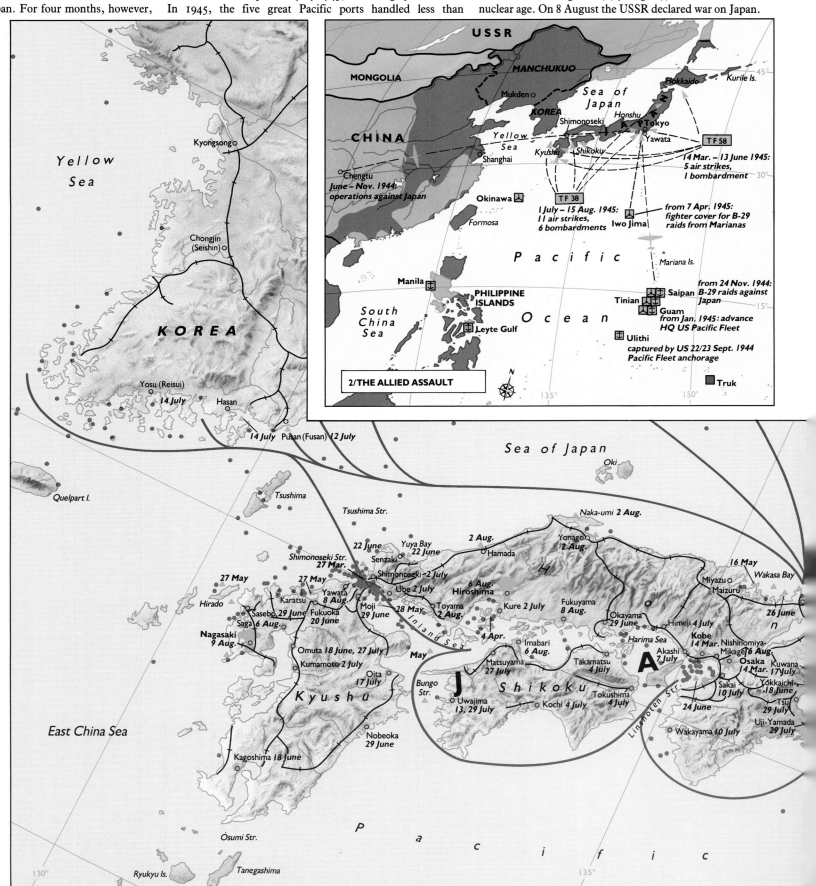

2/THE ALLIED ASSAULT

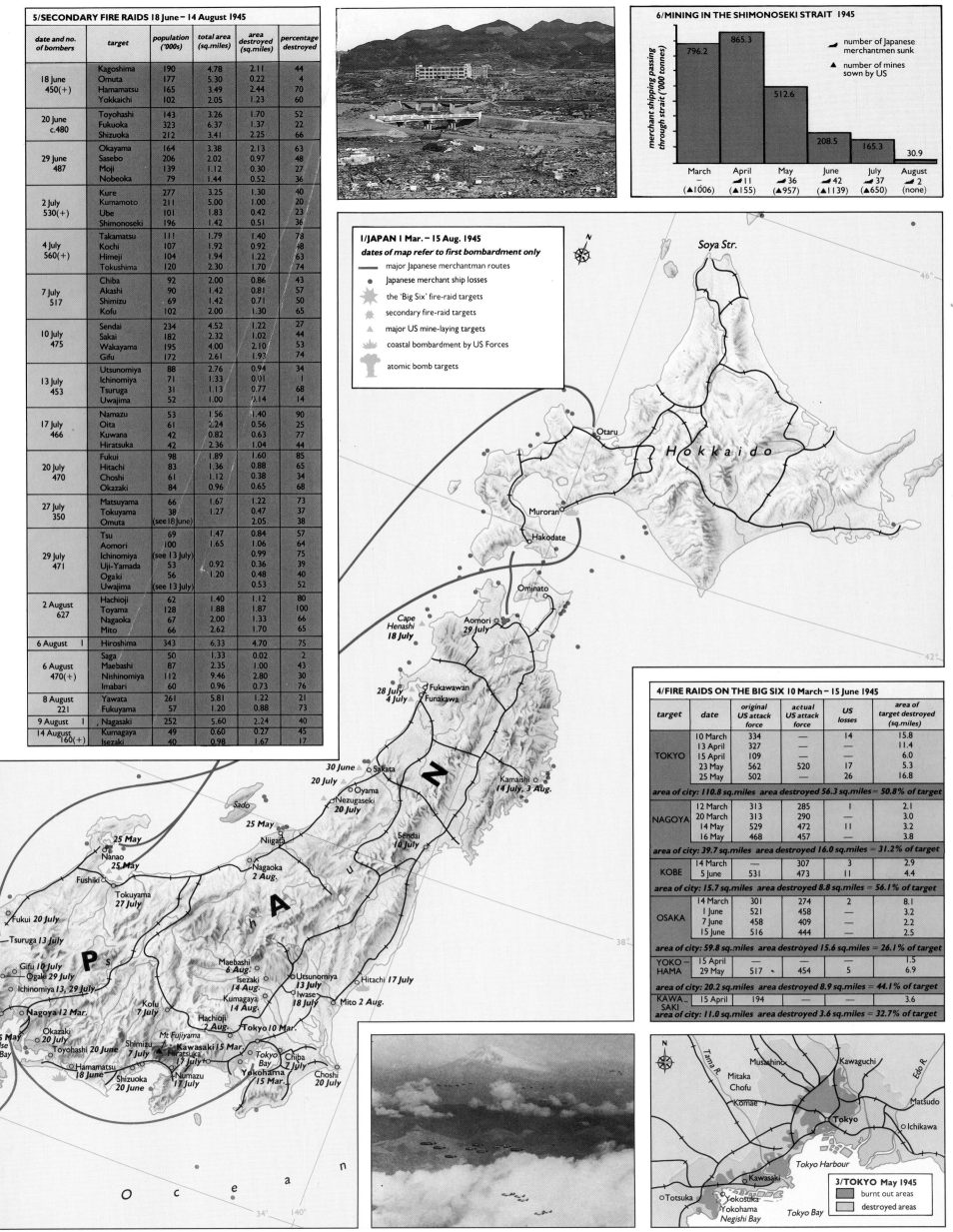

5/SECONDARY FIRE RAIDS 18 June – 14 August 1945

date and no. of bombers	target	population ('000s)	total area (sq.miles)	area destroyed (sq.miles)	percentage destroyed
18 June 450(+)	Kagoshima	190	4.78	2.11	44
	Omuta	177	5.30	0.22	4
	Hamamatsu	165	3.49	2.44	70
	Yokkaichi	102	2.05	1.23	60
20 June c.480	Toyohashi	143	3.26	1.70	52
	Fukuoka	323	6.37	1.37	22
	Shizuoka	212	3.41	2.25	66
29 June 487	Okayama	164	3.38	2.13	63
	Sasebo	206	2.02	0.97	48
	Moji	139	1.12	0.30	27
	Nobeoka	79	1.44	0.52	36
2 July 530(+)	Kure	277	3.25	1.30	40
	Kumamoto	211	5.00	1.00	20
	Ube	101	1.83	0.42	23
	Shimonoseki	196	1.42	0.51	36
4 July 560(+)	Takamatsu	111	1.79	1.40	78
	Kochi	107	1.92	0.92	48
	Himeji	104	1.94	1.22	63
	Tokushima	120	2.30	1.70	74
7 July 517	Chiba	92	2.00	0.86	43
	Akashi	90	1.42	0.81	57
	Shimizu	69	1.42	0.71	50
	Kofu	102	2.00	1.30	65
10 July 475	Sendai	234	4.52	1.22	27
	Sakai	182	2.32	1.02	44
	Wakayama	195	4.00	2.10	53
	Gifu	172	2.61	1.93	74
13 July 453	Utsunomiya	88	2.76	0.94	34
	Ichinomiya	71	1.33	0.01	1
	Tsuruga	31	1.13	0.77	68
	Uwajima	52	1.00	0.14	14
17 July 466	Namazu	53	1.56	1.40	90
	Oita	61	2.24	0.56	25
	Kuwana	42	0.82	0.63	77
	Hiratsuka	42	2.36	1.04	44
20 July 470	Fukui	98	1.89	1.60	85
	Hitachi	83	1.36	0.88	65
	Choshi	61	1.12	0.38	34
	Okazaki	84	0.96	0.65	68
27 July 350	Matsuyama	66	1.67	1.22	73
	Tokuyama	38	1.27	0.47	37
	Omuta	(see 18 June)		2.05	38
29 July 471	Tsu	69	1.47	0.84	57
	Aomori	100	1.65	1.06	64
	Ichinomiya	(see 13 July)		0.99	75
	Uji-Yamada	53	0.92	0.36	39
	Ogaki	56	1.20	0.48	40
	Uwajima	(see 13 July)		0.53	52
2 August 627	Hachioji	62	1.40	1.12	80
	Toyama	128	1.88	1.87	100
	Nagaoka	67	2.00	1.33	66
	Mito	66	2.62	1.70	65
6 August 1	Hiroshima	343	6.33	4.70	75
6 August 470(+)	Saga	50	1.33	0.02	2
	Maebashi	87	2.35	1.00	43
	Nishinomiya	112	9.46	2.80	30
	Imabari	60	0.96	0.73	76
8 August 221	Yawata	261	5.81	1.22	21
	Fukuyama	57	1.20	0.88	73
9 August 1	Nagasaki	252	5.60	2.24	40
14 August 160(+)	Kumagaya	49	0.60	0.27	45
	Isezaki	40	0.98	1.67	17

6/MINING IN THE SHIMONOSEKI STRAIT 1945

merchant shipping passing through strait ('000 tonnes)

⌐ number of Japanese merchantmen sunk
▲ number of mines sown by US

796.2	865.3	512.6	208.5	165.3	30.9
March – (▲1006)	April ⌐11 (▲155)	May ⌐36 (▲957)	June ⌐42 (▲1139)	July ⌐37 (▲650)	August ⌐2 (none)

1/JAPAN 1 Mar. – 15 Aug. 1945

dates of map refer to first bombardment only

— major Japanese merchantman routes
● Japanese merchant ship losses
✴ the 'Big Six' fire-raid targets
✴ secondary fire-raid targets
▲ major US mine-laying targets
🌴 coastal bombardment by US Forces
☁ atomic bomb targets

Soya Str.

Hokkaido

Otaru

Muroran

Hakodate

Ominato

Cape Henashi 18 July

Aomori 29 July

28 July 4 July — Fukawawan / Funakawa

30 June / 20 July — Sakata

Kamaishi 14 July, 3 Aug.

Oyama 20 July
Nezugaseki 20 July

25 May — Nanao
25 May
Fushiki
Tokuyama 27 July

Niigata

Nagaoka 2 Aug.

Sendai 10 July

Fukui 20 July
Tsuruga 13 July
Gifu 10 July
Ogaki 29 July
Ichinomiya 13, 29 July
Nagoya 12 Mar.
5 May Ise Bay
Okazaki 20 July
Toyohashi 20 June
Hamamatsu 18 June
Shizuoka 20 June

Maebashi 6 Aug.
Isezaki 14 Aug.
Iwase 14 Aug.
Kofu 7 July
Hachioji 2 Aug.
Kumagaya 14 Aug.
Mt Fujiyama
Kawasaki 15 Mar.
Hiratsuka 17 July
Shimizu 7 July
Numazu 17 July

Utsunomiya 13 July
Hitachi 17 July
Mito 2 Aug.
Tokyo 10 Mar.
Tokyo Bay
Yokohama 15 Mar.
Chiba 7 July
Choshi 20 July

Pacific Ocean

4/FIRE RAIDS ON THE BIG SIX 10 March – 15 June 1945

target	date	original US attack force	actual US attack force	US losses	area of target destroyed (sq.miles)
TOKYO	10 March	334	—	14	15.8
	13 April	327	—	—	11.4
	15 April	109	—	—	6.0
	23 May	562	520	17	5.3
	25 May	502	—	26	16.8
area of city: 110.8 sq.miles area destroyed 56.3 sq.miles = 50.8% of target					
NAGOYA	12 March	313	285	1	2.1
	20 March	313	290	—	3.0
	14 May	529	472	11	3.2
	16 May	468	457	—	3.8
area of city: 39.7 sq.miles area destroyed 16.0 sq.miles = 31.2% of target					
KOBE	14 March	—	307	3	2.9
	5 June	531	473	11	4.4
area of city: 15.7 sq.miles area destroyed 8.8 sq.miles = 56.1% of target					
OSAKA	14 March	301	274	2	8.1
	1 June	521	458	—	3.2
	7 June	458	409	—	2.2
	15 June	516	444	—	2.5
area of city: 59.8 sq.miles area destroyed 15.6 sq.miles = 26.1% of target					
YOKO-HAMA	15 April	—	—	—	1.5
	29 May	517	454	5	6.9
area of city: 20.2 sq.miles area destroyed 8.9 sq.miles = 44.1% of target					
KAWA-SAKI	15 April	194	—	—	3.6
area of city: 11.0 sq.miles area destroyed 3.6 sq.miles = 32.7% of target					

3/TOKYO May 1945

Tama R.
Musashino
Mitaka
Chofu
Komae
Kawaguchi
Kawasaki
Edo R.
Matsudo
Tokyo
Ichikawa
Tokyo Harbour
Totsuka
Yokosuka
Yokohama
Negishi Bay
Tokyo Bay

▓ burnt out areas
░ destroyed areas

Manchuria 1945

FOLLOWING THEIR non-aggression treaty of April 1941, both Japan and the Soviet Union enjoyed the benefits of the other's neutrality in the conduct of their respective wars. In April 1945, however, when the Russians indicated an unwillingness to consider a renewal of the 1941 treaty after April 1946 when it expired, the Japanese concluded correctly that the Soviet Union would enter the war against her at the earliest opportunity, once Germany was defeated.

It was indeed the Soviet Union's intention, first indicated to the Americans and British at the Teheran conference in November 1943, to enter the war against Japan despite her non-aggression treaty; the breach of the treaty was rationalized in 1945 as necessary both under the terms of Soviet responsibilities to the United Nations and due to the request of her allies at the Potsdam conference. But though they correctly divined Soviet intentions, the Japanese anticipated that the Soviets could not begin operations in Manchuria until September, when the ground would have dried after the seasonal summer rains. In fact the Soviets planned to open operations in mid-August, the better to secure a measure of surprise and a potentially critical advantage of timing.

This Japanese miscalculation virtually assured the defeat of their armies. Though numbering about a million men, the Japanese order of battle contained various non-Japanese units and garrison, as opposed to field, formations; many of the latter were little more than training cadre replacements for divisions transferred to the Home Islands and the Western Pacific in 1944 and 1945. Moreover, in terms of firepower, mobility, communications and air support, the Japanese were no match for the three Soviet fronts gathered around Manchuria, co-ordinated for a theatre of war the size of western Europe, under a new strategic level of command: the Far East Command. The Japanese also underestimated their adversary in one crucial respect: they anticipated that any Soviet offensive would be halted for want of resupply after 250 miles and therefore planned to marshal their forces for a defensive battle on the central Manchuria plain. The Soviets were to confound this intention by ensuring that depths of advance far beyond 250 miles could be achieved.

With the natural and obvious routes into Manchuria covered by defensive positions the Soviets planned to make their main effort from the west, through the Gobi Desert and Greater Khingan Range with the Trans-Baikal Front. A secondary effort was to be made in the east by the 1st Far Eastern Front, especially strengthened with artillery, engineers and infantry in order to overcome the defences of the border area. The 2nd Far Eastern Front was assigned to hold the Amur River. In order to secure strategic surprise the start line for the Trans-Baikal Front was 300 miles from the nearest railhead, and the Front planned to use the second-grade 36th Army in a frontal assault on Hailar in order to hold Japanese attention at a time when the breakthrough was attempted on the flank.

The Soviet declaration of war, three months after victory in Europe as promised at Yalta, and the start of the Manchurian campaign occurred within hours of one another, on either side of midnight, 8/9 August. The timing was perfect, allowing the Soviet Union to enter war against Japan before the Japanese could leave it after the US atomic bomb attacks. Within a week, as Soviet columns bit deep into Manchuria, Japan announced her decision to surrender, and on the 17th, following a direct order from Tokyo, the Kwantung Army signed the instrument of capitulation at Khabarovsk. Fighting in Manchuria and in the Kuriles nevertheless continued until 1 September.

Politically, the Manchurian campaign was of profound significance. Though not unexpected, the Soviet declaration of war came as a shock to the Japanese High Command. It ended Japanese hopes of securing a negotiated peace through Soviet auspices, and pointed to the hopelessness of Japan's position following the end of the war in Europe; the Allied resources thus released for redeployment in the Far East could not have been resisted. Moreover, though at the time defeat in Manchuria was incomplete, the Japanese High Command between 10-14 August rationalized the Emperor's decision to surrender in two ways: it was essential for Japan to capitulate while the United States remained her main enemy and it was imperative to avoid a final campaign on the Home Islands that could lead to social upheaval, revolution and Bolshevism. The fear of delaying a surrender until such a time as the Soviet Union would have a major voice in discussions regarding her future was also a strong factor. The Soviet Union was not a party to the 1951 peace treaty, and remains without a final settlement of the war with Japan, mainly because of her refusal to return (and Japan's refusal to cede) all or part of the Kurile Islands. Soviet commentators regard the destruction of Japan's last and largest concentration of ground forces as a cardinal factor in Japan's surrender. Western analysts maintain a particular interest in the campaign as a prototype for future Soviet strategic operations.

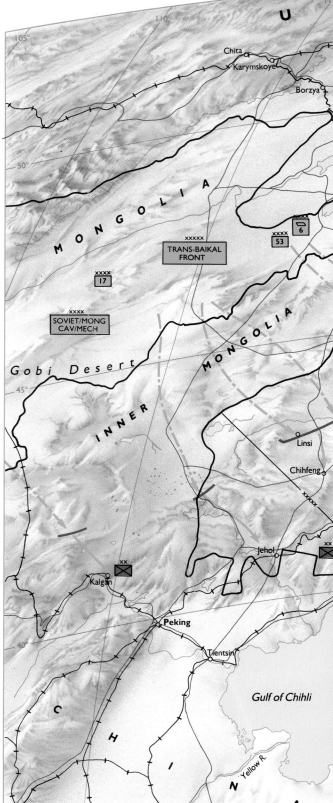

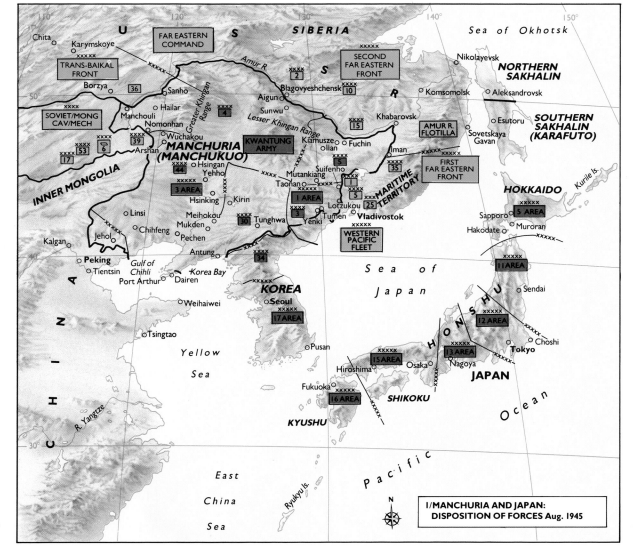

1/MANCHURIA AND JAPAN: DISPOSITION OF FORCES Aug. 1945

TO OPPOSE the 1 million men, 5360 guns, 1115 tanks and 1800 aircraft mustered by the Japanese for the defence of Korea and Manchuria *(1)*, the Soviets concentrated some 1.5 million men, 28,000 guns, 5500 tanks and 4370 aircraft across 3 fronts controlled by a theatre command. By moving material direct from factories, the Soviets were able to transfer combat-experienced formations from Europe in time for a Summer campaign, the 2nd Far Eastern Front being allocated the bulk of the second-grade formations already in the Far East. With formations that had fought in the close country and fixed defences of East Prussia (page 150) drafted to the 1st Far Eastern Front in readiness for operations on the Russia-Manchuria eastern border, in the west, the Trans-Baikal Front was assigned some 40% of overall Soviet strength and the greater part of the assembled armour. The Soviet offensive *(2)* was conceived as an envelopment by the Trans-Baikal and 1st Far Eastern Fronts, and the most obvious feature of the Manchurian campaign was the former's astonishing advance through the mountains to the central plain – a distance of 560 miles in 11 days. This advance was unopposed as the Japanese believed that the Soviets could not advance quickly and in strength through the mountains because of the problem of resupply. No less significant was the movement of light armour and cavalry of the mechanized group through the waterless Gobi Desert to positions from which Peking could be threatened. The main fighting in Manchuria came to an end on 17 Aug. but whilst isolated Japanese formations continued to fight until the end of the month, after 19 Aug. the Soviets used small airborne detachments to secure airfields, communications centres and local surrenders ahead of the main advances. The occupation of central Manchuria, of Port Arthur (22 Aug.) and of Korea north of the 38th parallel was unopposed for the most part. Elsewhere, however, hostilities were continued almost until the surrender in Tokyo Bay (1 Sept.). In the Kuriles *(3)* the Soviets opened their advance on 11 Aug.

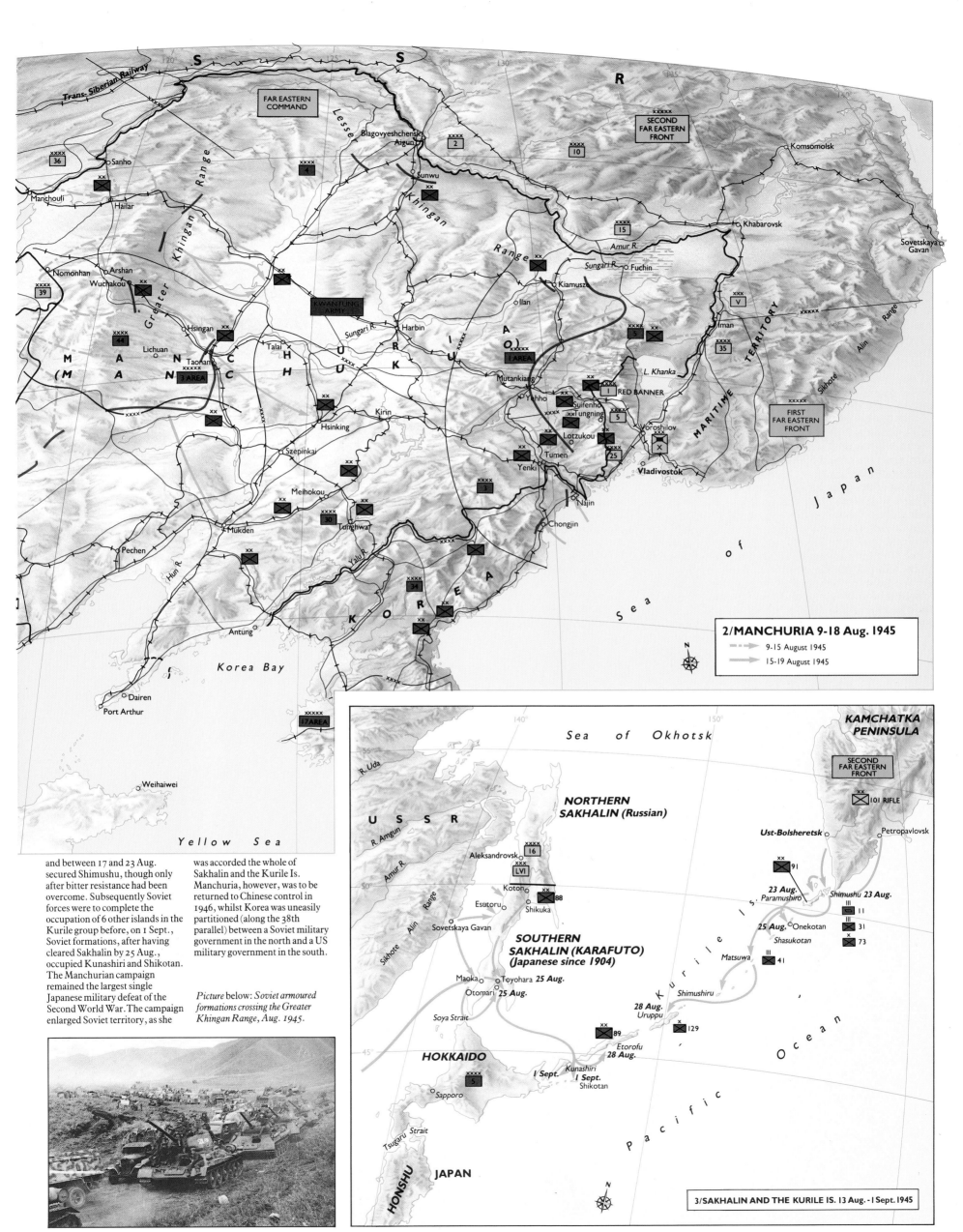

2/MANCHURIA 9-18 Aug. 1945

- - - → 9-15 August 1945

──→ 15-19 August 1945

and between 17 and 23 Aug. secured Shimushu, though only after bitter resistance had been overcome. Subsequently Soviet forces were to complete the occupation of 6 other islands in the Kurile group before, on 1 Sept., Soviet formations, after having cleared Sakhalin by 25 Aug., occupied Kunashiri and Shikotan. The Manchurian campaign remained the largest single Japanese military defeat of the Second World War. The campaign enlarged Soviet territory, as she

was accorded the whole of Sakhalin and the Kurile Is. Manchuria, however, was to be returned to Chinese control in 1946, whilst Korea was uneasily partitioned (along the 38th parallel) between a Soviet military government in the north and a US military government in the south.

Picture below: Soviet armoured formations crossing the Greater Khingan Range, Aug. 1945.

3/SAKHALIN AND THE KURILE IS. 13 Aug. - 1 Sept. 1945

Japan 1945

THE SECOND WORLD WAR was formally brought to an end on 2 September 1945 when Japanese representatives signed the instrument of their country's surrender on the starboard veranda deck of the battleship USS *Missouri* in Tokyo Bay. However, a host of related conflicts continued, at least in East and South-east Asia, until 1975, by which time the indigenous peoples of these areas had resolved most of their domestic affairs in a manner that suggested that they, not the great powers, now held the power of decision in such matters.

But these developments lay far beyond the reality that Japan faced in 1945. Such was her plight after the defeats at the hands of American forces in 1944 that court officials in early 1945 seriously, if discreetly, considered the possibility of the Emperor's abdication as the means of opening the way to peace, and in the Spring and Summer the American High Command was aware of Japan's hesitant and futile attempts to extricate herself from the war through Soviet mediation. The American decision to use atomic weapons against Japan (8 and 12 August 1945) was the result of a desire to bring about the quickest – and for the Allies, the most economical – end to the war, and to preclude effective Soviet intervention in the struggle. The Soviet invasion of Manchuria on 9 August (page 198), nevertheless proved a crucial factor in the Japanese decision to accept the terms of the Potsdam declaration of 27 July 1945 – unconditional surrender. While the Japanese High Command rationalized Emperor Hirohito's personal decision to surrender in terms of the need to end the war whilst the United States retained the power of decision amongst Japan's enemies, fear of social revolution was no less important. Nevertheless, despite an unprecedented broadcast by the Emperor on 15 August announcing the decision to accept Allied terms, sections of the armed forces opposed national surrender. Their resistance was quickly stifled. Under the supervision of General MacArthur, Japanese society was reconstituted. Hirohito retained his position as Emperor, but revoked his divine status. He was not accredited with responsibility for war crimes.

Six years were to elapse, however, before the end of the war was finalized with the Treaty of San Francisco (8 September 1951) between Japan and most of her former enemies, and by that time East and South-east Asia were in the process of a transformation. By exposing the fragility of the colonial empires Japan gave new impetus to the anti-imperial revolt of Asia, which would be a dominant feature of the post-war world. The Japanese had established governments in Burma (1942) and the East Indies and Indo-China (1945). After the Japanese defeat, these governments, enlarged or superseded by anti-Japanese nationalist elements, won much popular backing. The war had also unleashed the forces of Communism.

China after 1946 resumed full civil war between the Communists and Kuomintang that had been barely suspended since 1940; the civil war was settled in 1949 with the expulsion of the Kuomintang Nationalists from the mainland to Formosa (Taiwan). With this victory the influence of both Chinese and Soviet Communism began to infiltrate other areas of the former Japanese empire.

The various imperialist powers found their return to former colonies opposed by indigenous forces. A precedent was set in the post-war affairs of South Asia. India, once the target of Japanese subversion and propaganda, was rapidly conceded independence in 1947 by the newly elected British Labour government. Two separate territories formed the Muslim state of Pakistan. Ceylon and Burma became independent in 1948. Nationalists in Java proclaimed an Indonesian republic upon the Japanese surrender in 1945. They advanced into Sumatra, Dutch Borneo, Celebes and the Moluccas, until by 1956 they controlled the whole of the former Dutch East Indies except West New Guinea. The British in Malaya fought a long war against Communist insurgents and resisted Indonesian attempts to annex Sarawak and Brunei. Independence from the United States in 1946 did not spare the Philippines a Communist-inspired insurgency campaign on Luzon. Indeed the most costly wars of the post-1945 era were to be fought within the former Japanese empire: in Korea (1950-53) US military attempts to ease the way to independence brought secession, civil war, and eventual partition. In Indo-China (from 1948) a similar move by the French authorities produced the same result. The crisis in both countries resulted in foreign intervention and ideological confrontation between Communist northern states, and Western-backed southern governments. In Korea compromise was reached, but in Vietnam Western influence was utterly eradicated by 1975.

National independence on the part of the states of East and South-east Asia was accompanied neither by peace nor stability, and areas that are the most populous and heavily armed on the planet remain to this day beset by political, social and racial differences that seemingly remain intractable.

2/THE JAPANESE EMPIRE Aug.1945

ALLIED INVASION of the Home
Islands was planned as a 2-phase
undertaking; Operation *Downfall*
(*1*) would have represented the
greatest endeavour of the Pacific
war, involving the invasions of
Kyushu in Autumn 1945 and
Honshu in Spring 1946. The latter
would have required the
redeployment of US combat
troops from Europe, and
provisional planning assigned
some 14,000 combat aircraft and
about 100 aircraft carriers for this
single operation. The use of the
atom bomb made this
unnecessary. The Allied
occupation of Japan, ensuring the
surrender and repatriation of
Japanese forces that remained in
the scattered remnants of Japan's
former empire, was slow and
complicated (*2*). The aftermath of
the Greater East Asia war (*3*)
witnessed major political changes
in most of the region:

Japan The Home Islands were
placed under US military government, with General MacArthur at
its head, until independence
(1952). The armed forces were
completely disbanded. Various
Japanese pre-war territories were
reallocated. Japan's Pacific territories were variously removed to
US or UN control. Maintaining
close relations with the US, successive governments concentrated on
industrial development and new
technology until in the 1970s
Japan emerged as the world's
third industrial nation.
Burma British control restored
until independence granted in
1948. Communist guerrilla activity from 1948 leading to a series of
military coups (1958-62), and subsequent military government.
China Civil war between Communists and Nationalist (Kuomintang) forces resumed (1945-49);
Communists under Mao Tse-tung
emerged victorious to form the
People's Republic.
Indo-China French control restored until 1954; Laos and Cambodia granted independence; North
Vietnam declared a Communist
state (1954), South Vietnam an independent republic. Communist
insurgency became open civil war
in Vietnam in 1950s, with outside
military involvement (France,
UN, USA) which spread to Laos
and Cambodia. North Vietnam
invaded South (1975).
Indonesia Declared independence 1945; negotiated end to
Dutch control by 1949; effective
control of most Dutch East Indies
territory by 1956. Separatist and
Communist rebellions from 1950s.
Korea Under US and Soviet
military rule until 1948 when a
Communist Peoples Democracy
declared in North, and elected
constitutional government established in South. War between
North and South 1950-53, involving UN troops (under MacArthur)
and Chinese forces ended in stalemate.
Malaysia British colonial control restored (1945). Communist
insurgency from 1948s. Joined
with Sabah and Sarawak to form
Malaysia Federation (1963).
Philippines Short-lived US
military government followed by
independence (1946). Continuing
Communist and Muslim insurgency. Pervasive US influence grew
during Vietnam war.
Thailand (Siam) Continuing
constitutional monarchy (since
1932), with military governments
and intermittent coups. Territories gained during war years (page
192) stripped.

*Picture left: the Japanese surrender,
on USS* Missouri, *2 Sept. 1945.*

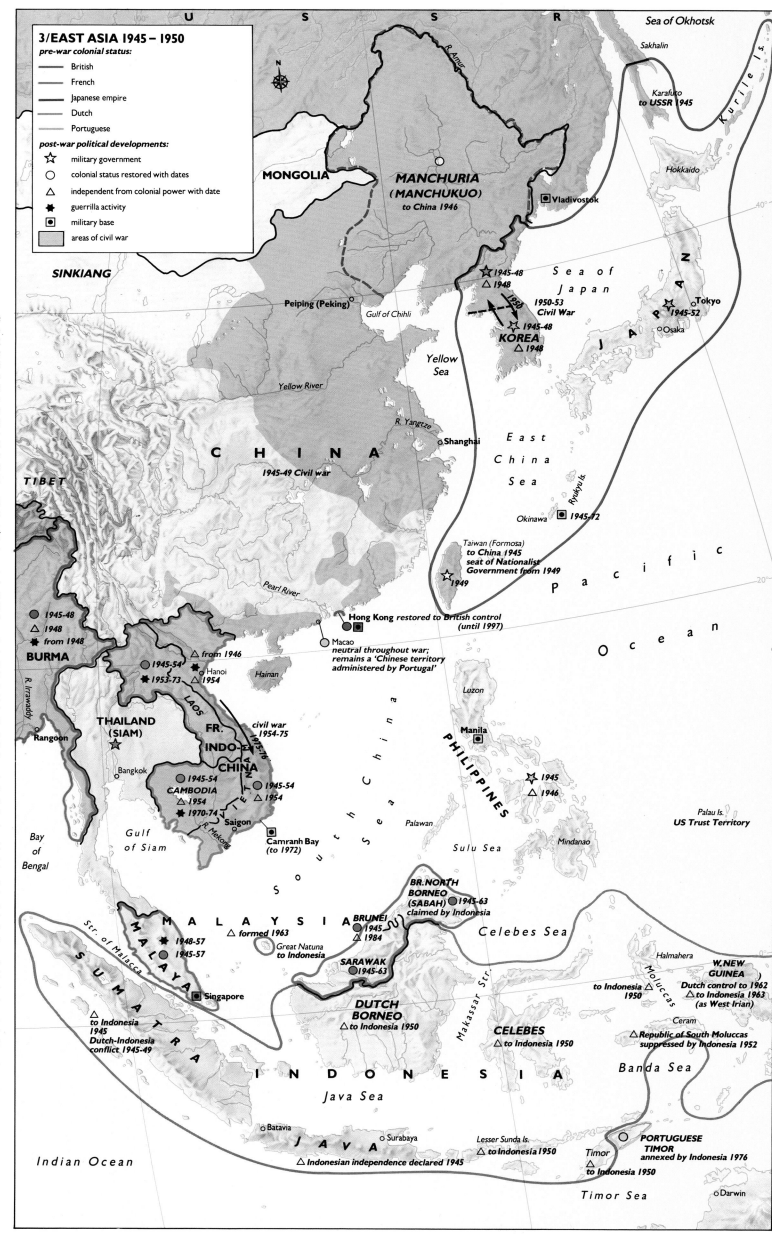

3/EAST ASIA 1945–1950

pre-war colonial status:
——— British
——— French
——— Japanese empire
——— Dutch
——— Portuguese

post-war political developments:
☆ military government
○ colonial status restored with dates
△ independent from colonial power with date
✳ guerrilla activity
⊡ military base
▨ areas of civil war

The world war economies 1939~1945

FROM THE BEGINNING the Second World War was about the mobilization and supply of economic resources. All the major powers involved in the conflict expected it to be a total war in which industry and agriculture would play as vital a part as the armed forces. The First World War had taught them that industrialized warfare could only be fought with industrial weapons – economic rationalization, the mass mobilization of the economy, and mass production in all essential fields. In the early stages of the war Germany was the largest economy, with access by 1941 to the resources of most of Europe. Britain was critically dependent on keeping open her worldwide supply lines which were threatened everywhere by submarine. The Soviet Union co-operated with Germany; the United States helped the British empire. The economic balance lay in the Axis favour. With Hitler's decision to attack Russia and then America's entry into the war in 1941 the balance swung massively in favour of the Allies. It would be wrong to assume that from then on Axis defeat was inevitable, but there is a real sense in which the sheer quantity of resources available for the Allied cause, and Allied domination of the seas, made the Axis task almost impossible. Japan, Germany and Italy became siege economies, forced to build their war efforts on the resources of their captured empires, subjected to naval blockade and, from 1943, to an increasingly heavy bombing offensive. The result was damaging pressure on production, the rapid decline of civilian living standards, and the savage exploitation of the captured areas.

The Axis problem can be expressed in a number of ways. In terms of population the Allied powers could still call on 360 million against 195 million for the Axis. But this gap was partly made good by access to the labour resources of captured Europe, or China and Korea, and by exceptionally high levels of female employment, much of it on farms, in both Germany and Japan. The real gap lay in manufacturing potential. In 1938 Britain, the USA and the USSR accounted for 60 per cent of the world's manufacturing capacity, the Axis for only 17 per cent. Even with the Axis occupation of western Russia in 1941 the gap was unbridgeable. The Allies had twice the steel output and three times the coal output of their adversaries. In 1938 Britain and France alone produced more motor vehicles and more shipping tonnage than the three Axis states together.

Though the Axis captured large additional resources, these only replaced overseas imports (the American embargo on steel and oil for Japan was not fully compensated for in Manchuria or the Dutch East Indies), or were exploited at well below optimum level. In the Soviet Union installations were so thoroughly destroyed by retreating Soviet forces that Germany acquired barely a fraction of the potential of the resources captured. In Fortress Europe hostility to Nazism, partisan activity and an increasingly disabled transport network reduced the gains from exploitation. The steel industry of Lorraine, for example, worked at no more than 50 per cent capacity; Germany's oil imports during the war averaged less than half the level of 1939 even with virtual control of Rumanian supplies. By contrast, the Allies had access to the resources of the whole western hemisphere, Africa, the Middle East, Australasia and South Asia. Only the submarine could undermine this economic advantage, and by 1943 that threat had been met (page 108). Moreover, the Allied states mobilized their economies more effectively than their enemies, leaving much of the task in the hands of industrialists and civilian experts rather than the military. The result was a degree of disparity in the output of finished weapons even greater than the gap in resources. In 1942 the Axis produced 26,000 aircraft, the Allies 101,000; the same year Allied tank production reached 58,000, Axis tank output a mere 11,000; the United States produced in 1943 ten times as many combat naval vessels as Japan and Germany together. Axis forces faced a relentless attrition cycle from 1942 onwards, which not even the revival of German production in 1944 could reverse.

The economic costs of the conflict were enormous. European industrial production was, by 1946, down to one-third of the pre-war level, food production to a half. France lost 46 per cent of her national wealth; Italy lost over one-third. The Soviet Union had 1700 towns and 70,000 villages completely destroyed. Bombing damaged or destroyed the central areas of almost all German, Italian and Japanese cities. All states were faced with enormous increases in public debt. The main beneficiaries of the war were those states not directly affected by conflict, where the huge inexhaustible demand for food, raw materials and weapons from the warring powers rapidly reversed the damage done by the Depression of the 1930s, and paved the way for the development of a more open and prosperous global economy under US leadership.

A CENTRAL ARGUMENT made by the Axis powers to justify their imperialism was the need to secure supplies of vital raw materials and foodstuffs. In 1939 much of the world's mineral and raw material supplies were found in the French and British empires or in the USA, or in areas which could be cut off from the Axis by Allied naval power (1). This forced the Axis states to fall back on the areas they conquered and explains why Russian oil and wheat, or the tin, rubber and oil of the colonial Far East were so important as targets for attack. In the captured areas living-standards were deliberately suppressed and resources taken for the war effort, though the home countries had to cut back on civilian consumption too. German daily intake of calories per day was higher than the occupied areas, but was well below levels in the United States or in neutral states (inset, 1). By 1944 Japanese imports of rice were down to one-tenth of the pre-war level. Germany had to depend on the programme of import-substitution set up in 1936 to make up for losses of oil, rubber and iron-ore supply. The occupied states of Europe were forced to pay more than 90 billion marks in war contributions, and to provide foodstuffs and labour for the Reich (3). By 1944 Germany owed the neutrals and her allies in Europe over 20 billion marks for goods bought during the war. The Allies had the advantage of being able to operate on a global scale after American entry into the war. The USA sent goods to every theatre and established a worldwide network of air bases and supply depots (2). The Allied powers had adequate access to oil supplies and their global tanker fleet expanded from 12 million to 21 million tons despite heavy losses to submarines (4). But even the Allies had problems with the loss of resources. The USA had to build up a synthetic rubber industry to replace losses from Malaya using technical know-how from Germany. The US economy grew by 50% during the war. The British, German and Japanese economies expanded more modestly. Growth was only reversed in countries hit by conquest and occupation; the French economy fell by 50%, the Soviet economy by 13% during the war (5). To compensate for losses the USA supplied large quantities of weapons and goods under Lend-Lease (6). A more modest reciprocal aid programme from the British empire helped to cover the very great costs of operating large US forces overseas (7).

Picture right: German citizens buying their bread ration.

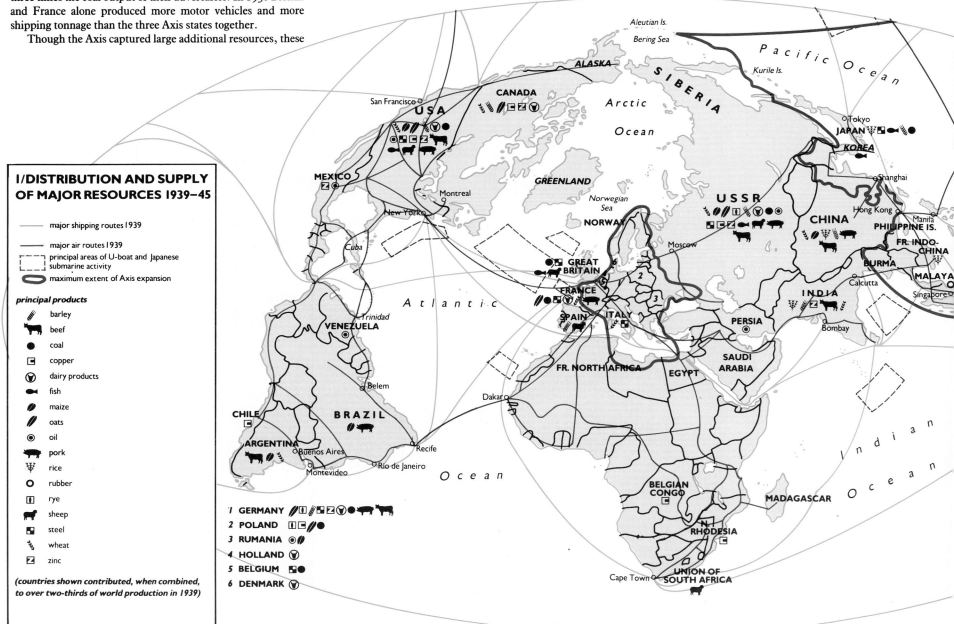

1/DISTRIBUTION AND SUPPLY OF MAJOR RESOURCES 1939–45

— major shipping routes 1939

--- major air routes 1939

principal areas of U-boat and Japanese submarine activity

⬭ maximum extent of Axis expansion

principal products

- barley
- beef
- coal
- copper
- dairy products
- fish
- maize
- oats
- oil
- pork
- rice
- rubber
- rye
- sheep
- steel
- wheat
- zinc

(countries shown contributed, when combined, to over two-thirds of world production in 1939)

1 GERMANY
2 POLAND
3 RUMANIA
4 HOLLAND
5 BELGIUM
6 DENMARK

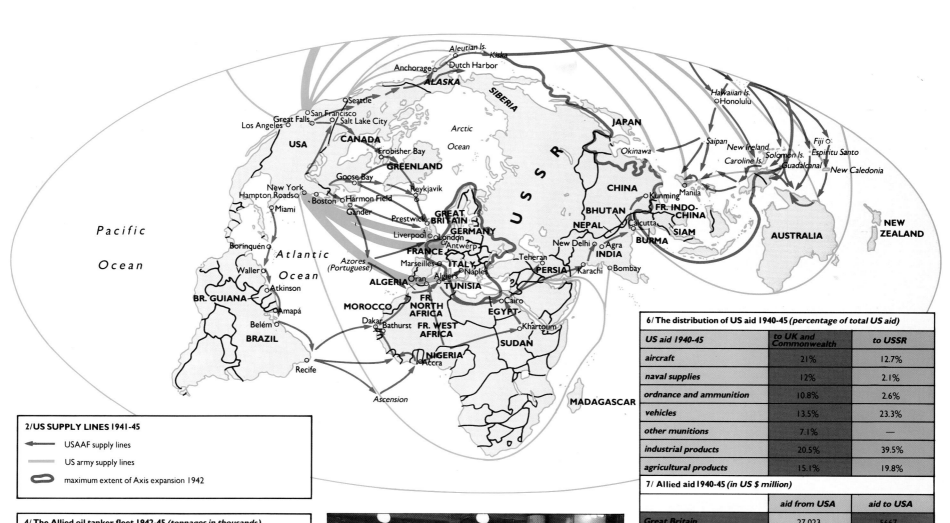

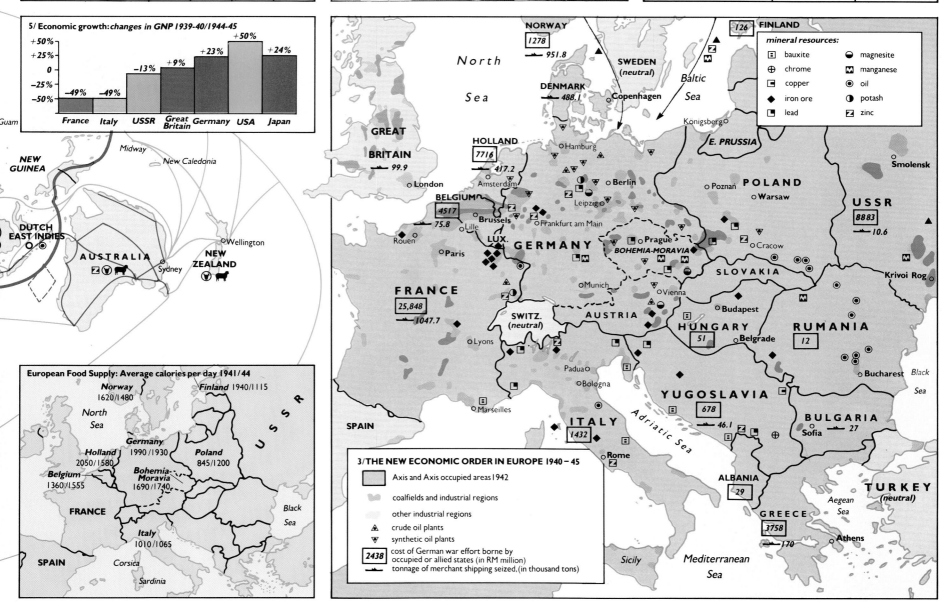

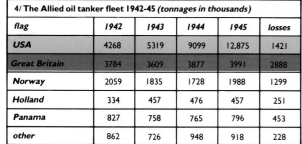

2/US SUPPLY LINES 1941-45

- ← USAAF supply lines
- US army supply lines
- ⬭ maximum extent of Axis expansion 1942

6/ The distribution of US aid 1940-45 (percentage of total US aid)

US aid 1940-45	to UK and Commonwealth	to USSR
aircraft	21%	12.7%
naval supplies	12%	2.1%
ordnance and ammunition	10.8%	2.6%
vehicles	13.5%	23.3%
other munitions	7.1%	—
industrial products	20.5%	39.5%
agricultural products	15.1%	19.8%

7/ Allied aid 1940-45 (in US $ million)

	aid from USA	aid to USA
Great Britain	27,023	5667
Australia	1570	1041
New Zealand	271	248
South Africa	296	1
India	913	610
USSR	10,670	—
other	2872	—
total	43,685	7567

4/ The Allied oil tanker fleet 1942-45 (tonnages in thousands)

flag	1942	1943	1944	1945	losses
USA	4268	5319	9099	12,875	1421
Great Britain	3784	3609	3877	3991	2888
Norway	2059	1835	1728	1988	1299
Holland	334	457	476	457	251
Panama	827	758	765	796	453
other	862	726	948	918	228

5/ Economic growth: changes in GNP 1939-40/1944-45

France	Italy	USSR	Great Britain	Germany	USA	Japan
-49%	-49%	-13%	+9%	+23%	+50%	+24%

European Food Supply: Average calories per day 1941/44

Norway 1620/1480
Finland 1940/1115
Holland 2050/1580
Germany 1990/1930
Poland 845/1200
Belgium 1360/1555
Bohemia-Moravia 1690/1740
France
Italy 1010/1065

3/ THE NEW ECONOMIC ORDER IN EUROPE 1940-45

- Axis and Axis occupied areas 1942
- coalfields and industrial regions
- other industrial regions
- ▲ crude oil plants
- ▽ synthetic oil plants
- 2438 cost of German war effort borne by occupied or allied states (in RM million)
- ⟷ tonnage of merchant shipping seized (in thousand tons)

mineral resources:
- ▣ bauxite
- ⊕ chrome
- ⊡ copper
- ◆ iron ore
- ▤ lead
- ◐ magnesite
- Ⓜ manganese
- ⊙ oil
- ◑ potash
- ⧄ zinc

NORWAY 1278 — 951.8
FINLAND 126
DENMARK — 488.1
HOLLAND 7716 — 417.2
GREAT BRITAIN — 99.9
BELGIUM 4517 — 75.8
LUX.
FRANCE 25,848 — 1047.7
BOHEMIA-MORAVIA
HUNGARY 51
RUMANIA 12
YUGOSLAVIA 678 — 46.1
BULGARIA 27
ITALY 1432
ALBANIA 29
GREECE 3758 — 170
USSR 8883 — 10.6

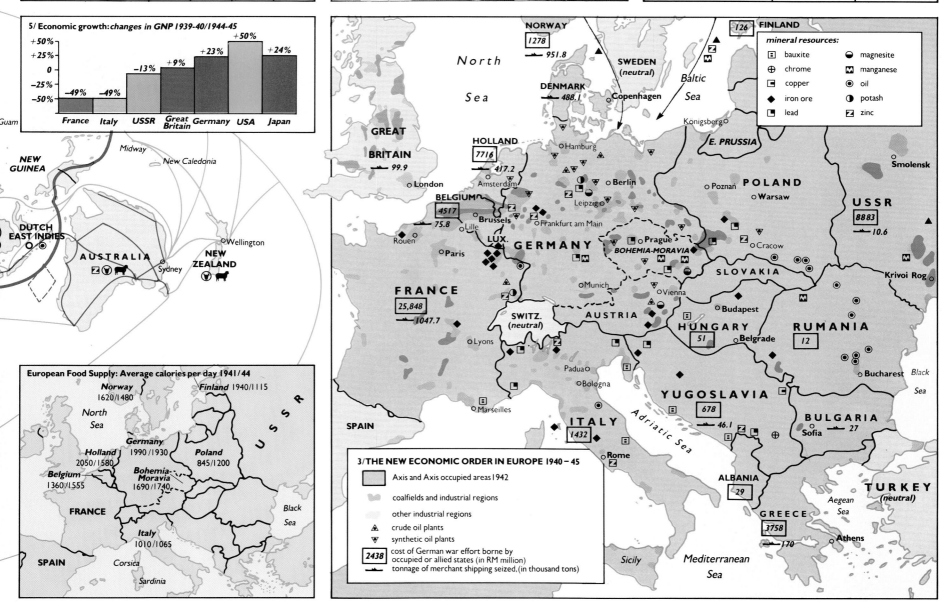

203

The casualties

THE COST of the Second World War in human life was the highest of any ever fought. It provoked a number of battles – Stalingrad, Normandy and Berlin – as destructive as the worst episodes of the First World War. It also caused very large loss of life away from the battlefield: by direct bombing attacks on the civilian population; by the deprivation imposed by siege (as at Leningrad, where over 500,000 civilians died between November 1941 and January 1944); by the disruption of agriculture and food supply; by massacre and reprisal in the course of guerrilla campaigns, particularly in Yugoslavia which lost over a million of its population between 1941 and 1945; by flight and forcible expulsion, which accounted for the death of two million Germans in 1945 alone; and by organized extermination, particularly of the European Jews in Poland, who suffered up to six million deaths between 1942 and 1945.

The campaigns fought by the Axis powers against the Western Allies were governed by observance of the Geneva convention, which ensured humane treatment of prisoners, wounded and non-combatants. Axis prisoners in Allied hands enjoyed particularly good treatment, since many were sent to locations in North America and Africa where food was plentiful. Western prisoners in Axis hands fared less well, but most were correctly treated until, at the very end of the war, many were sent on forced marches away from the advance of the liberating armies. Western prisoners in Japanese hands suffered varied ill-treatment, including semi-starvation, subjection to scientific experiment, forced labour and incarceration in camps close to bombing targets. Soviet prisoners in German hands died in millions, at first because their numbers overwhelmed arrangements made for their containment, later because many were deliberately worked to death, or left to starve. The Russians did not introduce regulations for dealing with prisoners of war until 1943. They took about two million Germans. Given shortages among Soviet troops, their treatment was at best perfunctory. Prior to the Japanese surrender in August 1945, the Allies took very few Japanese prisoners of war; they were determined to fight to the last man and most preferred suicide to the dishonour of captivity. However, in August-September 1945 the Soviets took over a million Japanese prisoners, most of whom were never seen again.

The monitoring of the treatment of prisoners was in the hands of the International Red Cross, based in Switzerland. Its representatives were allowed access to prisoner of war camps in Germany, and those operated by the Western Allies; they also gained limited access to concentration camps before the war. However, both the Japanese and Soviet governments persistently refused to admit teams of inspectors.

After 1941, all the belligerents abandoned any reservations about attacking large centres of population. The devastation wrought upon the cities of Europe alone are an index of this – only Rome and Paris were nominally declared open cities, on the basis of their cultural importance. Warsaw, however, was utterly destroyed (November-December 1944) by the retreating Germans. The large-scale bombing of cities caused the deaths of some 600,000 in Germany, 500,000 in Japan and 60,000 civilians in Britain. There was also serious loss of life by bombing in Poland, France, Italy, Belgium and Holland. In the combatant states where the administrative machinery remained intact, however, there was no repetition of the death toll by deprivation and epidemic which afflicted the Central Powers during the First World War. Efficient rationing and medical care ensured that the health of civilian populations in Germany and the western European states remained good; there were few war-related civilian deaths in the United States. In the USSR, eastern and southern Europe and China the toll of war-related civilian deaths was extremely high; some estimates put those killed by the Japanese in China at ten million.

Guerrilla warfare, internal disorder and forced movements of population, which afflicted the societies of eastern and southern Europe from 1939 to 1945 and wide areas of China from 1937 onwards, caused great loss of life. In Greece, where resistance to Axis occupation was strong, some 120,000 of the country's 140,000 war dead were victims of reprisal, factional fighting, massacre or deportation. A high proportion of the Soviet Union's seven million civilian dead were victims of direct oppression (page 172) or war-related deprivation. The largest single cause of death in the Second World War, however, was the battle between the *Wehrmacht* and the Soviet Army, which killed at least eleven million soldiers and wounded 25 million, of whom the vast majority were Soviet.

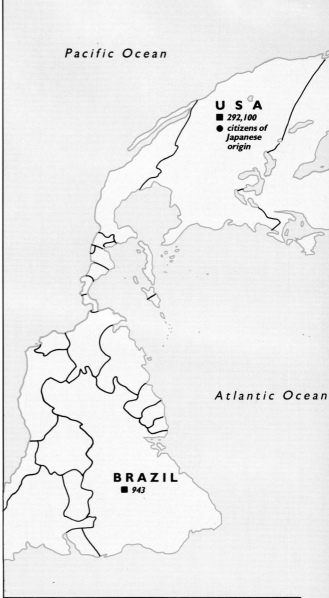

USA
■ 292,100
● citizens of Japanese origin

BRAZIL
■ 943

3/ POWs IN THE EAST 1941 – 45
- ● POW camps
- ▲ civilian internment camps
- <u>Macassar</u> labour camp

War dead of the Soviet Union (within post-1945 borders)

- - - pre-war western border of USSR

ESTONIANS 92,000
LATVIANS 181,500
LITHUANIANS 281,100
RUSSIANS and other Soviet nationalities 9 million
BYELORUSSIANS 1.5 million
POLES 1-2 million
JEWS 2 million
UKRAINIANS 4-5 million
RUMANIANS 500,000

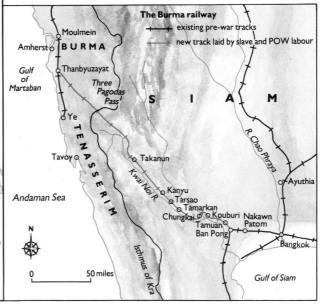

The Burma railway
—+— existing pre-war tracks
—++— new track laid by slave and POW labour

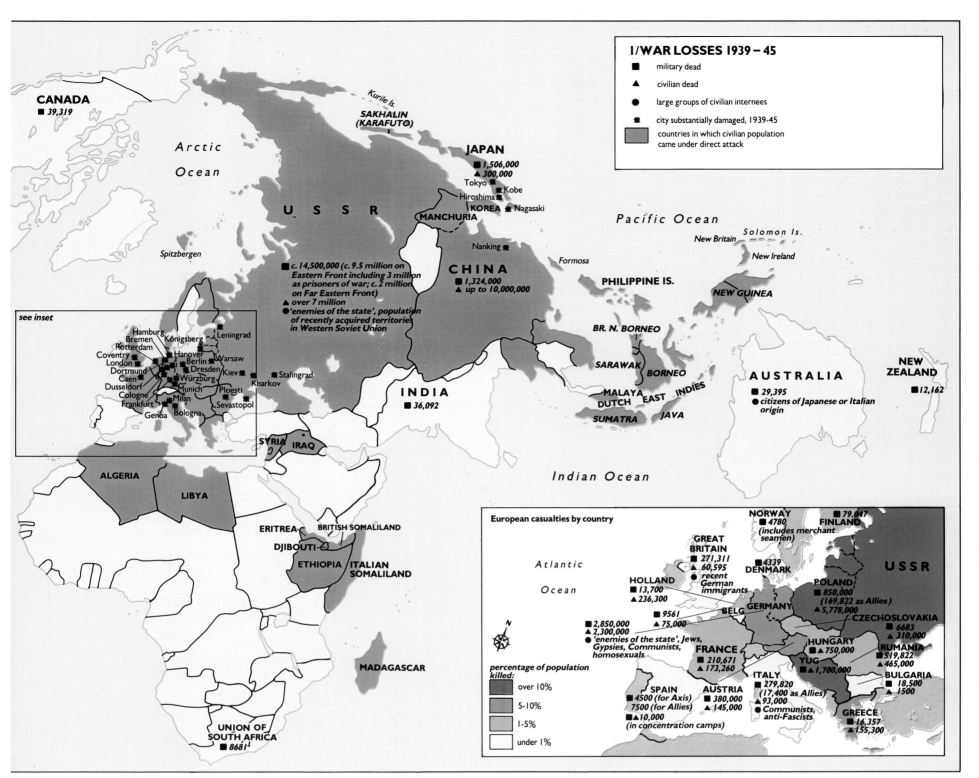

I/WAR LOSSES 1939 – 45

- ■ military dead
- ▲ civilian dead
- ● large groups of civilian internees
- ✳ city substantially damaged, 1939-45
- ▨ countries in which civilian population came under direct attack

CANADA
■ 39,319

Arctic Ocean

Spitzbergen

Kurile Is.
SAKHALIN (KARAFUTO)

JAPAN
■ 1,506,000
▲ 300,000
Tokyo ✳
Hiroshima ✳ ✳ Kobe
KOREA ✳ Nagasaki

Pacific Ocean

MANCHURIA

Nanking ✳

CHINA
■ 1,324,000
▲ up to 10,000,000

U S S R
■ c. 14,500,000 (c. 9.5 million on Eastern Front including 3 million as prisoners of war; c. 2 million on Far Eastern Front)
▲ over 7 million
● 'enemies of the state', population of recently acquired territories in Western Soviet Union

New Britain
Solomon Is.
New Ireland

PHILIPPINE IS.

NEW GUINEA

BR. N. BORNEO

SARAWAK
BORNEO

MALAYA
DUTCH **EAST** **INDIES**
SUMATRA **JAVA**

AUSTRALIA
■ 29,395
● citizens of Japanese or Italian origin

NEW ZEALAND
■ 12,162

see inset

Hamburg
Bremen
Königsberg
Leningrad
Rotterdam
Coventry
Hanover
London
Berlin
Warsaw
Dortmund
Dresden
Caen
Würzburg
Kiev
Dusseldorf
Munich
Ploesti
Cologne
Milan
Sevastopol
Frankfurt
Genoa
Bologna
Kharkov
Stalingrad

INDIA
■ 36,092

SYRIA
IRAQ

ALGERIA

LIBYA

ERITREA
BRITISH SOMALILAND
DJIBOUTI

ETHIOPIA **ITALIAN SOMALILAND**

Indian Ocean

MADAGASCAR

UNION OF SOUTH AFRICA
■ 8681

European casualties by country

Atlantic Ocean

NORWAY
■ 79,047 FINLAND
▲ 4780
(includes merchant seamen)

GREAT BRITAIN
■ 271,311
▲ 60,595
● recent German immigrants

DENMARK ▲ 4339

HOLLAND
■ 13,700
▲ 236,300

GERMANY
■ 2,850,000
▲ 2,300,000
● 'enemies of the state', Jews, Gypsies, Communists, homosexuals

BELG ■ 9561 ▲ 75,000

POLAND
■ 850,000 (169,822 as Allies)
▲ 5,778,000

U S S R

CZECHOSLOVAKIA
■ 6683
▲ 310,000

FRANCE
■ 210,671
▲ 173,260

HUNGARY
■ 750,000

RUMANIA
■ 519,822
▲ 465,000

YUG
▲ 1,700,000

BULGARIA
■ 18,500
▲ 1500

ITALY
■ 279,820 (17,400 as Allies)
▲ 93,000
● Communists, anti-Fascists

AUSTRIA
■ 380,000
▲ 145,000

SPAIN
■ 4500 (for Axis)
7500 (for Allies)

GREECE
■ 16,357
▲ 155,300

percentage of population killed:
- ▨ over 10%
- ▨ 5-10%
- ▨ 1-5%
- ▨ under 1%

■ 10,000 (in concentration camps)

THE TOTAL NUMBER OF WAR DEAD (*1*) defies accurate calculation but is usually estimated at between 40 and 50 million worldwide. The Second World War, unlike the First, caused very high direct civilian casualties – by bombing, deprivation, maltreatment or deliberate extermination – which may have equalled military battle deaths. Casualties, both military and civilian, were higher in Europe than in Asia and much higher in eastern than western Europe, an indication of the brutality of the East European campaigns. The Red Army suffered some 11.5 million battle deaths; another 3 million Russian soldiers died as German prisoners. The *Wehrmacht* suffered almost 3 million battle deaths and Japan 1.5 million. The highest totals of battle deaths among the Western Allies were some 250,000 in the British forces, 300,000 in the American and 200,000 in the French. Civilian deaths were highest in the Soviet Union (over 7 million, mostly non-Russians), China (many millions, but unverified) and Germany, where some 600,000 were killed by bombing and nearly 2 million died in the flight from the east in 1945. Among individual countries, Poland suffered worst, losing 6 million, or some 18% of its pre-war population; almost half of these were Jews, of whom 6 million

throughout Europe were killed by deliberate Nazi policy during the war. The largest number of prisoners taken in the war (*2*) was by the Germans from the Red Army; 4 million out of 5 million Russian prisoners captured died, at least 3 million in German hands; another million are believed to have died in labour camps on their return to the Soviet Union after 1945. About a million French prisoners were held by the Germans between 1940 and 1945, together with hundreds of thousands of Britons, Americans, Italians (after 1943) and Poles, as well as other nationalities in a network of camps within the Reich. In 1939 about 200,000 Polish soldiers became prisoners of the USSR; 15,000 officers disappeared, some 4500 officers being massacred at Katyn. In 1945 about 10 million Germans and 6 million Japanese became prisoners of the Allies. In the East (*3*), over 61,000 British, Australian and Dutch prisoners were taken by the Japanese in South-east Asia in their opening campaigns of 1941-42, of whom 12,000 died working alongside native slave labour to build the Burma Railway (*inset*). Of the 45,000 Indians captured in Malaya in 1942, nearly 40,000 agreed to join the Japanese-sponsored Indian National Army raised by the Indian nationalist, Subhas Chandra Bose (page 192).

2/POWs IN GERMANY 1939 – 45

- ▪ concentration camp
- ▲ camps for Soviet prisoners
- ● airmen's camp (*Stalag Luft*)
- ▪ officer's camp (*Oflag*)
- ◆ other ranks camp (*Stalag*)
- ☐ camps for persistent escapees
- △ internment camp (*Ilag*)
- ○ transit camp (*Dulag*)
- ⭕ collection centre for POWs during Allied invasions
- ✚ hospital (*Lazarett*)

DENMARK **SWEDEN**
North Sea *Baltic Sea*

Heydekrug

POLAND

Barth
Lübeck
Danzig
Gross Tychow
Marienburg
Wilhelmshaven
Hamburg
Westertimke naval prison
Bremen
Ravensbrück
Stargard
R. Vistula
Thorn

HOLLAND
The Hague
Altengrabow
Berlin
Sachsenhausen
Schubin
Warsaw

c. 5.5 million Soviet prisoners of war held in the East;
c. 4 million of these were killed by the Nazis;
c. 1 million were killed by Soviets following their liberation;
c. 800,000 avoided death by collaborating with the Nazis

from transit camps on Eastern Front

Biała Podlaska
Włodawa
Chełm

Fallingbostel
Luckenwalde
Posen
Querum
Steglitz
Fürstenberg
Elsterhorst
Schmorkau
Leipzig
Königswartha
R. Weser
Warburg
Spangenberg
Kirchnain
Mühlberg
Kunau
Brussels
Frankfurt am Main
Haina Kloster
Colditz
Bankau
Kreuzburg
R. Oder
Hartmannsdorf
Hadamar
Rotenburg
Hohnstein
Lamsdorf
Kloster Haina
Obermassfeld
Tost
Cosel
Teschen
Przemyśl
Zamość
Oberursel
Hammelburg
Bad Soden
Nuremberg
Prague
Mährisch-Trübau
Weissenburg
Weinsberg
Eichstätt
Vienna
Moosburg
Strassburg
Munich
Natzweiler
Offenburg
GERMANY

BELGIUM

FRANCE

Vittel
Biberach
Wurzach
Tittmoning
Freising
Dachau
Laufen
Besancon
Liebenau
Kaiserstein bei Bruch
Berne
Markt Pupp
AUSTRIA
Geneva
Spittal
Wolfsberg
SWITZERLAND
Marburg
Villach

from transit camps in N. Africa and (after 1942) Italy

from transit camps in the Balkans

c. 25,000 Russian POWs in France

ITALY
YUGOSLAVIA

Global war

THE SECOND WORLD WAR, unlike the First, eventually engulfed the globe. In 1939, in Asia, the Japanese were pursuing a continuing war designed to bring them effective control of China. In Europe, it began as a local war mounted by Hitler to complete his programme of frontier rectification on Germany's border with Poland. Though the armies mobilized in 1939 were large, numbering one million in Poland and three million each in France and Germany – Britain's regular army was only 200,000 strong – the numbers of men put into the field in the opening stage were smaller than in 1914.

The scale of the war grew apace thereafter. Britain continued its mobilization programme after the defeat of France in June 1940 and, though Hitler temporarily reduced the size of the *Wehrmacht* at that time, he raised it again later that year when he had decided to attack the Soviet Union. By the time he unleashed the invasion, in June 1941, his forces were twice the size they had been in 1939, while his offensive brought into the war a Russian force which was bigger still. It maintained a front-line strength alone of 11.5 million. Japan's decision to join Germany as an Axis combatant (enlarging the sphere of her ongoing war in China) further swelled fighting numbers, which would reach their fullest extent when the United States had completed the mobilization of almost twelve million active servicemen.

As the war spread and developed, the nature of the arena in which it was fought began to change. Although trans- and inter-continental conflicts had occurred before, the battlefield now assumed a spherical, global form, with varying implications for all the combatants.

As an imperial power, with garrisons stationed around the world before 1939, Britain was committed to fight on almost every front of the Second World War. British troops, and those of her colonies and associated dominions, consequently fought in South-east Asia, the Pacific islands, North and East Africa, southern and north-western Europe and the Middle East, as well as in the Atlantic, Pacific, Indian and Arctic Oceans and all the skies of the northern hemisphere.

By contrast, the Soviet war was limited to its own territory and contiguous areas, of which the most distant from the centre

was Manchuria, where it fought a victorious campaign against the Japanese in August 1945. Japanese forces ranged widely across the western Pacific and adjacent territories, penetrating by 1944 deep into China. Germany, largely a land-locked power, succeeded in projecting its military force across the Mediterranean and, with its U-boats and surface commerce raiders, in conducting a maritime campaign which reached as far as the Caribbean in the west and the Indian Ocean in the east. But it was the United States which eventually achieved the widest global outreach. In 1944 it was conducting major land, sea and air campaigns in western and southern Europe, in China, in South-east Asia, and in the central and southern Pacific. The Second World War, at its apogee, was truly an American war.

The extension of the 'killing zone' beyond the immediate battlefield was a further global characteristic of the war. Aside from the ideological nature of civilian persecutions by the Axis powers, notably in China and eastern Europe, civilians throughout Europe, western Russia and East Asia came under direct military attack, largely as a result of bombing strategies or when caught in the path of a mobile battle front.

The experience of war was neither clear-cut nor decisive for many peoples and nations, especially those chosen by the major powers as targets for ideological policies. This was true of none more so than the Poles. Their country was invaded by Germany on the first day of the war and its forces were still active in the field, in strength on three major fronts, at the moment of Germany's surrender. In the interim, the country had suffered invasion by the USSR, appalling social and ideological persecution by both occupying powers and virtual political extinction. Some Poles volunteered or were coerced into both the *Wehrmacht* and the Red Army; many served as slave labourers for the Reich. Nevertheless, Poles in exile fought with the greatest valour and effectiveness at the side of the French, the British and the Soviets, while in Poland itself the underground Home Army mounted the largest of all rebellions against German occupation forces (Warsaw 1944, page 170) to be staged by any resistance movement during the war.

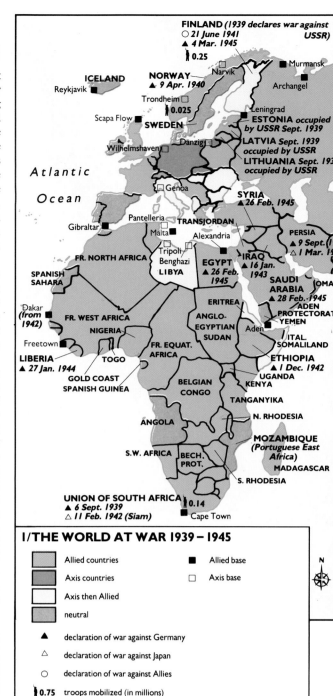

1/THE WORLD AT WAR 1939–1945

▢ Allied countries	■ Allied base	
▢ Axis countries	▢ Axis base	
▢ Axis then Allied		
▢ neutral		

▲ declaration of war against Germany

△ declaration of war against Japan

○ declaration of war against Allies

❚ 0.75 troops mobilized (in millions)

✚ declaration of war made by government in exile

BY 1945 almost every sovereign state in the world was actively or technically a combatant in the Second World War (*1*). The involvement of the great imperial powers ensured that of their colonies in Africa and Asia. At the moment of Germany's collapse (May 1945) only 9 sovereign states remained neutral. Every state in Latin America (including even previously pro-Axis Argentina) had joined the Allied cause; Brazil even maintained an expeditionary force in Italy. During the course of the war, several states changed sides from the Axis to the Allies – usually as they were overrun by the Allies. A number of Asian states, under sovereign or puppet governments, had meanwhile sided with Japan. They included Siam, the Philippines and Burma.

The war was geographically the most extensive ever fought (*2*). Its campaigns touched every continent except Antarctica. At the height of the Axis success, in the Summer of 1942, German troops controlled the whole of western Europe (less the neutrals Spain, Portugal, Sweden, Switzerland and Ireland) outside Great Britain, and much of European Russia, while Japan had occupied all the islands of the western Pacific (less Hawaii and Midway), the British, French and Dutch colonies of South-east Asia, and were poised to strike at northern Australia. The Allies, however, consistently retained greater control of both land masses and sea and air routes, allowing them to shift forces across the globe as required. Poland (*3*),

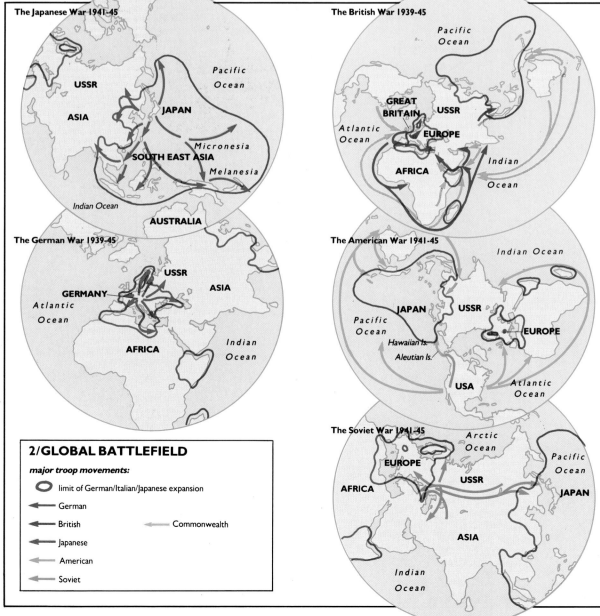

2/GLOBAL BATTLEFIELD

major troop movements:

⬭ limit of German/Italian/Japanese expansion

← German

← British ← Commonwealth

← Japanese

← American

← Soviet

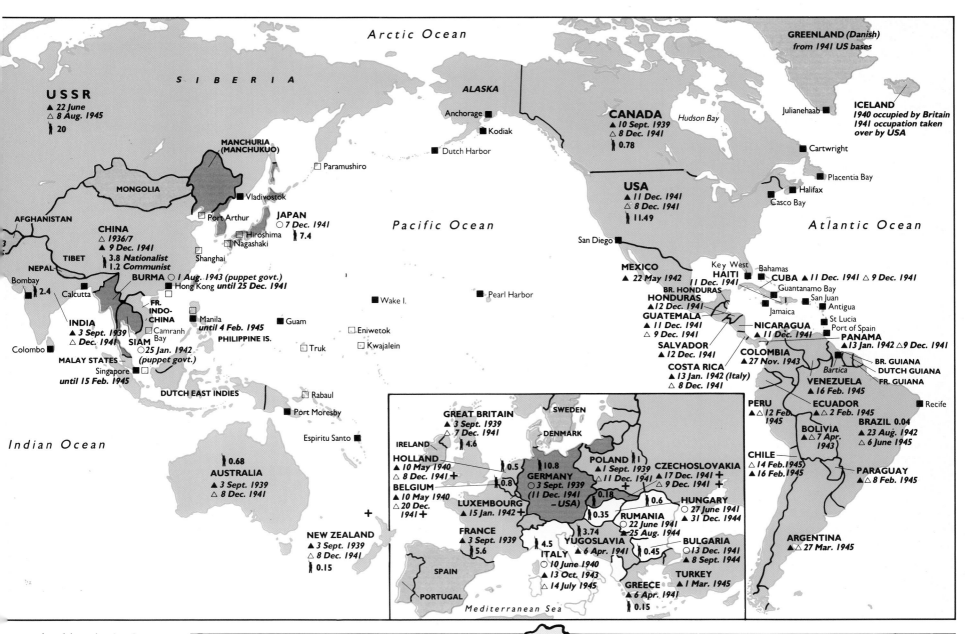

USSR
▲ 22 June
△ 8 Aug. 1945
👤 20

SIBERIA

Arctic Ocean

GREENLAND (Danish)
from 1941 US bases

MANCHURIA
(MANCHUKUO)
● Vladivostok
■ Port Arthur

● Paramushiro

ALASKA
● Anchorage
● Kodiak

■ Dutch Harbor

CANADA
▲ 10 Sept. 1939
△ 8 Dec. 1941
👤 0.78

● Cartwright

ICELAND
1940 occupied by Britain
1941 occupation taken
over by USA

MONGOLIA

● Julianehaab

AFGHANISTAN

CHINA
△ 1936/7
▲ 9 Dec. 1941
👤 3.8 Nationalist
1.2 Communist
■ Shanghai

JAPAN
○ 7 Dec. 1941
■ Hiroshima
■ Nagashaki

Pacific Ocean

● Placentia Bay

● Halifax

● Casco Bay

Atlantic Ocean

TIBET
NEPAL
Bombay ■ 2.4
BURMA ○ 1 Aug. 1943 (puppet govt.)
● Hong Kong until 25 Dec. 1941

👤 7.4

USA
▲ 11 Dec. 1941
△ 8 Dec. 1941
👤 11.49

● San Diego

Key West ■
Bahamas ■
■ Guantanamo Bay
● San Juan
Jamaica

CUBA ▲ 11 Dec. 1941 △ 9 Dec. 1941
HAITI 11 Dec. 1941
● Antigua
St Lucia ●
Port of Spain ●

INDIA
▲ 3 Sept. 1939
△ Dec. 1941
Colombo ■
MALAY STATES
Singapore
until 15 Feb. 1945

FR. INDO-CHINA
■ Manila
until 4 Feb. 1945
● Camranh Bay
SIAM ○ 25 Jan. 1942
(puppet govt.)
PHILIPPINE IS.

● Guam

● Wake I.

● Pearl Harbor

MEXICO
▲ 22 May 1942

BR. HONDURAS
11 Dec. 1941
HONDURAS ▲ 12 Dec. 1941
GUATEMALA ▲ 11 Dec. 1941
SALVADOR ▲ 12 Dec. 1941
NICARAGUA ▲ 11 Dec. 1941
△ 9 Dec. 1941
PANAMA ▲ 13 Jan. 1942 △ 9 Dec. 1941
COSTA RICA ▲ 13 Jan. 1942 (Italy)
△ 8 Dec. 1941
COLOMBIA ▲ 27 Nov. 1943
● Bartica
BR. GUIANA
DUTCH GUIANA
FR. GUIANA
VENEZUELA ▲ 16 Feb. 1945
● Recife

Indian Ocean

DUTCH EAST INDIES
● Rabaul
● Port Moresby

● Eniwetok
● Truk
● Kwajalein

PERU ▲△ 12 Feb 1945
ECUADOR ▲ 2 Feb. 1945
BRAZIL 0.04 ▲ 23 Aug. 1942 △ 6 June 1945
BOLIVIA ▲ 7 Apr. 1943

AUSTRALIA
👤 0.68
▲ 3 Sept. 1939
△ 8 Dec. 1941

● Espiritu Santo

CHILE ▲ 14 Feb.1945 △ 16 Feb.1945
PARAGUAY ▲ 8 Feb. 1945

NEW ZEALAND
▲ 3 Sept. 1939
△ 8 Dec. 1941
👤 0.15

ARGENTINA
▲△ 27 Mar. 1945

Inset: Europe

SWEDEN

GREAT BRITAIN
▲ 3 Sept. 1939
△ 7 Dec. 1941
👤 4.6

IRELAND
DENMARK

HOLLAND
▲ 10 May 1940
△ 8 Dec. 1941 👤 0.5

GERMANY
○ 3 Sept. 1939
(11 Dec. 1941
– USA) 👤 10.8

POLAND
▲ 1 Sept. 1939
▲ 11 Dec. 1941

CZECHOSLOVAKIA
▲ 17 Dec. 1941
▲ 9 Dec. 1941

BELGIUM
▲ 10 May 1940
△ 20 Dec. 1941 👤 0.8

LUXEMBOURG
△ 15 Jan. 1942

👤 0.18

HUNGARY
○ 27 June 1941
▲ 31 Dec. 1944

FRANCE
▲ 3 Sept. 1939
👤 5.6
👤 4.5

👤 0.35

RUMANIA
○ 22 June 1941
▲ 25 Aug. 1944

👤 0.6

ITALY
○ 10 June 1940
△ 13 Oct. 1943
△ 14 July 1945

👤 3.74
YUGOSLAVIA
● 6 Apr. 1941

BULGARIA
○ 13 Dec. 1941
▲ 8 Sept. 1944
👤 0.45

SPAIN
PORTUGAL

GREECE
▲ 6 Apr. 1941
👤 0.15

TURKEY
▲ 1 Mar. 1945

Mediterranean Sea

---

though its national territory was overrun and partitioned by Russo-German forces (Sept. 1939), and its civilians subjected to a ferocious array of persecutions, nevertheless succeeded in maintaining forces in the field throughout the war. In 1945 they were the 5th largest force – after those of the USSR, the USA, Britain and France – still engaged against Germany. After the defeat of the Polish Army in the field in 1939, emigré Polish units fought in Norway, France and the Battle of Britain (1940), in North Africa (where they had arrived from Russia 1942-43), in Italy (1943-45), in France, Belgium and Germany (1944-45), as part of the Red Army in Russia, Poland and Germany (1942-45), and as Allied seamen and aircrew.

Pictures left and centre: the global nature of the war, and of imperial ambitions, was recognized by propagandists on both sides. Below: atrocities of varying scales were committed by most participants and were often siezed upon as propaganda items. The massacre of 6000 Polish officers at Katyn (by the Soviets) was consistently accredited to the Germans by the Soviets themselves.

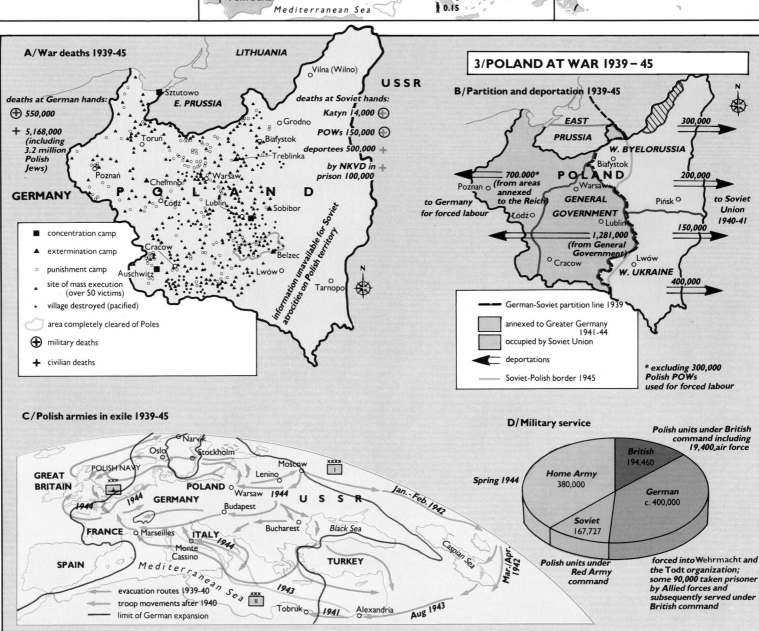

A/ War deaths 1939-45

LITHUANIA

● Vilna (Wilno)

USSR

deaths at German hands:
⊕ 550,000
+ 5,168,000 (including 3.2 million Polish Jews)

E. PRUSSIA
■ Sztutowo

● Grodno

deaths at Soviet hands:
Katyn 14,000 ⊕
POWs 150,000 ⊕
deportees 500,000 +
by NKVD in prison 100,000 +

Torun ○
● Białystok

▲ Treblinka

GERMANY

P O L A N D

Poznań ○
Warsaw
Chelmno ▲
Łódz ○
Lublin

▲ Sobibor

information unavailable for Soviet atrocities on Polish territory

Cracow ○
■ Auschwitz
● Belzec

● Lwów

● Tarnopo

■ concentration camp
▲ extermination camp
○ punishment camp
▲ site of mass execution (over 50 victims)
• village destroyed (pacified)
⬭ area completely cleared of Poles
⊕ military deaths
+ civilian deaths

N

3/POLAND AT WAR 1939 – 45

B/ Partition and deportation 1939-45

N

EAST PRUSSIA

300,000 →

W. BYELORUSSIA
● Białystok

700,000* (from areas annexed to the Reich)
Poznan ○
to Germany for forced labour

P O L A N D
● Warsaw

200,000 →

GENERAL GOVERNMENT

Łódz ○
● Pińsk
to Soviet Union 1940-41

1,281,000 (from General Government)

150,000 →

Cracow ○
● Lwów
W. UKRAINE

400,000 →

━━ German-Soviet partition line 1939

▨ annexed to Greater Germany 1941-44

▥ occupied by Soviet Union

◀ deportations

Soviet-Polish border 1945

* excluding 300,000 Polish POWs used for forced labour

C/ Polish armies in exile 1939-45

● Narvik
Oslo ●
● Stockholm
POLISH NAVY
GREAT BRITAIN

✕✕✕ 1944

● Moscow
● Lenino
✕✕✕✕ Jan.-Feb. 1942
POLAND
Warsaw 1944

GERMANY

1944

● Budapest

U S S R

● Bucharest

Jan.- Feb. 1942

FRANCE
● Marseilles
ITALY 1944
Monte Cassino

Black Sea

Caspian Sea

SPAIN

Mediterranean Sea

TURKEY

Mar./Apr. 1942

● Alexandria

Aug 1943
✕✕✕ II
● Tobruk
1941

→ evacuation routes 1939-40
→ troop movements after 1940
━━ limit of German expansion

D/ Military service

Katyn
e paradis sous terre

Polish units under British command including 19,400, air force

British 194,460

German c. 400,000

Home Army 380,000

Spring 1944

Soviet 167,727

Polish units under Red Army command

forced into Wehrmacht and the Todt organization; some 90,000 taken prisoner by Allied forces and subsequently served under British command

Bibliography

Among the large number of works consulted by the contributors, the following publications contain maps and other information which has proved particularly useful:

ATLASES

Chronology and Index of the Second World War (Royal Institute of International Affairs)   Reading, 1975

H.C. Darby and Harold Fullard: The New Cambridge Modern History Atlas Vol. XIV   Cambridge, 1970

Colonel Vincent J. Esposito: The West Point Atlas of American Wars Vol. II 1900-1953   New York, 1959

Atlas zur Geschichte Vols 1 & 2   Leipzig, 1976

Martin Gilbert: Atlas of the Holocaust   London, 1982

George Goodall: The War in Maps: Its Background and Course   London, 1941

Simon Goodenough: War Maps   London , 1982

Werner Hilgemann: Atlas zur deutschen Zeitgeschichte 1918-1968   Munich, 1984

F.W. Putzger: Historischer Weltatlas   Berlin and Bielefeld, 1961

The Times Atlas of World History   London, 1989

The Times Concise Atlas of World History   London, 1988

The Times Handy Atlas 3rd Ed.   Edinburgh and London, 1941

The West Point Atlas for the Second World War: Europe and the Mediterranean   New Jersey, 1985

The West Point Atlas for the Second World War: Asia and the Pacific   New Jersey, 1985

Georg Westermann: Grosser Atlas zur Weltgeschichte Braunschweig, 1972

OFFICIAL HISTORIES

History of the Second World War: United Kingdom Military Series

The Mediterranean and the Middle East, Vols I-VI HMSO London, 1954-1973

Victory in the West 1944-1945, Vols I-II   HMSO London

The War in France and Flanders 1939-1940, Vol 1   HMSO London, 1957-1965

The War against Japan, Vols I-V   HMSO London, 1957-1965

The War at Sea, Vols. I-III: S.W. Roskill   HMSO London, 1954-1961

History of the United States Naval Operations in World War II, 15 Vols: S.E. Morison   Oxford, 1960

Naval Staff History Second World War   London, 1952

United States Army in World War II

China-Burma-India Theater, 3 Vols.   Washington D.C. 1959

European Theater of Operations, 10 Vols   Washington D. C. 1951-1973

The War in the Pacific, 12 Vols.   Washington D.C. 1948-1960

Istoriya Velikoy Otechestvennoy voyny Socetskogo Soyuzo (IVOVS) (History of the Great Patriotic War of the Soviet Union) USSR Official History, 6 Vols.   Moscow, 1960

GENERAL PUBLICATIONS

Christopher Andrew: Codebreaking and Signals Intelligence   London, 1986

Catherine Andreyev: Vlasov and the Russian Liberation Movement   Cambridge, 1987

Mark Arnold-Forster: The World at War   Glasgow, 1973

Joan Beaumont: Comrades in Arms. British Aid to Russia 1941-1945   London, 1980

Gerda Beitter: Die Rote Armee im 2 Weltkrieg: Eine Bibliographie (The Red Army in World War II: A Bibliography)   Koblenz, 1984

Christopher D. Bellamy: Red God of War: Soviet Artillery and Rocket Forces   London, 1986

Omar N. Bradley: A Soldier's Story of the Allied Campaigns from Tunis to the Elbe   London, 1951

Peter Calvocoressi and Guy Wint: Total War Harmondsworth, 1985

E.H. Carr: International Relations between the Two World Wars 1919-1939   London, 1965

V.I. Chuikov: The End of the Third Reich   Moscow, 1985

Winston S. Churchill: The History of the Second World War Vols. 1-12   London, 1965

Alan Clark: Barbarossa: The Russian-German Conflict 1941-1945   London, 1965

Basil Collier: A Short History of The Second World War   London and Glasgow, 1969

Conway's All the World's Fighting Ships 1922-1946   London, 1980

John Costello: The Pacific War   London, 1985

Gordon A. Craig: Enemy at the Gates, The Battle for Stalingrad   London, 1973

Charles Cruickshank: SOE in the Far East   Oxford, 1987

R. Ernest Dupuy and Trevor N. Dupuy: The Encyclopedia of Military History   London, 1977

John Erickson: The Road to Stalingrad: Stalin's War with Germany Vol. 1   London, 1975

John Erickson: The Road to Berlin: Stalin's War with Germany Vol. 2   London, 1983

John Erickson: The Soviet High Command, 1918-1941. Moscow Notebooks (record of conversations with senior Soviet officers)   London, 1962-1965

Bryan I. Fugate: Operation Barbarossa. Strategy and Tactics on the Eastern Front, 1941   Novato, 1984

Col. David Glantz: August Storm: The Soviet 1945 Strategic Offensive in Manchuria (Leavenworth Paper No. 7). The Soviet Airborne Experience (Research Survey No. 4)   Fort Leavenworth, 1983-1984

Anthony Glees: The Secrets of the Service: British Intelligence and Communist subversion 1939-51   London, 1987

Ian Gow: Okinawa 1945: Gateway to Japan   London, 1986

Max Hastings: Bomber Command   London, 1981

Max Hastings: Overlord: D-Day and the Battle for Normandy   London, 1985

Alistair Horne: To Lose a Battle: France 1940   Harmondsworth, 1969

'Katyn' (discussion of latest research):Problems of Communism, November-December, 1988, p.49-57

William L. Langer: An Encyclopedia of World History   London, 1972

Col. E. Lederrey: Germany's Defeat in the East, 1941-45 HMSO London, 1955

Army General D.D. Lelyushenko: Moskva-Stalingrad-Berlin-Praga Zapiski komandarma (Moscow-Stalingrad-Berlin-Prague, An Army Commander's Notebook) 3rd ed. Moscow, 1975

James Lucas: World War Two Through German Eyes London, 1987

Donald Macintyre: The Battle of the Atlantic   London, 1983

Donald Macintyre: Narvik   London, 1962

Field Marshal Erich von Manstein: Lost Victories (Verlorene Siege), ed. and trans. Anthony Powell   London, 1958

David Marley: The Daily Telegraph Story of the War 1939-1945   London, 1942

Peter De Mendelssohn: Japan's Political Warfare   London, 1944

Karl August Muggenthaler: German Raiders of World War II   London, 1980

Professor Williamson Murray: 'Force Strategy, Blitzkrieg Strategy and the Economic Difficulties: Nazi Strategy in the 1930s', RUSI Journal, pp.39-43   March 1983

Gerd. Niepold: trans and commentary by Richard Simpkin: Battle for White Russia. The Destruction of Army Group Centre June 1944   London, 1987

H.C. O'Neill: History of the Second World War Vols. 1 and 2   London, 1951

R.J. Overy: The Air War 1939-1945   London, 1987

Michael Parrish: The USSR in World War II. An annotated bibliography of books published in the Soviet Union 1945-75, with an addenda for the years 1975-80 London, 1981

E.J. Passant: A Short History of Germany 1815-1945   Cambridge, 1959

Janusz Piekalkiewicz: Stalingrad: Anatomie einer Schlacht   Munich, 1977

Werner Rings: Life with the Enemy: Collaboration and Resistance in Hitler's Europe 1939-1945   London, 1982

Jurgen Rohwer: The Critical Convoy Battles of March 1943. The Battle for HX229/SC122   London, 1977

Marshal Konstantin Rokossovski: Velinkaya pobeda na volge (Great Victory on the Volga) 2 Vols.   Moscow, 1965

Marshal Konstantin Rokossovski: A Soldier's Duty Moscow, 1985

Cesare Salmaggi & Alfredo Pallavisini: 2194 Giorni Di Guerra   Milan, 1977

Albert Seaton: The Russo-German War 1941-45   London,1971

Sovetskaya Voyennaya Entisiklopediya (Soviet Military Encyclopaedia 8 Vols.) ed. Marshal A.A. Grechko, Vols. 1 and 2, then Marshal N.V. Ogarkov   Moscow, 1976-1980

Adrian Stewart: Guadalcanal: World War II's Fiercest Naval Campaign   London, 1985

R.J.S. Stolfi:'Equipment for Victory in France in 1940', History Vol. 55, No. 183, pp.1-20   February 1970

David Stafford: Britain and European Resistance 1940-1945   Oxford, 1983

A.J.P. Taylor: The Origins of the Second World War   Harmondsworth, 1985

Walter Theimer: The Penguin Political Dictionary   Harmondsworth, 1940

Tony Le Tissier: The Battle of Berlin 1945   London, 1988

Voyenny entsiklopedicheskiy slovar (Military Encyclopaedic Dictionary) 2nd ed., ed. Marshal Sergey Akhromeyev   Moscow, 1986

N. Voznesenski: Voyannaya ekonomika SSSR v periode otechestvennoy voyny (The War Economy of the USSR during the Patriotic War)   Moscow, 1948

Alexander Werth: Leningrad   London, 1944

Chester Wilmot: The Struggle for Europe   London, 1954

Brigadier Peter Young: The World Almanac Book of World War II   New York, 1981

Steven Zaloga & Victor Madej: The Polish Campaign 1939 New York, 1985

Col. Gen. Kurt Zeitzaler: 'Withdrawals of the German Army on the Eastern Front', Military Review, pp.73-74 March, 1960

Marshal Georgiy Zhukov: Reminiscences and Reflections, 2 Vols. (trans from Vospominaniya i razmyshleniya, Izdatel'stvo agenstva pechati 'Novosti' 1974, 1975)   Moscow, 1985

Acknowledgements

Most photographs have been reproduced by kind permission of the Imperial War Museum.

The publishers would also like to thank the following agencies for permission to reproduce their photographs:

Page	Credit
29	Weimar Archives
31	Barnaby's Picture Library
33	Süddeutscher Verlag, Bilderdienst
35	Popperfoto
37	Barnaby's Picture Library
50-51	E.C.P. Armées, Paris
57	Ullstein Bilderdienst, Berlin
58	Library of Congress
59	Novosti Press
61	Novosti Press
62	Novosti Press
63	Ullstein Bilderdienst, Berlin
64	Süddeutscher Verlag, Bilderdienst
65	Novosti Press
69	Robert Hunt Library
72	Robert Hunt Library
78	Ullstein Bilderdienst, Berlin
80	Bildarchiv Preussischer Kulturbesitz, Berlin
82	Robert Hunt Library
84-85	Süddeutscher Verlag, Bilderdienst
87	R. Overy
89	Süddeutscher Verlag, Bilderdienst
90 left	Musée Royale de L'Armée et d'Histoire Militaire
top right	Musée des Deux Guerres Mondiales
93	Sally Soames
95 top right	Musée des deux Guerres Mondiales
below	Archiv für Kunst und Geschichte, Berlin
96	National Archives ©
99 right	Robert Hunt Library
left	E.T. Archive
101	Süddeutscher Verlag, Bilderdienst
102 below	US Army
104	Ullstein Bilderdienst, Berlin
105	Novosti Press
108-109	Süddeutscher Verlag, Bilderdienst
110	Ullstein Bilderdienst, Berlin
118	National Archives ©
119	Australian War Museum
120	Robert Hunt Library
121	Robert Hunt Library
123	Robert Hunt Library
125	Novosti Press
127	Novosti Press
129	Robert Hunt Library
130	Robert Hunt Library
133	Süddeutscher Verlag, Bilderdienst
135 right	Deutsches Museum, Munich
below left	Robert Hunt Library
139	Ullstein Bilderdienst, Berlin
140	Robert Hunt Library
142	Offical US Navy Photograph
155	US Army
161	Ullstein Bilderdienst, Berlin
162 left	Popperfoto
top right	Robert Hunt Library
168	Official US Navy Photograph
169	Official US Navy Photograph
172	Library of Congress
174	Süddeutscher Verlag, Bilderdienst
176 right	Robert Hunt Library
180	National Archives ©
183 right	Robert Hunt Library
185	Robert Hunt Library
187	C.D. Bellamy
189	US Air Force
190-191	Ullstein Bilderdienst, Berlin
192 above	Popperfoto
below	Hoover Institute on War, Revolution and Peace
197 above	Robert Hunt Library
below	National Archives ©
199	Novosti Press
200	US Navy
203	Süddeutscher Verlag, Bilderdienst
206 left	Library of Congress
right	Musée des Deux Guerres Mondiales

Glossary

AA Anti-aircraft (British)

AAA Anti-aircraft (US)

ABDA American-British-Dutch-Australian Command

Abwehr The intelligence department of the German Armed Forces. *Abwehr* had three divisions: I espionage with specialist groups (military, technical, political and economic), II sabotage and III counter-espionage. From 1938, *Abwehr* was run by Admiral Wilhelm Canaris. After his implication in the plot against Hitler (1944), the organization was absorbed into the SS (RSHA VI).

ACC Allied Control Commission for the post-war government of Germany

Accolade Operational code name for Allied operations in the Aegean. The plan for the capture of Rhodes and other islands did not succeed

Acrobat Operational code name for the planned British advance from Cyrenaica to Tripoli, 1941.

Adlertag (Eagle Day) The mass German assault in the Battle of Britain, 15 September 1940.

AEAF Allied Expeditionary Air Force

AEF Allied Expeditionary Force

A-Go Operational code name for the Japanese counter-attack following the American capture of the Mariana Is., June 1944.

AIF Australian Imperial Forces

Alexander, Sir Harold, later 1st Earl Alexander of Tunis (1883-1963) British field marshal. He served in the Irish Guards during the First World War and, at the opening of the Second World War, commanded the 1st Division of the BEF in France. He was in charge of the Allied evacuation from Dunkirk in 1940 and, in 1942, took part in the British retreat from Rangoon. From August 1942 he was in command of Allied forces in the Middle East and compelled Rommel to evacuate North Africa. In the last year of the war he was Supreme Allied Commander, Mediterranean, a period which saw sustained strategic successes as German troops in Italy were driven north and finally forced to surrender following a brilliant envelopment at the foot of the Alps. He was overruled in his plan to strike north to Vienna, although he successfully established Trieste as an Allied command centre in the last days of the war. Later (1942-52) Alexander served as Governor-General of Canada. A patrician soldier of Anglo-Irish descent, he eschewed publicity and let others, notably Montgomery, take some credit for his considerable achievements.

Altmark incident Episode on 17 February 1940 when the British destroyer *Cossack* intercepted the German merchantman *Altmark* in neutral waters off the Norwegian coast and rescued a number of British prisoners originally taken in the South Atlantic by the pocket battleship *Graf Spee*. Hitler, incensed, pleading piracy and violation of international sea-law, shortly resolved on the occupation of Norway.

AMGOT Allied Military Government

AMMISCA American Military Mission in China

Anakim Operational code name for the Allied plan for the reoccupation of Burma, 1944.

Anders, Wladyslaw (1892-1970) a Polish commander who fought both the Nazis and Soviets at various times. He was captured during the Soviet invasion of Poland in 1939 but was released in July 1941, when he formed an army of some 5000 Polish exiles in Iran. Anders's most renowned military achievement was the part he and his men played in the capture of Monte Cassino (May 1944).

Anti-Comintern Pact Joint declaration by Germany and Japan, issued on 25 November 1936, that they would consult and collaborate in opposing the Comintern or Communist International. It was acceded to by Italy in October 1937, and later became the instrument by which Germany secured the loyalty of its Rumanian, Hungarian and Bulgarian satellites, and attempted to bind Yugoslavia. *See also* Comintern, Tripartite Pact.

Anton see Attila

Antonescu, Ion (1886-1946) A Rumanian officer, he became minister of war in 1932 and, in 1940, premier, in which capacity he seized absolute power, forced King Carol II's abdication and restored King Michael to the throne. In 1941, Antonescu aligned Rumania with Germany against the USSR. In August 1944, with Axis forces in terminal decline, King Michael ordered his arrest; he was tried, condemned to death and executed.

Anvil Later renamed *Dragoon*, operational code name for Allied landings in the south of France, 15 August 1944.

ANZAC Australia and New Zealand Army Corps

AOC Air Officer Commanding

Arcadia Code name for the First Washington Conference, 22 December 1941 to 14 January 1942.

Argonaut Code name for the Yalta Conference, 4-12 February 1945.

Argument Operational code name for Allied air attacks on German aircraft factories, 20-25 February 1944.

Arnold, Henry Harley ('Hap') (1886-1950) American general, known to his men as 'Hap'. He graduated from West Point in 1907 and was later (1911) assigned to the aviation section of the Signals Corps, aircraft at that time being considered suitable for reconnaissance only. Thereafter he served almost exclusively with the air arm. He was Chief of the Army Air Corps (1938-41), and from 1939 he was also a Deputy Chief of Staff under General Marshall. From June 1941, until the end of the war, Arnold was Chief of the newly created US Army Air Forces. He was an enthusiast for strategic bombardment, and took a keen interest in the supply side of the air war. After the war he became General of the new US Air Force in 1949; he had always championed a separate air force, and was responsible for making the Army Air Forces almost independent of army interference during the war.

AT Anti-tank (gun)

ATS Auxiliary Territorial Service (British women's army corps)

Attila Operational code name, known later as *Anton*, for the German occupation of Vichy France, 11 November 1942.

Auchinleck, Sir Claude (1884-1981) British general. He served with distinction in India, extricated British troops from the abortive Norway expedition in 1940 and then became Commander-in-Chief, India. Later, (July 1941-August 1942) he was Commander-in-Chief of British troops in the Middle East, taking personal command at the front when Rommel's Summer offensive (1942) almost broke through. Though he decisively defeated the Axis army at El Alamein (1-3 July 1942), he had withdrawn east of Tobruk, which Rommel invested and took. He was consequently replaced by Alexander in August and then again (1943-47) served as Commander-in-Chief, India. Auchinleck has been given little credit for the Second Battle of El Alamein (October-November 1942), where Montgomery made heavy use of his outline strategy, and subsequently declined an earldom on the grounds that too many British generals had already been ennobled.

Aufbau Ost (Build-up in the East) Operational cover name for the German build-up prior to *Operation Barbarossa*, 1940.

August Storm Operational code name for the Soviet invasion of Manchuria, 9 August 1945.

Autumn mist see Herbstnebel

Avalanche Operational code name for the Allied landings at Salerno, 9 September 1943.

AVG American Volunteer Group (Flying Tigers) of pilots fighting for Chiang Kai-shek.

Avonmouth Operational code name for the Allied expedition to Narvik, May 1940.

Axis see Pact of Steel, Tripartite Pact

Badoglio, Pietro (1871-1956) Italian marshal. He served (1928-34) as governor of Tripolitania and Cyrenaica and later as commander of troops invading Ethiopia. Badoglio, an anti-Fascist, resigned after the Italian invasion of Greece. In July 1943, after Mussolini's fall, the King appointed him Prime Minister. Badoglio signed Italy's unconditional surrender to the Allies and, on 30 October 1943, the document declaring war on Germany.

Bagration Operational code name for the Red Army's strategic offensive (23 June-29 August 1944), its greatest so far, designed to destroy German Army Group Centre and to liberate Byelorussia in preparation for the invasion of Poland, which it did.

Barbarossa Operational code name for the German invasion of the Soviet Union, 22 June 1941.

Battleaxe Operational code name for General Wavell's offensive (15-17 June 1941) in the Western Desert, designed to relieve the besieged fortress of Tobruk.

Baytown Operational code name for the Allied landings in southern Italy, 3 September 1943.

Beaverbrook, Lord (1879-1964) Formerly Max Aitken. A Canadian with an electric personality, Beaverbrook became a millionaire through his ownership of newspapers, in which capacity he exerted considerable energy in the British imperialist cause. In May 1940, Churchill appointed him Minister of Aircraft Production; energetic rationalization of small component-producing plants, assembly plants and recycling and repair programmes produced a massive supply of fighter aircraft, enabling Great Britain to resist the *Luftwaffe* in the Battle of Britain. He resigned in April 1941. In July he was appointed Minister of Supply but was replaced in February 1942 after a stormy relationship with his colleagues and the service chiefs.

BEF (British Expeditionary Force) Name given in both World Wars to British troops serving in France at the outbreak of hostilities and thereafter. In the Second World War, the BEF was evacuated by sea from Dunkirk (26 May-4 June 1940) and other parts of France in the face of overwhelming German strength.

Bestrafung (Punishment) German operational code name for terror air attacks (6-9 April 1941) on Belgrade, to punish the Yugoslavs for having overthrown the pro-Axis regency and to undermine resistance to the German invasion.

BEW Board of Economic Warfare (US)

Blitzkrieg (lightning war) Coined by an American newspaper, the term was in widespread use (in retrospect) from 1942, and described tactics for attack used by Germany in her invasions of Poland, France, the USSR and elsewhere. Objectives were selected and the weakest points in the enemy's front identified. Conventional attacks contained the sectors either side of each armoured thrust. The first tank attacks were preceded by air strikes to disrupt enemy communications; paratroopers were dropped at strategic points. After the armoured breakthrough, tanks fanned out, bypassing strongpoints, which were subdued by motorized divisions, with infantry in support. The process was repeated. Speed was crucial to ensure the capture of enemy formations before they could retreat and regroup.

Bock, Fedor von (1880-1945) German field marshal. He was Commander-in-Chief of Army Group North during the German invasion of Poland (1939) and Army Group B in France the following year. Bock commanded Army Group Centre during the invasion of the USSR in 1941 and, in 1942, Army Group South, but was dismissed by Hitler in July for being too cautious.

Bodenplatte (Base plate) Operational code name for the *Luftwaffe* offensive against Allied airfields in north-west Europe, January 1945.

Bolero Operational code name for the build-up of American forces in Britain, prior to the invasion of Europe, from 1942.

Bor-Komorowski, Tadeusz (1895-1966) Polish cavalry commander. He was acting commander of the Polish Home Army and in 1944 led the uprising against the Germans in Warsaw, believing that he would receive Russian support. From 1945 to 1947 he was commander of the Polish Army in Exile and from the latter date until 1949 was Prime Minister of the government in exile.

Bormann, Martin (1900-1945) German Nazi leader, an early adherent of Hitler. He became Hitler's personal political secretary in 1942 and in that capacity exerted enormous power, since virtually he alone could admit personages to the *Führer*'s presence. Shortly after Hitler's suicide on 30 April 1945, Bormann disappeared from the bunker and was never found. He was sentenced to death by hanging *in absentia* at the Nuremberg war crimes trials, but in 1973, despite alleged sightings of him in South America, the West German government declared him dead, probably on 2 May 1945.

Bradley, Omar (1893-1981) American general. He was selected by Eisenhower, his contemporary at West Point, for service in North Africa after the Anglo-American landings (Operation *Torch*) in 1942. He commanded the American II Corps in Tunisia and in Sicily (1943). Bradley led US 1st Army in the Normandy invasion and, from 1 August 1944, the 12th Army Group, which captured the Rhine crossings at Remagen. After the war, he was Chairman of the Joint Chiefs of Staff (1949-53).

Brandenburgers German Special Force set up by the *Abwehr* in 1939 and originally composed of small groups in civilian clothes who were sent in ahead of the main fighting force to seize or demolish key targets. The *Brandenburgers* later expanded to regimental size, and even had a parachute battalion. They were assigned to an extraordinary range of duties, working closely with conventional troops on the Eastern Front, but in the west conducting covert missions ranging from a daring raid, by glider, to rescue Mussolini from captivity in the Abruzzi mountains (1944) to insertion by parachute, in US military clothing, behind Allied lines in the Ardennes prior to the Battle of the Bulge. Many of their more colourful exploits were performed under the command of Colonel Otto Skorzeny.

Brauchitsch, Walther von (1881-1948) German general. He came of a Prussian army family and, in 1938, became army Commander-in-Chief. He was promoted field marshal in 1940 after the French capitulation but, in 1941, when the German armies failed to capture Moscow, he was dismissed by Hitler, who then replaced him in command of the German Army.

Brevity Operational code name for the British offensive against Rommel's Axis forces in the Halfaya Pass (15-17 May 1941), part of a larger operation.

Brimstone Operational code name for the projected Allied invasion of Sardinia, 1944.

Brooke, Sir Alan Francis, later Lord Alanbrooke (1883-1963) British field marshal. He led a corps of the BEF in France and, after the evacuation from Dunkirk, held (1940-41) the then supremely important command of the British Home Forces, his responsibility being to repel the expected German invasion, code-named Operation *Sealion*. Alanbrooke served as Chief of the Imperial General Staff from 1941 to 1946 and, from 1942, headed the Chiefs of Staff Committee. A consummate strategist, his advice, when pressed, was usually deferred to by Churchill and the American commanders.

Buccaneer Operational code name for the planned attack on the Andaman Islands, 1944.

Budenny, Semyon (1883-1973) Soviet marshal and vice-commissar of defence. He had served as an NCO in the Imperial Russian Army and rose to prominence in the Civil War and the Soviet-Polish War of 1920 when he commanded the 1st Cavalry Army. However, in 1941, while commanding the Soviet army group on the southwestern front, hundreds of thousands of his troops were encircled and captured by the Germans. Budenny was relieved of his command but later led the Soviet army group in the northern Caucasus front.

Bulganin, Nikolai Aleksandrovich (1895-1975) Soviet political and military leader. In 1939 he became a member of the Central Committee of the USSR and a political commissar on the Russian front. After the war, he was promoted to Marshal of the Soviet Union and served as defence minister under Stalin and then Malenkov. He became premier in 1955 but was dismissed by Khrushchev in 1958.

Canaris, Wilhelm (1887-1945) German admiral, appointed (1935) head of the *Abwehr*. In 1938 he headed the foreign branch of the OKW. An intelligent and humane man, Canaris gradually became an opponent of National Socialism and of Hitler's aggressive policies, but was opposed to any attempt to kill Hitler. In February 1944 he was dismissed from office and after the July Plot to assassinate Hitler was arrested and hanged.

Capital Operational code name for the reoccupation of northern Burma, 1944.

Cartwheel Operational code name for the Allied operations in the South-west Pacific which culminated in the isolation of Rabaul, 1943.

CAS Chief of Air Staff (British)

Catapult Operational code name for the British attack on the French fleet in North African ports, July 1940.

Catchpole Operational code name for American attacks on the Marshall Is., early 1944.

Catherine Operational code name for the British plan to force a passage into the Baltic to help Poland, 1939.

CBI China-Burma-India theatre of operations

CCAS Combined Civil Affairs Committee

CCS Combined Chiefs of Staff (Allied)

Cerberus Operational code name for the movements of the German warships *Scharnhorst*, *Gneisenau* and *Prinz Eugen* through the English Channel, 11-13 February 1942.

Chamberlain, (Arthur) Neville (1869-1940) British politician. He had served as Chairman of Birmingham City Council before becoming (1931-37) Chancellor of the Exchequer, when he curtailed expenditure on armaments, although he later reversed this policy, allowing a build-up of armaments to proceed in expectation of imminent war. Chamberlain became Prime Minister in 1937 and, Great Britain's military forces still being weak, signed the appeasement document, known as the Munich Pact, with Hitler, Mussolini and Daladier in September 1938. His decision to appease the dictators was a reflection of his Cabinet's and the nation's wishes, and the achievement of 'Peace in our time' was briefly held a diplomatic success. His highly-publicized flying visits to various 'Summit' conferences in an attempt to preserve European peace were an early example of shuttle diplomacy. Chamberlain later gave British guarantees to Poland, thereby bringing Great Britain into the war when Germany and the USSR attacked that country in 1939. Following the British debacle in Norway (1940) his Parliamentary majority fell from 250 votes to 81 in a crucial debate (7-8 May); he resigned two days later and was succeeded as Prime Minister by Winston Churchill.

Chennault, Claire Lee (1890-1958) USAAF major-general. He retired in 1937 and went to China as an aviation adviser. He returned to Washington in 1940, from where he recruited an aerial unit–known as the Flying Tigers–which saw service in Burma, destroying almost 300 Japanese aircraft within six months in 1941.

Chiang Kai-shek (1887-1975) Chinese Nationalist leader. He studied military affairs in Japan and later served briefly in the Japanese Army. He returned to China in 1911, where he became involved in the revolution against the Manchu (Ch'ing) dynasty. Chiang remained politically active from this time and in 1926, when he emerged as the successor to Sun Yat-sen as leader of the Nationalist party, he led the victorious Nationalist (Kuomintang) Army, co-operating with Communist elements and accepting aid from the USSR in an attempt to unify China. However, in 1927 he changed his stance and began the long civil war against Chinese Communists. By the end of that year he had become head of the Nationalist government in Nanking and was supreme warlord of all Nationalist forces. In 1937, the outbreak of the Sino-Japanese War left Chiang two options: to use his best troops against the Japanese or against the Communists. He chose the latter. His prestige increased dramatically during the Second World War and, in 1943, he attended the Cairo Conference as undisputed master of China. Nevertheless, he was often at odds with his allies, since his objective was not only to defeat Japan but also to destroy the Communist forces in his own country. After the war, however, his authority declined as the Nationalists were everywhere driven into retreat before Mao's Communists. In 1950, Chiang and the Nationalists were forced to remove to Formosa (Taiwan), from where he promised to reconquer the Chinese mainland. In 1972, the United Nations accepted the Communists as sole rulers of China and Chiang's influence was fatally undermined.

Chindits *see Wingate*

Chuikov, Vassili (1900-1982) Soviet general, the hero of Stalingrad where his 62nd Army was decisive in halting the Germans. He joined the army in 1919 and was quickly promoted, largely through his membership of the Communist Party. He later became an adviser to Chiang Kai-shek and was in China from 1926 to 1937. From then on, he studied mechanized warfare and commanded an army in the Finnish war. He returned to China but was recalled to the USSR after Germany attacked her in 1941. After Stalingrad, he commanded various large formations in the Red Army's westward drive and it was to Chuikov that a delegation from Hitler's bunker went to ask for peace terms. Tough and with unbreakable nerve, he also possessed great tactical skill but was a loyal subordinate rather than the initiator of strategy.

Churchill, Sir Winston Leonard Spencer (1874-1965) British statesman, soldier, author and journalist. A son of Lord Randolph Churchill, sometime Chancellor of the Exchequer, and grandson of the seventh Duke of Marlborough, Churchill was educated at Harrow and Sandhurst and in 1894 became an officer in the 4th Hussars. In 1895, while on leave, he saw his first military action in Cuba, where he served as a reporter for the London *Daily Graphic*. As a subaltern, he subsequently saw service in India and the Sudan, where he took part in the last great British cavalry charge at the Battle of Omdurman (1898). He then resigned his commission and reported the Boer War for the *Morning Post*. He was captured by the Boers in 1899 but escaped, an episode that made him a household name. In 1900, he was elected to Parliament as a Conservative; later, he crossed the floor of the House and joined the Liberals. He rose rapidly and served first as Under-Secretary for the Colonies, then (1908-10) as President of the Board of Trade and (1910-11) as Home Secretary. In the latter year he became First Lord of the Admiralty and completed the renovation of the British fleet. After the Spithead review in 1914, Churchill, convinced that war was imminent, ordered on his own initiative that the fleet, rather than disperse to its stations, should steam intact to Scapa Flow. This kept the German High Seas fleet in harbour for most of the First World War, and maintained an effective blockade of her merchant fleet. Churchill was the prime champion of the Dardanelles expedition (1915), one of the few imaginative Allied concepts of the war. The expedition proved a failure (ironically, the only professionally executed manoeuvre was the evacuation) through the indolence and timidity of commanders on the spot. Churchill took the blame, however, and lost his Admiralty post. In 1916, he commanded an infantry battalion on the Western Front as a major. Shortly after Lloyd George became Prime Minister in place of Asquith, Churchill returned to politics as Minister of Munitions (1917-19); after the war he was War Secretary (1919-21), then Colonial Secretary (1921-22). Between 1924 and 1929, once more a Conservative, he served as Chancellor of the Exchequer. During the years 1929 to 1939 - his period 'in the wilderness' - Churchill wrote some of his most monumental books, worked continuously as a journalist and remained in the public eye for his support of Edward VIII during the abdication crisis, his opposition to Indian independence and his reiterated, but largely ignored, warning of the rising Nazi menace. In 1939, at the outbreak of war, Chamberlain appointed him to his old post as First Lord of the Admiralty; then, on 10 May 1940, as German Panzers broke through in France, Churchill replaced him as Prime Minister. His stirring oratory, unremitting energy and refusal to make peace with Hitler, rallied and united British resolve and enabled Great Britain to hold out alone during the perilous period between May 1940 and June 1941. Churchill made many major contributions to Allied strategy, notably, with the support of the British staff but against the wishes of the Americans, persuading Roosevelt that Germany must be defeated first, then Japan. In his capacity as British leader and world statesman, he attended, and was hugely influential at, most of the major Allied conferences. Throughout the war, Churchill was possessed of more power than any British Prime Minister, before or since. But in July 1945, after the surrender of Germany, he and the Conservatives were defeated in the General Election by Attlee and the Labour Party. Churchill became leader of the Opposition. In 1946, anticipating Soviet imperial ambitions, he for the first time used the expression 'iron curtain' to describe the Soviet advance in eastern Europe. Churchill returned as Prime Minister after the 1951 election, but his mental and physical powers were much diminished. Nevertheless, his government ended nationalization of the steel and motor-car industries and he remained an internationally influential figure. He won the General Election in 1955, but shortly afterwards resigned the premiership and was succeeded by Eden. In 1953 he was appointed a Knight of the Garter and was awarded the Nobel Prize for Literature. At his death in 1965 he was given a state funeral, probably the last for any Briton other than a sovereign.

Ciano, Count Galeazzo (1903-1944) Italian Fascist leader. He began his career in the diplomatic service, but in 1930 married Mussolini's daughter and in 1936 was appointed Foreign Minister by his father-in-law. Ciano was instrumental in creating the Rome-Berlin Axis and encouraged Mussolini in his fatal attack on Greece (1940). Ciano, however, voted against Mussolini at the meeting of the Fascist Grand Council (1943) which led to the Duce's dismissal. Subsequently, he was arrested by the Germans (who occupied Italy), handed over to Fascists in northern Italy loyal to Mussolini and executed for treason.

CIGS Chief of the Imperial General Staff (British)

CINCAF Commander-in-Chief, Allied Forces

CINCMED Commander-in-Chief, Mediterranean Fleet (US)

CINCPAC Commander-in-Chief, Pacific Area Fleet (US)

CINCPOA Commander-in-Chief, Pacific Ocean Area (US)

CINCSWPA Commander-in-Chief, Southwest Pacific Area (US)

Clarion Operational code name for Allied air attacks on communications in Germany, 22-23 February 1945.

Clark, Mark Wayne (1896-1984) American general. He had a love of publicity and rarely travelled without an entourage of photographers and journalists. He led the US 5th Army during the landings at Salerno, but his decision to liberate rather than bypass the open city of Rome remains a matter of controversy. Later (December 1944-April 1945) Clark commanded the 15th Army Group in Italy, although its progress northwards was slow because of severe winter weather and stiff German resistance.

Clay, Lucius (1897-1977) American logistics authority and military engineer. After the successful Allied landings in Normandy, he commanded the base area. Following Germany's surrender, he was appointed Deputy Military Governor of the US zone of occupation, in which capacity he played an important part in the establishment of the new federal republic.

Cobra Operational code name for the American breakout from the Normandy bridgehead, 25 July 1944.

Cockade Operational code name for cover and deception in Western Europe in the Summer of 1944. The intention was to make the Germans think that the invasion of Europe would be from Brittany, Northern Norway or the Pas de Calais, and to distract attention from the real objective, Normandy.

Collins, Joseph L. (1896-1987) US general. In December 1941 he was sent to Hawaii to organize its defences and was in the Pacific theatre for the next three years. In February 1944, Collins was sent to Europe to command VII Corps in the D-Day invasions, which fought its way across the base of the Cotentin peninsula and (27 June) took Cherbourg, a crucial port for receiving Allied supplies. Collins' corps then led the breakout from the Normandy bridgehead at St Lô on 25 July. Later, soldiers of VII Corps were the first to reach German soil and captured Aachen, the first German town to fall. He subsequently captured Cologne (6 March

1945) and was involved in the fighting in the Remagen bridgehead on the Rhine. When the Germans there surrendered, Collins raced to the Elbe, which he reached on 25 April. Shortly thereafter, he returned to the USA to help plan the invasion of Japan.

Comintern Lenin inaugurated the Comintern at the Communist Third Socialist International in 1919, with the object of establishing Communist domination of all socialist movements throughout the world. The Comintern's endeavours to foster revolution, most especially in Germany, were generally unsuccessful. In 1943, during the Second World War, the USSR dissolved the Comintern to calm the misgivings of her western allies. *See also Anti-Comintern Pact.*

Commandos The British Special Force, composed of élite, all volunteer troops, was employed largely for raids along the coast of German-occupied Europe. They were formed into brigades, each usually comprising four units of about 500 men. The first brigades comprised British personnel only, but subsequently an international brigade of Free French, Dutch, Polish, Belgian and other volunteers, was formed. The Commandos fought in many theatres, including Norway, the Mediterranean, France and South-east Asia; they were also heavily involved in the 1944 campaigns in Italy, during the Normandy landings and in subsequent battles in the West. Hitler regarded them as saboteurs in uniform who should be shot on sight or on capture, an order not obeyed by all senior German commanders.

COMNAVEU Commander of US Naval Forces in Europe

Compass Operational code name for the British counter-offensive against the Italians in Egypt, December 1940.

COSSAC Chief of Staff to Supreme Allied Commander (Designate) and invasion planning staff.

Crerar, Henry (1888-1965) Canadian general. In the Summer of 1940 he was sent as Chief of General Staff to London, but subsequently, wishing to see active service, led the First Canadian Corps in Sicily. Later he commanded the 1st Canadian Army (this comprised units of European origin also), which saw service in France and, on 27 February 1945, broke through the Siegfried Line.

Crossbow Operational code name for Allied air attacks (1944) on German V-1 launching pads.

Crusader Operational code name for the attack by 8th Army, part of General Auchinleck's command, to relieve Tobruk (18 November-6 January 1942).

Cunningham, Sir Andrew Browne (1883-1963) British admiral and one of the ablest naval strategists of the Second World War. He had wide experience, having fought in both the Boer War and the First World War. Renowned for his imperturbable character, he commanded all British ships in the Mediterranean (1939-42), which, despite great difficulties, he kept open for the Allies. Later he served as naval commander for the *Torch* landings in North Africa (1942-43) and as First Sea Lord from 1943 to 1946.

Curtin, John (1885-1945) Australian politician. He was an active labour union official and editor of a labour weekly magazine before being elected to the Lower House in Parliament, where he served for all but three years between 1928 and 1941. In 1941 he became Prime Minister and, with American support, vigorously pursued the defence of Australia against the Japanese; he also strongly advocated a union with the nations of the British Empire to form a Commonwealth.

Darlan, Jean François (1881-1942) French admiral. He was made Commander of the French Navy in 1939 but, through his hatred of the British, joined the Vichy Government after the Fall of France in 1940 and was named Pétain's successor. He collaborated with the Germans in the Syrian campaign by placing Syrian airports at Germany's disposal, but during the Allied landings (7 November 1942) in North Africa, where he served as head of the French armed forces, he changed sides and ordered the cessation of all French resistance. On 24 December 1942 he was assassinated for treachery by a student acting on the order of the Resistance. He was succeeded as High Commissioner by General Giraud.

de Gaulle, Charles (1890-1970) French general and statesman. He graduated from the military college of St Cyr and then served in France during the First World War until wounded at Verdun (1916) and taken prisoner. Between the wars he wrote a prescient book, calling among other things for the formation of a mechanized battle corps. His writings were largely ignored. Nevertheless, the Prime Minister, Paul Reynaud, appointed him Under-Secretary of War in 1940, after he had commanded an armoured division in the Battle of France. De Gaulle opposed the Franco-German armistice and in June 1940 fled by airplane to London where he made his famous broadcast on 18 June: 'France has lost a battle, but not the war.' In London, he organized the Free French forces. In 1943 he became co-president with General Giraud of the French Committee of National Liberation in North Africa. In June 1944, having forced Giraud out of the governing committee, it was proclaimed the provisional government of France and his government was recognized by the Allies after his return to Paris upon the city's liberation (26 August). De Gaulle was elected provisional president of France in November 1945 but resigned early in the following year after an election filled the legislature with extreme left-wing elements antagonistic to his proposed reforms. In 1947 he became head of a new party (Rally of the French People) with the aim of terminating internal strife. De Gaulle retired in 1953 but in 1958, after the revolt in Algeria, he became Prime Minister and drew up a new constitution that strengthened the power of the president. He himself became President of the new Fifth Republic in 1959. Much of his subsequent policy was devised to restore France to her position as a world power, but in May 1968 student demonstrations in Paris and other cities, followed by strikes, discredited his administration. In 1969, de Gaulle was defeated in a referendum on constitutional reform and resigned. He played no further part in public affairs.

Demon Operational code name for the British evacuation of Greece, April 1941.

Dempsey, Lieutenant-General Sir Miles Christopher (1896-1969) first saw service as a young officer in France during the First World War. Between 1919 and 1920 he served during operations in Iraq. By 1939 he was only a lieutenant-colonel but promotion then came rapidly; in 1941 he was made acting major-general and in 1942 acting lieutenant-general. In 1940 he led an infantry brigade in northern France and was highly instrumental in safely extricating it through Dunkirk. After the battle of El Alamein, Dempsey joined the 8th Army as commander of XIII Corps. He landed with this unit in Sicily (July 1943) and subsequently in southern Italy. He was later appointed to command the British 2nd Army for the Normandy campaign. In 1945, he briefly commanded the 14th Army in Malaya.

Devers, Jacob (1887-1965) US general. He directed Operation *Dragoon* in August 1944, the Allied landings in the south of France made in support of the main landings in Normandy.

Diadem Operational code name for General Alexander's Italian offensive in the Spring of 1944, designed to secure the early capture of Rome.

Dill, Sir John Greer (1881-1944) British field marshal. He commanded I Corps in France in 1939 and in the following year (April) was appointed vice-CIGS; later he became CIGS. Churchill replaced him in this appointment with Alan Brooke. Dill was then sent to Washington as Head of the British Joint Staff Mission.

Dönitz, Karl (1891-1980) German admiral. He had served in U-boats during the First World War and was keenly aware of their potential. In 1935 he got his chance to devise strategy when he was appointed to re-create the U-boat fleet. He did so with great energy, while at the same time planning U-boat tactics, notably the use of 'Wolf packs'. Dönitz was never given the number of U-boats he needed during the Battle of the Atlantic but belatedly Hitler authorized a greater construction programme and Allied shipping losses rose dramatically. This, however, was reversed by May 1943, when the Allies used radar and more effective air patrols. In the same year, Dönitz succeeded Raeder as Commander-in-Chief of the Navy. In early 1945 he masterminded the seaborne evacuation of over two million German servicemen and civilians from pockets along the Baltic in the path of the Russian invasion, the largest such evacuation in history. On 1 May 1945, in accordance with Hitler's will, Dönitz succeeded him as *Führer*. He was arrested on 23 May, after Germany's surrender, and was sentenced at Nuremberg to 10 years' imprisonment.

Doolittle, James (1896-1988) US lieutenant-general. A keen experimental aviator, he was given responsibility in 1940 for converting the motor industry to the production of aircraft. He was active in air command throughout the war but is remembered principally for the raid by B-25 bombers that he led from aircraft carriers against Tokyo in 1942.

Dowding, Sir Hugh (1882-1970) Commander-in-Chief RAF Fighter Command from 1936 to 1940. A solitary man but with the ability to delegate responsibility, he steadily enhanced the morale of Fighter Command and was in large measure responsible for organizing the defeat of the *Luftwaffe* during the Battle of Britain. He realized the importance of a carefully co-ordinated air defence system linking early warning networks with fighter stations through a clearly defined chain of command. He was also aware of the importance of strong links with industry and technology, ensuring a steady supply of new and reconditioned aircraft and encouraging the use of newly developed aids such as radar. Although knighted in 1943, Dowding was never given his due credit and the reasons for his removal from command in 1940 remain a matter of conjecture.

Downfall Operational code name for the planned assault on Japan, 1945.

Dragoon *see Anvil*

DUKW Amphibious truck (duck)

Dynamo Operational code name for the Dunkirk evacuation, 26 May-4 June 1940.

EAC European Advisory Commission

Eaker, Ira (1898-) US Air Force general. He commanded US air forces in Great Britain from October 1943; then (January 1944) he became Commander-in-Chief Mediterranean Allied Air Forces. He was an insistent and highly effective exponent of precision strategic bombing of Germany and her allies.

Edelweiss Operational code name for the German Army Group A's manoeuvres in the Caucasus, Summer 1942.

Eden, Sir Anthony (1897-1977) British Conservative statesman. He served in the First World War and then entered Parliament in 1923 as a champion of the League of Nations. He served as Lord Privy Seal (1934-35) and between 1936 and 1938 as Foreign Secretary. He resigned in the latter year in opposition to Chamberlain's policy of appeasement towards the Axis powers. At the outbreak of the Second World War, however, he returned to the Cabinet as Secretary of State for Dominion Affairs. When Churchill became Prime Minister (May 1940), he quickly appointed Eden Secretary of War; then, in December 1940, he was again made Foreign Secretary. Eden was influential in forging the war-time Anglo-Soviet alliance and in establishing the United Nations Organization. After the war, he continued as a member of parliament during the Labour governments (1945-51) and on Churchill's return to power in the latter year was again appointed to the Foreign Office. Upon Churchill's resignation in 1955, Eden became Prime Minister. He himself resigned in January, 1957.

Eichmann, Adolf (1906-1962) An Austrian Nazi official, head of the Austrian office for Jewish emigration. He was energetic in deporting Jews and in 1939 became chief of the Gestapo's Jewish section. In that capacity, he was responsible for the deportation and killing of Jews during the Nazis' Final Solution exercise. He was arrested by the Allies in 1945, but escaped to Argentina. There he was ultimately found by Israeli agents in 1960, forcibly taken to Israel, tried and hanged for crimes against the Jewish people.

Einsatzgruppe German and Axis operational group of Germany security police for extermination missions in occupied territory. In the German-occupied territories of eastern Europe they formed punishment and extermination squads operating immediately behind conventional forces.

Eisenhammer Operational code name for the *Luftwaffe* plan to attack Soviet power stations, February 1945.

Eisenhower, Dwight David (1890-1969) American general, the Supreme Allied Commander for the Normandy landings and subsequent operations in Europe. He had served (1933-39) under General MacArthur in the Philippines but had never commanded troops until, in November 1942, he was put in charge of Operation *Torch*, the Anglo-American landings in Morocco and Algeria. The success of this operation, and President Roosevelt's need to retain a controlling influence in the European war, led to Eisenhower's appointment, despite opposition, as Supreme Commander Allied Forces in Europe. In this capacity, he oversaw the preparation and execution of Operation *Overlord*, the Allied landings in Normandy, for which he devised a system of unified command in which staff officers of many countries generally co-operated effectively. His other virtues as a commander were his strength of character, amiable temper and coolness in adversity. After the war, he served two consecutive terms (1953-61) as President of the United States.

Enabling Law (*Gesetz zur Behebung der Not von Volk und Reich*) - (Law for Removing the Distress of People and Reich) The basic law of Hitler's regime and of his absolute authority in Germany. The Enabling Act, passed by the Reichstag after the arrest of many Communist and other deputies, gave the government power for four years to enact laws without the consent of the Reichstag; to deviate from the constitutional laws as it thought necessary; to conclude treaties with other states. The act also provided that laws enacted by the government should be drafted by the chancellor (Hitler) and implemented immediately.

ETO European Theatre of Operations

ETOUSA European Theatre of Operations, US Army

Eureka Code name for the Teheran Conference, 28 November-1 December 1943.

Exporter Operational code name for the British and Free French occupation of Syria, 8 June-12 July 1941.

Falange Spanish political party, founded in 1933 by José Antonio Primo de Rivera, similar in outlook to the Italian Fascists. The party joined Franco's Nationalists in the Civil War but later lost almost all influence.

Fall Gelb (Yellow Plan) Operational code name for the German attack on the Low Countries and France, May 1940.

Far East Command (Soviet) New, theatre level of command, controlling three fronts (Army Groups) - Transbaikal, First and Second Far Eastern - set up for the Manchurian operation in August 1945, under Marshal Vasilevski. Previously the Fronts had been controlled directly from the *Stavka* in Moscow, but the distance of the theatre from Moscow and the problems of co-ordinating the operations of three fronts (1.5 million men) over an area the size of the whole of western Europe necessitated an 'intermediate, operational- strategic level of command'.

FCNL French Committee of National Liberation

Felix Operational code name for the German plan to capture Gibraltar, 1941.

FFI French Forces of the Interior

FHO (*Fremde heere ost* - Foreign armies east) German intelligence organization specializing in the Soviet Union, run first by Colonel Kinzel and then, from late Spring 1942, by General Gehlen. The organization held over 150 files on all aspects of Soviet equipment, organization and tactics as well as prisoner reports.

'Final Solution' (*Endlösung*) Decision reached by Hitler towards the end of 1941 and confirmed at the Wannsee conference (January 1942) to solve the 'Jewish question' by genocide, a policy of extermination that gathered in efficiency and ferocity as the war progressed.

Fischfang (Fish trap) Operational code name for the German counter-offensive (3-19 February 1944) against the Allied beach-head at Anzio.

Fish trap *see Fischfang*

Flintlock Operational code name for the American invasion of the Marshall Islands, 31 January - 7 February 1944.

Forager Operational code name for the American invasion of the Mariana Islands, 11 June 1944.

Franco, Francisco (1892-1975) Spanish dictator and general. Franco organized the revolt in Morocco (1936) that precipitated the Spanish Civil War, 1936-39. Although the beneficiary of German and Italian military aid, Franco refused to enter the Axis alliance with the other Fascist powers. He was declared head of state (*El Caudillo*) and regent for life in 1947. When he died, he was succeeded by the man he had proposed, Prince Juan Carlos of Bourbon.

Fraser, Peter (1884-1950) New Zealand politician. He was born in Scotland but emigrated to New Zealand in 1910, where he was elected to Parliament in 1918. He subsequently served in ministerial posts and, as Labour Party leader, was Prime Minister from 1940, during which time he mobilized his country's war effort, sending troops to the Mediterranean theatre from that year. He lost office a year before his death.

Freyberg, Bernard (1889-1963) New Zealand general. His parents emigrated from England when he was a child. In 1909 he joined the New Zealand Army and in the First World War served with the Royal Naval Division, notably at Gallipoli. Later he served in France and won the Victoria Cross. At 29, he became the youngest brigadier in the army. At the outbreak of the Second World War, Freyberg was given command of the New Zealand expeditionary force and led it in the early desert campaigns. He was then sent to command survivors from the expedition to Greece, who were assembling on Crete, but was overwhelmed by German paratroopers and dive bomb attacks. He returned to the desert to command the 2nd New Zealand Division but was badly wounded. He nevertheless returned to active service, first in the desert again, then in Italy. It was Freyberg who demanded that the Monte Cassino abbey should be destroyed, being acutely aware of New Zealand's limited manpower and therefore the future value of his men. Freyberg, a brave man and gifted tactician, was renowned for the care he took of his troops. His relatively low rank, however, gave him little scope as a strategist.

Galvanic Operational code name for the American occupation of the Gilbert Islands, 20 November 1943.

Gamelin, Maurice (1872-1958) French general. A senior staff officer of the First World War, he became Chief of Staff in 1938 and Commander-in-Chief of all French armies in 1940, but was replaced (19 May) by General Weygand after the German breakthrough in the West. Gamelin was incarcerated by the Germans and deported, but returned to France after the war.

Gandhi, Mohandas Karamchand (1869-1948) Indian politician and spiritual leader. Though he supported Great Britain during the First World War, in the hope of gaining Indian independence, he subsequently organized further acts of civil disobedience. In 1942, Gandhi called yet again for acts of civil disobedience against British rule in his 'Quit India' campaigns, (although had the Japanese occupied India he would almost certainly have been executed). After the war, he was prominent in the conferences that led to independence and the creation of the Muslim state of Pakistan, although he himself was opposed to partition. He was assassinated on 30 January 1948 by a fellow Hindu.

GAU (*Glavnoye Artilleriyskoye Upravleniye* - Russian Main Artillery Directorate) Commanded during the war by Colonel General of Artillery N.D. Yakovlev, the directorate was responsible not only for the design and supply of artillery pieces and shells, but also for small arms and ammunition, rockets and aircraft armament. GAU representatives supervised production in factories dispersed throughout the USSR.

GC&CS British Government Code and Cypher School, at Bletchley Park.

Gestapo (*Geheime Staatspolizei*) Originally part of the Prussian State Police, this force was moulded by Goering and Himmler into the primary security organization of the Third Reich. As part of the RSHA, it acted against political opponents of the Nazis both inside and outside Germany.

GHQ General Headquarters

Giraud, Henri Honoré (1879-1949) French general. He served in the First World War and then (1925-26) in the Moroccan Campaign. He later commanded the French 9th Army but was taken prisoner by the Germans on 18 May 1940. He escaped in April 1942, reached Gibraltar and took part in the Allied landings in North Africa. In December 1942, Admiral Darlan was assassinated and Giraud assumed his duties as High Commissioner of French North and West Africa. He soon came into conflict with General de Gaulle and, though serving as co-president with him on the French Committee of National Liberation, was quickly removed from office. Despite powerful American support, Giraud was virtually compelled to resign by de Gaulle on 8 April 1944.

GKO/GOKO Soviet State Defence Committee

GOC General Officer Commanding (Soviet)

Goebbels, Paul Joseph (1897-1945) German Nazi leader. He escaped national service during the First World War because of a club foot. His early career as a journalist was undistinguished, but his rise within the Nazi party was meteoric and in 1926 he was appointed District Party Leader in Berlin. He was instrumental in bringing Hitler to power by utilizing all modern methods of propaganda. Goebbels was elected to the Reichstag in 1928 and, when Hitler became Chancellor in 1933, was appointed Propaganda Minister. In this capacity he had absolute control over the radio, press, cinema and theatre, which he manipulated with utter cynicism. As an orator he was second only to Hitler, whom he served with unswerving devotion. He remained with Hitler in the Berlin bunker and, when the city was falling to Soviet forces, killed himself and his family.

Goering, Hermann Wilhelm (1893-1946) German air ace of the First World War and a National Socialist leader from 1933. An early confidant of Hitler, he was elected to the Reichstag in 1928 and became its president in 1932. In 1933, on coming to power, Hitler made him air minister, in which capacity Goering created the *Luftwaffe*. An advocate of air power as a decisive factor in war, Goering developed revolutionary techniques of tactical air support, but proved less able to maintain his air force on an economic basis. Despite this, from 1937 to 1942 he was virtual dictator of the German economy and, in 1939, was designated Hitler's successor. In the following year he was given the unique rank of *Reichsmarschall*. His great popularity in Germany waned, however, after Germany's lack of success in the Battle of Britain and, contrary to many of his bombastic predictions, Allied air forces bombed the Fatherland. Further promises concerning the relief of beleaguered troops at Stalingrad in 1942 caused his fall from favour with Hitler. Goering began to withdraw from public life, but remained head of the *Luftwaffe* to the last, his poor strategic judgement inhibiting the air force from making the most of the great increase in aircraft production in 1944. Goering surrendered to American troops in 1945 and, despite defending himself with brilliance at the Nuremberg Trials, was convicted and sentenced to death. Two hours before he was due to be hanged he committed suicide by swallowing poison.

Gomorrah Operational code name for the RAF bomber raids on Hamburg, July and August 1943.

Goodwood Operational code name for the British armoured offensive east of Caen, 18 July 1944.

Gort, Field Marshal John (6th Viscount) (1896-1946) British field marshal. Gort won the Victoria Cross during the First World War and was renowned in the army for his coolness under pressure. He was also a gifted staff officer and later (1937-39) served as Chief of the Imperial General Staff, in the latter year assuming command of the British Expeditionary Force in France. On 30 May, however, as the British and their allies were evacuating France from Dunkirk, Churchill ordered him home lest the Germans enjoyed a propaganda coup in his capture. Later (1941-42) he served as Governor of Malta, when that island was under intense Axis bombardment.

Granit Operational code name for the American offensive in the Central Pacific, beginning in March 1944.

Graziani, Rodolfo (1882-1955) Italian marshal. He commanded all Italian land forces in North Africa from 1 July 1940 to 25 March 1941, during which time his initially inspired attack towards Egypt was repulsed by General Wavell, with heavy losses and many thousands of prisoners taken. Graziani was driven westwards more than 500 miles and only escaped complete ignominy by Churchill's necessary decision to divert forces from North Africa to Greece. Graziani later became Minister of National Defence, but after the war, in 1950, an Italian military court sentenced him, then aged 66, to 19 years solitary confinement for his involvement with the Fascist government.

Grenade Operational code name given to the US 7th Army's thrust to the Upper Rhine, part of the US 6th Army Group's and other Allied army groups' offensive (7 February-28 March 1945) after the defeat of the German attack in the Ardennes.

Guderian, Heinz (1888-1954) German general. The creator of the *Panzerwaffe* (the armoured force of the German Army) and a forceful exponent of its *blitzkrieg* tactics, he commanded armoured corps in the invasion of Poland (1939), Belgium (1940) and the USSR (1941) with great daring and success. In all three operations the rapidity of his achievements often outstripped the extent of his orders. This brought him into conflict with his superiors. He was dismissed by Hitler in December 1941, when the Germans failed to take Moscow. In February 1943, however, he was appointed inspector-general of all armoured troops and in the following year, following the Bomb Plot (21 July), was made head of the general staff of land armies. On 28 March 1945, shortly before his suicide, Hitler relieved him of all responsibilites. Guderian's methods were uncommon for a man of his rank. When in action, he would leave his headquarters at dawn in an armoured car, with a signals officer, radio and Enigma cypher machine, thus able to direct operations at the front while keeping in contact with his headquarters.

Gymnast *see Torch*

Halder, Franz (1884-1971) German general. In the early years of the war he was Chief of the German Army General Staff but was dismissed by Hitler in 1942. He was instrumental in planning the invasions of Poland and the West, although he advised Hitler against the latter. He was implicated in the abortive plot on Hitler's life (July 1944) and was arrested, but escaped execution. Halder was captured by American troops in May 1945.

Halsey, William Frederick (1882-1959) American admiral. An aggressive commander, he led the early raids against the Marshall Islands and the Gilbert Islands in February 1942; he later commanded the task force in support of Doolittle's celebrated raid on Tokyo from the USS *Hornet* in April. From October 1942 to June 1944, Halsey commanded the Allied South Pacific naval forces. Subsequently (1944-45), as Third Fleet commander, he fought up to the Philippines and later in Japanese waters. After the war, he was promoted to Fleet Admiral. Despite his robust conduct of operations, which earned him great admiration, he was criticized for his inadequate response to two savage typhoons (December 1944 and June 1945), which severely damaged US ships.

Hardihood Later renamed *Saturn*, operational code name for proposed Allied assistance to Turkey.

Harris, Sir Arthur Travers (1892-1984) British air chief marshal. As Commander-in-Chief of Bomber Command (1942-45), a post he virtually created in order to improve the poor performance of the RAF bombers in the first years of the war, Harris directed the air offensives, notably against Germany. He was the leading exponent of sustained area bombing, despite this costing the lives of 50,000 airmen and countless enemy civilians. This policy was in contrast to the US preference for large-scale attacks on specific targets crucial to Germany's war effort. Harris organized the 1000-bomber raid on Cologne (30 May 1942) which, despite protests at its inhumanity, appeared to prove his contention that bombing non-military targets was more effective than costly strikes against military installations. a contention supported by Albert Speer in his memoirs. He was dismissed shortly after the war ended and retired to South Africa.

Heinrici, Gotthard (1886-1971) German general, an outstanding panzer commander, especially in defensive warfare. During the First World War he alternated between staff postings and front line duties. In the Second World War he first commanded XLIII Corps, then, in January 1943, 4th Army. On 15 August 1944 he was appointed to lead 1st Panzer Army and in March 1945, in the last weeks of the war, Army Group Vistula. Heinrici faced many crises on the Eastern Front during the war, the most serious being the final Russian assault towards Berlin of Zhukov and Koniev's superior forces, and managed to slow down the Soviets' overwhelming thrusts. At the dominant Seelow Heights, for example, he ordered the forward positions to be evacuated so that the Soviet barrage would fall on unoccupied land; when the barrage ceased, the Germans at once reoccupied the area and brought the Soviet attack to a halt. Nevertheless, Heinrici by now believed that Berlin was indefensible and refused to obey Hitler's orders, despite threats made against his family. He was one of the few who dared to challenge Hitler's orders when they seemed to him incompatible with the military situation.

Herbstnebel (Autumn mist) German operational code name for the thrust into the Ardennes (15 December 1944-7 February 1945), popularly known as the 'Battle of the Bulge'.

Hess, Rudolph (1894-1987) Prominent German Nazi leader, who was named deputy to the *Führer* in 1933 when Hitler came to power. A passionate adherent of Hitler, he shared his imprisonment after the abortive Munich putsch of 1923, during which time, from dictation, he transcribed Hitler's book *Mein Kampf* (*My Struggle*). In May 1941 he became prominent throughout the world when he flew solo to Scotland, ostensibly to negotiate peace terms with Great Britain prior to the German invasion of the Soviet Union. He was, however, incarcerated and at the Nuremberg war crimes trials was sentenced to life imprisonment in Spandau prison, despite doubts as to his sanity. The Western Allied occupying powers sought his release after he had served many years of imprisonment, but this was always vetoed by the Soviets. Hess remained in Spandau, ultimately a solitary inmate, until his death at the age of 93.

Heydrich, Reinhard (1904-42) German SS leader. Chosen by Himmler as his deputy, Heydrich became head of the Reich Main Security Office and, after Germany's invasion of the USSR, was in charge of the policy of exterminating Jews in occupied areas of eastern Europe. He was then appointed acting vice-Reichprotector of Bohemia-Moravia. He was assassinated in Prague by Czech agents who had been trained by SOE.

Himmler, Heinrich (1900-1945) German Nazi leader, appointed in 1929 head of the SS. On Hitler's assumption of power (1933), he was made Chief of Police in Munich and then of Bavaria. After Hitler eliminated Ernst Roehm in June 1934 (the 'Night of the Long Knives'), Himmler's SS became the dominant police arm of the Nazi state. From this powerful position, he terrorized not only the war-time occupied states of Europe but also the German people. Himmler was a hugely gifted administrator but a racial fanatic and, without compunction, sent millions (mainly Jews) to concentration camps and extermination centres. Himmler put down the conspiracy against Hitler after the attempt on the *Führer's* life in July 1944. As Germany's approaching collapse became evident early in 1945, he attempted for his own safety to negotiate a separate peace with the Western Allies. Hitler thereupon expelled him from the Nazi Party and stripped him of authority. Himmler was captured by the British in May 1945 but succeeded in committing suicide by taking poison.

Hirohito (1901-1989) Emperor of Japan. He became regent in 1921 and succeeded to the throne in 1926. For almost the next 20 years he played little part in politics, although he supported his various ministers in their prosecution of war in Manchuria, China and the Pacific. His inherited role as 'divine' ruler helped induce a fanatical devotion to duty among the armed forces, which became especially significant when the tide of the Second World War turned against Japan. In 1945, in company with a number of moderate politicians, Hirohito persuaded the Japanese High Command to accept unconditional surrender rather than fight to the finish on the Home Islands with heavy losses on both sides. In January 1946, at American insistence, he renounced the sacred concept of imperial divinity and served thenceforth as a constitutional monarch.

Hitler, Adolf (1889-1945) Reich Chancellor and *Führer*, German dictator. He was born in Linz in Austria (later he gained German citizenship), the son of a minor customs official. The young Hitler moved to Vienna in 1907, after the death of his adored mother. For a time he lived on a small inheritance and a modest income from the sale of watercolours and picture postcards which he copied, often with a degree of artistic skill. In these early years, he became increasingly anti-semitic. He moved to Munich in 1913 and in the following year, at the outbreak of war, joined the Bavarian Army. Hitler, who attained the rank of corporal, was both gassed and wounded, but received the Iron Cross, First Class, an award of which he was greatly proud; subsequently he always wore the medal on his uniform. By the armistice in 1918 he had become convinced that Germany's defeat had been brought about by Jewish and Marxist traitors. On demobilization, he returned to Munich, where he joined the small German Workers' Party, a group of veterans with nationalistic aspirations. In 1920, the party was renamed the National Socialist German Workers' Party (Nazis), over which Hitler shortly gained absolute control. Field Marshal Ludendorff, the strategic brains behind Hindenburg during the First World War, was one of his early adherents, lending him some respectability. On 8 November 1923, Hitler staged the so-called 'Beer-hall putsch' in Munich, hoping to overthrow the Bavarian government. He and his storm troopers were overcome and he himself arrested and sentenced to five years imprisonment in Landsberg fortress. He served, in relative comfort, only nine months of his sentence and during that time dictated to his follower and fellow prisoner, Rudolph Hess, the text of his book *Mein Kampf* (*My Struggle*), which clearly outlined his plans for world domination. The Nazi Party, even after Hitler's release from prison, grew slowly until the world economic depression, beginning in 1929; thereafter public support swelled rapidly in response to his magnetic oratory and his seeming ability, unique among German politicians, to solve the twin afflictions of inflation and unemployment. During this period, with consummate skill, he contrived to win the support of both workers and manufacturers, Protestants and Roman Catholics, city dwellers and farmers, with his anti-semitic and anti-Marxist diatribes. In 1932 he ran in the presidential election (he was the first politician to use an aircraft in a campaign) but lost to Field Marshal Paul von Hindenburg. However, in July 1932 the Nazis became the largest single party in the Reichstag; Hitler nevertheless declined the subordinate role offered him and Kurt von Schleicher was appointed chancellor. But on 28 January 1933, Schleicher resigned as civilian disorder and parliamentary impotence clearly heralded chaos in Germany. Hindenburg, by then senile, on the prompting of his desperate advisers, appointed Hitler chancellor on 30 January 1933. Hitler almost immediately set about crushing all opposition. The Communists were collectively blamed for the Reichstag fire (27 February) and they were shortly thereafter banned. The reduced Reichstag, under threats from storm troopers, voted Hitler dictatorial powers. Thereafter, political suspects were either murdered or simply 'disappeared'. Jews and left-wing sympathizers were arrested, executed or sent to concentration camps. His tyranny in the name of the 'Third Reich' had begun. Even his own supporters were at risk: Ernst Roehm, the head of the SA, was murdered, in company with many of his troops, after which the Army, individually and collectively, swore allegiance to Hitler personally. With Hindenburg's death in 1934, the presidency and chancellorship were united in the person of Adolf Hitler, who now assumed the title *Der Führer*. Thereafter, every aspect and feature of German life was made an adjunct of Nazi power and philosophy. Hitler's early successes, based on the reintroduction of conscription and a massive rearmament programme in defiance of the Treaty of Versailles, were remarkable. Austria was incorporated into Germany, as were large areas of Czechoslovakia in 1939 (the Munich Pact); Mussolini, the Italian dictator, became his ally, though as a junior partner, in the Axis Pact. German and Italian aid to Franco in the Spanish Civil War assured the establishment of a sympathetic Nationalist government. In August 1939, Hitler concluded with Stalin one of the most improbable diplomatic reversals in history: the signing of their non-aggression pact. This astute diplomatic act enabled Hitler, with Stalin, to attack and occupy

Poland in September 1939, thereby securing his eastern flank and beginning the Second World War. Germany next attacked and overran the Low Countries and France, beginning in May 1940, and in the following year (June 1941) attacked the USSR. This latter offensive was at first supremely successful, until in December it was brought to a halt immediately in front of Moscow. Hitler, dissatisfied with his generals, then assumed personal command of German war strategy. In 1942 Germany made further territorial gains in the east, but the battles of El Alamein and Stalingrad decisively turned the war in the favour of the Allies, joined, after Pearl Harbor, by the United States. Germany's position had so deteriorated by 1944 that, in July, a bomb attempt was made on the *Führer*. He escaped serious injury (the plotters were executed with the utmost cruelty) but his position was by then hopeless. On 30 April 1945, when Berlin was about to fall to the Russians, he and his newly-married mistress, Eva Braun, committed suicide in his bunker.

HIWI (*Hilfsfreiwillige*) Auxiliary (Russian) Volunteers in the German armed forces, 1941-45.

Hodges, Courtney Hicks (1887-1966) American general. He was Chief of Intelligence (1941-42) but in the latter year was appointed to head X Army Corps then, in 1943, to command the US 3rd Army. Subsequently he was appointed Bradley's deputy prior to the invasion of Normandy. As commander of the US 1st Army, he broke through the Siegfried Line and took Aachen.

Homma, Masaharu (1888-1946) Japanese lieutenant-general. Having studied military strategy and tactics in Great Britain, he was appointed (1918) Japanese observer of the BEF on the Western Front. In 1927 he became military secretary to Prince Chichibu, the Emperor's younger brother. In 1938, he commanded the 27th Division in China and in 1940 the Formosa Army. In November 1941 he was given command of the 14th Army, which invaded the Philippines as part of Terauchi's Southern Army. Nevertheless, Homma doubted the wisdom of going to war with the Western powers while Japan was still engaged in fighting the Chinese. Homma captured Manila in a lightning campaign and supervised the siege of the Bataan peninsula and Corregidor, eventually forcing General MacArthur to abandon the Philippines. However, some US elements remained scattered through the archipelago and the Filipinos were for the most part loyal to the Americans. Homma complained to Tokyo of his inadequate resources and the fatigued condition of his army; he even suspended further attacks, an unheard-of order from a Japanese general. He was given some replacement divisions but was henceforth held in low esteem. He was also considered too lenient to the Filipinos, particularly in his release of war prisoners. In August 1942 he was relieved of his command. In September 1945 he was tried for war crimes and executed by firing squad (3 April 1946).

Horrocks, Sir Brian Gwynne (1895-1985) British lieutenant-general. He served in the First World War, first in France and then (1919) in Russia. During the Second World War, he commanded a succession of corps, notably under Montgomery, first in northern France, then in Belgium and on the German frontier.

Horthy, Miklos (1868-1946) One time admiral in the Austro-Hungarian Navy, later regent of Hungary (1920-44). Though trying to keep Hungarian involvement to the minimum, he sided with Germany rather than the USSR. In August 1944, following Rumania's collapse, he started to negotiate with the Allies but was forced to abdicate and was removed to Germany, from where he was freed by American troops in May 1945.

Hoth, Hermann (1885-1971) German colonel-general. With Guderian, an early exponent of the potential of armoured warfare, he led the XV Panzer Corps in the Polish campaign (1939) and later distinguished himself during the invasion of France (1940), when his corps was the first to cross the River Meuse. Hoth, affectionately known to his men as 'Papa Hoth', commanded Panzer Group 3 in the German attack on the USSR (1941) and, with Guderian's and Hoepner's Panzer groups, was responsible for the huge, early encirclements of Soviet armies. He was involved in the unsuccessful attempts to break into the southern flank of the Kursk salient, in July 1943.

Hull, Cordell (1871-1955) US statesman, an unflinching opponent of aggression. Trained to the law, he was appointed circuit court judge in 1903. He then served in the House of Representatives for the state of Tennessee and was a strong supporter of Roosevelt and his 'New Deal'. In 1930 he was elected to the Senate and in 1933 Roosevelt appointed him Secretary of State. Hull was a dominant figure in the American pre-war conferences with the Japanese and placed great emphasis on the role of economic affairs in international relations. In July 1941 he was instrumental in freezing Japan's assets in the USA when the latter occupied part of French Indo-China. This produced a shortage of crucial war material for Japan, notably oil, and strengthened the war party in their argument that these necessities must now be obtained by military action. Hull generated the 'Good Neighbour' policy with Latin America and was energetic in providing aid and weaponry to the Allies, even before the USA was brought into the war in December 1941. In 1943 he visited Moscow, as part of his programme of securing co-operation among the Allies. He resigned in 1944 because of ill health; in the following year he was awarded the Nobel Peace Prize.

Husky Operational code name for the Allied landings, after Axis defeat in North Africa, on Sicily, 10 July 1943.

IA Indian Army

Ichi-Go Operational code name for the Japanese offensive in China, April 1944.

I-Go Operational code name for the Japanese counter-offensive in the South-west Pacific, April 1943.

Ilona *see Isabella*

INA Indian National Army, raised in Malaya following the Japanese invasion (1942), which served under Japanese command in Burma

Isabella (also called *Ilona*) German plans, abandoned, to occupy the Atlantic coasts of Spain and Portugal, 1941.

JCS Joint Chiefs of Staff (US)

JIC Joint Intelligence Committee

Jodl, Alfred (1890-1946) German general, and from 1939 to 1945 head of the *Oberkommando der Wehrmacht* operations bureau. In 1939 he was appointed Chief of Staff to Keitel, head of OKW, in which capacity he implemented Hitler's orders for all campaigns save in the USSR. A strong-willed and gifted strategist, he exerted much greater influence than his nominal superior, the ineffectual Keitel. Jodl signed the German surrender at Rheims on 7 May 1945 and, at the Nuremberg Trials, was condemned to death and subsequently hanged. He was a mesmerized devotee of Hitler.

JSM Joint Staff Mission (British)

Jubilee Operational code name for the Anglo-Canadian raid on Dieppe, 19 August 1942.

Juin, Alphonse (1888-1967) French marshal. He was captured in 1940 while leading a French division but was released at Pétain's request after the fall of France. He refused the post of Minister of War in the Vichy Government but went instead to North Africa as Commander-in-Chief. Then, in November 1942, he joined the Allies and distinguished himself against the Axis powers there and, later, in Italy. Subsequently he helped liberate France. Juin was posthumously promoted marshal by General de Gaulle.

Jupiter Operational code name for the projected Allied invasion of northern Norway, 1944.

Ka-Go Operational code name for the Japanese reinforcement of Guadalcanal, August 1942.

Kapp Putsch Named after Wolfgang Kapp (1858-1922), a German monarchist leader who, in 1920, led an armed uprising in Berlin to restore the Kaiser to his throne. The putsch proved abortive and Kapp fled to Sweden; he returned to Germany but, before being tried for treason by the republican government, he died.

Keitel, Wilhelm (1882-1946) German field marshal. An admirer of Hitler, he was appointed (1938) Chief of Staff of the *Oberkommando der Wehrmacht* (OKW), a new administrative body which directly subordinated the German armed forces to Hitler's authority. In this capacity he executed Hitler's commands to the letter, even when abhorrent. He ratified in Berlin Germany's unconditional surrender, was subsequently tried at Nuremberg and then hanged.

Kempf, Werner (1886-1964) German general. He served in the west during the First World War and in the inter-war years developed his theories on armoured warfare. He was so successful during the German invasion of Poland (1939) that he was given command of XLVIII Panzer Corps, which he led during the early stages of the invasion of the USSR, playing a major part in encircling the Soviet armies in the Uman pocket. His greatest achievement, however, was the part he played in the encirclement of Kiev, where he had a key role. He continued in command on the Eastern Front but when he was ordered into action in August 1943 to halt the advance of Vatutin's Voronezh Front towards Kharkov, he decided instead to evacuate the city and was immediately relieved of his command by Hitler. Thereafter he played little part in the war.

Kesselring, Albert (1885-1960) German field marshal. An army officer who transferred to the fledgling *Luftwaffe* in 1934, he was appointed in 1940 by Goering to command the German Second Air Fleet, stationed in Belgium and northern France, for the Battle of Britain. From 1941 to March 1945, Kesselring was Commander-in-Chief of the Southwest Army in the Italian and Mediterranean theatres, where he displayed his gift for improvization against a numerically superior enemy, notably during and after the Allied landings at Anzio when he fought a series of carefully planned retreats. In 1945, he was appointed Commander-in-Chief West. Kesselring was condemned to death by a British military court in 1947 but was pardoned in 1952.

Kido, Koichi (1889-1977) Japanese aristocrat and leading imperial adviser. He served in various domestic ministries and then, throughout the war, as Lord Keeper of the Privy Seal, the Emperor's principal source of information. In this capacity, Kido endeavoured to restrain the military government in its aggressive course. He played a crucial role in the peace overtures of 1945. Nonetheless, he was sentenced to life imprisonment by the Allies, but was released in 1953 because of poor health.

King, Ernest (1878-1956) American admiral. He was appointed Commander-in-Chief of the US Fleet in 1941 immediately following the Japanese attack on Pearl Harbor, replacing the sacked Admiral Kimmel; in the next year he was made Chief of Naval Operations. King's greatest achievements were to inspire and oversee major innovations in carrier-based air tactics and in conducting amphibious landings (notably at Guadalcanal, August 1942); his work in co-ordinating operations with his allies, most especially the British, was outstanding, despite his conviction that US resources should be directed to ending the Pacific war before deployment in Europe. The fleet he commanded was the largest ever brought together.

Kleist, Paul von (1885-1954) German field marshal. His greatest achievement was, as a Panzer group commander, to punch a hole in the Allied line at Sedan in 1940, allowing German Panzer formations rapidly to advance to the English Channel. Later he served on the Russian front with distinction (he had captured Belgrade in 1941) but in 1944 he was dismissed by Hitler for refusing to implement his orders unquestioningly.

Kluge, Günther von (1882-1944) German field marshal. He was Commander-in-Chief (1941) of the central front in Russia and, briefly during 1944, commanded the German armies in the West. Though obedient to Hitler, von Kluge was implicated in the attempt on the *Führer*'s life in July 1944 and was relieved of his command. Fearing that he would be put on trial, he committed suicide on 18 August of that year.

KMG (*Konno-Mekhanizirovannaya Gruppa* - Soviet Cavalry-Mechanized Group) The mixed mobile formation of cavalry, motor transport and armour used on the Eastern Front and in Manchuria. KMGs were formed in order to capitalize on the Red Army's large cavalry forces, which were of particular value in difficult terrain, but stiffened with armour and firepower.

Koenig, Marie Pierre (1898-1970) French general. He first saw service in the French colonial wars. At the fall of France, he escaped to England and joined de Gaulle's Free French Army. He was then sent to North Africa to command units of the Foreign Legion. Later he was entrusted with bringing all French resistance units under de Gaulle's control. He became the military governor of Paris after its liberation.

Koniev, Ivan Stepanovich (1897-1973) Soviet marshal. He barely escaped Stalin's purges of the higher military ranks in the 1930s and in the Second World War won renown for his reconquest (1944-45) of the Ukraine and southern Poland. Later he was instrumental in the Soviet victories in Czechoslovakia and in the final battle for Berlin. In 1945, he was appointed military governor of the Soviet occupation zone in Austria; then (1955-60) he commanded the military forces established by the Warsaw Treaty. In the following year (1961-62) he commanded Soviet forces in East Germany.

Konoye, Prince Fumimaro (1891-1945) Japanese prime minister and member of the 'peace party'. He was compelled to resign in October 1941 (he was replaced by the militarist Tojo) but after his successor's fall in 1944 he campaigned for an end to the war. In the first post-war cabinet he served as vice-president but committed suicide when the US sought to try him as a war criminal.

Konstantin Operational code name for the German occupation of the Italian-controlled Balkans, September 1943.

Kristallnacht On 9 November 1938, 'The night of broken glass'; 91 Jews were killed and many synagogues burned down in co-ordinated attacks against Jews and Jewish property throughout Germany and Austria.

Kuomintang (KMT) Also known as the Nationalist Party, the political party that governed mainland China from 1928 to 1949. The KMT became a political party in 1912 after the Chinese Republican Revolution (1911). It was outlawed in 1913, establishing three short-lived provisional governments under Sun Yat-sen (1917-23) before allying with the Chinese Communist Party in 1923. The allied forces wrested control of most of China from the warlords but split again (1927-28). Civil war ensued, but an uneasy truce was declared in the face of Japanese aggression from 1937. In 1946, following the Japanese capitulation, the KMT and Communists again took arms against one another, and this lasted until the Communist victory of 1949. The KMT fled to Taiwan, where they established a government under the leadership of Chiang Kai-shek.

Kutusov Operational code name for the Soviet offensive in the Kursk salient, July 1943.

Lammers, Hans Heinrich (1879-1962) Reich Minister and State Secretary in the Reich Chancery. A jurist, he was a member of Hitler's inner circle at Obersalzberg and was often consulted by him on legal matters. In 1943, together with Martin Bormann and Field Marshal Keitel, he was appointed to the Committee of Three, a triumvurate designed to lighten Hitler's tasks as head of state. Lammers was sentenced at Nuremberg to 20 years imprisonment but was released from Landsberg Prison in 1952.

Lattre de Tassigny, Jean de (1889-1952) French general, posthumously made marshal. He led the 14th Infantry Division during the German attack in 1940. In November 1942, he was arrested when he resisted the German occupation of the French 'Free' zone and sentenced to imprisonment by a Vichy court. He escaped, however, and joined General Giraud in North Africa. He then commanded the French 1st Army and, after the landings in the south of France, captured Marseilles and Toulon; subsequently his troops took Stuttgart and other German cities. De Tassigny, on behalf of France, signed the instrument of the German armed forces surrender.

Laval, Pierre (1883-1945) French politician. He served as foreign minister in the 1930s and, a staunch anti-Communist, sought to align France with Mussolini's Fascist Italy. Laval opposed the French declaration of war on Germany in 1939, and in June 1940 - following the German invasion of France - he promoted French collaboration with the occupying forces in his capacity as Pétain's prime minister. After the war, he was condemned to death for treason by the French High Court of Justice. Laval took poison, but was resuscitated and then hanged on 9 October 1945.

LCA Landing Craft Assault (US)

Lebensraum (Living space) The idea that Germany was too small to hold the German race had been current as early as the First World War, and Hitler adopted it as part of the justification for the expansion of Germany by the occupation of neighbouring European countries. Similar ideas were cited as the justification for Japanese expansion and Italian colonialism.

Leclerc, Philippe François Marie (1902-1947) General in the French Army. In 1940, he opposed the Vichy administration; he was imprisoned and twice escaped. On being sent to French Equatorial Africa, he raised a Free French force, which he led north across the Sahara Desert to join the British forces fighting in the Western Desert. In 1944, he commanded the 2nd French Armoured Division in the battle of Normandy, and then led his troops into Paris on the day the city was liberated. Leclerc was killed shortly after the war in a plane crash.

Leeb, Wilhelm Ritter von (1876-1956) German field marshal, promoted to that rank by Hitler for his part in the defeat of the French in Alsace-Lorraine in 1940 where he commanded Army Group C. A Bavarian gunner, Leeb had risen to the rank of general and retired in 1938, but was recalled by Hitler to command Army Group C in the Polish campaign (1939) which included Guderian's Panzer Korps, and which was responsible for closing the neck of the Polish Corridor, before sweeping through East Prussia to the Polish rear. Following his success in France, he led Army Group North in the invasion of the USSR, and saw his troops begin the long siege of Leningrad, but was relieved of his command during Hitler's purge of his generals in January 1942.

Leigh-Mallory, Sir Trafford (1892-1944) British air commander. He led the 12th Fighter Group during the Battle of Britain (1940), and used 'big wing' formations, with the resulting concentration of forces inland. He also led the 11th Fighter Group between 1940 and 1942 and then

Fighter Command (1942-43). Later he was appointed to command the Allied Expeditionary Air Force, comprising some 9000 aircraft, which supported the Allied landings in Normandy in 1944. Among Dowding's most assiduous denigrators, he aroused much animosity and, unlike Eisenhower, for example, caused friction with Britain's allies. He was killed in November 1944 when his aircraft crashed.

Le May, Curtis (1906-) US general. From 1942 he was one of the main exponents of the American bombing strategy against Germany and, later, Japan, through daytime bombing on specific targets. He also conceived the relatively safe aircraft tactic of flying formations at different heights. Against Japan he employed daytime assaults at low altitude with fire bombs.

Leopard Operational code name for the German attack on Leros, November 1944.

Lightfoot Code name for the Battle of Alamein, October 1942.

Lila Operational code name for the German plan to seize the French fleet at Toulon, 27 November 1942.

Lindemann, Ernst (1894-1941) German naval captain. A gunnery expert, he was appointed to command the mightily armed *Bismarck* early in 1940. After three hits on his ship during Operation *Rhine*, he argued forcefully with his superior, Admiral Lütjens, that the *Bismarck* should return to port. He was overruled and the *Bismarck* steamed on to her doom.

Little Entente Alliance formed (1920-21) between Czechoslovakia, Yugoslavia and Rumania, under French patronage, an economic and military grouping designed to maintain the territorial boundaries established by the Versailles treaties against Hungarian attempts to have them revised in her favour. Later the alliance disintegrated under German pressure after the *Anschluss* and the dismemberment of Czechoslovakia.

Little Saturn Operational code name for the Soviet offensive against the German forces trying to break through to the encircled 6th Army at Stalingrad, December 1942.

Locarno Pact (1925) An agreement made at a conference held in Switzerland, attended by Great Britain, France, Belgium, Germany, Italy, Poland and Czechoslovakia. A series of treaties was signed guaranteeing national boundaries, reiterating the terms of the Treaty of Versailles (1919). Germany signed treaties with, among others, Czechoslovakia and Poland, stipulating that boundary changes should be made only by agreement. Germany was promised membership of the League of Nations, but in 1936 Hitler denounced the pact and withdrew from the league.

LRDG Long-Range Desert Group (Allied)

LRPG Long-Range Penetration Group (US)

LSD Landing Ship Dock (US)

Lumberjack Code name for the offensive (1-7 March 1945) by the US 1st and 3rd Armies to push through the Eifel region, and Model's Army Group 'B', to reach the Rhine.

Lütjens, Gunther (1889-1941) German admiral. He joined the navy in 1907 and for most of his professional career worked with Torpedo Boat flotillas. During the Norwegian campaign in the Second World War he led the *Scharnhorst* and *Gneisenau*; in July 1940 he was promoted to command the *Bismarck* flotilla. A brave man, intelligent and generous, he was held in high regard in the service. He expressed reservations as to the wisdom of taking the flotilla to sea, yet when the *Bismarck*, on which he sailed, was hit three times he declined to turn for home; he perished with the ship.

MAAF Mediterranean Allied Air Force

MAC Mediterranean Air Command

MacArthur, Douglas (1880-1964) American five-star general. He was born into a military family and attended West Point, from which he graduated in 1903 top of his class. He then served in the Philippines and in Japan before becoming (1906-07) aide to President Theodore Roosevelt. From 1913 to 1917 he was attached to the US Army General Staff. As commander of the US 42nd (Rainbow) Division in France in the First World War, he was outstandingly successful during the Second Battle of the Marne (1918). He was superintendent of West Point (1919-22) and Chief of Staff of the Army (1930-35). In the intervening years (1928-30) he again served in the Philippines, preparing the islands for eventual independence. He retired from the army in 1937, but was recalled to active service on 26 July 1941, when war with Japan seemed probable. He was then appointed commander of the US and Philippine forces on the islands. Although he recognized the need for strong air support, the build-up of US bombers in the archipelago was incomplete when, after the Japanese attack on Pearl Harbor (7

December 1941), the numerically superior Japanese forces thrust into the Philippines. MacArthur's retreat was executed in so professional a manner that the Japanese advance was dangerously slowed down and it was not until May 1942 that the last resistance on the islands was overcome. Two months before this, however, President Roosevelt had ordered MacArthur to safety in Australia, where he was to prepare for counter-attacks as Commander-in-Chief, South-west Pacific. His area of direct responsibility embraced Australia, New Guinea, the Dutch East Indies and the Philippines. From Australia, MacArthur launched the New Guinea campaign, co-ordinated land forces in Operation *Cartwheel* leading to the isolation of Rabaul, and later (1944-45) the campaign that led to the reconquest of the Philippines. He accepted the Japanese surrender on behalf of the Allies in a ceremony on board USS *Missouri* in Tokyo Bay on 2 September 1945. He was then appointed commander of the Allied powers in Japan, which country he ruled virtually as a dictator, and for which he drew up a democratic constitution. His insistence that Emperor Hirohito should not be tried for war crimes but continue as nominal head of state contributed much to Japan's moral and economic recovery in post-war years. In 1950 he was appointed commander of UN military forces in South Korea during the Korean War. Despite early successes, a dispute with President Truman over whether to bomb Chinese bases led to his dismissal. It was suggested that MacArthur run as the Republican presidential candidate in 1952. Nothing came of this however, and he retired from active service and spent his last year as a director of a business corporation. MacArthur was one of the most brilliant strategists to emerge during the Second World War.

Magic The cover name for the American intelligence programme devoted to breaking Japanese codes.

Magnet Operational code name for the movement of American forces to Northern Ireland, February 1942.

Malinovski, Rodion Yakovlevich (1898-1967) Soviet marshal. Malinovski served in the Russian Army in the First World War, joined the Red Army in 1919 and the Communist Party in 1926. A graduate of the Frunze Military Academy (1930) he then served as Chief of Staff of a Cavalry Regiment, and in the headquarters of various Military Districts and as Chief of Staff of a Cavalry Corps. He served as a Soviet 'adviser' in the Spanish Civil War (1936-39), and was then an instructor at the Frunze Academy. In 1941 he commanded a Rifle Corps. In 1942 he was Deputy Commander of the Voronezh Front, and then commanded 2nd Guards Army during the battle of Stalingrad. In February 1943 he was appointed to command the Southern Front, then the South Western, 3rd and 2nd Ukrainian Fronts. He was promoted Marshal of the Soviet Union in 1944. From July to September 1945, during the Manchurian Campaign, he commanded the Transbaikal Front. After the war, he remained in the Far East to command the Transbaikal-Amur Military District and from 1947 he was Commander-in-Chief of Soviet Forces in the Far East. He held a number of very senior military posts, becoming Minister of Defence (1957-67) during which period he also became a senior Soviet politician.

Manhattan The cover name for the American atomic bomb project.

Mannerheim, Baron Carl Gustav von (1867-1951) Finnish field marshal. He led all Finnish forces in the Winter War (1939-40) against the USSR where he showed an exceptional ability to combine regular battlefield strategy with irregular, guerrilla-style tactics. He was again in command when Finland joined Germany in the war against the Soviet Union, from 1941 to 1944, and concluded an armistice in the latter year when Soviet might proved overwhelming. The 80-miles long Finnish defensive line on the Karelian frontier was built at his order and was named after him.

Manstein, Erich von (1887-1973) German field marshal. He passed out of the German Cadet Corps in 1906 and later saw action during the First World War, notably at the battles of Verdun and the Somme. In 1937 he was promoted major-general and appointed Deputy Chief of the General Staff. Manstein first came to prominence in the late autumn of 1939, when Hitler called for plans for an attack on the Low Countries and France. The most favoured option was an adaptation of the Schlieffen Plan employed by Germany in 1914; in the event, Manstein's plan to strike through the supposedly impassable Ardennes area was adopted by Hitler, with dramatically successful results; Holland and Belgium crumbled, France fell within seven weeks and the BEF was forced to evacuate Europe by way of Dunkirk. Manstein's greatest triumphs came, however, in the Russian campaigns when, in 1942, his 2nd Army overcame stiff Russian resistance in the Crimea and captured Sevastopol and, in 1943, when

he stabilized the German front after the surrender of the 6th Army at Stalingrad and, in an immaculately executed flank counter stroke, retook Kharkov. Arguably the most gifted battlefield commander to emerge during the European war, Manstein was nevertheless retired by Hitler for his outspokenness in March 1944. In 1950 he was sentenced by a British war crimes court to 18 years imprisonment, but was released on 6 May 1953.

Marita Operational code name for the German attack on Greece, 6 April 1941.

Market - Garden Twin operational code name for Montgomery's ill-fated airborne landings near Arnhem (September 1944). 'Market' was the code name for the airborne assault, 'Garden' for the supporting role of the infantry and armour.

Marshall, George Catlett (1880-1959) American soldier and statesman. He first distinguished himself as a staff officer during the First World War and then (1919-24) as aide to General Pershing. From 1939 to 1945 he was Chief of Staff of the American Army. After the war he served (1947-49) under President Truman as Secretary of State. Marshall directed strategy with great skill but his two greatest achievements were to support Churchill in his advocacy of defeating Germany before Japan, (though in this he was opposed by MacArthur and his own staff), and his post-war European Recovery Program (generally known as the Marshall Plan) by which huge sums in dollars were invested in bankrupt Europe to speed its economic recovery. For this last achievement he was awarded the Nobel Peace Prize in 1953.

Menace Operational code name for the British and Free French operation against Dakar, September 1940.

Mercury see Merkur

Merkur (Mercury) Operational code name for the German air attack on Crete, 20 April 1941.

Merrill, Frank D. (1903-1955) Major-general in the US Army and authority on the Japanese and their military tactics. Merrill graduated from West Point in 1929 and was assigned to the US embassy in Tokyo. In 1941, he was made operations officer under General Stilwell. Merrill organized and led a regiment-sized group of US volunteers who became known as 'Merrill's Marauders'. Trained in guerrilla tactics, the Marauders harassed Japanese positions in Burma, until in May 1944, with Chinese reinforcements, they captured the Myitkyina airfield. The city fell three months later. After serving as deputy commander of the US forces in the India-Burma theatre, Merrill became Chief of Staff of the 10th Army, Okinawa, in 1945, and then military adviser to the Republic of the Philippines (1947). He retired in 1948.

MI5 The British Security Service, responsible for counter-intelligence. Originally a branch of Military Intelligence, it came under the supervision of the Home Office. It acted against enemy agents attempting to operate in Britain and the Empire and monitored the activities of potentially subversive organizations and individuals. It proved itself to be particularly effective against German spies operating in Great Britain and consequently ran a highly sucessful series of double agents.

MI6 The British Secret Service, also known as the Secret Intelligence Service (SIS). Its function was to gather information from foreign sources and, with most of its European networks overrun by the German occupation, made extensive use of intelligence gathered by the Resistance. Once a branch of Military Intelligence, MI6 was under the administrative control of the Foreign Secretary. It was responsible for the important codebreaking establishment, the Government Code and Cypher School (GC&CS) and its most important product, *Ultra*.

Mihailović, Draža (1893-1946) Yugoslav resistance leader. Following the German invasion, he fled to Serbia, where he quickly raised a resistance group with the support of the king in exile (the Chetniks). This formation was pro-Serbian, passionately anti-Communist, and attacked Tito's partisans, but were defeated. The Allies then gave their support to Tito and, after the war, Mihailović was arrested and executed.

Millennium Operational code name for the RAF bomber attack on Cologne, 30-31 May 1942.

Mincemeat Operational code name for cover and deception in the Mediterranean, 1943.

Model, Walther (1891-1945) German field marshal. He was decorated for bravery at the Battle of Verdun during the First World War. A convinced Nazi, Model became one of Hitler's favourite generals, earning the nickname 'The Führer's Fireman' because Hitler repeatedly ordered him to take command in troublespots. His most notable achievement in this respect was on the Eastern Front when, as Commander of Army Group Centre, he

halted the Russian offensive near Warsaw in 1944. Following the Allied landings (1944) in Normandy, he was appointed to command Army Group B, in which capacity he prevented Allied paratroopers from establishing a bridgehead at Arnhem. In April 1945, finding his troops encircled in the Ruhr, he shot himself.

Molotov, Vyacheslav Mikhailovich (1890-1986) Soviet politician. He joined the Communist Party in 1906, and six years later was arrested for his political activities and exiled. He returned to St Petersburg in 1911 and in the following year became an editor on the Bolshevik daily newspaper *Pravda*. After the October Revolution of 1917, his promotion in the party was rapid, largely through his unswerving support of Stalin. In 1939, Molotov became Commissar of Foreign Affairs and in August of that year negotiated the Russo-German non-aggression pact with von Ribbentrop. After the German invasion of the USSR in 1941, Molotov strengthened his country's alliance with the West and attended all the war-time Allied conferences. In 1949, he was succeeded as Foreign Minister by Vyshinsky. However, in 1953, after Stalin's death, he was again appointed Foreign Minister, a post he held until 1956, when he was dismissed by Khrushchev. In the following year he was expelled from the central committee of the Communist Party after an abortive attempt, in which he played a prominent part, to remove Khrushchev from power. Thereafter he held only minor posts and was later expelled from the Communist Party. Throughout his political career, Molotov was an inflexible adherent to Soviet policies and was known in diplomatic circles for his uncompromising attitude.

Montgomery, Bernard Law (1887-1976) British field marshal. He served in France in the First World War, then in India and Palestine. At the outbreak of the Second World War he was posted to the BEF and was at Dunkirk, where he successfully extricated his division. In August 1942, following the death of General William Gort, he was appointed to command the British 8th Army in North Africa. To Churchill's irritation, he delayed his attack at El Alamein until he had assembled overwhelming material and numerical superiority in late October. Within seven months, under Alexander's supervision, 8th Army and Patton's US 7th Army had driven all Axis forces out of North Africa. Montgomery then led the army into Sicily and southern Italy, under Alexander, then Supreme Allied Commander in the Mediterranean theatre, before being recalled to Great Britain in readiness for the Normandy landings in 1944. From 6 June to 31 July, he commanded, under Eisenhower, all ground forces; thereafter, he commanded the 21st Army Group on the Allied left flank. His plan for airborne landings at Arnhem, to secure essential Rhine bridges ahead of the main forces, ended in disaster, but Montgomery was instrumental in stemming, then repulsing the ferocious German armoured offensive in the Ardennes in December 1944. Montgomery acccepted the surrender of all German armies in northwestern Europe on 4 May 1945. He later served as Chief of the Imperial General Staff. Mongomery was a self-publicist, with a strong belief in the value of central command. His success in North Africa may be attributed to this, the discipline and training he instigated and the sense of confidence with which he imbued those who served under him.

Motti tactics *Motti* is Finnish for a small log of firewood, specifically a reference to cutting up roadbound armoured columns into vulnerable sections, like a string of sausages. A tactic employed by the Finnish Army during the war with the USSR (1939-40). In these *motti* battles, Finnish troops, clad in white to camouflage them against the snow, and moving swiftly on skis, penetrated deep behind Soviet lines to destroy supply bases, disrupt communications and attack the enemy. Targets were usually first bypassed, then taken in rear.

Mountbatten, Lord Louis, 1st Earl Mountbatten of Burma (1900-1979) A great-grandson of Queen Victoria, he became a naval cadet in 1913 and saw service in the First World War. In September 1939 he was a commander in the destroyer service, but later (1942-43) served in Great Britain as Director of Combined Operations, in which capacity he organized exploratory commando raids on France and Norway, notably that at Dieppe in 1942. In 1943 he was appointed Head of the South-East Asia Command to organize Allied operations against the Japanese in Burma. In this role he was particularly successful, achieving co-operation between British, Empire, American and Chinese forces by tactful firmness. In 1947, Mountbatten became the last British viceroy of India and negotiated the creation of the states of India and Pakistan. Later (1959-65) he served as Chief of the British Defence Staff, where he sought to integrate the branches of the armed forces into a structure more suited to changing military and naval circumstances. He was murdered in 1979 by the IRA.

MT Motor Transport (US)

MTB Motor Torpedo Boat (US)

MTO Mediterranean Theatre of Operations

Mussolini, Benito (1883-1945) Italian dictator. The son of ardently socialist parents, Mussolini at first held left-wing views. He was a schoolteacher for a short time, then spent nearly two years (1902-04) in Switzerland and in 1909 edited a socialist newspaper. Later, in Milan, he became editor of the socialist *Avanti*. When the First World War broke out, he at first advocated Italian neutrality but quickly about-faced and demanded Italian intervention on the Allied side, particularly in *Il Popolo d'Italia*, a newspaper which he founded. His reasons for so abrupt a change are uncertain, but he was probably influenced by the French government's generosity in financing the pro-French press. Mussolini was called up for military service on 15 August 1914 and, like Hitler, attained the rank of corporal. He was wounded on the Isonzo but made a full recovery. He then returned to journalism and thereafter advocated an extreme form of nationalism; at the same time he founded the Fascist Party, which he led. He was elected to parliament in 1921. The National Fascist Party rapidly gained support under his inspiration and direction, and in October 1922 Mussolini was strong enough to order the Fascists to march on Rome, where King Victor Emmanuel III appointed him Prime Minister. He ended parliamentary government in 1928. In 1929, Mussolini - now called *Duce* (leader) - concluded the Lateran Treaty with the Papacy, ending the conflict between church and state. He inaugurated a massive building programme as part of his plan to restore Italy to the grandeur of Roman times. Mussolini was at first antagonistic to Hitler; however, he became diplomatically isolated after his attack on Ethiopia in 1935, and reached an agreement with Germany, his only potential ally. During the Spanish Civil War, he joined with the *Führer* in providing military support to General Franco and his Nationalists. In 1938, Mussolini stood aside when Hitler annexed Austria and in the same year took part in the Munich negotiations. Then, in April 1939, he ordered the Italian Army to occupy Albania. Subsequently (June 1940) he entered the war on Germany's side, but only when France was on the verge of collapse. Mussolini's failures in North Africa and in his invasion of Greece were temporarily relieved by German support, but by 1943, with the Italian mainland about to be invaded, his personal prestige collapsed and the Fascist Grand Council declined to support his policies. The King first dismissed him, then ordered his arrest. In September 1943, however, a brilliantly executed rescue operation by the Germans released him from captivity in the Abruzzi mountains and Hitler made him head of a puppet government based in Salo in north Italy. When Germany collapsed (April 1945), Mussolini was captured by Italian left-wing partisans and, with his mistress Clara Petacci, was shot. Mussolini was a demagogue, journalist and administrator of high order but brought himself and his country to ruin by his grandiose plans, which were wholly beyond Italy's industrial capability, and by the dominance, to which he reluctantly succumbed, of Hitler's 'Iron Will' and Germany's superior strength.

NAAF North Africa Air Force

Nagumo, Chuichi (1887-1944) Japanese vice-admiral and Yamamoto's First Air Fleet Commander. A talented and energetic officer, he led the attack on Pearl Harbor, but by the time of the Battle of Midway, when he lost four aircraft carriers to the US Navy within 24 hours, he had prematurely aged and approved readily, and without comment, plans submitted by his subordinates. Later he was appointed to command the Central Pacific Fleet with the task of defending the Marianas. When the Americans successfully landed on Saipan, he committed suicide.

NATO North Atlantic Treaty Organization, formed in 1949.

Nazi Party Acronymic form for Hitler's *National Sozialistische Deutsche Arbeitpartei* (National Socialist German Workers' Party), the only legal political movement in Germany between 1933 and May 1945.

Night of the Long Knives *see* SA

Nimitz, Chester W. (1885-1966) American admiral. A highly gifted administrator and naval strategist, Nimitz was appointed Commander-in-Chief of the US Pacific Fleet on 31 December 1941, immediately following the Japanese attack on Pearl Harbor. He retained all officers in their positions on the assumption that the disaster 'could have happened to anybody', an act of clemency that restored naval morale. Nimitz was chiefly responsible for the decisive American victory at Midway and for masterminding the ensuing destruction of Japanese naval strength by piecemeal operations, notably island landings, to push back Japanese forces to their mainland.

NKVD (*Narodny Komissariat Vnutrennykh Del* - Soviet People's Commissariat of Internal Affairs) The forerunner of the KGB. The NKVD were responsible for labour camps and exercised control over a large labour force which was used in the construction of fortifications. NKVD troops were also used as 'élite' forces to stiffen Red Army formations, not unlike the German use of the SS. Thus in July 1941, NKVD motorized troops were used to defend the approaches to Kiev, while 21st NKVD Division was used in the defence of Leningrad. The wartime controversy over the massacre of Polish officer prisoners at Katyn (Bialystok), which had serious implications for the alliance at the time, has been revived. Most authorities, including the Poles, now believe that the burden of proof lies with the Russians, and that the NKVD were probably responsible for most of the killings.

Noball Operational code name for the Allied air force offensive against German V-weapons sites, 1944.

Nordlicht (Northern Lights) Operational code name for the German offensive against Leningrad, Summer 1942.

Nordwind (North Wind) Operational code name for the German counter-attack (31 December 1944-26 January 1945) in Alsace, a doomed venture planned by Heinrich Himmler.

Northern Lights *see* Nordlicht

Ob *Oberbefehlshaber* (Commander-in-Chief)

Octagon Code name for the Second Quebec Conference, 10-16 September 1944.

O'Connor, Sir Richard Nugent (1899-1981) British general. He served with distinction during the First World War and later (1938-39) as military governor of Jerusalem. From 1940 to 1941 he was a corps commander in the Western Desert and defeated the Italians at Beda Fomm. He was later captured by the Germans but escaped in 1943 and was given command of the British VIII Corps in France.

OFEC Office of Foreign Economic Co-ordination (US)

OKH *see* OKW

OKW (*Oberkommando der Wehrmacht*) The High Command of all German armed forces created in 1938, with Hitler at its head. The OKH (*Oberkommando des Heeres*), the High Command of the German Army, together with the OKL (*Oberkommando der Luftwaffe*), the High Command of the Air Force, and the OKM (*Oberkommando der Kriegsmarine*), the High Command of the Navy, came under the authority of the OKW. After the Germans were held by the Soviets before Moscow (December 1941), Hitler personally assumed command of the German Army, taking direct responsibility for operations although he was not Chief of Staff. In addition, he commanded the Chancellery staff (Foreign Affairs, von Ribbentrop; Nazi Party affairs, Hess/Bormann; SS and Police Chief, Himmler, and Propaganda Minister, Goebbels), thereby holding absolute control of all aspects of German policy.

Olive Operational code name for the Allied attack on the Gothic Line, Italy, August 1944.

Olympic Operational code name for the Allied invasion of the Japanese island of Kyushu, planned for November 1945, but preempted by Japan's surrender. *See also* Downfall.

OPD Operations Division of the War Department(US)

OSS (Office of Strategic Services) US secret military agency, responsible to the Joint Chiefs of Staff. Created by President Roosevelt in 1942, its first director was General William Donovan (1883-1959), previously Co-ordinator of Information, who had studied resistance groups, and the British SOE. Under his leadership OSS worked closely with SOE, and developed a network of special units throughout the world, which gathered intelligence and sent agents to help resistance organizations.

Overcast Operational code name for the American plan to take German weapon scientists from Europe to work in the USA after the war.

Overlord Operational code name for the Allied invasion of Normandy, which started on 6 June 1944.

OWI Office of War Information (US)

Pact of Steel Formal alliance, signed on 22 May 1939, between Germany and Italy (Axis Pact).

Papagos, Alexander (1883-1955) Greek general. He commanded the Greek Army in its successful resistance to Italian invasion (1940) but was later captured by the Germans and incarcerated in Dachau concentration camp. He was freed in 1945, reinstated in his former position and led the struggle against Communist guerrillas in northern Greece.

Paris Peace Conferences (1919) *see Versailles, Treaty of*

Patch, Alexander McCarrell (1889-1945) US general. Early in 1942 he was appointed commander of the task force dispatched to help the French in New Caledonia. Then, in 1943, he led his American troops at the successful battle of Guadalcanal. In 1944 he commanded the US 7th Army in the invasion of southern France.

Patton, George Smith (1885-1945) American general. He graduated from West Point in 1909 and was soon after appointed *aide de camp* to General Pershing during his expedition against Mexico in 1916. Patton accompanied Pershing when the latter was given command of the US expeditionary force in the First World War. His experience as a tank officer in the St Mihiel offensive and in the Meuse-Argonne sector (1918) led him to appreciate the tank's potential against static defence formations. His first important role in the Second World War came in March 1943, when he was given command of the US II Corps with the task of restoring its morale after its defeat by Rommel in the Kasserine Pass in North Africa. He then led the US 7th Army in Sicily. For the next year, however, Patton, despite his mastery of aggressive tank warfare, was out of favour. His anti-British attitudes, his personal dislike of Montgomery and his indiscreet political pronouncements led to his being reprimanded by Eisenhower, the Allied supreme commander. His ruin was nearly brought about when, visiting a hospital, he slapped a shell-shocked soldier. He was quickly recalled to Great Britain and given the minor command of diversionary forces prior to Operation *Overlord*. He was again given active command following the Allied landings in Normandy (June 1944), and he distinguished himself by leading US 3rd Army from the breakout at Avranches (August 1944) in a race to the Seine and then to the Meuse, which was halted only through shortage of fuel. In December 1944, his army moved at great speed to relieve German pressure on Bradley's formations during the Ardennes offensive. This accomplished, Patton's next attacks took him across the Rhine, with the loss of only 34 men killed or wounded. Finally, he pushed down the Danube into Austria. However, his brutal policy of destroying any village that offered even the slightest resistance to his advance again brought him into disrepute. Distrust of his judgement was further heightened by his repeated recommendations that the Western Allies should attack Soviet armies in the east. Eisenhower transferred him to the token command of l5th Army, which was not a fighting formation. Shortly after the end of the war, Patton was killed in a car accident. Opinion remains divided as to Patton's stature. Patton's outspokenness, his love of personal display (he habitually wore a Colt 45 pistol on each hip) and his mindless brutality were balanced by his undoubted gifts for organization and the rapid deployment of armour in lightning thrusts. Further, Patton, like Montgomery, inspired devotion and loyalty of a high order among his troops.

Paulus, Friedrich (1890-1957) German field marshal. Sent by Hitler to supervize the activities of Rommel's *Deutsches Afrika Korps* in 1941, Paulus displayed caution in overriding Rommel's plans to destroy the Allied pocket at Tobruk, and in the interim commanded the 6th Army at Stalingrad. Shortly before his capitulation, being encircled and unsupplied by the *Luftwaffe* (despite Goering's promises to the contrary), he was promoted to Field Marshal by Hitler, since no German of that rank had ever surrendered. In captivity, Paulus joined the National Committee for a Free Germany, a Soviet-sponsored organization, and called on Germans to surrender. He was released in 1953 and spent the rest of his life in East Germany. Paulus was a gifted, diligent staff officer but was placed in an impossible situation when all his requests for permission to withdraw his army intact from Stalingrad were overruled by Berlin.

PCNL Polish Committee of National Liberation

Pedestal Operational code name for a great convoy of 14 merchantmen and escorts, dispatched from northern England on 2 August 1942 to the beleaguered island fortress of Malta. Five merchant vessels reached the harbour of Valletta on 13 August, enabling Maltese resistance to continue.

Percival, Sir Arthur (1887-1966) British lieutenant-general. He was commissioned in the infantry and during the First World War was awarded the DSO, the MC and the *Croix de Guerre* for bravery. He was Chief of Staff (1936-37) in Malaya and for this reason was appointed General Officer Commanding Malaya in April 1941. After the fall of Singapore, for which he was held responsible, Percival was imprisoned by the Japanese. He was released in 1945 and, at General MacArthur's special invitation, watched the Japanese sign the instrument of surrender on the USS *Missouri* in Tokyo Bay.

Pétain, Henri Philippe (1856-1951) French marshal. Though an industrious officer, his undisguised contempt for French politicians hindered his promotion. He made his name during the First World War at Verdun and in 1917 was appointed French Commander-in-Chief. He emerged from the war as France's hero and served (1934) as war minister before becoming ambassador to Franco's Spain in 1939. In 1940, when France was on the verge of collapse, he was recalled by Paul Reynaud, the Prime Minister, to be Vice Premier. Pétain, however, advocated seeking an armistice. On 16 June 1940 he succeeded Reynaud as Prime Minister, agreed to Hitler's armistice terms and became Chief of State of the Vichy government, in control of temporarily unoccupied France. For his collaboration with the Nazis he was tried by a French court after the war and sentenced to death, later commuted to life imprisonment.

Plunder Operational code name for Montgomery's British and Canadian 21st Army Group thrust across the Rhine, north of the Ruhr, 23 March 1945.

Pluto (Pipe Line Under The Ocean) Code name for the oil pipeline laid under the English Channel to supply the Allied armies in North West Europe, 1944.

Pointblank Operational code name for the Anglo/American Combined Bombing Offensive against Germany in 1943 and thereafter.

Portal, Sir Charles (1893-1971) Air Chief Marshal of the RAF and British Chief of Air Staff from 1940 to 1945. Though an early advocate of saturation area bombing, he co-operated in the Combined Anglo-American bombing offensive of precision daytime bombing, bringing him into conflict with Harris.

Pound, Sir Dudley (1877-1943) British Admiral of the Fleet. He was First Sea Lord in September 1939 and, until 1942, Chairman of the British Chiefs of Staff Committee. He worked so continuously that his judgement is thought to have been impaired, but by his death (generally attributed to overwork) his professionalism and diligence had greatly contributed to Allied mastery of the seas.

PPR Polish Worker's Party

Priceless Operational code name for Allied operations in the Mediterranean, 1943.

Punishment *see Bestrafung*

Quadrant Code name for the First Quebec Conference, 17-24 August 1943.

Quisling, Vidkun (1887-1945) Norwegian Fascist leader and head of the *Nasjonal Samling* (National Unity) party. An army officer, he became Norwegian Minister for Defence (1931-33) and in 1940 helped prepare for the German invasion of his country. From 1942 to 1945 he served as Prime Minister under Josef Terboven, Nazi *Reichskommissar* for Norway. He was arrested in May 1945, convicted of high treason and shot. His name is today universally synonymous with 'traitor'.

RAAF Royal Australian Air Force

Raeder, Erich (1876-1960) German grand admiral, the architect of the Third Reich's navy. He entered the imperial navy in 1894 and, during the First World War, served at the Battle of the Dogger Bank. He was rapidly promoted and in 1935 Hitler appointed him Supreme Naval Commander. In this capacity, he instigated an intensive building programme, notably of 'pocket' battleships for surface raiding. During the war, his strategy relied on commerce raiders (both conventional and disguised) and U-boats to starve Great Britain into submission rather than risk a confrontation of the scale of the Battle of Jutland (1916). The *Führer* lost confidence in surface ships and considered scrapping them and using their guns on land. Raeder consequently resigned and was replaced by Dönitz. Raeder was tried at Nuremberg and sentenced to life imprisonment, but was released in 1955.

RAF Royal Air Force (British)

Rainbow Operational code name for the United States' pre-war operational plans.

Ramsay, Sir Bertram Home (1883-1945) British admiral. He organized the naval aspects of the Dunkirk evacuation and then in 1942 was deputy to Admiral Cunningham for the *Torch* landings. Later (1943) he masterminded the landings in Sicily and in 1944 was made Naval Commander-in-Chief for the Normandy landings. He was killed (2 Jan. 1945) in an aircraft crash while on his way to a military conference.

RAN Royal Australian Navy

Rangers American Special Force formed and organized into battalions. Unlike the British Commandos, the Rangers usually operated in concert with conventional forces, being detailed specific tasks within combined operations. In this capacity, they played a crucial role in the development of amphibious landing techniques in numerous operations in the Pacific. Their most outstanding exploits - by the 2nd and 5th battalions -

were the assaults on the Pointe du Hoc and the Pointe de la Percée during the Normandy landings (June 1944) when, equipped with grapnels, ropes and ladders, they scaled the cliffs, intending to silence heavy German defensive guns.

Rapallo, Treaty of (1922) An agreement signed by Germany and the USSR in which Germany recognized the Soviet state. Soviet agreements allowed Germany to produce weapons in the USSR, forbidden by the Treaty of Versailles.

RCAF Royal Canadian Air Force

RCN Royal Canadian Navy

RCT Regimental Combat Team (US)

Reckless Operational code name for the American operation against Hollandia, New Guinea, April 1944.

Red *see Rot*

Reynaud, Paul (1878-1966) French politician. He was Prime Minister, Minister of War and Foreign Minister between March and June 1940, having succeeded Daladier. One of his earliest acts was to meet Churchill and sign a declaration that neither Great Britain nor France would conclude a separate peace agreement with Nazi Germany. On 18 May 1940, Reynaud replaced Gamelin with Weygand and appointed Pétain Deputy Prime Minister. Both appointees, however, became ardent for surrender after German successes and on 16 June he resigned and was succeeded by Pétain. Reynaud was arrested by the puppet Vichy Government and deported to Germany. He was freed by the Allies in 1945.

RFSS *Reichsführer SS* (Reich Leader SS) The formal title of Himmler

Rhubarb Operational code name for the RAF sweeps over the English Channel and occupied French coastline, 1940 onwards.

Ribbentrop, Joachim von (1893-1946) Prominent Nazi leader. He joined the National Socialist Party in 1932 and soon became Hitler's expert on foreign affairs. He was German ambassador (1936-38) to Great Britain and, by the time he was recalled to Germany, had become a passionate Anglophobe. Hitler appointed him Foreign Minister in 1938, and in this capacity he concluded the Russo-German non-aggression pact of August 1939. He was entirely loyal to Hitler and was promptly dismissed by Dönitz on his succession as *Führer*. He was arrested by the Allies, found guilty of war crimes at the Nuremberg trials and hanged.

Richard Operational code name for the planned German intervention in Spain if there was a Republican victory in the Civil War.

Riga, Treaties of (1920, 1921) The first, between Latvia and the USSR, acknowledged Latvian independence; the second, between the USSR and Poland, established the Russo-Polish frontier after the war between them.

RIN Royal Indian Navy

Ring Operational code name for the Soviet manoeuvres to destroy the German 6th Army at Stalingrad, January 1943.

RN Royal Navy (British)

RNZAF Royal New Zealand Air Force

RNZN Royal New Zealand Navy

Roesselsprung (Knight's move) Operational code name for the German attack on Tito's HQ at Hvar, 25 May 1944.

Rokossovski, Konstantin (1896-1968) Soviet marshal. A Tsarist cavalry NCO, he joined the Red Army in 1918 and commanded cavalry divisions in the 1930s. During the purges, he was arrested by the NKVD, very badly beaten up and imprisoned, but in 1940 he was released as one of the Red Army's new major-generals, to command IX Mechanized Corps. He commanded the Briansk Front (from July 1942), the Don (from September 1942), the Central (from February 1943), the Byelorussian (from October 1943), the lst Byelorussian (from February 1944) and the 2nd Byelorussian (from November 1944). At Stalingrad, as commander of the Don Front, he was instrumental in the destruction of the encircled 6th Army. He narrowly escaped death in an air strike on his HQ because he decided on a whim to hold his final briefing in the officers' mess. Promoted marshal in 1944, Rokossovski captured Warsaw (14-18 January 1945) and, in Berlin, was a signatory to German surrender.

Rommel, Erwin (1891-1944) German field marshal. A dashing, courageous officer, he won the Iron Cross and Prussia's highest military award, the *Pour le Mérite*, during the First World War. He was made a general in 1939 and took part in many early campaigns, notably the invasion of France where his Panzer division swept through to Cherbourg. He proved himself a master of *blitzkrieg* tactics. When Hitler agreed to support Mussolini's ailing North African adventure, Rommel was given command of the newly created *Deutsches Afrika Korps*; he arrived in Africa in February 1941. Rommel was by nature impatient and difficult to work with, but in the Western Desert campaigns he became idolized by his men and his cunning and tactical skill earned him the nickname of 'The Desert Fox'. Although much of his tactical success was a result of the Italian monitoring of British signal traffic, Rommel's audacity and flair in conducting first an offensive, then a defensive campaign against enormously superior numbers cannot be doubted. By 23 October 1942, immediately prior to the Battle of El Alamein, Montgomery had accumulated 195,000 men to Rommel's 104,000 and 1000 tanks to his 500. Following the Axis defeat in Africa, Rommel supervised the build-up of defences on the Channel coast in preparation for a possible Allied invasion. During the Battle of Normandy he commanded Army Group B. Rommel at first held Hitler in awe and was fascinated by his phenomenal memory and ability to reach decisions by intuition rather than by reasoned argument. Nevertheless, Rommel was falsely implicated in the abortive attempt (20 July 1944) to assassinate the *Führer*. Given the options of trial by a people's court or suicide, he chose the latter and took poison on 14 October.

Roosevelt, Franklin Delano (1882-1945) 32nd President of the United States, the only man to be elected to that office four times. From both sides of his family he inherited wealth. His early career was in the law but in 1910 he was elected to the New York state senate. Roosevelt, a Democrat, allied himself with reform groups in the party. Between 1913 and 1920 he served as Assistant Secretary of the Navy, during which period he earned his reputation as a sound administrator. In 1921, while on holiday, he was stricken with poliomyelitis and was thereafter scarcely able to walk. In 1928, however, he won the governorship of New York State. In 1932, Roosevelt was chosen as the presidential candidate by the Democratic Party and was duly elected, replacing the Republican incumbent, Herbert C. Hoover. He immediately set himself the awesome task of conquering the worst effects of the Depression, by fiscal measures rushed through Congress and by the establishment of several government agencies, notably the National Recovery Administration. Moreover, strenuous efforts were made to develop the country's natural resources, with the establishment of such bodies as the Tennessee Valley Authority (1933). These and other measures were all part of Roosevelt's 'New Deal'; their success led to his re-election in 1936. In foreign affairs, Roosevelt developed his 'Good Neighbour' policy towards the countries of South America and denounced both the growing power and aggression of the Axis nations in Europe and Japanese expansion in Manchuria and China. When the Second World War broke out, Roosevelt, though the USA was neutral, made his country and its military output an 'arsenal for democracy'. In 1941, 'Lend-Lease' aid to the Allies was inaugurated. Roosevelt was re-elected president in 1940. In August 1941, Roosevelt met Winston Churchill, the British Prime Minister, at sea and together they drafted the Atlantic Charter. On 7 December of that year, when the Japanese bombed Pearl Harbor, the United States was finally brought into the war. Thereafter Roosevelt devoted his considerable energies primarily to the conflict, rapidly increasing American fighting strength. He attended all the Allied international conferences with Churchill, Stalin, Smuts, de Gaulle, Chiang Kai-shek and others and worked tirelessly for the establishment of the United Nations. He was re-elected for a fourth term as president in November 1944, but died from a cerebral haemorrhage on 12 April 1945, less than a month before Hitler's suicide and Germany's surrender. He was succeeded by his vice-president, Harry S. Truman.

Rot (Red) Operational code name for the German plans in the event of the takeover of Czechoslovakia (1938) being resisted.

Rotmistrov, Pavel Alekseyevich (1901-1982) Soviet General, later Chief Marshal of Armour (equivalent to Marshal of the Soviet Union) (1962). Rotmistrov joined the Red Army and Communist Party in 1919 and fought in the ranks during the Civil War. He went to a command school in 1924 and became a platoon commander, rising to battalion command by 1931 when he attended the Frunze Academy. From 1931-37 he served in divisional and army HQs and commanded a rifle regiment. During the Russo-Finnish War of 1939-40 he commanded a tank battalion and was Chief of Staff of 35th Tank Brigade. From May 1941 he was Chief of Staff of 3rd Mechanized Corps, one of the new giant formations which were dismantled as the Germans tore through Soviet territory. In September he commanded 8th (later 3rd Guards) Tank Brigade, which was involved in heavy fighting at Staraya Russa, Rogachev and then in the counter-offensive at Moscow. From April 1942 he commanded 7th Tank (later 3rd Guards Tank) Corps, one of the first powerful armoured formations to be reintroduced after Moscow. As its commander he saw service at Stalingrad. In January 1943 it fought against von Manstein's counter-offensive and in the recapture of Rostov. From February 1943 he commanded 5th Guards Tank Army, again a relatively new type of formation, and led it at Prokhorovka during the battle of Kursk, the largest tank battle of the war. He took the crucial decision to order close fighting, since German tanks' guns outranged his. He continued to lead 5th Guards Tank Army as a strike force of the Voronezh and Steppe (later 2nd Ukrainian) Fronts through the Belgorod-Kharkov, and Korsun-ShevchenkovskiyOperations. In Summer 1944 it was part of 3rd Byelorussian Front in the Byelorussian Operation. From August 1944 he was deputy commander of Soviet Armoured and Mechanized Forces. After the war Rotmistrov commanded the armoured and mechanized forces of the Group of Soviet Forces, Germany and the Far East. From 1948-58 he taught at the General Staff Academy and from 1958 was head of the Tank Academy. From 1964 to 1968 he was deputy Minister of Defence, and then a senior Inspector-General of the Armed Forces. He was uniquely qualified to take a broad but informed view of the development of armour, and his published works and possession of the distinguished Degree of Doctor of Military Science (1956) indicate that he was more academic in his outlook than some other front line commanders. Fusing theory and practice (like Guderian), he was one of the outstanding tank commanders of the war.

RSHA (*Reichssicherheitshauptamt*) The Reich Central Security Department that was the co-ordinating body for the activities of Nazi Germany's police, security and intelligence organizations.

Rumyantsev Operational code name for the Soviet counter-offensive mounted at the southern end of the Kursk salient, August 1943. It followed Operation *Citadel*.

Runstedt, Gerd von (1875-1953) German field marshal. A Prussian officer, he was retired by 1939, but was recalled to command Army Group A for the invasion of Poland in September. In May 1940, commanding the same formations, he was responsible for the German breakthrough at Sedan, which cut off the BEF. For this, he was promoted field marshal. In 1941, Runstedt commanded Army Group South in its drive through the Ukraine but, in November, was dismissed by Hitler when he advocated withdrawal to shorten the German front. In 1942, however, he was reinstated and appointed Commander-in-Chief West, with responsibility for all German defences from the Netherlands to the Spanish frontier. On 1 July 1944, after the Allied invasion, he was again dismissed and replaced by Kluge, and later Model. In September of that year, Runstedt was recalled by Hitler to command in the west but by then, even an officer of his consummate skills could not avert the coming German disaster. He was in nominal command of the Ardennes offensive (in which he had little confidence) and after its failure, retired from active service in March 1945. He was captured on 1 May by American troops and interned, but was subsequently released because of ill-health. Runstedt was one of the few German commanders whose views Hitler listened to with respect.

SA (*Sturmabteilung*) Storm troopers, the street fighters of the Nazi Party before Hitler came to power, led by Ernst Roehm. It was a million strong by 1933, committed to Socialist revolution in Germany. The SA did not accept Hitler's declaration in Feb. 1934 that their function, now that the Nazi Party was in power, had come to an end. Its influence was eroded after the 'Night of the Long Knives' (30 June 1934), when Hitler ordered it to be purged. Roehm and many others were murdered by the SS, after which the SS under Himmler became the predominant uniformed political force in Germany and, later, occupied Europe.

SACEUR Supreme Allied Commander Europe

SACMED Supreme Allied Commander Mediterranean

Salmon Trap Operational code name for the German plan to sabotage the Murmansk railway, 1943.

SAS Special Air Service (British)

Saturn *see Hardihood*

SCAEF Supreme Commander Allied Expeditionary Force

Scorched earth The policy of destroying, mainly by fire, everything in the path of an advancing army, to prevent their living off occupied land; it was adopted by Stalin during the German invasion of the USSR in 1941.

Scorcher Operational code name for the British occupation of Crete, May-June 1941.

SD (*Sicherheitsdienst*) The SS's own security service formed in 1932 under Reinhard Heydrich; later part of the state security organization.

SEAC Southeast Asia Command

Sealion *see Seelöwe*

Secret Intelligence Service (SIS) *see MI6*.

Seelöwe (Sealion) German operational code name for their planned, but not implemented, invasion of Great Britain during the Summer of 1940.

Sextant Code name for the Cairo Conference, 22-26 November 1943.

SHAEF Supreme Headquarters Allied Expeditionary Force

Shimonoseki, Treaty of Signed on 17 April 1895, ending the war between China and Japan. By its terms, the victorious Japanese abolished Chinese suzerainty over Korea and acquired Taiwan and Port Arthur among other possessions. However, France, Germany and Russia combined to make Japan relinquish her claim to Port Arthur. Japan nevertheless regarded the Treaty as a cornerstone and precedent for subsequent territorial claims on mainland Asia.

Shingle Operational code name for Allied amphibious landings at Anzio, 22 January 1944, designed to hasten the advance of General Mark Clark's US 5th Army up the west coast of Italy towards Rome.

Sho-Go (Victory) Operational code name for the Japanese defence plan, Summer 1944. The plan included the defence of the Philippines, Formosa and the Ryukyus, Japan itself and the Kuriles. The battle of Leyte Gulf followed.

Sickle Operational code name for the build-up in Britain of the US 8th Air Force, 1942.

Sikorski, Wladyslaw (1881-1943) Polish soldier and statesman. After the collapse of his country in 1939, he became prime minister of the Polish Government in exile, in which capacity he assembled an army of some 100,000 men in Great Britain. He was killed in an aircraft crash.

Simpson, William H. (1888-1980) US general, leader of the 9th Army during the fighting in north-west Europe in 1944 and 1945. He served in France during the First World War and, in the inter-war years, commanded the 30th and then the 35th Divisions; subsequently he headed XII Corps. In 1943 he was promoted Lieutenant-General and later given command of the 9th Army. Simpson's army was transferred from Bradley's 12th Army Group to Montgomery's 21st Army Group in December 1944 during the German offensive in the Ardennes. After the German thrust had been contained, Simpson's army remained under Montgomery, forming the right wing of his advance towards the Rhine. He served his British superior with unswerving loyalty. Early in April 1945, however, 9th Army was again placed under Bradley's command, but Simpson was instructed not to advance from his positions on the Elbe, since the Allies had agreed–with momentous consequences for the post-war world–that the Soviets should capture Berlin. Simpson was a man of high intelligence, was meticulous in his planning and had sound military judgement. In contrast to many commanders of the war, he was utterly professional and without vanity.

SIS (Secret Intelligence Service) US Army cryptographic unit formed in the inter-war years under the leadership of Wiliam Friedman. Renamed the Signal Security Service and, later, the Signal Security Agency, it was responsible for unravelling the Japanese *Purple* diplomatic cipher and handling the intelligence they obtained, codenamed *Magic*.

SIS Secret Intelligence Service (British) *see MI6*

Slapstick Operational code name for the British 1st Airborne Division landing at Taranto, 9 September 1943.

Sledgehammer Operational code name for a planned Allied landing on the French coast in late 1942 in the event of a Russian crisis on the Eastern Front.

Slim, Sir William (1891-1970) British field marshal. He had seen action during the First World War at Gallipoli and at Baghdad, where he was awarded the Military Cross. Subsequently he served in India, the Sudan and the Near East. In 1942 he commanded the I Burma Corps and masterminded the retreat of British and colonial troops in the face of overwhelming Japanese superiority. On 16 October 1943 he was appointed to command the 14th Army in Burma. His decisive achievements were his victories over the Japanese at the battles of Kohima/Imphal (7 March-22 June 1944) and Meiktila/Mandalay (14 January-28 March 1945). A strong-willed man of outstandingly clear mind, Slim imbued all who served under him with total confidence. After the war he served first as Chief of the Imperial General Staff, and then as Governor-General of Australia.

Smuts, Jan Christiaan (1870-1950) South African political leader and general. He fought against the British from 1899 to 1902 in the Boer War but was later reconciled to them and fought on their side against the Germans in East Africa during the First World War. From 1917 to 1918 he was a member of the British War Cabinet. He served two terms as South Africa's Prime Minister; his second election to office (1939-48) was based largely upon his avowed commitment to bringing his country into the war on the Allied side. Under his direction South African units played a significant role notably in the air war and in North Africa and subsequently in Italy and north-west Europe. His advice on military and Commonwealth matters was highly valued by Churchill, and Smuts attended many of the major Allied war conferences.

SOE *see Special Operations Executive*

SOS Service of Supply (US)

Spaatz, Carl (1891-1974) US general in command of American army air forces in Europe during the Second World War. After training at a flying school (1915-16), he saw action on the Western Front during the First World War. In 1939 he was on the staff of Air Force Combat Command, and the following year was sent to England as observer during the Battle of Britain. He became Chief of Staff of the new Army Air Forces in 1941, and then Commanding General of the Air Force Combat Command in 1942, when he helped to organize the establishment and deployment of the 8th Air Force in Britain. Like General Arnold he was an enthusiast for strategic bombardment. When Eisenhower appointed him Theatre Air Officer (Europe) in August 1942, he assumed overall responsibility for American air strategy against Italy and Germany. Unlike the British he favoured the bombing of selected targets through precision attacks on key industrial sectors, particularly oil, aviation industry and transportation. American forces attacked by day increase accuracy, but sustained heavy losses. To reduce these Spaatz introduced 'aircraft boxes', layer upon layer of bombers flying in close formation to increase their defensive fire-power against fighters. Only with the introduction of long-range fighters, however, was it possible to inflict serious damage on the German economy and air force. From 1944 precision bombing was very effective in reducing aircraft production, fuel oil output and the German transport system. Bombing placed a ceiling on German war production and by Autumn 1944 had brought the German economy close to the point of collapse. Spaatz was also a champion of close co-operation between air forces and the ground army, and developed a close working relationship with Eisenhower, the army commander. When the European war was finished he was transferred to the Japanese theatre, where strategic bombardment, culminating with the atomic bomb attacks in August 1945, successfully destroyed the Japanese will-to-resist without the need for invasion.

Spartacus Party A left-wing group of Germans, named after the Roman gladiator who had led a slave revolt against Rome in the first century BC. The leading figures were Rosa Luxemburg and Karl Liebknecht. Their object was to conclude peace with the Allies in 1916 and establish a working-class dictatorship. After the Treaty of Versailles, they committed various terrorist attacks against the government of the new republic. On 6 January 1919, when a general strike was called, they occupied a number of government offices. They were overcome and both Luxemburg and Liebknecht were arrested, and later killed.

Special Operations Executive (SOE) Formed in July 1940 out of two small SIS and War Office departments, SOE's remit was, in Churchill's words, to 'Set Europe Ablaze' and to foment resistance in German and, later, Japanese occupied territories. It supplied organizers, instructors, communications, weapons and equipment to tens of thousands of resisters throughout the war. Its relations with other government bodies and the military establishment were not always harmonious and this contributed to its disbandment in 1946.

Speer, Albert (1905-1981) German architect and Nazi leader. He joined the party in 1931 and was later appointed by Hitler official architect. Among his work was the grandiose stadium at Nuremberg. Speer was a highly gifted organizer and in 1942 Hitler appointed him Minister for Armaments, on the death of Fritz Todt. From 1943 onwards, he assumed many of the discredited Goering's responsibilities as head of the German war economy. Despite Allied bombing, Speer rejuvenated German production, so that in September 1944 it reached its greatest output. Speer, who always had access to Hitler, did much in the last months of the war to thwart the *Führer*'s scorched-earth policy. He was condemned by the Nuremberg war criminals court to 20 years imprisonment. He was freed in 1966. Speer was one of the few Nazi leaders to admit any guilt for war crimes, to which he freely alluded in his writing, notably *Inside the Third Reich* (1970), after his release from captivity.

Spruance, Raymond A. (1886-1969) American admiral. A calm, decisive officer, but receptive to advice from his subordinates, Spruance commanded Task Force 16 at the battle of Midway and, given freedom of movement by his immediate superior, Admiral Fletcher, was able to employ his great ability to anticipate an enemy's intentions while disguising his own. Spruance, unlike many commanders of the Second World War, disliked personal publicity and gave no interviews until after his retirement.

SS (*Schützstaffel*) Elite arm of the Nazi Party, established by Hitler in 1925 from his personal guard units and shock troops. By 1929 it comprised some 50,000 men and had become the security arm of the Nazi Party, under Heinrich Himmler. Combat formations, the Waffen SS, were developed as an élite force operating as a Nazi wing with the German Army. Formed in 1935, by 1943 there were only four divisions, principally armoured. Following SS Adolf Hitler division's success in halting a Soviet advance at Kharkov, the Waffen SS was rapidly expanded by conscripting throughout the Reich and occupied territories, reaching a strength of 40 divisions by 1945. They were noted for their ruthless efficiency and cruelty, especially in participating in the realization of Hitler's Final Solution, and in quelling both the ghetto and 1944 uprisings in Warsaw. They saw action as front line troops in every theatre of the German war.

SSS *see* **SIS**

Stalin, Josef Vissarionovich (1879-1953) Dictator of the USSR who established his supremacy after the death (1924) of Lenin. Born in Georgia, Stalin became a revolutionary in 1899 and was first arrested for conspiracy in 1902. The son of a shoemaker, Stalin (his adopted name, meaning 'man of steel' - his original name was Dzhugashvili) continued his subversive activities in the Caucasus on his release from prison. He was repeatedly arrested between 1902 and 1913 but always managed to escape. In 1912, by then in St Petersburg, he became one of the first editors of *Pravda*. He was again arrested in 1913 and exiled for life to Siberia, but was released under amnesty after the February 1917 revolution. Stalin quickly emerged as a leading Bolshevik and assembled a group of politicians loyal to him. In 1917, he became People's Commissar for Nationalities in the Soviet government and was General Secretary of the Soviet Union from 1922 until his death. Stalin eliminated all rivals after the death of Lenin in 1924, and embarked on a savage purge of the higher military ranks, the terror reaching its height in the years 1937-38. From 1928 he inaugurated a series of Five Year Plans designed to transform Soviet industry and to collectivize Soviet agriculture. These were only partly successful, the latter resulting in enormous loss of life and forcible resettlement in the eastern republics. This period saw the emergence of a repressive, authoritarian state, bolstered by the political machinery of a full police state. Stalin signed a non-aggression pact with Nazi Germany in August 1939, which resulted in the Russian invasion of eastern Poland and Finland, and led ultimately to the successful resistance to German invasion. Nevertheless, like Hitler, Stalin soon assumed personal control of all military operations, and demanded unquestioning obedience. Stalin's contribution to ultimate victory over Germany is a matter of keen dispute; probably, his forceful leadership and brutal indifference to the suffering of his people, notably during the siege of Leningrad, made a greater contribution than his military expertise. He was undoubtedly served well by talented military commanders such as Zhukov, Chuikov and Koniev. Stalin was a talented diplomat and at the various Allied conferences during and after the European war he won considerable concessions, especially from the ailing Roosevelt, which ensured Soviet domination of large parts of eastern Europe and inaugurated the Cold War. At home, his repressions and persecutions were resumed. Three years after his death his regime was denounced by Khrushchev and de-Stalinization programmes began, although his political legacy remained. Only in the late 1980s did a full reassessment of his role in modern Russian history begin to emerge.

Starvation Operation code name for the American mining of the Japanese home waters, begun March 1945.

Stauffenberg, Claus von (1907-44) German colonel. He had served with distinction and bravery (he was badly wounded in North Africa) in the early campaigns but later became disenchanted with Hitler and his regime and was involved in the July Plot conspiracy to kill the *Führer* (1944). It was Stauffenberg who carried the bomb into Hitler's headquarters. When Hitler escaped the ensuing blast, Stauffenberg, who had flown to Berlin, was seized and shot.

Stavka (of the Supreme High Command (Soviet)). *Stavka* is an old Russian word for a warrior chief's encampment, and implies the highest military-political authority. In the First World War, the *Stavka* had been the headquarters of the Russian Supreme Commander, first Grand Duke Nikolay Nikolayevich, then Tsar Nicholas II himself. In the Second World War, the *Stavka* of the Main Command (*Stavka glavnogo komandovaniya*) was set up on 23 June 1941, by an order of the USSR Council of People's Commissars and the Party Central Committee. It included People's Commissar of Defence Timoshenko (President), Voroshilov, Molotov, Stalin, Zhukov (Chief of the General Staff), Budenny and Admiral Kuznetsov. On 10 July it was renamed *Stavka* of the Supreme Command (*Verkhovnogo Komandovaniya*) and on 8 August *Stavka* of the Supreme High Command (*Verkhovnogo Glavnokomandovaniya*) when Stalin adopted that title. *Stavka* controlled military activity of all the Soviet Union's Armed Forces, but under the direction of the State Defence Committee (GKO), thus fulfilling the Leninist principle of 'unity of political and military direction of armed struggle'. Communication between *Stavka* and commanders of fronts was accomplished by inviting the latter to *Stavka* briefings, and also by sending *Stavka* representatives to supervise and advise Front headquarters and co-ordinate operations on more than one front. Eminent *Stavka* representatives were Zhukov, Vasilevskiy, Voroshilov, Timoshenko, Shaposhnikov, Antonov, Novikov, Kuznetsov and Voronov.

Steinbock Operational code name for the series of German air raids against London and other cities, especially on the English south coast, between 21 January and 29 May 1944, ordered by Hitler to take the war to the British Isles once again. German losses were heavy and the 'Baby Blitz' was abandoned when the Allied invasion of northern Europe seemed imminent.

Stilwell, Joseph Warren (1883-1946) American general. He fought in the First World War and then, for about 13 years, served in China, into which country he gained a deep insight. Between 1942 and 1944 he was Chief of Staff to Chiang Kai-shek and commander of all US land forces in the area of China, Burma and India. After the Japanese overran much of the area, the Joint Chiefs of Staff wanted him to take command of all Chinese forces. Stilwell, however, though an astute commander, was opinionated, tactless and difficult to work with (he was known as 'Vinegar Joe') and Chiang had him recalled to the US in October 1944. In 1945, Stilwell was made Chief of Army Ground Forces and commanded the 10th Army on Okinawa after the death of Buckner.

Stimson, Henry (1867-1950) American politician, Secretary of War throughout the Second World War. A Republican, though serving in Roosevelt's administration, he strongly advocated sending aid to Great Britain and, after Pearl Harbor, supported the British view that Germany should be defeated first, Japan later. Stimson, who attended all the Allied conferences, was among those who urged President Truman to use the atom bomb against Japan.

Strangle Operational code name for Allied air attacks on communications targets in central Italy, March 1944.

Student, Kurt (1891-1973) German general, creator of the German airborne forces. He served in the First World War as a fighter pilot and subsequently helped plan and develop the *Luftwaffe*. He, more than any other, devised the tactic commonly known as 'vertical envelopment', by which paratroopers were dropped or landed behind enemy lines. Sophisticated weaponry and equipment were developed under his direction to meet the paratroopers' needs. In all this he had the support of Goering, and in July 1938 Student was appointed by him to command the 7th Parachute Division. His first opportunity to prove the soundness of his theories came during the invasion of the Low Countries and France (1940), when some of his men were designated to capture the crucial Belgian fortress of Eben Emael, guarding a crucial crossing of the Meuse; all objectives were swiftly reached. In 1941, Student drew up plans for an airborne attack on Crete; this received Hitler's endorsement and was successfully accomplished, but almost a quarter of the landing force was killed. His formations, though increased in number, thereafter played a ground role in the war–mainly in Sicily, Italy, Normandy and the Ardennes–but elsewhere they were employed as elite infantry. Student was one of the ablest innovators of the war, adapting new technologies to form an original, largely successful tactical arm.

Symbol Code name for the Casablanca Conference, 14-23 January 1943.

TAF Tactical Air Force (US)

Taifun (Typhoon) Operational code name for the German drive towards Moscow, September 1941.

Tanaka, Raizo (1892-1969) Japanese rear-admiral. A veteran destroyer commander, he led the landing force at the battle of Midway and was later placed in command of the Guadalcanal Reinforcement Force. Though known in the Japanese Navy as 'Tanaka the tenacious', he became convinced, after the Americans gained control of Henderson Field, that Guadalcanal was indefensible and that Japanese forces should be withdrawn. His advice was ignored with inevitable results: after six months of costly fighting on both land and sea, what remained of the Japanese force was evacuated. His sound appraisal of the situation on Guadalcanal brought about his dismissal.

TBS Talk Between Ships

Tedder, Sir Arthur William (1890-1967) British air commander. He flew in France during the First World War and later (1941-43) commanded the Royal Air Force in the Middle East, where, with consummate skill, he made best use of limited strength in the early months against German forces in the Balkans and North Africa. He was appointed commander-in-chief of the Mediterranean Air Command in 1943, in which capacity he worked with Eisenhower and was responsible for co-ordinating land and air operations during the invasion of Sicily and Italy. In 1944 he acted as Eisenhower's deputy in preparing Operation *Overlord*, planning the preparatory bombing operations and tactical air support during and after the Normandy landings. In May 1945 he signed the instrument of surrender of the German forces on Eisenhower's behalf. A man of cool mind, wit and untiring energy, in 1946 Tedder became Chief of Air Staff and was elevated to the peerage.

Ten-Go Operational code name for the Japanese naval offensive off Okinawa and Iwo Jima, April-July 1945.

Terminal Code name for the Potsdam Conference, 17 July-2 August 1945.

TF Task Force (Allied, navy)

TG Task Group (Allied, navy)

Thunderclap Operational code name for the Allied air attack on Dresden, February 1945.

Tidal Wave Operational code name for the USAAF bombing of the Ploesti oilfields, Rumania, 1 August 1943.

Tiger Operational code name for the offensive (13-22 June 1940) by the 1st Army of General von Leeb's Army Group C through the Maginot Line, the northern pincer of the German attack on France; also the code name for a British merchant convoy carrying aircraft and tanks to Egypt (5-12 May 1941) for deployment in Operation *Battleaxe*.

Timoshenko, Semyon Konstantinovich (1895-1970) Soviet marshal. He was a cavalry commander during the Russian civil war (1918-20) and later (1940) commanded Soviet troops in their final offensives against the Finns. He was Vice-Commissar for Defence from 1941 to 1945 under Stalin. He replaced the discredited Budenny on the Southern Front and in November recaptured Rostov. In the next three years he commanded on various fronts - the North-west (1942), the Caucasus (1943) and Bessarabia (1944) - but is chiefly remembered for his skill in relieving Moscow in 1941.

Tito, born Josip Broz (1892-1980) Yugoslav Communist partisan leader and later (1945-80) President of Yugoslavia. A blacksmith's son, he fought with the Imperial Austro-Hungarian Army in the First World War, during which he was captured by the Russians. He then served with the Bolshevik Army during the Russian civil war (1918-20), after which he returned to Croatia, where he became a leading organizer of labour unions. Between 1929 and 1934 he was imprisoned as a political agitator, but in 1937 he was assigned the task of reorganizing the Yugoslav Communist Party. In 1941, he emerged as leader of guerrilla resistance to the occupying Axis powers, despite the support which the Yugoslav government in exile gave to Mihailović, the Serbian resistance leader. Tito's success as a guerrilla leader may be attributed to his lightning tactics, his dynamic personality, his stamina and, above all, to his ruthlessness in the cause of Communism and Yugoslav independence. During his leadership of the partisans he received little aid from the USSR but, from 1944 onwards, great airborne assistance from the USA and Great Britain. Tito was proclaimed marshal in December 1943 and in 1944 his partisans worked with the Red Army in driving the Germans out of Yugoslavia. Tito then became the dominant figure in the Federal People's Republic of Yugoslavia. The monarchy was abolished, Mihailović was summarily executed and other opposition figures, notably the Archbishop of Zagreb, were imprisoned. Tito, thereafter virtual dictator of Yugoslavia, co-operated with the USSR but frequently took an independent line. In 1948 his intransigence led to Yugoslavia's being expelled from the Comintern. He subsequently tried to evolve common policies with other non-aligned leaders, notably Nehru and Nasser. He was nevertheless repeatedly re-elected president and in 1963 he was granted the appointment for life.

Tojo, Hideki (1884-1948) Japanese military commander and statesman. He became Prime Minister in October 1941, his accession marking the triumph of the pro-war military party. A chairman rather than a despot, Tojo nevertheless strongly advocated war against the USA and Great Britain. He supported the attack on Pearl Harbor and subsequent Japanese expansion in the Pacific, but neither he nor his German counterparts proved capable of devising a uniform grand strategy during the war. In July 1944 Tojo, a gifted organizer but without superlative military gifts, resigned when the Americans captured Saipan in the Mariana Islands. The war was clearly lost but as late as April 1945 he was recommending that it should be fought to the last. In September of that year he made an abortive attempt at suicide, was arrested by the Allies, tried, found guilty of war crimes and executed.

Tolbukhin, Fedor I. (1894-1949) Russian marshal. He commanded the 57th Army at the battle of Stalingrad and then the Third Ukrainian Front. In this capacity he played a significant role in the major battles for the recovery of the Ukraine, and led his Front into eastern Europe. In 1945 he commanded Soviet occupation forces in Austria.

Torch Operational code name for the Allied landings in French North Africa, 8 November 1942.

Totalize Operational code name for the Canadian First Army's attack towards Falaise, 8 August 1944.

Trident Code name for the Third Washington Conference, 11-17 May 1943.

Tripartite Pact Agreement signed on 27 September 1940 between Germany, Italy and Japan, setting up full military and political alliance (the Rome-Berlin-Tokyo Axis) to support one another in the event of the war spreading beyond Europe.

Truman, Harry S. (1884-1972) 33rd President of the USA. He grew up on a Missouri farm and his family's poverty prevented his attending college. During the First World War he served as a captain on the Western Front. After the war, Truman worked for a time as co-partner in a haberdashery store but soon turned to politics. In 1934 he won a seat in the Senate as a Democrat. By 1940 he was a renowned figure in American politics for his chairmanship of a committee that revealed gross instances of fraud in the national defence budget. Truman was nominated for vice-president in 1944 and was duly elected in Roosevelt's shadow. In the following year (12 April) he succeeded Roosevelt as president on the latter's death. As with most American vice-presidents, he had been largely kept in ignorance of high matters of state and had at first heavily to rely on advisers, but he soon proved himself his own master and of independent mind. When told of the first successful atomic bomb test, he immediately authorized its military use against Japan to save both Allied and enemy lives by bringing the war swiftly to an end. After the war, Truman used America's great economic strength to resuscitate the devastated countries of Europe, notably through the European Recovery Program (the Marshall Plan) of financial assistance. Despite general predictions to the contrary, Truman was re-elected president in 1948. During his second term in office he supported the formation of the North Atlantic Treaty Organization (NATO) in response to the Soviet-inspired Warsaw Pact, and in 1950 authorized the entry of the USA into the Korean conflict.

Turner, Richmond K. (1885-1961) American vice-admiral, commander of the US Amphibious Force. Ordered to the Pacific in 1942, he developed the perilous art of ship-to-shore landings under fire, supervising notable operations at Guadalcanal (the first major US amphibious operation in the Pacific against a hostile coast) and at Iwo Jima, where he commanded Task Force 52. Able but opinionated, he frequently caused friction among his colleagues by giving unsolicited advice in the form of instructions.

Typhoon *see* Taifun

U-Go Operational code name for the Japanese drive on India from Burma, March-July 1944.

Ultra The code name (and attached security classification) given to the British system for intercepting, decrypting, interpreting and distributing German signals encyphered on the Enigma machine. The product of the system was known as '*Ultra* intelligence'. The system control on the Government Code and Cypher School (GCCS) of Bletchley Park.

Uranus Operational code name for the Soviet offensive at Stalingrad, which encircled the German 6th Army, 19 November 1942.

USAAF US Army Air Force (formerly US Army Air Corps)

USAAC US Army Air Corps *see* USAAF

USN US Navy

USS US Ship

USSTAF US Strategic Air Force

Valkyrie Operational code name for the security operations if there were to be a revolt by slave labour in Germany. Also used by the Stauffenberg conspirators as a cover name for the July Bomb Plot 1944.

Vanguard Operational code name for the Allied plan to capture Rangoon, 1944.

Varsity Operational code name for the Allied airborne crossing of the Rhine, 24 March 1945.

Vasilevski, Aleksandr Mikhailovich (1895-1977) Soviet Marshal. Vasilevski served in the First World War and joined the Red Army in 1919. After serving as a regimental commander, in 1937 he went to the General Staff and in 1940 became head of its Operational Directorate (War Planning). He continued to serve there in the opening phases of the war, and in June 1942 became Chief of the General Staff and a Deputy People's Commissar for Defence. He played a major part in the plan for the counter-offensive at Stalingrad. Although a *Stavka* representative, he believed in leading from the front and was actually wounded in the recapture of Sevastopol. In 1943 he was promoted Marshal, and was made a Hero of the Soviet Union twice (29 July 1944 and 8 May 1945). In June 1945, he was nominated Commander-in-Chief of Soviet forces in the Far East, controlling three fronts in the invasion of Manchuria. After the war, Vasilevski became Chief of the General Staff, and from 1949 to March 1953 Minister for the Armed Forces, as well as holding a number of Deputy Minister of Defence posts.

Vatutin, Nikolai F. (1901-1944) Soviet general. He distinguished himself, through personal bravery and coolness in adversity, in many sectors of the Russian Front and, during the Battle of Stalingrad, when he was the Commander-in-Chief of the Voronezh Front. In 1944, while commanding the First Ukrainian Front, he was killed in an ambush, reputedly mounted by Ukrainian Nationalist partisans.

Veritable Initially called *Valediction*, operational code name for Montgomery's British and Canadian offensive between the Maas and Rhine rivers, (8-21 February 1945), to give the Allies an entry to Germany through the Netherlands.

Versailles, Treaty of (1919) The most important of five treaties between the Allies and the Central Powers and their satellites that concluded the First World War, collectively known as the Treaty of Paris. The Treaty of Versailles, between the Allies and Germany (which was not consulted as to its terms) dubbed Germany the aggressor. Alsace and Lorraine were restored to France, former German colonies were placed under League of Nations mandate, and most of west Prussia was given to Poland; in addition, the Saar territory was placed under French administration and the Rhineland occupied by the Allies, both for 15 years. The German Army was henceforth restricted to 100,000 men and she was forbidden to build major warships, or possess U-boats and military aircraft. For Germany, the most ruinous clause of the treaty was the imposition of reparations, which she could not subsequently meet. The very harshness of the treaty's terms, largely imposed at French insistence, assisted Hitler and the Nazis in their rise to power. The Treaty of Saint-Germain (1919) with Austria declared the Austro-Hungarian Empire dissolved and instituted the new republic of Austria, largely comprising German-speaking members of the old empire. The Treaty of Trianon (1920) between the Allies and Hungary reduced the size of the latter by some two-thirds; Rumania received Transylvania, for which she had imprudently entered the war. Hungarian military strength was restricted to 35,000 men. The Treaty of Neuilly (1919) compelled Bulgaria to relinquish territory and population to Greece, Yugoslavia and Rumania, while the Treaty of Lausanne (1923) gave Turkey most of her modern territory; the Arab provinces were partitioned between Britain and France; Italy secured only the Dodecanese, while the 'independent Arab state' in Damascus fell to the French in July 1920.

Vlasov, Andrei (1900-46) Soviet lieutenant-general and leader of a German puppet army. His first ambition was to be a priest but he was conscripted into the Soviet infantry after the October Revolution. He was rapidly promoted and in 1929, the year he joined the Communist Party, he rose to command a regiment. By 1940 he had become one of the youngest generals in the Red Army. Late in 1941, having distinguished himself as commander of IV Tank Corps in the Lwów area during the German invasion, he was posted to Moscow to assume command of the newly-raised 20th Army, an élite formation of Siberian units designated by Stalin as part of a strategic reserve for the Winter counter-attack. Vlasov remained confident, even when the Germans were within 18 miles of Moscow. His first infantry attacks were launched on 4 December, followed, when weak German sections were identified, by Soviet armour. The advance of 20th Army, though slow, was irresistible. By 23 January 1942, the Germans had been driven back along the northern approaches to Moscow and the capital had been saved. Vlasov was now a Soviet hero but in his next appointment, command of 2nd Shock Army, fighting to relieve Leningrad, he was captured by the Germans on the Volkhov Front. In captivity, he became an ardent anti-Communist and volunteered to raise an army of Russian prisoners of war to fight against the Soviets. Hitler allowed him to raise a Russian Liberation Army (KONR) but used it mainly for its propaganda value. In 1945 the Americans handed him over to the Russians, who took him to Moscow, where he was tried *in camera* as a traitor and executed.

Volksdeutsche People of German extraction who lived outside Germany, especially in the former Habsburg empire. Hitler was concerned to gather those *Volksdeutsche* who had settled in other countries back into the Reich. The *Volksdeutsche* who lived in occupied countries were given special privileges and positions of authority.

Voronov, Nikolay Nikolayevich (1899-1968) Soviet Chief Marshal of Artillery. Voronov joined the Red Army in 1918 and fought in the Civil War. Between 1937 and 1940 he was Chief of Red Army Artillery, and then for a short while a Deputy Chief of the Main Artillery Directorate (a temporary fall from favour). He also gained combat experience in Mongolia (Khalkin Gol) and in the 1939-40 Soviet Finnish War. As a *Stavka* representative and Colonel General of Artillery, he signed the ultimatum to Paulus to surrender at Stalingrad, and was put in charge of the destruction of the encircled grouping. In 1944 he became the first of only three holders to date of the rank of Chief Marshal of Artillery (equivalent to Marshal of the Soviet Union). After the war, from 1950-53, he was president of the Academy of Artillery Sciences, the organization which fronted ballistic missile, nuclear warheads and space research.

Voroshilov, Kliment Yefremovich (1881-1969) Soviet Marshal and senior State and Party functionary. Son of a railway worker, he joined the Communist Party (1903), making him alongside Stalin one of the oldest generation of Soviet Communists to hold office during the Second World War. He was active before the First World War, first meeting Lenin in 1906. He participated in the February Revolution of 1917 and was active in forming Red Guard Units before the October Revolution. Commissar for Petrograd from November, 1917, he organized the Lugansk Detachment which helped defend Kharkov against German forces in early 1918, and paid particular attention to the organization of cavalry forces. In 1919 he commanded 14th Army and was an organizer and staff member of the First Cavalry Army from 1919-21. He was thus, alongside Budenny, a member of the old Bolshevik-cavalry clique which survived when many of the former Tsarist officers and military intellectuals were purged. From 1921-24 he commanded forces in the North Caucasus Military District, rooting out armed guerrilla opposition to the Soviet regime. He worked with Frunze on the 1924-25 Military reforms, and after the latter's untimely and suspicious death became People's Commissar for Military and Naval Affairs and from 1934 to 1940 People's Commissar for Defence. He was one of the first five Marshals of the Soviet Union created in 1935, and, with Budenny, one of only two to survive into World War II. Voroshilov was the Soviet defence supremo during the crucial period of military reform and industrialization, though ably advised and assisted by such first rate minds as Tukhachevski. He made an important contribution to modernising the Red Army and equipping it to fight a mechanized war of manoeuvre, although the most radical and futuristic ideas came from others. In August 1939 Voroshilov headed the Soviet delegation which negotiated with Britain and France about the possibility of an anti-Hitler coalition. On the outbreak of war in 1941 he became a member of the State Defence Committee (GKO) and the *Stavka*. Were it not for his close association with Stalin, he might have suffered savagely for the Red Army's lack of preparedness. From 10 July to 31 August, 1941 he commanded the North West 'Strategic Direction', a higher command concept involving control of multiple Fronts, and from 5 to 12 September 1941 briefly commanded the Leningrad Front. He found a more natural niche as an adviser to the partisan effort and, from 6 September to 19 November, 1942, as its formal commander. He briefed partisan commanders personally before their insertion behind German lines. In January 1943 he was *Stavka* co-ordinator of the Leningrad and Volkhov Fronts during the breakthrough of the Leningrad blockade. From December 1943 he supervised a naval and military operations during the recapture of the Crimea. He also participated in the Moscow (1941) and Teheran (1943) conferences. After the war he was president of the Soviet control commission in Hungary (1945-47). From 1946-53 he was deputy President of the Council of Ministers and on Stalin's death, in 1953, became President of the USSR. In 1960 Khrushchev forced him to take a back seat in the Praesidium of the Party Central Committee.

Vulcan Operational code name for the final Allied offensive in Tunisia, 6 May 1943.

WAAC Women's Auxiliary Army Corps (US)

WAAF Women's Auxiliary Air Force (British)

Wacht am Rhein (Watch on the Rhine) First operational code name for the German attack on the Ardennes, December 1944; *Herbstnebel* replaced it.

Waffen SS *see SS*

WASP Women's Airforce Service Pilot (British)

WAVE Women accepted for Voluntary Emergency Service (British navy)

Wavell, Archibald Percival, Ist Earl Wavell (1883-1950) British field marshal. He served (1901) in South Africa during the Boer War and in France during the First World War. Later he fought under General Allenby in Palestine, where he learned the desert tactics that in the Second World War were to equip him so well for command in North Africa. In July 1939 he was given the Middle East command and in the Winter of 1940-41 he drove the Italians from both Cyrenaica and Ethiopia. Early in 1941, however, having been ordered to divert forces to Greece, he lost Cyrenaica. Though no blame attached to him (his limited forces were also operating in Iraq and Syria) he was ordered to change places with Auchinleck, then military commander in India. He had no option but to abandon Burma in the face of massive Japanese formations, particularly as he had little assistance from home. Nevertheless, in June 1943, to his surprise, he was appointed Viceroy. By then Indian independence was inevitable and he worked ceaselessly to find terms that would enable Muslims and Hindus to work harmoniously together in a united India, but their bitter intransigence frustrated him. In February 1947 he relinquished his post to Lord Mountbatten and retired to write his reminiscences and military studies and edit poetry.

Wehrmacht The armed forces of Germany. *See OKW*

Weimar Republic (1919-1933) The state set up under the democratic constitution adopted in Germany after the abdication and flight of the Kaiser (1918) and the Treaty of Versailles following the First World War. The first president was Friedrich Ebert, who successfully sought to suppress extremists of both right and left. After his death, Field Marshal Paul von Hindenburg was elected president in 1925 and from then until 1929, under various chancellors, and despite the crippling terms of the Versailles treaty, Germany made a remarkable return to economic prosperity and was admitted to the League of Nations. But the world depression, beginning in 1929, reduced Germany to chaos, with massive inflation, companies daily rendered bankrupt and unemployment rising without check. Hindenburg, faced with the alternative of authorizing a military dictatorship or appointing Hitler Chancellor, chose the latter option and the short-lived parliamentary system of the Weimar Republic was abruptly brought to an end in 1934.

Weiss (White) Operational code name for the German invasion of Poland, 1 September 1939.

Weserübung (River exercise) Operational code name for the German invasion of Denmark and Norway, begun 9 April 1940.

Weygand, Maxime (1867-1965) French general. He had been Head of Marshal Foch's Chiefs of Staff in the First World War and, in 1935, was appointed Inspector-General of the French Army. He became Commander-in-Chief of all French armies on 19 May 1940, after Germany's breakthrough on the Western Front, in succession to the discredited Gamelin. On his appointment, he pessimistically remarked 'I do not guarantee success'. Indeed, he was shortly urging Marshal Pétain to seek an armistice. It must be said that his defence of France, using troops already dispirited by defeat in the Low Countries, was valiant, though short-lived, for it proved incapable of containing German armoured thrusts. With French units encircled by *Blitzkrieg* tactics, the end for France was inevitable. In 1941, Weygand was deported to Germany and was freed by American troops in May 1945.

Wilson, Henry Maitland, 1st Baron (1881-1964) British field marshal. He served in the Boer War and the First World War; in 1939 he became Commander of British forces in Egypt. He commanded in the Western Desert (1940-41) and Greece and Syria (1941); later (1944-45), when danger to the Allies in the area was past, he was made Supreme Allied Commander in the Mediterranean. Between 1945 and 1947, he headed the British joint staff mission in Washington.

Wingate, Orde Charles (1903-1944) British general. Wingate showed early promise as an original and unconventional commander. He served under Wavell on special duty in Palestine (1936-39), where he led a Jewish militia which used guerrilla tactics in aid of the British army during the Arab rebellion of 1936-39. In 1941, then a major, he contributed to the ousting of Italian forces from Ethiopia. In 1942 he was sent to India as a brigadier; there he created and led long-range penetration troops (known as 'Chindits') behind Japanese lines. While in command of a second operation, he was killed in an air crash. Wavell considered him to be endowed with 'military genius'.

Wintergewitter (Winter storm) General von Manstein's unsuccessful operation to relieve Stalingrad, December 1942.

Winter storm see *Wintergewitter*

WPD War Plans Division of the US War Department; effectively Marshall's operations staff

WRNS Women's Royal Naval Service (British)

WVS Women's Voluntary Service (British)

Yamamoto, Isoroku (1884-1943) Japanese fleet admiral. He knew the Americans well, having studied at Harvard and (1925-27) served as Japanese naval attaché in Washington. In 1939 he was appointed Commander-in-Chief of the Japanese Combined Fleet. He was opposed to Japan's alliance with Germany but was a forceful advocate of war with the British and American presence in Asia. Yamamoto masterminded the attack on Pearl Harbor and for the next 18 months directed Japanese naval operations in the Pacific, including the battles of the Coral Sea and Midway. On 18 April 1943, the Americans having broken the Japanese naval code knowing of his journey, his aircraft was shot down by American fighter planes over Bougainville. His death was rightly regarded as a major blow to Japanese morale at a time when their fortunes were turning, and news of his death was for a time suppressed in Japan.

Yamashita, Tomoyuki (1888-1946) Japanese general. He passed out of the Hiroshima Military Academy with honours in 1908 and was commissioned in the infantry. He further studied the military art as a military attaché in Europe. Yamashita commanded the Japanese 4th Division in northern China (1938-40) and in 1941 was appointed to lead the 25th Army for the invasion of Malaya. A well-planned and tactically inspired campaign was crowned between 8-15 February 1942, when his units captured the great British fortress port of Singapore. Later in the war (October 1944-August 1945) he commanded Japanese forces in their unsuccessful defence of the Philippines against the invading Americans. Yamashita surrendered the Philippines in September 1945, was put on trial for atrocities committed by his troops and hanged the following year.

Yellow Plan see *Fall Gelb*

Yeremenko, Andrei (1892-1970) Soviet general. He was conscripted into the army during the First World War and reached the rank of corporal. Later he fought against the White Russians in the civil war and took part in the invasion of Poland. In 1940 he was in command of an army in the Far East but was summoned to Moscow by Stalin when the Germans invaded and given command of West Front. The situation was desperate but Yeremenko, by force of personality, backed by threats, got every available aircraft into the air in his area to attack the advancing Panzer columns of Guderian and Hoth. Then he counter-attacked with a tank group equipped with the new T34 and KV models, whose armour could not be penetrated by German anti-tank guns. This was temporarily successful, helped save Moscow and badly disjointed the timetable of Operation *Barbarossa*. Yeremenko was later involved in the fighting before Moscow (where he was wounded) and then at Stalingrad. His troops liberated Prague in May 1945. He possessed outstanding tactical

skills, but was overshadowed by Zhukov and given little opportunity as a strategist.

Zeitzler, Kurt (1895-1963) German Chief of Staff of the Army from September 1942 until July 1944, when he suffered a nervous collapse. A keen admirer of Hitler, he and his master at first worked harmoniously together. They disagreed, however, over the question of withdrawal from Stalingrad. Once Zeitzler was proved correct in his analysis, after the surrender of the 6th Army, he exerted considerable influence, but later was discredited by his support for the failed counter-offensive at Kursk.

Zeppelin Operational code name for cover and deception in the Balkans, 1943.

Zhukov, Georgi Konstantinovich (1896-1974) Soviet Marshal. Son of a village cobbler. Apprenticed to a Moscow furrier, he was conscripted into the Imperial Russian Army in 1915 and assigned to the cavalry, in which he served continuously until 1938. In 1918 he joined the Red Army and in 1919 the Communist Party. During the Civil War served as Company and Squadron commander in action against counter-revolutionary guerrilla units. He remained in the Red Army after the Civil War, and in 1923 was promoted to command 39th Buzuluk Cavalry Regiment. At this stage he became acquainted with the need for a modern approach to military science, and in 1925 completed the Cavalry Higher Command course along with Rokossovski, Bagramyan and Yeremenko, who would also rise to prominence in World War II. In 1930 he was appointed to command 2nd Cavalry Brigade, and then to Assistant Cavalry Inspector of the Red Army. He then commanded 4th Cavalry Division, 3rd and 6th Cavalry Corps, and in 1938 was made deputy commander of the Byelorussian Military District. In Summer 1939 he took command of 57th Special Corps, which when reinforced was renamed 1st Army Group, to repel the Japanese incursion into Mongolia. This carried promotion to *komkor* (Lt. Gen.). His victory at the Khalkin Gol was a classic combined arms battle by a reinforced corps and a much needed shot in the arm for a Red Army beaten and bloody after Stalin's purges, which Zhukov luckily escaped. He was made a Hero of the Soviet Union for the first time, and, now an Army (full) General, was appointed to command the Kiev Special Military District, a prestigious command on the western frontier where he could put his new ideas and experience into practice. From January to July, 1941 he was Chief of the General Staff and a Deputy Minister (People's Commissar) of Defence. Zhukov correctly criticized the positioning of the fortified regions too close to the new western border prior to *Barbarossa*. On 23 June, he was appointed a member of the *Stavka*. As a *Stavka* representative he was sent to the South-West front to help organize the counterstroke by several mechanized corps in the Brody region. In August-September he commanded forces of the Reserve Front, which executed a counter offensive on the River Elni. On 12 September he took command of the Leningrad Front from Voroshilov, where, in co-operation with the Baltic Front he helped stall the German attack. In October he moved to the Western Front, where, with the Kalinin and South-West fronts he commanded a resolute defence and then the counter-attack before Moscow. In 1942-43 he coordinated the actions of several fronts at Stalingrad, Leningrad, Kursk and on the Battle of the Dnieper. Promoted a Marshal of the Soviet Union in 1943, in March to May 1944 he commanded 1st Ukrainian Front. In Summer 1944 he coordinated the actions of 1st and 2nd Byelorussian Fronts in the vast Byelorussian Strategic Offensive Operation. From November, 1944 to May 1945 he commanded 1st Byelorussian Front in the Vistula-Oder and Berlin operations. In the final assault on Berlin he temporarily incurred Stalin's ire, as his attack stalled and he committed two tank armies early, against *Stavka* instructions, but Stalin nevertheless ruled that Zhukov and not Koniev should seize the centre of the Nazi capital. It was men of Zhukov's Front who seized the Reichstag, and one of his generals, Chuikov, who reported Hitler's suicide to him on 1 May. Zhukov immediately telephoned Stalin, who had to be woken up to hear the news. On 8 May Zhukov was the first Allied commander to sign the instrument of surrender at Karlshorst, outside Berlin. Zhukov remained Commander-in-Chief of the Group of Soviet Forces, Germany, from June 1945 to March 1946, and took part in the great Victory Parade in Red Square, riding a magnificent white horse. A Deputy Minister of Defence (March-July, 1946), Zhukov then commanded the Odessa and Ural Military Districts, a period of isolation from the centre of power, in which he made only two brief public appearances (1950, 1951). He was significantly absent from the list of alleged victims of the 'Doctors' Plot' (January, 1953), by which

time he had secretly returned to be a Deputy Minister and Inspector-General. With Stalin's death, Zhukov joined Vasilevkski and Kuznetsov as a First Deputy Minister. In July, 1953, Beria, notorious head of the Secret Police was purged: it is rumoured that Zhukov and Koniev personally played a role in his arrest. Zhukov was nominated to Beria's seat on the Central Committee. Between February 1955 and October, 1957 Zhukov was in alliance with Khrushchev, and in June 1957, when Khrushchev's opponents attempted to depose him, Zhukov pledged the military's support. Although Khrushchev owed his survival to Zhukov, in October 1957, he went on a trip to Yugoslavia and returned to find himself dismissed for fostering a personal cult and attempting to remove the armed forces from party control.

Zitadelle (Citadel) Operational code name for the German attack on the Kursk salient, July 1943.

Index

THE UNDERLYING PRINCIPLE behind the spellings of geographical names in this atlas is that they should follow the forms commonly used in the years 1919-1945, so that they may be more readily related to contemporary records. Conventional English names (e.g. Moscow, Warsaw, Belgrade, Peking) are used wherever possible but the reader will notice many differences from spellings found in present-day atlases. These differences fall generally into three categories:–

1 Changes of sovereignty. The atlas reflects the political boundaries as they existed or were changed between 1919 and 1945. Thus, Italian names are used in those parts of Dalmatia subsequently transferred to Yugoslavia; Japanese names are used for places in southern Sakhalin and the Kurile Islands which are now part of the USSR. Poland is the area where differences are most marked, since the atlas uses Polish forms of names within the 1939 boundaries of the country both before and after it was dismembered by German and Russian aggression and subsequently restored with very different boundaries. The consequence is that many places in what was then eastern Poland now have Russian names (e.g. Wlodzimierz is now Vladimir-Volynskiy), while many places in then eastern Germany now have Polish names (e.g. Breslau is now Wrocław). All cases of changed sovereignty are noted in the index, which gives the present-day names in brackets, e.g. Königsberg (n/c Kaliningrad, in USSR).

2 Changes of romanization system. Many of the romanization systems in current use were devised and implemented *after* 1945. Names in Libya, for example, are transliterated by a system for Arabic introduced in the 1950s but the atlas follows the Italian romanizations used earlier (e.g. El Agheila is now spelled Al 'Uqaylah). The present system used for Russian names was introduced only in 1947; though differences are less marked than in the case of Arabic, some spellings in the atlas will be unfamiliar (e.g. Briansk, Bielgorod and Zaporozhe are now spelled Bryansk, Belgorod and Zaporozh'ye respectively). The most profound differences will be noticed in the case of Chinese names, which have been re-spelled twice since 1939. The atlas spells Chinese names in what is generally known as the Post Office System. After the war there was a rewriting of Chinese names following the Wade-Giles System, and at the end of the 1970s they all underwent yet another change to the current Pinyin System. The three forms are often very different, e.g. Tsinkong/Ch'ien-chiang/Qianjiang. Wherever spellings have changed because of new romanization systems the present-day spelling is given in brackets in the index and is also cross-referred to the spelling used in the atlas.

3 Changes of name. A number of names, particularly in eastern Europe, were changed in the years after 1945, e.g. Stalingrad is now Volgograd, Marijampole (in Lithuania) is now Kapsukas, Petrovgrad (Yugoslavia) is now Zrenjanin. In all such cases the index gives the present name in brackets and cross-refers from this to the name used in the atlas.

Every name in the atlas that falls within the 'action' covered by the map is indexed; only those few names added peripherally to a map for locational purposes are not indexed. Some commonly recurring names, in France, Italy and Poland, for example, have distinguishing elements added to them for which there is not always room on the maps; in such cases the index gives the full name with the distinguishing element in brackets, e.g. St. Laurent (-sur-Mer), Peschiera (del Garda). Many places in eastern Europe have German names; most are historical (e.g. Posen for Poznan) but some were apparently invented during the war (e.g. Gumpolds for Humpolec, in Czechoslovakia). All are given in the index in brackets after the correct form of the name and are also cross-referred to this. Other foreign-language forms of names which may be useful are also given in brackets in the index.

Places are located generally by reference to the country or major area in which they lie, or by island groups or sea areas, this being narrowed down as necessary by location as E(ast), N(orth), C(entral), etc. Reference is generally to page number/map number (e.g. 156/2), unless the subject is dealt with over the plate as a whole, when the reference occurs as 116-117 (i.e. pages 116 and 117).

Abbreviations

a/c	also called
Alb.	Albania
Ar.	Arabic
a/s	also spelled
C	central
Chin.	Chinese
Cz.	Czech
Dut.	Dutch
E	eastern
f/c	formerly called
Finn.	Finnish
form.	former(ly)
Fr.	French
f/s	formerly spelled
Ger.	German
Hung.	Hungarian
I.	island
Is.	islands
It.	Italian
Jap.	Japanese
Lith.	Lithuanian
N	northern
n/c	now called
Nor.	Norwegian
n/s	now spelled
Pol.	Polish
Pt.	point
R.	river
Rum.	Rumanian
Russ.	Russian
S	southern
S.Cr.	Serbo-Croat
USA	United States of America
USSR	Union of Soviet Socialist Republics
W	western
W/G	Wade-Giles

A

Aa, R. S Holland 159/4
Aachen NW Germany separatist declaration 1923 28/2; 42/2; 44/1; bombed by RAF 53/3, 112/1; 160/1,2; 161/3; captured by US forces 183/2
Aalborg (a/s Ålborg) N Denmark German airborne landing 41/3; sabotage attacks 95/4
Aalesund C Norway 40/3
Aardenburg W Holland captured by Canadians 158/6
Aarhus (a/s Århus) C Denmark 41/3; sabotage attacks 95/4
Abadan W Persia oil production 79/4
Abau SE Papua 75/1; 119/1,5; Allied control 120/1,2, 122/1
Abbassia NE Egypt British air base 81/6, 115/4
Abbeville NE France 42/1,2; 43/6; 44/1; German fighter station 52/1; bombed by USAAF 112/1; 155/1
Aberdeen Hong Kong 69/7
Aberdeen NE Scotland industrial centre 46/1; 88/4, 136/4
Abingdon S England Bomber Command group HQ 53/3, 112/1, 138/1
Abinskaya (n/c Abinsk) W Caucasus 103/3
Åbo see Turku
Abrene see Jaunlatgale
Abucay C Philippines, Bataan 73/2,3
Abu Dhabi country of SE Arabia 79/4
Abu Kemal (n/s Abu Kamal) E Syria 79/3
Abu Qir NE Egypt 81/6
Abu Suweir NE Egypt British air base 81/6, 115/4
Abuyog Leyte, C Philippines 164/2, 167/2
Abyar al Hakim see Bir Hakeim
Abyssinia see Ethiopia
Acre (n/s 'Akko, in Israel) N Palestine 79/3
Acroma (n/s 'Ikrimah) NE Libya 50/3; 80/2,6
Acqualagna N Italy 157/3
Adadle (n/s Cadadley) Brit.Somaliland 51/2
Adak Aleutian Is. 68; US garrison established 96/1, 181/1
Adana C Turkey Churchill/Inönü meeting 134/1
Addis Ababa (n/s Adis Abeba) C Ethiopia captured by Italians 37/4; captured by British forces 51/2; British intelligence 82/1
Addis Derra (n/s Adis Dera) C Ethiopia 37/4
Adelaide S Australia 67
Adel-Neuendorf E Prussia 151/2
Adelup Pt. Guam, Mariana Is. US landing 143/6
Aden S Arabia 51/2; supply routes 78/1; Allied base 206/1
Aden Protectorate (later called Federation of South Arabia n/c Peoples' Democratic Republic of South Yemen) 37/4; 50/1, 51/2
Adige, R. N Italy German defensive position 157/5
Adigrat N Ethiopia captured by Italians 37/4
Adis Abeba see Addis Ababa
Adis Dera see Addis Derra
Admiralty Is. SW Pacific 68, 75/1; 166/1; US landings 122/1, 141/1
Adowa see Aduwa
Adrano E Sicily 131/2
Adrianople (n/c Edirne) NW Turkey occupied by Greeks 28/1; 54/1, 55/3
Aduwa (a/s Adowa n/s Adwa) N Ethiopia 37/4
Aegean Is. Greece surrender of German garrisons 190/1
Afetna Pt. Saipan, Mariana Is. US landings 143/4,7
Africa political and military situation 1940-1941 50-51; supply routes 1940 78/1; Desert War 78-81, 114-115; convoy routes 88-89, 108-109, 136-137; air and sea routes 202/1; US Air Force supply lines 203/2
Agana Guam, Mariana Is. 69/6
Agat Guam, Mariana Is. 69/6
Agat Bay Guam, Mariana Is. US landing 143/6
Agedabia (n/s Ajdabiya) NE Libya 50/3; retaken by Germans 78/2; retaken by British 80/6, 115/4; SAS raid 111/2
Agingan Pt. Saipan, Mariana Is. 143/4, 7
Agira C Sicily 131/2
Agnez NE France 43/5
Agny NE France 43/5
Agon NW France 154/2
Agram see Zagreb
Agrigento W Sicily 130/2
Agropoli S Italy 131/3
Aguijan Mariana Is. 142/2,3
Aguni I. (Jap.Aguni-jima) W Okinawa US attack 169/4
Aha N Okinawa captured by US 169/4
Ahonwa S Burma 76/2
Ahvenanmaa see Åland Is.
Ahwaz (n/s Ahvaz) W Persia oil production 79/4
Aichi prefecture of C Japan population 192/1
Aigun (n/c Heihe) N Manchuria treaty port 32/1; 35/4; captured by Russians 199/2
Aimara E Papua 119/5
Ainaži (Ger.Hainasch) N Latvia 151/1
Airel NW France Normandy invasion 153/2,4; 154/2,3
Aiscia (n/s Aysha) E Ethiopia 51/2
Aisne department of NE France German military administration 90/1
Aisne, R. NW France French defensive line 44/1
Aitape NE New Guinea 75/1; Japanese control 119/1; captured by US forces 140/1,2; 166/1
Aizpute (Ger.Hasenpoth) W Latvia 148/2, 151/1
Ajdabiya see Agedabia
Akamaruno Cape (Jap.Akamaruno-misaki) N Okinawa 169/4
Akashi C Japan US air raid 196/1
Akatovka SE Russia battle of Stalingrad 105/2
Akhtari (n/c Primorsko-Akhtarsk) S Ukraine 63/1, 147/3
Akhtyrka NE Ukraine 63/1; battle of Kharkov 107/3; 124/1,125/3; 126/2
Akimovka S Ukraine 63/1, 146/3
Akita N Japan population 192/1
Akkerman (n/c Belgorod-Dnevstrovskiy Rum.Cetatea-Alba) S USSR 57/1; 146/3; 147/2
'Akko see Acre
Ak-Mechet (n/c Chernomorskoye) S Ukraine Crimea 62/1, 146/3
Akmolinsk (n/c Tselinograd) Kazakhstan industry 172/1
Aksai (n/s Aksay) SE Russia battle of Stalingrad 104/1
Ak-Sheikh (n/c Razdol'noye) S Ukraine Crimea 62/1, 146/3
Aksum N Ethiopia 37/4
Aktyubinsk C USSR industry 172/1
Akureyri N Iceland 88/4 (inset); US air base 180/1
Akyab (n/c Sittwe) W Burma abandoned by British 77/3; 162/1, 163/2
Alabama S USA war industries 98/1
Alamagan Mariana Is. 142/2,3
Alameda W USA shipbuilding 99/2
Alamogordo S USA atomic bomb test 189
Alabat C Philippines 167/3, 4
Al Abyar see El Abiar
Al Adam see El Adem
Alakamisy C Madagascar 79/5
Alamein see El Alamein
Alam el Halfa Ridge NE Egypt 114/1, 115/2
Aland I. (Finn. Ahvenanmaa) SW Finland neutralized 1921 28/1
Alaska USA 68; 96/1; US bases for Lend-Lease 181/1
Alaska Highway USA 181/1
Alavuokki E Finland 41/2
Albacete E Spain Civil War 37/3
Albanella S Italy 131/3
Albaneta Farm C Italy 132/1
Alban Hills C Italy 133/2
Albania alliance with Italy 29/5; 37/2; annexed by Italy 54/1,2; SOE operations 84/1; 90/1; extermination of Jews 93/2; Kosovo annexed by Italians 128/1; strikes and demonstrations 170/1; Communist government 191/2
Albano (Laziale) C Italy 133/2-4
Al Bardi see Bardia
Al Basrah see Basra
Albay Gulf C Philippines 167/3, 4
Albert Canal S Belgium 43/3
Al Birkah see Berka
Ålborg see Aalborg
Al Burayqah see Mersa Brega
Alconbury S England SOE airfield 85/2
Aldrich Bay Hong Kong Japanese landing 69/7
Aleksandrovka SE Russia battle of Stalingrad 100/2, 105/2
Aleksandrovsk E USSR 199/3
Alekseyevka C USSR 125/1
Alekseyevka S Ukraine 62/2, 63/1
Alekseyevo-Lozovskoye SE Russia Upper Don offensive 107/2
Alençon NW France 44/1; German bomber station 52/1; Normandy invasion 152/2; 155/3
Aleppo (n/c Halab) N Syria 79/3
Alès S France 156/2
Alessandria N Italy Allied bombing 157/4
Aleutian Is. Alaska 68; attacked by Japanese 96/1; Japanese expelled by US forces 181/1
Alexandretta (n/c Iskenderun) SE Turkey ceded to Syria 28/1
Alexandria N Egypt British base 50/1, 51/4; 79/6, 81/5, 81/6, 115/4; British intelligence 82/1; 117/5; 206/1
Alexandroupolis NE Greece captured by Germans 55/3
Alexishafen NE New Guinea Japanese control 119/1, 120/1; captured by Allies 122/1, 122/2, 140/1, 140/2
Al Fallujah see Falluja
Alger see Algiers
Algeria Vichy administration 37/3; 45/3, 50/1; Allied landings 116/1; base for Allied invasion of S France 156/1
Algiers (Fr.Alger) N Algeria French air base 51/4, 79/6, 81/5; foreign intelligence activities 82/1; SOE base 84/1; Allied landings 116/1; RAF base 156/1
Al Hasakah see Hassetché
Al Husayyat see El Huseiat
Alicante SE Spain Civil War 37/3
Al Khums see Homs
Al Ladhiqiyah see Latakia
Allenstein (n/c Olsztyn, in Poland) SE Prussia plebiscite 1920 28/1,2; 39/2; 148/2, 151/1; 175/1
Allerton N England Bomber Command group HQ 112/1, 138/1
Alma-Ata S Ukraine Kazakhstan industry 172/1
Alma-Tarkhan (n/c Krasnoarmeyskoye) S USSR Crimea 146/3
Al Maqrun see El Magrun
Al Marj see Barce
Al Mawsil see Mosul
Almaza NE Egypt British air base 81/6, 115/4
Almeria S Spain Civil War 37/3
Al Mukhaylib see Mekili
Alola E Papua 119/5
Alor Gajah S Malaya 71/4
Alor Star (n/s Alor Setar) N Malaya British airbase 70/1; Japanese airfield 71/2
Alpenland S Germany SS region 91/3
Alpha Beach S France US landings 156/2
Alpine Line Italy-Yugoslavia German defensive position 157/5
Al Qamishli see Kameshli
Al Qubbah see Giovanni Berta
Al Qunaytirah see Kuneitra
Alsace-Lorraine (Ger.Elsass-Lothringen) provinces of E France incorporated into Germany 45/2; ceded to France 28/1,2; German military administration 90/1; US offensive 158/1, 159/7
Al Tamimi see El Tmimi
Altamura S Italy 131/2
Altavilla (Silentina) S Italy 131/3
Altenberg E Prussia 151/2
Altengrabow N Germany POW camp 205/2
Althammer W Poland German labour camp 93/5
Altkanischa see Magyarkanizsa
Al 'Uqaylah see El Agheila
Alupka S Ukraine Crimea 146/3
Alushta S Ukraine Crimea 63/1, 146/3
Alytus E Lithuania 148/2, 151/1
Amagusan Pt. Leyte, C Philippines 165/3
Ama Keng Singapore I. 71/5
Amalfi S Italy taken by Americans 131/3
Amba Alagi (n/s Amba Alage) N Ethiopia Italian surrender 51/2
Ambalavao S Madagascar battle with Vichy French 79/5
Ambanja N Madagascar 79/5
Ambarchik E USSR naval and convoy port 181/1
Ambès W France bombed by RAF 53/3
Ambleteuse NE France Commando raid 110/1
Amboina (n/s Ambon) S Moluccas 69/1; Japanese landing 74/1; 166/1; Japanese port 194-195; POW camp 204/3
Ambon see Amboina
Ambositra C Madagascar 79/5
Ambunti NE New Guinea Japanese control 119/1
Amcenis NW France 154/1
Amchitka Aleutian Is. 68; US troops land 96/1, 181/1
American Samoa S Pacific 66
Amersfoort S Holland German detention centre 94/1
Amhara region of N Ethiopia 37/4
Amiens NE France 42/2,43/6; 44/1; German fighter station 52/1; escape route centre 95/2; bombed by USAAF 112/1, 138/1; Normandy invasion 152/1; 155/1
Amindaion see Amyntaion
Amiriya (n/s El Amiriya) NE Egypt British air base 81/6
Amman N Trans-Jordan 79/3
Ämmänsaari E Finland 41/2
Amoy (n/c Xiamen a/s Hsia-men) SE China treaty port 32/1; taken by Japanese 35/4; 69/1; Japanese bridgehead 169/3; POW camp 204/3
Ampasimanolotra see Brickaville
Amsterdam W Holland 42/2; German bomber station 53/1, 113/6; bombed by RAF 53/3; strikes and demonstrations 94/1; 95/2; bombed by USAAF 112/1; 138/1
Amur, R. (Chin.Heilong Jiang) USSR/China 32/1; Russian invasion of Manchuria 199/2
Amyntaion (n/s Amindaion) N Greece 54/2
Ananyev C Ukraine, USSR Einsatzgruppe operations 93/4;126/2
Anapa W Caucasus, USSR 103/3,147/3
Anatahan Mariana Is. 142/2, 3
An-ch'ing see Anking
Anchorage S Alaska US base 181/1, 207/1
Ancona N Italy 55/3; 133/4
Ancourt N France Dieppe raid 86/2
Andalsnes (Nor. Åndalsnes) C Norway Allied landing 40/3
Andaman Is. Indian Ocean Japanese surrender 200/2
Andizhan S USSR C Asia industry 172/1
Andreapol NW USSR battle for Moscow 60-61;
Andreyevka SE Russia battle of Stalingrad 104/1
Andreyevka NE Ukraine, USSR battle for Kharkov 107/4, 5
Andriba NW Madagascar 79/5
Angangki (n/s Ang'angxi) C China taken by Japanese 35/1
Angeles C Philippines captured by Japanese 73/2
Angers W France 45/1; Normandy invasion 152/1; 154/1
Anglo-Egyptian Sudan (n/c Sudan) 37/4; Italian attack 50/1, 51/2; air reinforcement route 78/1
Angola (a/c Portuguese West Africa) 50/1
Angoulême SW France 44/1
Anhsiang see Ansiang
Anhui see Anhwei
Anhwei (n/s Anhui) province of C China warlord control 32/2, 33/3-5; 33/7; Japanese occupation 34/2, 35/4
Aniene, R. C Italy 133/4
Aninoasa NW Rumania anti-German strikes 170/1
Anjen (n/s Anren) C China taken by Japanese 145/3
Ankara C Turkey 29/5; foreign intelligence activities 82/1
Ankazobe C Madagascar 79/5
Ankenes N Norway 40/4
Anking (a/s An-ch'ing, n/s Anqing) C China taken by Japanese 35/4
Anklam N Germany bombed by USAAF 112/1
Annaba see Bône
Annanberg NE New Guinea Japanese control 119/1
An Nawfaliyah see Nofilia
Annecy E France sabotage 85/3
Annopol C Poland German invasion 39/2
Anqing see Anking
Anren see Anjen
Anshan S Manchukuo Japanese garrison 35/1; 66
Ansiang (a/s Anhsiang, n/s Anxiang) C China taken by Japanese 145/3
Ansty C England aircraft factory 46/1
Antalaha N Madagascar battle against Vichy French 79/5
Antananarivo see Tananarive
Antelat (n/s Antalat) NE Libya 50/3; 78/2
Antigua island of West Indies Allied base 207/1
Antikythera island S Greece occupied by Germans 90/1
Antimonan N Philippines 165/2, 167/3,4
Antivari see Bar
Antseranana see Diego Suarez
Antsirabe N Madagascar 79/5
Antung Formosa 66
Antung (n/c Dandong a/s Tan-tung) NE China treaty port 32/1; taken by Japanese 35/1,4; 199/2
Antwerp (Fr. Anvers Dut. Antwerpen) N Belgium 42/1,2; 43/6; German bomber station 52/1, 113/6; bombed by RAF 53/3; escape route 95/2; bombed by USAAF 112/1, 138/1; captured by British 158/1, 159/6; 160/1,2
Anxiang see Ansiang
Anyang N China taken by Japanese 34/2, 35/4
Anyi C China taken by Japanese 34/2
Anzin NE France 43/5
Anzio C Italy German special forces operations 111/3; 131/2; US landing 133/2,3; 133/4
Aola Bay Guadalcanal, Solomon Is. US landing 121/8
Aomori NE Japan population 193/1; US air raid 197/1
Aosta NW Italy 44/1
Aparri N Philippines captured by Japanese 72/1; air base 165/2, 167/3,4
Apollonia (n/c Susah) NE Libya 50/3; 78/2; Commando raid 111/2
Apra Harbor Guam US naval base 69/6
Arad NW Rumania anti-German demonstrations 170/1; 177/3

B

C

Ciechanów (Ger.Zichenau) C Poland 148/2, 151/1; 175/1
Cieszyn see Teschen
Cili see Tzeli
Cilli see Celje
Cirene see Cyrene
Cisterna (di Latina) C Italy 133/2
Citta Vecchia (n/c Mdina) W Malta 81/4
Civitavecchia C Italy 131/2, 133/4
Clark Field C Philippines US air base 73/2, 168/1, 169/3
Cleethorpes E England evacuation area 47/4
Clelles SW France Vercors uprising 95/3
Clermont N France 42/2; 44/1; German bomber station 52/1, 113/6
Clermont-Ferrand S France 44/1; sabotage 85/3; 95/2
Clervaux N Luxembourg battle of the Bulge 161/3
Cleveland C USA war industries 98/1
Clipperton I. E Pacific Free French control 45/3
Cluj see Kolozsvár
Cluny SE France 44/1
Clydebank S Scotland evacuation area 47/4
Cobh see Queenstown
Coblenz (n/s Koblenz) NW Germany Allied occupation 28/2; Nazi land court 36/1; 44/1; Allied bombing 53/3, 138/1; captured by US forces 182/3, 183/2
Coburg E Germany 28/2
Cocanada (n/s Kakinada) E India Japanese air raid 77/4
Cogolin S France US landing 156/2
Cöka N Serbia German detention centre 170/1
Colchester E England German air raids 113/6
Colditz C Germany POW camp 205/2
Colerne W England Fighter Command group HQ 52/1
Colleville-sur-Mer NW France Normandy invasion 153/2,4
Collingwood Bay E Papua 119/5,6
Colmar E France captured by Germans 44/1; 183/2
Cologne (Ger. Köln) W Germany Nazi economy 36/1; 42/2; bombed by RAF 53/3; Allied bombing 112/1, 113/2, 138/1; taken by US forces 182/3, 183/2
Colombelles Normandy battle for Caen 153/5
Colombia declaration of war against Germany 207/1
Colombo W Ceylon Japanese air raid 77/4; Allied base 207/1
Colorado W USA war industries 98/1
Coltishall E England RAF fighter station 52/1
Comilla NE India (now Bangladesh) 76/1
Comiso S Sicily 131/2
Commercy NE France 158/1
Commonwealth Keep NE Libya 80/2
Compiègne NE France 44/1; German Fliegerkorps HQ 52/1; German detention centre 94/1; 155/1; 158/1
Conches N France 155/3
Condé (-sur-Noireau) NW France Normandy invasion 152/2; 154/1,2,3
Condroz Plateau S Belgium battle of the Bulge 161/3
Conical Hill S Okinawa 169/5
Connage NE France 43/4
Connecticut NE USA war industries 98/1
Constanţa E Rumania 54/1; naval base 57/1; 146/3; 177/3
Constantine NE Algeria 116/1
Continental Hotel C Italy, Cassino 132/1
Copenhagen (Dan.København) E Denmark 29/5; 41/3; Scandinavian conference 86/1; German SS and SD base 94/1; escape route 95/2; sabotage attacks 95/4
Coquelles NE France German fighter station 52/1
Coral Sea SW Pacific naval battle 75/2-5; 118/1;
Corbeil N France taken by US forces 155/1
Cordillera Central mts. of N Philippines Japanese resistance 167/3,4
Córdoba S Spain Civil War 37/3
Cordova Alaska US air base 181/1
Corfu (Gk. Kerkyra) W Greece 28/1; Greek naval base 54/2; surrendered to Germans 55/3; occupied by Germans 128/1
Cori C Italy 133/2
Coriano N Italy captured by British 157/3
Corigliano S Italy 131/2
Corinth S Greece captured by Germans 55/3; 128/1, 129/2
Cork S Ireland 28/1
Corleone W Sicily 130/2
Cormeilles-en-Vexin N France German bomber station 52/1, 113/6
Corregidor island C Philippines 73/3; 167/3,4; POW camp 204/3
Corrençon SW France Vercors uprising 95/3
Corsica (Fr. Corse) occupied by Germany 45/2; Vichy French garrison 45/3; evacuated by German

forces 130/1; base for Allied invasion of S France 156/1
Cos (a/s Kos) SE Greece Dodecanese captured by British 128/1
Cosel (n/c Koźle, in Poland) SE Germany POW hospital 205/2
Cosenza S Italy 131/2
Cospicua NE Malta 81/4
Costa Rica declarations of war against Italy and Japan 207/1
Coswig E Germany Nazi economy 36/1
Cotabato S Philippines 73/1; attacked by Japanese 73/4; Japanese air base 164/2
Cotentin Peninsula NW France Allied invasion 153/2
Cottbus E Germany 150/1, 174/1
Courbevoie N France sabotage 85/3
Courland region of W Latvia 151/1; German Army surrenders 190/1
Courland Lagoon (Ger.Kurisches Haff) E Prussia 151/1
Courseulles NW France landing by Canadian forces 152/2; 154/1
Courtrai (Dut.Kortrijk) W Belgium 42/2,43/6
Coutances N France 45/1; Normandy invasion 153/2; taken by US forces 154/1,2,3
Coventry C England industrial centre 46/1; evacuation area 47/4; air defences 52/1; German air raids 53/6
Cowes S England German air raids 113/6
Cox's Bazar NE India (now Bangladesh) 76/1
Cracow (Pol. Kraków Ger.Krakau) C Poland 38/1; German invasion 39/2,4; 57/1; German administration 90/1; 148/2, 151/1; German SS and SD base 170/1; Polish partisans 171/2; 174/2; 207/3
Craiova S Rumania 55/3; taken by Russians 177/3
Cranz (n/c Zelenogradsk, in USSR) E Prussia 148/2, 151/1
Crécy-en-Ponthieu NE France German fighter station 52/1
Crefeld (n/s Krefeld) W Germany 42/2; bombed by RAF 53/3, 112/1
Creil N France German bomber station 113/6
Cremona N Italy Allied bombing 157/4
Crepon N France German fighter station 52/1
Crest S France 156/2
Crete occupied by British 54/1; German invasion and British evacuation 55/4; SOE operations 84/1; German military administration 90/1; British special forces operations 111/2; held by Germans 115/4; surrender of German garrison 190/1
Cretin, Cape NE New Guinea Australian landing 122/2
Cricklewood NW London aircraft factory 46/1
Crimea (Russ.Krym) taken by Germans 62/1,3; German military administration 90/1 126/2; retaken by Russians 146/3; Soviet deportations 173/4
Croatia province of C Yugoslavia 28/1; region of N Yugoslavia 55/3; puppet Axis state 90/1; extermination of gypsies 92/3; extermination of Jews 93/2; German and Italian administration 128/1; German detention centres 170/1
Croce N Italy captured by British 157/3
Croix Haute, Col de la S France US invasion route 156/2
Crossen (n/c Krosno Odrzańskie, in Poland) E Germany 174/1
Crotone S Italy 131/2
Croydon SE England RAF fighter station 52/1, 53/5
Cruz, Pt. Guadalcanal, Solomon Is. 118/2,4
Csáktornya (n/c Čakovec, in Yugoslavia) SW Hungary 128/1
Csepreg NW Hungary 178/2, 187/2
Csongrád S Hungary 179/2
Csurgó W Hungary 178/2
Cuba declaration of war against Axis 207/1
Curzon Line proposed frontier demarcation USSR/Poland 28/1
Cuxhaven N Germany bombed by RAF 53/3; bombed by USAAF 112/1
Cyprus garrisoned by British forces 79/3, 115/4; MI6 outstation 82/1
Cyrenaica region of NE Libya 50/3; Desert War 78/2, 80/6, 115/4
Cyrene (It.Cirene n/c Shahhat) NE Libya 50/3; 78/2
Czechoslovakia independence 1918 28/1; First World War debts 29/3; alliances 1921-1934 29/5; emigration of Germans and Hungarians 29/6; dismemberment 1938-39 36/1, 37/2; 38/1 (inset); SOE operations 84/1; extermination of Jews 93/2; anti-German demonstrations 170/1; Communist coup 191/2; war casualties 205/1; declaration of war against Axis 207/1. See also Bohemia-Moravia, Slovakia
Czechowice S Poland German labour camp 93/5
Czerniaków district of SE Warsaw uprising 171/4
Czernowitz see Chernovtsy

Czersk N Poland 148/2, 151/1
Częstochowa (Ger.Tschenstochau) SW Poland German invasion 39/2,4; 151/1; Jewish ghetto uprising 171/2; 174/2, 175/1
Człuchów see Schlochau
Czyżew NE Poland 175/1

D

Dachang see Tachang
Dachau S Germany SS enterprise 91/3; concentration camp 92/1,3, 205/2
Daet C Philippines 72/1; 165/2
Dagabur (n/s Degeh Bur) E Ethiopia captured by Italians 37/4
Dagami C Philippines 167/2
Dagenham E London German air raids 53/4
Dagupan N Philippines 72/1
Daik-U S Burma captured by Japanese 76/2; retaken by British 163/2
Dairen (n/s Dalian) NE China Japanese treaty port 32/1; Japanese garrison 35/1; 66; 199/2
Daito Is. (Jap.Daito-jima) N Pacific radar station 169/3
Daixian see Taihsien
Dakar W Africa Senegal Free French landing 50/1; Allied base 206/1
Dakiton (n/s Taketomi) S Okinawa 169/5
Dakovo see Djakovo
Dala S Burma 163/2
Dalai see Talai
Dale S Wales Coastal Command airfield 88/4, 108/4
Daletme W Burma 77/3
Dalian see Dairen
Dallas S USA war industries 98/1
Dalmatia region of W Yugoslavia 28/1; 55/3
Dalmuir S Scotland Royal Ordnance Factory 46/1
Dalnyaya Igumenka C USSR 125/2
Damascus (Fr.Damas a/c Esh Sham Ar.Dimashq) SW Syria 50/1; British attack 79/3
Danao C Philippines 73/5
Danan (n/s Denan) SE Ethiopia 37/4
Dandong see Antung
Dangtu see Tangtu
Dangyang see Tangyang
Danica N Yugoslavia German concentration camp 92/1
Danshui see Tanshui
Dante (n/c Xaafuun a/s Hafun) It.Somaliland 37/4
Danube, R. Allied crossing 182/3
Danyang see Tanyang
Danzig (n/c Gdańsk) N Poland Free City 28/1, 29/2; 36/1, 37/2; German occupation 38/1, 39/2; German naval base 56/1, 58/1; extermination of Jews 93/2; 148/2, 151/1; SS and SD base 170/1; 171/2; bombed by USAAF 112/1; ceded to Poland 191/2,3
Danzig-West Prussia (Ger. Danzig-Westpreussen) province of Germany 90/1
Dapitan S Philippines 73/4
Daqian see Tachien
Dar'a see Dera
Dardanelles (Turk.Çanakkale Bogazi) NW Turkey de-and re-militarization 28/1
Darfeld NW Germany V2 HQ 139/6
Darmstadt W Germany Nazi economy 36/1; Allied bombing 138/1
Darnah see Derna
Daru S Papua 75/1; 119/1; Allied control 120/1
Darwin N Australia 66; 69/1; Japanese air raid 74/1
Dashiqiao see Tashihkiao
Datong see Tatung
Daugavpils (Ger. Dünaburg, former Russ. Dvinsk) NW USSR Latvia German attack 56/1, 57/2; 64/1; 106/1; 149/2, 151/1; 171/2
Daunia Mts. S Italy 131/2
Davao S Philippines Japanese attack 69/1; US air base captured by Japanese 73/1; 73/4; Japanese staging base 74/1; 166/1; POW camp 204/3
Davidston Moor SW England Coastal Command airfield 108/4
Dawa see Tawa
Deal SE England Dunkirk evacuation 43/6
De'an see Teian
Death Valley Saipan, Mariana Is. 143/7
Deauville NW France German Fliegerkorps HQ 52/1; Normandy invasion 152/2
Debaltsevo NE Ukraine battle for Kharkov 107/4,5
Debden E England RAF fighter station 52/1
Dębica S Poland German invasion 39/2,4; 175/1
Dęblin C Poland German invasion 39/2; 148/2, 175/1
Dębno see Neudamm

G

233

Korea (Jap.Chosen) under Japanese control 32/1; 35/1,4; 66; 68; US mining targets 196/1; disposition of Japanese forces 1945 198/1, 199/2; Japanese garrison 200/1; Japanese surrender 200/2; independence and civil war 201/3; food resources 202/1; POW camps 204/3
Korenevo C USSR 124/1, 125/3
Koritsa (Alb.Korçë) C Albania Italian occupation 54/2
Körmend NW Hungary 178/2
Korneuberg NE Austria 186/1
Kornin W Ukraine 127/4
Korobochkino NE Ukraine battle for Kharkov 107/3
Korocha C USSR 124/1, 125/3; 126/2
Korop W Ukraine 126/2
Korosten W Ukraine 106/1; 126/2; 127/4; 147/2
Korpona see Krupina
Korsakov see Otomari
Kortrijk see Courtrai
Koryukovka W Ukraine 126/2
Kos see Cos
Kościan (Ger.Kosten) W Poland 174/1,2
Kościerzyna (Ger.Berent) NW Poland 148/2, 151/1
Koshan (n/s Keshan) NE Manchuria taken by Japanese 35/1
Košice (Hung.Kassa, Ger.Kaschau) E Slovakia 179/2
Koskovo NW Russia siege of Leningrad 64/2
Kosovo region of SW Yugoslavia incorporated into Albania by Italians 90/1, 128/1
Kosów (n/s Kosov, in USSR) SE Poland 176/2
Kostelec (Ger.Kosteletz) N Moravia 187/2
Kosten see Kościan
Kőszeg (Ger.Güns) NW Hungary 178/2
Kota Bharu (n/s Kota Baharu) C Malaya British air base 70/1,71/2
Kota Kinabalu see Jesselton
Kota Tinggi S Malaya 71/4
Kotelnich NE Russia 106/1
Kotelnikovski (n/c Kotelnikovo) SE Russia 63/1; battle of Stalingrad 104/1
Kotelva NE Ukraine battle for Kharkov 107/3; 124/1, 125/3
Kotka SE Finland 41/1; 64/1
Kotlas N Russia 106/1; industry 172/1
Kotlin I. NW Russia siege of Leningrad 64/2
Kotlyarka W Ukraine 127/4
Koton (n/c Pobedino, in USSR) N Japan 199/3
Kotor (It.Cattaro) SW Yugoslavia 129/2
Kotovskoye see Gancheshty
Kouang-Tchéou-Wan see Kwangchowwan
Kouburi S Siam Burma railway 204
Kouri I. (Jap. Kouri-jima) NW Okinawa captured by US 169/4
Kouvola S Finland 64/1
Kovel' see Kowel
Kovno see Kaunas
Kowel (n/s Kovel', in USSR) E Poland 39/2; 146/2; 149/2; 176/2; 171/3
Kowloon Hong Kong treaty port 32/1; 69/7; POW camp 204/3
Kozani N Greece 55/3
Kozelsk C USSR 125/3
Koźle see Cosel
Kozlovka C USSR 125/2
Kra (n/c Kra Buri) S Siam 70-71
Krabbendijke SW Holland captured by Canadians 159/6
Kragan N Java Japanese landing 74/1
Kragujevac E Yugoslavia 55/3; 128/1
Krainburg see Kranj
Krakau see Cracow
Kraków see Cracow
Kramatorsk NE Ukraine Nazi industry 91/2; battle for Kharkov 107/4,5; 126/2
Kranj (Ger.Krainburg) W Slovenia liberated by partisans 129/2
Kranji Singapore 71/5
Krasilovka W Ukraine 127/4
Krasnaya Polyana NW USSR battle for Moscow 60-61
Krasnaya Sloboda SE Russia battle of Stalingrad 104-105
Krasnik C Poland German invasion 39/2; 175/1, 176/2
Krasnoarmeisk SE Russia battle of Stalingrad 104/1, 105/2
Krasnoarmeiskoye NE Ukraine battle for Kharkov 107/4,5
Krasnoarmeyskoye see Alma-Tarkhan
Krasnoborka W Ukraine 127/4
Krasnodar W Caucasus 102/2; industry 172/1
Krasnograd NE Ukraine 62/2, 63/1; battle for Kharkov 107/3,4,5; 126/2; 147/2
Krasnogvardeisk W USSR Einsatzgruppe operations 93/4
Krasnogvardeyskoye see Kurman-Kemelchi
Krasnokutsk NE Ukraine 124/1, 125/3
Krasnopavlovka NE Ukraine battle for Kharkov 107/4,5
Krasnopolye C USSR 124/1, 125/3
Krasnopolye NE Ukraine battle for Kharkov 107/3

Krasnovodsk S USSR industry 172/1
Krasnoyarsk C USSR industry 172/1
Krasnoye see Ulan-Erge
Krasnoye Selo NW Russia siege of Leningrad 64/2, 65/4
Krasny Liman (f/c Liman) E Ukraine 147/2
Krasny Luch SE Ukraine 127/2
Krasnystaw C Poland 148/2, 151/1, 176/2
Krasnyy Oktyabr' see Red October
Krasnyy Sulin see Sulin
Krefeld see Crefeld
Kremenchug S USSR 57/1; 63/1; 102/2, 103/1; 126/2; 147/2; 171/3
Kremenets see Krzemieniec
Krems NE Austria 186/1, 187/2
Krestovy Pass (Russ.Pereval Krestovyy) S Caucasus 103/1,2
Kreuz (n/c Krzyż, in Poland) NE Germany 174/1
Kreuzberg S suburb of Berlin 185/2
Kreuzburg (n/c Kluczbork, in Poland) E Germany 39/2; 175/1; POW camp 205/2
Kreuzburg see Krustpils
Krian R. (n/s Kerian) N Malaya crossed by Japanese 71/2
Krichev C USSR battle for Moscow 60-61
Krieglach E Austria Nazi industry 91/2
Kristiansand S Norway German landing 41/3
Krivoi Rog (n/s Krivoy Rog) S USSR Nazi industry 91/2; 126/2; retaken by Russians 147/2; industry 172/1
Krivoye W Ukraine 127/4
Krnov see Jägerndorf
Kroh (n/s Keroh) N Malaya 71/2
Kroll Opera battle for Berlin 185/3
Krompachy Nazi industry 91/2
Kromy NE Ukraine 124/1, 125/3; 147/2
Kronstadt (n/s Kronshtadt) N USSR Russo-Finnish war 41/1; Russian naval base 56/1; 64/1,2; 151/1
Kropotkin NW Caucasus 102/2, 103/1; industry 172/1
Krośniewice C Poland German invasion 38/3
Krosno SE Poland 175/1, 176/2, 177/4
Krosno Odrzańskie see Crossen
Krupina (Hung.Korpona Ger.Karpfen) C Slovakia 179/2
Kruščica C Yugoslavia German concentration camp 92/1
Kruševac C Serbia 129/2; German detention centre 170/1
Krustpils (Ger.Kreuzburg) C Latvia 149/2, 151/1
Krutoy Gully SE Russia battle of Stalingrad 100/2
Krym see Crimea
Krymskaya W Caucasus 102/2, 103/3
Krynki NE Poland Jewish ghetto uprising 171/3
Kryukovo NW USSR battle for Moscow 60-61
Krzemieniec (n/c Kremenets, in USSR) SE Poland Kovpak's raid 171/3
Krzyż see Kreuz
Kuala Kangsar N Malaya captured by Japanese 71/2
Kuala Krai (n/s Kuala Kerai) C Malaya British withdrawal 71/2
Kuala Kubu C Malaya captured by Japanese 71/3
Kuala Lipis C Malaya 70/1; British defensive position 71/3
Kuala Lumpur C Malaya 67; 69/1; British air base 71/1; captured by Japanese 71/3; 74/1
Kuala Selangor C Malaya captured by Japanese 71/3
Kuala Trengganu (n/s Kuala Terengganu) C Malaya 71/2
Kuang-chou see Canton
Kuanghaicheng (n/c Guanghai) S China taken by Japanese 35/4
Kuang-te see Kwangteh
Kuantan S Malaya British air base 71/1; captured by Japanese 71/3
Kuba S Okinawa 169/4
Kuban, R. W Caucasus 102/2, 103/1
Kubinka NW Russia 60-61
Kuching Sarawak, NE Borneo 69/1; Japanese landing 74/1; 167/5; Japanese surrender 200/2; POW camp 204/3
Kudaka-jima see Kutaka I.
Kudat British North Borneo 167/5
Kugo-Yeya, R. NW Caucasus 102/2, 103/1
Kuhmo E Finland 41/1
Kuibyshev (n/s Kuybyshev) C USSR industry 172/1
Kukës N Albania Italian occupation 54/2
Kukui NW Russia siege of Leningrad 64/2
Kukum Guadalcanal, Solomon Is. Japanese landing 118/4
Kul NE New Guinea captured by Australians 122/2
Kulai S Malaya captured by Japanese 71/4
Kuldīga (Ger.Goldingen) W Latvia 148/2, 151/1

Kulm see Chelmno
Kuma I. Makin atoll, Gilbert Is. .141/3
Kuma, R . S USSR 103/1,2
Kumagaya C Japan US air raid 197/1
Kumamoto W Japan population 192/1; US air raid 196/1
Kumanovo S Yugoslavia attacked by Germans 55/3; 128/1, 129/2
Kume I. (Jap.Kume-shima) W Okinawa US attack 169/4
Kunashiri (n/c Ostrov Kunashir, in USSR) Kurile Is. Japan Russian occupation 199/3
Kunau C Germany POW camp 205/2
Kunda N Estonia taken by Germans 64/1
Kuneitra (n/s Al Qunaytirah) SW Syria 79/3
Kungyangon S Burma 76/2
Kunming W China 32/1; 35/4; 66; Chinese air base 77/4
Kunshan E China taken by Japanese 34/2,3
Kunzeik S Burma captured by Japanese 76/2
Kuolajärvi, Kuoloyarvi see Salla
Kuporosnoye SE Russia battle of Stalingrad 100/2
Kupyansk NE Ukraine 63/1; battle for Kharkov 107/3; 124/1; 126/2
Kurawa C Okinawa 169/4 .verpitch 3 '16
Kure Japan 96/1; population 192/1
Kure I. (f/c Ocean I.) W Japan N Pacific Japanese attack 96-97; US air raid 196/1
Kurgan C USSR industry 172/1
Kurile Is. (Jap.Chishima-retto Russ.Kuril'skiye Ostrova) 66; 68; 96/1; Russian occupation 199/3
Kuril'skiye Ostrova see Kurile Is.
Kurisches Haff see Courland Lagoon
Kurman-Kemelchi (n/c Krasnogvardeyskoye) S Ukraine Crimea 63/1
Kursk S USSR Russian air base 27/1, 58/1; battle for Moscow 60-61; 61/1; 63/1; 63/4; 106/1; German offensive 124-125; 147/2; industry 172/1
Kurtlak, R. SE Russia battle of Stalingrad 104/1
Kurume W Japan population 192/1
Kushchevskaya S Ukraine 63/1, 147/2
Kustanai (n/s Kustanay) Kazakhstan industry 172/1
Küstrin E Germany Army uprising 1923 28/2; 150/1, 174/1; Russian bridgehead over the Oder 184/1
Kutaisi S Caucasus 102/2, 103/1; industry 172/1
Kutaka I. (Jap.Kudaka-jima) SE Okinawa 169/4
Kutná Hora (Ger.Kuttenberg) C Bohemia 187/2
Kutno W Poland German invasion 38/3, 39/2,4; 146/2; 148/2; 175/1
Kuttenberg see Kutná Hora
Kuwait 79/4
Kuwana C Japan US air raid 197/1
Kuybyshev see Kuibyshev
Küyung (a/s Chüyung n/s Jurong) E China taken by Japanese 34/3
Kuzmichi SE Russia battle of Stalingrad 105/2
Kvam S Norway 40/3
Kwai Noi, R. Burma railway 204
Kwajalein C Pacific, Marshall Is. 66; 68; bombed by US 74/6; US landings 141/1,3; Japanese base 207/1
Kwangchowwan (Fr. Kouang-Tchéou-Wan n/c Zhanjiang a/s Chan-chiang) S China French treaty port 32/1; Free French administration 45/3
Kwangsi (n/s Guangxi) province of S China warlord control 32/2, 33/3-5; 33/7; Japanese invasion 35/4; USAAF bases 144/2; Japanese Ichi-Go offensive 145/3; reoccupied by Kuomintang 145/4
Kwangteh (a/s Kuang-te n/s Guangde) E China taken by Japanese 34/2,3
Kwangtung (n/s Guangdong) province of S China warlord control 32/2, 33/3-5; 33/7; Japanese invasion 35/4; Japanese Ichi-Go offensive 145/3; reoccupied by Kuomintang 145/4
Kwazon W Burma 162/2
Kweichow (n/s Guizhou) province of SW China warlord control 32/2, 33/3-5; 33/7; 35/4; USAAF base 144/2; Japanese offensive 145/3
Kweihsien (n/s Guixian) S China taken by Japanese 145/3
Kweilin (n/s Guilin) S China 33/6; taken by Japanese 145/3
Kweiping (n/s Guiping) S China taken by Japanese 145/3
Kweisui see Hohohoto
Kweiyang (n/s Guiyang) W China 32/1; 35/4; 145/3
Kwidzyn see Marienwerder
Kyaiklat SW Burma 76/2
Kyaikto S Burma captured by Japanese 76/2
Kyaukme NE Burma 163/2
Kyaukpadaung C Burma 77/3; 163/2
Kyaukpyu W Burma 163/2
Kyaukse C Burma 77/3
Kyauktan S Burma 76/2; retaken by British 163/2
Kyauktaw NW Burma 163/2
Kyondo C Burma 76/2
Kyongsong see Seoul
Kyoto C Japan 68; population 192/1

Kythera island S Greece occupied by Germans 90/1
Kyushu island of W Japan 68; US air raids 169/3, industry and raw materials 192/1; 196/1; disposition of forces 198/1; Japanese military dispositions 200/1

La Bagnolle – Longling

L

La Bagnolle NE France 43/4
Labinskaya (n/c Labinsk) W Caucasus 102/2, 103/1
Labis S Malaya captured by Japanese 71/4
Labuan British North Borneo 167/5
La Chapelle NE France 43/4
La Chapelle (-en-Vercors) SW France Vercors uprising 95/3
Łachwa (n/s Lakhva, in USSR) E Poland Soviet partisans 171/2
La Coruña NW Spain Civil War 37/3; 108/4
Ladoga, Lake N USSR Russo-Finnish war 41/1; 56/1, 57/3, 59/1; siege of Leningrad 64-65
Lae E New Guinea Japanese landing 75/1; bombed by US 74/6; Japanese base 119/1; Japanese control 120/1; captured by Allies 122/1, 122/1, 140/2, 141/1; 166/1
La Fère NE France 42/2
Laferug (n/s Lafaruug) Brit.Somaliland 51/2
La Flèche N France 155/1
Lagonoy Gulf C Philippines 167/3,4
Lagos S Nigeria aircraft reinforcement route 78/1
Laguna de Bay C Philippines 167/3,4
La Haye-du-Puits NW France Normandy invasion 153/2; 154/1
La Horgne NE France 43/4
Lahti S Finland 64/1
Laibach *see* Ljubljana
Laibin *see* Laipin
Laie N Oahu, Hawaiian Is. 69/2,3
Laipin (n/s Laibin) S China taken by Japanese 145/3
Laiyuan N China taken by Japanese 34/2
Lakhva *see* Lachwa
Lalo Pt Tinian, Mariana Is. 143/5
Lambeth S London German air raids 53/4
Lambeti New Georgia, Solomon Is. captured by US forces 123/3
La-meng W China 77/3
Lamezia S Italy bombed by USAAF 113/3
Lamia C Greece 128/1
Lamon Bay C Philippines Japanese landing 72/1; 167/3,4
Lampang (a/c Meng Lampang n/s Muang Lampang) NW Siam 77/3
Lampedusa island C Mediterranean 81/3, 114/4
Lampun (a/c Meng Lampun n/s Muang Lamphun) 66
Lamsdorf SE Germany POW camp 205/2
Lancaster NW England industrial centre 46/1
Lanchow (n/s Lanzhou) NW China 32/1
Lanciano C Italy 131/2
Landsberg (n/c Gorzów Wielkopolski, in Poland) E Germany 174/1
Lanfeng C China taken by Japanese 34/2
Lang-ch'i *see* Langki
Langenbielau (n/c Bielawa, in Poland) SE Germany 150/1
Langki (a/s Lang-ch'i n/s Langxi) E China taken by Japanese 34/3
Langxi *see* Langki
Langres E France 44/1
Lannemezan SW France sabotage 85/3
Lans (-en-Vercors) SW France Vercors uprising 95/3
Lanuvio C Italy 133/2
Lanzhou *see* Lanchow
Laoag N Philippines 72/1; air base 165/2, 167/3,4
Laoet (n/s Laut) island, SE Borneo Japanese landing 74/1
Laohokow (n/c Guanghua) C China 144/1
Laon NE France 42/2; 44/1; German bomber station 53/6, 113/6; 155/1
Laoyao *see* Lienyün
La Pallice W France bombed by RAF 53/3; U-boat base 108/4; bombed by USAAF 113/1
La Panne W Belgium 43/6
Lapland N Finland/USSR 180/3
Lapphaugen N Norway 40/4
Lapstone W Australia UNRRA conference 189/1
Łapy NE Poland 175/1
La Rivière SW France Vercors uprising 95/3
La Roche (-en-Ardennes) SE Belgium battle of the Bulge 161/3
La Rochelle W France 45/1; bombed by USAAF 113/1
Laruni E Papua taken by Allies 119/6, 120/2
Laruns SW France sabotage 85/3
Lashio C Burma 67; British air base 76/1,77/3,4; 162/1; retaken 163/2
La Spezia *see* Spezia
Las Vegas SW USA 98/1
Latakia (n/s Al Ladhiqiyah) NW Syria 79/3
Latina *see* Littoria
Latvia independence from Russia 28/1; First World War debts 29/3; Baltic Entente 29/5; refugees from USSR 29/6; 36/1; neutrality 86/1; German administration 90/1; German mass-murder sites 92/1; extermination of gypsies 92/3; extermination of Jews 93/2; Einsatzgruppe operations 93/4; Russian offensive 149/2, 151/1; German SS and SD bases 170/1; Soviet deportations 173/4; annexed by USSR 191/2; occupied by USSR 206/1
Lauban (n/c Lubań, in Poland) E Germany 174/1
Laufen S Germany POW camp 205/2
Laumant N Belgium 43/3
Laurahütte S Poland German labour camp 93/5
Lauria S Italy 131/2
Lausanne W Switzerland treaty of 1923 28/1
Laut *see* Laoet
Lauterbach C Germany 182/3
Laut Strait (a/s Laoet Strait) S Borneo 167/5
Laval N France taken by US forces 154/1
Lavelanet SW France sabotage 85/3
Lavrova (n/s Lavrovo) NW Russia siege of Leningrad 64/2
Layang Layang S Malaya captured by Japanese 71/4
Laysan I. C Pacific 96/1
Leavesden SE England aircraft factory 46/1
Lebanon Vichy administration 45/3; Allied occupation and defeat of Vichy French 79/3
Lebedin NE Ukraine battle for Kharkov 107/3; 124/1, 125/3; 126/2
Le Bény-Bocage N France Normandy invasion 153/2; taken by US forces 154/2,3
Le Bourget N France bombed by USAAF 112/1
Lecce S Italy 117/5; 131/2
Le Creusot C France 44/1; sabotage 85/3
Łęczyca C Poland German invasion 38/3; 175/1
Ledge S Siam captured by Japanese 71/2
Lednevo NW Russia siege of Leningrad 64/2, 65/4
Ledo NE India 77/3,4; 162/1; Chindit forces 163/3
Ledo Road N Burma 76/1
Leeds N England industrial centre 46/1; civil defence HQ 47/3; evacuation area 47/4; 112/1
Leegebruch NE Germany Nazi economy 36/1
Leeuwarden N Holland 42/2
Legaspi C Philippines 72/1; air base 165/2, 167/3,4
Leghorn *see* Livorno
Legnica *see* Liegnitz
Le Grand Hameau NW France Normandy invasion 152/4
Le Havre N France captured by Germans 44/1; German base 52/1; bombed by RAF 53/3; strikes 94/1; 155/1; bombed by USAAF 112/1, 138/1; Normandy invasion 152/1,2; captured by Allies 158/1
Leicester C England industrial centre 46/1; air defences 52/1; V1 attack 139/6
Leiden W Holland V2 launching area 139/6
Leipe *see* Lipno
Leipzig E Germany 28/2; Allied bombing 138/1; captured by US forces 182/3
Leitmeritz (n/c Litoměřice, in Czechoslovakia) Sudetenland Nazi work seat 36/1
Le Kef N Tunisia 114/4; 116/1
Lelle W Estonia 151/1
Le Luc S France 156/1
Le Mans NW France 44/1; bombed by USAAF 113/1, 138/1; Normandy invasion 152/1; taken by US forces 155/1
Lemberg *see* Lwów
Lemery C Philippines 72/1; 165/2
Lemnos island N Aegean Greek naval base captured by Germans 55/3, 128/1
Le Muy S France 156/2
Lenggong N Malaya 71/2
Lengo Channel Guadalcanal, Solomon Is. 118/2,3
Leninakan S Caucasus 103/1
Leningrad N USSR Russo-Finnish war 41/1; German and Finnish attack 56/1, 57/2,3, 59/1,2; 61/1; siege 64-65; 106/1; 151/1; 170/1; industry 172/1; 180/1,3
Leninsk SE Russia battle of Stalingrad 104/1
Lens NE France 43/5,6
León NW Spain Civil War 37/3
Leopold Canal NW Belgium 158/6
Lepel W USSR 149/2, 151/1
Lepini Mts. C Italy 133/2, 3
Le Pont-de-Claix SW France Vercors uprising 95/3
Leppäsilta (n/s Leppyasil'ta, in USSR) E Finland occupied by Russians 41/1
Leppyasil'ta *see* Leppäsilta
Leros SE Aegean German special forces operations 111/3
Leros (It.Lero) island of Dodecanese captured by British 128/1
Lerwick Shetland Is. 40/3
Lesbos island E Aegean captured by Germans 55/3, 128/1
Leskovac SE Yugoslavia 129/2
Leslau *see* Wloclawek
Les Moulins NW France Normandy invasion 152/4
Les Quatre Vents Farm N France Dieppe raid 86/2
Lessay NW France Normandy invasion 153/2; 154/1,2,3
L'Estaque S France sabotage 85/3
Leszno (Ger.Lissa) W Poland 174/1
Le Touquet NE France German base 52/1
Letpadan S Burma British raid 76/2; 163/2
Le Trait N France 112/1
Leuven *see* Louvain
Levallois-Perret N France sabotage 85/3
Levanger C Norway 40/3
Levant I. S France 156/2
Levoča E Slovakia 179/2
Lewisham SE London German air raids 53/4
Leyte island S Philippines 72/1; surrendered to Japanese 73/5; US landings 164/2, 167/2
Leyte Gulf C Philippines US naval base 196/2
Leżajsk SE Poland 148/2, 151/1
Lgov C USSR battle for Moscow 60-61; 124/1, 125/3
Liaoning province of NE China 33/7
Lianyungang *see* Lienyün
Liaoyang SW Manchuria Japanese garrison 35/1
Libau *see* Liepāja
Liberec *see* Reichenberg
Liberia W Africa 50/1; OSS base 82/1; declaration of war against Germany 206/1
Libo *see* Lipo
Libramont E Belgium 42/2
Libya Commonwealth operation against Italian forces 50/1,3; 51/4; Axis supply routes 78/1; Desert War 78-81, 114-115; British special forces operations 111/2; Axis reinforcement routes 117/5
Licata W Sicily US landing 130/2
Lichtenberg E suburb of Berlin 185/2
Lichterfelde S suburb of Berlin 185/2
Lichuan (n/c Tuquan) NE Manchuria captured by Russians 199/2
Lida NW Poland 149/2, 151/1; Soviet partisans 171/2
Lidice W Bohemia German reprisals 170/1
Liebenau SW Germany POW camp 205/2
Liebenfelde *see* Mehlauken
Liège E Belgium 42/2; 44/1; captured by US forces 158/1; 160/1,2; battle of the Bulge 161/3
Liegnitz (n/c Legnica, in Poland) E Germany Nazi land court 36/1; 39/2; 150/1; 174/1
Lienhwa (n/s Lienhua) C China taken by Japanese 145/3
Lienshan (a/c Chinsi, n/s Jinxi) SW Manchuria taken by Japanese 35/1
Lienyün (f/c Laoyao n/c Lianyungang) NE China taken by Japanese 35/4
Liepāja (Ger. Libau) Latvia, NW USSR 38/2; 56/1; 64/1; 106/1; 148/2, 151/1
Lieven NE France sabotage 85/2
Ligao C Philippines 165/2
Lihir Is. SW Pacific 75/1
Lihsien (n/s Lixian) C China taken by Japanese 145/3
Likhovskoi SE Russia Upper Don offensive 107/2
Liling C China taken by Japanese 145/3
Lille NE France 42/2; French surrender to Germans 43/6; 44/1; German bomber station 52/1, 53/6, 113/6; sabotage 85/3; strikes 94/1; escape route centre 95/2; bombed by USAAF 112/1, 138/1; Normandy invasion 152/1; 158/1
Lillebo (n/s Litlabo) S Norway Commando raid 110/1
Lillehammer S Norway 40/3
Liman *see* Krasny Liman
Limay Bataan, C Philippines 73/3
Limoges C France sabotage 85/3; escape route 95/2
Limon Leyte, C Philippines 165/2
Limoux S France 95/2
Lincoln E England industrial centre 46/1; German air raids 113/6
Line Is. S Pacific 68
Linfen N China taken by Japanese 34/2, 35/4
Lingayen N Philippines 72/1; air base 165/2, 167/3,4
Lingayen Gulf N Philippines Japanese landing 72/1; US landing 167/3
Lingchwan (n/s Lingchuan) S China 145/3
Lin-hsi *see* Linsi
Linyi E China taken by Japanese 34/2
Linsi (a/s Lin-hsi) W Manchuria Russian attack 198/2
Linz N Austria Nazi land court 36/1; Nazi industry 91/2; Führerstadt 91/4; 187/2; captured by US forces 190/1
Lion-sur-Mer Normandy British landings 152/2; 154/1
Lipa N Philippines 165/2; 167/3,4
Lipetsk C USSR battle for Moscow 60-61; 63/1; 125/1
Lipno (Ger.Leipe) N Poland 175/1
Lipo (n/s Libo) SW China taken by Japanese 145/3
Lipovy Rog (n/s Lipovyy Rog) NW Ukraine 127/3
Lippstadt NW Germany captured by US forces 182/3
Liri, R. S Italy German defence 131/2, 132/1
Lisbon (Port.Lisboa) C Portugal 37/3; SOE base 84/1; courier route 95/2
Lishan E China taken by Japanese 34/2
Lishih (n/s Lishi) N China taken by Japanese 34/2
Lishui E China taken by Japanese 34/3
Lisianski I. C Pacific 96/1
Lisichansk NE Ukraine 63/1; battle for Kharkov 107/4,5; 127/2
Lisieux NW France Normandy invasion 152/2; 155/1,3
Liski (n/c Georgiu-Dezh) C USSR 125/1
Lison Normandy taken by US forces 153/2
Lissa *see* Leszno
Litan NE India 162/5
Litani R. Lebanon Layforce raid 111/2
Lithuania independence from Russia 28/1; First World War debts 29/3; Baltic Entente 29/5; refugees from USSR 29/6; Memel territory annexed to Germany 36/1, 37/2; 38/1,2; neutrality 86/1; German administration 90/1; German concentration camps 92/1; extermination of gypsies 92/3; extermination of Jews 93/2; Russian offensive 149/2, 151/1; German SS and SD bases 170/1; Soviet deportations 173/4; annexed by USSR 191/2; occupied by USSR 206/1
Litin SW Ukraine 126/2
Litlabo *see* Lillebo
Litoměřice *see* Leitmeritz
Littoria (n/c Latina) C Italy bombed by USAAF 113/3; 133/2
Litzmannstadt *see* Łódź
Liuan (n/c Lu'an) E China taken by Japanese 34/2
Liuchai (n/s Liuzhai) S China taken by Japanese 145/3
Liucheng S China taken by Japanese 145/3
Liuchow (n/s Liuzhou) S China taken by Japanese 145/3
Liuyang C China taken by Japanese 145/3
Liuzhai *see* Liuchai
Liuzhou *see* Liuchow
Liverpool N England industries 46/1; evacuation area 47/4; Atlantic convoys 48/1; air defences 52/1; German air raids 53/6; 112/1; convoy routes 136/4, 137/2
Livny C USSR 63/1; 124/1, 125/3
Livorno (a/c Leghorn Eng.Leghorn) N Italy Allied bombing 113/3; 156/1
Livron SE France 44/1
Lixian *see* Lihsien
Liyang E China taken by Japanese 34/3
Ljubinje W Yugoslavia 128/1
Ljubljana (Ger. Laibach It.Lubiana) NW Yugoslavia 55/3; incorporated into Italy 90/1; annexed to Italy 128/1; liberated by partisans 129/2; 156/1
Loborgrad N Yugoslavia German concentration camp 92/1
Loches N France 155/1
Lodeinoye Pole N USSR 57/3
Łódź (Ger.Litzmannstadt) W Poland German invasion 38/3, 39/2,4; 148/2, 151/1; taken by Russians 174/2, 175/2; German SS and SD base 170/1; Polish partisans 171/2; 207/3
Lofoten Is. N Norway 40/3; Commando raid 110/1
Loiano N Italy 157/3
Loikaw E Burma captured by Japanese 77/3
Loilem C Burma 76/1,77/3
Loire, R. N France crossed by US forces 155/1
Lokhvitsa S USSR 58/1; 63/1; 147/2
Lombok Strait Dutch East Indies naval battle 74/1
Lomonosov *see* Oranienbaum
Łomża NE Poland German invasion 39/2; 175/1
London S England 29/5; Free French base 45/2; industries 46/1; civil defence HQ 47/3; evacuationa area 47/4; air defences 52/1; German air raids 53/3-6, 113/6; SOE HQ 84/1; Allied conferences 86/1, 189/1; V1 and V2 attacks 139/6; Normandy invasion 152/1
London, City of German air raids 53/4
Londonderry N Ireland 28/1; Atlantic convoys 48/1,49/2; transatlantic convoys 88-89, 136/4
Long Beach SW USA aircraft manufacturing 99/2
Long I. NE New Guinea 122/2
Longkou *see* Lungkow
Longling *see* Lungling

Longoskawayan Pt. Bataan, C Philippines Japanese landing 73/3
Longueuil N France Dieppe raid 87/2
Longuyon E France 42/2; 44/1
Longvilly SE Belgium battle for Bastogne 161/4
Longwy NE France 42/2
Longzhou see Lungchow
Lonkin N Burma 77/3; 163/3
Lopera C Spain Civil War 37/3
Lorengau Manus I. SW Pacific 119/1; Japanese control 120/1
Lorient NW France 45/1; U-boat base 48/4; bombed by RAF 53/3; bombed by USAAF 113/1; U-boat base 108/4; Germans hold out 154/1
Lorraine E France German military administration 90/1
Los Angeles SW USA Japanese intelligence 82/1; war industries 98/1, 99/2
Los Baños N Philippines POW camp 204/3
Loshan (n/s Luoshan) E China taken by Japanese 34/2
Losheim NW Germany battle of the Bulge 161/3
Los Negros Bismarck Archipelago 141/1
Lottinghem NE France V1 bunker 139/6
Lötzen (n/c Giżycko, in Poland) E Prussia 148/2, 151/1
Lotzukou (n/s Luozigou) E Manchuria captured by Russians 199/2
Loudéac N France taken by US forces 154/1
Louisiade Archipelago SW Pacific 75/1,2,3, 119/1
Louisiana S USA war industries 98/1
Loukhi NW USSR 180/3
Louvain (Dut.Leuven) C Belgium 42/2
Louvières NW France Normandy invasion 152/4
Louviers N France 155/1
Löwenstadt see Brzeziny
Lower Saxony (Ger. Niedersachsen) province of NW Germany 191/3
Lower Styria SE Austria German province 90/1
Łowicz (Ger.Lowitsch) C Poland German invasion 39/2,3,4; 148/2, 151/1; 174/2, 175/1
Loyang (n/s Luoyang) C China 34/2
Lozovaya NE Ukraine 62/2; 63/1; battle for Kharkov 107/4,5
Lu'an see Liuan
Luang Prabang Laos 69/1
Lubań see Lauban
Lubang C Philippines 72/1; 167/3,4
Lübars N suburb of Berlin 185/2
Lubartów E Poland 175/1
Lübben E Germany 150/1, 174/1
Lübeck N Germany 28/2; 41/3; bombed by RAF 53/3, 112/1; 184/1; POW camp 205/2
Lüben (n/c Lubin, in Poland) E Germany 174/1
Lubiana see Ljubljana
Lubień C Poland German invasion 38/3
Lublin E Poland German invasion 39/2,4; 56/1; German administration 90/1; 146/2; 148/2, 151/1; German SS and SD base 170/1; 175/1; taken by Russians 176/2; 207/3
Lubny C Ukraine 147/2
Lubuagan N Philippines 72/1
Lucban N Philippines 167/3,4
Lucca N Italy Italian air base 79/6, 81/3,5; 157/3
Lucena N Philippines air base 165/2, 167/3,4
Lucera S Italy 131/2
Łuck (n/s Lutsk, in USSR) E Poland 39/2; Russian defence 57/1; 146/2; 149/2; Kovpak's raid 171/3; 176/2
Luckau E Germany 174/1
Luckenwalde N Germany POW camp 205/2
Ludwigshafen S Germany Nazi economy 36/1; Allied bombing 112/1, 138/1; captured by US forces 183/2
Lufeng (a/s Lukfung) SE China taken by Japanese 35/4
Luga NW Russia 65/4; 151/1
Luga, R. NW USSR German bridgehead 56/1, 59/1
Lugansk see Voroshilovgrad
Lugh Ferrandi (n/c Luuq) S It. Somaliland 37/4; 51/2
Lukfung see Lufeng
Lukou C China taken by Japanese 145/3
Łuków SE Poland 146/2; 148/2, 151/1; 175/1
Luleå N Sweden 40/4
Lumut C Malaya 71/3
Lüneburg 182/3; 184/1
Lüneburg Heath N Germany surrender of German forces to Montgomery 190/1
Lünen NW Germany bombed by RAF 53/3 (inset)
Lunéville E France 44/1; sabotage 85/3; 159/7
Lunga (n/s Lungga) Guadalcanal, Solomon Is. Japanese airfield captured by US and renamed Henderson 118/2-4; US landing 121/8
Lunga Pt. (n/s Lungga Pt.) Guadalcanal, Solomon Is. Japanese landing 18/4
Lungchow (n/s Longzhou) S China treaty port 32/1

Lungkow (n/s Longkou) E China treaty port 32/1
Lungling (n/s Longling) W China 77/3; 162/1
Łuniniec (n/c Luninets, in USSR) SE Poland 149/2
Luoshan see Loshan
Luoyang see Loyang
Luozigou see Lotzukou
Lupeni NW Rumania anti-German strikes 170/1
Lupków S Poland 175/1
Luqa C Malta British air base 81/4
Lushun see Port Arthur
Luton SE England aircraft factory 46/1
Lutong Sarawak 167/5
Lutsenki C USSR 125/2
Lutsk see Łuck
Luuq see Lugh Ferrandi
Luxembourg 28-29; 36/1; German invasion 42/2; 44/1; SOE operations 84/1; absorbed into Germany 90/1; extermination of Jews 93/2; German air defences 112/1; battle of the Bulge 161/3; 182/3, 183/2
Luxembourg city German SS and SD base 94/1
Luzon island N Philippines 69/1; Japanese invasion 72/1; 140/1; US air strikes 164/1; Japanese bases 165/2; US landings 1945 167/3,4
L'vov see Lwów
Lwów (n/s L'vov, in USSR Ger.Lemberg) E Poland surrendered to Germans, occupied by Russians 39/4; Russian defence 57/1; Einsatzgruppe operations 93/4; 146/2; German SS and SD base 170/1; 171/3; taken by Russians 176/2; annexed by USSR 191/2
Lychkovo NW USSR battle for Moscow 60-61
Lyck (n/c Elk, in Poland) E Prussia 39/2,4; 148/2, 151/1
Lympne SE England RAF fighter station 52/1, 53/5
Lyons (Fr. Lyon) SE France captured by Germans 44/1; 45/2; sabotage 85/3; mass demonstrations 94/1; escape route 95/2
Lyuban NW Russia 64/2; Russian counter-offensive 65/4,5
Lyubotin NE Ukraine 124/1, 125/3
Lyudinovo C USSR 125/3
Lyutezh NW Ukraine 126/2

Maalöy (n/s Måloy) C Norway Commando raid 111/4
Maas, R. (Fr.Meuse) 159/4
Maasin C Philippines 73/5
Maastricht SW Holland 42/2; 138/1; 158/1, 159/7; 160/2, 161/3
Maas-Waal Canal S Holland 159/4
Mabuni S Okinawa Japanese defensive position 169/5
Macao (Port.Macau) S China treaty port 32/1; Portuguese colony 33/7; 35/4; 69/1
Macassar (a/s Makassar) S Celebes Japanese landing 74/1; Japanese propaganda radio station 193/2; POW camp 204/3
Macedonia province of N Greece 28/1; territory of S Yugoslavia occupied by Bulgaria 90/1, 128/1; extermination of Jews 93/2
Machang C Malaya captured by Japanese 71/2
Machang NE China taken by Japanese 34/2
Machilipatnam see Masulipatam
Machinato S Okinawa Japanese air base 169/4,5
Madagascar Vichy administration 45/3, 50/1; British occupation 79/5
Madang NE New Guinea 75/1; Japanese control 119/1, 120/1; captured by Allies 122/1, 122/2, 140/1, 140/2; 166/1
Madauk S Burma 76/2
Madaya C Burma 77/3
Maddalena NE Libya 81/6
Madrid C Spain bombed by Nationalists in Spanish Civil War 37/3; escape route 95/2
Maebashi C Japan population 192/1; US air raid 197/1
Maevatanana NW Madagascar 79/5
Maezato see Mezado
Magadan E USSR naval base and convoy port 181/1
Magdeburg C Germany Nazi economy 36/1; Allied bombing 53/3, 138/1; 182/3
Magdeburg-Anhalt district of N Germany 36/1
Magicienne Bay Saipan, Mariana Is. 143/7
Maginot Line E France French defensive line 42/2; 44/1
Maglie SE Italy 131/2
Magnitogorsk C Russia industry 172/1
Magok NE Burma 163/2
Magwe C Burma 76/1,77/3
Magyarkanizsa (Ger.Altkanischa, n/c Stara Kanjiža, in Yugoslavia) S Hungary 179/2
Mahajanga see Majunga
Mahang S Siam 71/2
Mahe French colony, S India Free French administration 45/3
Mahitsy C Madagascar 79/5
Mahón Balearic Is. Civil War 37/3
Mährisch-Ostrau see Ostrava
Mährisch-Trübau (n/c Moravská Třebová) Moravia POW camp 205/2
Mai Chio (It.Mai Ceu n/s Maych'ew) N Ethiopia captured by Italians 37/4
Maidan-i Naftun (n/s Meydan-e Naftun) W Persia 79/4
Maidstone SE England Observer Corps centre 53/5
Maikop (n/s Maykop) W Caucasus 102/2
Main C Germany SS region 91/3
Maine NE USA war industries 99/1
Mainfranken district of C Germany 36/1
Maingkwan N Burma 77/3; 163/3
Mainz W Germany Allied occupation 28/2; Allied bombing 112/1, 138/1; captured by US forces 183/2; 191/3
Maiori S Italy US landing 131/3
Maisoncelle NE France 43/4
Maisons-Lafitte N France bombed by USAAF 138/1; V-weapon storage depot 139/6
Maizuru C Japan US minelaying 196/1
Majdanek E Poland German extermination camp 92/1
Majola Hill C Italy 132/1
Majorca (Sp.Mallorca) Balearic Is. Civil War 37/3
Majunga (n/c Mahajanga) NW Madagascar British landing 79/5
Majuro Marshall Is. captured by US forces 141/1

Makale (n/s Mek'ele) N Ethiopia captured by Italians 37/4
Makassar see Macassar
Makedony NW Ukraine 127/3
Makeyevka (a/s Makeevka) SE Ukraine 127/2; industry 172/1
Makhach Kala (n/c Makhachkala) E Caucasus Russian supply port 103/1; 106/1
Makin atoll, Gilbert Is. 68; US landings 141/1, 3
Maknassy (n/s Meknassy) C Tunisia 114/4; 117/3
Makó S Hungary 179/2
Maków N Poland 175/1
Malabang S Philippines 73/4
Malacca (n/s Melaka) S Malaya 71/1,4; Japanese propaganda radio station 193/2
Málaga S Spain Civil War 37/3
Malaita Solomon Is. 75/3-5, 118/1, 121/4, 123/3
Malang E Java Japanese propaganda radio station 193/2
Malaya (n/c Peninsular Malaysia a/c Malay States) 67; 69/1; Japanese invasion 70-71; build-up for Japanese invasion of East Indies 74/1,6; under Japanese occupation 77/4, 193/2; 166/1; Japanese surrender 200/2; independence 201/3; rubber 203/1; POW camps 204/3
Malaya Rossoshka SE Russia battle of Stalingrad 105/2
Malaybalay S Philippines 73/4
Malbork see Marienburg
Maleme W Crete Greek air base captured by Germans 55/4; German air base 79/6, 117/5
Malgobek C Caucasus 103/1,2
Malin NW Ukraine 127/4
Málinec E Slovakia 179/2
Malines W Belgium 42/2
Małkinia (Górna) NE Poland 175/1
Mallorca see Majorca
Malmédy W Germany ceded to Belgium 28/1,2; battle of the Bulge 161/3
Malmö S Sweden 41/3
Maloarkhangelsk C USSR 124/1, 125/3
Maloelap Marshall Is. Japanese garrison 141/1
Malolos C Philippines 73/2
Måloy see Maalöy
Maloyaroslavets NW USSR battle for Moscow 60-61; 124/1, 125/3
Malta British air and naval base 51/4, 55/5, 79/6, 81/3-5, 117/5, 130/1, 206/1; MI6 outstation 82/1; British carrier force leaves for invasion of S France 156/1; Roosevelt-Churchill meeting 189/1
Maltby C England Royal Ordnance Factory 46/1
Maluko see Tankulan
Maluku see Moluccas
Malye Derbety (n/s Malyye Derbety) SE Russia battle of Stalingrad 104/1
Maly Trostenets (n/s Malyy Trostenets) W Russia German extermination camp 92/1
Mamara Guadalcanal, Solomon Is. 121/8
Mamayev Kurgan SE Russia battle of Stalingrad 100/2
Mamison Pass (Russ.Maminsonskiy Pereval) S Caucasus 103/1,2
Manchester N England industries 46/1; civil defence HQ 47/3; evacuation area 47/4; air defences 52/1; German air raids 53/6; 112/1; 138/1
Manchouli (n/s Manzhouli) NW Manchuria treaty port 32/1; 35/1,4; captured by Russians 199/2
Manchukuo (a/c Manchuria) Japanese puppet state 66; 68; Japanese garrison 168/1, 169/3
Manchuria warlord control 32/2-5; invaded by Japanese 32/7, 35/1, 35/4; Japanese puppet state of Manchukuo 193/2; Russian invasion 198-199; Japanese surrender 200/2; restored to China 201/3; POW camp 204/3; 207/1. See also Manchukuo
Mandai Singapore 71/5
Mandalay C Burma 76/1; captured by Japanese 77/3; 77/4; 162/1, 163/2; Chindit operations 163/3
Manduria SE Italy 131/2
Manell Pt. Guam, Mariana Is. Japanese landing 69/6
Mang-shih (n/s Mangshi) W China 77/3
Manhay SE Belgium battle of the Bulge 161/3
Manila C Philippines 69/1; 72/1; 73/2; 140/1; 165/2; 166/1; 167/3,4; Japanese base 193/2; Japanese propaganda radio station 193/2; Japanese port 194-195; Japanese surrender 200/2; postwar US base 201/3
Mankovo SE Russia Upper Don offensive 107/2
Mannerheim Line E Finland Finnish defensive line 41/1
Manneville Normandy battle for Caen 153/5
Mannheim SW Germany Nazi economy 36/1; 44/1; Allied bombing 53/3, 112/1, 138/1; 160/1; captured by US forces 182/3
Manokwari NW New Guinea Japanese landing 74/1; 140/1
Manston SE England RAF fighter station 52/1, 53/5
Mantes N France sabotage 85/3; 155/1

Mong Long C Burma 77/3
Möng Mit NE Burma retaken by British 163/2
Mong Nai C Burma 77/3
Mong Nawng (a/s Monong) E Burma 77/3
Mongolia (f/c Outer Mongolia) 32-33; conflict between Japan and USSR 35/4; base for Russian invasion of Manchuria 198/1,2
Mong Pawn (a/s Mongpaung) C Burma 77/3
Mong Ping E Burma 77/3
Monheim NW Germany bombed by RAF 53/3
Monong see Mong Nawng
Monopoli SE Italy 131/2; SOE base 84/1
Monor C Hungary 179/3
Monowitz-Buna S Poland German labour camp 93/5
Mons W Belgium 42/2; 44/1; escape route 95/2; 158/1
Monschau W Germany 42/2; 160/2
Montalban C Philippines 72/1; 73/2
Montana NW USA worker mobility 98/1
Montataire N France sabotage 85/3
Montbartier SW France sabotage 85/3
Montbéliard E France sabotage 85/3
Montcarnet NE France 42/2
Montdidier N France German bomber station 52/1, 113/6
Monte Artemisio C Italy 133/4
Montebourg Normandy taken by US forces 153/2,4
Monte Cairo (a/s Caira) C Italy 132/1, 133/3
Monte Camino S Italy 131/2
Monte Cassino S Italy battle for 132/1, 133/3
Monte Castellone C Italy 132/1
Montecchio Emilia N Italy Allied bombing 157/4; 157/5
Montélimar SE France 44/1; captured by US forces 156/2
Montenegro (S.Cr. Crna Gora) province of S Yugoslavia 28/1; 55/3; 90/1; Italian occupation 128/1; 170/1
Monte Sant'Angelo S Italy 131/2
Monte Trocchio S Italy 131/2
Montevideo Uruguay Graf Spee scuttled 49/7
Monte Villa C Italy 132/1
Montherme E France 42/2; 44/1
Montigny NE France 43/4
Montluçon C France sabotage 85/3; 95/2
Montmedy NE France 44/1
Montoire (-sur-la-Loire) N France Axis conference 86/1; 90/1
Montpellier S France escape route 95/2
Montreal E Canada UNNRA meeting 189/1
Montreuil NE France 43/6; German fighter station 52/1
Montreux W Switzerland conference of 1936 28/1
Montrichard N France 155/1
Mont-St.Eloi NE France 43/5
Monywa NW Burma captured by Japanese 77/3; 163/2
Moosburg S Germany POW camp 205/2
Mór C Hungary 178/2, 186/1
Moramanga C Madagascar 79/5
Moravia province of central Czechoslovakia 28/1
Moravská Ostrava see Ostrava
Moravská Třebová (Ger. Mährisch-Trübau) C Moravia 187/2
Moreh NE India 162/5
Morlaix NW France bombed by USAAF 113/1; 154/1
Morobe E Papua 75/1; 119/1, 120/2; 122/1,2
Morocco Vichy administration 45/3, 50/1; American landings 116/1
Moron C Philippines, Bataan captured by Japanese 73/3
Morondava W Madagascar 79/5
Morotai island of E Indies 164/1; 166/1; 167/5; captured by US forces 140/1
Morozovsk SE Russia Upper Don offensive 107/2
Mortagne NW France Normandy invasion 152/2; 155/1,3
Mortain N France German counter-offensive 154/3
Mosalsk NW USSR battle for Moscow 60-61
Moscow (Russ. Moskva, Ger. Moskau) NW USSR 29/5; German air raids 56/1, 59/1; German plan of attack 57/2; 59/2; German attack 60-61; 65/4; Japanese intelligence 82/1; SOE base 82/1, 84/1; Axis conferences 86/1; Allied conferences 86/1, 189/1; 106/1; 171/2; industry 172/1
Moselland district of W Germany 36/1
Mosit NE Burma 163/2
Mosjöen N Norway 40/3
Moskau see Moscow
Moskva see Moscow
Moson NW Hungary 186/1
Mosonmagyaróvár NW Hungary 178/2, 179/4
Moss S Norway 41/3
Most see Brüx
Mosta see Musta
Mostar S Yugoslavia 128/1, 129/2
Mosty E Poland (now in USSR) 148/2, 151/1

Mosul (n/s Al Mawsil) N Iraq German air base 79/3
Motobu Peninsula (Jap. Motobu-hanto) NW Okinawa Japanese resistance 169/4
Motoyami C Iwo Jima 168/2
Moulmein S Burma British air base 76/1; captured by Japanese 76/2; Japanese air base 77/3; POW camp 204/3
Mount Batten SW England Coastal Command airfield 88/4, 108/4
Mouzon NE France 43/4
Moyale N Kenya 37/4; captured by Italians 51/2
Mozambique (a/c Portuguese East Africa) 50/1
Mozdok C Caucasus Germans cross R.Terek 103/1; 106/1
Mozhaisk (n/s Mozhaysk) NW USSR battle for Moscow 60-61; 65/4
Mozyr W Russia 106/1; 147/2; 149/2; Soviet partisans 171/2
Mshinskaya NW Russia 151/1
Msus (n/c Zawiyat Masus) NE Libya captured by Allies 50/3; recaptured by Germans 78/2; retaken by British 80/6, 115/4
Mtsensk C USSR 125/3
Muang Lampang see Lampang
Muang Lamphun see Lampun
Muar S Malaya captured by Japanese 71/4
Muda R. N Malaya crossed by Japanese 71/2
Mudanjiang see Mutankiang
Mühlberg C Germany POW camp 205/2
Mühlhausen see Milevsko
Mukachevo (Cz. Mukačevo, Hung. Munkács) SW Ukraine 177/3
Mukden (a/c Fengtien n/c Shenyang) S Manchuria treaty port 32/1; taken by Japanese 35/1,4; 66,68; Japanese propaganda radio station 193/2; captured by Russians 199/2; POW camp 204/3
Mulberry Harbour Normandy, France 152/2, 153/3
Mulhouse (Ger. Mülhausen) E France 44/1; 159/7; 183/2
Mulong S Siam 71/2
Müncheberg E Germany 150/1, 174/1
München see Munich
München-Gladbach (n/s Mönchengladbach) NW Germany Allied bombing 53/3, 138/1; captured by US forces 183/2
Munda Pt. Solomon Is. Japanese base 120/1, 121/4; Allied assault 123/3
Mu Nggava see Rennell I.
Munich (Ger. München) S Germany Hitler's Putsch of 1923 28/2; Nazi economy 36/1; Allied bombing 53/3, 112/1, 138/1; listening post 83/2; Führerstadt 91/4; captured by Allies 182/3; resistance to Hitler 188/2; 191/3
Münichkirchen S Austria Hitler HQ 134/2
Munich-Upper Bavaria district of S Germany 36/1
Munkács see Mukachevo
Münster N Germany Nazi work seat 36/1; 42/2; Allied bombing 53/3, 112/1, 138/1; listening post 83/2
Münsterberg (n/c Ziębice, in Poland) SE Germany 150/1
Muntok S Sumatra POW camp 204/3
Muqdisho see Mogadishu
Muraköz see Medjumurje
Murmansk N USSR base for attack on Finland 41/1; 57/3; industry 172/1; convoy port 180/1; 180/3; naval base 206/1
Mūrmuiža C Latvia 148/2, 151/1
Muroran NE Japan population 193/2; port 194-195; US naval bombardment 196/2, 197/1
Murzuk (n/s Murzuq) S Libya LRDG raid 111/2
Mürzzuschlag E Austria 186/1
Musashino C Japan US air raids 197/3
Muscovy NW Russia post-war province planned by Germany 91/4
Mussolini Canal C Italy 133/2
Musta (n/s Mosta) NW Malta 81/4
Mutankiang (a/s Mu-tan-chiang n/s Mudanjiang) E Manchuria captured by Russians 199/2
Mutcho Pt. Saipan, Mariana Is. 143/4,7
Myanaung SW Burma 76/1,2
Myaungmya SW Burma 76/2
Myaungtanga S Burma 76/2
Myawaddy (a/s Myawadi) S Burma captured by Japanese 76/2
Myebon W Burma 163/2
Myingun C Burma 163/2
Myingyan C Burma captured by Japanese 77/3; retaken by British 163/2
Myinmu N Burma retaken by British 163/2
Myitche N Burma 163/2
Myitkyina N Burma captured by Japanese 77/3; Chindit operations 163/2,3
Myitson NE Burma 77/3; retaken by British 163/2
Myjava NW Slovakia 186/1
Myohaung NW Burma 163/2
Myothit NE Burma 163/2
Mysen SE Norway German detention centre 94/1
Myskhako W Caucasus 103/4

Myślenice S Poland 175/1
Myślibórz see Soldin
Mysłowice (Ger. Myslowitz) S Poland 175/1
Mytho S Indo-China POW camp 204/3
Mytishchi NW USSR battle for Moscow 60-61;

Náchod N Bohemia 174/1
Nadzab NE New Guinea 119/1; 122/1,2; captured by Allies 140/1,2
Nafutan Pt. Saipan, Mariana Is. 143/7
Naga C Philippines air base 165/2, 167/3,4
Nagano C Japan population 192/1
Nagaoka NE Japan US air raid 197/1
Nagasaki W Japan 68; 96/1; industry 192/1; atomic bomb attack 196/1; POW Camp 204/3; Japanese base 207/1
Nago NW Okinawa captured by US 169/4
Nagoya C Japan 66; population 192/1; US air raid 197/1
Nagybecskerek see Petrovgrad
Nagyberezna see Veliki Berezny
Nagybocsko see Veliki Bochkov
Nagykáta C Hungary 179/2
Nagykőrös C Hungary 179/2
Nagymihály see Michalovce
Nagyvárad (n/c Oradea, in Rumania; Ger. Grosswardein) SE Hungary taken by Russians 177/3; 179/2
Naha S Okinawa Japanese air base 169/4,5
Nairobi S Kenya 51/2
Najin (Jap. Rashin) N Korea Japanese port 194-195; Russian attack 199/2
Nakagusuku Bay (Jap. Nakagusuku-Wan) S Okinawa 169/4,5
Nakawn Patom (n/s Nakhon Pathom) S Siam Burma railway 204
Nakawn Sritamarat (n/c Nakhon Si Thammarat) S Siam 70/1
Nakhon Pathom see Nakawn Patom
Nakhon Si Thammarat see Nakawn Sritamarat
Nakło (nad Nolecią) (Ger. Nakel) NW Poland German invasion 39/2; 175/1
Nalchik C Caucasus reached by Germans 103/1
Nalong NE Burma 163/2
Namhkam NE Burma 163/2
Namhkan C Burma 77/3
Namhpakka C Burma 77/3
Namibia see South West Africa
Namsang C Burma 77/3
Namsos C Norway Allied landing 40/3; 41/5
Namtu C Burma 77/3; 163/2
Namudi Papua 120/2
Namur C Belgium 42/2; 44/1; 160/2, 161/3
Namur I. Kwajalein atoll, Marshall Is. 141/5
Nanao C Japan US minelaying 197/1
Nanchang SE China taken by Kuomintang forces 33/6; Communist rising 33/7; taken by Japanese 34/2, 35/4
Nancy E France 44/1; 112/1; 158/1
Nandan see Nantan
Naniagassa I. Saipan, Mariana Is. 143/4
Nanjing see Nanking
Nanking (n/s Nanjing a/s Nan-ching) E China treaty port 32/1; taken by Kuomintang and made Nationalist capital 33/6,7; taken by Japanese 34/2, 34/3, 35/4; occupied by Japanese 66; 68; Japanese puppet government 144/3; Chinese national government 193/2; Japanese surrender 200/2
Nankow (n/s Nankou) N China taken by Japanese 34/2
Nanning S China treaty port 32/1; 69/1; taken by Japanese 35/4; taken by Japanese 145/3
Nantan (n/s Nandan) SW China taken by Japanese 145/3
Nantes W France captured by Germans 45/1; bombed by USAAF 113/1; German bomber station 113/6; Normandy invasion 152/1; taken by US forces 154/1
Naples (It. Napoli) S Italy Italian naval base 51/4; RAF raid on naval base 55/5; Italian air base 79/6, 81/3,5; Allied bombing 113/3; Axis base 117/5; taken by British 131/2; 156/1
Nara C Japan population 192/1
Narew, R. C Poland 39/3
Naro-Fominsk NW USSR battle for Moscow 60-61
Narsarssuak S Greenland 109/2
Narva Estonia, NW USSR 56/1; taken by Germans 64/1
Narvik N Norway Allied attack 40/3,4; Allied evacuation 41/5; German air base and weather station 180/1, 181,2; German base 206/1

O

Oahu Hawaiian Is. Japanese attack 68,69/2,3; 96/1/
Oban W Scotland port 48/4
Obbia (n/s Hobyo) It.Somaliland 37/4
Oberhausen NW Germany Communist uprising 1920 28/2; Allied bombing 112/1, 138/1
Obermassfeld W Germany POW hospital 205/2
Oberursel W Germany POW camp 205/2
Obiam, Cape Saipan, Mariana Is. 143/4,7
Oboyan C USSR 124/1, 125/3
Obrovac (It.Obbrovazzo) NW Yugoslavia 129/2
Obukhov NW Ukraine 127/4
Ocean I. (n.c Kure I.) S Pacific 66; Japanese surrender 200/2
Ochakov S USSR Russian naval base 57/1; 126/2
Ochota district of S Warsaw uprising 171/4
Ochrida see Ohrid
Ödenburg see Sopron
Odense C Denmark 41/3; sabotage attacks 95/4
Odessa S USSR Russian naval base 57/1; evacuation to Crimea 58/1; 61/1; 62/1; 106/1; 126/2; 146/3; 147/2; 170/1, 171/2; industry 172/1; 177/3
Odon, R. Normandy, France 152/2; battle for Caen 153/5
O'Donnell N Philippines POW camp 204/3
Odweina (n/s Oodweyne) Brit.Somaliland captured by Italians 51/2
Oels (n/s Oleśnica, in Poland) E. Germany 175/1
Offenburg SW Germany 28/2; POW camp 205/2
Offranville N France Dieppe raid 86/2
Ofotfjord N Norway inlet naval battle 40/4
Ogaden region of SE Ethiopia claimed by Italy 37/4
Ogaki C Japan US air raid 197/1
Ogasawara-gunto see Bonin Is.
Ogliastro (Cilento) S Italy 131/3
Ohio N USA war industries 98/1
Ohrid (a/s Ochrida) S Yugoslavia 128/1, 129/2
Oita W Japan copper resources 192/1; US air raid 196/1
Okayama W Japan population 192/1; US air raid 196/1
Okazaki C Japan US air raid 197/1
Okhocheye NE Ukraine battle for Kharkov 107/4,5
Okhotsk, Sea of Japanese shipping losses 194-195
Oki see Ouki
Okinawa Ryukyu Is. S Japan 66,68; US invasion 169/3,4,5; postwar US base 201/3
Oklahoma C USA war industries 98/1
Oktwin C Burma 163/2
Okulovka NW Russia 65/4
Oldenburg N Germany Communist uprising 1919 28/2; 36/1; 42/2; bombed by RAF 53/3
Olenegorsk NW USSR 180/3
Olenino NW USSR battle for Moscow 60-61
Oleśnica see Oels
Olevsk Soviet partisans 171/2; Kovpak's raid 171/3
Olkhovatka C USSR 125/2
Olonets (Finn. Aunus) NW USSR 41/1 captured by Finns 64/1
Olongapo C Philippines 72/1, 73/2; 167/3,4
Olshany NE Ukraine 124/1, 125/3
Olsztyn see Allenstein
Omaha Beach Normandy US landings 152/4, 153/2
Oman country of SE Arabia 79/4
Ombrone, R. N Italy 133/4
Omicourt NE France 43/4
Ominato NE Japan 96/1/; 197/1
Ommen E Holland German detention centre 94/1
Omont NE France 43/4
Omsk C Russia industry 172/1
Omuta W Japan US air raid 196/1
Ona see Wana
Onega NW USSR 180/1
Onega, Lake NW USSR 56/1, 57/3, 59/1
Onekotan (now in USSR) Kurile Is., Japan Russian occupation 199/3
Onival NE France Commando raids 110/1
Oodweyne see Odweina

Oosterbeek S Holland British airborne landing 159/4,5
Oostmalle N Belgium 159/6
Opava (Ger.Troppau) Bohemia-Moravia 39/2; 175/1; 187/2
Opheusden S Holland captured by British 159/4
Opochka W Russia 149/2, 151/1
Opoczno C Poland 175/1
Opole see Oppeln
Oporto N Portugal 37/3
Oposhnya NE Ukraine battle for Kharkov 107/4,5
Oppeln (n/c Opole, in Poland) E Germany Nazi land court 36/1; 151/1; 174/2; 175/1
Oppenheim W Germany US bridgehead over R.Rhine 183/2
Oradea see Nagyvárad
Oradour-sur-Glane C France German reprisal massacre 94/1
Oran NW Algeria French base 50/1, 51/4, 79/6, 81/5; Allied landings 116/1; base for Allied invasion of S France 156/1
Oranienbaum (n/c Lomonosov) NW Russia taken by Germans 64/2, 65/4
Oranienburg NE Germany Nazi land court 36/1, 150/1, 174/1
Orcia, R. N Italy 133/4
Ordzhonikidze (a/c Dzaudzhikau) C Caucasus 103/2; 106/1
Ordzhonikidze see Yenakiyevo
Oregon NW USA worker mobility 98/1
Orekhov S Ukraine 63/1
Orekhovo-Zuyevo NW USSR battle for Moscow 60-61
Orel C USSR 57/1, 58/1; battle for Moscow 60-61; 61/1; German offensive against Kursk 106/1; 124/1; liberated 125/3; 171/2; industry 172/1
Orenburg see Chkalov
Orgeyev (Rum. Orhei) SW Ukraine 177/3
Orgon S France liberated by US forces 156/2
Orhei see Orgeyev
Orion Bataan, C Philippines 73/2,3
Orkney Is. 41/5
Orléans C France 44/1; sabotage 85/3; German bomber station 113/6; taken by US forces 155/1; 158/1
Orlovka SE Russia battle of Stalingrad 101/2; 125/2
Ormoc C Philippines 73/5; 164/2, 167/2
Orne, R. NW France Normandy invasion 152/2, 153/5
Oro Bay E Papua 119/5,6; Allied base 122/1,2
Oroku Peninsula S Okinawa 169/4,5
Orote Peninsula Guam, Mariana Is. 143/6
Orsogna C Italy taken by British 131/2
Orsha NW USSR 56/1; battle for Moscow 60-61; 61/1; 106/1; 149/2; 151/1
Orsk C Russia industry 172/1
Ortelsburg (n/c Szczytno, in Poland) E Prussia 148/2, 151/1, 175/1
Ortheuville SE Belgium battle for Bastogne 161/4
Ortona C Italy taken by British 131/2
Osaka C Japan 66; 68; industry 192/1; Japanese propaganda radio station 193/2; US air raid 196/1; POW camp 204/3
Oschersleben N Germany bombed by USAAF 112/1
Oseshchino NW Ukraine 127/4
Osipenko S Ukraine 63/1; 147/2
Osipovichi W Russia 149/2,4; 151/1
Osjaków W Poland 174/2
Oskol, R. C USSR 125/1,3
Oslo (f/c Christiania) S Norway 29/5; German airborne landing 41/3; German SS and SD base 94/1
Oslo Fjord S Norway 41/3
Osnabrück N Germany Nazi work seat 36/1; 42/2; Allied bombing 53/3, 112/1, 138/1; 182/3
Osnochnoe C USSR 125/2
Oss S Holland 159/4
Ostashkov NW USSR battle for Moscow 60-61; 65/4
Ostenburg see Pułtusk
Ostend (Dut. Oostende Fr. Ostende) W Belgium 42/2,43/6; German invasion base 52/1; bombed by RAF 53/3; Normandy invasion 152/1; captured by Allies 158/1; 160/1
Osterode (n/c Ostróda in Poland) E Prussia 39/2; 175/1
Ostiglia N Italy 157/5
Ostland German territory embracing Estonia, Latvia, Lithuania and W Byelorussia 90/1, 91/4; extermination of gypsies 92/3; 170/1
Ostpreussen see East Prussia
Ostrava Bohemia-Moravia 39/2, 91/2, 4, 170/1 175/1, 187/2
Ostróda see Osterode
Ostrołęka NE Poland 175/1
Ostrov NW Russia 64/1; 149/2; 151/1
Ostrów W Poland 150/1, taken by Russians 174/2, 175/1
Ostrowiec S Poland 146/2, 148/2, 151/1, 175/1, 176/2

Ostrów Mazowiecka E Poland 148/2, 151/1, 175/1
Ostsee N Germany SS region 91/4
Oświęcim see Auschwitz
Otaru N Japan population 193/2; port 194-195; NE Japan 197/1
Otočac NW Yugoslavia 128/1
Otomari (n/c Korsakov, in USSR) N Japan occupied by Russians 199/3
Otranto SE Italy 131/2
Otsu C Japan population 192/1
Ottawa E. Canada Russian intelligence 82/1; Commonwealth Conference 87/1
Oudenaarde see Audenarde
Ouistreham Normandy, France battle for Caen 153/5
Ouki (n/s Oki) S Okinawa 169/5
Oulu C Finland 41/1; 180/3
Outer Mongolia see Mongolia
Ouville-la-Rivière N France Dieppe raid 87/2
Ovidiopol SW Ukraine 126/2, 146/3, 147/2, 177/3
Oviedo N Spain Civil War 37/3
Ovruch W Ukraine Kovpak's raid 171/3
Owen Stanley Range E Papua 119/1,5,6; 120/2
Oxford S England air defences 52/1; 112/1; 138/1; V1 and V2 attacks 139/6
Oyama NE Japan US minelaying 197/1
Oye-Plage NE France German fighter station 52/1
Öyjord N Norway 40/4
Ozamiz S Philippines 73/4
Özd N Hungary 179/2
Ozerechnya NW USSR battle for Moscow 60-61
Ozorków C Poland German invasion 39/2

P

Pa-an S Burma 76/2
Pabjanice (Ger.Pabianitz) C Poland 175/1
Pabradė see Podbrodzie
Pacific Ocean German surface raiders 49/7; spheres of control 1941 66; Japanese occupation 74,75/1-6; battle of Midway 96-97; convoy routes 99/3; battles for south-west Pacific 118-119; 122-123, 140-141; US convoy routes to USSR 181/1; Japanese mandated islands 193/2; Japanese shipping losses 194-195; shipping routes 202/1; US Army and Air Force supply lines 203/2; troop movements 206/1
Pacijan island of C Philippines 167/2
Padang S Sumatra Japanese propaganda radio station 193/2; Japanese port 194-195; Japanese surrender 200/2; POW camp 204/3
Paddington W London German air raids 53/4
Paderborn NW Germany bombed by RAF 53/3; 182/3
Padiglione Woods C Italy, Anzio, 133/2
Padua (It.Padova) N Italy anti-German strike 94/1; captured by US forces 157/5
Paestum S Italy German airfield 131/3
Pag (It.Pago) NW Yugoslavia 128/1
Pagan C Burma 77/3
Pagan Mariana Is. 66; 168/1,169/3
Pagat Pt. Guam, Mariana Is. 143/6
Pago Bay Guam, Mariana Is. 143/6
Pahang state of C Malaya 71/3,4
Pahsien (n/s Baxian) N China taken by Japanese 34/2
Paide (Ger.Weissenstein) C Estonia 151/1
Paihokang (n/s Baihegang) E China taken by Japanese 34/3
Paimaokou E China taken by Japanese 34/2
Paingkyon S Burma 76/2
Pakhoi (n/c Beihai a/s Pei-hai) S China treaty port 32/1; taken by Japanese 35/4
Pakokku C Burma 77/3; retaken by British 163/2
Paks C Hungary 178/2
Palaiokhora W Crete captured by Germans 54/4
Palanga (Ger.Polangen) W Latvia 148/2, 151/1
Palatinate (Ger.Pfalz) district of W Germany occupied by US forces 183/2
Palau Is. W Pacific 66; Japanese base 68; captured by US forces 140/1; 166/1; Japanese shipping routes 195/5; Japanese surrender 200/2; US trust territory 201/3
Palawan island of W Philippines 164/2, 166/1
Paldiski (Ger.Baltischport) NW Estonia 151/1
Palel NE India 77/3; 162/5
Palembang S Sumatra 69/1; Japanese landing 74/1; 166/1; Japanese propaganda radio station 193/2; Japanese port 194-195; POW camp 204/3
Palermo W Sicily Italian air and naval bases 51/4, 54/1, 79/6, 81/3,5; German air base 130/2
Palestine 50/1, 51/4; 79/3; British and US intelligence 82/1
Palestrina C Italy 133/2
Paletwa W Burma 77/3
Palma Balearic Is. Civil War 37/3
Palmi S Italy bombed by USAAF 113/3; 131/2
Palmyra (n/c Tadmur) C Syria bombed by RAF 79/3
Palmyra I. C Pacific 66
Palo C Philippines 167/2
Palompon Leyte, C Philippines 164/2, 167/2
Panama Japanese intelligence 82/1; tanker fleet 203/4; declaration of war against Axis 207/1
Pan-American neutrality zone Atlantic Ocean 48/1, 49/2
Panaon island of C Philippines 165/3
Panay island S Philippines 72/1; surrendered to Japanese 73/5; Japanese air bases 164/2; Japanese propaganda radio station 193/2
Pančevo (Ger.Pantschowa) SE Yugoslavia 129/2; German detention centre 170/1
Pangdan C Philippines Leyte 167/2
Pangfow (a/s Pengpu n/s Bengbu) E China taken by Japanese 34/2, 35/4
Pankow E suburb of Berlin 185/2
Panshino SE Russia battle of Stalingrad 104/1
Pantschowa see Pančevo
Pantelleria island C Mediterranean 81/5, 114/4; bombed by Allies 130/1; Axis base 206/1
Paochi (n/s Baoji) W China 34/2, 35/4

Paola – Port Moresby

Paola S Italy bombed by USAAF 113/3
Paoshan (n/s Baoshan) W China 77/3
Paoting (n/s Baoding a/c Tsingyüan) NE China 35/4
Paotow (a/s Pao-tou n/s Baotou) N China taken by Japanese 34/2, 35/4
Pápa NW Hungary 178/2, 179/4, 186/1
Papua 75/1; 74/6; Japanese landings 119/1,5; Allied landings 119/1,6; Australian offensive 120/2,3; 166/1
Papun S Burma 76/2
Paradiso NE Sicily 131/2
Paraguay declaration of war against Axis 207/1
Parajd (n/s Praid, in Rumania) E Hungary 177/3
Paramushiro (n/s Ostrov Paramushir, in USSR) Kurile Is. 96/1; Russian attack 199/3; Japanese base 207/1
Parang S Philippines Japanese landing 73/4
Parczew Forest C Poland partisan activity 171/2
Parichi W USSR 149/4
Paris N France Treaty of Versailles 28/1; 42/2; captured by Germans 44/1; Japanese intelligence 82/1; German military HQ 83/2; strikes and demonstrations 94/1; reprisals 94/1; escape route centre 95/2; bombed by USAAF 112/1, 138/1; Hitlers visit 134/2; Normandy invasion 152/1; liberation 155/1,4; anti-Hitler plot 188/2
Parit Sulong S Malaya captured by Japanese 71/4
Parma N Italy captured by US forces 157/5
Pärnu (Ger.Pernau) W Estonia 151/1
Pas-de-Calais district of NE France German administration from Belgium 90/1; Normandy invasion 152/1
Pasir Laba Singapore 71/5
Pasir Panjang Singapore 71/5
Passau SE Germany 187/2
Passero, Cape S Sicily British landings 131/2
Pastrana Leyte, C Philippines 167/2
Pásztó N Hungary 179/2
Patani (n/s Pattani) S Siam Siamese air base 71/1 Japanese landing 71/2
Pati Pt. Guam, Mariana Is. 143/6
Patras S Greece occupied by Germans 55/3; 128/1, 129/2; anti-German strikes 170/1
Patricroft NW England Royal Ordnance Factory 46/1 (inset)
Pau SW France sabotage 85/3
Pauk W Burma 77/3; 163/2
Paukkaung S Burma 77/3
Paung S Burma 76/2
Paungbyin NW Burma 77/3
Paunggyi S Burma 76/2
Pavelets NW USSR battle for Moscow 60-61
Pavia N Italy Allied bombing 157/4
Pävilosta W Latvia 148/2, 151/1
Pavlodar Kazakhstan 172/1
Pavlograd NE Ukraine 62/2; 63/1; Nazi industry 91/2; battle for Kharkov 107/4,5; 147/2
Pavlov House Stalingrad 100/2
Pavlovo NW Russia siege of Leningrad 64/2
Pavlovsk NW Russia siege of Leningrad 64/2
Pavlovsk S Ukraine 63/1
Pavlovskaya S USSR 63/1, 147/2
Paya Lebar Singapore 71/5
Pearl City S Oahu, Hawaiian Is. 69/2,3
Pearl Harbor Hawaiian Is. US naval base 66, 207/1; Japanese attack 68, 69/4; 96/1
Pearl and Hermes Reef N Pacific 96/1
Peć (Alb.Pejë) S Yugoslavia 129/2
Pechen (a/s Pei-chen n/s Beizhen) SW Manchuria 199/2
Pechenegi NE Ukraine battle for Kharkov 107/3
Pechenga *see* Petsamo
Pécs (Ger.Fünfkirchen) SW Hungary 178/2
Peenemünde NE Germany captured by Russians 190/1
Pegnitz C Germany Nazi industry 91/2
Pegu S Burma captured by Japanese 76/2; retaken by British 163/2
Pei-chen *see* Pechen
Pei-hai *see* Pakhoi
Peiping *see* Peking
Peipus, Lake NW Russia 64/1; 149/2; 151/1
Peisern *see* Pyzdry
Pejë *see* Pec
Pekari NW Ukraine 127/3
Pekanbaru S Sumatra POW camp 204/3
Peking (n/s Beijing, called Peiping 1928-1949) NE China taken by Japanese 34/2, 35/1; taken by Kuomintang forces 33/6; under Japanese occupation 66; 68; Japanese intelligence 82/1; North China Political Council 144/2; 198/2; POW camp 204/3
Pembrey S Wales Royal Ordnance Factory 46/1
Pembroke SW Wales shipbuilding and naval base 46/1; Coastal Command airfield 88/4, 108/4
Penang N Malaya 74/1; Japanese propaganda radio station 193/2
Pengpu *see* Pangfow
Peninsular Malaysia *see* Malaya
Pennsylvania E USA war industries 98/1
Penza W USSR industry 172/1
Perak state of N Malaya 71/2,3
Perak R. N Malaya crossed by Japanese 71/2
Percy N France 154/2
Perekop S USSR 62/1; 106/1; 126/2; 146/3; 147/2
Peremyshl NW USSR battle for Moscow 60-61
Pereshchepino NE Ukraine battle for Kharkov 107/4,5
Pereslavl-Zalessky NW USSR battle for Moscow 60-61
Pereyaslav (n/c Pereyaslav-Khmel'nitskiy) C Ukraine 147/2
Périers NW France Normandy invasion 153/2; 154/1,2,3
Périgueux SW France 95/2
Peringat S Siam airfield captured by Japanese 71/2
Perm C USSR industry 172/1
Pernau *see* Pärnu
Peronne NE France 42/2; 44/1
Perpignan S France escape route 95/2
Persia (a/c Iran) 50/1; oil production 79/4; supply routes to USSR 79/4; declaration of war against Axis 206/1
Perth W Australia 67
Perth C Scotland industrial centre 46/1
Peru declaration of war against Axis 207/1
Pervomaisk (n/s Pervomaysk) C Ukraine Einsatzgruppe operations 93/4; 126/2, 147/2
Pervomaiskoye SE Russia Upper Don offensive 107/2
Pesaro N Italy 157/3
Pescara C Italy German defence 131/2, 133/4
Peschanka SE Russia battle of Stalingrad 100/2, 105/2
Peschanoye *see* Yashkul
Peschici S Italy 131/2
Peschiera (del Garda) N Italy Allied bombing 157/4; 157/5
Peski NW Russia siege of Leningrad 64/2
Peskovatka SE Russia battle of Stalingrad 104/1
Pesye W USSR Einsatzgruppe operations 93/4
Peter Beach C Italy Anzio, US landing 133/2
Petrikau *see* Piotrków
Petrila NW Rumania anti-German strikes 170/1
Petropavlovka NE Ukraine battle for Kharkov 107/4,5
Petropavlovsk (n/c Petropavlovsk-Kamchatskiy) E USSR 66; industry 172/1; Russian air and naval base 181/1; base for invasion of Kurile Is. 199/3
Petroskoi *see* Petrozavodsk
Petrovgrad (Ger.Grossbetschkerek, Hung.Nagybecskerek, n/c Zrenjanin) NE Yugoslavia occupied by Germans 128/1; liberated by partisans 129/2; German detention centre 170/1
Petrovichi W USSR 149/4
Petrovsk (n/c Petrovsk-Zabaykal'skiy) E USSR industry 173/1
Petrovskaya W Caucasus 103/3
Petrozavodsk (Finn.Petroskoi) NW USSR 56/1, 57/3; 106/1; industry 172/1; occupied by Finns 180/3
Petsamo (n/c Pechenga, in USSR) N Finland 90/1; nickel deposits 180/1; retaken by Finns 180/3; German air base 181/2
Pfalz *see* Palatinate
Pforzheim SW Germany Allied bombing 138/1; 182/3
Phantom Ridge C Italy Cassino, 132/1
Philippeville S Belgium 42/2
Philippeville (n/c Skikda) NE Algeria 116/1
Philippine Is. 66; Japanese invasion 69/1, 72-73; build-up for Japanese invasion of East Indies and Pacific 74/1,6; under Japanese occupation 77/4; Japanese intelligence 82/1; 140/1; Japanese air bases 142/1; American landings 1944-5 164-167; Japanese defence 168/1, 169/3; puppet government under Japanese control 193/2; 200/2; independence 201/3; POW camps 204/3
Philippine Sea US-Japanese carrier battle 142/1,2,3
Phlorina *see* Florina
Phnom-penh *see* Pnom-penh
Phoenix Is. C Pacific 66
Phuket *see* Puket
Phu-kwok I. (n/s Phu Quoc) S Indo-China Japanese air base 70/1
Piacenza N Italy Allied bombing 157/4; captured by US forces 157/5
Piątek C Poland German invasion 38/3
Piatra Neamt E Rumania Einsatzgruppe operations 93/4; taken by Russians 177/3
Pichon (n/c Haffouz) N Tunisia 117/2
Piešt'any (Ger.Pistyan) W Slovakia 186/1
Pikit S Philippines 73/4
Piła *see* Schneidemühl
Pilar Bataan, C Philippines 73/3
Pilsen (Cz.Plzeň) W Czechoslovakia Bohemia Nazi industry 91/2; taken by Russians 187/2; captured by US forces 190/1
Pinamopoan C Philippines 167/2
Pinbaw NE Burma retaken by Chinese forces 163/2
Pinbon NW Burma captured by Japanese 77/3
Pinghu E China taken by Japanese 34/3
P'ing-ka W China 77/3
Pingkiang (n/s Pingjiang) C China taken by Japanese 145/3
Pinglu C China taken by Japanese 34/2
Pingnan S China taken by Japanese 145/3
Pingtichuan *see* Tsining
P'ing-tung *see* Heito
Pingwang E China taken by Japanese 34/3
Pingyao N China changed hands 34/2, 35/4
Pingyüan NE China taken by Japanese 34/2
Pinlebu NE Burma 163/3
Pińsk (now Pinsk, in USSR) E Poland 39/2; occupied by Russians 39/4; 56/1; 149/2; Soviet partisans 171/2
Pinwe NE Burma 163/3
Pinyang S China taken by Japanese 145/3
Piotrków (n/c Piotrków Trybunalski Ger.Petrikau) C Poland German invasion 39/2; 151/1, 175/1
Piraeus (n/s Piraievs) SE Greece 51/4; Greek naval base captured by Germans 55/3; German supply port 79/6; 81/5; German base 117/5
Pirgos S Crete 55/4
Pirna E Germany 174/1
Pirot SE Yugoslavia 55/3; 128, 129/2
Piryatin S Ukraine 147/2
Pisa N Italy Italian air base 79/6, 81/3,5; bombed by USAAF 113/3; 133/4; German defensive line 157/3; 157/4-5
Pisticci S Italy 131/2
Pistoia N Italy 133/4; 157/3
Pistyan *see* Piešt'any
Pisz *see* Johannisburg
Piti Guam, Mariana Is. 69/6
Pitkäranta (n/s Pitkyaranta, now in USSR) E Finland occupied by Russians 41/1
Pitomnik SE Russia battle of Stalingrad 104/1; German airfield 105/2
Placentia Bay E Canada Allied base 207/1
Plan-de-Baix SW France Vercors uprising 95/3
Plaridel C Philippines 73/2
Plaški NW Yugoslavia 129/2
Plaszów C Poland German concentration camp 92/1
Plate, River S America Graf Spee scuttled 49/7
Platonovski SE Russia battle of Stalingrad 105/2
Plauen C Germany 182/3
Pļaviņas (Ger.Stockmannshof) C Latvia 149/2, 151/1
Pławy S Poland German labour camp 93/5
Plesz *see* Pszczyna
Pleszew (Ger.Pleschen) W Poland 175/1
Pleven N Bulgaria 55/3; 177/3
Ploče (n/c Kardeljevo) W Yugoslavia 128/1
Płock (Ger.Schröttersburg) N Poland German invasion 38/3, 39/2,4; 175/1
Plodovitoye SE Russia battle of Stalingrad 104/1
Ploeşti (n/s Ploieşti) C Rumania 54/1; taken by Russians 177/3
Plöhnen *see* Płońsk
Płońsk (Ger.Plöhnen) C Poland 148/2, 151/1, 175/1
Plouha NW France escape route centre 95/2
Plouézec, Pointe de NW France Commando raid 110/1
Plovdiv C Bulgaria 55/3; anti-German strikes 170/1; 177/3
Plymouth SW England industrial centre and naval base 46/1; port 48/4; air defences 52/1; 112/1; German air raids 53/6, 113/6; 136/4; Normandy invasion 152/1
Plzeň *see* Pilsen
Pnom-penh (n/s Phnom-penh) Cambodia 69/1; 70/1
Po, R. N Italy 133/4
Pobedino *see* Koton
Podbrodzie (n/c Pabradė , in Lithuania) NE Poland 149/2, 151/1
Podgora N Slovenia 129/2
Podgorica (n/c Titograd) SW Yugoslavia 128/1
Podolsk NW USSR battle for Moscow 60-61
Pogoreloye Gorodishche NW USSR battle for Moscow 60-61
Pogradec C Albania Italian occupation 54/2, 55/3
Pohsien (n/s Boxian) C China taken by Japanese 34/2
Pointe du Hoe NW France Normandy invasion 153/2,4; 154/1
Poix N France bombed by USAAF 112/1, 138/1
Poix-Terron NE France 43/4
Pokrovski C USSR 125/2
Pokrovskoye NE Ukraine battle for Kharkov 107/4,5
Pola (n/s Pula) NE Italy (now Yugoslavia) Italian naval base 55/3; liberated by Yugoslav partisans 129/2
Poland independence 1918 28/1; First World War debts 29/3; alliances 1921-1934 29/5; influx of refugees 1919-1939 29/6; 36/1; Czechoslovak territory annexed 1938 37/2; German invasion 38-39; German invasion of USSR 56/1; SOE operations 84/1; dismemberment by Germany 90/1: German concentration camps 92/1; extermination of gypsies 92/3; extermination of Jews 93/2; German special forces operations 111/3; Russian offensive 148-151, 174-5, 176/2; resistance movements and partisan operations 170-171; Soviet persecution and deportations 173/4; front line April 1945 187/3; incorporation of territory from Germany 191/2,3; loss of territory to USSR 191/3; agriculture and industry 202/1, 203/3; war casualties 205/1; declaration of war against Axis 207/1; dismemberment and persecutions by Germany and USSR 207/3; Polish armies in exile 207/3 (inset)
Polangen *see* Palanga
Połczyn *see* Polzin
Poleshoev C USSR 125/2
Polgár NE Hungary 179/2
Poligny E France escape route 95/2
Polillo Is. E Philippines 165/2
Po Line N Italy German defensive position 157/5
Polish Corridor territory of E Germany ceded to Poland 28/1; 37/2; German invasion 38/1,2
Pologi (f/c Chubarovka) S Ukraine 63/1, 147/2
Polotsk NW USSR Russian defence 57/1; 106/1; 149/2; 151/1
Poltava S USSR 57/1; 63/1; Einsatzgruppe operations 93/4; battle for Kharkov 107/4,5; 126/2; 147/2; 171/2,3
Polyarny (n/s Polyarnyy) N USSR naval base 57/3; 180/1, 181/2
Polzin (a/c Bad Polzin, n/c Połczyn, in Poland) NE Germany Hitler HQ 134/2
Pomerania (Ger.Pommern) province of NE Germany 36/1; ceded to Poland 191/3
Pommern *see* Pomerania
Ponape island of W Pacific 141/1; 166/1
Ponar E Lithuania German mass-murder site 92/1
Pondicherry (Fr. Pondichéry) French colony, S India Free French administration 45/3
Pongani E Papua taken by Allies 119/6, 120/2
Ponson island of C Philippines 167/2
Pontaix SW France Vercors uprising 95/3
Pontarlier SE France captured by Germans 44/1
Pontassieve N Italy German defence 157/3
Pont du Fahs N Tunisia 117/4
Ponte alla Scarfa S Italy 131/3
Pontedera N Italy 157/3
Pont-en-Royans SW France Vercors uprising 95/3
Ponte Sele S Italy naval bombardment 131/3
Pontfarcy N France 154/2
Pontianak W Borneo Japanese landing 74/1
Pontian Kechil S Malaya 71/4
Pontivy N France 154/1
Pont-l'Abbé Normandy, France taken by US forces 152/4, 153/2
Pontoise N France 44/1; 155/1
Pontorson N France taken by US forces 154/1
Ponyri Station C USSR 124/1, 125/3
Poole S England Royal Ordnance Factory 46/1; German air raids 113/6; Normandy invasion 152/1
Popasnoye NE Ukraine battle for Kharkov 107/4,5
Popelnya NW Ukraine 127/4
Poperinghe S Belgium 43/6
Poplar E London German air raids 53/4
Poprad (Ger.Deutschendorf) N Slovakia 175/1; 179/2
Porajärvi *see* Porosozero
Pori SW Finland 40/1; 64/1
Porkhov NW Russia taken by Germans 64/1; 149/2; 151/1
Poro island of C Philippines 167/2
Porogi NW Russia siege of Leningrad 64/2
Poronaysk *see* Shikuka
Porosozero (Finn.Porajärvi) N USSR 41/1
Porquerolles I. S France 156/2
Porretta N Italy 157/3
Port Arthur (n/c Lushun) NE China Japanese treaty port 32/1; Japanese garrison 35/1,4; Japanese base & propaganda radio station 193/2; 199/2; 207/1
Port Bello Leyte, C Philippines 167/2
Port-Cros I. S France 156/2
Port Dickson C Malaya 71/1,2,3
Porte di Ferro S Italy 131/3
Port-en-Bessin NW France Normandy invasion 152/4, 153/2
Port Inarajan Guam, Mariana Is. 143/6
Portland S England port 48/4; German air raids 113/6; base for Normandy invasion 152/1
Portland NW USA 99/2
Port-Lyautey (n/c Kénitra) NW Morocco American landing 116/1
Port Merizo Guam, Mariana Is. 143/6
Port Moresby SE Papua 68; Allied base 74/1-6, 207/1; Australian landing 119/1,5,6; Australian base 120/1,2; 122/1; 166/1; Japanese port 194-195

Q

R

T

Titov Veles see Veles
Titovo Užice see Užice
Tittmoning S Germany POW camp 205/2
Tiyan Guam 69/6
Tjeldöy island N Norway 40/4
Toamasina see Tamatave
Tobang C Philippines 73/3
Tobiishi Pt. (Jap.Tobiishi-hana) S Iwo Jima 168/2
Toboso W Philippines Japanese air base 164/2
Tobruk (n/s Tubruq) NE Libya Italian naval base 50/1,51/4; captured by Australians 50/3; German attack 78/1,2; held by Allies 80/1,2; evacuated by Allies 80/6; 81/5; Layforce raid 111/2; recaptured 115/4; German naval base 117/5
Tochigi prefecture of C Japan population 192/1
Tocra (n/s Tukrah) NE Libya 50/3; 78/2
Töging S Germany Nazi economy 36/1
Tokaj NE Hungary 179/2
Tokelau Is. C Pacific 66
Tóketerebes see Trebisov
Tokushima W Japan population 192/1; US air raid 196/1
Tokuyama C Japan US air raid 197/1
Tokyo C Japan 66; 68; US air raids 74/6, 196-197; Axis conference 87/1; Russian intelligence 82/1; war crimes trials 189/1; industry 192/1; Japanese propaganda radio station 193/2; Japanese surrender 200/1; port 195/5; 197/1,3; POW camp 204/3
Toledo C Philippines 73/5
Toledo C Spain Civil War 37/3
Toliara see Tuléar
Tolna S Hungary 178/2
Tolochin W Russia 149/2, 151/1
Tolvayarvi (Finn.Tolvajärvi) N USSR Finns stop Russian advance 41/1
Tomakovka SW Ukraine 63/1
Tomarovka C USSR 124/1, 125/2,3
Tomaszów Lubelski S Poland German invasion 39/2; 176/2
Tomaszów Mazowiecki C Poland 175/1
Tomsk E Russia industry 172/1
Tomuri (n/s Tomori) S Okinawa 169/5
Tonaki (Jap.Tonaki-jima) island, W Okinawa 169/4
Tönder SW Denmark sabotage attacks 95/4
Tonga S Pacific 66
Tongcheng see Tungcheng
Tonghua see Tunghwa
Tongliao see Tungliao
Tongres N Belgium 42/2
Tongshan see Tungshan
Tongzang NW Burma 162/5
Topoľčany C Slovakia 179/2
Topolica N Albania German detention centre 170/1
Torbung NE India 162/5
Torgau C Germany US and Russian forces meet 182/3, 184/1
Torigny N France 154/2
Tori I. (Jap. Tori-shima) W Okinawa US capture 169/4
Torkovichi NW Russia Volkhov offensive 65/5
Tormosin SE Russia Upper Don offensive 107/2
Tornio C Finland 41/1
Torokina Bougainville, Solomon Is. 118/1; Japanese control 120/1, 122/1; Allied beachhead 123/3
Törökszentmiklós E Hungary 179/2
Toropets NW USSR battle for Moscow 60-61; 65/4, 149/2, 151/1
Torquay SW England German air raids 113/6
Torres Strait NE Australia 119/1
Tortorici N Sicily 131/2
Toruń (Ger.Thorn) NW Poland German invasion 39/2,4; ;148/2, 151/1; 175/1; 207/3; POW camp 205/2
Torzhok NW USSR battle for Moscow 60-61
Tosno NW Russia taken by Germans 64/1, 64/2, 65/4, 65/5
Tost (n/c Toszek, in Poland) SE Germany POW camp 205/2
Toszek see Tost
Totis see Tata
Toto Guam 69/6
Totore E Papua taken by Allies 119/6, 120/2
Tottori W Japan population 192/1
Toulon S France French naval base 44/1; French fleet scuttled 45/2; French naval base 79/6, 81/3, 81/5; Vichy fleet scuttled 117/5; captured by Free French forces 156/2
Toulouse S France 44/1, 45/2; mass demonstrations 94/1; escape route centre 95/2
Toungoo S Burma British air base 76/1; captured by Japanese 77/3; retaken by British 163/2
Tournai W Belgium 44/1; 158/1
Tours C France seat of French government 45/2; captured by Germans 44/1; German bomber station 113/6; 155/1
Toushan S China taken by Japanese 35/4
Townsville NE Australia Allied base 119/1
Toyama W Japan population 192/1; US air raid 196/1

Toyohara (n/c Yuzhno-Sakhalinsk, in USSR) N Japan occupied by Russians 199/3
Toyohashi C Japan population 192/1; US air raid 197/1
Tozeur C Tunisia 114/4; 116/1
Trach (a/c Kompong Trach) Cambodia Japanese air base 70/1
Trachenberg (n/c Žmigród, in Poland) E Germany 174/1
Tragino Viaduct S Italy SAS raid 111/2
Trakhtemirov NW Ukraine Bukrin bridgehead 127/3
Tramecourt NE France German bomber station 52/1
Trang S Siam 70/1
Trans-Jordan (n/c Jordan) base for Allied invasion of Syria and occupation of Baghdad 79/3
Transnistria territory of SW Ukraine occupied by Rumania 90/1
Transylvania transferred from Hungary to Rumania 28/1; returned to Hungary 90/1
Trapani W Sicily Italian naval base 51/4; Axis naval base 117/5; 130/2
Trasimene Line N Italy German defensive position 133/4
Treasury Is. Solomon Is. 118/1; captured by New Zealanders 123/3, 141/1
Trebišov (Hung.Tóketerebes) E Slovakia 179/2
Treblinka NE Poland German extermination camp 92/1,3; Jewish ghetto uprising 171/2; 207/3
Trebnitz (n/s Trzebnica, in Poland) E Germany 39/2; 174/1
Třeboň (Ger.Wittingau) SE Bohemia 187/2
Trekhostrovskaya SE Russia battle of Stalingrad 104/1
Trenčín (Ger.Trentschin) W Slovakia 175/1
Trengganu (n/s Terengganu) state of C Malaya 71/1,2
Trepča N Albania German detention centre 170/1
Trévières Normandy taken by US forces 153/2,4; 154/1
Treviso N Italy 157/4
Tricase SE Italy 131/2
Trier NW Germany 42/2; 44/1; Allied bombing 138/1; 160/2; 159/7; 161/3; captured by US forces 183/2
Trieste (S.Cr. Trst) NE Italy transferred from Austria 28/1; 54/1, 55/3; Italian naval base 51/4, 79/6, 81/3,5, 117/5; German detention centre 94/1; 128/1; liberated by Yugoslav partisans 129/2; 170/1; captured by British 157/5; Italo-Yugoslav dispute 191/2
Trigh Bir Hakeim NE Libya 80/2
Trigh Capuzzo NE Libya 78/2 (inset), 80/1,2
Trigh el Abd NE Libya 80/1,2
Trikkala NW Greece 54/2; captured by Germans 55/3
Trincomalee E Ceylon Japanese air raid 77/4
Trinidad MI6 outstation 82/1; 89/2
Tripoli (n/c Tarabulus) NW Libya Italian naval base 50/1,51/4, 206/1; Axis supply port 78/2, 79/6; Axis air base 79/6, 81/3,5; 114/4; German air base 117/5
Tripoli N Lebanon oil terminal 79/3; German air base 117/5
Tripolitania region of NW Libya 78/2, 114/4
Trnovo (n/s Tŭrnovo) N Bulgaria 177/3
Troarn Normandy battle for Caen 153/5
Trois-Ponts SE Belgium battle of the Bulge 161/3
Trobriand Is. (a/c Kiriwina Is.) E New Guinea 75/1, 119/1
Tromsö N Norway 40/3; German air base 180/1, 181/2
Trondheim C Norway Allied landing 40/3; 41/5; planned German naval port 91/4; German air base 180/1; German base 206/1
Trondheim Fjord C Norway 40/3
Troppau see Opava
Trostyanets NE Ukraine battle for Kharkov 107/3
Trouville NW France Normandy invasion 152/2; 155/1
Troyes E France 44/1; 155/1
Trst see Trieste
Trstená N Slovakia 175/1
Truk W Pacific Caroline Is. 66; 68; Japanese base 75/2, 207/1; 96/1; 141/1; 166/1; Japanese base 193/2; Japanese ships destroyed 195/3; Japanese surrender 200/2
Trzebinia S Poland German labour camp 93/5
Trzebnica see Trebnitz
Tsanghsien (n/c Cangzhou) NE China taken by Japanese 34/2
Tsaochwang (n/s Zaozhuang) E China taken by Japanese 34/2
Tsaritsa,R. SE Russia battle of Stalingrad 100/2
Tsaritsyn see Stalingrad
Tschenstochau see Częstochowa
Tselinograd see Akmolinsk
Tsimlyanskaya (n/c Tsimlyansk) S Russia 63/1, 147/3
Tsinan (a/s Chi-nan n/s Jinan) NE China treaty port 32/1 taken by Japanese 34/2, 35/4

Tsingpu (a/s Ch'ing-p'u n/s Qingpu) E China taken by Japanese 34/3
Tsingsing (a/s Ching-hsing n/s Tingxing) N China taken by Japanese 34/2
Tsingtao (n/s Qingdao) E China taken by Japanese 34/2; under Japanese occupation 66-67; 68; Japanese port 194-195; POW camp 204/3
Tsingyüan see Paoting
Tsining (a/s Chi-ning n/s Jining f/c Pingtichuan) N China taken by Japanese 34/2
Tsinkong (a/s Chienchiang n/s Qianjiang) S China taken by Japanese 145/3
Tsinyang (a/s Ch'in-yang n/s Qinyang) N China taken by Japanese 34/2
Tsitsihar (n/s Qiqihar) C Manchuria treaty port 32/1; taken by Japanese 35/1,4
Tsowhsien (n/s Zouxian) E China taken by Japanese 34/2
Tsu C Japan population 192/1; US air raid 197/1
Tsugen I. (Jap.Tsuken-jima) SE Okinawa captured by US 169/4
Tsuha see Tsuwa
Tsuhako see Tsuwanuku
Tsuruga C Japan US air raid 197/1
Tsushima island NW Japan 196/1
Tsuwa (n/s Tsuha) S Okinawa 169/5
Tsuwanuku (n/s Tsuhako) S Okinawa 169/5
Tsybenko SE Russia battle of Stalingrad 105/2
Tsyurupinsk SW Ukraine 62/1
Tuamotu Archipelago S Pacific Free French administration 45/3
Tuan (n/s Du'an) SW China 145/3
Tuapse W Caucasus 102/2, 103/1
Tubruq see Tobruk
Tubuai Is. see Austral Is.
Tuckum see Tukums
Tufi SE Papua 75/1; 119/1,5,6; 120/2
Tuguegarao N Philippines captured by Japanese 72/1; air base 165/2, 167/3,4
Tuhshan see Tushan
Tukerere I. Makin atoll, Gilbert Is. 141/3
Tukrah see Tocra
Tukums (Ger.Tuckum) NW Latvia 148/2, 151/1
Tula N USSR 56/1; battle for Moscow 60-61; 106/1; industry 172/1
Tulagi (n/s Tulaghi) Solomon Is. Japanese landing 75/1; Japanese base 75/3-5; bombed by US 75/2; US land 118/1-3
Tulcea NE Rumania 146/2,3
Tulchin SW Ukraine 57/1; 126/2; 177/3
Tuléar (n/c Toliara) SW Madagascar British landing 79/5
Tulle C France sabotage 85/3
Tulsa C USA war industries 98/1
Tumen E Manchuria captured by Russians 199/2
Tumon Bay Guam Japanese landing 69/6
Tunbridge Wells SE England civil defence HQ 47/3
Tungcheng (n/s Tongcheng) C China taken by Japanese 145/3
Tunghai (n/s Donghai) E China taken by Japanese 34/2, 35/2
Tunghwa (n/s Tonghua) S Manchuria 199/2
Tung-kou see Tatungkow
Tunglan (n/s Donglan) SW China 145/3
Tungliao (n/s Tongliao) C Manchuria taken by Japanese 35/1
Tungning (n/s Dongning) NE Manchuria captured by Russians 199/2
Tungshan (n/s Tongshan) C China taken by Japanese 34/2; 145/3
Tung Song (n/s Thung Song) S Siam 70/1
Tunhwa (n/s Tun-hua, n/s Dunhua) E Manchuria taken by Japanese 35/1
Tunis French North Africa 79/6, 81/3, 81/5; German defence 116/1, 117/4
Tunisia Vichy administration 45/3, 50/1; German special forces operations 111/3; Afrika Korps arrives 114/4; defeat of Axis forces 116-117; Allied base for invasion of Sicily 130/1; neutral in war 206/1
Tuquan see Lichuan
Turcoing NE France 44/1
Turek C Poland German invasion 38/3
Turgel see Türi
Türi (Ger.Turgel) N Estonia taken by Germans 64/1; 151/1
Turin (It.Torino) NW Italy 45/1; bombed by RAF 53/3, anti-German strike 94/1; 113/3; 133/4; Allied bombing 157/4
Turkestan C USSR post-war province planned by Germany 91/4
Turkey break-up of Ottoman Empire and Greek occupation 28/1; alliances 1921-1934 29/5; refugees to and from Greece and Bulgaria 29/6; 54/1; 79/3; neutral during war 90/1; Germany's 'Final Solution' for Jews 93/2; 103/1; declaration of war against Germany 203/3, 207/1
Turku (Sw.Åbo) SW Finland bombed by Russians 40/1; 64/1
Turnhout W Belgium 42/2
Turnhout Canal N Belgium 159/6
Tŭrnovo see Trnovo
Turnu-Severin SW Rumania 177/3

Tushan (a/s Tuhshan n/s Dushan) SW China taken by Japanese 145/3
Tuvinskaya ASSR see Tannu Tuva
Tuyün (n/s Duyun) SW China taken by Japanese 145/3
Tuzla N Yugoslavia 128/1, 129/2
Tver see Kalinin
Twante S Burma 76/2
Twinnge N Burma retaken by British 163/2
Tychowo see Gross Tychow
Tynemouth NE England evacuation area 47/4
Tynset C Norway 40/3
Tyre (n/c Sour) S Lebanon British landing 79/3
Tyumen C Russia industry 172/1
Tzeli (n/c Cili) C China taken by Japanese 145/3
Tzeyang (n/c Yanzhou) E China taken by Japanese 34/2

U

Ualual see Walwal
Uban C Philippines 167/2
Ube W Japan US air raid 196/1
Uberi E Papua 119/5, 120/2
Uchitomari S Okinawa 169/5
Uden S Holland 159/4
Udvard (n/c Dvory nad Žitavou, in Czechoslovakia) N Hungary 186/1
Ufa C Russia industry 172/1
Uganda 50/1, 51/2
Ugine E France sabotage 85/3
Uglegorsk see Esutoru
Uglich NW USSR battle for Moscow 60-61
Uglovka NW Russia 65/4
Uji-Yamada C Japan US air raid 197/1
Újpest C Hungary 179/2,4; 186/1
Újvidék see Novi Sad
Ukhrul NE India 76/1
Ukiangong Makin atoll, Gilbert Is. US landings 141/3
Ukraine emigration of refugees from Russian Revolution 29/6; German invasion 57/1,2, 58/1, 62-63; German military administration 90/1; post-war province planned by Germany 91/4; German concentration camps 92/1; extermination of gypsies 92/3; extermination of Jews 93/2; Einsatzgruppe operations 93/4; Don and Kharkov offensives 106-107; regained by Russians 126-127, 146-147; Russian operations Dec 43 - May 44 147/2 (inset); Soviet repression 173/4; German SS and SD bases 170/1; partisan areas 171/2; partisan raids 171/3; deportation of Poles 207/3; conquered by Germans 62-63;
Ulan-Erge (a/c Krasnoye) N Caucasus 103/1
Ulan Hot see Hsingan
Ulan-Ude E Russia industry 173/1
Ulithi Caroline Is. captured by US forces 140/1; 168/1, 169/3; 166/1; US air base 196/2
Ulm S Germany Allied bombing 138/1
Ulster (a/c Northern Ireland) area of dispute 28/1
Ulyanov C USSR 125/2
Ulyanovka NW Russia siege of Leningrad 64/2
Ulyanovsk C Russia 106/1
Uman SW USSR Russian defensive pocket 58/1; 126/2, 147/2
Umatac Guam, Mariana Is. 69/6
Umatac Bay Guam, Mariana Is. 143/6
Umnak Aleutian Is. 68; 96/1
Unalaska Aleutian Is. 96/1
Unecha C USSR battle for Moscow 60-61
Ungvár see Uzhgorod
Uniejów C Poland German invasion 38/3; 175/1
Unimak Aleutian Is. 96/1
U.S.S.R independence of Finland and Baltic States 28/1; First World War debts 29/3; alliances 1921-1934 29/5; refugees to West 29/6; 32-33; conflict with Japan in Manchuria 35/4; occupation of E Poland 39/4; Russo-Finnish war 41/1,2; German invasion 56-59; disposition of German and Russian forces at Sept. 1941 61/1; battle for Moscow 60-61; siege of Leningrad 64-65; front line: May-July 1942 63/4, Aug.-Dec. 1943 127/1, Dec. 43-May 44 146/1, Sep 1944 178/1; supply routes from Middle East 79/4; intelligence organizations 82/1; German administration 90-91; Nazi industry 91/2; post-war territorial plan 91/4; extermination of Jews 93/2; aircraft delivery routes from USA 99/3; Lend-lease Aid 99/5; Stalingrad 100-101, 104-105; German offensive in Caucasus 102-103; German special forces operations 111/3; recovery of Ukraine 126-127, 146-147; German SS and SD bases 170/1; partisan areas 171/2; Kovpak's raid 171/3; industry and raw materials 172-173; evacuation of industry 173/5; Soviet persecutions 173/4; territorial losses to Finland 180/3; Allied convoy routes 180-181; trade with Japan 195/5; invasion of Manchuria 198/1,2; occupation of Southern Sakhalin and Kurile Is. 199/3; agriculture and mineral resources 202/1; US aid 203/7; global troop movements 206/2; declaration of war against Axis 207/1; number of troops mobilized 207/1; war casualties 204/1 (inset), 205/1
U.S.A. exports to Britain 47/2D; intelligence organizations 82/1; German intelligence 82/1; Allied conferences 86-87, 134-135, 188-189; coastal convoy routes 89/2, 108-109, 136-137; economy 1941-45 98-99; convoy routes to USSR 181/1;

agricultural products and raw materials 202/1; air routes 202/1; US Army and Air Force supply lines 203/2; tanker fleet 203/4; aid to Allies 203/6,7; global troop movements 206/2; declaration of war against Axis 207/1; number of troops mobilized 207/1; war casualties 204/1
Upper Sheikh (n/s Shiikh) Brit.Somaliland 51/2
Upper Silesia divided by plebiscite 1921 between Germany and Poland 28/1, 29/2
Uppsala S Sweden 41/3
Urawa NE Japan POW camp 204/3
Urbania N Italy 157/3
Urbino N Italy 157/3
Uritsk NW Russia siege of Leningrad 64/2
Urukh, R. C Caucasus 103/1
Urup, R. C Caucasus 102/2, 103/1
Uruppu (n/c Urup, in USSR) Kurile Is. Japan Russian attack 199/3
Ushi Pt Tinian, Mariana Is. US air base 143/5
Ussel C France sabotage 85/3
Usson S France sabotage 85/3
Usti nad Labem see Aussig
Ust-Khoperski SE Russia battle of Stalingrad 104/1
Ussuriysk see Voroshilov
Ust-Bolsheretsk E USSR 199/3
Utah W USA worker mobility 98/1
Utah Beach Normandy, France US landings 152/4, 153/2
Utan Melintang (n/s Hutan Melintang) C Malaya captured by Japanese 71/3
Utekhina (n/s Utekhino) NW Russia 149/2, 151/1
Utena E Lithuania 149/2, 151/1
Utrecht C Holland 42/2
Utsunomiya C Japan population 192/1; US air raid 197/1
Uvarovo S Russia 63/1
Uwajima W Japan US air raid 196/1
Uzhgorod (Cz.Užhorod, Hung. Ungvár) SW Ukraine 176/2
Uzhok Pass SW USSR 177/3
Užice (n/c Titovo Užice) C Yugoslavia 55/3; 128/1

V

Vaagsfjord (n/s Vågsfjord) inlet N Norway 40/4
Vaagsö (n/s Vågsøy) C Norway Commando raid 110/1, 111/4
Vaasa W Finland 40/1
Vác (Ger.Waitzen) C Hungary 179/2,4
Vado Ligure NW Italy 44/1
Vaenga (n/s Vayenga) NW USSR Russian air base 180/1, 181/2
Vaernes C Norway 40/3
Vaganovo NW Russia siege of Leningrad 64/2
Vágfarkasd (n/c Vlčany, in Czechoslovakia) N Hungary 186/1
Vågsøy see Vaagsö/Valchevrière SW France Vercors uprising 95/3
Valdai NW USSR battle for Moscow 60-61; 65/4
Valdai Hills NW USSR 56/1, 59/1; 65/4
Valence SE France 44/1; 156/2
Valencia E Spain Civil War 37/3
Valenciennes NE France 42/2
Valetta (n/s Valletta) Malta British naval base 81/4
Valjevo E Yugoslavia 55/3; 129/2
Valki NE Ukraine battle for Kharkov 107/4,5; 124/1, 125/3
Valladolid N Spain Republican air raid in Civil War 37/3
Valletta see Valetta
Valmiera (Ger. Wolmar) C Latvia 151/1
Valmontone C Italy 133/2-4
Valognes Normandy, France taken by US forces 153/2; 154/1
Valona (Alb.Vlonë a/s Vlorë) S Albania Italian occupation 54/2, 55/3
Valuiki (n/s Valuyki) C USSR 62/2; 63/1; battle for Kharkov 107/3; 125/1
Vammelsuu see Serovo
Vamos W Crete captured by Germans 55/4
Vancouver W Canada 99/2
Vandsburg see Więcbork
Vangunu island of C Solomons 121/4; US landings 123/3
Vannes NW France German bomber staion 53/6, 113/6; 154/1
Vanuatu see New Hebrides
Varaville Normandy, France battle for Caen 153/5
Varaždin (Ger.Warasdin, Hung.Varasd) N Yugoslavia 128/1, 129/2
Varengeville-sur-Mer N France Dieppe raid 86/2
Varenikovskaya W Caucasus 103/3
Varna E Bulgaria German troops arrive 54/1; taken by Russians 177/3
Varvarovka SE Russia battle of Stalingrad 105/2
Vasilkov W Russia 106/1
Vasilyevka SW Ukraine 63/1
Vassieux (-en-Vercors) SW France Vercors uprising 95/3
Vasterival N France Dieppe raid 87/2
Vasto C Italy 131/2
Vasvár (Ger.Eisenburg) NW Hungary 178/2, 186/1
Vatican City C Italy Japanese intelligence 82/1
Vatra Dornei N Rumania 177/3
Vayenga see Vaenga
Vecsés C Hungary 179/3
Vega island N Norway 40/3
Vegesack N Germany bombed by USAAF 112/1
Veghel S Holland 159/4
Vejle C Denmark sabotage attacks 95/4
Veles (n/c Titov Veles) S Yugoslavia 54/2
Veliki Berezny (Hung. Nagyberezna) SW Ukraine 176/2
Veliki Bochkov (Hung. Nagybocsko) SW Ukraine 176/2
Veliki Bukrin (n/s Velikiy Bukrin) NW Ukraine Russian bridgehead 126/2, 127/3
Velikiye Luki NW USSR 56/1; battle for Moscow 60-61; taken by Russians 65/4; 106/1; 149/2; 151/1
Velizh NW USSR battle for Moscow 60-61; 65/4
Vella Lavella (a/c Mbilua) island of C Solomons 121/4; US landing 123/3, 141/1

Velletri C Italy 133/2
Velsk N Russia 106/1
Vemork S Norway raid by Royal Engineers 110/1
Vendôme N France 155/1
Venetian Line N Italy German defensive position 157/5
Venezuela 89/2; oil 202/1; declaration of war against Germany 207/1
Venice (It.Venezia) N Italy 54/1, 55/3; anti-German strike 94/1; captured by British 157/5
Venlo SE Holland 95/2
Venray S Holland 159/4
Ventimiglia NW Italy 156/2
Ventspils (Ger.Windau) NW Latvia 64/1; 148/2, 151/1
Veprik NE Ukraine battle for Kharkov 107/3; 125/3
Veprin NW Ukraine 127/4
Verahue Guadalcanal, Solomon Is. 118/2; US landing 121/9
Vercors district of SW France resistance uprising 95/3
Verde I. C Philippines 167/3,4
Verdun E France 42/1,2; 44/1; 160/1
Veretski Pass SW USSR 177/3
Vergato N Italy 157/3
Verkhne-Bakanski (n/s Verkhnebakanskiy) W Caucasus 103/3
Verkhne-Dneprovsk S Ukraine 63/1, 126/2, 147/2
Verkhne-Yelshanka SE Russia battle of Stalingrad 100/2
Verkhni Mamon SE Russia Upper Don offensive 107/2
Verkhni Olshanets (n/s Verkhniy Ol'shanets) C USSR 125/2
Verkhnyaya Syrovatka NE Ukraine 124/1, 125/3
Verkhovye C USSR battle for Moscow 60-61
Vermont NE USA worker mobility 98/1
Verneuil N France 155/3
Vernon N France 155/1
Verona N Italy Axis conference 135/1,2; captured by US forces 157/5
Verson Normandy, France battle for Caen 153/5
Vertyachi SE Russia battle of Stalingrad 104/1
Verviers N Belgium 42/2
Vervins NE France 42/2
Vesely (n/s Vesëlyy) S USSR 102/2, 103/1; 125/2
Veshenskaya SE Russia Upper Don offensive 107/2
Vesoul E France 44/1
Vest Fjord (n/s Vestfjorden) N Norway 40/3
Veszprém W Hungary 178/2, 179/4
Veurey SW France Vercors uprising 95/3
Via Balbia NE Libya 80/1,2
Vianden Luxembourg 42/2
Vianos E Crete 55/4
Viborg N Denmark 41/3
Vibo Valentia S Italy 131/2
Vicenza N Italy 157/4,5
Vichy C France French Government 1940-42 45/2; 95/2
Vichy France occupied by Germany 90/1; strikes and demonstrations 94/1
Victoria Hong Kong Japanese attack 69/7
Victoria Harbour Hong Kong British naval yards 69/7
Victory Road Leningrad siege 65/7
Vidin NW Bulgaria 55/3; 177/3
Vielsalm SE Belgium battle of the Bulge 161/3
Vienna (Ger.Wien) NE Austria 29/5; Nazi ecomony 36/1; Axis conference 86/1; Nazi industry 91/2; planned financial capital 91/4; 112/1; Allied bombing 138/1; 178/2; captured by Russians 186/1; 187/2; anti-Hitler plot 188/2; Allied occupation 191/2
Vienne SE France 44/1; 156/2
Vientiane Laos 69/1
Vierville (-sur-Mer) NW France Normandy invasion 153/2,4
Vierzon C France 44/1
Vietri sul Mare S Italy 131/3
Vigan N Philippines captured by Japanese 72/1; air base 165/2, 167/3,4
Vigo NW Spain 108/4
Viipuri SE Finland (n/c Vyborg, in USSR) occupied by Russians 41/1; 57/3; retaken by Finns 64/1; 106/1; 180/3
Vikna island C Norway 40/3
Vila Pt. Solomon Is. Japanese air base 121/4, 123/3
Villacoublay N France German Fliegerkorps HQ 52/1; bombed by USAAF 112/1; German bomber station 113/6
Villaggio Duca degli Abruzzi It.Somaliland 37/4
Villard-de-Lans SW France Vercors uprising 95/3
Villa Santa Lucia C Italy 132/1
Villebaudon N France 154/2
Villedieu NE France 155/1

Willems Canal S Holland 159/4
Willenberg (n/c Wielbark, in Poland) E Prussia 39/2,4; 148/2 151/1; 175/1
Willesden NW London German air raids 53/4
Wilmersdorf SW suburb of Berlin 184/2
Wilno (a/c Vilna n/c Vilnius) E Lithuania annexed by Poland 28/1. See also Vilna
Wiltz N Luxembourg battle of the Bulge 161/3
Windau see Ventspils
Wingen E France 183/2
Winkowitz see Vinkovci
Winslow S England Bomber Command group HQ 112/1, 138/1
Winter Position see Gustav Line
Wisley SE England aircraft factory 46/1
Wisconsin N USA war industries 98/1
Wisła, R. see Vistula
Wismar N Germany 41/3; bombed by RAF 53/3; 184/1
Wissant NE France German fighter station 52/1
Wittenau N suburb of Berlin 184/2
Wittenberg E Germany 184/1
Wittering C England RAF fighter station 52/1
Wittingau see Třeboň
Włocławek (Ger.Leslau) N Poland German invasion 38/3, 39/2; 175/1
Włodawa E Poland 39/2; POW camp 205/2
Włodzimierz (n/c Vladimir-Volynskiy, in USSR E Poland) 148/2; 171/3
Włoszczowa W Poland 174/2, 175/1
Woensdrecht W Holland captured by Canadians 159/6
Wola district of Warsaw uprising 171/4
Wolbrom S Poland 175/1
Woleai Caroline Is. 140/1; Japanese air base 142/1
Wolfberg S Germany POW camp 205/2
Wolfheze S Holland 159/4
Wolfsburg N Germany Nazi economy 36/1; planned industrial capital 91/2
Wo Li Hop (n/c Wo Yi Hop) Hong Kong Japanese attack 69/7
Wołkowysk (n/c Volkovysk, in USSR) E Poland 149/2
Wolmar see Valmiera
Wołomin C Poland 148/2, 151/1
Wolverhampton C England industrial centre 46/1
Wongrowitz see Wągrowiec
Wonsan (Jap. Gensan) N Korea Japanese port 194-195; 200/1
Woodford NW England aircraft factory 46/1 (inset)
Woodlands Singapore 71/5
Woodlark I. Solomon Sea captured by Australians 122/1
Woodleigh Singapore 71/5
Woolwich SE London Royal Ordnance Factory 46/1; German air raids 53/4
Woosung (n/s Wusong) E China treaty port 32/1
Wormhoudt NE France 43/6
Worms W Germany US forces cross Rhine 183/2
Wotitz see Votice
Wotje Marshall Is. Japanese garrison 141/1
Wo Yi Hop see Wo Li Hop
Wrangell Alaska US base 181/1
Wreschen see Września
Wrexham NW England Royal Ordnance Factory 46/1 (inset)
Wrocław see Breslau
Września (Ger.Wreschen) NW Poland 175/1
Wuan N China taken by Japanese 34/2
Wuchakou (n/s Wuchagou) NW Manchuria captured by Russians 199/2
Wuchang C China taken by Kuomintang forces 33/6; taken by Japanese 34/2, 35/4
Wuchin see Wutsin
Wuchow (n/s Wuzhou a/s Wu-chou) S China treaty port 32/1; taken by Japanese 145/3
Wugang see Wukang
Wuhan E China 66
Wuhing see Wuhsing
Wuhsi see Wusih
Wuhsing (a/s Wuhing n/s Wuxing) E China taken by Japanese 34/2,3
Wuhu NE China treaty port 32/1; taken by Japanese 34/2,3
Wukang (n/s Wugang) C China taken by Japanese 145/3
Wuming S China 35/4; taken by Japanese 145/3
Wundwin C Burma 77/3
Wuning C China taken by Japanese 34/2
Wuntho NW Burma 77/3; 163/3
Wuppertal NW Germany bombed by RAF 112/1
Württemberg province of S Germany 28/2; 36/1
Württemberg-Baden province of S Germany 191/3
Württemberg-Hohenzollern province of S Germany 191/3
Wurzach SW Germany POW camp 205/2

Würzburg S Germany Nazi land court 36/1; Allied bombing 138/1; 182/3
Wusih (a/s Wu-hsi, n/s Wuxi) E China taken by Japanese 34/2,3
Wusong see Woosung
Wutsin (a/s Wuchin n/c Changzhou) E China taken by Japanese 34/2,3
Wuvulu Is. NE New Guinea 140/2
Wuxi see Wusih
Wuxing see Wuhsing
Wuzhou see Wuchow
Wyler E Holland 159/4
Wyoming W USA worker mobility 98/1
Wysokie Mazowieckie NE Poland 148/2, 151/1, 175/1
Wyszków N Poland German invasion 39/2,4; 148/2, 151/1, 175/1
Wyszogród N Poland German invasion 39/2,3
Wyton E England USAAF group HQ 112/1

Xaafuun see Dante
Xanten NW Germany 183/2
Xanthi NE Greece captured by Germans 55/3
Xiamen see Amoy
Xi'an see Sian
Xiangtan see Siangtan
Xiangxiang see Siangsiang
Xiangzhou see Hsiangchou
Xianning see Sienning
Xiaochikou see Hsiaochihkou
Xiaofan see Hsiaofanchen
Xing'an see Hsingan
Xingtai see Singtai
Xinjiang see Sinkiang
Xinkou see Hsinkouchen
Xinning see Sinning
Xinxiang see Sinsiang
Xinyang see Sinyang
Xinzheng see Sincheng
X-ray Beach C Italy, Anzio US landing 133/2
Xuancheng see Süancheng
Xuchang see Hsüchow
Xuguan see Fuhsukuan

Yabelo S Ethiopia 37/4
Yafo see Jaffa
Yagachi I. (Jap. Yagachi-shima) NW Okinawa captured by US 169/4
Yakhroma NW USSR battle for Moscow 60-61
Yakovlevo C USSR 125/2
Yalta S Ukraine Crimea 62/1, 146/3, 147/2; Roosevelt-Churchill-Stalin meeting 189/1
Yamagata N Japan population 192/1
Yamaguchi prefecture of W Japan 192/1
Yamanashi prefecture of C Japan population 192/1
Yamethin C Burma 77/3; retaken by British 163/2
Yaminsk W Russia 149/4
Yam-Izhora NW Russia siege of Leningrad 64/2, 65/4
Yanam French colony, E India Free French administration 45/3
Yan'an see Yenan
Yangchiang S China taken by Japanese 35/4
Yangchow (n/s Yangzhou) E China 35/4; POW camp 204/2
Yangjiang see Yangchiang
Yangkii N China taken by Japanese 34/2
Yangtze, R. Japanese advance 34/3
Yanji see Yenki
Yantai see Chefoo
Yanzhou see Tzeyang
Yap island, W Pacific 66; Japanese base 68, 142/1; 140/1, 166/1; 168/1, 169/3
Yapen see Japen
Yarmouth E England port 48/4
Yaroslavl N USSR 59/1; battle for Moscow 60-61; 61/1; 64/1, 106/1; industry 172/1
Yartsevo NW USSR battle for Moscow 60-61; 65/4
Yashkul (a/c Peschanoye) N Caucasus 103/1
Yasnaya Polyana NW USSR battle for Moscow 60-61
Yasnogorodka NW Ukraine 127/4
Yawata W Japan population 192/1; US air raid 196/1,2
Ye S Burma 76/2
Yedashe S Burma 77/3
Yedintsy see Edineţi
Yefremov C USSR battle for Moscow 60-61
Yegorlyk, R. NW Caucasus 102/2
Yegoryevsk NW USSR battle for Moscow 60-61
Yehho E Manchuria captured by Russians 199/2
Yeisk (n/s Yeysk) 63/1; S Russia 106/1, 127/2, 147/2
Yelets C USSR battle for Moscow 60-61; 63/1; 106/1; 124/1 147/2
Yelizavetgrad see Kirovograd
Yelkhi SE Russia battle of Stalingrad 105/2
Yellow Beach C Italy, Anzio US landing 133/2
Yelshanka SE Russia battle of Stalingrad 100/2, 105/2
Yel'nya see Elnya
Yemen 37/4; 51/2; neutral in war 206/1
Yenakiyevo (f/c Ordzhonikidze) C Ukraine industry 172/1
Yenan (n/s Yan'an) NW China Communist stronghold 34/2
Yenangyaung C Burma 76/1, 77/3; retaken by British 163/2
Yen-chi see Yenki
Yenki (a/s Yen-chi n/s Yanji) E Manchuria captured by Russians 199/2; Japanese garrison 35/1,4
Yeovil SW England aircraft factory 46/1
Yerevan see Erivan
Yёrzovka see Erzovka
Yetsovka SE Russia battle of Stalingrad 105/2
Yeu NW Burma 76/1,77/3
Yevpatoriya S Ukraine Crimea 146/3
Yeya, R. NW Caucasus 102/2, 103/1
Yeysk see Yeisk
Yibei see Ipeh
Yichang see Ichang
Yihsien (n/s Yixian) N China taken by Japanese 34/2
Yi-hsing see Ihing
Yilan see Ilan
Yimianpo see Imienpo
Yingcheng C China taken by Japanese 34/2

Z

40 ▶

40

▪ Na

Vaagso 110

46

94

52
▶ 112

108

42 ◀
158 ▶

184

Königsberg

London 52
42
158   158

Berlin 184

38

▶ Dunkirk 42
44 ▼

182

Dresden 138

152 ▼
Arras 42
Cologne 112

St. Lo 154   ▪ Caen 152
▪ Dieppe 86
Eban Emael 42

186
Prague 186

Auschwit

Sedan 42   Bastogne 160
160 ▼

▪ Paris 154

Vienna 186

154

▪ Be

132 156
178

L.Balat

156
▪ Vercors 94

36

130

Anzio
▶ 132   Monte Cassino 132

130 ▶   Salerno

■ Oran 50

130

116 ◀   Kasserine
Pass

▪ Malta 80

116 ◀
Mareth

78

116 ◀

116 ◀